THE OXFORD AUTHORS

General Editor: Frank Kermode

WILLIAM WORDSWORTH was born in 1770 at Cockermouth in the Lake District. After education at Hawkshead Grammar School and St John's College, Cambridge, he lived an unsettled life in France, London and the West Country, meeting radical thinkers and in his writings identifying himself with their cause. Intimacy with Coleridge and the poetry of the *annus mirabilis* 1797–8 confirmed his vocation as a poet and in 1799 he returned to the Lake District. Here he made his home until his death in 1850. Retirement and marriage in 1802, however, did not signal retreat. *Lyrical Ballads* (1798–1805) and *Poems in Two Volumes* (1807) provoked much hostility and Wordsworth had to fight to establish himself as the first poet of the age. In 1843 he was appointed Poet Laureate, in public recognition of the veneration in which he had long been held.

STEPHEN GILL is a Fellow of Lincoln College, Oxford, a Trustee of Dove Cottage and Honorary Librarian of the Wordsworth Library in Grasmere. His publications include *The Salisbury Plain Poems*, which inaugurated the Cornell Wordsworth Series.

THE OXFORD AUTHORS

WILLIAM WORDSWORTH

EDITED BY
STEPHEN GILL

Oxford   New York
OXFORD UNIVERSITY PRESS
1984

Oxford University Press, Walton Street, Oxford OX2 6DP

London Glasgow New York Toronto
Delhi Bombay Calcutta Madras Karachi
Kuala Lumpur Singapore Hong Kong Tokyo
Nairobi Dar es Salaam Cape Town
Melbourne Auckland

and associated companies in
Beirut Berlin Ibadan Mexico City Nicosia

Oxford is a trade mark of Oxford University Press

British Library Cataloguing in Publication Data
Wordsworth, William, 1770–1850
William Wordsworth.—(The Oxford authors)
I. Title   II. Gill, Stephen
821'.7   PR5050
ISBN 0–19–254175–7
ISBN 0–19–281333–1 Pbk

Library of Congress Cataloguing in Publication Data
Wordsworth, William, 1770–1850.
William Wordsworth.
(The Oxford authors)
Bibliography: p.
Includes index.
I. Gill, Stephen Charles.   II. Title.
PR5853.G54 1984   821'.7   83–17278
ISBN 0–19–254175–7
ISBN 0–19–281333–1 (pbk.)

Set by Wyvern Typesetting Ltd.
Printed in Great Britain by
Cox & Wyman Ltd., Reading

PREFACE

THIS edition must begin with what may seem an immodest claim. Here for the first time a selection of Wordsworth's work is offered in which the poems are ordered according to the date of their composition, and presented in texts which give as nearly as possible their earliest completed state. That such a claim can be made so long after Wordsworth's death in 1850 and in the face of so many editions since then may seem amazing. To appreciate why it is justified, and what the importance of this edition is, one must understand the problem of Wordsworth's text and the reader is, therefore, referred at once to the Note on the Text below, pp. xxxi–xxxiii. It should be read by all who use this edition, and not just by those who already have an interest in textual matters.

Wordsworth lived to old age and never stopped writing and publishing. The last Collected Edition he saw through the press was in six volumes and even so did not include all that he had written. In the year of his death *The Prelude* was published and scholarly investigation has since added many more poems to the canon. For a one-volume edition selection was, therefore, necessary, and in a broad sense not difficult to make. Most readers, from his contemporaries onwards, have found the later poetry less compelling than the earlier, and scholars and critics have not really dissented from the common judgement. Most of the poems in this volume belong to the early period which closed with the publication of *The Excursion* in 1814. Selection within this period, however, has not been easy and I am aware that I have had to omit much that is vital for full understanding of Wordsworth's achievement in his greatest years. The list is dismayingly long: *Descriptive Sketches*, 'Adventures on Salisbury Plain', *The Borderers*, *Benjamin, the Waggoner*, 'The White Doe of Rylstone', *The Excursion*. Wordsworth's powers as a prose writer are likewise not fully represented. The major public statements about poetry are all included, but not the fine insights scattered throughout the letters nor the very important writings on more general matters such as *A Letter to the Bishop of Llandaff*, *The Convention of Cintra*, *Essays Upon Epitaphs*, *A Guide Through the District of the Lakes* or the Postscript to *Yarrow Revisited*. None the less, although all of these absences are to be regretted, this volume presents enough of the evidence for the reader to assess

Coleridge's judgement on Wordsworth that 'in imaginative power, he stands nearest of all modern writers to Shakespeare and Milton; and yet in a kind perfectly unborrowed and his own'.

CONTENTS

Introduction   xiii

Acknowledgements   xxvi

Chronology   xxvii

Note on the Text   xxx

POETRY

An Evening Walk	1
Salisbury Plain	13
Old Man Travelling	29
Lines left upon a Seat in a Yew-tree	29
The Ruined Cottage	31
[A Night-Piece]	44
[The Discharged Soldier]	45
The Old Cumberland Beggar	49
Lines Written at a Small Distance from my House	54
Goody Blake and Harry Gill	56
The Thorn	59
'A whirl-blast from behind the hill'	66
The Idiot Boy	67
Lines written in Early Spring	80
Anecdote for Fathers	81
We Are Seven	83
Simon Lee, the Old Huntsman	85
The Last of the Flock	88
Peter Bell	91
Expostulation and Reply	129
The Tables Turned	130
Lines written a few miles above Tintern Abbey	131
To a Sexton	136
'If Nature, for a favorite Child'	137
The Fountain	138
The Two April Mornings	140

[Five Elegies]
   'Could I the priest's consent have gained'   142
   'Just as the blowing thorn began'   143
   Elegy   144
   'Carved, Mathew, with a master's skill'   145
   Dirge   146
'A slumber did my spirit seal'   147
Song ('She dwelt among th' untrodden ways')   147
'Strange fits of passion I have known'   148
Lucy Gray   149
A Poet's Epitaph   151
Nutting   153
'Three years she grew in sun and shower'   154
The Brothers   155
Hart-Leap Well   168
Home at Grasmere   174
Poems on the Naming of Places   199
   'It was an April Morning: fresh and clear'   199
   To Joanna   201
   'There is an Eminence,—of these our hills'   203
   'A narrow girdle of rough stones and crags'   203
   To M.H.   205
Rural Architecture   206
The Childless Father   207
Inscription: For the Spot where the Hermitage stood   208
''Tis said, that some have died for love'   208
Lines: Written with a Slate-pencil   210
The Oak and the Broom   211
The Waterfall and the Eglantine   214
The Two Thieves   216
The Idle Shepherd-Boys   217
'When first I journeyed hither'   220
A Character   223
Michael   224
'I travelled among unknown Men'   237
Louisa   237
To a Sky-Lark   238

The Sparrow's Nest   239
The Sailor's Mother   239
Alice Fell   241
Beggars   243
To a Butterfly ('Stay near me')   244
To the Cuckoo   245
'My heart leaps up when I behold'   246
To H.C., Six Years Old   246
'Among all lovely things my Love had been'   247
Written in March   248
The Green Linnet   248
To the Daisy ('In youth')   250
To the Daisy ('With little here')   252
To the Same Flower ('Bright Flower')   253
To a Butterfly ('I've watched you')   254
'These chairs they have no words to utter'   255
The Tinker   256
To the Small Celandine   257
To the Same Flower ('Pleasures newly found')   259
Resolution and Independence   260
Travelling   265
'Within our happy Castle there dwelt one'   265
'I grieved for Buonaparte'   267
On the Extinction of the Venetian Republic   268
'How sweet it is, when mother Fancy rocks'   268
'I am not One who much or oft delight'   269
'The world is too much with us'   270
To the Memory of Raisley Calvert   271
'Where lies the Land to which yon Ship must go?'   271
'With Ships the sea was sprinkled far and nigh'   272
'It is no Spirit who from Heaven hath flown'   272
'Methought I saw the footsteps of a throne'   273
'Are souls then nothing?'   273
' "Beloved Vale!" I said, "when I shall con" '   274
'Brook, that hast been my solace days and weeks'   274
'Dear Native Brooks your ways have I pursued'   275
'England! the time is come when thou shouldst wean'   275

'Great Men have been among us'   276
'It is not to be thought of that the Flood'   276
'There is a bondage which is worse to bear'   277
'When I have borne in memory what has tamed'   277
'Farewell, thou little Nook of mountain ground'   278
'The Sun has long been set'   280
Calais, August, 1802   280
Composed by the Sea-Side, near Calais   281
'It is a beauteous Evening, calm and free'   281
To Toussaint L'Ouverture   282
To a Friend, Composed near Calais   282
Calais, August 15th, 1802   283
September 1st, 1802   283
Composed in the Valley, near Dover   284
September, 1802   284
Composed Upon Westminster Bridge   285
Written in London, September, 1802   285
London, 1802   286
'Nuns fret not at their Convent's narrow room'   286
Composed after a Journey across the Hamilton Hills   287
'These words were uttered in a pensive mood'   287
The Small Celandine   288
Sonnet. September 25th, 1803   289
To the Men of Kent   289
Anticipation. October, 1803   290
Yarrow Unvisited   290
'She was a Phantom of delight'   292
October, 1803 ('One might believe')   293
October, 1803 ('When, looking on')   294
October, 1803 ('These times')   294
October, 1803 ('Six thousand Veterans')   295
Ode to Duty   295
Ode ('There was a time')   297
'Who fancied what a pretty sight'   303
'I wandered lonely as a Cloud'   303
The Matron of Jedborough and Her Husband   304
To the River Duddon   306

To the Daisy ('Sweet Flower!')   307
'I only looked for pain and grief'   308
'Distressful gift! this Book receives'   311
Glen-Almain   312
Stepping Westward   313
Rob Roy's Grave   314
Address to the Sons of Burns   318
The Solitary Reaper   319
Character of the Happy Warrior   320
Star Gazers   322
Power of Music   323
'By their floating Mill'   325
Elegiac Stanzas   326
'Yes! full surely 'twas the Echo'   328
Lines, Composed at Grasmere   329
A Complaint   330
Thought of a Briton on the Subjugation of Switzerland   330
November, 1806   331
'O Nightingale! thou surely art'   331
Gipsies   332
St Paul's   332
Characteristics of a Child three Years old   333
'Surprized by joy—impatient as the Wind'   334
Yew-Trees   334
Yarrow Visited   335
Composed at Cora Linn   338
To B. R. Haydon, Esq.   340
November 1, 1815   340
'While not a leaf seems faded'   341
Ode.—1817   341
Ode. The Pass of Kirkstone   345
Ode. Composed Upon an Evening of Extraordinary Splendor
     and Beauty   347
Sequel to [Beggars]   350
The River Duddon: Conclusion   351
Bruges ('Bruges I saw')   352
Bruges ('The Spirit of Antiquity')   352

Mutability   353
To the Torrent at the Devil's Bridge   353
Composed Among the Ruins of a Castle   353
To — ('O dearer far')   354
To — ('Let other Bards')   354
'Once I could hail (howe'er serene the sky)'   355
'Scorn not the Sonnet'   356
Incident at Bruges   357
On the Power of Sound   358
Yarrow Revisited   365
On the Departure of Sir Walter Scott   368
'Calm is the fragrant air, and loth to lose'   369
Airey-Force Valley   369
Extempore Effusion Upon the Death of James Hogg   370
November, 1836   371
'I know an aged Man constrained to dwell'   372

The Prelude (1805)   375

PROSE

Advertisement to *Lyrical Ballads* (1798)   591
Note to *The Thorn* (1800)   593
Preface to *Lyrical Ballads* (1802)   595
Appendix to Preface to *Lyrical Ballads* (1802)   616
Letter to John Wilson (7 June 1802)   620
Preface to *Poems* (1815)   626
Essay, Supplementary to the Preface to *Poems* (1815)   640
A Letter to a Friend of Robert Burns (1816)   663

Appendix   676
Notes   682
Further Reading   741
Index of Titles and First Lines   744

INTRODUCTION

(i)

MANY attempts have been made to analyse Wordsworth's power: the first was made in 1799 by Wordsworth himself. The previous year had been rich in achievement. 'The Ruined Cottage', to Coleridge 'one of the most beautiful poems in the language',[1] had been completed. Poems such as 'Simon Lee' and 'Goody Blake and Harry Gill' had demonstrated Wordsworth's command of the dramatic-lyric form; *Peter Bell* and 'The Idiot Boy' had shown his capacity to sustain interest in narrative unseasoned by highly-wrought incidents. 'Tintern Abbey', a *confessio fidei* whose power Wordsworth was never to surpass, had moved Coleridge to believe that he 'possessed more of the genius of a great philosophic poet than any man I ever knew',[2] and plans for *The Recluse*, a philosophical poem to give 'pictures of Nature, Man, and Society'[3] had been laid. A great poet was entering his kingdom. 'Tintern Abbey' itself, however, is built on questions which pull as an undertow against the energy of the poem's affirmations and once Wordsworth began to reflect on the philosophic song that beckoned him hesitations such as, 'If this be but a vain belief . . .', were bound to lead to the more wide-ranging questioning which became the two-part *Prelude* of 1799.

This poem (not published in this selection but essentially present in the first two books of the 1805 *Prelude*)[4] is an attempt to explain to Coleridge—and to Wordsworth himself—'how the heart was framed | Of him thou lovest' and it culminates in a declaration of the greatest importance. At the end of the Second Part Wordsworth describes his perception of the unity of creation—'in all things | I saw one life, and felt that it was joy'—acknowledges that this faith might be 'error' but nonetheless goes on to make this claim:

[1] Recorded under 21 July 1832 in *Specimens of the Table Talk of the late Samuel Taylor Coleridge*, ed. H. N. Coleridge (1835).

[2] Ibid.

[3] W to J. W. Tobin, 6 March 1798. All future references to letters of W and C (Coleridge) will be given in the text. Full citation of the standard editions of the letters and other texts used will be found on p. 682. When the source of a quotation from, e.g. the Preface to *Lyrical Ballads* is clear from the text further detailed reference will not be given.

[4] The most important difference is that the 'spots of time' passage was part of the 1799 poem, before it was incorporated into *The Prelude* (1805), xi. 257–388. See *The Prelude* eds. Wordsworth, Abrams, Gill, and Parrish's edition, full citations p. 741.

> if in these times of fear
> This melancholy waste of hopes o'erthrown,
>
> .   .   .   .
>
> if, in this time
> Of dereliction and dismay, I yet
> Despair not of our nature, but retain
> A more than Roman confidence, a faith
> That fails not, in all sorrow my support,
> The blessing of my life, the gift is yours
> Ye mountains, thine O Nature. Thou hast fed
> My lofty speculations, and in thee
> For this uneasy heart of ours I find
> A never-failing principle of joy
> And purest passion.

In this affirmation, which is both a credo and a prayer of thanksgiving, the private life of William Wordsworth and the public world of Britain at war in the 1790s intermingle. Coleridge would have had no difficulty in understanding the link between them or why it was that as they both watched the 'hopes expire | Of a low dishonest decade' Wordsworth, like Auden in 'September 1, 1939', felt able to 'Show an affirming flame'.

Wordsworth was right to conclude the 1799 autobiography in this way, for the 1790s were the most active years of his life and they certainly shaped him as a poet. In a famous passage in *The Prelude*, iv. 319-45, Wordsworth pin-points in 'the sweetness of a common dawn' the moment at which he became 'A dedicated spirit' and the passage justly celebrates the splendour of the mountain scenery which witnessed the unspoken vows. 'Fair seed-time had my soul' begins another passage (i. 305), one of the many which depict the raptures of childhood in a Lake District no less beautiful than it is today, but more alive with people in farming, commerce, mining, quarrying and allied trades. Had Wordsworth remained there he might have continued to celebrate it in poems such as *An Evening Walk*, a masterly exercise in a familiar eighteenth-century genre. But 1790 saw Wordsworth travelling on foot across France, a year after the first Revolution, joyfully responding to the movement of the spirit of a whole people. He would not have used the words, but certainly would have echoed the sentiments of another writer, Anna Seward, the 'Swan of Lichfield': 'So France has dipt her lilies in the living streams of American freedom, and bids her sons be slaves no longer. In such a contest the vital sluices must be wastefully opened—but few English hearts . . . there are, that do not wish victory may sit upon the

swords that freedom has unsheathed.'[5] Succeeding years revealed what
follows the unsheathing of swords: the execution of the French King, the
Terror, war between England and France, the suspension of civil
liberties at home, when men were jailed or transported for speaking their
minds, soaring food prices, near famine amongst the rural poor. 'The
misery of the last four years', declared the *Analytical Review* in 1797, 'has
been greater than at any former period . . . if we except the momentary
rage of plague or of famine.'

Wordsworth's feelings during these 'times of fear' are recalled in Book
Ten of *The Prelude*, which is not just an account of a private or an exceptional anguish but a vivid reliving of the experiences of so many who had
been possessed by hope 'when Europe was rejoiced | France standing on
the top of golden hours | And human nature seeming born again' (vi.
352–4). The evidence of *The Prelude* clearly has to be treated with caution,
for in the composition of 1804–5 Wordsworth is shaping his earlier
experiences to a particular end, to the affirmation that beneath the
turmoil ran steady the stream of his true self. But his writings in the years
1793–6 and what we know of his life support *The Prelude*'s depiction of
this as a period when the 'ravage of this most unnatural strife' (x. 250)
between Britain and France and between Government and Radicals
drove Wordsworth to extremes. His passionate republican tract, *A Letter
to the Bishop of Llandaff*, was followed by 'Salisbury Plain' (printed in this
selection) in which contemporary authority is identified with the Druids
and their lust for human sacrifice. Nevertheless Wordsworth did not
welcome the idea of violent revolution. A series of letters to William
Mathews, a Cambridge friend, shows that Wordsworth thought that the
way to combat the 'infatuation, profligacy and extravagance of men in
power' was for the 'enlightened friend of mankind' to 'diffuse by every
method a knowledge of those rules of political justice, from which the
farther any government deviates the more effectually must it defeat the
object for which government was ordained' (8 June 1794). In 1795
Wordsworth frequently met William Godwin, whose great work *An
Enquiry concerning Political Justice* (1793) was clearly in Wordsworth's
mind as he wrote to Mathews. He mixed more widely in radical circles,
thought of entering the polemical fray with his own journal, translated
Juvenal and reworked 'Salisbury Plain' into a more complex dramatic

---

[5] 3 July 1789. *Letters of Anna Seward, Written between the Years 1784 and 1807* (1811).
Anna Seward (1747–1809) is a barometer of changing attitudes towards the
Revolution in France. By 1792 she is exclaiming 'What legions of fiends rise up in
Paris' and by 1794 inveighing against 'the increasing force of our internal miscreants,
whose dire ambition raises and stimulates the discontents of the lower classes'.

narrative called 'Adventures on Salisbury Plain', which highlights the effects of war and state tyranny on individuals. In 1795 too he sought out Coleridge and Southey, not just because they were poets but because of their spreading fame as political activists.

Much remains unclear about the latter stages of this period. In *The Prelude* Wordsworth compresses into one marvellously tormented passage (x. 805–940) what must have taken many months, the process in which he came to realize that for him political agitation and rationalist procedures of enquiry were not the way to Truth. What is clear is that his play *The Borderers*, written in 1796–7, reveals greater creative power than Wordsworth had yet displayed. The tragedy subjects what he saw as the essential tendency of rationalist thought, that identified most closely with Godwin, to the test of human feelings, to embodiment in dramatic relationships, and in doing so explores for the first time questions about man's moral nature which are to be the ground of all, not just of his greatest work.

In early June 1797 the Wordsworths were joined at Racedown by Coleridge who thrilled them, as he did everyone he met, by his talk. 'His conversation', Dorothy wrote, 'teems with soul, mind and spirit.' This meeting, and sharing of poetry—'The first thing that was read after he came was William's new poem 'The Ruined Cottage' with which he was much delighted; and after tea he repeated to us two acts and a half of his tragedy *Osorio*. The next morning William read his tragedy *The Borderers* . . .' (June 1797)—marked the beginning of the most fortunate confluence of minds in English literature. Throughout the 1790s Coleridge had responded more actively than Wordsworth to political events, even entering with Robert Southey into plans for an egalitarian society to be founded in America by a few like-minded idealists. After the collapse of that scheme he wrote, lectured, preached, drawing no line between religion and politics and bringing to bear on every subject the resources of a genuinely philosophic as well as a naturally poetic mind. Poems such as 'Religious Musings' and 'The Aeolian Harp', the lectures delivered in Bristol in 1795, the periodical *The Watchman*, with its motto 'That All may know the TRUTH | And that the TRUTH may make us FREE!!'—all testified to the passionate commitment of a poet and thinker who had absorbed current theories of mind, who was in touch with contemporary science and who saw the search for Truth as inextricable from the search to know God.[6] Personal attraction between him and

---

[6] See C's letters, the poetry ed. E. H. Coleridge (Oxford, 1912), *Lectures 1795 On Politics and Religion*, eds. Lewis Patton and Peter Mann (1971) and *The Watchman*, ed. Lewis Patton (1970). Useful introductions to C in this period are W. J. Bate, *Coleridge*

Wordsworth warmed to a love that, however tested by later misunder-standings, remained with both for their lifetimes.

To Coleridge, Wordsworth was 'a very great man—the only man to whom *at all times* and *in all modes of excellence* I feel myself inferior' (17 July 1797). To Wordsworth, Coleridge was always 'The rapt One, of the godlike forehead',[7] one of the two beings, he later declared, 'to whom my intellect is most indebted' (25 June 1832). It was a love that fused their minds during the *annus mirabilis* 1797-8 into a symbiotic creative power.[8] A phrase in one letter, for example (17 July 1797), shows how deeply Coleridge has been affected by Wordsworth's 'Yew-Tree Lines'. In another Coleridge declares that he has 'snapped my squeaking baby-trumpet of Sedition' and that 'I love fields & woods & mountains with almost a visionary fondness—and because I have found bene-volence & quietness growing within me as that fondness [has] increased, therefore I should wish to be the means of implanting it in others—& to destroy the bad passions not by combating them but by keeping them in inaction' (10 March 1798). Then to explain the associationist action which brings about this amelioration, Coleridge copies out Words-worth's lines, 'Not useless do I deem' (printed in the Appendix). The revisions to 'The Ruined Cottage' show how far Wordsworth's thought has developed under the stimulus of Coleridge's speculative conversa-tion, as does 'Tintern Abbey' when, to give only a detail, it echoes at a vital moment Coleridge's earlier use in 'Religious Musings' of the word 'interfused'. In summer 1798 Joseph Cottle was anxious to publish some of Wordsworth's longer poems, but Wordsworth resisted and it was a joint volume, *Lyrical Ballads*, which finally appeared.[9]

'The Ruined Cottage', 'Tintern Abbey', the blank verse in the Appen-dix and other less obviously ambitious poems in *Lyrical Ballads* embody

---

(1968); John Cornwell, *Coleridge, Poet and Revolutionary 1772–1804* (1973); Kelvin Everest, *Coleridge's Secret Ministry: The Context of the Conversation Poems 1795–1798* (1979). The advanced student should read Southey's early poems, in the early unrevised texts if possible, and see Geoffrey Carnall, *Southey and His Age: The Development of a Conservative Mind* (Oxford, 1960).

[7] The phrase is from the tribute to Coleridge in 'Extempore Effusion . . .' (1835). Occasioned by the death of James Hogg, this, the most moving of Wordsworth's later verse, is a lament for a whole generation of friends.

[8] For an invaluable account, see Thomas McFarland, 'The Symbiosis of Coleridge and Wordsworth', *Studies in Romanticism*, xi (1972), 263–303.

[9] The events which led to the publication of *Lyrical Ballads* are confusing. For the best unravelling see Mark L. Reed, 'Wordsworth, Coleridge, and the "Plan" of the *Lyrical Ballads*', *University of Toronto Quarterly*, xxxiv (1964–5), 238–53 and the introduction to Owen's edition of *Lyrical Ballads 1798*, listed under Further Reading.

the convictions which Wordsworth was struggling both to express in poetry and to live by. What were they? The philosophical verse beginning 'Not useless do I deem . . .' offers a sequential exposition: the universe is not mechanical and dead, but alive and vitally connected with the human mind; awakened consciousness leads to an awakened moral sense and must lead to communion with the divine. In the profoundest sense, love of nature leads to love of Man and awareness of God. Such philosophical verse, however, was not Wordsworth's real strength. The power of the other poems of 1797–8 is that they do not propose a chain of reasoning but draw the reader to share Wordsworth's thought through lyrical utterance and dramatic narrative which embody a sense of reverence for Man and nature. They everywhere assert the vital significance of feeling both as a bond between men and as a means of discovering truth and declare as in 'Tintern Abbey' the unity of the individual consciousness with the divine. Above all these poems declare by their very form as poetry Wordsworth's newly confident belief in poetry's special power to teach by incorporating 'itself with the blood & vital juices of our minds'[10] and by appealing to the imagination and to the 'grand elementary principle of pleasure, by which man knows, and feels, and lives, and moves'. Much in these poems, especially their emphasis on the inherent worth of simple men, can be related to the political and social ferment of the times. Hazlitt was not the only one to see that Wordsworth's poetry 'partakes of, and is carried along with, the revolutionary movement of our age . . . His Muse . . . is a levelling one'.[11] Much of the thought can be traced to eighteenth-century philosophy and psychology. The particular nature of many of the poems is determined by Wordsworth's quarrel with prevailing literary modes. But what made the achievement of 1797–8 so great and, when all the scholarly footnotes have been written, still a new beginning in English poetry, is that the poems of whatever kind embodied a coherent and unified vision of man and nature which had been tested and found firm by a man searching not only for poetry but for a basis to his life. Turbulent years of conflicting experience brought, finally, not the somnolent peace of a closed mind, but certain calm assurances. It is not surprising that Wordsworth should have ended this first period with thanks for his 'more than Roman confidence' and hymns of praise to the Power that gave him 'A never-failing principle of joy | And purest passion'.

[10] From W's *Essay on Morals* (Prose, i. 103), in which he takes as impotent 'such books as Mr Godwyn's, Mr Paley's, & those of the whole tribe of authors of that class'.

[11] William Hazlitt, 'Mr Wordsworth', in *The Spirit of the Age* (1825).

(ii)

When Wordsworth entered Dove Cottage in December 1799 he began a new phase of life which was to be, in essentials, the pattern until he died. Financial uncertainty remained, but the years of wandering were over. Grasmere and then nearby Rydal was to be his home, and domestic life with an extended family which included Dorothy Wordsworth and his wife's sister Sara, was to be the secure personal base on which his creative life rested. Greater shocks than most families have to suffer tested them: the overwhelming blow of John Wordsworth's death by shipwreck in 1805; the deaths of two infant children in 1812; the bitter breach with Coleridge in 1810–12; the recurrent mental illness in later life of Dorothy; the death in 1847 of the beloved daughter named after the beloved sister. But it has always been clear from Dorothy's Journal and from Wordsworth's recorded tributes how strong the Dove Cottage community was, and the recent discovery of the letters which passed between William and Mary in 1810–12 has provided further evidence of the power of the love that united them.

Crossing the threshold of Dove Cottage marked a new phase in Wordsworth's creative life as well. From one point of view 1800–15 might be called the years of *The Recluse*. This philosophical poem was conceived in 1798. Wordsworth's announcement on 6 March that he has already 'written 1300 lines of a poem in which I contrive to convey most of the knowledge of which I am possessed. My object is to give pictures of Nature, Man, and Society. Indeed I know not any thing which will not come within the scope of my plan', suggests both the speed with which he embraced the idea of a comprehensive philosophic work and the grandeur of the conception which was, undoubtedly, Coleridge's. In later life he recalled the 'plan laid out, and, I believe, partly suggested by me', that 'Wordsworth should assume the station of a man in mental repose, one whose principles were made up, and so prepared to deliver upon authority a system of philosophy'. [12]

Wordsworth always suspected and resisted *systems* of any sort, however, and it is not surprising that after the summer at Alfoxden sustained composition towards *The Recluse* eluded him. First came the 1799 autobiographical poem—welcomed by Coleridge to whom it was addressed, but only if it were to be 'the tail-piece of "The Recluse!", for of nothing but "The Recluse" can I hear patiently' (21 October 1799). Work on *Home at Grasmere* in 1800 included the lines 'On Man, on

---

[12] *Table Talk*, 21 July 1832. C's fascinating recollection, which is too long to quote here, is reprinted in *PW*, v. 364.

Nature, and on human Life', which give substance to what was only vague ambition in March 1798, 'I know not any thing that will not come within the scope of my plan'. But *Home at Grasmere* proved a false dawn at that time, as did extensive revision to 'The Ruined Cottage' and 'The Pedlar'. *The Prelude* itself reveals the poet's consciousness of a greater mission yet to be accomplished. In the opening section this consciousness is an 'awful burthen' from which the poet takes refuge, beguiling himself 'with trust | That mellower years will bring a riper mind | And clearer insight' (i. 235–8). At the end of the poem it has become a beacon, beckoning both Wordsworth and Coleridge, 'Prophets of Nature', to the fulfilment of their vocation. Only after *The Prelude* was completed did work on *The Recluse* take first place. But when *The Excursion* (the only part of *The Recluse* to be published) appeared in 1814 it fell far short of achieving what had been hoped for in 1798. The Preface announced the design of the whole work for the first time and offered the lines 'On Man, on Nature, and on human Life' as a 'kind of *Prospectus* of the design and scope of the whole Poem', but the poem only really lives in passages which Wordsworth had retrieved from poetry written long before in 1798. Though to Keats *The Excursion* was one of the 'three things to rejoice at in this Age', it disappointed Coleridge and remained for Wordsworth a life-long reminder of unrealized ambition.[13]

Looked at from another point of view, however, and judged not by what Coleridge wanted Wordsworth to achieve but on what he actually did achieve, the years 1800–15 are years of triumph. By 1815 the poet who had echoed in 1800 Milton's 'Fit audience let me find though few' had declared his purpose, won an audience, and demonstrated in his own way the rightness of Coleridge's perception that he was 'a thinking feeling Philosopher habitually—that your Poetry was your Philosophy under the action of strong winds of Feeling—a sea rolling high' (23 July 1803).

The period opens and closes with critical and theoretical prose (all printed in this selection). The 1798 *Lyrical Ballads* had been published anonymously. In 1800 Wordsworth acknowledged authorship of the bulk of the poems and prefaced the greatly expanded second edition with his first defence of his art. He touches on both the intention to trace 'the primary laws of our nature' and on the peculiarities of the medium, poetry in which 'the feeling therein developed gives importance to the

[13] References to *The Recluse* in progress crop up long after the project had in reality died. In November 1829, for example, Dora Wordsworth wrote of their mixed feelings about *On the Power of Sound*: 'We all think there is a grandeur in this Poem but it ought to have been in the "Recluse" . . .'

action and situation and not the action and situation to the feeling'. The account given of how these poems originate and how they can work to ameliorate a reader's understanding and affections raises so many issues, which Coleridge certainly wanted clarified, that it was inevitable that Wordsworth would have to pursue them. For the next edition of 1802 he made considerable additions, reiterating and heightening the claims made for poetry as a mode of Truth and introducing a discussion of 'What is a Poet?' which defines him as both 'a man speaking to men' and as someone out of the ordinary, 'endued with more lively sensibility, more enthusiasm and tenderness'. Both of these Prefaces caused trouble. It was not that they were startlingly original. As W. J. B. Owen and others have shown, many of the ideas in them were current in eighteenth-century aesthetics. But never before had they been uttered with such confidence or supported by such a body of verse that evidently took itself seriously. Critics sensed a conspiracy against canons of taste in these manifestos and knew that they were right when *Poems in Two Volumes* appeared in 1807. But neither the scorn which greeted this collection nor the criticisms of friends such as Lamb and Coleridge shook Wordsworth in his belief that his poetry was defensible on principled grounds and that it ought to be defended. In 1815 he therefore prefaced his first Collected Edition with an entirely new justification both of his work and of the manner in which he intended to present it, and in a supplementary essay challenged his critics with the declaration: 'Of genius, in the fine arts, the only infallible sign is the widening the sphere of human sensibility, for the delight, honour and benefit of human nature. Genius is the introduction of a new element into the intellectual universe . . .'

Framed by these theoretical writings is the poetry. In narratives such as 'Michael' and 'The Brothers' Wordsworth justified his claim to be the celebrant of 'the great and simple affections of our nature'. Focusing in a particular manner on incidents of common life, the *Lyrical Ballads* as a whole seek to rid them of the condescension, sentimentality and sensationalism found in many eighteenth-century treatments of the rural poor and show in what way Wordsworth interpreted the task he outlined to John Wilson: 'You have given me praise for having reflected faithfully in my poems the feelings of human nature. I would fain hope that I have done so. But a great Poet ought to do more than this[,] he ought to a certain degree to rectify men's feelings, to give them new compositions of feeling, to render them more sane pure and permanent . . . He ought to travel before men occasionally as well as at their sides' (7 June 1802). The lyrical poems published in 1807 are Wordsworth's most challenging demonstration that a poet is a man 'who rejoices more than other men in the spirit of life that is in him; delighting to contemplate similar volitions and passions as manifested in the goings-on of the Universe, and habitually impelled to create them where he does not find them'. Coleridge hesitated, troubled by their 'daring Humbleness of Language & Versification, and a strict adherence to matter of fact' (29 July 1802), and reviewers in 1807 were outraged by the impertinence of a poet who would publish addresses to daisies and butterflies. But these lyrics are central to Wordsworth's achievement, continuing testimony to his perception of 'joy in widest commonalty spread'. The poems of the Scotch Tour and the eloquent political sonnets reveal the intensity with which Wordsworth fused life and art. Literature, especially Milton's poetry, colours his reading of contemporary politics: daily life, a chance remark, a meeting on the road, call forth poetry.

Most important of all, perhaps, these are the years of 'Resolution and Independence', 'Ode: Intimations of Immortality', 'Ode to Duty', 'Elegiac Stanzas . . . Peele Castle', and *The Prelude*. In this series of poems—closely linked in origin to Coleridge's 'Dejection: An Ode'—Wordsworth explores both as private man and as Poet the dark passages of anxiety, self-doubt, and imaginative weakening. Here the anguish of the Romantic poet is expressed for the first time, the solitariness of the knowledge 'By our own spirits are we deified'. Here too are voiced the fears of a poet no more immune than other men to the shocks of ageing and loss:

> The days gone by
> Come back upon me from the dawn almost
> Of life; the hiding-places of my power
> Seem open, I approach, and then they close;
> I see by glimpses now, when age comes on
> May scarcely see at all; and I would give
> While yet we may, as far as words can give,
> A substance and a life to what I feel . . .

> (*Prelude*, xi. 333–40)

But against the profound sadness of the ending of the 'Ode: Intimations', whose last word is 'tears', or of 'Elegiac Stanzas', 'Not without hope we suffer and we mourn', must be placed the triumphant close of *The Prelude*, with its continuing re-affirmation of the mystery and strength of

> the mind of man . . .
> A thousand times more beautiful than the earth
> On which he dwells . . .

In beauty exalted, as it is itself
Of substance and of fabric more divine.

The Prelude explicitly traces the growth of the poet's mind from birth to that never-to-be-forgotten summer of 1798 when 'on Quantock's grassy hills | Far ranging, and among the sylvan coombs' Wordsworth and Coleridge had 'Together wantoned in wild poesy' (xiii. 393–4, 414). But it is also implicitly a record of Wordsworth's intellectual journey between 1799 and 1805. In its growth from two, to five, to eight and finally to thirteen books it expands to include developing ideas about the nature and function of the creative imagination and about the powers and limitations of language, and becomes the triumphant embodiment of Wordsworth's 'last and favourite aspiration ... some philosophic song | Of truth that cherishes our daily life' (i. 229–31). It was not *The Recluse* and so it remained unpublished in Wordsworth's lifetime, always anticipating the never-to-be-written work, but it was, as M. H. Abrams has said, a poem of 'radical novelty',[14] the first truly great achievement of a new era in English poetry.

(iii)

1815 was the year of Waterloo. 1851, the year after Wordsworth's death and the year in which the official biography was published, saw also the opening by Queen Victoria of the Great Exhibition. Those dates and events give some indication of the national transformation Wordsworth lived through. The final defeat of Napoleon established Britain as the most powerful and stable European nation. The Great Exhibition demonstrated to an admiring world the industrial fruits of that stability and power. In the years between, the pace of industrial growth had quickened. Cities grew—the population of Manchester, for example, increased by 45 per cent between 1821–31—and presented marvels for the many who undertook the new version of the tour in search of the sublime. For such travellers railways shortened distance, reaching in Wordsworth's lifetime even into the Lake District itself and making it a convenient second home for many notable figures whose public life was elsewhere. There was a quickening of religious life and a hesitant movement towards reform, signalled by Catholic emancipation in 1829 and electoral reform in 1832. The increasingly urgent demands of the working classes, allied to new political groupings, threatened (or seemed to threaten) the structure of society, raising in many older people

14 M. H. Abrams, *Natural Supernaturalism* (1971), 74.

memories of the French Revolution. When Carlyle called the workhouses, the symbols of the New Poor Law, 'Bastilles' the effect was not lost on anyone with memory or imagination.

These were important years of change in the literary market-place as well. In 1825 Hazlitt published a series of character studies, *The Spirit of the Age*. In 1844 Richard Horne emulated it with his *A New Spirit of the Age*. Wordsworth appears in both, but in what different company. Hazlitt opens with Bentham and includes only one novelist, Scott. Horne opens with Dickens and includes G. P. R. James, Marryat, Mrs Trollope, Bulwer Lytton, Ainsworth. A new readership was demanding prose fiction. When Clough declared in 1853 that, faced with poetry 'there is no question . . . people much prefer *Vanity Fair* and *Bleak House*',[15] he was lamenting a process which had been taking place for fully thirty years. As Wordsworth indignantly reported in 1842, 'Dr Arnold told me that his lads seemed to care for nothing but Bozzy's [Dickens's] next number . . .' (1 April).

Wordsworth was not untouched by all of these changes. He feared the growth of radical influence in Parliament and campaigned forcefully in the Tory interest in the General Election of 1818. He was deeply troubled by Catholic emancipation and by the reform agitation of the 1830s and 1840s. In the 'Prelude' to *Poems, Chiefly of Early and Late Years*, published in 1842 in the worst year of the 'hungry forties', Wordsworth declares that his purpose is to awaken 'Kindly emotion tending to console | And reconcile' at a time 'When unforeseen distress spreads far and wide | Among a People mournfully cast down . . .'. He feared, above all, the spread of utilitarian ideas in social and educational matters, and in a very striking 'Postscript' to 'Yarrow Revisited' (1835) joined with the young Dickens of *Oliver Twist* in assault on the New Poor Law. Like Coleridge he embraced the Anglican Church, not like him as a result of years of thought and enquiry, but as a natural return to an institution whose stability as a repository of wisdom and as a formal expression of man's unchanging needs seemed more and more attractive.

Throughout these years, of course, Wordsworth's main concern was his writing. He continued to produce new poems and to husband the old. As one Collected Edition followed another he laboured with obsessive attention to detail to perfect his life's work. Some revision prepared for the press for the first time poems written long before, such as *Peter Bell* (1798, published 1819), *The Waggoner* (1806, published 1819), *The Borderers* and 'Guilt and Sorrow' (1796–7 and 1793–5, published 1842).

15 In a review of contemporary verse. See Isobel Armstrong, ed. *Victorian Scrutinies: Reviews of Poetry 1830–1870* (1972), 154.

Other revisions markedly changed poems such as *The Excursion* and (unbeknown to the public because unpublished) *The Prelude*. The new work reflects Wordsworth's travels abroad and in Scotland, records public events and draws on Wordsworth's growing interest in the history of his country's religious life. Some of the poems are of the highest quality, such as the conclusion to 'The River Duddon' sonnet sequence or the lament for dead friends, 'Extempore Effusion Upon the Death of James Hogg', or the farewell 'On the Departure of Sir Walter Scott'. In some the inherent poignancy of the subject matter is intensified by Wordsworth's recollection of his own earlier, more powerful verse—for example, the Yarrow poems, the 'Sequel to [Beggars]' and the very fine companion to 'Ode: Intimations', the 'Ode. Composed Upon an Evening of Extraordinary Splendor and Beauty'. The last poem in this selection, 'I know an aged man', recalls 'The Old Cumberland Beggar' and reminds us that on some fundamental matters Wordsworth's beliefs did not change.

These poems are all examples of the poetic power which remained to Wordsworth when some experience touched him deeply, but they are drawn from a mass of undistinguished verse. Faced with this fact most lovers of Wordsworth become uncertain or defensive. Some wonder wistfully what would have become of Shelley or Keats had they outlived the first fine careless rapture. Others point out that much of Wordsworth's later verse is at least as good as Tennyson's or Browning's. Some find in Wordsworth's political move to the right and in his more orthodox religious position the reason for his poetic decline, although the examples of Yeats and Eliot suggest that right-wing views and Christianity are not in themselves a blight on imagination. The most persuasive point, in poems such as 'Resolution and Independence', the 'Ode: Intimations', and *The Prelude*, to Wordsworth's own premonition of the time when the glory of Imagination might fade before the 'light of common day'.

What is clear is that, in one sense, the years of Wordsworth's decline do not matter, for a split had inevitably occurred between the William Wordsworth of Rydal Mount and the poet who, like Tennyson's Ulysses, had 'become a name'. The ageing poet who campaigned for the Tory cause was certainly, in Browning's phrase, 'The Lost Leader'. Keats visited him in 1818 only to find that he was out electioneering for the greatest landowner in the district. Byron scorched him in the Preface to the opening cantos of *Don Juan* for selling himself to Lord Lonsdale. From Shelley, Wordsworth's defection from the cause of 'truth and liberty' wrung an eloquent sonnet which concludes, 'thou leavest me to grieve, | Thus having been, that thou shouldst cease to be'. But none of these poets was untouched by what Wordsworth had already achieved. In his own lifetime the writings up to 1815 became the Wordsworth who mattered, for it was their power which influenced first these younger Romantics and then the next generation of early Victorian writers. By 1838 Elizabeth Gaskell is quoting from 'The Old Cumberland Beggar' to support her own contention that 'the beauty and poetry of many of the common things and daily events of life in its humblest aspect does not seem to me sufficiently appreciated'.[16] In 1841 John Sterling recommended Wordsworth's poetry as a medicine for the 'dry, hard spirit' of contemporary ideologies, directly anticipating *Hard Times*, whose author alluded to 'The world is too much with us' as the novel was germinating in his mind.[17] By 1831 Wordsworth's poems were being used in schools. They influenced Tennyson and more profoundly Arnold and George Eliot. They significantly affected Emerson and Thoreau and were enjoyed by a wider American audience as well, many of whom, including Emerson, made the pilgrimage to Rydal Mount. In his 'Reply to "Mathetes"' (1809–10) Wordsworth had written of the choice to be made between the allurements of the World and the demands of Truth. Pursuit of the latter, he said, would involve 'solitary and unremitting labour, a life of entire neglect perhaps, or assuredly a life exposed to scorn, insult, persecution, and hatred; but cheared by encouragement from a grateful few, by applauding Conscience, and by a prophetic anticipation, perhaps of fame—a late though lasting consequence'. By 1850 he had long outfaced the scorn. More important, he had lived to see the 'grateful few' become the many, amongst them some of the greatest intellects of the century.

Acknowledgements

I am deeply indebted to many scholars and especially to the editors of the Cornell Wordsworth series not just for scholarly assistance, but for friendship and encouragement over many years. The Trustees of Dove Cottage have been most helpful in allowing me access to manuscripts and granting permission to publish. I am above all grateful to Jonathan Wordsworth of St Catherine's College, Oxford, who was my first tutor and has since been my best Wordsworthian guide.

[16] 18 August 1838. *The Letters of Mrs Gaskell*, eds. J. A. V. Chapple and Arthur Pollard (Manchester, 1966), 33.

[17] See Horace N. Pym, ed. *Memories of old Friends: Journals of Caroline Fox* (1882), 121. Dickens's letter to W. H. Wills, 27 July 1853.

CHRONOLOGY

1770   W born 7 April at Cockermouth.

1771   Dorothy Wordsworth (DW) born 25 September at Cockermouth.

1778   Mother, Ann Wordsworth, dies c.8 March.

1779   W enters Hawkshead Grammar School, lodging with Hugh and Ann Tyson.

1783   Father, John Wordsworth, dies 30 December.

1785–6   First surviving verse, 'Lines Written as a School Exercise at Hawkshead' (1785) and more sustained composition towards 'The Vale of Esthwaite', not published by W.

1787   W's first published poem, 'Sonnet, on Seeing Miss Helen Maria Williams Weep at a Tale of Distress' appears in *The European Magazine* in March. October: W enters St John's College, Cambridge.

1788–9   Composition of 'An Evening Walk', published 1793. Storming of the Bastille, 14 July 1789.

1790   Walking tour in France and Switzerland with Robert Jones, July–October. Edmund Burke's *Reflections on the Revolution in France* published.

1791–2   W in London. In November 1791 returns to France and sees Revolutionary fervour in Paris. Is influenced by Michel Beaupuy. Love affair with Annette Vallon and birth of their daughter, Caroline, 15 December 1792. Composes *Descriptive Sketches*, published 1793. Returns to England to seek a livelihood.

1793   Louis XVI executed in January. War declared between England and France in February. W feels an outcast in his own country. Writes, but does not publish, a seditious *Letter to the Bishop of Llandaff* and after wandering penniless across Salisbury Plain into Wales composes 'Salisbury Plain'. Sees Tintern Abbey. William Godwin's *Political Justice* published, as Government repression of dissent intensifies.

1794   W reunited with DW in stay at Windy Brow, Keswick. In August–September stays at Rampside and sees Peele Castle. Nurses Raisley Calvert, who leaves W £900 on his death in January 1795. Execution of Robespierre 28 July.

1795   C lectures in Bristol on politics and religion. W a familiar figure in radical circles in London in spring and summer and regularly visits Godwin. Meets C and Southey in Bristol in August. Settles with DW at Racedown in Dorset and rewrites 'Salisbury Plain'.

1797   Completes play, *The Borderers* and moves to Alfoxden to be nearer C, with whom period of greatest intimacy begins. First version of 'The Ruined Cottage' and plans for joint composition with C.

1798   The *annus mirabilis*. W completes 'The Ruined Cottage' and composes the bulk of the verse published anonymously in September as *Lyrical Ballads*. Plans for *The Recluse* first mentioned. W, DW, and C go to Germany and over winter W writes autobiographical verse, the foundation of *The Prelude*.

1799   By end April W back in England. Move into Dove Cottage, Grasmere in December.

1800   Begins *Home at Grasmere* and probably composes lines printed in 1814 as a 'Prospectus' to *The Recluse*. Works on poems for second edition of *Lyrical Ballads*, published January 1801, and writes *Preface*.

1802   Much lyrical poetry composed. Publication in April of further edition of *Lyrical Ballads*, with revised *Preface*. Peace of Amiens enables W's to visit Annette and Caroline in August. W marries Mary Hutchinson (b. 1770, d. 1859) 4 October.

1803   War begins again and fear of invasion grows. Birth of first son, John. W, DW, and C tour Scotland from mid-August. The Ws meet Sir Walter Scott 17 September. C ill and planning to leave for better climate.

1804   Much composition, especially on *The Prelude*, enlarged after March from planned five-book structure. 'Ode to Duty' and completion of 'Ode: Intimations of Immortality'. C sails to Malta. 18 May: Napoleon crowned Emperor.

1805   5–6 February: John Wordsworth (b. 1772), Captain of the *Earl of Abergavenny*, drowned. W circle very deeply affected. W completes *The Prelude*.

1806–7 Visits London. Sees Sir George Beaumont's picture of Peele Castle in a storm. Ws spend winter in a Beaumont house at Coleorton, Leicestershire. C at last returns, much changed by ill-health. W reads *The Prelude* to him. *Poems in Two Volumes* published in 1807 and ridiculed in reviews. W composes 'The White Doe of Rylstone', but does not publish it till 1815.

1808–9 Ws leave Dove Cottage for larger house in Grasmere, Allan Bank. Publishes, 1809, *The Convention of Cintra*.

1810   Son, William, born 12 May. Misunderstanding leads to breach with C—healed in 1812. First version of *Guide to the Lakes* published as anonymous Preface to Joseph Wilkinson's *Select Views in Cumberland, Westmorland and Lancashire*.

1811–12 Deaths of Children, Thomas (b. 1806) and Catherine (b. 1808). Ws move from Allan Bank to Rectory, Grasmere.

1813   Becomes Distributor of Stamps for Westmorland, a post in the revenue service. Moves to Rydal Mount, home for the rest of his life. Completes *The Excursion*.

1814   *The Excursion* published, prefaced by an account of the plan for *The Recluse*. Further attack by reviewers. Tour of Scotland, including a visit to the Yarrow.

1815–20   First Collected Edition of Poems published, with Preface, in 1815. The argument and classification advanced here spurs C to complete his own theoretical statement, *Biographia Literaria*, published 1817. 'The White Doe of Rylstone' also published in 1815. W issues a *Letter to a Friend of Robert Burns*, 1816, and in 1819 *The Waggoner* and *Peter Bell*, written in 1806 and 1798 respectively. W moves more widely in London circles and meets Keats in 1817. For the General Election of 1818 W campaigned hard in the Tory interest to the distress of many admirers.

1820–8   Publishes *The River Duddon* sonnet sequence in 1820. Tours Europe and revisits places last seen in 1790. Publishes in 1822 *Memorials of a Tour on the Continent, 1820* and *Ecclesiastical Sketches*. Enlarged Collected Editions published 1820 and 1827. Tours the Rhine with C and much loved daughter Dora (b. 1804).

1829–35   Catholic emancipation issue greatly troubles W. Tours Scotland again September–October 1831 and sees Sir Walter Scott (d. 1832) for last time. Further Collected Edition 1832. C dies 25 July 1834. *Yarrow Revisited* published 1835, with important Postscript.

1836–43   Further Collected Edition, revised as always, 1836. Tours France and Italy 1837. Sonnets gathered into one volume in 1838. In 1839 W revises *The Prelude* for the last time. Poems written in youth (notably *The Borderers* and 'Salisbury Plain') revised for publication in *Poems, Chiefly of Early and Late Years*, 1842. Resigns Stamp distributorship in 1842 and becomes Poet Laureate on Southey's death in 1843. Dictates Fenwick Notes. W now a widely celebrated figure, receiving honorary degrees from Durham and Oxford. Steady increase in American reputation.

1844–50   Supervises with great care one-volume Collected Edition of 1845 and the final edition in six volumes of 1849–50. W deeply stricken by the death of Dora, 9 July 1847. W dies 23 April 1850. *The Prelude* published in July by his wife and executors.

NOTE ON THE TEXT

'A CORRECT text is the first object of an editor,' Wordsworth declared to Sir Walter Scott (7 November 1805), and he is clearly right. Deciding on a 'correct text' and an order of presentation for Wordsworth's own poems, however, is not a straightforward matter. I have discussed the issues at length in 'Wordsworth's Poems: The Question of Text', *Review of English Studies*, NS xxxiv (1983), 172–90 and can only outline them here.

During his long writing life Wordsworth published a great deal: between 1793 and 1849–50 fifteen new volumes of verse (excluding from consideration reprint editions, selections and pamphlets), and from 1815 nine collected editions (again excluding reprints, American and other unauthorized editions). Each new collection contained fresh verse added to the canon and presented Wordsworth's latest revision of the old. Over revision the poet expended enormous labour and vigilance and the labour did not end until his death. The Collected Edition of 1849–50 must, therefore, be regarded as the poet's final authorized text, and Wordsworth's view of such texts were stated firmly to Alexander Dyce: 'You know what importance I attach to following strictly the last copy text of an author' (*c.*19 April, 1830).

For the reader interested in the development of Wordsworth's art, however, this last edition is most unsatisfactory. Many poems have been considerably revised from their first published state, altered moreover not in one creative burst of revision, but at various times throughout Wordsworth's lifetime. Some poems which were not published soon after composition, such as 'Salisbury Plain', only appear in a text which fundamentally changes the original conception. Others, such as 'The Ruined Cottage' or the elegies on John Wordsworth, are incorporated into other works or dismembered to make new ones. Some poems which were published are excised from the canon, while others, much excellent poetry which includes *The Prelude*, were not published by Wordsworth at all. The 1849–50 edition might have canonical status from some bibliographical points of view, but it does not present all of the poetry, nor the poems as they appeared to Wordsworth's first readers.

There is a further objection to the last authorized edition, namely that its organization deliberately prevents a chronological reading. From 1815 onwards Wordsworth arranged his poems in groupings designed to 'assist the attentive Reader in perceiving their connection with each other', as he explained in the *Preface*. New categories were added after *Poems* (1815) and poems were moved from one to another, but overall this remained Wordsworth's preferred arrangement. What determines the relation of poems within his classification is not chronology of composition, but the powers of mind predominant in their creation, or relationship of subject-matter.

In the belief that a chronological presentation can best reveal the growth of the poet's mind (the subject, after all, of his greatest poem, *The Prelude*) and the unfolding of his imagination, this volume is ordered according to date of composition. It follows—and here I break with all of the editorial pioneers, Dowden, Knight, Hutchinson, De Selincourt, Darbishire—that one *must* print a text which comes as close as possible to the state of a poem when it was first completed. To place a poem under 1795 in a text encrusted with the revisions of perhaps forty years—the practice of the current Penguin edition—is, to say the least, confusing.

The decision to break with the poet's wishes both as to text and arrangement means that for the majority of the poems I have taken the text of the first appearance in a Wordsworth volume, i.e. not in a newspaper or magazine. When a significant time elapsed between the completion of a poem and its publication I have returned to the manuscript text. *Peter Bell* (1798), for example, is taken from the earliest completed version and not from the much revised first edition of 1819. For poems which Wordsworth did not publish at all, a category which includes *Home at Grasmere* and *The Prelude*, my text is similarly drawn from the first completed manuscript. The source of a text is always indicated in the notes, either by reference to the date of first publication or to a manuscript. Obvious printing errors have been silently corrected. Ampersands and 'd have been expanded, but Wordsworth's spelling has been retained. The punctuation of published texts has only been altered when absolutely necessary and in texts taken from manuscript I have punctuated lightly, trying to follow my source wherever possible. [   ] indicates a word missing in the manuscript; [word] indicates material supplied by the editor.

The date of composition for many of the poems can be established quite accurately. Some, on the other hand—'Yew-Trees' or *Home at Grasmere* for example—pose problems, the major one being that surviving manuscripts are not contemporaneous with what seems a likely date for first composition. In such cases I have established the text on the principles already outlined and placed it in the chronological order, drawing attention to the conflicting evidence in the notes. I have relied heavily and with immense gratitude on the scholarship of Mark L. Reed,

Jonathan Wordsworth and the editors of the individual volumes in the Cornell Wordsworth series.

The Prelude has been printed outside the chronological sequence to emphasize the fact that its composition spanned 1799–1805, Wordsworth's greatest years. The text is that of the first completed thirteen-book version of 1805, but to place it under 1805 would have been as misleading as to place *The Prelude* under 1799 or 1803–4. In this edition it stands apart, but it is, of course, closely related to all of the poems in the chronological sequence 1799–1805.

The degree sign (°) indicates a note at the end of the book. More general notes and headnotes are not cued.

An Evening Walk

AN EVENING WALK. AN EPISTLE; IN VERSE. ADDRESSED TO A YOUNG LADY,
FROM THE LAKES OF THE NORTH OF ENGLAND.

ARGUMENT

General Sketch of the Lakes—Author's Regret of his Youth passed amongst
them—Short description of Noon—Cascade Scene—Noontide Retreat—
Precipice and Sloping Lights—Face of Nature as the Sun declines—Mountain
Farm, and the Cock—Slate Quarry—Sunset—Superstition of the Country,
connected with that Moment—Swans—Female Beggar—Twilight Objects—
Twilight Sounds—Western Lights—Spirits—Night—Moonlight—Hope—
Night Sounds—Conclusion.

Far from my dearest friend, 'tis mine to rove
Thro' bare grey dell, high wood, and pastoral cove;
His wizard course where hoary Derwent takes
Thro' craggs, and forest glooms, and opening lakes,
Staying his silent waves, to hear the roar
That stuns the tremulous cliffs of high Lodore:
Where silver rocks the savage prospect chear
Of giant yews that frown on Rydale's mere;
Where peace to Grasmere's lonely island leads,
To willowy hedgerows, and to emerald meads;   10
Leads to her bridge, rude church, and cottaged grounds,
Her rocky sheepwalks, and her woodland bounds;
Where, bosomed deep, the shy Winander peeps
'Mid clust'ring isles, and holly-sprinkled steeps;
Where twilight glens endear my Esthwaite's shore,
And memory of departed pleasures, more.

Fair scenes! with other eyes, than once, I gaze,
The ever-varying charm your round displays,
Than when, erewhile, I taught, 'a happy child,'°
The echoes of your rocks my carols wild: 20
Then did no ebb of chearfulness demand
Sad tides of joy from Melancholy's hand;
In youth's wild eye the livelong day was bright,
The sun at morning, and the stars of night,
Alike, when first the vales the bittern fills
Or the first woodcocks roamed the moonlight hills.°

Return Delights! with whom my road begun,
When Life reared laughing up her morning sun;
When Transport kissed away my april tear,
'Rocking as in a dream the tedious year;'   30
When linked with thoughtless Mirth I coursed the plain,
And hope itself was all I knew of pain.
For then, ev'n then, the little heart would beat
At times, while young Content forsook her seat,
And wild Impatience, panting upward, showed
Where tipped with gold the mountain-summits glowed.
Alas! the idle tale of man is found
Depicted in the dial's moral round;
With Hope Reflexion blends her social rays
To gild the total tablet of his days;   40
Yet still, the sport of some malignant Pow'r,
He knows but from its shade the present hour.

While, Memory at my side, I wander here,
Starts at the simplest sight th' unbidden tear,
A form discovered at the well-known seat,
A spot, that angles at the riv'let's feet,
The cot the ray of morning trav'ling nigh,°
And sail that glides the well-known alders by.

But why, ungrateful, dwell on idle pain?
To shew her yet some joys to me remain,   50
Say, will my friend, with soft affection's ear,
The history of a poet's ev'ning hear?

When, in the south, the wan noon brooding still,
Breathed a pale steam around the glaring hill,
And shades of deep embattled clouds were seen
Spotting the northern cliffs with lights between;
Gazing the tempting shades to them denyed,
When stood the shortened herds amid the tide,
Where, from the barren wall's unsheltered end,
Long rails into the shallow lake extend;   60
When schoolboys stretched their length upon the green,
And round the humming elm, a glimmering scene!
In the brown park, in flocks, the troubled deer
Shook the still twinkling tail and glancing ear;

When horses in the wall-girt intake stood,°
Unshaded, eying far below, the flood,
Crouded behind the swain, in mute distress,
With forward neck the closing gate to press;
And long, with wistful gaze, his walk surveyed
Till dipped his pathway in the river shade;   70

—Then Quiet led me up the huddling rill,
Bright'ning with water-breaks the sombrous gill;°
To where, while thick above the branches close,
In dark-brown bason its wild waves repose,
Inverted shrubs, and moss of darkest green,
Cling from the rocks, with pale wood-weeds between;
Save that, atop, the subtle sunbeams shine,
On withered briars that o'er the craggs recline;
Sole light admitted here, a small cascade,
Illumes with sparkling foam the twilight shade.   80
Beyond, along the visto of the brook,
Where antique roots its bustling path o'erlook,
The eye reposes on a secret bridge°
Half grey, half shagged with ivy to its ridge.

—Sweet rill, farewel! To-morrow's noon again,
Shall hide me wooing long thy wildwood strain;
But now the sun has gained his western road,
And eve's mild hour invites my steps abroad.

While, near the midway cliff, the silvered kite
In many a whistling circle wheels her flight;   90
Slant wat'ry lights, from parting clouds a-pace,
Travel along the precipice's base;
Chearing its naked waste of scattered stone
By lychens grey, and scanty moss o'er-grown,
Where scarce the foxglove peeps, and thistle's beard,
And desert stone-chat, all day long, is heard.

How pleasant, as the yellowing sun declines,
And with long rays and shades the landscape shines;
To mark the birches' stems all golden light,
That lit the dark slant woods with silvery white!   100

The willows weeping trees, that twinkling hoar,
Glanced oft upturned along the breezy shore,
Low bending o'er the coloured water, fold
Their moveless boughs and leaves like threads of gold;
The skiffs with naked masts at anchor laid,
Before the boat-house peeping thro' the shade;
Th' unwearied glance of woodman's echoed stroke;
And curling from the trees the cottage smoke.

    Their panniered train a groupe of potters goad,
Winding from side to side up the steep road;   110
The peasant from yon cliff of fearful edge
Shot, down the headlong pathway darts his sledge;
Bright beams the lonely mountain horse illume,
Feeding 'mid purple heath, 'green rings,' and broom;°
While the sharp slope the slackened team confounds,
Downward the pond'rous timber-wain resounds;°
Beside their sheltering cross of wall, the flock°
Feeds on in light, nor thinks of winter's shock;
In foamy breaks the rill, with merry song,
Dashed down the rough rock, lightly leaps along;   120
From lonesome chapel at the mountain's feet,
Three humble bells their rustic chime repeat;
Sounds from the water-side the hammered boat;
And blasted quarry thunders heard remote.

    Ev'n here, amid the sweep of endless woods,
Blue pomp of lakes, high cliffs, and falling floods,
Not undelightful are the simplest charms
Found by the verdant door of mountain farms.

    Sweetly ferocious round his native walks,°
Gazed by his sister-wives, the monarch stalks;   130
Spur-clad his nervous feet, and firm his tread,
A crest of purple tops his warrior head.
Bright sparks his black and haggard eye-ball hurls
Afar his tail he closes and unfurls;
Whose state, like pine-trees, waving to and fro,
Droops, and o'er canopies his regal brow,
On tiptoe reared he blows his clarion throat,
Threatened by faintly answering farms remote.

Bright'ning the cliffs between where sombrous pine,
And yew-trees o'er the silver rocks recline,   140
I love to mark the quarry's moving trains,
Dwarf panniered steeds, and men, and numerous wains:
How busy the enormous hive within,
While Echo dallies with the various din!
Some, hardly heard their chissel's clinking sound,
Toil, small as pigmies, in the gulph profound;
Some, dim between th' aereal cliffs descryed,
O'erwalk the viewless plank from side to side;
These by the pale-blue rocks that ceaseless ring
Glad from their airy baskets hang and sing.   150

Hung o'er a cloud, above the steep that rears
It's edge all flame, the broadening sun appears;
A long blue bar it's ægis orb divides,
And breaks the spreading of it's golden tides;
And now it touches on the purple steep
That flings his shadow on the pictured deep.
Cross the calm lake's blue shades the cliffs aspire,
With tow'rs and woods a 'prospect all on fire;'
The coves and secret hollows thro' a ray
Of fainter gold a purple gleam betray;   160
The gilded turf arrays in richer green
Each speck of lawn the broken rocks between;
Deep yellow beams the scattered boles illume,
Far in the level forest's central gloom;
Waving his hat, the shepherd in the vale
Directs his winding dog the cliffs to scale,
That, barking busy 'mid the glittering rocks,
Hunts, where he points, the intercepted flocks;
Where oaks o'erhang the road the radiance shoots
On tawny earth, wild weeds, and twisted roots;   170
The Druid stones their lighted fane unfold°
And all the babbling brooks are liquid gold;
Sunk to a curve the day-star lessens still,°
Gives one bright glance, and sinks behind the hill.

In these lone vales, if aught of faith may claim,
Thin silver hairs, and ancient hamlet fame;
When up the hills, as now, retreats the light,
Strange apparitions mock the village sight.

A desperate form appears, that spurs his steed,
Along the midway cliffs with violent speed;   180
Unhurt pursues his lengthened flight, while all
Attend, at every stretch, his headlong fall.
Anon, in order mounts a gorgeous show
Of horsemen shadows winding to and fro;
And now the van is gilt with evening's beam,
The rear thro' iron brown betrays a sullen gleam;
Lost gradual o'er the heights in pomp they go,°
While silent stands th' admiring vale below;
Till, but the lonely beacon all is fled,
That tips with eve's last gleam his spiry head.   190

Now while the solemn evening Shadows sail,
On red slow-waving pinions down the vale,
And, fronting the bright west in stronger lines,
The oak its dark'ning boughs and foliage twines,
I love beside the glowing lake to stray,
Where winds the road along the secret bay;
By rills that tumble down the woody steeps,
And run in transport to the dimpling deeps;
Along the 'wild meand'ring' shore to view,
Obsequious Grace the winding swan pursue,   200
He swells his lifted chest, and backward flings
His bridling neck between his tow'ring wings;
Stately, and burning in his pride, divides
And glorying looks around, the silent tides:
On as he floats, the silvered waters glow,
Proud of the varying arch and moveless form of snow.
While tender Cares and mild domestic Loves,
With furtive watch pursue her as she moves;
The female with a meeker charm succeeds,
And her brown little ones around her leads,   210
Nibbling the water lilies as they pass,
Or playing wanton with the floating grass:
She in a mother's care, her beauty's pride
Forgets, unwearyed watching every side,
She calls them near, and with affection sweet
Alternately relieves their weary feet;
Alternately they mount her back, and rest°
Close by her mantling wings' embraces prest.

Long may ye roam these hermit waves that sleep,
In birch besprinkled cliffs embosomed deep;   220
These fairy holms untrodden, still, and green,
Whose shades protect the hidden wave serene;
Whence fragrance scents the water's desart gale,
The violet, and the lily of the vale;°
Where, tho' her far-off twilight ditty steal,
They not the trip of harmless milkmaid feel.

Yon tuft conceals your home, your cottage bow'r,
Fresh water rushes strew the verdant floor;
Long grass and willows form the woven wall,
And swings above the roof the poplar tall.   230
Thence issuing oft, unwieldly as ye stalk,
Ye crush with broad black feet your flow'ry walk;
Safe from your door ye hear at breezy morn,
The hound, the horse's tread, and mellow horn;
At peace inverted your lithe necks ye lave,
With the green bottom strewing o'er the wave;
No ruder sound your desart haunts invades,
Than waters dashing wild, or rocking shades.
Ye ne'er, like hapless human wanderers, throw
Your young on winter's winding sheet of snow.   240

Fair swan! by all a mother's joys caressed,°
Haply some wretch has eyed, and called thee blessed;
Who faint, and beat by summer's breathless ray,
Hath dragged her babes along this weary way;
While arrowy fire extorting feverish groans,
Shot stinging through her stark o'er-laboured bones,
—With backward gaze, locked joints, and step of pain,
Her seat scarce left, she strives, alas! in vain,
To teach their limbs along the burning road
A few short steps to totter with their load,   250
Shakes her numb arm that slumbers with its weight,
And eyes through tears the mountain's shadeless height;
And bids her soldier come her woes to share,
Asleep on Bunker's charnel hill afar;
For hope's deserted well why wistful look?
Choked is the pathway, and the pitcher broke.

    I see her now, denied to lay her head,
On cold blue nights, in hut or straw-built shed;
Turn to a silent smile their sleepy cry,
By pointing to a shooting star on high: 260
I hear, while in the forest depth he sees,
The Moon's fixed gaze between the opening trees,
In broken sounds her elder grief demand,
And skyward lift, like one that prays, his hand,
If, in that country, where he dwells afar,
His father views that good, that kindly star;
—Ah me! all light is mute amid the gloom,
The interlunar cavern of the tomb.
—When low-hung clouds each star of summer hide,
And fireless are the valleys far and wide,   270
Where the brook brawls along the painful road,
Dark with bat haunted ashes stretching broad,
The distant clock forgot, and chilling dew,
Pleased thro' the dusk their breaking smiles to view,
Oft has she taught them on her lap to play
Delighted, with the glow-worm's harmless ray
Tossed light from hand to hand; while on the ground
Small circles of green radiance gleam around.

    Oh! when the bitter showers her path assail,
And roars between the hills the torrent gale,   280
—No more her breath can thaw their fingers cold,
Their frozen arms her neck no more can fold;
Scarce heard, their chattering lips her shoulder chill,
And her cold back their colder bosoms thrill;
All blind she wilders o'er the lightless heath,
Led by Fear's cold wet hand, and dogged by Death;
Death, as she turns her neck the kiss to seek,
Breaks off the dreadful kiss with angry shriek.
Snatched from her shoulder with despairing moan,
She clasps them at that dim-seen roofless stone—   290
'Now ruthless Tempest launch thy deadliest dart!
Fall fires—but let us perish heart to heart.'
Weak roof a cow'ring form two babes to shield,
And faint the fire a dying heart can yield;
Press the sad kiss, fond mother! vainly fears
Thy flooded cheek to wet them with its tears;

Soon shall the Light'ning hold before thy head
His torch, and shew them slumbering in their bed,
No tears can chill them, and no bosom warms,
Thy breast their death-bed coffined in thine arms.   300

Sweet are the sounds that mingle from afar,
Heard by calm lakes, as peeps the folding star,
Where the duck dabbles 'mid the rustling sedge,
And feeding pike starts from the water's edge,
Or the swan stirs the reeds, his neck and bill
Wetting, that drip upon the water still;
And heron, as resounds the trodden shore,
Shoots upward, darting his long neck before.
While, by the scene composed, the breast subsides,
Nought wakens or disturbs its tranquil tides;   310
Nought but the char that for the may-fly leaps,
And breaks the mirror of the circling deeps;
Or clock, that blind against the wanderer born
Drops at his feet, and stills his droning horn.
—The whistling swain that plods his ringing way
Where the slow waggon winds along the bay;
The sugh of swallow flocks that twittering sweep,°
The solemn curfew swinging long and deep;
The talking boat that moves with pensive sound,
Or drops his anchor down with plunge profound;   320
Of boys that bathe remote the faint uproar,
And restless piper wearying out the shore;
These all to swell the village murmurs blend,
That softened from the water-head descend.
While in sweet cadence rising small and still
The far-off minstrels of the haunted hill,
As the last bleating of the fold expires,
Tune in the mountain dells their water lyres.

Now with religious awe the farewell light
Blends with the solemn colouring of the night;   330
Mid groves of clouds that crest the mountain's brow,
And round the West's proud lodge their shadows throw,
Like Una shining on her gloomy way,°
The half seen form of Twilight roams astray;

Thence, from three paly loopholes mild and small,
Slow lights upon the lake's still bosom fall,
Beyond the mountain's giant reach that hides
In deep determined gloom his subject tides,
—Mid the dark steeps repose the shadowy streams,
As touched with dawning moonlight's hoary gleams,   340
Long streaks of fairy light the wave illume
With bordering lines of intervening gloom,
Soft o'er the surface creep the lustres pale
Tracking with silvering path the changeful gale,
—'Tis restless magic all; at once the bright
Breaks on the shade, the shade upon the light,
Fair Spirits are abroad; in sportive chase
Brushing with lucid wands the water's face,
While music stealing round the glimmering deeps
Charms the tall circle of th' enchanted steeps.   350
—As thro' th' astonished woods the notes ascend,
The mountain streams their rising song suspend;
Below Eve's listening Star the sheep walk stills
Its drowsy tinklings on th' attentive hills;
The milkmaid stops her ballad, and her pail
Stays its low murmur in th' unbreathing vale;
No night-duck clamours for his wildered mate,
Awed, while below the Genii hold their state.
—The pomp is fled, and mute the wondrous strains,
No wrack of all the pageant scene remains,   360
So vanish those fair Shadows, human Joys,°
But death alone their vain regret destroys.
Unheeded Night has overcome the vales,
On the dark earth the baffled vision fails,
If peep between the clouds a star on high,
There turns for glad repose the weary eye;
The latest lingerer of the forest train,
The lone black fir, forsakes the faded plain;
Last evening sight, the cottage smoke no more,
Lost in the deepened darkness, glimmers hoar;   370
High towering from the sullen dark-brown mere,
Like a black wall, the mountain steeps appear,
Thence red from different heights with restless gleam
Small cottage lights across the water stream,
Nought else of man or life remains behind

To call from other worlds the wildered mind,
Till pours the wakeful bird her solemn strains
Heard by the night-calm of the wat'ry plains.°
—No purple prospects now the mind employ
Glowing in golden sunset tints of joy,   380
But o'er the soothed accordant heart we feel
A sympathetic twilight slowly steal,
And ever, as we fondly muse, we find
The soft gloom deep'ning on the tranquil mind.
Stay! pensive, sadly-pleasing visions, stay!
Ah no! as fades the vale, they fade away.
Yet still the tender, vacant gloom remains,
Still the cold cheek its shuddering tear retains.

    The bird, with fading light who ceased to thread
Silent the hedge or steaming rivulet's bed,   390
From his grey re-appearing tower shall soon
Salute with boding note the rising moon,
Frosting with hoary light the pearly ground,
And pouring deeper blue to Æther's bound;
Rejoiced her solemn pomp of clouds to fold
In robes of azure, fleecy white, and gold,
While rose and poppy, as the glow-worm fades,
Chequer with paler red the thicket shades.
    Now o'er the eastern hill, where Darkness broods
O'er all its vanished dells, and lawns, and woods   400
Where but a mass of shade the sight can trace,
She lifts in silence up her lovely face;
Above the gloomy valley flings her light,
Far to the western slopes with hamlets white;
And gives, where woods the chequered upland strew,
To the green corn of summer autumn's hue.
    Thus Hope, first pouring from her blessed horn
Her dawn, far lovelier than the Moon's own morn;
'Till higher mounted, strives in vain to chear
The weary hills, impervious, black'ning near;   410
—Yet does she still, undaunted, throw the while
On darling spots remote her tempting smile.
—Ev'n now she decks for me a distant scene,
(For dark and broad the gulph of time between)

Gilding that cottage with her fondest ray,
(Sole bourn, sole wish, sole object of my way;
How fair its lawn and silvery woods appear!
How sweet its streamlet murmurs in mine ear!)
Where we, my friend, to golden days shall rise,
'Till our small share of hardly-paining sighs   420
(For sighs will ever trouble human breath)
Creep hushed into the tranquil breast of Death.

But now the clear-bright Moon her zenith gains,
And rimy without speck extend the plains;
The deepest dell the mountain's breast displays,
Scarce hides a shadow from her searching rays;
From the dark-blue 'faint silvery threads' divide
The hills, while gleams below the azure tide;
The scene is wakened, yet its peace unbroke,
By silvered wreaths of quiet charcoal smoke,   430
That, o'er the ruins of the fallen wood,
Steal down the hills, and spread along the flood.

The song of mountain streams unheard by day,
Now hardly heard, beguiles my homeward way.
All air is, as the sleeping water, still,
List'ning th' aëreal music of the hill,
Broke only by the slow clock tolling deep,
Or shout that wakes the ferry-man from sleep,
Soon followed by his hollow-parting oar,
And echoed hoof approaching the far shore;   440
Sound of closed gate, across the water born,
Hurrying the feeding hare thro' rustling corn;
The tremulous sob of the complaining owl;
And at long intervals the mill-dog's howl;
The distant forge's swinging thump profound;
Or yell in the deep woods of lonely hound.

Salisbury Plain

1

Hard is the life when naked and unhouzed
And wasted by the long day's fruitless pains,
The hungry savage, 'mid deep forests, rouzed
By storms, lies down at night on unknown plains
And lifts his head in fear, while famished trains
Of boars along the crashing forests prowl,
And heard in darkness, as the rushing rains
Put out his watch-fire, bears contending growl
And round his fenceless bed gaunt wolves in armies howl.

2

Yet is he strong to suffer, and his mind   10
Encounters all his evils unsubdued;
For happier days since at the breast he pined
He never knew, and when by foes pursued
With life he scarce has reached the fortress rude,
While with the war-song's peal the valleys shake,
What in those wild assemblies has he viewed
But men who all of his hard lot partake,
Repose in the same fear, to the same toil awake?

3

The thoughts which bow the kindly spirits down
And break the springs of joy, their deadly weight   20
Derive from memory of pleasures flown
Which haunts us in some sad reverse of fate,
Or from reflection on the state
Of those who on the couch of Affluence rest
By laughing Fortune's sparkling cup elate,
While we of comfort reft, by pain depressed,
No other pillow know than Penury's iron breast.

4

Hence where Refinement's genial influence calls
The soft affections from their wintry sleep
And the sweet tear of Love and Friendship falls   30
The willing heart in tender joy to steep,

When men in various vessels roam the deep
Of social life, and turns of chance prevail
Various and sad, how many thousands weep
Beset with foes more fierce than e'er assail
The savage without home in winter's keenest gale.

5

The troubled west was red with stormy fire,
O'er Sarum's plain the traveller with a sigh
Measured each painful step, the distant spire
That fixed at every turn his backward eye   40
Was lost, tho' still he turned, in the blank sky.
By thirst and hunger pressed he gazed around
And scarce could any trace of man descry,
Save wastes of corn that stretched without a bound,
But where the sower dwelt was nowhere to be found.

6

No shade was there, no meads of pleasant green,
No brook to wet his lips or soothe his ear,
Huge piles of corn-stack here and there were seen
But thence no smoke upwreathed his sight to cheer;
And see the homeward shepherd dim appear   50
Far off—He stops his feeble voice to strain;
No sound replies but winds that whistling near
Sweep the thin grass and passing, wildly plain;
Or desert lark that pours on high a wasted strain.

7

Long had each slope he mounted seemed to hide
Some cottage whither his tired feet might turn,
But now, all hope resigned, in tears he eyed
The crows in blackening eddies homeward borne,
Then sought, in vain, a shepherd's lowly thorn
Or hovel from the storm to shield his head.   60
On as he passed more wild and more forlorn
And vacant the huge plain around him spread;
Ah me! the wet cold ground must be his only bed.

8

Hurtle the rattling clouds together piled
By fiercer gales, and soon the storm must break.
He stood the only creature in the wild
On whom the elements their rage could wreak,
Save that the bustard of those limits bleak,
Shy tenant, seeing there a mortal wight
At that dread hour, outsent a mournful shriek   70
And half upon the ground, with strange affright.
Forced hard against the wind a thick unwieldy flight.

9

The Sun unheeded sunk, while on a mound
He stands beholding with astonished gaze,
Frequent upon the deep entrenched ground,
Strange marks of mighty arms of former days,
Then looking up at distance he surveys
What seems an antique castle spreading wide.
Hoary and naked are its walls and raise
Their brow sublime; while to those walls he hied   80
A voice as from a tomb in hollow accents cried:

10

'Oh from that mountain-pile avert thy face
Whate'er betide at this tremendous hour.
To hell's most cursed sprites the baleful place
Belongs, upreared by their magic power.
Though mixed with flame rush down the crazing shower
And o'er thy naked bed the thunder roll
Fly ere the fiends their prey unwares devour
Or grinning, on thy endless tortures scowl
Till very madness seem a mercy to thy soul.   90

11

'For oft at dead of night, when dreadful fire
Reveals that powerful circle's reddening stones,°
'Mid priests and spectres grim and idols dire,
Far heard the great flame utters human moans,

Then all is hushed: again the desert groans,
A dismal light its farthest bounds illumes,
While warrior spectres of gigantic bones,
Forth-issuing from a thousand rifted tombs,
Wheel on their fiery steeds amid the infernal glooms.'

12

The voice was from beneath but face or form   100
He saw not, mocked as by a hideous dream.
Three hours he wildered through the watery storm
No moon to open the black clouds and stream
From narrow gulph profound one friendly beam;
No watch-dog howled from shepherd's homely shed.
Once did the lightning's pale abortive beam
Disclose a naked guide-post's double head,
Sole object where he stood had day its radiance spread.

13

'Twas dark and waste as ocean's shipless flood
Roaring with storms beneath night's starless gloom.   110
[   ]
Where the wet gypsey in her straw-built home
Warmed her wet limbs by fire of fern and broom.
No transient meteor burst upon his sight
Nor taper glimmered dim from sick man's room.
Along the moor no line of mournful light
From lamp of lonely toll-gate streamed athwart the night.

14

At length, deep hid in clouds, the moon arose
And spread a sickly glare. With flight unwilled,
Worn out and wasted, wishing the repose   120
Of death, he came where, antient vows fulfilled,
Kind pious hands did to the Virgin build
A lonely Spital, the belated swain
From the night-terrors of that waste to shield.
But there no human being could remain
And now the walls are named the dead house of the plain.

15

Till then as if his terror dogged his road
He fled, and often backward cast his face;
And when the ambiguous gloom that ruin shewed
How glad he was at length to find a place   130
That bore of human hands the chearing trace:
Here shall he rest till Morn her eye unclose.
Ah me! that last of hopes is fled apace;
For, entering in, his hair in horror rose
To hear a voice that seemed to mourn in sorrow's throes.

16

It was the voice of one that sleeping mourned,
A human voice! and soon his terrors fled;
At dusk a female wanderer hither turned
And found a comfortless half-sheltered bed.
The moon a wan dead light around her shed;   140
He waked her and at once her spirits fail
Thrilled by the poignant dart of sudden dread,
For of that ruin she had heard a tale
That might with a child's fears the stoutest heart assail.

17

Had heard of one who forced from storms to shroud
Felt the loose walls of this decayed retreat
Rock to his horse's neighings shrill and loud,
While the ground rang by ceaseless pawing beat,
Till on a stone that sparkled to his feet
Struck and still struck again the troubled horse.   150
The man half raised that stone by pain and sweat,
Half raised; for well his arm might lose its force
Disclosing the grim head of a new murdered corse.

18

Such tales of the lone Spital she had learned,
And when that shape with eyes in sleep half-drowned
By the moon's sullen lamp she scarce discerned,
Cold stony horror all her senses bound.

But he to her low words of chearing sound
Addressed. With joy she heard such greeting kind
And much they conversed of that desert ground,   160
Which seemed to those of other worlds consigned
Whose voices still they heard as paused the hollow wind.

19

The Woman told that through a hollow deep
As on she journeyed, far from spring or bower,
An old man beckoning from the naked steep
Came tottering sidelong down to ask the hour;
There never clock was heard from steeple tower.
From the wide corn the plundering crows to scare
He held a rusty gun. In sun and shower,
Old as he was, alone he lingered there,   170
His hungry meal too scant for dog that meal to share.

20

Much of the wonders of that boundless heath
He spoke, and of a swain who far astray
Reached unawares a height and saw beneath
Gigantic beings ranged in dread array.
Such beings thwarting oft the traveller's way
With shield and stone-ax stride across the wold.
Or, throned on that dread circle's summit gray
Of mountains hung in air, their state unfold,
And like a thousand Gods mysterious council hold.   180

21

And oft a night-fire mounting to the clouds
Reveals the desert and with dismal red
Clothes the black bodies of encircling crowds.
It is the sacrificial altar fed
With living men. How deep it groans—the dead
Thrilled in their yawning tombs their helms uprear;
The sword that slept beneath the warriour's head
Thunders in fiery air: red arms appear
Uplifted thro' the gloom and shake the rattling spear.

22

Not thus where clear moons spread their pleasing light.   190
—Long bearded forms with wands uplifted shew
To vast assemblies, while each breath of night
Is hushed, the living fires that bright and slow
Rounding th'aetherial field in order go.
Then as they trace with awe their various files
All figured on the mystic plain below,
Still prelude of sweet sounds the moon beguiles
And charmed for many a league the hoary desert smiles.

23

While thus they talk the churlish storms relent;
And round those broken walls the dying wind   200
In feeble murmurs told his rage was spent.
With sober sympathy and tranquil mind
Gently the Woman gan her wounds unbind.
Might Beauty charm the canker worm of pain
The rose on her sweet cheek had ne'er declined:
Moved she not once the prime of Keswick's plain
While Hope and Love and Joy composed her smiling train?

24

Like swans, twin swans, that when on the sweet brink
Of Derwent's stream the south winds hardly blow,
'Mid Derwent's water-lillies swell and sink   210
In union, rose her sister breasts of snow,
(Fair emblem of two lovers' hearts that know
No separate impulse) or like infants played,
Like infants strangers yet to pain and woe.
Unwearied Hope to tend their motions made
Long Vigils, and Delight her cheek between them laid.

25

And are ye spread ye glittering dews of youth
For this,—that Frost may gall the tender flower
In Joy's fair breast with more untimely tooth?
Unhappy man! thy sole delightful hour   220

Flies first; it is thy miserable dower
Only to taste of joy that thou may'st pine
A loss, which rolling suns shall ne'er restore.
New suns roll on and scatter as they shine
No second spring, but pain, till death release thee, thine.

26

'By Derwent's side my father's cottage stood,'
The mourner thus her artless story told.
'A little flock and what the finny flood
Supplied, to him were more than mines of gold.
Light was my sleep; my days in transport rolled: 230
With thoughtless joy I stretched along the shore
My parent's nets, or watched, when from the fold
High o'er the cliffs I led his fleecy store,
A dizzy depth below! his boat and twinkling oar.

27

'Can I forget my seat beneath the thorn,
My garden stored with peas and mint and thyme,
And rose and lilly for the sabbath morn;
The church-inviting bell's delightful chime,
The merriment and song at shearing time,
My hen's rich nest with long grass overgrown,   240
The cowslip gathering at the morning prime,
The hazel copse with teeming clusters brown,
[   ]

28

'Can I forget the casement where I fed
The red-breast when the fields were whitened o'er,
My snowy kerchiefs on the hawthorn spread
My humming wheel and glittering table store,
The well-known knocking at the evening door,
The hunted slipper and the blinded game,
The dance that loudly beat the merry floor,   250
The ballad chaunted round the brightening flame
While down the ravaged hills the storm unheeded came?

29

'The suns of eighteen summers danced along
Joyous as in the pleasant morn of May.
At last by cruel chance and wilful wrong
My father's substance fell into decay.
Oppression trampled on his tresses grey:
His little range of water was denied;°
Even to the bed where his old body lay
His all was seized; and weeping side by side   260
Turned out on the cold winds, alone we wandered wide.°

30

'Can I forget that miserable hour
When from the last hill-top my sire surveyed,
Peering above the trees, the steeple-tower
That on his marriage-day sweet music made?
There at my birth my mother's bones were laid
And there, till then, he hoped his own might rest.
Bidding me trust in God he stood and prayed:
I could not pray, by human grief oppressed,
Viewing our glimmering cot through tears that never ceased. 270

31

'There was a youth whose tender voice and eye
Might add fresh happiness to happiest days.
At uprise of the sun when he was by
The birds prolonged with joy their choicest lays,
The soft pipe warbled out a wilder maze,
The silent moon of evening, hung above,
Showered through the waving lime-trees mellower rays;
Warm was the breath of night: his voice of love
Charmed the rude winds to sleep by river, field or grove.

32

'His father bid him to a distant town   280
To ply remote from groves the artist's trade.
What tears of bitter grief till then unknown,
What tender vows our last sad kiss delayed!

To him our steps we turned, by hope upstayed.
Oh with what bliss upon his neck I wept;
And her whom he had loved in joy, he said,
He well could love in grief: his faith he kept,
And sheltered from the winds once more my father slept.

33

'Four years each day with daily bread was blessed,
By constant toil and constant prayer supplied.   290
Three lovely infants lay within my breast
And often viewing their sweet smiles I sighed
And knew not why. My happy father died
Just as the children's meal began to fail.
For War the nations to the field defied.
The loom stood still; unwatched, the idle gale
Wooed in deserted shrouds the unregarding sail.

34

'How changed at once! for Labor's chearful hum
Silence and Fear, and Misery's weeping train.
But soon with proud parade the noisy drum   300
Beat round to sweep the streets of want and pain.
My husband's arms now only served to strain
Me and his children hungering in his view.
He could not beg: my prayers and tears were vain;
To join those miserable men he flew.
We reached the western world a poor devoted crew.°

35

'Oh dreadful price of being! to resign
All that is dear in being; better far
In Want's most lonely cave till death to pine
Unseen, unheard, unwatched by any star.   310
Better before proud Fortune's sumptuous car
Obvious our dying bodies to obtrude,
Than dog-like wading at the heels of War
Protract a cursed existence with the brood
That lap, their very nourishment, their brother's blood.

36

'The pains and plagues that on our heads came down,
Disease and Famine, Agony and Fear,
In wood or wilderness, in camp or town,
It would thy brain unsettle even to hear.
All perished, all in one remorseless year,   320
Husband and children one by one, by sword
And scourge of fiery fever: every tear
Dried up, despairing, desolate, on board
A British ship I waked as from a trance restored.'

37

Here paused she of all present thought forlorn,
Living once more those hours that sealed her doom.
Meanwhile he looked and saw the smiling morn
All unconcerned with their unrest resume
Her progress through the brightening eastern gloom.
Oh when shall such fair hours their gleams bestow   330
To bid the grave its opening clouds illume?
Fled each fierce blast and hellish fiend, and lo!
Day fresh from ocean wave uprears his lovely brow.

38

'Oh come,' he said, 'come after weary night
So ruinous far other scene to view.'
So forth she came and eastward looked. The sight
O'er her moist eyes meek dawn of gladness threw
That tinged with faint red smile her faded hue.
Not lovelier did the morning star appear
Parting the lucid mist and bathed in dew,   340
The whilst her comrade to her pensive chear
Tempered sweet words of hope and the lark warbled near.

39

They looked and saw a lengthening road and wain
Descending a bare slope not far remote.
The downs all glistered dropt with freshening rain;
The carman whistled loud with chearful note;

The cock scarce heard at distance sounds his throat;
But town or farm or hamlet none they viewed,
Only were told there stood a lonely cot
Full two miles distant. Then, while they pursued   350
Their journey, her sad tale the mourner thus renewed.

40

'Peaceful as this immeasurable plain
By these extended beams of dawn impressed,
In the calm sunshine slept the glittering main.
The very ocean has its hour of rest
Ungranted to the human mourner's breast.
Remote from man and storms of mortal care,
With wings which did the world of waves invest,
The Spirit of God diffused through balmy air
Quiet that might have healed, if aught could heal, Despair. 360

41

'Ah! how unlike each smell, each sight and sound
That late the stupor of my spirit broke.
Of noysome hospitals the groan profound,
The mine's dire earthquake, the bomb's thunder stroke;
Heart sickening Famine's grim despairing look;
The midnight flames in thundering deluge spread;
The stormed town's expiring shriek that woke
Far round the griesly phantoms of the dead,
And pale with ghastly light the victor's human head.

42

'Some mighty gulf of separation passed   370
I seemed transported to another world:
A dream resigned with pain when from the mast
The impatient mariner the sail unfurled,
And whistling called the wind that hardly curled
The silent seas. The pleasant thoughts of home
With tears his weather-beaten cheek impearled:
For me, farthest from earthly port to roam
Was best; my only wish to shun where man might come.

43

'And oft, robbed of my perfect mind, I thought
At last my feet a resting-place had found.   380
"Here will I weep in peace," so Fancy wrought,
"Roaming the illimitable waters round,
Here gaze, of every friend but Death disowned,
All day, my ready tomb the ocean flood."
To break my dream the vessel reached its bound
And homeless near a thousand homes I stood,
And near a thousand tables pined and wanted food.

44

'Three years a wanderer round my native coast
My eyes have watched yon sun declining tend
Down to the land where hope to me was lost;   390
And now across this waste my steps I bend:
Oh! tell me whither, for no earthly friend
Have I, no house in prospect but the tomb.'
She ceased. The city's distant spires ascend
Like flames which far and wide the west illume,
Scattering from out the sky the rear of night's thin gloom.

45

Along the fiery east the Sun, a show
More gorgeous still! pursued his proud career.
But human sufferings and that tale of woe
Had dimmed the traveller's eye with Pity's tear,   400
And in the youthful mourner's doom severe
He half forgot the terrors of the night,
Striving with counsel sweet her soul to chear,
Her soul for ever widowed of delight.
He too had withered young in sorrow's deadly blight.

46

But now from a hill summit down they look
Where through a narrow valley's pleasant scene
A wreath of vapour tracked a winding brook
Babbling through groves and lawns and meads of green.

A smoking cottage peeped the trees between,   410
The woods resound the linnet's amorous lays,
And melancholy lowings intervene
Of scattered herds that in the meadows graze,
While through the furrowed grass the merry milkmaid strays.

47

Adieu ye friendless hope-forsaken pair!
Yet friendless ere ye take your several road,
Enter that lowly cot and ye shall share
Comforts by prouder mansions unbestowed.
For you yon milkmaid bears her brimming load,
For you the board is piled with homely bread,   420
And think that life is like this desart broad,
Where all the happiest find is but a shed
And a green spot 'mid wastes interminably spread.

48

Though from huge wickers paled with circling fire°
No longer horrid shrieks and dying cries
To ears of Dæmon-Gods in peals aspire,
To Dæmon-Gods a human sacrifice;
Though Treachery her sword no longer dyes
In the cold blood of Truce, still, reason's ray,
What does it more than while the tempests rise,   430
With starless glooms and sounds of loud dismay,
Reveal with still-born glimpse the terrors of our way?

49

For proof, if man thou lovest, turn thy eye
On realms which least the cup of Misery taste.
For want how many men and children die?
How many at Oppression's portal placed
Receive the scanty dole she cannot waste,
And bless, as she has taught, her hand benign?
How many by inhuman toil debased,
Abject, obscure, and brute to earth incline   440
Unrespited, forlorn of every spark divine?

50

Nor only is the walk of private life
Unblessed by Justice and the kindly train
Of Peace and Truth, while Injury and Strife,
Outrage and deadly Hate usurp their reign;
From the pale line to either frozen main
The nations, though at home in bonds they drink
The dregs of wretchedness, for empire strain,
And crushed by their own fetters helpless sink,
Move their galled limbs in fear and eye each silent link.   450

51

Lo! where the Sun exulting in his might
In haste the fiery top of Andes scales
And flings deep silent floods of purple light
Down to the sea through long Peruvian vales,
At once a thousand streams and gentle gales
Start from their slumber breathing scent and song.
But now no joy of man or woman hails
That star as once, ere with him came the throng
Of Furies and grim Death by Avarice lashed along.

52

Oh that a slave who on his naked knees   460
Weeps tears of fear at Superstition's nod,
Should rise a monster Tyrant and o'er seas
And mountains stretch so far his cruel rod
To bruise meek nature in her lone abode.
Is it for this the planet of the pole
Sends through the storms its stedfast light abroad?
Through storms we ride with Misery to her goal:
Nor star nor needle know the tempests of the soul.

53

How changed that paradise, those happy bounds
Where once through his own groves the Hindoo strayed;   470
No more the voice of jocund toil resounds
Along the crowded banyan's high arcade.

[*Lines 473–504 are missing*]

57

How weak the solace such fond thoughts afford,
When with untimely stroke the virtuous bleed.
Say, rulers of the nations, from the sword
Can ought but murder, pain, and tears proceed?
Oh! what can war but endless war still breed?°
Or whence but from the labours of the sage   510
Can poor benighted mortals gain the meed
Of happiness and virtue, how assuage
But by his gentle words their self-consuming rage?

58

Insensate they who think, at Wisdom's porch
That Exile, Terror, Bonds, and Force may stand:
That Truth with human blood can feed her torch,
And Justice balance with her gory hand
Scales whose dire weights of human heads demand
A Nero's arm. Must Law with iron scourge
Still torture crimes that grew a monstrous band   520
Formed by his care, and still his victim urge,
With voice that breathes despair, to death's tremendous verge?

[*Lines 523–539 are missing*]

Who fierce on kingly crowns hurled his own lightning blaze.   540

61

Heroes of Truth pursue your march, uptear
Th'Oppressor's dungeon from its deepest base;
High o'er the towers of Pride undaunted rear
Resistless in your might the herculean mace
Of Reason; let foul Error's monster race
Dragged from their dens start at the light with pain
And die; pursue your toils, till not a trace
Be left on earth of Superstition's reign,
Save that eternal pile which frowns on Sarum's plain.

Old Man Travelling

ANIMAL TRANQUILLITY AND DECAY, A SKETCH

The little hedge-row birds,
That peck along the road, regard him not.
He travels on, and in his face, his step,
His gait, is one expression; every limb,
His look and bending figure, all bespeak
A man who does not move with pain, but moves
With thought—He is insensibly subdued
To settled quiet: he is one by whom
All effort seems forgotten, one to whom
Long patience has such mild composure given,   10
That patience now doth seem a thing, of which
He hath no need. He is by nature led
To peace so perfect, that the young behold
With envy, what the old man hardly feels.
—I asked him whither he was bound, and what
The object of his journey; he replied
'Sir! I am going many miles to take
A last leave of my son, a mariner,
Who from a sea-fight has been brought to Falmouth,
And there is dying in an hospital.'   20

Lines left upon a Seat in a Yew-tree

WHICH STANDS NEAR THE LAKE OF ESTHWAITE,
ON A DESOLATE PART OF THE SHORE,
YET COMMANDING A BEAUTIFUL PROSPECT

—Nay, Traveller! rest. This lonely yew-tree stands
Far from all human dwelling: what if here
No sparkling rivulet spread the verdant herb;
What if these barren boughs the bee not loves;
Yet, if the wind breathe soft, the curling waves,
That break against the shore, shall lull thy mind
By one soft impulse saved from vacancy.
————————————Who he was

That piled these stones, and with the mossy sod
First covered o'er, and taught this aged tree,   10
Now wild, to bend its arms in circling shade,
I well remember.—He was one who owned
No common soul. In youth, by genius nursed,
And big with lofty views, he to the world
Went forth, pure in his heart, against the taint
Of dissolute tongues, 'gainst jealousy, and hate,
And scorn, against all enemies prepared,
All but neglect: and so, his spirit damped
At once, with rash disdain he turned away,
And with the food of pride sustained his soul   20
In solitude.—Stranger! these gloomy boughs
Had charms for him; and here he loved to sit,
His only visitants a straggling sheep,
The stone-chat, or the glancing sand-piper;
And on these barren rocks, with juniper,
And heath, and thistle, thinly sprinkled o'er,
Fixing his downward eye, he many an hour
A morbid pleasure nourished, tracing here
An emblem of his own unfruitful life:
And lifting up his head, he then would gaze   30
On the more distant scene; how lovely 'tis
Thou seest, and he would gaze till it became°
Far lovelier, and his heart could not sustain
The beauty still more beauteous. Nor, that time,
Would he forget those beings, to whose minds,
Warm from the labours of benevolence,
The world, and man himself, appeared a scene
Of kindred loveliness: then he would sigh
With mournful joy, to think that others felt
What he must never feel: and so, lost man!   40
On visionary views would fancy feed,
Till his eye streamed with tears. In this deep vale
He died, this seat his only monument.

If thou be one whose heart the holy forms
Of young imagination have kept pure,
Stranger! henceforth be warned; and know, that pride,
Howe'er disguised in its own majesty,
Is littleness; that he, who feels contempt

For any living thing, hath faculties
Which he has never used; that thought with him   50
Is in its infancy. The man, whose eye
Is ever on himself, doth look on one,
The least of nature's works, one who might move
The wise man to that scorn which wisdom holds
Unlawful, ever. O, be wiser thou!
Instructed that true knowledge leads to love,
True dignity abides with him alone
Who, in the silent hour of inward thought,
Can still suspect, and still revere himself,
In lowliness of heart.   60

The Ruined Cottage

'Twas summer and the sun was mounted high.
Along the south the uplands feebly glared
Through a pale stream, and all the northern downs
In clearer air ascending shewed far off
Their surfaces with shadows dappled o'er
Of deep embattled clouds: far as the sight
Could reach those many shadows lay in spots
Determined and unmoved, with steady beams
Of clear and pleasant sunshine interposed;
Pleasant to him who on the soft cool moss   10
Extends his careless limbs beside the root
Of some huge oak whose aged branches make
A twilight of their own, a dewy shade
Where the wren warbles while the dreaming man,
Half-conscious of that soothing melody,
With side-long eye looks out upon the scene,
By those impending branches made more soft,
More soft and distant. Other lot was mine.
Across a bare wide Common I had toiled
With languid feet which by the slipp'ry ground   20
Were baffled still, and when I stretched myself
On the brown earth my limbs from very heat
Could find no rest nor my weak arm disperse
The insect host which gathered round my face

And joined their murmurs to the tedious noise
Of seeds of bursting gorse that crackled round.
I rose and turned towards a group of trees
Which midway in that level stood alone,
And thither come at length, beneath a shade
Of clustering elms that sprang from the same root   30
I found a ruined house, four naked walls
That stared upon each other. I looked round
And near the door I saw an aged Man,
Alone, and stretched upon the cottage bench;
An iron-pointed staff lay at his side.
With instantaneous joy I recognized
That pride of nature and of lowly life,
The venerable Armytage, a friend
As dear to me as is the setting sun.
                    Two days before   40
We had been fellow-travellers. I knew
That he was in this neighbourhood and now
Delighted found him here in the cool shade.
He lay, his pack of rustic merchandize
Pillowing his head—I guess he had no thought°
Of his way-wandering life. His eyes were shut;
The shadows of the breezy elms above
Dappled his face. With thirsty heat oppressed
At length I hailed him, glad to see his hat
Bedewed with water-drops, as if the brim   50
Had newly scooped a running stream. He rose
And pointing to a sun-flower bade me climb
The [   ] wall where that same gaudy flower
Looked out upon the road. It was a plot
Of garden-ground, now wild, its matted weeds
Marked with the steps of those whom as they passed,
The goose-berry trees that shot in long lank slips,
Or currants hanging from their leafless stems
In scanty strings, had tempted to o'erleap
The broken wall. Within that cheerless spot,   60
Where two tall hedgerows of thick willow boughs
Joined in a damp cold nook, I found a well
Half-choked [with willow flowers and weeds.]
I slaked my thirst and to the shady bench
Returned, and while I stood unbonneted

To catch the motion of the cooler air
The old Man said, 'I see around me here
Things which you cannot see: we die, my Friend,
Nor we alone, but that which each man loved
And prized in his peculiar nook of earth   70
Dies with him or is changed, and very soon
Even of the good is no memorial left.
The Poets in their elegies and songs
Lamenting the departed call the groves,
They call upon the hills and streams to mourn,
And senseless rocks, nor idly; for they speak
In these their invocations with a voice
Obedient to the strong creative power
Of human passion. Sympathies there are
More tranquil, yet perhaps of kindred birth,   80
That steal upon the meditative mind
And grow with thought. Beside yon spring I stood
And eyed its waters till we seemed to feel
One sadness, they and I. For them a bond
Of brotherhood is broken: time has been
When every day the touch of human hand
Disturbed their stillness, and they ministered
To human comfort. When I stooped to drink,
A spider's web hung to the water's edge,
And on the wet and slimy foot-stone lay   90
The useless fragment of a wooden bowl;
It moved my very heart. The day has been
When I could never pass this road but she
Who lived within these walls, when I appeared,
A daughter's welcome gave me, and I loved her
As my own child. O Sir! the good die first,
And they whose hearts are dry as summer dust
Burn to the socket. Many a passenger
Has blessed poor Margaret for her gentle looks°
When she upheld the cool refreshment drawn   100
From that forsaken spring, and no one came
But he was welcome, no one went away
But that it seemed she loved him. She is dead,
The worm is on her cheek, and this poor hut,
Stripped of its outward garb of houshold flowers,
Of rose and sweet-briar, offers to the wind

A cold bare wall whose earthy top is tricked
With weeds and the rank spear-grass. She is dead,
And nettles rot and adders sun themselves
Where we have sate together while she nursed   110
Her infant at her breast. The unshod Colt,
The wandring heifer and the Potter's ass,
Find shelter now within the chimney-wall
Where I have seen her evening hearth-stone blaze
And through the window spread upon the road
Its chearful light.—You will forgive me, Sir,
But often on this cottage do I muse
As on a picture, till my wiser mind
Sinks, yielding to the foolishness of grief.
    She had a husband, an industrious man,   120
Sober and steady; I have heard her say
That he was up and busy at his loom
In summer ere the mower's scythe had swept
The dewy grass, and in the early spring
Ere the last star had vanished. They who passed
At evening, from behind the garden-fence
Might hear his busy spade, which he would ply
After his daily work till the day-light
Was gone and every leaf and flower were lost
In the dark hedges. So they passed their days   130
In peace and comfort, and two pretty babes
Were their best hope next to the God in Heaven.
—You may remember, now some ten years gone,
Two blighting seasons when the fields were left
With half a harvest. It pleased heaven to add
A worse affliction in the plague of war:
A happy land was stricken to the heart;
'Twas a sad time of sorrow and distress:
A wanderer among the cottages,
I with my pack of winter raiment saw   140
The hardships of that season: many rich
Sunk down as in a dream among the poor,
And of the poor did many cease to be,
And their place knew them not. Meanwhile, abridged
Of daily comforts, gladly reconciled
To numerous self-denials, Margaret
Went struggling on through those calamitous years

With chearful hope: but ere the second autumn
A fever seized her husband. In disease
He lingered long, and when his strength returned   150
He found the little he had stored to meet
The hour of accident or crippling age
Was all consumed. As I have said, 'twas now
A time of trouble; shoals of artisans
Were from their daily labour turned away
To hang for bread on parish charity,
They and their wives and children—happier far
Could they have lived as do the little birds
That peck along the hedges or the kite
That makes her dwelling in the mountain rocks.   160
Ill fared it now with Robert, he who dwelt
In this poor cottage; at his door he stood
And whistled many a snatch of merry tunes
That had no mirth in them, or with his knife
Carved uncouth figures on the heads of sticks,
Then idly sought about through every nook
Of house or garden any casual task
Of use or ornament, and with a strange,
Amusing but uneasy novelty
He blended where he might the various tasks   170
Of summer, autumn, winter, and of spring.
But this endured not; his good-humour soon
Became a weight in which no pleasure was,
And poverty brought on a petted mood
And a sore temper: day by day he drooped,
And he would leave his home, and to the town
Without an errand would he turn his steps
Or wander here and there among the fields.
One while he would speak lightly of his babes
And with a cruel tongue: at other times   180
He played with them wild freaks of merriment:
And 'twas a piteous thing to see the looks
Of the poor innocent children. "Every smile,"
Said Margaret to me here beneath these trees,
"Made my heart bleed." ' At this the old Man paused
And looking up to those enormous elms
He said, ' 'Tis now the hour of deepest noon.
At this still season of repose and peace,

This hour when all things which are not at rest
Are chearful, while this multitude of flies   190
Fills all the air with happy melody,
Why should a tear be in an old man's eye?
Why should we thus with an untoward mind
And in the weakness of humanity
From natural wisdom turn our hearts away,
To natural comfort shut our eyes and ears,
And feeding on disquiet thus disturb
The calm of Nature with our restless thoughts?'

SECOND PART

He spake with somewhat of a solemn tone:
But when he ended there was in his face   200
Such easy chearfulness, a look so mild
That for a little time it stole away
All recollection, and that simple tale
Passed from my mind like a forgotten sound.
A while on trivial things we held discourse,
To me soon tasteless. In my own despite
I thought of that poor woman as of one
Whom I had known and loved. He had rehearsed
Her homely tale with such familiar power,
With such a[n active] countenance, an eye   210
So busy, that the things of which he spake
Seemed present, and, attention now relaxed,
There was a heartfelt chillness in my veins.
I rose, and turning from that breezy shade
Went out into the open air and stood
To drink the comfort of the warmer sun.
Long time I had not stayed ere, looking round
Upon that tranquil ruin, I returned
And begged of the old man that for my sake
He would resume his story. He replied,   220
'It were a wantonness and would demand
Severe reproof, if we were men whose hearts
Could hold vain dalliance with the misery
Even of the dead, contented thence to draw
A momentary pleasure never marked
By reason, barren of all future good.

But we have known that there is often found
In mournful thoughts, and always might be found,
A power to virtue friendly; were't not so,
I am a dreamer among men, indeed   230
An idle dreamer. 'Tis a common tale,
By moving accidents uncharactered,°
A tale of silent suffering, hardly clothed
In bodily form, and to the grosser sense
But ill adapted, scarcely palpable
To him who does not think. But at your bidding
I will proceed.
           While thus it fared with them
To whom this cottage till that hapless year
Had been a blessed home, it was my chance
To travel in a country far remote.   240
And glad I was when, halting by yon gate
That leads from the green lane, again I saw
These lofty elm-trees. Long I did not rest:
With many pleasant thoughts I cheered my way
O'er the flat common. At the door arrived,
I knocked, and when I entered with the hope
Of usual greeting, Margaret looked at me
A little while, then turned her head away
Speechless, and sitting down upon a chair
Wept bitterly. I wist not what to do   250
Or how to speak to her. Poor wretch! at last
She rose from off her seat—and then, oh Sir!
I cannot tell how she pronounced my name:
With fervent love, and with a face of grief
Unutterably helpless, and a look
That seemed to cling upon me, she enquired
If I had seen her husband. As she spake
A strange surprize and fear came to my heart,
Nor had I power to answer ere she told
That he had disappeared—just two months gone.   260
He left his house; two wretched days had passed,
And on the third by the first break of light,
Within her casement full in view she saw
A purse of gold. "I trembled at the sight,"°
Said Margaret, "for I knew it was his hand
That placed it there, and on that very day

By one, a stranger, from my husband sent,
The tidings came that he had joined a troop
Of soldiers going to a distant land.
He left me thus—Poor Man! he had not heart   270
To take a farewell of me, and he feared
That I should follow with my babes, and sink
Beneath the misery of a soldier's life."
This tale did Margaret tell with many tears:
And when she ended I had little power
To give her comfort, and was glad to take
Such words of hope from her own mouth as served
To cheer us both: but long we had not talked
Ere we built up a pile of better thoughts,
And with a brighter eye she looked around   280
As if she had been shedding tears of joy.
We parted. It was then the early spring;
I left her busy with her garden tools;
And well remember, o'er that fence she looked,
And while I paced along the foot-way path
Called out, and sent a blessing after me
With tender chearfulness and with a voice
That seemed the very sound of happy thoughts.
      I roved o'er many a hill and many a dale
With this my weary load, in heat and cold,   290
Through many a wood, and many an open ground,
In sunshine or in shade, in wet or fair,
Now blithe, now drooping, as it might befal,
My best companions now the driving winds
And now the "trotting brooks" and whispering trees°
And now the music of my own sad steps,
With many a short-lived thought that passed between
And disappeared. I came this way again
Towards the wane of summer, when the wheat
Was yellow, and the soft and bladed grass   300
Sprang up afresh and o'er the hay-field spread
Its tender green. When I had reached the door
I found that she was absent. In the shade
Where now we sit I waited her return.
Her cottage in its outward look appeared
As chearful as before; in any shew
Of neatness little changed, but that I thought

The honeysuckle crowded round the door
And from the wall hung down in heavier wreathes,
And knots of worthless stone-crop started out   310
Along the window's edge, and grew like weeds
Against the lower panes. I turned aside
And strolled into her garden.—It was changed:
The unprofitable bindweed spread his bells
From side to side and with unwieldy wreaths
Had dragged the rose from its sustaining wall
And bent it down to earth; the border-tufts—
Daisy and thrift and lowly camomile
And thyme—had straggled out into the paths
Which they were used to deck. Ere this an hour   320
Was wasted. Back I turned my restless steps,
And as I walked before the door it chanced
A stranger passed, and guessing whom I sought
He said that she was used to ramble far.
The sun was sinking in the west, and now
I sate with sad impatience. From within
Her solitary infant cried aloud.
The spot though fair seemed very desolate:
The longer I remained more desolate.
And, looking round, I saw the corner-stones,°   330
Till then unmarked, on either side the door
With dull red stains discoloured and stuck o'er
With tufts and hairs of wool, as if the sheep
That feed upon the commons thither came
Familiarly and found a couching-place
Even at her threshold.—The house-clock struck eight;
I turned and saw her distant a few steps.
Her face was pale and thin, her figure too
Was changed. As she unlocked the door she said,
"It grieves me you have waited here so long,   340
But in good truth I've wandered much of late
And sometimes, to my shame I speak, have need
Of my best prayers to bring me back again."
While on the board she spread our evening meal
She told me she had lost her elder child,
That he for months had been a serving-boy
Apprenticed by the parish. "I perceive
You look at me, and you have cause. Today

I have been travelling far, and many days
About the fields I wander, knowing this   350
Only, that what I seek I cannot find.
And so I waste my time: for I am changed;
And to myself," said she, "have done much wrong,
And to this helpless infant. I have slept
Weeping, and weeping I have waked; my tears
Have flowed as if my body were not such
As others are, and I could never die.
But I am now in mind and in my heart
More easy, and I hope," said she, "that heaven
Will give me patience to endure the things   360
Which I behold at home." It would have grieved
Your very heart to see her. Sir, I feel
The story linger in my heart. I fear
'Tis long and tedious, but my spirit clings
To that poor woman: so familiarly
Do I perceive her manner, and her look
And presence, and so deeply do I feel
Her goodness, that not seldom in my walks
A momentary trance comes over me;
And to myself I seem to muse on one   370
By sorrow laid asleep or borne away,
A human being destined to awake
To human life, or something very near
To human life, when he shall come again
For whom she suffered. Sir, it would have grieved
Your very soul to see her: evermore
Her eye-lids drooped, her eyes were downward cast;
And when she at her table gave me food
She did not look at me. Her voice was low,
Her body was subdued. In every act   380
Pertaining to her house-affairs appeared
The careless stillness which a thinking mind
Gives to an idle matter—still she sighed,
But yet no motion of the breast was seen,
No heaving of the heart. While by the fire
We sate together, sighs came on my ear;
I knew not how, and hardly whence they came.
I took my staff, and when I kissed her babe
The tears stood in her eyes. I left her then

With the best hope and comfort I could give;   390
She thanked me for my will, but for my hope
It seemed she did not thank me.
                          I returned
And took my rounds along this road again
Ere on its sunny bank the primrose flower
Had chronicled the earliest day of spring.
I found her sad and drooping; she had learned
No tidings of her husband: if he lived
She knew not that he lived; if he were dead
She knew not he was dead. She seemed the same
In person [   ] appearance, but her house   400
Bespoke a sleepy hand of negligence;
The floor was neither dry nor neat, the hearth
Was comfortless [   ],
The windows too were dim, and her few books,
Which, one upon the other, heretofore
Had been piled up against the corner-panes
In seemly order, now with straggling leaves
Lay scattered here and there, open or shut
As they had chanced to fall. Her infant babe
Had from its mother caught the trick of grief   410
And sighed among its playthings. Once again
I turned towards the garden-gate and saw
More plainly still that poverty and grief
Were now come nearer to her: the earth was hard,
With weeds defaced and knots of withered grass;
No ridges there appeared of clear black mould,
No winter greenness: of her herbs and flowers
It seemed the better part were gnawed away
Or trampled on the earth; a chain of straw
Which had been twisted round the tender stem   420
Of a young apple-tree lay at its root;
The bark was nibbled round by truant sheep.
Margaret stood near, her infant in her arms,
And seeing that my eye was on the tree
She said, "I fear it will be dead and gone
Ere Robert come again." Towards the house
Together we returned, and she inquired
If I had any hope. But for her Babe
And for her little friendless Boy, she said,

She had no wish to live, that she must die   430
Of sorrow. Yet I saw the idle loom
Still in its place. His sunday garments hung
Upon the self-same nail, his very staff
Stood undisturbed behind the door. And when
I passed this way beaten by Autumn winds
She told me that her little babe was dead
And she was left alone. That very time,
I yet remember, through the miry lane
She walked with me a mile, when the bare trees
Trickled with foggy damps, and in such sort   440
That any heart had ached to hear her begged
That wheresoe'er I went I still would ask
For him whom she had lost. We parted then,
Our final parting, for from that time forth
Did many seasons pass ere I returned
Into this tract again.
                          Five tedious years
She lingered in unquiet widowhood,
A wife and widow. Needs must it have been
A sore heart-wasting. I have heard, my friend,
That in that broken arbour she would sit   450
The idle length of half a sabbath day—
There, where you see the toadstool's lazy head—
And when a dog passed by she still would quit
The shade and look abroad. On this old Bench
For hours she sate, and evermore her eye
Was busy in the distance, shaping things
Which made her heart beat quick. Seest thou that path?
(The green-sward now has broken its grey line)
There to and fro she paced through many a day
Of the warm summer, from a belt of flax°   460
That girt her waist spinning the long-drawn thread
With backward steps.—Yet ever as there passed
A man whose garments shewed the Soldier's red,
Or crippled Mendicant in Sailor's garb,
The little child who sate to turn the wheel
Ceased from his toil, and she with faltering voice,
Expecting still to learn her husband's fate,
Made many a fond inquiry; and when they
Whose presence gave no comfort were gone by,

Her heart was still more sad. And by yon gate   470
Which bars the traveller's road she often stood
And when a stranger horseman came, the latch
Would lift, and in his face look wistfully,
Most happy if from aught discovered there
Of tender feeling she might dare repeat
The same sad question. Meanwhile her poor hut
Sunk to decay, for he was gone whose hand
At the first nippings of October frost
Closed up each chink and with fresh bands of straw
Chequered the green-grown thatch. And so she lived   480
Through the long winter, reckless and alone,
Till this reft house by frost, and thaw, and rain
Was sapped; and when she slept the nightly damps
Did chill her breast, and in the stormy day
Her tattered clothes were ruffled by the wind
Even at the side of her own fire. Yet still
She loved this wretched spot, nor would for worlds
Have parted hence; and still that length of road
And this rude bench one torturing hope endeared,
Fast rooted at her heart, and here, my friend,   490
In sickness she remained, and here she died,
Last human tenant of these ruined walls.'
    The old Man ceased: he saw that I was moved;
From that low Bench, rising instinctively,
I turned aside in weakness, nor had power
To thank him for the tale which he had told.
I stood, and leaning o'er the garden-gate
Reviewed that Woman's suff'rings, and it seemed
To comfort me while with a brother's love
I blessed her in the impotence of grief.   500
At length [   ] the [   ]
Fondly, and traced with milder interest
That secret spirit of humanity
Which, 'mid the calm oblivious tendencies
Of nature, 'mid her plants, her weeds, and flowers,
And silent overgrowings, still survived.
The old man, seeing this, resumed and said,
'My Friend, enough to sorrow have you given,
The purposes of wisdom ask no more;
Be wise and chearful, and no longer read   510

The forms of things with an unworthy eye.
She sleeps in the calm earth, and peace is here.
I well remember that those very plumes,
Those weeds, and the high spear-grass on that wall,
By mist and silent rain-drops silvered o'er,
As once I passed did to my heart convey
So still an image of tranquillity,
So calm and still, and looked so beautiful
Amid the uneasy thoughts which filled my mind,
That what we feel of sorrow and despair   520
From ruin and from change, and all the grief
The passing shews of being leave behind,
Appeared an idle dream that could not live
Where meditation was. I turned away
And walked along my road in happiness.'
    He ceased. By this the sun declining shot
A slant and mellow radiance which began
To fall upon us where beneath the trees
We sate on that low bench, and now we felt,
Admonished thus, the sweet hour coming on.   530
A linnet warbled from those lofty elms,
A thrush sang loud, and other melodies,
At distance heard, peopled the milder air.
The old man rose and hoisted up his load.
Together casting then a farewell look
Upon those silent walls, we left the shade
And ere the stars were visible attained
A rustic inn, our evening resting-place.

[A Night-Piece]

        The sky is overspread
With a close veil of one continuous cloud
All whitened by the moon, that just appears,
A dim-seen orb, yet chequers not the ground
With any shadow—plant, or tower, or tree.
At last a pleasant instantaneous light
Startles the musing man whose eyes are bent
To earth. He looks around, the clouds are split

Asunder, and above his head he views
The clear moon and the glory of the heavens.   10
There in a black-blue vault she sails along
Followed by multitudes of stars, that small,
And bright, and sharp along the gloomy vault
Drive as she drives. How fast they wheel away!
Yet vanish not! The wind is in the trees;
But they are silent. Still they roll along
Immeasurably distant, and the vault
Built round by those white clouds, enormous clouds,
Still deepens its interminable depth.
At length the vision closes, and the mind   20
Not undisturbed by the deep joy it feels,
Which slowly settles into peaceful calm,
Is left to muse upon the solemn scene.

[*The Discharged Soldier*]

                              I love to walk
Along the public way when for the night,
Deserted in its silence, it assumes
A character of deeper quietness
Than pathless solitudes. At such a time
I slowly mounted up a steep ascent
Where the road's watry surface to the ridge
Of that sharp rising glittered in the moon
And seemed before my eyes another stream
Stealing with silent lapse to join the brook   10
That murmured in the valley. On I passed
Tranquil, receiving in my own despite
Amusement, as I slowly passed along,
From such near objects as from time to time
Perforce disturbed the slumber of the sense
Quiescent, and disposed to sympathy,
With an exhausted mind worn out by toil
And all unworthy of the deeper joy
Which waits on distant prospect, cliff or sea,
The dark blue vault, and universe of stars.   20
Thus did I steal along that silent road,

My body from the stillness drinking in
A restoration like the calm of sleep
But sweeter far. Above, before, behind,
Around me, all was peace and solitude:
I looked not round, nor did the solitude
Speak to my eye, but it was heard and felt.
Oh happy state! What beauteous pictures now
Rose in harmonious imagery—they rose
As from some distant region of my soul   30
And came along like dreams, yet such as left
Obscurely mingled with their passing forms
A consciousness of animal delight,
A self-possession felt in every pause
And every gentle movement of my frame.
    While thus I wandered, step by step led on,
It chanced a sudden turning of the road
Presented to my view an uncouth shape
So near that, stepping back into the shade
Of a thick hawthorn, I could mark him well,   40
Myself unseen. He was in stature tall,
A foot above man's common measure tall,
And lank, and upright. There was in his form
A meagre stiffness. You might almost think
That his bones wounded him. His legs were long,
So long and shapeless that I looked at them
Forgetful of the body they sustained.
His arms were long and lean; his hands were bare;
His visage, wasted though it seemed, was large
In feature; his cheeks sunken; and his mouth   50
Shewed ghastly in the moonlight. From behind
A mile-stone propped him, and his figure seemed
Half-sitting and half-standing. I could mark
That he was clad in military garb,
Though faded yet entire. His face was turned
Towards the road, yet not as if he sought
For any living thing. He appeared
Forlorn and desolate, a man cut off
From all his kind, and more than half detached
From his own nature.   60
                          He was alone,
Had no attendant, neither dog, nor staff,

Nor knapsack—in his very dress appeared
A desolation, a simplicity
That appertained to solitude. I think
If but a glove had dangled in his hand
It would have made him more akin to man.
Long time I scanned him with a mingled sense
Of fear and sorrow. From his lips meanwhile
There issued murmuring sounds as if of pain   70
Or of uneasy thought; yet still his form
Kept the same fearful steadiness. His shadow
Lay at his feet and moved not. In a glen
Hard by a village stood, whose silent doors
Were visible among the scattered trees,
Scarce distant from the spot an arrow's flight.
I wished to see him move, but he remained
Fixed to his place, and still from time to time
Sent forth a murmuring voice of dead complaint,
A groan scarce audible. Yet all the while   80
The chained mastiff in his wooden house
Was vexed, and from among the village trees
Howled never ceasing. Not without reproach
Had I prolonged my watch, and now confirmed,
And my heart's specious cowardice subdued,
I left the shady nook where I had stood
And hailed the Stranger. From his resting-place
He rose, and with his lean and wasted arm
In measured gesture lifted to his head
Returned my salutation. A short while   90
I held discourse on things indifferent
And casual matter. He meanwhile had ceased
From all complaint—his station had resumed,
Propped by the mile stone as before, and when erelong
I asked his history, he in reply
Was neither slow nor eager, but unmoved,
And with a quiet uncomplaining voice,
A stately air of mild indifference,
He told a simple fact: that he had been
A Soldier, to the tropic isles had gone,   100
Whence he had landed now some ten days past;
That on his landing he had been dismissed,
And with the little strength he yet had left

Was travelling to regain his native home.
At this I turned and through the trees looked down
Into the village—all were gone to rest,
Nor smoke nor any taper light appeared,
But every silent window to the moon
Shone with a yellow glitter. 'No one there,'
Said I, 'is waking; we must measure back   110
The way which we have come. Behind yon wood
A labourer dwells, an honest man and kind;
He will not murmur should we break his rest,
And he will give you food if food you need,
And lodging for the night.' At this he stooped,
And from the ground took up an oaken staff
By me yet unobserved, a traveller's staff,
Which I suppose from his slack hand had dropped,
And, such the languor of the weary man,
Had lain till now neglected in the grass,   120
But not forgotten. Back we turned and shaped
Our course toward the cottage. He appeared
To travel without pain, and I beheld
With ill-suppressed astonishment his tall
And ghostly figure moving at my side.
As we advanced I asked him for what cause
He tarried there, nor had demanded rest
At inn or cottage. He replied, 'In truth
My weakness made me loth to move, and here
I felt myself at ease and much relieved,   130
But that the village mastiff fretted me,
And every second moment rang a peal
Felt at my very heart. There was no noise,
Nor any foot abroad—I do not know
What ailed him, but it seemed as if the dog
Were howling to the murmur of the stream.'
While thus we travelled on I did not fail
To question him of what he had endured
From war and battle and the pestilence.
He all the while was in demeanor calm,   140
Concise in answer: solemn and sublime
He might have seemed, but that in all he said
There was a strange half-absence and a tone
Of weakness and indifference, as of one

Remembering the importance of his theme,
But feeling it no longer. We advanced
Slowly, and ere we to the wood were come
Discourse had ceased. Together on we passed
In silence through the shades gloomy and dark,
Then turning up along an open field   150
We gained the cottage. At the door I knocked,
And called aloud, 'My Friend, here is a man
By sickness overcome; beneath your roof
This night let him find rest, and give him food—
The service if need be I will requite.'
Assured that now my comrade would repose
In comfort, I entreated that henceforth
He would not linger in the public ways
But at the door of cottage or of inn
Demand the succour which his state required,   160
And told him, feeble as he was 'twere fit
He asked relief or alms. At this reproof
With the same ghastly mildness in his look
He said, 'My trust is in the God of heaven,
And in the eye of him that passes me.'
By this the labourer had unlocked the door,
And now my comrade touched his hat again
With his lean hand, and in a voice that seemed
To speak with a reviving interest
Till then unfelt, he thanked me. I returned   170
The blessing of the poor unhappy man,
And so we parted.

The Old Cumberland Beggar

A DESCRIPTION

The class of Beggars to which the old man here described belongs, will probably
soon be extinct. It consisted of poor, and, mostly, old and infirm persons, who
confined themselves to a stated round in their neighbourhood, and had certain
fixed days, on which, at different houses, they regularly received charity;
sometimes in money, but mostly in provisions.

I saw an aged Beggar in my walk,
And he was seated by the highway side
On a low structure of rude masonry

Built at the foot of a huge hill, that they
Who lead their horses down the steep rough road
May thence remount at ease. The aged man
Had placed his staff across the broad smooth stone
That overlays the pile, and from a bag
All white with flour the dole of village dames,
He drew his scraps and fragments, one by one,   10
And scanned them with a fixed and serious look
Of idle computation. In the sun,
Upon the second step of that small pile,
Surrounded by those wild unpeopled hills,
He sate, and eat his food in solitude;
And ever, scattered from his palsied hand,
That still attempting to prevent the waste,
Was baffled still, the crumbs in little showers
Fell on the ground, and the small mountain birds,
Not venturing yet to peck their destined meal,   20
Approached within the length of half his staff.

Him from my childhood have I known, and then
He was so old, he seems not older now;
He travels on, a solitary man,
So helpless in appearance, that for him
The sauntering horseman-traveller does not throw
With careless hands his alms upon the ground,
But stops, that he may safely lodge the coin
Within the old Man's hat; nor quits him so,
But still when he has given his horse the rein   30
Towards the aged Beggar turns a look,
Sidelong and half-reverted. She who tends
The toll-gate, when in summer at her door
She turns her wheel, if on the road she sees
The aged Beggar coming, quits her work,
And lifts the latch for him that he may pass.
The Post-boy when his rattling wheels o'ertake
The aged Beggar, in the woody lane,
Shouts to him from behind, and, if perchance
The old Man does not change his course, the Boy   40
Turns with less noisy wheels to the road-side,
And passes gently by, without a curse

Upon his lips, or anger at his heart.
He travels on, a solitary Man,
His age has no companion. On the ground
His eyes are turned, and, as he moves along,
They move along the ground; and evermore,
Instead of common and habitual sight
Of fields with rural works, of hill and dale,
And the blue sky, one little span of earth   50
Is all his prospect. Thus, from day to day,
Bowbent, his eyes for ever on the ground,
He plies his weary journey, seeing still,
And never knowing that he sees, some straw,
Some scattered leaf, or marks which, in one track,
The nails of cart or chariot wheel have left
Impressed on the white road, in the same line,
At distance still the same. Poor Traveller!
His staff trails with him, scarcely do his feet
Disturb the summer dust, he is so still   60
In look and motion that the cottage curs,
Ere he have passed the door, will turn away
Weary of barking at him. Boys and girls,
The vacant and the busy, maids and youths,
And urchins newly breeched all pass him by:
Him even the slow-paced waggon leaves behind.

But deem not this man useless.—Statesman! ye
Who are so restless in your wisdom, ye
Who have a broom still ready in your hands
To rid the world of nuisances; ye proud,   70
Heart-swoln, while in your pride ye contemplate
Your talents, power, and wisdom, deem him not
A burthen of the earth. 'Tis Nature's law
That none, the meanest of created things,
Of forms created the most vile and brute,
The dullest or most noxious, should exist
Divorced from good, a spirit and pulse of good,
A life and soul to every mode of being
Inseparably linked. While thus he creeps
From door to door, the Villagers in him   80
Behold a record which together binds

Past deeds and offices of charity
Else unremembered, and so keeps alive
The kindly mood in hearts which lapse of years,
And that half-wisdom half-experience gives
Make slow to feel, and by sure steps resign
To selfishness and cold oblivious cares.
Among the farms and solitary huts
Hamlets, and thinly-scattered villages,
Where'er the aged Beggar takes his rounds,   90
The mild necessity of use compels
To acts of love; and habit does the work
Of reason, yet prepares that after joy
Which reason cherishes. And thus the soul,
By that sweet taste of pleasure unpursued
Doth find itself insensibly disposed
To virtue and true goodness. Some there are,
By their good works exalted, lofty minds
And meditative, authors of delight
And happiness, which to the end of time   100
Will live, and spread, and kindle; minds like these,
In childhood, from this solitary being,
This helpless wanderer, have perchance received,
(A thing more precious far than all that books
Or the solicitudes of love can do!)
That first mild touch of sympathy and thought,
In which they found their kindred with a world
Where want and sorrow were. The easy man
Who sits at his own door, and like the pear
Which overhangs his head from the green wall,   110
Feeds in the sunshine; the robust and young,
The prosperous and unthinking, they who live
Sheltered, and flourish in a little grove
Of their own kindred, all behold in him
A silent monitor, which on their minds
Must needs impress a transitory thought
Of self-congratulation, to the heart
Of each recalling his peculiar boons,
His charters and exemptions; and perchance,
Though he to no one give the fortitude   120
And circumspection needful to preserve
His present blessings, and to husband up

The respite of the season, he, at least,
And 'tis no vulgar service, makes them felt.

Yet further.—Many, I believe, there are
Who live a life of virtuous decency,
Men who can hear the Decalogue and feel
No self-reproach, who of the moral law
Established in the land where they abide
Are strict observers, and not negligent,   130
Meanwhile, in any tenderness of heart
Or act of love to those with whom they dwell,
Their kindred, and the children of their blood.
Praise be to such, and to their slumbers peace!
—But of the poor man ask, the abject poor,
Go and demand of him, if there be here,
In this cold abstinence from evil deeds,
And these inevitable charities,
Wherewith to satisfy the human soul.
No—man is dear to man: the poorest poor   140
Long for some moments in a weary life
When they can know and feel that they have been
Themselves the fathers and the dealers out
Of some small blessings, have been kind to such
As needed kindness, for this single cause,
That we have all of us one human heart.
—Such pleasure is to one kind Being known,
My Neighbour, when with punctual care, each week
Duly as Friday comes, though pressed herself
By her own wants, she from her chest of meal   150
Takes one unsparing handful for the scrip
Of this old Mendicant, and, from her door
Returning with exhilarated heart,
Sits by her fire and builds her hope in heaven.

Then let him pass, a blessing on his head!
And while, in that vast solitude to which
The tide of things has led him, he appears
To breathe and live but for himself alone,
Unblamed, uninjured, let him bear about
The good which the benignant law of heaven   160
Has hung around him, and, while life is his,
Still let him prompt the unlettered Villagers

To tender offices and pensive thoughts.
Then let him pass, a blessing on his head!
And, long as he can wander, let him breathe
The freshness of the vallies, let his blood
Struggle with frosty air and winter snows,
And let the chartered wind that sweeps the heath
Beat his grey locks against his withered face.
Reverence the hope whose vital anxiousness   170
Gives the last human interest to his heart.
May never House, misnamed of industry,
Make him a captive; for that pent-up din,
Those life-consuming sounds that clog the air,
Be his the natural silence of old age.
Let him be free of mountain solitudes,
And have around him, whether heard or not,
The pleasant melody of woodland birds.
Few are his pleasures; if his eyes, which now
Have been so long familiar with the earth,   180
No more behold the horizontal sun
Rising or setting, let the light at least
Find a free entrance to their languid orbs.
And let him, *where* and *when* he will, sit down
Beneath the trees, or by the grassy bank
Of high-way side, and with the little birds
Share his chance-gathered meal, and, finally,
As in the eye of Nature he has lived,
So in the eye of Nature let him die.

Lines

WRITTEN AT A SMALL DISTANCE FROM MY HOUSE,
AND SENT BY MY LITTLE BOY TO THE
PERSON TO WHOM THEY ARE
ADDRESSED

It is the first mild day of March:
Each minute sweeter than before,
The red-breast sings from the tall larch
That stands beside our door.

There is a blessing in the air,
Which seems a sense of joy to yield
To the bare trees, and mountains bare,
And grass in the green field.

My Sister! ('tis a wish of mine)
Now that our morning meal is done,   10
Make haste, your morning task resign;
Come forth and feel the sun.

Edward will come with you, and pray,
Put on with speed your woodland dress,
And bring no book, for this one day
We'll give to idleness.

No joyless forms shall regulate
Our living Calendar:
We from to-day, my friend, will date
The opening of the year.   20

Love, now an universal birth,
From heart to heart is stealing,
From earth to man, from man to earth,
—It is the hour of feeling.

One moment now may give us more
Than fifty years of reason;
Our minds shall drink at every pore
The spirit of the season.

Some silent laws our hearts may make,
Which they shall long obey;   30
We for the year to come may take
Our temper from to-day.

And from the blessed power that rolls
About, below, above;
We'll frame the measure of our souls,
They shall be tuned to love.

Then come, my sister! come, I pray,
With speed put on your woodland dress,
And bring no book; for this one day
We'll give to idleness.   40

Goody Blake and Harry Gill

A TRUE STORY

Oh! what's the matter? what's the matter?
What is't that ails young Harry Gill?
That evermore his teeth they chatter,
Chatter, chatter, chatter still.
Of waistcoats Harry has no lack,
Good duffle grey, and flannel fine;
He has a blanket on his back,
And coats enough to smother nine.

In March, December, and in July,
'Tis all the same with Harry Gill;   10
The neighbours tell, and tell you truly,
His teeth they chatter, chatter still.
At night, at morning, and at noon,
'Tis all the same with Harry Gill;
Beneath the sun, beneath the moon,
His teeth they chatter, chatter still.

Young Harry was a lusty drover,
And who so stout of limb as he?
His cheeks were red as ruddy clover,
His voice was like the voice of three.   20
Auld Goody Blake was old and poor,
Ill fed she was, and thinly clad;
And any man who passed her door,
Might see how poor a hut she had.

All day she spun in her poor dwelling,
And then her three hours' work at night!
Alas! 'twas hardly worth the telling,
It would not pay for candle-light.
—This woman dwelt in Dorsetshire,
Her hut was on a cold hill-side,   30
And in that country coals are dear,
For they come far by wind and tide.

By the same fire to boil their pottage,
Two poor old dames, as I have known,
Will often live in one small cottage,
But she, poor woman, dwelt alone.
'Twas well enough when summer came,
The long, warm, lightsome summer-day,
Then at her door the *canty* dame
Would sit, as any linnet gay.   40

But when the ice our streams did fetter,
Oh! then how her old bones would shake!
You would have said, if you had met her,
'Twas a hard time for Goody Blake.
Her evenings then were dull and dead;
Sad case it was, as you may think,
For very cold to go to bed,
And then for cold not sleep a wink.

Oh joy for her! when e'er in winter
The winds at night had made a rout,   50
And scattered many a lusty splinter,
And many a rotten bough about.
Yet never had she, well or sick,
As every man who knew her says,
A pile before-hand, wood or stick,
Enough to warm her for three days.

Now, when the frost was past enduring,
And made her poor old bones to ache,
Could any thing be more alluring,
Than an old hedge to Goody Blake?   60
And now and then, it must be said,
When her old bones were cold and chill,
She left her fire, or left her bed,
To seek the hedge of Harry Gill.

Now Harry he had long suspected
This trespass of old Goody Blake,
And vowed that she should be detected,
And he on her would vengeance take.

And oft from his warm fire he'd go,
And to the fields his road would take,   70
And there, at night, in frost and snow,
He watched to seize old Goody Blake.

And once, behind a rick of barley,
Thus looking out did Harry stand;
The moon was full and shining clearly,
And crisp with frost the stubble-land.
—He hears a noise—he's all awake—
Again?—on tip-toe down the hill
He softly creeps—'Tis Goody Blake,
She's at the hedge of Harry Gill.   80

Right glad was he when he beheld her:
Stick after stick did Goody pull,
He stood behind a bush of elder,
Till she had filled her apron full.
When with her load she turned about,
The bye-road back again to take,
He started forward with a shout,
And sprang upon poor Goody Blake.

And fiercely by the arm he took her,
And by the arm he held her fast,   90
And fiercely by the arm he shook her,
And cried, 'I've caught you then at last!'
Then Goody, who had nothing said,
Her bundle from her lap let fall;
And kneeling on the sticks, she prayed
To God that is the judge of all.

She prayed, her withered hand uprearing,
While Harry held her by the arm—
'God! who art never out of hearing,
Oh may he never more be warm!'   100
The cold, cold moon above her head,
Thus on her knees did Goody pray,
Young Harry heard what she had said,
And icy-cold he turned away.

He went complaining all the morrow
That he was cold and very chill:
His face was gloom, his heart was sorrow,
Alas! that day for Harry Gill!
That day he wore a riding-coat,
But not a whit the warmer he: 110
Another was on Thursday brought,
And ere the Sabbath he had three.

'Twas all in vain, a useless matter,
And blankets were about him pinned;
Yet still his jaws and teeth they clatter,
Like a loose casement in the wind.
And Harry's flesh it fell away;
And all who see him say 'tis plain,
That, live as long as live he may,
He never will be warm again.   120

No word to any man he utters,
A-bed or up, to young or old;
But ever to himself he mutters,
'Poor Harry Gill is very cold.'
A-bed or up, by night or day;
His teeth they chatter, chatter still.
Now think, ye farmers all, I pray,
Of Goody Blake and Harry Gill.

The Thorn

There is a thorn; it looks so old,
In truth you'd find it hard to say,
How it could ever have been young,
It looks so old and grey.
Not higher than a two-years' child,
It stands erect this aged thorn;
No leaves it has, no thorny points;
It is a mass of knotted joints,
A wretched thing forlorn.
It stands erect, and like a stone   10
With lichens it is overgrown.

Like rock or stone, it is o'ergrown
With lichens to the very top,
And hung with heavy tufts of moss,
A melancholy crop:
Up from the earth these mosses creep,
And this poor thorn they clasp it round
So close, you'd say that they were bent
With plain and manifest intent,
To drag it to the ground;   20
And all had joined in one endeavour
To bury this poor thorn for ever.

High on a mountain's highest ridge,
Where oft the stormy winter gale
Cuts like a scythe, while through the clouds
It sweeps from vale to vale;
Not five yards from the mountain-path,
This thorn you on your left espy;
And to the left, three yards beyond,
You see a little muddy pond   30
Of water, never dry;
I've measured it from side to side:
'Tis three feet long, and two feet wide.

And close beside this aged thorn,
There is a fresh and lovely sight,
A beauteous heap, a hill of moss,
Just half a foot in height.
All lovely colours there you see,
All colours that were ever seen,
And mossy network too is there,   40
As if by hand of lady fair
The work had woven been,
And cups, the darlings of the eye,
So deep is their vermilion dye.

Ah me! what lovely tints are there!
Of olive-green and scarlet bright,
In spikes, in branches, and in stars,
Green, red, and pearly white.
This heap of earth o'ergrown with moss,

Which close beside the thorn you see,   50
So fresh in all its beauteous dyes,
Is like an infant's grave in size
As like as like can be:
But never, never any where,
An infant's grave was half so fair.

Now would you see this aged thorn,
This pond and beauteous hill of moss,
You must take care and chuse your time
The mountain when to cross.
For oft there sits, between the heap   60
That's like an infant's grave in size,
And that same pond of which I spoke,
A woman in a scarlet cloak,
And to herself she cries,
'Oh misery! oh misery!
Oh woe is me! oh misery!'

At all times of the day and night
This wretched woman thither goes,
And she is known to every star,
And every wind that blows;
And there beside the thorn she sits   70
When the blue day-light's in the skies,
And when the whirlwind's on the hill,
Or frosty air is keen and still,
And to herself she cries,
'Oh misery! oh misery!
Oh woe is me! oh misery!'

'Now wherefore thus, by day and night,
In rain, in tempest, and in snow,
Thus to the dreary mountain-top   80
Does this poor woman go?
And why sits she beside the thorn
When the blue day-light's in the sky,
Or when the whirlwind's on the hill,
Or frosty air is keen and still,
And wherefore does she cry?—
Oh wherefore? wherefore? tell me why
Does she repeat that doleful cry?'

I cannot tell; I wish I could;
For the true reason no one knows,   90
But if you'd gladly view the spot,
The spot to which she goes;
The heap that's like an infant's grave,
The pond—and thorn, so old and grey,
Pass by her door—'tis seldom shut—
And if you see her in her hut,
Then to the spot away!—
I never heard of such as dare
Approach the spot when she is there.

'But wherefore to the mountain-top   100
Can this unhappy woman go,
Whatever star is in the skies,
Whatever wind may blow?'
Nay rack your brain—'tis all in vain,
I'll tell you every thing I know;
But to the thorn, and to the pond
Which is a little step beyond,
I wish that you would go:
Perhaps when you are at the place
You something of her tale may trace.   110

I'll give you the best help I can:
Before you up the mountain go,
Up to the dreary mountain-top,
I'll tell you all I know.
'Tis now some two and twenty years,
Since she (her name is Martha Ray)
Gave with a maiden's true good will
Her company to Stephen Hill;
And she was blithe and gay,
And she was happy, happy still   120
Whene'er she thought of Stephen Hill.

And they had fixed the wedding-day,
The morning that must wed them both;
But Stephen to another maid
Had sworn another oath;
And with this other maid to church

Unthinking Stephen went—
Poor Martha! on that woful day
A cruel, cruel fire, they say,
Into her bones was sent: 130
It dried her body like a cinder,
And almost turned her brain to tinder.

They say, full six months after this,
While yet the summer-leaves were green,
She to the mountain-top would go,
And there was often seen.
'Tis said, a child was in her womb,
As now to any eye was plain;
She was with child, and she was mad,
Yet often she was sober sad   140
From her exceeding pain.
Oh me! ten thousand times I'd rather
That he had died, that cruel father!

Sad case for such a brain to hold
Communion with a stirring child!
Sad case, as you may think, for one
Who had a brain so wild!
Last Christmas when we talked of this,
Old Farmer Simpson did maintain,
That in her womb the infant wrought   150
About its mother's heart, and brought
Her senses back again:
And when at last her time drew near,
Her looks were calm, her senses clear.

No more I know, I wish I did,
And I would tell it all to you;
For what became of this poor child
There's none that ever knew:
And if a child was born or no,
There's no one that could ever tell;   160
And if 'twas born alive or dead,
There's no one knows, as I have said,
But some remember well,
That Martha Ray about this time
Would up the mountain often climb.

And all that winter, when at night
The wind blew from the mountain-peak,
'Twas worth your while, though in the dark,
The church-yard path to seek:
For many a time and oft were heard   170
Cries coming from the mountain-head,
Some plainly living voices were,
And others, I've heard many swear,
Were voices of the dead:
I cannot think, whate'er they say,
They had to do with Martha Ray.

But that she goes to this old thorn,
The thorn which I've described to you,
And there sits in a scarlet cloak,
I will be sworn is true.   180
For one day with my telescope,
To view the ocean wide and bright,
When to this country first I came,
Ere I had heard of Martha's name,
I climbed the mountain's height:
A storm came on, and I could see
No object higher than my knee.

'Twas mist and rain, and storm and rain,
No screen, no fence could I discover,
And then the wind! in faith, it was   190
A wind full ten times over.
I looked around, I thought I saw
A jutting crag, and off I ran,
Head-foremost, through the driving rain,
The shelter of the crag to gain,
And, as I am a man,
Instead of jutting crag, I found
A woman seated on the ground.

I did not speak—I saw her face,
Her face it was enough for me;   200
I turned about and heard her cry,
'O misery! O misery!'
And there she sits, until the moon

Through half the clear blue sky will go,
And when the little breezes make
The waters of the pond to shake,
As all the country know,
She shudders and you hear her cry,
'Oh misery! oh misery!'

'But what's the thorn? and what's the pond?   210
And what's the hill of moss to her?
And what's the creeping breeze that comes
The little pond to stir?'
I cannot tell; but some will say
She hanged her baby on the tree,
Some say she drowned it in the pond,
Which is a little step beyond,
But all and each agree,
The little babe was buried there,
Beneath that hill of moss so fair.   220

I've heard the scarlet moss is red
With drops of that poor infant's blood;
But kill a new-born infant thus!
I do not think she could.
Some say, if to the pond you go,
And fix on it a steady view,
The shadow of a babe you trace,
A baby and a baby's face,
And that it looks at you;
Whene'er you look on it, 'tis plain   230
The baby looks at you again.

And some had sworn an oath that she
Should be to public justice brought;
And for the little infant's bones
With spades they would have sought.
But then the beauteous hill of moss
Before their eyes began to stir;
And for full fifty yards around,
The grass it shook upon the ground;
But all do still aver   240

The little babe is buried there,
Beneath that hill of moss so fair.

I cannot tell how this may be,
But plain it is, the thorn is bound
With heavy tufts of moss, that strive
To drag it to the ground.
And this I know, full many a time,
When she was on the mountain high,
By day, and in the silent night,
When all the stars shone clear and bright,   250
That I have heard her cry,
'Oh misery! oh misery!
O woe is me! oh misery!'

'A whirl-blast from behind the hill'

A whirl-blast from behind the hill
Rushed o'er the wood with startling sound:
Then all at once the air was still,
And showers of hail-stones pattered round.
Where leafless Oaks towered high above,
I sate within an undergrove
Of tallest hollies, tall and green,
A fairer bower was never seen.
From year to year the spacious floor
With withered leaves is covered o'er,   10
You could not lay a hair between:
And all the year the bower is green.
But see! where'er the hailstones drop
The withered leaves all skip and hop,
There's not a breeze—no breath of air—
Yet here, and there, and every where
Along the floor, beneath the shade
By those embowering hollies made,
The leaves in myriads jump and spring,
As if with pipes and music rare   20
Some Robin Good-fellow were there,

And all those leaves, that jump and spring,
Were each a joyous, living thing.

Oh! grant me Heaven a heart at ease
That I may never cease to find,
Even in appearances like these
Enough to nourish and to stir my mind!

The Idiot Boy

'Tis eight o'clock,—a clear March night,
The moon is up—the sky is blue,
The owlet in the moonlight air,
He shouts from nobody knows where;
He lengthens out his lonely shout,
Halloo! halloo! a long halloo!

—Why bustle thus about your door,
What means this bustle, Betty Foy?
Why are you in this mighty fret?
And why on horseback have you set   10
Him whom you love, your idiot boy?

Beneath the moon that shines so bright,
Till she is tired, let Betty Foy
With girt and stirrup fiddle-faddle;
But wherefore set upon a saddle
Him whom she loves, her idiot boy?

There's scarce a soul that's out of bed;
Good Betty! put him down again;
His lips with joy they burr at you,
But, Betty! what has he to do   20
With stirrup, saddle, or with rein?

The world will say 'tis very idle,
Bethink you of the time of night;
There's not a mother, no not one,
But when she hears what you have done,
Oh! Betty she'll be in a fright.

But Betty's bent on her intent,
For her good neighbour, Susan Gale,
Old Susan, she who dwells alone,
Is sick, and makes a piteous moan,   30
As if her very life would fail.

There's not a house within a mile,
No hand to help them in distress:
Old Susan lies a bed in pain,
And sorely puzzled are the twain,
For what she ails they cannot guess.

And Betty's husband's at the wood,
Where by the week he doth abide,
A woodman in the distant vale;
There's none to help poor Susan Gale,   40
What must be done? what will betide?

And Betty from the lane has fetched
Her pony, that is mild and good,
Whether he be in joy or pain,
Feeding at will along the lane,
Or bringing faggots from the wood.

And he is all in travelling trim,
And by the moonlight, Betty Foy
Has up upon the saddle set,
The like was never heard of yet,   50
Him whom she loves, her idiot boy.

And he must post without delay
Across the bridge that's in the dale,
And by the church, and o'er the down,
To bring a doctor from the town,
Or she will die, old Susan Gale.

There is no need of boot or spur,
There is no need of whip or wand,
For Johnny has his holly-bough,
And with a hurly-burly now   60
He shakes the green bough in his hand.

And Betty o'er and o'er has told
The boy who is her best delight,
Both what to follow, what to shun,
What do, and what to leave undone,
How turn to left, and how to right.

And Betty's most especial charge,
Was, 'Johnny! Johnny! mind that you
Come home again, nor stop at all,
Come home again, whate'er befal,   70
My Johnny do, I pray you do.'

To this did Johnny answer make,
Both with his head, and with his hand,
And proudly shook the bridle too,
And then! his words were not a few,
Which Betty well could understand.

And now that Johnny is just going,
Though Betty's in a mighty flurry,
She gently pats the pony's side,
On which her idiot boy must ride,   80
And seems no longer in a hurry.

But when the pony moved his legs,
Oh! then for the poor idiot boy!
For joy he cannot hold the bridle,
For joy his head and heels are idle,
He's idle all for very joy.

And while the pony moves his legs,
In Johnny's left-hand you may see,
The green bough's motionless and dead;
The moon that shines above his head   90
Is not more still and mute than he.

His heart it was so full of glee,
That till full fifty yards were gone,
He quite forgot his holly whip,
And all his skill in horsemanship,
Oh! happy, happy, happy John.

And Betty's standing at the door,
And Betty's face with joy o'erflows,
Proud of herself, and proud of him,
She sees him in his travelling trim;   100
How quietly her Johnny goes.

The silence of her idiot boy,
What hopes it sends to Betty's heart!
He's at the guide-post—he turns right,
She watches till he's out of sight,
And Betty will not then depart.

Burr, burr—now Johnny's lips they burr,
As loud as any mill, or near it,
Meek as a lamb the pony moves,
And Johnny makes the noise he loves,   110
And Betty listens, glad to hear it.

Away she hies to Susan Gale:
And Johnny's in a merry tune,
The owlets hoot, the owlets curr,
And Johnny's lips they burr, burr, burr,
And on he goes beneath the moon.

His steed and he right well agree,
For of this pony there's a rumour,
That should he lose his eyes and ears,
And should he live a thousand years,   120
He never will be out of humour.

But then he is a horse that thinks!
And when he thinks his pace is slack;
Now, though he knows poor Johnny well,
Yet for his life he cannot tell
What he has got upon his back.

So through the moonlight lanes they go,
And far into the moonlight dale,
And by the church, and o'er the down,
To bring a doctor from the town,   130
To comfort poor old Susan Gale.

And Betty, now at Susan's side,
Is in the middle of her story,
What comfort Johnny soon will bring,
With many a most diverting thing,
Of Johnny's wit and Johnny's glory.

And Betty's still at Susan's side:
By this time she's not quite so flurried;
Demure with porringer and plate
She sits, as if in Susan's fate   140
Her life and soul were buried.

But Betty, poor good woman! she,
You plainly in her face may read it,
Could lend out of that moment's store
Five years of happiness or more,
To any that might need it.

But yet I guess that now and then
With Betty all was not so well,
And to the road she turns her ears,
And thence full many a sound she hears,   150
Which she to Susan will not tell.

Poor Susan moans, poor Susan groans,
'As sure as there's a moon in heaven,'
Cries Betty, 'he'll be back again;
They'll both be here, 'tis almost ten,
They'll both be here before eleven.'

Poor Susan moans, poor Susan groans,
The clock gives warning for eleven;
'Tis on the stroke—'If Johnny's near,'
Quoth Betty 'he will soon be here,   160
As sure as there's a moon in heaven.'

The clock is on the stroke of twelve,
And Johnny is not yet in sight,
The moon's in heaven, as Betty sees,
But Betty is not quite at ease;
And Susan has a dreadful night.

And Betty, half an hour ago,
On Johnny vile reflections cast;
'A little idle sauntering thing!'
With other names, an endless string,   170
But now that time is gone and past.

And Betty's drooping at the heart,
That happy time all past and gone,
'How can it be he is so late?
The doctor he has made him wait,
Susan! they'll both be here anon.'

And Susan's growing worse and worse,
And Betty's in a sad quandary;
And then there's nobody to say
If she must go or she must stay: 180
—She's in a sad quandary.

The clock is on the stroke of one;
But neither Doctor nor his guide
Appear along the moonlight road,
There's neither horse nor man abroad,
And Betty's still at Susan's side.

And Susan she begins to fear
Of sad mischances not a few,
That Johnny may perhaps be drowned,
Or lost perhaps, and never found;   190
Which they must both for ever rue.

She prefaced half a hint of this
With, 'God forbid it should be true!'
At the first word that Susan said
Cried Betty, rising from the bed,
'Susan, I'd gladly stay with you.

I must be gone, I must away,
Consider, Johnny's but half-wise;
Susan, we must take care of him,
If he is hurt in life or limb'—   200
'Oh God forbid!' poor Susan cries.

'What can I do?' says Betty, going,
'What can I do to ease your pain?
Good Susan tell me, and I'll stay;
I fear you're in a dreadful way,
But I shall soon be back again.'

'Good Betty go, good Betty go,
There's nothing that can ease my pain.'
Then off she hies, but with a prayer
That God poor Susan's life would spare,   210
Till she comes back again.

So, through the moonlight lane she goes,
And far into the moonlight dale;
And how she ran, and how she walked,
And all that to herself she talked,
Would surely be a tedious tale.

In high and low, above, below,
In great and small, in round and square,
In tree and tower was Johnny seen,
In bush and brake, in black and green,   220
'Twas Johnny, Johnny, every where.

She's past the bridge that's in the dale,
And now the thought torments her sore,
Johnny perhaps his horse forsook,
To hunt the moon that's in the brook,
And never will be heard of more.

And now she's high upon the down,
Alone amid a prospect wide;
There's neither Johnny nor his horse,
Among the fern or in the gorse;   230
There's neither doctor nor his guide.

'Oh saints! what is become of him?
Perhaps he's climbed into an oak,
Where he will stay till he is dead;
Or sadly he has been misled,
And joined the wandering gypsey-folk.

Or him that wicked pony's carried
To the dark cave, the goblins' hall,
Or in the castle he's pursuing,
Among the ghosts, his own undoing;   240
Or playing with the waterfall.'

At poor old Susan then she railed,
While to the town she posts away;
'If Susan had not been so ill,
Alas! I should have had him still,
My Johnny, till my dying day.'

Poor Betty! in this sad distemper,
The doctor's self would hardly spare,
Unworthy things she talked and wild,
Even he, of cattle of the most mild,   250
The pony had his share.

And now she's got into the town,
And to the doctor's door she hies;
'Tis silence all on every side;
The town so long, the town so wide,
Is silent as the skies.

And now she's at the doctor's door,
She lifts the knocker, rap, rap, rap,
The doctor at the casement shews,
His glimmering eyes that peep and doze;   260
And one hand rubs his old night-cap.

'Oh Doctor! Doctor! where's my Johnny?'
'I'm here, what is't you want with me?'
'Oh Sir! you know I'm Betty Foy,
And I have lost my poor dear boy,
You know him—him you often see;

He's not so wise as some folks be,'
'The devil take his wisdom!' said
The Doctor, looking somewhat grim,
'What, woman! should I know of him?'   270
And, grumbling, he went back to bed.

'O woe is me! O woe is me!
Here will I die; here will I die;
I thought to find my Johnny here,
But he is neither far nor near,
Oh! what a wretched mother I!'

She stops, she stands, she looks about,
Which way to turn she cannot tell.
Poor Betty! it would ease her pain
If she had heart to knock again;   280
—The clock strikes three—a dismal knell!

Then up along the town she hies,
No wonder if her senses fail,
This piteous news so much it shocked her,
She quite forgot to send the Doctor,
To comfort poor old Susan Gale.

And now she's high upon the down,
And she can see a mile of road,
'Oh cruel! I'm almost three-score;
Such night as this was ne'er before,   290
There's not a single soul abroad.'

She listens, but she cannot hear
The foot of horse, the voice of man;
The streams with softest sound are flowing,
The grass you almost hear it growing,
You hear it now if e'er you can.

The owlets through the long blue night
Are shouting to each other still:
Fond lovers, yet not quite hob nob,
They lengthen out the tremulous sob.   300
That echoes far from hill to hill.

Poor Betty now has lost all hope,
Her thoughts are bent on deadly sin;
A green-grown pond she just has passed,
And from the brink she hurries fast,
Lest she should drown herself therein.

And now she sits her down and weeps;
Such tears she never shed before;
'O dear, dear pony! my sweet joy!
Oh carry back my idiot boy!   310
And we will ne'er o'erload thee more.'

A thought is come into her head;
'The pony he is mild and good,
And we have always used him well;
Perhaps he's gone along the dell,
And carried Johnny to the wood.'

Then up she springs as if on wings;
She thinks no more of deadly sin;
If Betty fifty ponds should see,
The last of all her thoughts would be,   320
To drown herself therein.

Oh reader! now that I might tell
What Johnny and his horse are doing!
What they've been doing all this time,
Oh could I put it into rhyme,
A most delightful tale pursuing!

Perhaps, and no unlikely thought!
He with his pony now doth roam
The cliffs and peaks so high that are,
To lay his hands upon a star,   330
And in his pocket bring it home.

Perhaps he's turned himself about,
His face unto his horse's tail,
And still and mute, in wonder lost,
All like a silent horseman-ghost,
He travels on along the vale.

And now, perhaps, he's hunting sheep,
A fierce and dreadful hunter he!
Yon valley, that's so trim and green,
In five months' time, should he be seen.   340
A desert wilderness will be.

Perhaps, with head and heels on fire,
And like the very soul of evil,
He's galloping away, away,
And so he'll gallop on for aye,
The bane of all that dread the devil.

I to the muses have been bound,
These fourteen years, by strong indentures;
Oh gentle muses! let me tell
But half of what to him befel.   350
For sure he met with strange adventures.

Oh gentle muses! is this kind?
Why will ye thus my suit repel?
Why of your further aid bereave me?
And can ye thus unfriended leave me?
Ye muses! whom I love so well.

Who's yon, that, near the waterfall,
Which thunders down with headlong force,
Beneath the moon, yet shining fair,
As careless as if nothing were,   360
Sits upright on a feeding horse?

Unto his horse, that's feeding free,
He seems, I think, the rein to give;
Of moon or stars he takes no heed;
Of such we in romances read,
—'Tis Johnny! Johnny! as I live.

And that's the very pony too.
Where is she, where is Betty Foy?
She hardly can sustain her fears;
The roaring water-fall she hears,   370
And cannot find her idiot boy.

Your pony's worth his weight in gold,
Then calm your terrors, Betty Foy!
She's coming from among the trees,
And now, all full in view, she sees
Him whom she loves, her idiot boy.

And Betty sees the pony too:
Why stand you thus Good Betty Foy?
It is not goblin, 'tis no ghost,
'Tis he whom you so long have lost,   380
He whom you love, your idiot boy.

She looks again—her arms are up—
She screams—she cannot move for joy;
She darts as with a torrent's force,
She almost has o'erturned the horse,
And fast she holds her idiot boy.

And Johnny burrs and laughs aloud,
Whether in cunning or in joy,
I cannot tell; but while he laughs,
Betty a drunken pleasure quaffs,   390
To hear again her idiot boy.

And now she's at the pony's tail,
And now she's at the pony's head,
On that side now, and now on this,
And almost stifled with her bliss,
A few sad tears does Betty shed.

She kisses o'er and o'er again,
Him whom she loves, her idiot boy,
She's happy here, she's happy there,
She is uneasy every where;   400
Her limbs are all alive with joy.

She pats the pony, where or when
She knows not, happy Betty Foy!
The little pony glad may be,
But he is milder far than she,
You hardly can perceive his joy.

'Oh! Johnny, never mind the Doctor;
You've done your best, and that is all.'
She took the reins, when this was said,
And gently turned the pony's head   410
From the loud water-fall.

By this the stars were almost gone,
The moon was setting on the hill,
So pale you scarcely looked at her:
The little birds began to stir,
Though yet their tongues were still.

The pony, Betty, and her boy,
Wind slowly through the woody dale:
And who is she, be-times abroad,
That hobbles up the steep rough road?   420
Who is it, but old Susan Gale?

Long Susan lay deep lost in thought,
And many dreadful fears beset her,
Both for her messenger and nurse;
And as her mind grew worse and worse,
Her body it grew better.

She turned, she tossed herself in bed,
On all sides doubts and terrors met her;
Point after point did she discuss;
And while her mind was fighting thus,   430
Her body still grew better.

'Alas! what is become of them?
These fears can never be endured,
I'll to the wood.'—The word scarce said,
Did Susan rise up from her bed,
As if by magic cured.

Away she posts up hill and down,
And to the wood at length is come,
She spies her friends, she shouts a greeting;
Oh me! it is a merry meeting,   440
As ever was in Christendom.

The owls have hardly sung their last,
While our four travellers homeward wend;
The owls have hooted all night long,
And with the owls began my song,
And with the owls must end.

For while they all were travelling home,
Cried Betty, 'Tell us Johnny, do,
Where all this long night you have been,
What you have heard, what you have seen,   450
And Johnny, mind you tell us true.'

Now Johnny all night long had heard
The owls in tuneful concert strive;
No doubt too he the moon had seen;
For in the moonlight he had been
From eight o'clock till five.

And thus to Betty's question, he
Made answer, like a traveller bold,
(His very words I give to you,)
'The cocks did crow to-whoo, to-whoo,   460
And the sun did shine so cold.'
—Thus answered Johnny in his glory,
And that was all his travel's story.

Lines written in Early Spring

I heard a thousand blended notes,
While in a grove I sate reclined,
In that sweet mood when pleasant thoughts
Bring sad thoughts to the mind.

To her fair works did nature link
The human soul that through me ran;
And much it grieved my heart to think
What man has made of man.

Through primrose-tufts, in that sweet bower,
The periwinkle trailed its wreathes;   10
And 'tis my faith that every flower
Enjoys the air it breathes.

The birds around me hopped and played:
Their thoughts I cannot measure,
But the least motion which they made,
It seemed a thrill of pleasure.

The budding twigs spread out their fan,
To catch the breezy air;
And I must think, do all I can,
That there was pleasure there.   20

If I these thoughts may not prevent,
If such be of my creed the plan,
Have I not reason to lament
What man has made of man?

Anecdote for Fathers

SHEWING HOW THE ART OF LYING MAY BE TAUGHT

I have a boy of five years old,
His face is fair and fresh to see;
His limbs are cast in beauty's mould,
And dearly he loves me.

One morn we strolled on our dry walk,
Our quiet house all full in view,
And held such intermitted talk
As we are wont to do.

My thoughts on former pleasures ran;
I thought of Kilve's delightful shore,   10
My pleasant home, when spring began,
A long, long year before.

A day it was when I could bear
To think, and think, and think again;
With so much happiness to spare,
I could not feel a pain.

My boy was by my side, so slim
And graceful in his rustic dress!
And oftentimes I talked to him,
In very idleness.   20

The young lambs ran a pretty race;
The morning sun shone bright and warm;
'Kilve,' said I, 'was a pleasant place,
And so is Liswyn farm.

My little boy, which like you more,'
I said and took him by the arm—
'Our home by Kilve's delightful shore,
Or here at Liswyn farm?'

'And tell me, had you rather be,'
I said and held him by the arm,   30
'At Kilve's smooth shore by the green sea,
Or here at Liswyn farm?'

In careless mood he looked at me,
While still I held him by the arm,
And said, 'At Kilve I'd rather be
Than here at Liswyn farm.'

'Now, little Edward, say why so;
My little Edward, tell me why;'
'I cannot tell, I do not know.'
'Why this is strange,' said I.   40

'For, here are woods and green-hills warm;
There surely must some reason be
Why you would change sweet Liswyn farm
For Kilve by the green sea.'

At this, my boy, so fair and slim,
Hung down his head, nor made reply;
And five times did I say to him,
'Why? Edward, tell me why?'

His head he raised—there was in sight,
It caught his eye, he saw it plain—　　50
Upon the house-top, glittering bright,
A broad and gilded vane.

Then did the boy his tongue unlock,
And thus to me he made reply;
'At Kilve there was no weather-cock,
And that's the reason why.'

O dearest, dearest boy! my heart
For better lore would seldom yearn,
Could I but teach the hundredth part
Of what from thee I learn.　　60

We Are Seven

A simple child, dear brother Jim,
That lightly draws its breath,
And feels its life in every limb,
What should it know of death?

I met a little cottage girl,
She was eight years old, she said;
Her hair was thick with many a curl
That clustered round her head.

She had a rustic, woodland air,
And she was wildly clad;　　10
Her eyes were fair, and very fair,
—Her beauty made me glad.

'Sisters and brothers, little maid,
How many may you be?'
'How many? seven in all,' she said,
And wondering looked at me.

'And where are they, I pray you tell?'
She answered, 'Seven are we,
And two of us at Conway dwell,
And two are gone to sea.   20

Two of us in the church-yard lie,
My sister and my brother,
And in the church-yard cottage, I
Dwell near them with my mother.'

'You say that two at Conway dwell,
And two are gone to sea,
Yet you are seven; I pray you tell
Sweet Maid, how this may be?'

Then did the little Maid reply,
'Seven boys and girls are we;   30
Two of us in the church-yard lie,
Beneath the church-yard tree.'

'You run about, my little maid,
Your limbs they are alive;
If two are in the church-yard laid,
Then ye are only five.'

'Their graves are green, they may be seen,'
The little Maid replied,
'Twelve steps or more from my mother's door,
And they are side by side.   40

'My stockings there I often knit,
My 'kerchief there I hem;
And there upon the ground I sit—
I sit and sing to them.

And often after sunset, Sir,
When it is light and fair,
I take my little porringer,
And eat my supper there.

The first that died was little Jane;
In bed she moaning lay,   50
Till God released her of her pain,
And then she went away.

So in the church-yard she was laid,
And all the summer dry,
Together round her grave we played,
My brother John and I.

And when the ground was white with snow,
And I could run and slide,
My brother John was forced to go,
And he lies by her side.'   60

'How many are you then,' said I,
'If they two are in Heaven?'
The little Maiden did reply,
'O Master! we are seven.'

'But they are dead; those two are dead!
Their spirits are in heaven!'
'Twas throwing words away; for still
The little Maid would have her will,
And said, 'Nay, we are seven!'

Simon Lee, the Old Huntsman

WITH AN INCIDENT IN WHICH HE WAS CONCERNED

In the sweet shire of Cardigan,
Not far from pleasant Ivor-hall,
An old man dwells, a little man,
I've heard he once was tall.
Of years he has upon his back,
No doubt, a burthen weighty;
He says he is three score and ten,
But others say he's eighty.

A long blue livery-coat has he,
That's fair behind, and fair before;   10
Yet, meet him where you will, you see
At once that he is poor.
Full five and twenty years he lived
A running huntsman merry;
And, though he has but one eye left,
His cheek is like a cherry.

No man like him the horn could sound,
And no man was so full of glee;
To say the least, four counties round
Had heard of Simon Lee;   20
His master's dead, and no one now
Dwells in the hall of Ivor;
Men, dogs, and horses, all are dead;
He is the sole survivor.

His hunting feats have him bereft
Of his right eye, as you may see:
And then, what limbs those feats have left
To poor old Simon Lee!
He has no son, he has no child,
His wife, an aged woman,   30
Lives with him, near the waterfall,
Upon the village common.

And he is lean and he is sick,
His little body's half awry;
His ancles they are swoln and thick;
His legs are thin and dry.
When he was young he little knew
Of husbandry or tillage;
And now he's forced to work, though weak,
—The weakest in the village.   40

He all the country could outrun,
Could leave both man and horse behind;
And often, ere the race was done,
He reeled and was stone-blind.

And still there's something in the world
At which his heart rejoices;
For when the chiming hounds are out,
He dearly loves their voices!

Old Ruth works out of doors with him,
And does what Simon cannot do;   50
For she, not over stout of limb,
Is stouter of the two.
And though you with your utmost skill
From labour could not wean them,
Alas! 'tis very little, all
Which they can do between them.

Beside their moss-grown hut of clay,
Not twenty paces from the door,
A scrap of land they have, but they
Are poorest of the poor.   60
This scrap of land he from the heath
Enclosed when he was stronger;
But what avails the land to them,
Which they can till no longer?

Few months of life has he in store,
As he to you will tell,
For still, the more he works, the more
His poor old ancles swell.
My gentle reader, I perceive
How patiently you've waited,   70
And I'm afraid that you expect
Some tale will be related.

O reader! had you in your mind
Such stores as silent thought can bring,
O gentle reader! you would find
A tale in every thing.
What more I have to say is short,
I hope you'll kindly take it;
It is no tale; but should you think,
Perhaps a tale you'll make it.   80

One summer-day I chanced to see
This old man doing all he could
About the root of an old tree,
A stump of rotten wood.
The mattock tottered in his hand;
So vain was his endeavour
That at the root of the old tree
He might have worked for ever.

'You're overtasked, good Simon Lee,
Give me your tool' to him I said;   90
And at the word right gladly he
Received my proffered aid.
I struck, and with a single blow
The tangled root I severed,
At which the poor old man so long
And vainly had endeavoured.

The tears into his eyes were brought,
And thanks and praises seemed to run
So fast out of his heart, I thought
They never would have done.   100
—I've heard of hearts unkind, kind deeds
With coldness still returning.
Alas! the gratitude of men
Has oftner left me mourning.

The Last of the Flock

In distant countries I have been,
And yet I have not often seen
A healthy man, a man full grown,
Weep in the public roads alone.
But such a one, on English ground,
And in the broad high-way, I met;
Along the broad high-way he came,
His cheeks with tears were wet:

Sturdy he seemed, though he was sad;
And in his arms a lamb he had.   10

He saw me, and he turned aside,
As if he wished himself to hide:
Then with his coat he made essay
To wipe those briny tears away.
I followed him, and said, 'My friend,
What ails you? wherefore weep you so?'
—'Shame on me, Sir! this lusty lamb,
He makes my tears to flow.
To-day I fetched him from the rock;
He is the last of all my flock.   20

When I was young, a single man,
And after youthful follies ran,
Though little given to care and thought,
Yet, so it was, a ewe I bought;
And other sheep from her I raised,
As healthy sheep as you might see;
And then I married, and was rich
As I could wish to be;
Of sheep I numbered a full score,
And every year encreased my store.   30

Year after year my stock it grew;
And from this one, this single ewe,
Full fifty comely sheep I raised,
As sweet a flock as ever grazed!
Upon the mountain did they feed;
They throve, and we at home did thrive:
—This lusty lamb of all my store
Is all that is alive:
And now I care not if we die,
And perish all of poverty.   40

Six children, Sir! had I to feed,
Hard labour in a time of need!
My pride was tamed, and in our grief
I of the parish asked relief.

They said I was a wealthy man;
My sheep upon the mountain fed,
And it was fit that thence I took
Whereof to buy us bread:'
'Do this: how can we give to you,'
They cried, 'what to the poor is due?'   50

I sold a sheep as they had said,
And bought my little children bread,
And they were healthy with their food;
For me it never did me good.
A woeful time it was for me,
To see the end of all my gains,
The pretty flock which I had reared
With all my care and pains,
To see it melt like snow away!
For me it was a woeful day.   60

Another still! and still another!
A little lamb, and then its mother!
It was a vein that never stopped,
Like blood-drops from my heart they dropped.
Till thirty were not left alive
They dwindled, dwindled, one by one,
And I may say that many a time
I wished they all were gone:
They dwindled one by one away;
For me it was a woeful day.   70

To wicked deeds I was inclined,
And wicked fancies crossed my mind,
And every man I chanced to see,
I thought he knew some ill of me.
No peace, no comfort could I find,
No ease, within doors or without,
And crazily, and wearily,
I went my work about.
Oft-times I thought to run away;
For me it was a woeful day.   80

Sir! 'twas a precious flock to me,
As dear as my own children be;
For daily with my growing store
I loved my children more and more.
Alas! it was an evil time;
God cursed me in my sore distress,
I prayed, yet every day I thought
I loved my children less;
And every week, and every day,
My flock, it seemed to melt away.   90

They dwindled, Sir, sad sight to see!
From ten to five, from five to three,
A lamb, a weather, and a ewe;
And then at last, from three to two;
And of my fifty, yesterday
I had but only one,
And here it lies upon my arm,
Alas! and I have none;
To-day I fetched it from the rock;
It is the last of all my flock.'   100

Peter Bell, a Tale

PROLOGUE

There's something in a flying horse,
There's something in a huge balloon,
But through the clouds I'll never float
Until I have a little boat
In shape just like the crescent moon.

And now I have a little boat
In shape just like the crescent moon.
Fast through the clouds my boat can sail,
But if perchance your faith should fail,
Look up and you shall see me soon.   10

The woods, my friends, are round you roaring,
The woods are roaring like a sea;
The noise of danger's in your ears,
And you have all a thousand fears
Both for my little boat and me.

Meanwhile I from the helm admire
The pointed horns of my canoe,
And did not pity touch my breast
To see how you are all distressed,
Till my ribs ached I'd laugh at you.   20

Away we go, my boat and I,
Sure never man had such another,
Whether among the winds we strive
Or deep into the heavens we drive
We're both contented with each other.

Away we go, and what care we
For treasons, tumults and for wars?
We are as calm in our delight
As is the crescent moon so bright
Among the scattered stars.   30

Up goes my boat between the stars,
Through many a breathless field of light,
Through many a long blue field of ether,
Leaving ten thousand stars beneath her:
Up goes my little boat so bright.

The towns in Saturn are ill built,
But Jove has very pretty bowers;
The evening star is not amiss,
But what are all of them to this
This little earth of ours?   40

Then back again to our green earth.
What business had I here to roam?
The world for my remarks and me
Will not a whit the better be;
I've left my heart at home.

And that is then the dear green earth,
And that's the dear Pacific ocean,
And that is Caucasus so dear:
To think that I again am here,
Oh! my poor heart's commotion!   50

And there is little Tartary,
And there's the famous river Dnieper,
And there amid the ocean green
Is that sweet isle, of isles the queen,
Ye Fairies! from all evil keep her.

And there's the town where I was born,
And that's the house of Parson Swan.
My heart is touched, I must avow,
Consider where I've been, and now
I feel I am a man.   60

Never did fifty things at once
Appear so lovely, never, never.
The woods how sweetly do they ring
To hear the earth's sweet murmuring,
Thus could I hang for ever.

'Oh shame upon you! cruel shame!
Was ever such a heartless loon,
In such a lovely boat to sit,
And make no better use of it;
A boat that's like the crescent moon!   70

Out, out, and like a brooding hen
Beside your sooty hearth-stone cower.
Go creep along the dirt and pick
Your way with your good walking stick,
Just three good miles an hour.

Sure in the breast of full grown poet
So faint a heart was n'er before;
Come to the poet's wild delights,
I have ten thousand lovely sights,
Ten thousand sights in store.   80

I am a pretty little barge,
Then come I pray you come with me.
I want a comrade and for you
There's nothing which I would not do,
There's nothing which you shall not see.

Come, and above the land of snow
We'll sport amid the boreal morning,
Where thousand forms of light are riding
Among the stars, the stars now hiding
And now the stars adorning.   90

I know a deep romantic land,
A land that's deep and far away,
And fair it is as evening skies,
And in the farthest heart it lies
Of deepest Africa.

Or we'll into the world of fairy
Among the lovely shades of things,
The shadowy forms of mountains bare
And streams and bowers and ladies fair,
The shades of palaces and kings'.   100

'My pretty little form of light,
My sweet and beautiful canoe,
Now though it grieves me to the heart
I feel, I feel that we must part;
I must take leave of you.

You are a pretty little barge,
But while your pleasure you're pursuing
Without impediment or let,
My little barge, you quite forget
What in the world is doing.   110

Suppose now in the land of Fairy
That we should play our sportive pranks
Above those shadowy streams and there
Should make discoveries rich and rare,
The world would count us little thanks.

There was a time, a time indeed,
A time when poets lived in clover.
What boots it now to to keep the key
Of Fairyland? for, woe is me!
Those blessed days are over. 120

There is a party in the Bower,
Round the stone table in my garden;
The squire is there, and as I guess,
His pretty little daughter Bess,
With Harry the church-warden.

They were to come this very evening,
They know not I have been so far,
I see them, in number nine,
All in the bower of Weymouth pine,
I see them, there they are. 130

And there's the wife of Parson Swan,
And there's my good friend Stephen Otter.
And, ere the light of evening fail,
To them I must relate the tale
Of Peter Bell the Potter'.

Off flew my pretty little barge
All in a trance of indignation,
And I, as well as I was able,
On two poor legs to my stone table
Limped on with some vexation. 140

'Oh here he is!' cried little Bess,
She saw me at the garden door,
'Oh here he is!' cried Mistress Swan,
And all at once around me ran
Full nine of them or more.

'Sit down, I beg you would be seated',
Said I, no doubt with visage pale.
'And if my friends it pleases you,
This instant without more ado,
We'll have the promised tale'. 150

And so though somewhat out of breath
With lips, no doubt, and visage pale,
And sore too from a slight contusion,
Did I, to cover my confusion,
Begin the promised tale.

TALE OF PETER BELL

All by the moonlight river side
It gave three miserable groans
"'Tis come then to a pretty pass',
Said Peter to the groaning Ass,
'But I will bang your bones'.   160

'My dearest Sir', cried Mistress Swan,
'You've got at once into the middle'.
And little Bess with accents sweeter
Cried, 'Oh, dear Sir! but who is Peter?'
Said Harry, ''tis a downright riddle'.

The Squire cried, 'Sure as Paradise
Was lost to us by Adam's sinning,
We all are wandering in a wood,
And therefore, Sir, I wish you would
Begin at the beginning'.   170

'A Potter, Sir, he was by trade',
Cried I, becoming quite collected,
'And wheresoever he appeared
Full twenty times was Peter feared
For once that Peter was respected.

He two and thirty years or more
Had been a wild and woodland rover;
Had been in furthest Pembrokeshire,
And he had been at Exeter,
In Kent, Sir, and at Dover.   180

And he had been at Nottingham,
And well he knew the spire of Sarum;
And he had been where Lincoln's bell
To Shepherds in the distant dell
Rings out his loud alarum.

At York and at the hill of Brough
And merry Carlisle had he been,
And all along the lowlands fair,
And through the bonny shire of Ayr
As far as Aberdeen   190

And he had been at Inverness,
And Peter by the moonlight rills
Had danced his round with Highland lasses,
And he had lain beside his asses
On lofty Cheviot hills.

And he had trudged through Yorkshire dales
Among the rocks and winding scars,
Where deep and low the hamlets lie
Beneath their little patch of sky
And little lot of stars.   200

And all along the winding coast
Bespattered with the salt-sea foam;
Where'er a knot of houses lay
On headland or in hollow bay;
Sure never man like him did roam!

As well might Peter in the Fleet
Have been fast bound, a begging debtor.
He travelled here, he travelled there,
But Peter never was a hair
In heart or head the better.   210

He roved among the vales and streams,
In the green wood and hollow dell;
They were his dwellings night and day,
But Nature ne'er could find the way
Into the heart of Peter Bell.

In vain through every changeful year
Did Nature lead him as before;
A primrose by a river's brim
A yellow primrose was to him,
And it was nothing more.   220

Small change it made in Peter's heart
To see his gentle panniered train
With more than vernal pleasure feeding,
Where'er the tender grass was leading
Its earliest green along the lane.

In vain through water, earth, and air,
The soul of happy sound was spread,
When Peter on some April morn
Beneath the broom or budding thorn
Made the warm earth his lazy bed.   230

At noon, when by the forest's edge
He lay beneath the branches high,
The soft blue sky did never melt
Into his heart, he never felt
The witchery of the soft blue sky.

On a fair prospect some have looked
And felt, as I have heard them say,
As if the moving time had been
A thing as stedfast as the scene
On which they gazed themselves away.   240

With Peter Bell I need not tell
That this had never been the case;
He was a carl as wild and rude
As ever hue and cry pursued,
As ever ran a felon's race.

Of all that lead a lawless life,
Of all that *love* their lawless lives,
In city or in village small,
He was the wildest far of all;
He had a dozen wedded wives'.   250

'Oh monster!' cried the Parson's Lady.
'Poor fellow!' echoed Stephen Otter.
'Poor fellow!' say you, Mistress Swan,
I do assure you such a man
Was Peter Bell the Potter.

He had a dozen wedded wives,
But how *one* wife could e'er come near him,
Upon my faith I cannot tell,
For I can say of Peter Bell
To see him was to fear him.   260

Though Nature ne'er could touch his heart
By lovely forms, and silent weather,
And tender sounds, yet you could see
At once that Peter Bell and she
Had often been together.

A savage wildness round him hung,
As of a dweller out of doors,
In his whole figure and his mien
A savage character was seen
Of mountains and of dreary moors.   270

To all the unshaped half-human thoughts
Which solitary Nature feeds
'Mid summer's storms or winter's ice,
Had Peter joined whatever vice
The cruel city breeds.

His face was keen as is the wind
That cuts along the hawthorn fence;
Of courage you saw little there
But, in its stead, a medley air
Of cunning and of impudence.   280

He had a dark and sidelong walk,
And long and slouching was his gait;
Between his looks so bare and bold,
You might perceive his spirit cold
Was playing with some inward bait.

His forehead wrinkled was and furred;
A work, one half of which was done
By thinking of his 'whens' and 'hows',
And half of wrinkling of his brows
Beneath the glaring sun.   290

There was a hardness in his cheek,
There was a hardness in his eye,
As if the man had fixed his face,
In many a solitary place,
Against the wind that sweeps the sky.

One night, (and now my little Bess
I'm coming to the promised tale),
One beautiful November night,
When the full moon was shining bright,
Upon the rapid river Swale,   300

Close by the river's winding banks
Was Peter travelling all alone;—
Whether to buy or sell, or led
By pleasure running in his head,
To me was never known.

Along the turf, and through the fern,
And in the mire he travelled on;
If he had left that night or day
His wife or wives I cannot say,
But wife or comrade he had none.   310

Some chuse to travel with a dog,
And Peter had a savage elf,
A lurcher, and he loved him well,
But sure it is that Peter Bell
That evening travelled by himself.

He trudged along through copse and brake,
He trudged along o'er hill and dale;
Nor for the moon cared he a tittle,
And for the stars he cared as little,
And for the murmuring river Swale.   320

Quoth Peter, 'Here's a nearer cut.
'Twill save a mile as sure as day'.
He took the path; the path did lead
Across a smooth and grassy mead
And a tall wood before him lay.

And now he to a wood is come,
And Peter there in whole cart loads
Is heaping curses on them all,
Commissioners both great and small,
Who made the zig-zag roads.   330

For while he drives among the boughs,
With head and hands and cheeks that burn,
With downright fury and with wrath,
There's little sign that Peter's path
Will to the road return.

The path grows dim, and dimmer still,
Now up, now down, his way he wends,
With all the sail that he can carry,
Till he is brought to an old quarry;
And there the path-way ends.   340

'What, back again, old grimface-no,
I'll grapple with the devil first!
Stretch like a yawning wolf your paws
But dam'me if by any laws
Of your's I'll e'er be cursed.'

And so where on the huge rough stones
The black and massy shadows lay,
And through the dark, and through the cold,
And through the yawning fissures old
Did Peter boldly press his way.   350

And in a moment opened out
A scene of soft and lovely hue,
Where blue and grey and tender green
Together made as sweet a scene
As ever human eye did view.

Beneath the clear blue sky you saw
A little plot of meadow ground;
But oh! far rather name it not,
Call it of earth a small green plot
With rocks encompassed round.   360

The Swale flowed under the green rocks,
But he flowed quiet and unseen.
You need a strong and stormy gale
To bring the noises of the Swale
To that green spot, so calm and green.

Now you'll suppose that Peter Bell
Had some temptation here to tarry,
And so it was, but I must add,
His heart was not a little glad
That he was out of the old quarry.   370

And is there no one dwelling here,
No hermit, with his beads and glass?
And does no little cottage look
Upon this green and silent nook?
Does no one live near this green grass?

Across that deep and quiet spot
Is Peter driving through the grass,
And now he is among the trees,
And turning round his head he sees
The solitary Ass.   380

'No doubt I'm foundered in these woods.
For once', quoth he 'I will be wise.
Upon my faith, I'll back again
And not to make my journey vain,
I'll take the Ass likewise'.

So off he goes, as you'll suppose,
With thought as blithe as my dream,
To where the Ass beside the bed
Of that green meadow hung his head
Over the silent stream.   390

'A pretty beast! though we'll allow
Not quite so fat as he might be.
Upon my soul, with such a platter
You should have been a little fatter;
But come Sir, come with me'.

But first friend Peter deems it fit
To spy about him far and near.
There's not a single house in sight,
No woodman's hut, no cottage light;
Peter you need not fear.   400

There's nothing to be seen but woods,
And rocks that spread a hoary gleam,
And this poor Ass, which near the bed
Of the green meadow hangs his head
Over the silent stream.

Close to the river's bank he stands;
His head is with a halter bound.
Now Peter's purpose did not alter
And so at once he seized the halter
And would have turned him round.   410

He pulled, the creature did not move.
Upon his back then Peter leapt,
And with his staff and heels he plied
The little Ass on either side,
But still the Ass his station kept.

Quoth Peter, 'You're a beast of mettle.
I see you'll suit me to an ace'.
And now the Ass through his left eye
On Peter turned most quietly,
Looked quietly in his face.   420

'What's this?' cries Peter, brandishing
A new peeled sapling white as cream,
The Ass knew well what Peter said,
But as before hung down his head
Over the silent stream.

Then Peter gave another jerk,
A jerk that from a dungeon floor
Would have pulled up an iron ring;
But still the heavy headed thing
Stood just as he had stood before.   430

Quoth Peter, leaping from the Ass,
'There is some plot against me laid',
Once more the little meadow ground,
And all the hoary cliffs around,
He cautiously surveyed.

There's nothing, Peter, far or near;
There's nothing with your purpose jars.
Only the full moon's in the sky,
And with her a fair company
The fairest of the stars.   440

All, all is silent, rocks and woods;
All, all is silent, far and near;
Only the Ass, with motion dull,
Upon the pivot of his skull
Turns round his long left ear.

Thought Peter, What can mean all this?
There is some ugly witchcraft here.
Once more the Ass, with motion dull,
Upon the pivot of his skull
Turned round his long left ear.   450

Quoth Peter, 'By the devil's beard,
I'll root you up you mongrel hound'.
And both his arms did pass
Beneath the belly of the Ass;
With both his arms he clasped him round.

Cried Peter, 'You'll be wise, I hope,
Before we're both five minutes older'.
Upon the Ass the sapling rings;
Each blow the arm of Peter stings
Up to the elbow and the shoulder.   460

At last, poor patient thing, at last
His sides they heaved, his belly stirred,
He gave a groan, and then another
Of that which went before the brother,
And then he gave a third.

All by the moonlight river side
He gave three miserable groans.
' 'Tis come then to a pretty pass',
Said Peter to the groaning Ass,
'But I will bang your bones'.   470

And now the little harmless beast
Gently, as if to take his ease,
The Ass whom Peter thus had bruised,
Whom he so cruelly had used,
Dropped gently down upon his knees.

And then upon his sides he fell,
And now to Peter's eye was shewn,
What till this time he had not seen,
That the poor ass was gaunt and lean
And almost wasted to the bone.   480

The meagre beast lay still as death;
No word of kind commiseration
Fell at the sight from Peter's tongue;
With hard contempt his heart was wrung,
With hatred, and with new vexation.

For Peter's merriment is flown,
His lips with rage and fury quiver.
Quoth he, 'You little mulish dog',
Quoth he, 'I'll fling you like a log
Head foremost down the river.   490

By God I will'. When this was said,
As stretched upon his side he lay,
To all the echoes, south and north,
And east and west, the Ass sent forth
A loud and horrible bray.

This outcry on the heart of Peter
Seems like a note of joy to strike.
Joy on the heart of Peter knocks,
But in the echo of the rocks
Was something Peter did not like.   500

Whether to cheer his coward heart,
Or that he felt a wicked chain
Twined round him like a magic spell,
Upon my faith I cannot tell,
But to the work he fell again.

Among the rocks and winding crags,
Among the mountains far away,
Once more the Ass did lengthen out,
Just like a sounding trumpet shout,
The long dry see-saw of his horrible bray.   510

What is there now in Peter's heart,
Or what's the power of that strange sound?
The moon uneasy looked, and dimmer
The broad blue heavens appeared to glimmer,
And the rocks staggered all around.

Yet in a fit of dastard rage
He stoops the Ass's neck to seize,
And in the clear deep stream below
He spies an ugly sight I trow,
Among the shadows of the trees.   520

Is it the shadow of the moon?
Is it the shadow of the cloud?
Is it a gallows there pourtrayed?
Is Peter of himself afraid?
Is it a coffin or a shroud?

Is it a fiend, that to a stake
Of red-hot fire himself is tethering?
Some solitary ward or cell,
Where lies a damned soul in hell,
Ten thousand miles from all his brethren?   530

Is it some party in a parlour
Crammed, just as they on earth were cramming,
Some sipping punch, some sipping tea,
But, as you by their faces see,
All silent and all damned?

'Tis no such thing, I do assure you,
Which Peter sees in the clear flood.
It is no ugly apprehension
Of eyes and ears, 'tis no invention;
It is a thing of flesh and blood.   540

It cannot be a water-rat,
No, Peter is not such a noddy.
The flesh and blood which Peter sees
Among the shadows of the trees
It is a dead man's body.

And Peter looks, and looks again,
Just like a man whose brain is haunted.
He looks, he cannot chuse but look,
Like one that's reading in a book,
A book that is enchanted.   550

He grasps the poor Ass by the jaws;
His hands and body shake and shiver;
And up and down, and to and fro,
The Ass's head and mouth they go,
Dimpling the surface of the river.

Sure uglier sights were never seen
By good or bad, by sad or simple,
Than Peter, while he holds the Ass,
Sees clearly in that wat'ry glass,
Where the still moonlight waters dimple.   560

Ah! well-a-day for Peter Bell,
He will be turned to iron soon.
Flesh, sinew, fibre, bone and gristle
His hat is up, his hairs they bristle,
Bristle and whiten in the moon.

And see him now fast bound like iron;
Head, joints and hands, his lips and teeth,
You'd think that he was looking at you,
But no, this uncouth iron statue
Is looking at the stream beneath.   570

And now poor Peter is convinced,
While still he holds the Ass's head,
That 'tis a fiend with visage wan,
A live man-fiend, a living man,
That's lying in the river's bed.

He looks, he looks, he looks again,
He sees a motion, hears a groan,
His eyes will burst, his heart will break,
He gives a loud and frightful shriek,
And back he falls just like a stone.   580

PART SECOND

We left poor Peter in a trance;
We left the dead man in the river;
The Ass is by the river-side,
And where the feeble breezes glide
Upon the stream the moonbeams quiver.

And Peter wakes, he wakes at last;
He feels the glimmerings of the moon,
And to stretch forth his hand he's trying,
Sure when he knows where he is lying
He'll sink into a second swoon.   590

He lifts his head, he sees his staff;
He touches, 'tis to him a treasure.
To find that he is not in hell,
As you'll suppose to Peter Bell
Doth give a sweet and languid pleasure.

And while upon his side he lies,
His head upon his elbow raised,
Almost you'd say as in a dream
His eyes are settling on the stream
Where he before had gazed.   600

No dimple now disturbs the stream,
In Peter's brain there is no riot.
His eye upon the stream he fixes,
And with the sight no terror mixes,
His heart is calm and quiet.

Quoth he, 'That is a dead man's face
Among the shadows of the trees.
Those are no doubt a dead man's knuckles,
And there you see his brass shoe buckles,
And there his breeches knees'.   610

At last he rises from his side,
And sits upright upon the ground,
And o'er the stream he hangs his nose
And points his staff, as you'd suppose
The river's depth to sound.

This sees the Ass, while on the grass
Close by the river's brink he lies,
And strait with a transition tragic,
That seems just like the touch of magic,
Up from the ground the Ass doth rise.   620

At this friend Peter round him looks,
And sees the poor and patient creature
Close to him, in his uncouth way,
Expressing all the joy he may
In every limb and every feature.

His meagre bones all shake with joy,
And close by Peter's side he stands;
While Peter o'er the river bends,
The little Ass his neck extends
And fondly licks his hands.   630

Such life is in the Ass's eyes,
Such life is in his limbs and ears,
That Peter Bell, if he had been
The veriest coward ever seen,
Must now have thrown aside his fears.

With caution Peter eyes the stream;
The sapling deep and deeper goes.
'The body is no doubt', quoth he,
'The thing which it appears to be,
It moves not, neither limbs nor clothes'.   640

The Ass looks on, and to his work
Is Peter quietly resigned.
He touches here, he touches there,
And now among the dead man's hair
His sapling Peter has entwined.

He pulls, and pulls, and pulls again,
And he whom the poor Ass had lost,
The man who had been four days dead,
Head foremost from the river's bed
Uprises like a Ghost.   650

And Peter draws him to dry land,
And lays him strait upon the grass.
And Peter feels some ugly pains
Across his liver, heart, and reins
In quick succession pass.

He sees the poor man's blue swoln face,
And through the brain of Peter pass,
Those ugly twitches fast and faster,
'No doubt', quoth he, 'he is the master
Of this poor miserable Ass'.   660

Then on the Ass did Peter look,
And all those ugly pains encreased,
To see her wasted to the bone,
To see the meagre skeleton
Of that poor faithful beast.

And scanning him from limb to limb,
'I've played with you an ugly game',
Quoth Peter to the Ass, 'but still
I did not mean to use you ill,
You must allow you were to blame'.   670

But the poor shadow, all this while,
The little Ass, what is he doing?
His joy is passed, his joy is flown,
He on his knees had laid him down
As if he were his grief renewing.

That Peter on his back should mount,
He's showing all the wish he can.
'I'll go, I'll go, if life forsake me,
No doubt he to his home will take me,
The cottage of this drowned man'.   680

This said, Friend Peter mounts forthwith
Upon that good and faithful Ass,
And strait, without a moment's stay,
The Ass turns quietly away,
Leaving the body on the grass.

The little Ass is strong at heart,
And firm he walks and bolt upright,
And well may the poor beast be wasted,
For four long days he has not tasted
Of food a single bite.   690

Amid that green and quiet spot
He four long days and nights had passed.
A sweeter meadow ne'er was seen,
And there the Ass four days had been
And never once had broke his fast.

Across the meadow they are gone,
And now are at the quarry's mouth;
The little Ass, who is the guide,
Into a thicket turns aside
And takes his way towards the south.   700

When in the silent woods they hear
A cry of lamentable sort;
Though there is nothing he should start at,
Yet in the middle of the thicket
The little Ass stops short.

And Peter hears the doleful sound,
And he in honest truth may say
The like came never to his ears,
Though he has been full thirty years
A rover night and day.   710

'Tis not a plover of the moors;
'Tis not a bittern of the fern;
Nor is it like a barking fox,
Nor like a night bird of the rocks,
Or wild cat in a woody glen.

The cry grows loud, and louder still,
The little Ass, who meant to climb
That lofty mountain which you see,
Beneath the shadow of the tree
Is listening all this time.   720

And Peter on the Ass's back
Is in the middle of the thicket,
And though he's used to whistle loud,
Whether alone or in a croud,
He's silent as a silent cricket.

Now should it be a crazy ghost,
One who must sing in doleful pain,
Through a long vision to be broken
When time shall snap the true love token
To which she sings her doleful strain?   730

What ails you now my pretty Bess?
What is't that makes you look so grave?
The cry which sets your heart a throbbing,
It is a little boy that's sobbing
Beside the entrance of a cave.

A blooming wood-boy of the woods,
And Bess, I will be bold to say,
If once you knew but whose he is
Your heart would be as sad as his,
Till you had kissed his tears away.   740

A branch of hawthorn's in his hands,
The haws they are both ripe and red.
And now toward the cave he creeps,
And now into its mouth he peeps,
And then draws back in fear and dread.

He is bewitched by some strange hope
And shows a wondrous self-command;
Yet though his heart is bold and staunch,
The berries on the hawthorn branch
All rattle in his hand.   750

Beneath the ivy now he creeps
Upon his hands and knees and then,
Like swans when pinched by hunger make
Their moan beside a frozen lake,
He sobs and sobs and sobs again.

Ah well, my pretty little Bess,
To hear that miserable sound
The tears into your eyes may gather.
The boy is seeking his dead father,
His father dead and drowned.   760

Poor Robin loved his father well,
For often by the hand he led
Sweet Robin to the [   ] and he
Gave Robin many a halfpenny,
And many a crust of bread.

Since five o'clock hath Robin sought
O'er heath and hill, through copse and lane,
Through gypsey-scenes of rocks and woods,
Soothed day and night by murmuring floods,
As wild as any place in Spain.   770

And hither he is come at last,
When he through such a day has gone,
By this dark cave to be distressed,
Where like a bird about its nest
He flutters off and on.

At last, both in despair and fear,
Along the wood his road he takes,
And, like a little child that's lost
And thinks he's followed by a ghost,
A wild and doleful cry he makes.   780

The Ass, when first he caught the noise,
Stopped short and soon he knew it well,
And towards the cave, whence Robin sent
All through the wood that sad lament,
He has been carrying Peter Bell.

But soon as Peter saw the Ass
His road all on a sudden change
And turn right upwards from the hollow,
That lamentable noise to follow,
It wrought in him conviction strange.   790

A sober and a firm belief
Is in the heart of Peter Bell
That something will to him befall,
Some visitation worse than all,
Which ever till this night befell.

Meanwhile, the Ass in Robin's track
Is following stoutly as he may,
But while he climbs the woody hill
The cry grows weak, and weaker still,
And now at last dies quite away.   800

Fain would he overtake the boy,
He loves him with a dear delight,
But, finding 'tis an idle hope,
Down the close pathway's rugged slope
He quietly turns towards the right.

With Peter on his back he turns
Into a gloomy grove of beech,
Along the shade with footsteps true
Descending slowly, till the two
The open moonlight reach.   810

And then along a narrow dell
A fair smooth pathway you discern,
A verdant and an open road,
As any little river broad
Winding away among the fern.

And Peter hears the rustling leaf,
And many a time he turns his face,
Both here and there, ere he can find
What 'tis which follows close behind
Along that solitary place.   820

At last he spies the withered leaf,
And Peter's in a sore distress:
'Where there is not a bush or tree
The very leaves they follow me,
So huge hath been my wickedness'.

Along the [   ] down they go,
And to a broad highway are come,
They quit the turf and on the gravel,
Upon the broad highway they travel,
A pair both sad and dumb.   830

For Peter Bell he looks, I vow,
With his dull face of ashy white,
Just like a creature that pertains
To some strange world of silent pains,
A creature of a moonlight night.

And now they to a lane are come;
And still the little, meagre, Ass
Moves on without a moment's stop,
Nor once turns round his head to crop
A bramble leaf or blade of grass.   840

Between the hedges on they go,
The dusty road is white as bone,
When Peter, casting down his eyes,
Towards the moonlight road espies
A drop of blood upon a stone.

Peter has little power to move;
Upon the Ass remain he must.
He travels on and now and then
He sees that drop of blood again
Upon a stone, or in the dust.   850

Did Peter e'er with club or stake
Smite some poor traveller on the head,
Or beat his father in a rage,
Or spill the blood of his old age,
Or kick a child till he was dead?

Did Peter ever kill his man
With fist or staff in single duel,
Or stab with some inhuman wound
A soldier bleeding on the ground?
No, Peter never was so cruel.   860

Then why to see this drop of blood
Doth Peter look so pale and wan?
Why is he in this sad despair?
He knows not how the blood comes there—
And Peter is a wicked man.

At length he spies a bleeding wound,
Where he had struck the Ass's head;
He sees the blood—sees what it is—
A glimpse of sudden joy was his,
But then it quickly fled.   870

He thought—he could not help but think—
Of that poor beast, that faithful Ass,
And once again those ugly pains
Across his liver, heart, and reins,
Just like a weaver's shuttle pass.

PART THIRD

I've heard of one, a gentle soul,°
Though giv'n to sadness and to gloom,
And, for the fact I'll vouch, one night
It chanced that by a taper's light
This man was reading in his room.   880

Reading, as you or I might read
At night in any pious book,
When sudden blackness overspread
The snow-white page in which he read
And made the good man round him look.

The chamber all was dark all round,
And to his book he turned again,
The light had left the good man's taper
And formed itself upon the paper
Into large letters bright and plain.   890

The godly book was in his hand,
And on the page, as black as coal,
Those ghostly letters formed a word
Which till his dying day, I've heard,
Perplexed the good man's gentle soul.

The wondrous word which thus he saw
Did never from his lips depart,
But he has said, poor gentle wight,
It brought full many a sin to light
Out of the bottom of his heart.   900

Dread Spirits! thus to vex the good,
How can ye with your functions jar,
Disordering colour, form and stature!
Let good men feel the soul of Nature
And see things as they are.

I know you, potent Spirits, well,
How with the feeling and the sense
Ye play, both with your foes and friends,
Most fearful work for fearful ends,
And this I speak in reverence.   910

But might I give advice to you,
Whom in my fear I love so well,
From men of pensive virtue go,
Dread beings! and your empire show
To hearts like that of Peter Bell.

Your presence I have often felt
In darkness and the stormy night,
And well I know, if need there be,
Ye can put forth your agency
Beneath the sweet moonlight.   920

Then coming from the wayward world,
That powerful world in which ye dwell,
Come, Spirits of the mind, to try
Tonight beneath the moonlight sky,
What may be done with Peter Bell.

Oh! would that any, friend or foe,
My further labour would prevent.
Oh me, it cannot easy sit,
I feel that I am all unfit
For such high argument.   930

I've played, I've danced with my narration,
A happy and a thoughtless man;
I've moved to many a giddy measure,
But now, my friends, for your good pleasure
I'll do the best I can.

The Ass, as you remember well,
Is travelling now along a lane,
And Peter many tricks is trying,
And many anodynes applying,
To ease his stomach of its pain.   940

Quoth Peter, 'Wounds will bleed we know,
And blood is blood, and fools have fears'.
But yet the leaf he can't deny
It dogged him, and that doleful cry
Is ringing in his ears.

But Peter is a deep logician,
And hath no lack of wit mercurial,
'Why, after all, 'tis plain', quoth he,
'This poor man never but for me
Could have had christian burial'.   950

So from his pocket Peter takes
His shining horn tobacco-box,
And in a careless way, as you,
Or I, good Mr Swan, might do,
Upon the lid he knocks.

There's some of you, my Friends, perhaps,
There's some of you in yawning weather,
Who may have seen an ass's grin—
'Tis uglier far than death and sin
And all the devils together.   960

And just as Peter struck the box
—It might be to recruit his wind,
Or from some more important cause—
The quiet creature made a pause,
Turned round his head, and grinned.

You know that Peter is resolved
His drooping spirits to repair,
And though no doubt a sight like this
To others might have come amiss,
It suited Peter to a hair.   970

And Peter, grinning with a joke,
His teeth in approbation shewed,
When, cruel blow to Peter's mirth,
He heard a murmur in the earth,
In the dead earth beneath the road.

Beneath the Ass's feet it passed,
A murmur and a rumbling sound,
'Twas by a crew of miners made
Who plied with gunpowder their trade
Some hundred fathoms underground.   980

And I will venture to affirm
If ever any king or cotter
Did think as sure as five is five,
That he'd be swallowed up alive,
'Twas Peter Bell the Potter.

And while the little silent Ass,
Requiring neither rein nor goad,
Moves on beneath the moonlight skies,
And the grey dust in silence lies
Upon the moonlight road,   990

Poor Peter by an ugly fiend
Is troubled, more and more; quoth he,
'I know the truth, I know it well,
Through meadow ground, to rock and dell,
A devil is following me'.

At this how poor Peter gave a moan,
And straightway from a cottage door
A little cur came barking out,
Barking and making such a rout
As never cur had made before.   1000

This barking cur, as you suppose,
Must needs have been a joyful sight.
You think, no doubt, it must have cut
The thread of Peter's trance and put
The subterraneous devil to flight.

The barking cur, he might have been
A roaring lion just as well
For any good that he has wrought,
For any comfort he has brought
For poor unhappy Peter Bell.   1010

Upon the Ass's back he sits
Like one that's riding in a swoon,
Or as a ghost that cannot see,
Whose face, if any such there be,
Is like the eyeless moon.

And every twenty yards, or less,
Poor Peter, well may he look grim,
Whether on rising ground or level,
Still feels the subterraneous devil
Heave up the little Ass and him.   1020

And now the patient Ass is come
To where beneath a mountain cove
A little chapel stands alone.
With greenest ivy overgrown,
And tufted with an ivy grove.

A building dying half away
From human thoughts and purposes,
It seems, both wall and roof and tower,
To bow to some transforming power
And blend with the surrounding trees.   1030

Deep sighing as he passed along,
Quoth Peter, 'In the Shire of Fife,
'Twas just in such a place as that,
Not knowing what I would be at,
I married my sixth wife'.

Thus Peter communed with himself;
By this time he is somewhat weaned,
I think, from his delirous notion
That the road's giddy with commotion
Made by a subterranean fiend.   1040

The little Ass moves slowly on,
And now is passing by an inn
That's full of a carousing crew,
Making with curses not a few
An uproar and a drunken din.

I cannot well express the thoughts
Which Peter in those noises found.
A stifling power compressed his frame,
'Twas just as if a darkness came
Over that dull and dreary sound.   1050

For well did Peter know the sound.
The language of those drunken joys
To him, a jovial soul I ween,
But a few hours ago had been
A gladsome and a welcome noise.

But now 'tis plain that Peter's thoughts
Have taken a far different course,
Whate'er he sees, whate'er he hears,
Gives him new sorrow or new fears,
Deepens his anguish and remorse.   1060

And passing by a twisted elm
Again poor Peter thus began,
''Twas just by such another inn
I robbed of sixpence-halfpenny
A boy that led a poor blind man.

And close by such a gate as that
Did I, by a most heinous murther,
Destroy my good dog Ruffian, he
Who gladly would have gone for me
To the world's end and further.   1070

And faithful beast like this poor Ass
Whom I have bruised so cruelly,
Just such another animal,
Made by the God that made us all,
And fitter far to live than I.'

But more than all his heart is stung
To think of one, almost a child,
A sweet and playful Highland Girl,
As light and beauteous as a squirrel,
As beauteous, and as wild.   1080

A lonely house her dwelling was,
A cottage in a heathy dell,
And she put on her gown of green,
And left her mother at sixteen,
And followed Peter Bell.

But many a good and pious thought
Had she and in the Kirk to pray,
Two long Scotch miles through rain and snow,
To Kirk she had been used to go,
Twice every Sabbath day.   1090

And when she followed Peter Bell
It was to live an honest life,
For he with tongue not used to falter,
Had pledged his troth before the altar,
To love her as his wedded wife.

A child was in her womb, but soon
She drooped and seemed like one forlorn,
From scripture she a name did borrow;
Benoni, or the child of sorrow,°
She called her babe unborn.   1100

For she had learned how Peter lived,
And took it in most grievous part,
She to the bone was worn,
And ere that little child was born
Died of a broken heart.

And now the Spirits of the Mind
Are busy with poor Peter Bell;
And from the Ass's back he sees
I think as ugly images
As ever eye did see in hell.   1110

Close by a brake of flowering furze
He sees himself, as plain as day,
He sees himself, a man in figure
Just like himself, nor less nor bigger,
Not five yards from the broad highway.

And stretched beneath the furze he sees
The highland girl—it is no other—
And hears her crying, as she cried,
The very moment that she died,
'My mother! oh! my mother!'   1120

The sweat pours down from Peter's face,
So grievous is his heart's contrition;
With agony his eye-balls ache,
While he beholds by the furze-brake
This miserable vision.

The Ass is pacing down a hill,
By this he had not far to go;
And now, while down the slope he wends,
A voice to Peter's ears ascends
From the deep woody dell below.   1130

It is a voice just like a voice
Re-echoed from a naked rock,
It comes from that low chapel, list,
It is a pious Methodist
That's preaching to his pious flock.

'Repent, repent', he cries aloud,
'God is a God of mercy—strive
To love him, then, with all your might,
Do that which lawful is and right,
And save your souls alive.   1140

My friends, my brethren, though you're gone
Through paths of wickedness and woe
After the babylonian harlot,
And though your sins be red as scarlet,
They shall be white as snow'.

Just as he passed the door these words
Did plainly come to Peter's ears,
And they such joyful tidings were
The joy was more than he could bear;
He melted into tears.   1150

Sweet tears of hope and tenderness,
And fast they fell a plenteous shower,
His nerves, his sinews seemed to melt,
Through all his iron frame was felt
A gentle, a relaxing power.

Each nerve, each fibre of his frame,
And all the animal within
Was weak, perhaps, but it was mild
And gentle as an infant child,
An infant that has known no sin.   1160

But now the little, patient Ass
Towards a gate that's full in view
Turned up a narrow lane, his chest
Against the yielding gate he pressed,
And quietly passed through.

And up the stony lane he goes,
No ghost more softly ever trod,
Among the stones and pebbles he
Sets down his hoofs inaudibly,
As if with felt his hoofs were shod.   1170

Along the lane the little Ass
Had gone two hundred yards, not more,
When to a lonely house he came;
He turned aside towards the same,
And stopped before the door.

Thought Peter, 'tis the poor man's house.
He listens—not a sound is heard.
But ere you could count half a score
It chanced that at the cottage door
A little girl appeared.   1180

Towards the chapel she was going
With hope that she some news might gather.
She saw the pair, and with a scream
Cried out, like one that's in a dream,
'My father, here's my father'.

The very word was plainly heard,
Heard plainly by the wretched mother;
Her joy was like a deep affright
And forth she ran into the light—
And saw it was another.   1190

And instantly upon the earth,
Beneath the full moon shining bright,
Just at the Ass's feet she fell,
And from the Ass poor Peter Bell
Dismounts in most unhappy plight.

What would he do? the woman lay
Dead, as it seemed, both breath and limb.
Poor Peter sadly was confused;
To scenes like these he was not used,
'Twas all together new to him.   1200

He raised her up, and while he held
Her body propped against his knee,
She waked, and when the woman spied
The poor Ass standing by her side,
She moaned most bitterly.

'Oh, God be praised! my heart's at ease,
For he is dead, I know it well'.
Of tears she poured a bitter flood,
And in the best way that he could
His tale did Peter tell.   1210

He trembled, he was pale as death,
His voice is weak with perturbation.
He turns aside his head, he pauses.
Poor Peter from a thousand causes
Is crippled sore in his narration.

At last she learned how he espied
The Ass in that small meadow ground,
And that beside the river bed
Her husband now was lying dead,
That he was dead and drowned.   1220

The wretched mother looks and looks
Upon the Ass that near her stands.
She sees 'tis he, that 'tis the same,
She calls the poor Ass by his name,
And wrings and wrings her hands.

'Oh, woe is me! he was so stout;
If he had died upon his bed.
He knew no sickness, knew no pain,
He never will come home again
He's dead, for ever dead'.   1230

Beside the woman Peter stands;
His heart is opening more and more;
A holy sense is in his mind;
He feels what he for human-kind
Had never felt before.

At length, by Peter's arm sustained,
The woman rises from the ground.
'Oh, mercy! something must be done,
My little Rachael, you must run
Across the meadow by the pound.   1240

Make haste, my little Rachael, do,
Bid Mathew Simpson hither come.
Ask him to lend his horse tonight
And this good man, whom heaven requite,
Will help to bring the body home'.

Away goes Rachael, weeping loud;
An infant, waked by her distress,
Makes in the house a piteous cry,
And Peter hears the mother sigh,
'Poor thing, 'tis fatherless'.   1250

And now does Peter deeply feel
The heart of man's a holy thing;
And nature, through a world of death,
Breathes into him a second breath
Just like the breath of spring.

Upon a stone the woman sits
In agony of silent grief.
From his own thought does Peter start,
He longs to press her to his heart,
From love that cannot give relief.   1260

At last, upspringing from her seat,
As with a sudden fear and dread,
The woman through the threshold flies,
And up the cottage stairs she hies,
And flings herself upon the bed.

And Peter turns his steps aside
Towards a shade of alder trees,
And he sits down, he knows not how,
With his hands pressed against his brow,
And his head fixed between his knees.   1270

In silence there does Peter sit,
Not any sign of life he makes,
As if his mind were sinking deep
Through years that have been long asleep;
At last as from a trance he wakes.

He turns his head and sees the Ass
Yet standing in the clear moonshine.
'When shall I be as good as thou?
Oh! would poor beast that I had now
A heart but half as good as thine'.   1280

But hark, that doleful cry again!
'Tis travelling up the woody slope.
Once more while Peter hears the sound,
With stifling pain his heart is bound,
He feels like one that has no hope.

'Tis little Robin, he who sought
His father with such grief and pain,
And, after many perils past,
Has found his way safe home at last,
And now is coming up the lane.   1290

He's coming towards the door and now
He sees the Ass—and nothing living
Had ever such a fit of joy,
As has this little orphan boy,
For he has no misgiving.

Towards the gentle Ass he springs,
And up about his neck he climbs;
In loving words he talks to him,
He kisses, kisses face and limb,
He kisses him a thousand times.   1300

This Peter sees, where in the shade
He stood beside the cottage door,
And Peter, he the ruffian wild,
Sobs loud, he sobs, just like a child,
'Oh God! I can endure no more'.

Here ends my tale: for in a trice
Came Mathew Simpson with his horse.
Peter set out with him straightway
And, two hours ere the break of day,
Together they brought back the corse.   1310

And many years did this poor Ass,
Whom once it was my luck to see
Not many miles from Leming Lane,°
Help by his labour to maintain
The widow and her family.

And Peter Bell, who till that night
Had been the wildest of his clan,
Forsook his crimes, forsook his folly,
And after ten months' melancholy
Became a good and honest man.   1320

Expostulation and Reply

'Why William, on that old grey stone,
Thus for the length of half a day,
Why William, sit you thus alone,
And dream your time away?

Where are your books? that light bequeathed
To beings else forlorn and blind!
Up! Up! and drink the spirit breathed
From dead men to their kind.

You look round on your mother earth,
As if she for no purpose bore you;   10
As if you were her first-born birth,
And none had lived before you!'

One morning thus, by Esthwaite lake,°
When life was sweet I knew not why,
To me my good friend Matthew spake,
And thus I made reply.

'The eye it cannot chuse but see,
We cannot bid the ear be still;
Our bodies feel, where'er they be,
Against, or with our will.   20

Nor less I deem that there are powers,
Which of themselves our minds impress,
That we can feed this mind of ours,
In a wise passiveness.

Think you, 'mid all this mighty sum
Of things for ever speaking,
That nothing of itself will come,
But we must still be seeking?

—Then ask not wherefore, here, alone,
Conversing as I may,   30
I sit upon this old grey stone,
And dream my time away.'

The Tables Turned

AN EVENING SCENE, ON THE SAME SUBJECT

Up! up! my friend, and clear your looks,
Why all this toil and trouble?
Up! up! my friend, and quit your books,
Or surely you'll grow double.

The sun above the mountain's head,
A freshening lustre mellow,
Through all the long green fields has spread,
His first sweet evening yellow.

Books! 'tis a dull and endless strife,
Come, hear the woodland linnet,   10
How sweet his music; on my life
There's more of wisdom in it.

And hark! how blithe the throstle sings!
And he is no mean preacher;
Come forth into the light of things,
Let Nature be your teacher.

She has a world of ready wealth,
Our minds and hearts to bless—
Spontaneous wisdom breathed by health,
Truth breathed by chearfulness.   20

One impulse from a vernal wood
May teach you more of man;
Of moral evil and of good,
Than all the sages can.

Sweet is the lore which nature brings;
Our meddling intellect
Mis-shapes the beauteous forms of things;
—We murder to dissect.

Enough of science and of art;
Close up these barren leaves;   30
Come forth, and bring with you a heart
That watches and receives.

Lines written a few miles above Tintern Abbey

ON REVISITING THE BANKS OF THE WYE DURING A TOUR,
JULY 13, 1798

Five years have passed; five summers, with the length°
Of five long winters! and again I hear
These waters, rolling from their mountain-springs
With a sweet inland murmur. —Once again
Do I behold these steep and lofty cliffs,
Which on a wild secluded scene impress
Thoughts of more deep seclusion; and connect
The landscape with the quiet of the sky.
The day is come when I again repose

Here, under this dark sycamore, and view   10
These plots of cottage-ground, these orchard-tufts,
Which, at this season, with their unripe fruits,
Among the woods and copses lose themselves,
Nor, with their green and simple hue, disturb
The wild green landscape. Once again I see
These hedge-rows, hardly hedge-rows, little lines
Of sportive wood run wild; these pastoral farms
Green to the very door; and wreathes of smoke°
Sent up, in silence, from among the trees,
With some uncertain notice, as might seem,   20
Of vagrant dwellers in the houseless woods,
Or of some hermit's cave, where by his fire
The hermit sits alone.

              Though absent long,
These forms of beauty have not been to me,
As is a landscape to a blind man's eye:
But oft, in lonely rooms, and mid the din
Of towns and cities, I have owed to them,
In hours of weariness, sensations sweet,
Felt in the blood, and felt along the heart,
And passing even into my purer mind   30
With tranquil restoration:—feelings too
Of unremembered pleasure; such, perhaps,
As may have had no trivial influence
On that best portion of a good man's life;
His little, nameless, unremembered acts
Of kindness and of love. Nor less, I trust,
To them I may have owed another gift,
Of aspect more sublime; that blessed mood,
In which the burthen of the mystery,
In which the heavy and the weary weight   40
Of all this unintelligible world
Is lightened:—that serene and blessed mood,
In which the affections gently lead us on,
Until, the breath of this corporeal frame,
And even the motion of our human blood
Almost suspended, we are laid asleep
In body, and become a living soul:
While with an eye made quiet by the power

Of harmony, and the deep power of joy,
We see into the life of things.°

                       If this   50
Be but a vain belief, yet, oh! how oft,
In darkness, and amid the many shapes
Of joyless day-light; when the fretful stir
Unprofitable, and the fever of the world,
Have hung upon the beatings of my heart,
How oft, in spirit, have I turned to thee
O sylvan Wye! Thou wanderer through the woods,
How often has my spirit turned to thee!

And now, with gleams of half-extinguished thought,
With many recognitions dim and faint,   60
And somewhat of a sad perplexity,
The picture of the mind revives again:
While here I stand, not only with the sense
Of present pleasure, but with pleasing thoughts°
That in this moment there is life and food
For future years. And so I dare to hope
Though changed, no doubt, from what I was, when first°
I came among these hills; when like a roe
I bounded o'er the mountains, by the sides
Of the deep rivers, and the lonely streams,   70
Wherever nature led; more like a man
Flying from something that he dreads, than one
Who sought the thing he loved. For nature then
(The coarser pleasures of my boyish days,°
And their glad animal movements all gone by,)
To me was all in all.—I cannot paint
What then I was. The sounding cataract
Haunted me like a passion: the tall rock,
The mountain, and the deep and gloomy wood,
Their colours and their forms, were then to me   80
An appetite: a feeling and a love,
That had no need of a remoter charm,
By thought supplied, or any interest
Unborrowed from the eye.—That time is past,
And all its aching joys are now no more,
And all its dizzy raptures. Not for this

Faint I, nor mourn nor murmur: other gifts
Have followed, for such loss, I would believe,
Abundant recompence. For I have learned
To look on nature, not as in the hour   90
Of thoughtless youth, but hearing oftentimes
The still, sad music of humanity,
Not harsh nor grating, though of ample power
To chasten and subdue. And I have felt
A presence that disturbs me with the joy
Of elevated thoughts; a sense sublime
Of something far more deeply interfused,°
Whose dwelling is the light of setting suns,
And the round ocean, and the living air,
And the blue sky, and in the mind of man,   100
A motion and a spirit, that impels
All thinking things, all objects of all thought,
And rolls through all things. Therefore am I still
A lover of the meadows and the woods,
And mountains; and of all that we behold
From this green earth; of all the mighty world
Of eye and ear, both what they half-create,°
And what perceive; well pleased to recognize
In nature and the language of the sense,
The anchor of my purest thoughts, the nurse,   110
The guide, the guardian of my heart, and soul
Of all my moral being.

                Nor, perchance,
If I were not thus taught, should I the more
Suffer my genial spirits to decay:
For thou art with me, here, upon the banks
Of this fair river; thou, my dearest Friend,
My dear, dear Friend, and in thy voice I catch
The language of my former heart, and read
My former pleasures in the shooting lights
Of thy wild eyes. Oh! yet a little while   120
May I behold in thee what I was once,
My dear, dear Sister! And this prayer I make,
Knowing that Nature never did betray
The heart that loved her; 'tis her privilege,
Through all the years of this our life, to lead

From joy to joy: for she can so inform
The mind that is within us, so impress
With quietness and beauty, and so feed
With lofty thoughts, that neither evil tongues,°
Rash judgments, nor the sneers of selfish men,   130
Nor greetings where no kindness is, nor all
The dreary intercourse of daily life,
Shall e'er prevail against us, or disturb
Our chearful faith that all which we behold
Is full of blessings. Therefore let the moon
Shine on thee in thy solitary walk;
And let the misty mountain winds be free
To blow against thee: and in after years,
When these wild ecstasies shall be matured
Into a sober pleasure, when thy mind   140
Shall be a mansion for all lovely forms,
Thy memory be as a dwelling-place
For all sweet sounds and harmonies; Oh! then,
If solitude, or fear, or pain, or grief,
Should be thy portion, with what healing thoughts
Of tender joy wilt thou remember me,
And these my exhortations! Nor, perchance,
If I should be, where I no more can hear
Thy voice, nor catch from thy wild eyes these gleams
Of past existence, wilt thou then forget   150
That on the banks of this delightful stream
We stood together; and that I, so long
A worshipper of Nature, hither came,
Unwearied in that service: rather say
With warmer love, oh! with far deeper zeal
Of holier love. Nor wilt thou then forget,
That after many wanderings, many years
Of absence, these steep woods and lofty cliffs,
And this green pastoral landscape, were to me
More dear, both for themselves, and for thy sake.   160

To a Sexton

Let thy wheel-barrow alone.
Wherefore, Sexton, piling still
In thy bone-house bone on bone?
'Tis already like a hill
In a field of battle made,
Where three thousand skulls are laid.
—These died in peace each with the other,
Father, Sister, Friend, and Brother.

Mark the spot to which I point!
From this platform eight feet square   10
Take not even a finger-joint:
Andrew's whole fire-side is there.
Here, alone, before thine eyes,
Simon's sickly Daughter lies
From weakness now, and pain defended,
Whom he twenty winters tended.

Look but at the gardener's pride,
How he glories, when he sees
Roses, lilies, side by side,
Violets in families.   20
By the heart of Man, his tears,
By his hopes and by his fears,
Thou, old Grey-beard! art the Warden
Of a far superior garden.

Thus then, each to other dear,
Let them all in quiet lie,
Andrew there and Susan here,
Neighbours in mortality.
And should I live through sun and rain
Seven widowed years without my Jane,   30
O Sexton, do not then remove her,
Let one grave hold the Loved and Lover!

'If Nature, for a favorite Child'

In the School of—— is a tablet on which are inscribed, in gilt letters, the names of
the several persons who have been Schoolmasters there since the foundation of
the School, with the time at which they entered upon and quitted their office.
Opposite one of those names the Author wrote the following lines.

If nature, for a favorite Child
In thee hath tempered so her clay,
That every hour thy heart runs wild
Yet never once doth go astray,

Read o'er these lines; and then review
This tablet, that thus humbly rears
In such diversity of hue
Its history of two hundred years.

—When through this little wreck of fame,
Cypher and syllable, thine eye   10
Has travelled down to Matthew's name,
Pause with no common sympathy.

And if a sleeping tear should wake
Then be it neither checked nor stayed:
For Matthew a request I make
Which for himself he had not made.

Poor Matthew, all his frolics o'er,
Is silent as a standing pool,
Far from the chimney's merry roar,
And murmur of the village school.   20

The sighs which Matthew heaved were sighs
Of one tired out with fun and madness;
The tears which came to Matthew's eyes
Were tears of light, the oil of gladness.

Yet sometimes when the secret cup
Of still and serious thought went round
It seemed as if he drank it up,
He felt with spirit so profound.

—Thou soul of God's best earthly mould,
Thou happy soul, and can it be   30
That these two words of glittering gold
Are all that must remain of thee?

The Fountain

A CONVERSATION

We talked with open heart, and tongue
Affectionate and true,
A pair of Friends, though I was young,
And Matthew seventy-two.

We lay beneath a spreading oak,
Beside a mossy seat,
And from the turf a fountain broke,
And gurgled at our feet.

Now, Matthew, let us try to match
This water's pleasant tune   10
With some old Border-song, or catch
That suits a summer's noon.

Or of the Church-clock and the chimes
Sing here beneath the shade,
That half-mad thing of witty rhymes
Which you last April made!

In silence Matthew lay, and eyed
The spring beneath the tree;
And thus the dear old Man replied,
The grey-haired Man of glee.   20

'Down to the vale this water steers,
How merrily it goes!
'Twill murmur on a thousand years,
And flow as now it flows.

And here, on this delightful day,
I cannot chuse but think
How oft, a vigorous Man, I lay
Beside this Fountain's brink.

My eyes are dim with childish tears,
My heart is idly stirred,
For the same sound is in my ears,
Which in those days I heard.

Thus fares it still in our decay:
And yet the wiser mind
Mourns less for what age takes away
Than what it leaves behind.

The blackbird in the summer trees,
The lark upon the hill,
Let loose their carols when they please,
Are quiet when they will.

With Nature never do *they* wage
A foolish strife; they see
A happy youth, and their old age
Is beautiful and free:

But we are pressed by heavy laws,
And often, glad no more,
We wear a face of joy, because
We have been glad of yore.

If there is one who need bemoan
His kindred laid in earth,
The household hearts that were his own,
It is the man of mirth.

My days, my Friend, are almost gone,
My life has been approved,
And many love me, but by none
Am I enough beloved.'

'Now both himself and me he wrongs,
The man who thus complains!
I live and sing my idle songs
Upon these happy plains,   60

And, Matthew, for thy Children dead
I'll be a son to thee!'
At this he grasped his hands, and said,
'Alas! that cannot be.'

We rose up from the fountain-side,
And down the smooth descent
Of the green sheep-track did we glide,
And through the wood we went,

And, ere we came to Leonard's Rock,
He sang those witty rhymes   70
About the crazy old church-clock
And the bewildered chimes.

The Two April Mornings

We walked along, while bright and red
Uprose the morning sun,
And Matthew stopped, he looked, and said,
'The will of God be done!'

A village Schoolmaster was he,
With hair of glittering grey;
As blithe a man as you could see
On a spring holiday.

And on that morning, through the grass,
And by the steaming rills,   10
We travelled merrily to pass
A day among the hills.

'Our work,' said I, 'was well begun;
Then, from thy breast what thought,
Beneath so beautiful a sun,
So sad a sigh has brought?'

A second time did Matthew stop,
And fixing still his eye
Upon the eastern mountain-top
To me he made reply.   20

'Yon cloud with that long purple cleft
Brings fresh into my mind
A day like this which I have left
Full thirty years behind.

And on that slope of springing corn
The self-same crimson hue
Fell from the sky that April morn,
The same which now I view!

With rod and line my silent sport
I plied by Derwent's wave,°   30
And, coming to the church, stopped short
Beside my Daughter's grave.

Nine summers had she scarcely seen
The pride of all the vale;
And then she sang!—she would have been
A very nightingale.

Six feet in earth my Emma lay,
And yet I loved her more,
For so it seemed, than till that day
I e'er had loved before.   40

And, turning from her grave, I met
Beside the church-yard Yew
A blooming Girl, whose hair was wet
With points of morning dew.

A basket on her head she bare,
Her brow was smooth and white,
To see a Child so very fair,
It was a pure delight!

No fountain from its rocky cave
E'er tripped with foot so free,   50
She seemed as happy as a wave
That dances on the sea.

There came from me a sigh of pain
Which I could ill confine;
I looked at her and looked again;
—And did not wish her mine.'

Matthew is in his grave, yet now
Methinks I see him stand,
As at that moment, with his bough
Of wilding in his hand.   60

[*Five Elegies*]

I

'Could I the priest's consent have gained'

Could I the priest's consent have gained,
Or his who tolled thy passing bell,
Then, Mathew, had thy bones remained
Beneath this tree we loved so well.

Yet in our thorn will I suspend
Thy gift, this twisted oaken staff;
And here, where trunk and branches blend,
Will I engrave thy epitaph.

II

'Just as the blowing thorn began'

Just as the blowing thorn began
To spread again its vernal shade,
This village lost as good a man
As ever handled book or spade.

Stop, thou that travellest o'er the green,
Thy course a single moment stay,
Though here no mouldering heap be seen
To tell thee thou art kindred clay.

A schoolmaster by title known,
Long Mathew penned his little flock   10
Within yon pile, that stands alone,
In colour like its native rock.

Learning will often dry the heart,
The very bones it will distress,
But Mathew had an idle art
Of teaching love and happiness.

The neat trim house, the cottage rude,
All owed to Mathew gifts of gold,
Light pleasures every day renewed,
Or blessings half a century old.   20

His fancy played with endless play,
So full of mother wit was he;
He was a thousand times more gay
Than any dunce has power to be.

Yet when his hair was white as rime
And he twice thirty years had seen,
Would Mathew wish from time to time
That he a graver man had been.

But nothing could his heart have bribed
To be as sad as mine is now,   30
As I have been, while I inscribed
This verse beneath the hawthorn bough.

III

Elegy

written in the same place upon the same occasion

Remembering how thou didst beguile
With thy wild ways our eyes and ears,
I feel more sorrow in a smile
Than in a waggon load of tears.
I smile to hear the hunter's horn,
I smile at meadow, rock, and shore,
I smile too at this silly thorn
Which blooms as sweetly as before.

I think of thee in silent love
And feel, just like a wavering leaf,   10
Along my face the muscles move,
Nor know if 'tis with joy or grief.
But oft, when I look up and view
Yon huts upon the mountain-side,
I sigh and say it was for you
An evil day when Mathew died.

Ye little girls, Ye loved his name,
Come here and knit your gloves of yarn;
Ye loved him better than your dame,
—The schoolmaster of fair Glencarn.   20
For though to many a wanton boy
Did Mathew act a father's part,
Ye tiny maids, *Ye* were his joy,
Ye were the favourites of his heart!

Ye ruddy damsels past sixteen,
Weep now that Mathew's race is run;
He wrote your love-letters, I ween,
Ye kissed him when the work was done.
Ye Brothers gone to towns remote,
And ye upon the ocean tost,   30
Ye many a good and pious thought
And many a [   ] have lost.

Staid men may weep, from him they quaffed
Such wit as never failed to please,
While at his [   ] they laughed
Enough to set their hearts at ease.
Ye Mothers, who for jibe or jest
Have little room in heart or head,
The child that lies upon your breast
May make you think of Mathew dead.   40

Old Women in your elbow chairs,
Who now will be your fence and shield,
When wintry blasts and cutting airs
Are busy in both house and field?
And weep, thou School of fair Glencarn,
No more shalt thou in a stormy weather
Be like a play-house in a barn,
Where Punch and Hamlet play together.

Ye sheep-curs, a mirth-loving corps!
Now let your tails lie still between   50
Your drooping hips—You'll never more
Bark at his voice upon the green.
—Remembering how thou didst beguile
With thy wild ways our eyes and ears,
I feel more sorrow in a smile
Than in a waggon-load of tears.—

IV

'Carved, Mathew, with a master's skill'

Carved, Mathew, with a master's skill,
Thy name is on the hawthorn tree,
'Twill live, and yet it seemed that still
I owed another verse to thee.
I sate upon thy favourite stool,
And this, my last memorial song,
We sang together in the school
I and thy little tuneful throng.

These rhymes, so homely in attire,
With learned ears may ill agree,   10
But chaunted by thy orphan quire
They made a touching melody—
Thus did I sing, thy little brood
All followed me with voice and hand,
Moved both by what they understood
And what they did not understand.

V

Dirge

I bring ye little noisy crew!
Fulfilling a most kind intent,
The pious blessing which to you
Our common friend and father sent.
I kissed his cheek before he died,
I raised his hand up from his side,
And down it dropped like lead;
Like clay it fell—your hands, do all
That can be done, will never fall
Like his till they are dead.   10
Oh never more, blow foul or fair,
Ne'er shall the best of all your train,
Have Mathew's hand upon his hair
Or stand between his knees again.

He taught in this his humble state
What happiness a man of worth,
A single mortal, may create
Upon a single spot of earth.
Among the distant stars we view
The hand of God, in rain and dew   20
And in the summer heat,
And Mathew's little works we trace
All round his happy native place
In every eye we meet.
The neat trim house, the cottage rude
Allowed to Mathew gifts of gold,
Light pleasures every day renewed
Or blessings half a century old.

Here did he sit for hours and hours,
But then he saw the woods and plains,   30
He heard the wind and saw the showers
Come streaming down the streaming panes.
He lies beneath the grass-green mound,
A prisoner of the silent ground.
He loved the breathing air,
He loved the sun; he does not know
Whether the sun be up or no,
He lies for ever there.
If he to you did aught amiss,
Forgive him now that he is dead;   40
Both in your sorrow and your bliss
Remember him and his grey head.

'A slumber did my spirit seal'

A slumber did my spirit seal;
    I had no human fears:
She seemed a thing that could not feel
    The touch of earthly years.

No motion has she now, no force;
    She neither hears nor sees,
Rolled round in earth's diurnal course
    With rocks and stones and trees.

Song

She dwelt among th' untrodden ways
    Beside the springs of Dove,
A Maid whom there were none to praise
    And very few to love.

A Violet by a mossy stone
    Half-hidden from the Eye!
—Fair, as a star when only one
    Is shining in the sky!

She *lived* unknown, and few could know
   When Lucy ceased to be;   10
But she is in her Grave, and Oh!
   The difference to me.

'Strange fits of passion I have known'

Strange fits of passion I have known,
And I will dare to tell,
But in the lover's ear alone,
What once to me befel.

When she I loved, was strong and gay
And like a rose in June,
I to her cottage bent my way,
Beneath the evening moon.

Upon the moon I fixed my eye
All over the wide lea;   10
My horse trudged on, and we drew nigh
Those paths so dear to me.

And now we reached the orchard plot,
And, as we climbed the hill,
Towards the roof of Lucy's cot
The moon descended still.

In one of those sweet dreams I slept,
Kind Nature's gentlest boon!
And, all the while, my eyes I kept
On the descending moon.   20

My horse moved on; hoof after hoof
He raised and never stopped:
When down behind the cottage roof
At once the planet dropped.

What fond and wayward thoughts will slide
Into a Lover's head—
'O mercy!' to myself I cried,
'If Lucy should be dead!'

Lucy Gray

Oft had I heard of Lucy Gray,
And when I crossed the Wild,
I chanced to see at break of day
The solitary Child.

No Mate, no comrade Lucy knew;
She dwelt on a wide Moor,
The sweetest Thing that ever grew
Beside a human door!

You yet may spy the Fawn at play,
The Hare upon the Green;   10
But the sweet face of Lucy Gray
Will never more be seen.

'To-night will be a stormy night,
You to the Town must go,
And take a lantern, Child, to light
Your Mother thro' the snow.'

'That, Father! will I gladly do;
'Tis scarcely afternoon—
The Minster-clock has just struck two,
And yonder is the Moon.'°   20

At this the Father raised his hook
And snapped a faggot-band;
He plied his work, and Lucy took
The lantern in her hand.

Not blither is the mountain roe,
With many a wanton stroke
Her feet disperse the powd'ry snow
That rises up like smoke.

The storm came on before its time,
She wandered up and down,   30
And many a hill did Lucy climb
But never reached the Town.

The wretched Parents all that night
Went shouting far and wide;
But there was neither sound nor sight
To serve them for a guide.

At day-break on a hill they stood
That overlooked the Moor;
And thence they saw the Bridge of Wood
A furlong from their door.   40

And now they homeward turned, and cried
'In Heaven we all shall meet!'
When in the snow the Mother spied
The print of Lucy's feet.

Then downward from the steep hill's edge
They tracked the footmarks small;
And through the broken hawthorn-hedge,
And by the long stone-wall;

And then an open field they crossed,
The marks were still the same;   50
They tracked them on, nor ever lost,
And to the Bridge they came.

They followed from the snowy bank
The footmarks, one by one,
Into the middle of the plank,
And further there were none.

Yet some maintain that to this day
She is a living Child,
That you may see sweet Lucy Gray
Upon the lonesome Wild.   60

O'er rough and smooth she trips along,
And never looks behind;
And sings a solitary song
That whistles in the wind.

A Poet's Epitaph

Art thou a Statesman, in the van
Of public business trained and bred,
—First learn to love one living man;
Then may'st thou think upon the dead.

A Lawyer art thou?—draw not nigh;
Go, carry to some other place
The hardness of thy coward eye,
The falshood of thy sallow face.

Art thou a man of purple cheer?
A rosy man, right plump to see?   10
Approach; yet Doctor, not too near:
This grave no cushion is for thee.

Art thou a man of gallant pride,
A Soldier, and no man of chaff?
Welcome!—but lay thy sword aside,
And lean upon a Peasant's staff.

Physician art thou? One, all eyes,
Philosopher! a fingering slave,
One that would peep and botanize
Upon his mother's grave?   20

Wrapped closely in thy sensual fleece
O turn aside, and take, I pray,
That he below may rest in peace,
Thy pin-point of a soul away!

—A Moralist perchance appears;
Led, Heaven knows how! to this poor sod:
And He has neither eyes nor ears;
Himself his world, and his own God;

One to whose smooth-rubbed soul can cling
Nor form nor feeling great nor small,   30
A reasoning, self-sufficing thing,
An intellectual All in All!

Shut close the door! press down the latch:
Sleep in thy intellectual crust,
Nor lose ten tickings of thy watch,
Near this unprofitable dust.

But who is He with modest looks,
And clad in homely russet brown?
He murmurs near the running brooks
A music sweeter than their own.   40

He is retired as noontide dew,
Or fountain in a noonday grove;
And you must love him, ere to you
He will seem worthy of your love.

The outward shews of sky and earth,
Of hill and valley he has viewed;
And impulses of deeper birth
Have come to him in solitude.

In common things that round us lie
Some random truths he can impart   50
The harvest of a quiet eye
That broods and sleeps on his own heart.

But he is weak, both man and boy,
Hath been an idler in the land;
Contented if he might enjoy
The things which others understand.

—Come hither in thy hour of strength,
Come, weak as is a breaking wave!
Here stretch thy body at full length;
Or build thy house upon this grave.—   60

Nutting

——————————————It seems a day,
One of those heavenly days which cannot die,
When forth I sallied from our cottage-door,
And with a wallet o'er my shoulder slung,
A nutting crook in hand, I turned my steps
Towards the distant woods, a Figure quaint,
Tricked out in proud disguise of Beggar's weeds
Put on for the occasion, by advice
And exhortation of my frugal Dame.°
Motley accoutrements! of power to smile   10
At thorns, and brakes, and brambles, and, in truth,
More ragged than need was. Among the woods,
And o'er the pathless rocks, I forced my way
Until, at length, I came to one dear nook
Unvisited, where not a broken bough
Drooped with its withered leaves, ungracious sign
Of devastation, but the hazels rose
Tall and erect, with milk-white clusters hung,
A virgin scene!—A little while I stood,
Breathing with such suppression of the heart   20
As joy delights in; and with wise restraint
Voluptuous, fearless of a rival, eyed
The banquet, or beneath the trees I sate
Among the flowers, and with the flowers I played;
A temper known to those, who, after long
And weary expectation, have been blessed
With sudden happiness beyond all hope.—
—Perhaps it was a bower beneath whose leaves
The violets of five seasons re-appear
And fade, unseen by any human eye,   30
Where fairy water-breaks do murmur on
For ever, and I saw the sparkling foam,
And with my cheek on one of those green stones
That, fleeced with moss, beneath the shady trees,
Lay round me scattered like a flock of sheep,
I heard the murmur and the murmuring sound,
In that sweet mood when pleasure loves to pay
Tribute to ease, and, of its joy secure
The heart luxuriates with indifferent things,

Wasting its kindliness on stocks and stones,   40
And on the vacant air. Then up I rose,
And dragged to earth both branch and bough, with crash
And merciless ravage; and the shady nook
Of hazels, and the green and mossy bower,
Deformed and sullied, patiently gave up
Their quiet being: and unless I now
Confound my present feelings with the past,
Even then, when from the bower I turned away,
Exulting, rich beyond the wealth of kings
I felt a sense of pain when I beheld   50
The silent trees and the intruding sky.—

    Then, dearest Maiden! move along these shades
In gentleness of heart; with gentle hand
Touch,——for there is a Spirit in the woods.

'Three years she grew in sun and shower'

Three years she grew in sun and shower,
Then Nature said, 'A lovelier flower
On earth was never sown;
This Child I to myself will take,
She shall be mine, and I will make
A Lady of my own.

Myself will to my darling be
Both law and impulse, and with me
The Girl in rock and plain,
In earth and heaven, in glade and bower,   10
Shall feel an overseeing power
To kindle or restrain.

She shall be sportive as the fawn
That wild with glee across the lawn
Or up the mountain springs,
And hers shall be the breathing balm,
And hers the silence and the calm
Of mute insensate things.

The floating clouds their state shall lend
To her, for her the willow bend,   20
Nor shall she fail to see
Even in the motions of the storm
A beauty that shall mould her form
By silent sympathy.

The stars of midnight shall be dear
To her, and she shall lean her ear
In many a secret place
Where rivulets dance their wayward round,
And beauty born of murmuring sound
Shall pass into her face.   30

And vital feelings of delight
Shall rear her form to stately height,
Her virgin bosom swell,
Such thoughts to Lucy I will give
While she and I together live
Here in this happy dell.'

Thus Nature spake—The work was done—
How soon my Lucy's race was run!
She died and left to me
This heath, this calm and quiet scene,   40
The memory of what has been,
And never more will be.

The Brothers

These Tourists, Heaven preserve us! needs must live°
A profitable life: some glance along,
Rapid and gay, as if the earth were air,
And they were butterflies to wheel about
Long as their summer lasted; some, as wise,
Upon the forehead of a jutting crag
Sit perched with book and pencil on their knee,
And look and scribble, scribble on and look,
Until a man might travel twelve stout miles,

Or reap an acre of his neighbour's corn.
But, for that moping son of Idleness
Why can he tarry *yonder?*—In our church-yard
Is neither epitaph nor monument,
Tomb-stone nor name, only the turf we tread,
And a few natural graves. To Jane, his Wife,
Thus spake the homely Priest of Ennerdale.
It was a July evening, and he sate
Upon the long stone-seat beneath the eaves
Of his old cottage, as it chanced that day,
Employed in winter's work. Upon the stone
His Wife sate near him, teasing matted wool,
While, from the twin cards toothed with glittering wire,
He fed the spindle of his youngest child,
Who turned her large round wheel in the open air
With back and forward steps. Towards the field
In which the parish chapel stood alone,
Girt round with a bare ring of mossy wall,
While half an hour went by, the Priest had sent
Many a long look of wonder, and at last,
Risen from his seat, beside the snowy ridge
Of carded wool which the old Man had piled
He laid his implements with gentle care,
Each in the other locked; and, down the path
Which from his cottage to the church-yard led,
He took his way, impatient to accost
The Stranger, whom he saw still lingering there.

'Twas one well known to him in former days,
A Shepherd-lad: who ere his thirteenth year
Had changed his calling, with the mariners
A fellow-mariner, and so had fared
Through twenty seasons; but he had been reared
Among the mountains, and he in his heart
Was half a Shepherd on the stormy seas.
Oft in the piping shrouds had Leonard heard
The tones of waterfalls, and inland sounds
Of caves and trees; and when the regular wind
Between the tropics filled the steady sail
And blew with the same breath through days and weeks,
Lengthening invisibly its weary line

Along the cloudless main, he, in those hours   50
Of tiresome indolence would often hang
Over the vessel's side, and gaze and gaze,
And, while the broad green wave and sparkling foam°
Flashed round him images and hues, that wrought
In union with the employment of his heart,
He, thus by feverish passion overcome,
Even with the organs of his bodily eye,
Below him, in the bosom of the deep,
Saw mountains, saw the forms of sheep that grazed
On verdant hills, with dwellings among trees,   60
And Shepherds clad in the same country grey
Which he himself had worn.
                    And now at length,
From perils manifold, with some small wealth
Acquired by traffic in the Indian Isles,
To his paternal home he is returned,
With a determined purpose to resume
The life which he lived there, both for the sake
Of many darling pleasures, and the love
Which to an only brother he has borne
In all his hardships, since that happy time   70
When, whether it blew foul or fair, they two
Were brother Shepherds on their native hills.
—They were the last of all their race; and now,
When Leonard had approached his home, his heart
Failed in him, and, not venturing to inquire
Tidings of one whom he so dearly loved,
Towards the church-yard he had turned aside,
That, as he knew in what particular spot
His family were laid, he thence might learn
If still his Brother lived, or to the file   80
Another grave was added.—He had found
Another grave, near which a full half hour
He had remained, but, as he gazed, there grew
Such a confusion in his memory,
That he began to doubt, and he had hopes
That he had seen this heap of turf before,
That it was not another grave, but one,
He had forgotten. He had lost his path,
As up the vale he came that afternoon,

Through fields which once had been well known to him. 90
And Oh! what joy the recollection now
Sent to his heart! he lifted up his eyes,
And looking round he thought that he perceived
Strange alteration wrought on every side
Among the woods and fields, and that the rocks,
And the eternal hills, themselves were changed.

  By this the Priest who down the field had come
Unseen by Leonard, at the church-yard gate
Stopped short, and thence, at leisure, limb by limb
He scanned him with a gay complacency.　　　　　100
Aye, thought the Vicar, smiling to himself,
'Tis one of those who needs must leave the path
Of the world's business, to go wild alone:
His arms have a perpetual holiday,
The happy man will creep about the fields
Following his fancies by the hour, to bring
Tears down his cheek, or solitary smiles
Into his face, until the setting sun
Write Fool upon his forehead. Planted thus
Beneath a shed that overarched the gate　　　　　110
Of this rude church-yard, till the stars appeared
The good man might have communed with himself
But that the Stranger, who had left the grave,
Approached; he recognized the Priest at once,
And after greetings interchanged, and given
By Leonard to the Vicar as to one
Unknown to him, this dialogue ensued.

LEONARD

You live, Sir, in these dales, a quiet life:
Your years make up one peaceful family;
And who would grieve and fret, if, welcome come　　　120
And welcome gone, they are so like each other,
They cannot be remembered. Scarce a funeral
Comes to this church-yard once in eighteen months;
And yet, some changes must take place among you:
And you, who dwell here, even among these rocks
Can trace the finger of mortality,
And see, that with our threescore years and ten

We are not all that perish.—I remember,
For many years ago I passed this road,
There was a foot-way all along the fields   130
By the brook-side—'tis gone—and that dark cleft!
To me it does not seem to wear the face
Which then it had.

                           PRIEST
                       Why, Sir, for aught I know,
That chasm is much the same—

                    LEONARD
                                     But, surely, yonder—

                    PRIEST
Aye, there indeed, your memory is a friend°
That does not play you false.—On that tall pike,
(It is the loneliest place of all these hills)
There were two Springs which bubbled side by side
As if they had been made that they might be
Companions for each other: ten years back,   140
Close to those brother fountains, the huge crag
Was rent with lightning—one is dead and gone,
The other, left behind, is flowing still.—
For accidents and changes such as these,
Why we have store of them! a water–spout
Will bring down half a mountain; what a feast
For folks that wander up and down like you,
To see an acre's breadth of that wide cliff
One roaring cataract—a sharp May storm
Will come with loads of January snow,   150
And in one night send twenty score of sheep
To feed the ravens, or a Shepherd dies
By some untoward death among the rocks:
The ice breaks up and sweeps away a bridge—
A wood is felled:—and then for our own homes!
A child is born or christened, a field ploughed,
A daughter sent to service, a web spun,
The old house clock is decked with a new face;
And hence, so far from wanting facts or dates
To chronicle the time, we all have here   160
A pair of diaries, one serving, Sir,
For the whole dale, and one for each fire-side—

Your's was a stranger's judgment; for historians
Commend me to these vallies.

LEONARD

                    Yet your church-yard
Seems, if such freedom may be used with you,
To say that you are heedless of the past.
Here's neither head nor foot-stone, plate of brass,
Cross-bones or skull, type of our earthly state
Or emblem of our hopes: the dead man's home
Is but a fellow to that pasture field.   170

PRIEST

Why there, Sir, is a thought that's new to me.
The Stone-cutters, 'tis true, might beg their bread
If every English church-yard were like ours:
Yet your conclusion wanders from the truth.
We have no need of names and epitaphs,
We talk about the dead by our fire-sides.
And then for our immortal part, *we* want
No symbols, Sir, to tell us that plain tale:
The thought of death sits easy on the man
Who has been born and dies among the mountains:°   180

LEONARD

Your dalesmen, then, do in each other's thoughts
Possess a kind of second life: no doubt
You, Sir, could help me to the history
Of half these Graves?

PRIEST

With what I've witnessed, and with what I've heard,
Perhaps I might, and, on a winter's evening,
If you were seated at my chimney's nook
By turning o'er these hillocks one by one,
We two could travel, Sir, through a strange round,
Yet all in the broad high-way of the world.   190
Now there's a grave—your foot is half upon it,
It looks just like the rest, and yet that man
Died broken hearted.

LEONARD

            'Tis a common case,
We'll take another: who is he that lies

Beneath yon ridge, the last of those three graves,
It touches on that piece of native rock
Left in the church-yard wall.

PRIEST

That's Walter Ewbank.
He had as white a head and fresh a cheek
As ever were produced by youth and age
Engendering in the blood of hale fourscore.   200
For five long generations had the heart
Of Walter's forefathers o'erflowed the bounds
Of their inheritance, that single cottage,
You see it yonder, and those few green fields.
They toiled and wrought, and still, from sire to son
Each struggled, and each yielded as before
A little—yet a little—and old Walter,
They left to him the family heart, and land
With other burthens than the crop it bore.
Year after year the old man still preserved   210
A chearful mind, and buffeted with bond,
Interest and mortgages; at last he sank,
And went into his grave before his time.
Poor Walter! whether it was care that spurred him
God only knows, but to the very last
He had the lightest foot in Ennerdale:
His pace was never that of an old man:
I almost see him tripping down the path
With his two Grandsons after him—but you,
Unless our Landlord be your host to-night,   220
Have far to travel, and in these rough paths
Even in the longest day of midsummer—

LEONARD

But these two Orphans!

PRIEST

Orphans! such they were—
Yet not while Walter lived—for, though their Parents
Lay buried side by side as now they lie,
The old Man was a father to the boys,
Two fathers in one father: and if tears
Shed, when he talked of them where they were not,

And hauntings from the infirmity of love,
Are aught of what makes up a mother's heart,   230
This old Man in the day of his old age
Was half a mother to them.—If you weep, Sir,
To hear a stranger talking about strangers,
Heaven bless you when you are among your kindred!
Aye. You may turn that way—it is a grave
Which will bear looking at.

                    LEONARD
                              These Boys I hope
They loved this good old Man—

                    PRIEST
                                        They did—and truly,
But that was what we almost overlooked,
They were such darlings of each other. For
Though from their cradles they had lived with Walter,   240
The only kinsman near them in the house,
Yet he being old, they had much love to spare,
And it all went into each other's hearts.
Leonard, the elder by just eighteen months,
Was two years taller: 'twas a joy to see,
To hear, to meet them! from their house the School
Was distant three short miles, and in the time
Of storm and thaw, when every water-course
And unbridged stream, such as you may have noticed
Crossing our roads at every hundred steps,   250
Was swoln into a noisy rivulet,
Would Leonard then, when elder boys perhaps
Remained at home, go staggering through the fords
Bearing his Brother on his back.—I've seen him,
On windy days, in one of those stray brooks,
Aye, more than once I've seen him mid-leg deep,
Their two books lying both on a dry stone
Upon the hither side:—and once I said,
As I remember, looking round these rocks
And hills on which we all of us were born,   260
That God who made the great book of the world
Would bless such piety—

                    LEONARD
                              It may be then—

PRIEST

Never did worthier lads break English bread:
The finest Sunday that the Autumn saw,
With all its mealy clusters of ripe nuts,
Could never keep these boys away from church,
Or tempt them to an hour of sabbath breach.
Leonard and James! I warrant, every corner
Among these rocks and every hollow place
Where foot could come, to one or both of them   270
Was known as well as to the flowers that grew there.
Like roe-bucks they went bounding o'er the hills:
They played like two young ravens on the crags:
Then they could write, aye and speak too, as well
As many of their betters—and for Leonard!
The very night before he went away,
In my own house I put into his hand
A Bible, and I'd wager twenty pounds,
That, if he is alive, he has it yet.

LEONARD

It seems, these Brothers have not lived to be   280
A comfort to each other.—

PRIEST

                    That they might
Live to that end, is what both old and young
In this our valley all of us have wished,
And what, for my part, I have often prayed:
But Leonard—

LEONARD

            Then James still is left among you—

PRIEST

'Tis of the elder Brother I am speaking:
They had an Uncle, he was at that time
A thriving man, and trafficked on the seas:
And, but for this same Uncle, to this hour
Leonard had never handled rope or shroud.   290
For the Boy loved the life which we lead here;
And, though a very Stripling, twelve years old;
His soul was knit to this his native soil.
But, as I said, old Walter was too weak

To strive with such a torrent; when he died,
The estate and house were sold, and all their sheep,
A pretty flock, and which, for aught I know,
Had clothed the Ewbanks for a thousand years.
Well—all was gone, and they were destitute.
And Leonard, chiefly for his brother's sake,   300
Resolved to try his fortune on the seas.
'Tis now twelve years since we had tidings from him.
If there was one among us who had heard
That Leonard Ewbank was come home again,
From the great Gavel, down by Leeza's Banks,°
And down the Enna, far as Egremont,
The day would be a very festival,
And those two bells of ours, which there you see
Hanging in the open air—but, O good Sir!
This is sad talk—they'll never sound for him   310
Living or dead—When last we heard of him
He was in slavery among the Moors
Upon the Barbary Coast—'Twas not a little
That would bring down his spirit, and, no doubt,
Before it ended in his death, the Lad
Was sadly crossed—Poor Leonard! when we parted,
He took me by the hand and said to me,
If ever the day came when he was rich,
He would return, and on his Father's Land
He would grow old among us.

LEONARD

                                   If that day   320
Should come, 'twould needs be a glad day for him;
He would himself, no doubt, be as happy then
As any that should meet him—

PRIEST

                                   Happy, Sir—

LEONARD

You said his kindred all were in their graves,
And that he had one Brother—

PRIEST

                                   That is but
A fellow tale of sorrow. From his youth

James, though not sickly, yet was delicate,
And Leonard being always by his side
Had done so many offices about him,
That, though he was not of a timid nature,   330
Yet still the spirit of a mountain boy
In him was somewhat checked, and when his Brother
Was gone to sea and he was left alone
The little colour that he had was soon
Stolen from his cheek, he drooped, and pined and pined:

LEONARD

But these are all the graves of full grown men!

PRIEST

Aye, Sir, that passed away: we took him to us.
He was the child of all the dale—he lived
Three months with one, and six months with another:
And wanted neither food, nor clothes, nor love,   340
And many, many happy days were his.
But, whether blithe or sad, 'tis my belief
His absent Brother still was at his heart.
And, when he lived beneath our roof, we found
(A practice till this time unknown to him)
That often, rising from his bed at night,
He in his sleep would walk about, and sleeping
He sought his Brother Leonard—You are moved!
Forgive me, Sir: before I spoke to you,
I judged you most unkindly.

LEONARD
                              But this youth,   350
How did he die at last?

PRIEST
                         One sweet May morning,
It will be twelve years since, when Spring returns,
He had gone forth among the new-dropped lambs,
With two or three companions whom it chanced
Some further business summoned to a house
Which stands at the Dale-head. James, tired perhaps,
Or from some other cause remained behind.
You see yon precipice—it almost looks
Like some vast building made of many crags,

And in the midst is one particular rock   360
That rises like a column from the vale,
Whence by our Shepherds it is called, the Pillar.
James, pointing to its summit, over which
They all had purposed to return together,
Informed them that he there would wait for them:
They parted, and his comrades passed that way
Some two hours after, but they did not find him
At the appointed place, a circumstance
Of which they took no heed: but one of them,
Going by chance, at night, into the house   370
Which at this time was James's home, there learned
That nobody had seen him all that day:
The morning came, and still, he was unheard of:
The neighbours were alarmed, and to the Brook
Some went, and some towards the Lake; ere noon
They found him at the foot of that same Rock
Dead, and with mangled limbs. The third day after
I buried him, poor lad, and there he lies.

LEONARD

And that then *is* his grave!—Before his death
You said that he saw many happy years?   380

PRIEST

Aye, that he did—

LEONARD

                    And all went well with him—

PRIEST

If he had one, the Lad had twenty homes.

LEONARD

And you believe then, that his mind was easy—

PRIEST

Yes, long before he died, he found that time
Is a true friend to sorrow, and unless
His thoughts were turned on Leonard's luckless fortune,
He talked about him with a chearful love.

LEONARD

He could not come to an unhallowed end!

PRIEST

Nay, God forbid! You recollect I mentioned
A habit which disquietude and grief   390
Had brought upon him, and we all conjectured
That, as the day was warm, he had lain down
Upon the grass, and, waiting for his comrades
He there had fallen asleep, that in his sleep
He to the margin of the precipice
Had walked, and from the summit had fallen head-long,
And so no doubt he perished: at the time,
We guess, that in his hands he must have had
His Shepherd's staff; for midway in the cliff
It had been caught, and there for many years   400
It hung—and mouldered there.
                              The Priest here ended.
The Stranger would have thanked him, but he felt
Tears rushing in; both left the spot in silence,
And Leonard, when they reached the church-yard gate,
As the Priest lifted up the latch, turned round,
And, looking at the grave, he said, 'My Brother'.
The Vicar did not hear the words: and now,
Pointing towards the Cottage, he entreated
That Leonard would partake his homely fare:
The other thanked him with a fervent voice,   410
But added, that, the evening being calm,
He would pursue his journey. So they parted.

It was not long ere Leonard reached a grove
That overhung the road: he there stopped short,
And, sitting down beneath the trees, reviewed
All that the Priest had said: his early years
Were with him in his heart: his cherished hopes,
And thoughts which had been his an hour before,
All pressed on him with such a weight, that now,
This vale, where he had been so happy, seemed   420
A place in which he could not bear to live:
So he relinquished all his purposes.
He travelled on to Egremont; and thence,
That night, addressed a letter to the Priest
Reminding him of what had passed between them;
And adding, with a hope to be forgiven,

That it was from the weakness of his heart,
He had not dared to tell him, who he was.

This done, he went on shipboard, and is now
A Seaman, a grey headed Mariner.   430

Hart-Leap Well

Hart-Leap Well is a small spring of water, about five miles from Richmond in
Yorkshire, and near the side of the road which leads from Richmond to Askrigg.
Its name is derived from a remarkable chace, the memory of which is preserved by
the monuments spoken of in the second Part of the following Poem, which
monuments do now exist as I have there described them.

The Knight had ridden down from Wensley moor
With the slow motion of a summer's cloud;
He turned aside towards a Vassal's door,
And, 'Bring another Horse!' he cried aloud.

'Another Horse!'—That shout the Vassal heard,
And saddled his best steed, a comely Grey;
Sir Walter mounted him; he was the third
Which he had mounted on that glorious day.

Joy sparkled in the prancing Courser's eyes,
The horse and horsemen are a happy pair;   10
But, though Sir Walter like a falcon flies,
There is a doleful silence in the air.

A rout this morning left Sir Walter's Hall,
That as they galloped made the echoes roar;
But horse and man are vanished, one and all;
Such race, I think, was never seen before.

Sir Walter, restless as a veering wind,
Calls to the few tired dogs that yet remain:
Brach, Swift and Music, noblest of their kind,
Follow, and weary up the mountain strain.   20

The Knight hallooed, he chid and cheered them on
With suppliant gestures and upbraidings stern;
But breath and eye-sight fail, and, one by one,
The dogs are stretched among the mountain fern.

Where is the throng, the tumult of the chace?
The bugles that so joyfully were blown?
—This race it looks not like an earthly race;
Sir Walter and the Hart are left alone.

The poor Hart toils along the mountain side;
I will not stop to tell how far he fled,   30
Nor will I mention by what death he died;
But now the Knight beholds him lying dead.

Dismounting then, he leaned against a thorn;
He had no follower, dog, nor man, nor boy:
He neither smacked his whip, nor blew his horn,
But gazed upon the spoil with silent joy.

Close to the thorn on which Sir Walter leaned,
Stood his dumb partner in this glorious act;
Weak as a lamb the hour that it is yeaned,
And foaming like a mountain cataract.   40

Upon his side the Hart was lying stretched:
His nose half-touched a spring beneath a hill,
And with the last deep groan his breath had fetched
The waters of the spring were trembling still.

And now, too happy for repose or rest,
Was never man in such a joyful case,
Sir Walter walked all around, north, south and west,
And gazed, and gazed upon that darling place.

And turning up the hill, it was at least
Nine roods of sheer ascent, Sir Walter found   50
Three several marks which with his hoofs the beast
Had left imprinted on the verdant ground.

Sir Walter wiped his face, and cried, 'Till now
Such sight was never seen by living eyes:
Three leaps have borne him from this lofty brow,
Down to the very fountain where he lies.

I'll build a Pleasure-house upon this spot,
And a small Arbour, made for rural joy;
'Twill be the traveller's shed, the pilgrim's cot
A place of love for damsels that are coy.   60

A cunning Artist will I have to frame
A bason for that fountain in the dell;
And they, who do make mention of the same,
From this day forth, shall call it Hart-leap Well.

And, gallant brute, to make thy praises known,
Another monument shall here be raised;
Three several pillars, each a rough hewn stone,
And planted where thy hoofs the turf have grazed.

And in the summer-time when days are long,
I will come hither with my paramour,   70
And with the dancers, and the minstrel's song,
We will make merry in that pleasant bower.

Till the foundations of the mountains fail
My mansion with its arbour shall endure,
—The joy of them who till the fields of Swale,
And them who dwell among the woods of Ure.'

Then home he went, and left the Hart, stone-dead,
With breathless nostrils stretched above the spring.
And soon the Knight performed what he had said,
The fame whereof through many a land did ring.   80

Ere thrice the moon into her port had steered,
A cup of stone received the living well;
Three pillars of rude stone Sir Walter reared,
And built a house of pleasure in the dell.

And near the fountain, flowers of stature tall,
With trailing plants and trees were intertwined,
Which soon composed a little sylvan hall,
A leafy shelter from the sun and wind.

And thither, when the summer days were long,
Sir Walter journeyed with his paramour;   90
And with the dancers and the minstrel's song
Made merriment within that pleasant bower.

The Knight, Sir Walter, died in course of time,
And his bones lie in his paternal vale.
But there is matter for a second rhyme,
And I to this would add another tale.

PART SECOND

The moving accident is not my trade,°
To curl the blood I have no ready arts;°
'Tis my delight, alone in summer shade,
To pipe a simple song to thinking hearts.   100

As I from Hawes to Richmond did repair,
It chanced that I saw standing in a dell
Three aspins at three corners of a square,
And one, not four yards distant, near a well.

What this imported I could ill divine,
And, pulling now the rein my horse to stop,
I saw three pillars standing in a line,
The last stone pillar on a dark hill-top.

The trees were grey, with neither arms nor head;
Half-wasted the square mound of tawny green;   110
So that you just might say, as then I said,
'Here in old time the hand of man has been.'

I looked upon the hills both far and near;
More doleful place did never eye survey;
It seemed as if the spring-time came not here,
And Nature here were willing to decay.

I stood in various thoughts and fancies lost,
When one who was in Shepherd's garb attired,
Came up the hollow. Him did I accost,
And what this place might be I then inquired.

The Shepherd stopped, and that same story told
Which in my former rhyme I have rehearsed.
'A jolly place,' said he, 'in times of old,
But something ails it now; the spot is cursed.   120

You see these lifeless stumps of aspin wood,
Some say that they are beeches, others elms,
These were the Bower; and here a Mansion stood,
The finest palace of a hundred realms.

The arbour does its own condition tell,
You see the stones, the fountain, and the stream,
But as to the great Lodge, you might as well
Hunt half a day for a forgotten dream.

There's neither dog nor heifer, horse nor sheep,
Will wet his lips within that cup of stone;   130
And, oftentimes, when all are fast asleep,
This water doth send forth a dolorous groan.

Some say that here a murder has been done,
And blood cries out for blood: but, for my part,
I've guessed, when I've been sitting in the sun,
That it was all for that unhappy Hart.

What thoughts must through the creature's brain have
    passed!
To this place from the stone upon the steep
Are but three bounds, and look, Sir, at this last!
O Master! it has been a cruel leap.   140

For thirteen hours he ran a desperate race;
And in my simple mind we cannot tell
What cause the Hart might have to love this place,
And come and make his death-bed near the well.

Here on the grass perhaps asleep he sank,
Lulled by this fountain in the summer-tide;
This water was perhaps the first he drank
When he had wandered from his mother's side.

In April here beneath the scented thorn
He heard the birds their morning carols sing,   150
And he, perhaps, for aught we know, was born
Not half a furlong from that self-same spring.

But now here's neither grass nor pleasant shade;
The sun on drearier hollow never shone:
So will it be, as I have often said,
Till trees, and stones, and fountain all are gone.'

'Grey-headed Shepherd, thou hast spoken well;
Small difference lies between thy creed and mine;
This beast not unobserved by Nature fell,
His death was mourned by sympathy divine.   160

The Being, that is in the clouds and air,
That is in the green leaves among the groves,
Maintains a deep and reverential care
For them the quiet creatures whom he loves.

The Pleasure-house is dust:—behind, before,
This is no common waste, no common gloom;
But Nature, in due course of time, once more
Shall here put on her beauty and her bloom.

She leaves these objects to a slow decay
That what we are, and have been, may be known;   170
But, at the coming of the milder day,
These monuments shall all be overgrown.

One lesson, Shepherd, let us two divide,
Taught both by what she shews, and what conceals,
Never to blend our pleasure or our pride
With sorrow of the meanest thing that feels.'

Home at Grasmere

Once on the brow of yonder Hill I stopped°
While I was yet a School-boy (of what age
I cannot well remember, but the hour
I well remember though the year be gone),
And, with a sudden influx overcome
At sight of this seclusion, I forgot
My haste, for hasty had my footsteps been
As boyish my pursuits; and sighing said,
'What happy fortune were it here to live!
And if I thought of dying, if a thought   10
Of mortal separation could come in
With paradise before me, here to die.'
I was no Prophet, nor had even a hope,
Scarcely a wish, but one bright pleasing thought,
A fancy in the heart of what might be
The lot of others, never could be mine.
    The place from which I looked was soft and green,
Not giddy yet aerial, with a depth
Of Vale below, a height of Hills above.
Long did I halt; I could have made it even   20
My business and my errand so to halt.
For rest of body 'twas a perfect place,
All that luxurious nature could desire,
But tempting to the Spirit; who could look
And not feel motions there? I thought of clouds
That sail on winds; of breezes that delight
To play on water, or in endless chase
Pursue each other through the liquid depths
Of grass or corn, over and through and through,
In billow after billow, evermore;   30
Of Sunbeams, Shadows, Butterflies and Birds,
Angels and winged Creatures that are Lords
Without restraint of all which they behold.
I sate and stirred in Spirit as I looked,
I seemed to feel such liberty was mine,
Such power and joy; but only for this end,
To flit from field to rock, from rock to field,
From shore to island, and from isle to shore,

From open place to covert, from a bed
Of meadow-flowers into a tuft of wood, 40
From high to low, from low to high, yet still
Within the bounds of this huge Concave; here
Should be my home, this Valley be my World.
    From that time forward was the place to me
As beautiful in thought, as it had been
When present to my bodily eyes; a haunt
Of my affections, oftentimes in joy
A brighter joy, in sorrow (but of that
I have known little) in such gloom, at least,
Such damp of the gay mind as stood to me 50
In place of sorrow, 'twas a gleam of light.
And now 'tis mine for life: dear Vale,
One of thy lowly dwellings is my home!
    Yes, the Realities of Life—so cold,
So cowardly, so ready to betray,
So stinted in the measure of their grace,
As we report them, doing them much wrong,
Have been to me more bountiful than hope,
Less timid than desire. Oh bold indeed
They have been, bold and bounteous unto me 60
Who have myself been bold, not wanting trust
Nor resolution, nor at last the hope
Which is of wisdom, for I feel it is.
    And did it cost so much, and did it ask
Such length of discipline, and could it seem
An act of courage, and the thing itself
A conquest? Shame that this was ever so,
Not to the Boy or Youth, but shame to thee,
Sage Man, thou Sun in its meridian strength,
Thou flower in its full blow, thou King and Crown 70
Of human Nature; shame to thee, sage Man,
Thy prudence, thy experience, thy desires,
Thy apprehensions—blush thou for them all.
But I am safe, yes, one at least is safe;
What once was deemed so difficult, is now
Smooth, easy, without obstacle; what once
Did to my blindness seem a sacrifice,
The same is now a choice of the whole heart.
If e'er the acceptance of such dower was deemed

A condescention or a weak indulgence   80
To a sick fancy, it is now an act
Of reason that exultingly aspires.
This solitude is mine; the distant thought
Is fetched out of the heaven in which it was.
The unappropriated bliss hath found
An owner, and that owner I am he.
The Lord of this enjoyment is on Earth
And in my breast. What wonder if I speak
With fervour, am exalted with the thought
Of my possessions, of my genuine wealth   90
Inward and outward? What I keep, have gained,
Shall gain, must gain, if sound be my belief
From past and present, rightly understood,
That in my day of childhood I was less
The mind of Nature, less, take all in all,
Whatever may be lost, than I am now.
For proof behold this Valley, and behold
Yon Cottage, where with me my Emma dwells.
    Aye, think on that, my Heart, and cease to stir,
Pause upon that, and let the breathing frame   100
No longer breathe, but all be satisfied.
Oh, if such silence be not thanks to God
For what hath been bestowed, then where, where then
Shall gratitude find rest? Mine eyes did ne'er
Rest on a lovely object, nor my mind
Take pleasure in the midst of happy thoughts,
But either She whom now I have, who now
Divides with me this loved abode, was there,
Or not far off. Where'er my footsteps turned,
Her Voice was like a hidden Bird that sang;   110
The thought of her was like a flash of light
Or an unseen companionship, a breath
Or fragrance independent of the wind;
In all my goings, in the new and old
Of all my meditations, and in this
Favorite of all, in this the most of all.
What Being, therefore, since the birth of Man
Had ever more abundant cause to speak
Thanks, and if music and the power of song
Make him more thankful, then to call on these   120

To aid him, and with these resound his joy.
The boon is absolute; surpassing grace
To me hath been vouchsafed; among the bowers
Of blissful Eden this was neither given,
Nor could be given, possession of the good
Which had been sighed for, antient thought fulfilled
And dear Imaginations realized,
Up to their highest measure, yea, and more.
    Embrace me, then, ye Hills, and close me in,
Now in the clear and open day I feel   130
Your guardianship; I take it to my heart;
'Tis like the solemn shelter of the night.
But I would call thee beautiful, for mild,
And soft, and gay, and beautiful thou art,
Dear Valley, having in thy face a smile
Though peaceful, full of gladness. Thou art pleased,
Pleased with thy crags, and woody steeps, thy Lake,
Its one green Island and its winding shores,
The multitude of little rocky hills,
Thy Church and Cottages of mountain stone—   140
Clustered like stars, some few, but single most,
And lurking dimly in their shy retreats,
Or glancing at each other chearful looks,
Like separated stars with clouds between.
What want we? Have we not perpetual streams,
Warm woods, and sunny hills, and fresh green fields,
And mountains not less green, and flocks and herds,
And thickets full of songsters, and the voice
Of lordly birds—an unexpected sound
Heard now and then from morn to latest eve,   150
Admonishing the man who walks below
Of solitude and silence in the sky?
These have we, and a thousand nooks of earth
Have also these, but no where else is found—
No where (or is it fancy?) can be found—
The one sensation that is here; 'tis here,
Here as it found its way into my heart
In childhood, here as it abides by day,
By night, here only; or in chosen minds
That take it with them hence, where'er they go.   160
'Tis (but I cannot name it) 'tis the sense

Of majesty, and beauty, and repose,
A blended holiness of earth and sky,
Something that makes this individual Spot,
This small abiding-place of many men,
A termination, and a last retreat,
A Centre, come from wheresoe'er you will,
A Whole without dependence or defect,
Made for itself, and happy in itself,
Perfect Contentment, Unity entire.   170
    Long is it since we met, to part no more,°
Since I and Emma heard each other's call
And were Companions once again, like Birds
Which by the intruding Fowler had been scared,
Two of a scattered brood that could not bear
To live in loneliness; 'tis long since we,
Rememb'ring much and hoping more, found means
To walk abreast, though in a narrow path,
With undivided steps. Our home was sweet;
Could it be less? If we were forced to change,   180
Our home again was sweet; but still, for Youth,
Strong as it seems and bold, is inly weak
And diffident, the destiny of life
Remained unfixed, and therefore we were still

[*Lines 185–191 are missing*]

We will be free, and, as we mean to live
In culture of divinity and truth,
Will chuse the noblest Temple that we know.
Not in mistrust or ignorance of the mind
And of the power she has within herself
To enoble all things made we this resolve;
Far less from any momentary fit
Of inconsiderate fancy, light and vain;
But that we deemed it wise to take the help   200
Which lay within our reach; and here, we knew,
Help could be found of no mean sort; the spirit
Of singleness and unity and peace.
In this majestic self-sufficing world,
This all in all of nature, it will suit,
We said, no other [   ] on earth so well,
Simplicity of purpose, love intense,

Ambition not aspiring to the prize
Of outward things, but for the prize within—
Highest ambition; in the daily walks   210
Of business, 'twill be harmony and grace
For the perpetual pleasure of the sense,
And for the Soul—I do not say too much,
Though much be said—an image for the soul,
A habit of Eternity and God.
    Nor have we been deceived; thus far the effect
Falls not below the loftiest of our hopes.
Bleak season was it, turbulent and bleak,
When hitherward we journeyed, and on foot,
Through bursts of sunshine and through flying snows, 220
Paced the long Vales, how long they were, and yet
How fast that length of way was left behind,
Wensley's long Vale and Sedbergh's naked heights.
The frosty wind, as if to make amends
For its keen breath, was aiding to our course
And drove us onward like two Ships at sea.
Stern was the face of nature; we rejoiced
In that stern countenance, for our souls had there
A feeling of their strength. The naked trees,
The icy brooks, as on we passed, appeared   230
To question us. 'Whence come ye? To what end?'
They seemed to say. 'What would ye?' said the shower,
'Wild Wanderers, whither through my dark domain?'
The Sunbeam said, 'Be happy.' They were moved,
All things were moved; they round us as we went,
We in the midst of them. And when the trance
Came to us, as we stood by Hart-leap Well,
The intimation of the milder day
Which is to come, the fairer world than this,
And raised us up, dejected as we were   240
Among the records of that doleful place
By sorrow for the hunted beast who there
Had yielded up his breath, the awful trance—
The vision of humanity, and of God
The Mourner, God the Sufferer when the heart
Of his poor Creatures suffers wrongfully—
Both in the sadness and the joy we found
A promise and an earnest that we twain,

A pair seceding from the common world,
Might in that hallowed spot to which our steps   250
Were tending, in that individual nook,
Might even thus early for ourselves secure,
And in the midst of these unhappy times,
A portion of the blessedness which love
And knowledge will, we trust, hereafter give
To all the Vales of earth and all mankind.
   Thrice hath the winter moon been filled with light°
Since that dear day when Grasmere, our dear Vale,
Received us; bright and solemn was the sky
That faced us with a passionate welcoming,   260
And led us to our threshold, to a home
Within a home, what was to be, and soon,
Our love within a love. Then darkness came,
Composing darkness, with its quiet load
Of full contentment, in a little shed
Disturbed, uneasy in itself as seemed,
And wondering at its new inhabitants.
It loves us now, this Vale so beautiful
Begins to love us! By a sullen storm,
Two months unwearied of severest storm,   270
It put the temper of our minds to proof,
And found us faithful through the gloom, and heard
The Poet mutter his prelusive songs
With chearful heart, an unknown voice of joy
Among the silence of the woods and hills,
Silent to any gladsomeness of sound
With all their Shepherds.
                    But the gates of Spring
Are opened; churlish Winter hath giv'n leave
That she should entertain for this one day,
Perhaps for many genial days to come,   280
His guests, and make them happy. They are pleased,
But most of all the birds that haunt the flood,
With the mild summons; inmates though they be
Of Winter's household: they are jubilant
This day, who drooped, or seemed to droop, so long;
They shew their pleasure, and shall I do less?
Happier of happy though I be, like them
I cannot take possession of the sky,

Mount with a thoughtless impulse and wheel there
One of a mighty multitude, whose way   290
And motion is a harmony and dance
Magnificent. Behold them, how they shape
Orb after orb their course still round and round
Above the area of the Lake, their own
Adopted region, girding it about
In wanton repetition, yet therewith
With that large circle evermore renewed:
Hundreds of curves and circlets high and low,
Backwards and forwards, progress intricate,
As if one spirit was in all and swayed   300
Their indefatigable flight. 'Tis done,
Ten times or more I fancied it had ceased,
And lo! the vanished company again
Ascending,—list again—I hear their wings
Faint, faint at first; and then an eager sound
Passed in a moment—and as faint again!
They tempt the sun to sport among their plumes;
They tempt the water, and the gleaming ice,
To shew them a fair image,—'tis themselves,
Their own fair forms, upon the glimm'ring plain,   310
Painted more soft and fair as they descend,
Almost to touch,—then up again aloft,
Up with a sally and a flash of speed,
As if they scorned both resting-place and rest.
Spring! for this day belongs to thee, rejoice!
Not upon me alone hath been bestowed,
Me blessed with many onward-looking thoughts,
The sunshine and mild air; oh surely these
Are grateful, not the happy Quires of love,
Thine own peculiar family, Sweet Spring,   320
That sport among green leaves so blithe a train.
    But two are missing—two, a lonely pair
Of milk-white Swans—ah, why are they not here?
These above all, ah, why are they not here
To share in this day's pleasure? From afar
They came, like Emma and myself, to live
Together here in peace and solitude,
Chusing this Valley, they who had the choice
Of the whole world. We saw them day by day,

Through those two months of unrelenting storm,   330
Conspicuous in the centre of the Lake,
Their safe retreat; we knew them well—I guess
That the whole Valley knew them—but to us
They were more dear than may be well believed,
Not only for their beauty and their still
And placid way of life and faithful love
Inseparable, not for these alone,
But that their state so much resembled ours,
They also having chosen this abode;
They strangers, and we strangers; they a pair,   340
And we a solitary pair like them.
They should not have departed; many days
I've looked for them in vain, nor on the wing
Have seen them, nor in that small open space
Of blue unfrozen water, where they lodged,
And lived so long in quiet, side by side.
Companions, brethren, consecrated friends,
Shall we behold them yet another year
Surviving, they for us, and we for them,
And neither pair be broken?—nay, perchance   350
It is too late already for such hope;
The Shepherd may have seized the deadly tube,
And parted them, incited by the prize
Which, for the sake of those he loves at home
And for the Lamb upon the mountain tops,
He should have spared; or haply both are gone,
One death, and that were mercy giv'n to both.

    I cannot look upon this favoured Vale
But that I seem, by harbouring this thought,
To wrong it, such unworthy recompense   360
Imagining, of confidence so pure.
Ah! if I wished to follow where the sight
Of all that is before my eyes, the voice
Which is as a presiding Spirit here
Would lead me, I should say unto myself:
They who are dwellers in this holy place
Must needs themselves be hallowed; they require
No benediction from the Stranger's lips,
For they are blessed already; none would give
The greeting 'Peace be with you' unto them   370

For peace they have, it cannot but be theirs,
And mercy, and forbearance—nay—not these;
There is no call for these; that office Love
Performs, and charity beyond the bounds
Of charity—an overflowing love,
Not for the creature only, but for all
Which is around them; love for every thing
Which in this happy Valley we behold!
   Thus do we soothe ourselves, and when the thought
Is passed, we blame it not for having come.   380
What if I floated down a pleasant stream
And now am landed, and the motion gone,
Shall I reprove myself? Ah no, the stream
Is flowing, and will never cease to flow,
And I shall float upon that stream again.
By such forgetfulness the soul becomes,
Words cannot say how beautiful: then hail,
Hail to the visible Presence, hail to thee,
Delightful Valley, habitation fair!
And to whatever else of outward form   390
Can give us inward help, can purify,
And elevate, and harmonize, and soothe,
And steal away, and for a while deceive
And lap in pleasing rest, and bear us on
Without desire in full complacency,
Contemplating perfection absolute
And entertained as in a placid sleep.
   But not betrayed by tenderness of mind
That feared, or wholly overlooked, the truth
Did we come hither, with romantic hope   400
To find in midst of so much loveliness
Love, perfect love, of so much majesty
A like majestic frame of mind in those
Who here abide, the persons like the place.
Nor from such hope, or aught of such belief,
Hath issued any portion of the joy
Which I have felt this day. An awful voice,
'Tis true, I in my walks have often heard,
Sent from the mountains or the sheltered fields,
Shout after shout—reiterated whoop   410
In manner of a bird that takes delight

In answering to itself, or like a hound
Single at chace among the lonely woods—
A human voice, how awful in the gloom
Of coming night, when sky is dark, and earth
Not dark, nor yet enlightenened, but by snow
Made visible, amid the noise of winds
And bleatings manifold of sheep that know
Their summons, and are gathering round for food—
That voice, the same, the very same, that breath   420
Which was an utterance awful as the wind,
Or any sound the mountains ever heard.
      That Shepherd's voice, it may have reached mine ear
Debased and under prophanation, made
An organ for the sounds articulate
Of ribaldry and blasphemy and wrath,
Where drunkenness hath kindled senseless frays.
I came not dreaming of unruffled life,
Untainted manners; born among the hills,
Bred also there, I wanted not a scale   430
To regulate my hopes; pleased with the good,
I shrink not from the evil in disgust,
Or with immoderate pain. I look for man,
The common Creature of the brotherhood,
But little differing from the man elsewhere,
For selfishness and envy and revenge,
Ill neighbourhood—pity that this should be—
Flattery and double-dealing, strife and wrong.
      Yet is it something gained, it is in truth
A mighty gain, that Labour here preserves   440
His rosy face, a Servant only here
Of the fire-side or of the open field,
A Freeman, therefore sound and unimpaired;
That extreme penury is here unknown,
And cold and hunger's abject wretchedness,
Mortal to body and the heaven-born mind;
That they who want, are not too great a weight
For those who can relieve; here may the heart
Breathe in the air of fellow-suffering
Dreadless, as in a kind of fresher breeze   450
Of her own native element, the hand
Be ready and unwearied without plea

From task too frequent and beyond its power,
For languor or indifference or despair.
And as these lofty barriers break the force
Of winds,—this deep vale, as it doth in part
Conceal us from the storm, so here there is
A Power and a protection for the mind,
Dispensed indeed to other solitudes
Favoured by noble privilege like this,   460
Where kindred independence of estate
Is prevalent, where he who tills the field,
He, happy Man! is Master of the field
And treads the mountain which his Father trod.
Hence, and from other local circumstance,
In this enclosure many of the old
Substantial virtues have a firmer tone
Than in the base and ordinary world.
    Yon Cottage, would that it could tell a part
Of its own story. Thousands might give ear,   470
Might hear it and blush deep. There few years past
In this his Native Valley dwelt a Man,
The Master of a little lot of ground,
A man of mild deportment and discourse,
A Scholar also (as the phrase is here),
For he drew much delight from those few books
That lay within his reach, and for this cause
Was by his Fellow-dalesmen honoured more.
A Shepherd and a Tiller of the ground,
Studious withal, and healthy in his frame   480
Of body, and of just and placid mind,
He with his consort and his Children saw
Days that were seldom touched by petty strife,
Years safe from large misfortune, long maintained
That course which men the wisest and most pure
Might look on with entire complacency.
Yet in himself and near him were there faults
At work to undermine his happiness
By little and by little. Active, prompt,
And lively was the Housewife; in the Vale   490
None more industrious; but her industry
Was of that kind, 'tis said, which tended more
To splendid neatness, to a shewy, trim,

And overlaboured purity of house,
Than to substantial thrift. He, on his part,
Generous and easy-minded, was not free
From carelessness, and thus, in course of time,
These joint infirmities, combined perchance
With other cause less obvious, brought decay
Of worldly substance and distress of mind,   500
Which to a thoughtful man was hard to shun
And which he could not cure. A blooming Girl
Served them, an Inmate of the House. Alas!
Poor now in tranquil pleasure he gave way
To thoughts of troubled pleasure; he became
A lawless Suitor of the Maid, and she
Yielded unworthily. Unhappy Man!
That which he had been weak enough to do
Was misery in remembrance; he was stung,
Stung by his inward thoughts, and by the smiles   510
Of Wife and Children stung to agony.
His temper urged him not to seek relief
Amid the noise of revellers nor from draught
Of lonely stupefaction; he himself
A rational and suffering Man, himself
Was his own world, without a resting-place.
Wretched at home he had no peace abroad;
Ranged through the mountains, slept upon the earth,
Asked comfort of the open air, and found
No quiet in the darkness of the night,   520
No pleasure in the beauty of the day.
His flock he slighted: his paternal fields
Were as a Clog to him, whose Spirit wished
To fly, but whither? And yon gracious Church,
That has a look so full of peace and hope
And love, benignant Mother of the Vale,
How fair amid her brood of Cottages!
She was to him a sickness and reproach.
I speak conjecturing from the little known,
The much that to the last remained unknown;   530
But this is sure: he died of his own grief,
He could not bear the weight of his own shame.
      That Ridge, which elbowing from the mountain-side
Carries into the Plain its rocks and woods,

Conceals a Cottage where a Father dwells
In widowhood, whose Life's Co-partner died
Long since, and left him solitary Prop
Of many helpless Children. I begin
With words which might be prelude to a Tale
Of sorrow and dejection; but I feel,   540
Though in the midst of sadness, as might seem,
No sadness, when I think of what mine eyes
Have seen in that delightful family.
Bright garland make they for their Father's brows,
Those six fair Daughters budding yet, not one,
Not one of all the band a full-blown flower!
Go to the Dwelling: there Thou shalt have proof
That He who takes away, yet takes not half
Of what he seems to take, or gives it back,
Not to our prayer, but far beyond our prayer;   550
He gives it—the boon-produce of a soil
Which Hope hath never watered. Thou shalt see
A House, which, at small distance, will appear
In no distinction to have passed beyond
Its Fellows, will appear, like them, to have grown
Out of the native Rock; but nearer view
Will shew it not so grave in outward mien
And soberly arrayed as for the most
Are these rude mountain-dwellings—Nature's care,
Mere friendless Nature's—but a studious work   560
Of many fancies and of many hands,
A play thing and a pride; for such the air
And aspect which the little Spot maintains
In spite of lonely Winter's nakedness.
They have their jasmine resting on the Porch,
Their rose-trees, strong in health, that will be soon
Roof-high; and here and there the garden wall
Is topped with single stones, a shewy file
Curious for shape or hue, some round, like Balls,
Worn smooth and round by fretting of the Brook   570
From which they have been gathered, others bright
And sparry, the rough scatterings of the Hills.
These ornaments the Cottage chiefly owes
To one, a hardy Girl, who mounts the rocks;
Such is her choice; she fears not the bleak wind;

Companion of her Father, does for him
Where'er he wanders in his pastoral course
The service of a Boy, and with delight
More keen and prouder daring: yet hath She,
Within the garden, like the rest, a bed   580
For her own flowers or favorite Herbs, a space
Holden by sacred charter; and I guess
She also helped to frame that tiny Plot
Of garden ground which one day 'twas my chance
To find among the woody rocks that rise
Above the House, a Slip of smoother earth
Planted with goose-berry bushes, and in one,
Right in the centre of the prickly shrub,
A mimic Bird's-nest, fashioned by the hand,
Was stuck, a staring Thing of twisted hay,   590
And one quaint Fir-tree towered above the Whole.
But in the darkness of the night, then most
This Dwelling charms me. Covered by the gloom,
Then, heedless of good manners, I stop short
And (who could help it?) feed by stealth my sight
With prospect of the company within,
Laid open through the blazing window: there
I see the eldest Daughter at her wheel
Spinning amain, as if to overtake
She knows not what, or teaching in her turn   600
Some little Novice of the sisterhood
That skill in this or other household work
Which from her Father's honored hands, herself
While She was yet a Little-one, had learned.
Mild Man! he is not gay, but they are gay,
And the whole House is filled with gaiety.

From yonder grey-stone that stands alone
Close to the foaming Stream, look up and see,
Not less than half-way up the mountain-side,
A dusky Spot, a little grove of firs   610
And seems still smaller than it is; the Dame
Who dwells below, she told me that this grove,
Just six weeks younger than her eldest Boy,
Was planted by her Husband and herself
For a convenient shelter which in storm
Their sheep might draw to. 'And they knew it well,'

Said she, 'for thither do we bear them food
In time of heavy snow.' She then began
In fond obedience to her private thoughts
To speak of her dead Husband: is there not   620
An art, a music, and a stream of words
That shall be life, the acknowledged voice of life,
Shall speak of what is done among the fields,
Done truly there, or felt, of solid good
And real evil, yet be sweet withal,
More grateful, more harmonious than the breath,
The idle breath of sweetest pipe attuned
To pastoral fancies? Is there such a stream,
Pure and unsullied, flowing from the heart
With motions of true dignity and grace?   630
Or must we seek these things where man is not?
Methinks I could repeat in tuneful verse
Delicious as the gentlest breeze that sounds
Through that aerial fir-grove, could preserve
Some portion of its human history
As gathered from that Matron's lips, and tell
Of tears that have been shed at sight of it
And moving dialogues between this Pair,
Who in the prime of wedlock, with joint hands
Did plant this grove, now flourishing, while they   640
No longer flourish; he entirely gone,
She withering in her loneliness. Be this
A task above my skill: the silent mind
Has its own treasures, and I think of these,
Love what I see, and honour humankind.
    No, We are not alone, we do not stand,
My Emma, here misplaced and desolate,
Loving what no one cares for but ourselves.
We shall not scatter through the plains and rocks
Of this fair Vale, and o'er its spatious heights,   650
Unprofitable kindliness, bestowed
On Objects unaccustomed to the gifts
Of feeling, that were cheerless and forlorn
But few weeks past, and would be so again
If we were not; we do not tend a lamp
Whose lustre we alone participate,
Which is dependent upon us alone,

Mortal though bright, a dying, dying flame.
Look where we will, some human heart has been
Before us with its offering; not a tree   660
Sprinkles these little pastures, but the same
Hath furnished matter for a thought; perchance
To some one is as a familiar Friend.
Joy spreads and sorrow spreads; and this whole Vale,
Home of untutored Shepherds as it is,
Swarms with sensation, as with gleams of sunshine,
Shadows or breezes, scents or sounds. Nor deem
These feelings, though subservient more than ours
To every day's demand for daily bread,
And borrowing more their spirit and their shape   670
From self-respecting interests, deem them not
Unworthy therefore, and unhallowed—no,
They lift the animal being, do themselves
By nature's kind and ever present aid
Refine the selfishness from which they spring,
Redeem by love the individual sense
Of anxiousness with which they are combined.
Many are pure, the best of them are pure;
The best, and these, remember, most abound,
Are fit associates of the [   ] joy,   680
Joy of the highest and the purest minds.
They blend with it congenially: meanwhile,
Calmly they breathe their own undying life,
Lowly and unassuming as it is,
Through this their mountain sanctuary (long,
Oh long may it remain inviolate),
Diffusing health and sober chearfulness,
And giving to the moments as they pass
Their little boons of animating thought
That sweeten labour, make it seem and feel   690
To be no arbitrary weight imposed,
But a glad function natural to Man.
    Fair proof of this, Newcomer though I be,
Already have I seen; the inward frame,
Though slowly opening, opens every day.
Nor am I less delighted with the show
As it unfolds itself, now here, now there,
Than is the passing Traveller, when his way

Lies through some region then first trod by him
(Say this fair Valley's self), when low-hung mists   700
Break up and are beginning to recede.
How pleased he is to hear the murmuring streams,
The many Voices, from he knows not where,
To have about him, which way e'er he goes,
Something on every side concealed from view,
In every quarter some thing visible,
Half-seen or wholly, lost and found again,
Alternate progress and impediment,
And yet a growing prospect in the main.
    Such pleasure now is mine, and what if I,   710
Herein less happy than the Traveller,
Am sometimes forced to cast a painful look
Upon unwelcome things, which unawares
Reveal themselves? Not therefore is my mind
Depressed, nor do I fear what is to come;
But confident, enriched at every glance,
The more I see the more is my delight.
Truth justifies herself, and as she dwells
With Hope, who would not follow where she leads?
    Nor let me overlook those other loves   720
Where no fear is, those humbler sympathies
That have to me endeared the quietness
Of this sublime retirement. I begin
Already to inscribe upon my heart
A liking for the small grey Horse that bears
The paralytic Man; I know the Ass
On which the Cripple, in the Quarry maimed,
Rides to and fro: I know them and their ways.
The famous Sheep-dog, first in all the vale,
Though yet to me a Stranger, will not be   730
A Stranger long; nor will the blind Man's Guide,
Meek and neglected Thing, of no renown.
Who ever lived a Winter in one place,
Beneath the shelter of one Cottage-roof,
And has not had his Red-beast or his Wren?
I have them both; and I shall have my Thrush
In spring-time, and a hundred Warblers more;
And if the banished Eagle Pair return,
Helvellyn's Eagles, to their antient Hold,°

Then shall I see, shall claim with those two Birds   740
Acquaintance, as they soar amid the Heav'ns.
The Owl that gives the name to Owlet-crag
Have I heard shouting, and he soon will be
A chosen one of my regards. See there
The Heifer in yon little Croft belongs
To one who holds it dear; with duteous care
She reared it, and in speaking of her Charge
I heard her scatter once a word or two,
Domestic and in spirit Motherly,
She being herself a Mother; happy Beast,   750
If the caresses of a human voice
Can make it so, and care of human hands.
    And Ye as happy under Nature's care,
Strangers to me and all men, or at least
Strangers to all particular amity,
All intercourse of knowledge or of love
That parts the individual from the kind.
Whether in large communities ye keep
From year to year, not shunning man's abode,
A settled residence, or be from far,   760
Wild creatures, and of many homes, that come
The gift of winds, and whom the winds again
Take from us at your pleasure—yet shall ye
Not want for this, your own subordinate place
According to your claim, an underplace
In my affections. Witness the delight
With which erewhile I saw that multitude
Wheel through the sky and see them now at rest,
Yet not at rest, upon the glassy lake.
They cannot rest—they gambol like young whelps;   770
Active as lambs, and overcome with joy,
They try all frolic motions, flutter, plunge,
And beat the passive water with their wings.
Too distant are they for plain view, but lo!
Those little fountains, sparkling in the sun,
Which tell what they are doing, which rise up,
First one and then another silver spout,
As one or other takes the fit of glee,
Fountains and spouts, yet rather in the guise
Of plaything fire-works, which on festal nights   780

Hiss hiss about the feet of wanton boys.
How vast the compass of this theatre,
Yet nothing to be seen but lovely pomp
And silent majesty. The birch-tree woods
Are hung with thousand thousand diamond drops
Of melted hoar-frost, every tiny knot
In the bare twigs, each little budding-place
Cased with its several bead; what myriads there
Upon one tree, while all the distant grove
That rises to the summit of the steep   790
Is like a mountain built of silver light:
See yonder the same pageant, and again
Behold the universal imagery
At what a depth, deep in the Lake below.
Admonished of the days of love to come,
The raven croaks and fills the sunny air
With a strange sound of genial harmony;
And in and all about that playful band,
Incapable although they be of rest,
And in their fashion very rioters,   800
There is a stillness; and they seem to make
Calm revelry in that their calm abode.
I leave them to their pleasure, and I pass,
Pass with a thought the life of the whole year
That is to come: the Throngs of mountain flowers
And lillies that will dance upon the lake.
    Then boldly say that solitude is not
Where these things are: he truly is alone,
He of the multitude whose eyes are doomed
To hold a vacant commerce day by day   810
With that which he can neither know nor love,
Dead things, to him thrice dead, or worse than this,
With swarms of life, and worse than all, of men,
His fellow men, that are to him no more
Than to the Forest Hermit are the leaves
That hang aloft in myriads—nay, far less,
Far less for aught that comforts or defends
Or lulls or chears. Society is here:
The true community, the noblest Frame
Of many into one incorporate;   820
That must be looked for here; paternal sway,

One Household, under God, for high and low,
One family and one mansion; to themselves
Appropriate, and divided from the world
As if it were a cave, a multitude
Human and brute, possessors undisturbed
Of this recess, their legislative Hall,
Their Temple, and their glorious dwelling-place.
   Dismissing therefore all Arcadian dreams,
All golden fancies of the golden age,   830
The bright array of shadowy thoughts from times
That were before all time, or are to be
When time is not, the pageantry that stirs
And will be stirring when our eyes are fixed
On lovely objects and we wish to part
With all remembrance of a jarring world,
Give entrance to the sober truth; avow
That Nature to this favourite Spot of ours
Yields no exemption, but her awful rights
Enforces to the utmost and exacts   840
Her tribute of inevitable pain,
And that the sting is added, man himself
For ever busy to afflict himself.
Yet temper this with one sufficient hope,
What need of more? that we shall neither droop
Nor pine for want of pleasure in the life
Which is about us, nor through dearth of aught
That keeps in health the insatiable mind;
That we shall have for knowledge and for love
Abundance; and that, feeling as we do,   850
How goodly, how exceeding fair, how pure
From all reproach is this aetherial frame
And this deep vale, its earthly counterpart,
By which, and under which, we are enclosed
To breathe in peace; we shall moreover find
(If sound, and what we ought to be ourselves,
If rightly we observe and justly weigh)
The Inmates not unworthy of their home,
The Dwellers of the Dwelling.
                     And if this
Were not, we have enough within ourselves,   860
Enough to fill the present day with joy

And overspread the future years with hope,
Our beautiful and quiet home, enriched
Already with a Stranger whom we love°
Deeply, a Stranger of our Father's house,
A never-resting Pilgrim of the Sea,
Who finds at last an hour to his content
Beneath our roof. And others whom we love
Will seek us also, Sisters of our hearts,°
And one, like them, a Brother of our hearts,   870
Philosopher and Poet, in whose sight
These mountains will rejoice with open joy.
Such is our wealth: O Vale of Peace, we are
And must be, with God's will, a happy band.
   But 'tis not to enjoy, for this alone
That we exist; no, something must be done.
I must not walk in unreproved delight
These narrow bounds and think of nothing more,
No duty that looks further and no care.
Each Being has his office, lowly some   880
And common, yet all worthy if fulfilled
With zeal, acknowledgement that with the gift
Keeps pace a harvest answering to the seed.
Of ill-advised ambition and of pride
I would stand clear, yet unto me I feel
That an internal brightness is vouchsafed
That must not die, that must not pass away.
Why does this inward lustre fondly seek
And gladly blend with outward fellowship?
Why shine they round me thus, whom thus I love?   890
Why do they teach me, whom I thus revere?
Strange question, yet it answers not itself.
That humble Roof embowered among the trees,
That calm fireside, it is not even in them,
Blessed as they are, to furnish a reply
That satisfies and ends in perfect rest.
Possessions have I wholly, solely, mine,
Something within, which yet is shared by none,
Not even the nearest to me and most dear,
Something which power and effort may impart.   900
I would impart it; I would spread it wide,
Immortal in the world which is to come.

I would not wholly perish even in this,
Lie down, and be forgotten in the dust,
I and the modest partners of my days
Making a silent company in death.
It must not be, if I divinely taught
Am privileged to speak as I have felt
Of what in man is human or divine.
    While yet an innocent little-one, a heart   910
That doubtless wanted not its tender moods,
I breathed (for this I better recollect)
Among wild appetites and blind desires,
Motions of savage instinct, my delight
And exaltation. Nothing at that time
So welcome, no temptation half so dear
As that which urged me to a daring feat.
Deep pools, tall trees, black chasms, and dizzy crags,
I loved to look at them, to stand and read
Their looks forbidding, read and disobey,   920
Sometimes in act, and evermore in thought.
With impulses which only were by these
Surpassed in strength, I heard of danger met
Or sought with courage, enterprize forlorn
By one, sole keeper of his own intent
Or by a resolute few, who for the sake
Of glory fronted multitudes in arms.
Yea, to this day I swell with like desire;
I cannot at this moment read a tale
Of two brave Vessels matched in deadly fight   930
And fighting to the death, but I am pleased
More than a wise Man ought to be; I wish,
I burn, I struggle, and in soul am there.
But me hath Nature tamed and bade me seek
For other agitations or be calm,
Hath dealt with me as with a turbulent Stream—
Some Nurseling of the Mountains which she leads
Through quiet meadows after it has learned
Its strength and had its triumph and its joy,
Its desperate course of tumult and of glee.   940
That which in stealth by Nature was performed
Hath Reason sanctioned: her deliberate Voice
Hath said, 'Be mild and love all gentle things;

Thy glory and thy happiness be there.
Yet fear (though thou confide in me) no want
Of aspirations which have been—of foes
To wrestle with and victory to complete,
Bounds to be leapt and darkness to explore.
That which enflamed thy infant heart, the love,
The longing, the contempt, the undaunted quest,   950
These shall survive, though changed their office, these
Shall live—it is not in their power to die.'
Then farewell to the Warrior's deeds, farewell
All hope which once and long was mine, to fill
The heroic trumpet with the Muse's breath!
Yet in this peaceful Vale we will not spend
Unheard-of days, though loving peaceful thoughts;
A Voice shall speak, and what will be the Theme?
  On Man, on Nature, and on human Life,
Thinking in solitude, from time to time   960
I feel sweet passions traversing my Soul
Like Music; unto these, where'er I may,
I would give utterance in numerous verse.
Of truth, of grandeur, beauty, love, and hope—
Hope for this earth and hope beyond the grave;
Of virtue and of intellectual power;
Of blessed consolations in distress;
Of joy in widest commonalty spread;
Of the individual mind that keeps its own
Inviolate retirement, and consists   970
With being limitless, the one great Life;
I sing: fit audience let me find though few.°
  'Fit audience find though few'—thus prayed the Bard,
Holiest of Men. Urania, I shall need
Thy guidance, or a greater Muse, if such
Descend to earth or dwell in highest heaven.
For I must tread on shadowy ground, must sink
Deep, and, aloft ascending, breathe in worlds
To which the Heaven of heavens is but a veil.
All strength, all terror, single or in bands,   980
That ever was put forth in personal form—
Jehovah, with his thunder, and the quire
Of shouting angels, and the empyreal thrones—
I pass them unalarmed. The darkest Pit

Of the profoundest Hell, chaos, night,
Nor aught of [   ] vacancy scooped out
By help of dreams can breed such fear and awe
As fall upon us often when we look
Into our minds, into the mind of Man,
My haunt, and the main region of my song.   990
Beauty, whose living home is the green earth,
Surpassing the most fair ideal Forms
The craft of delicate spirits hath composed
From earth's materials, waits upon my steps,
Pitches her tents before me where I move,
An hourly Neighbour. Paradise, and groves
Elysian, fortunate islands, fields like those of old
In the deep ocean, wherefore should they be
A History, or but a dream, when minds
Once wedded to this outward frame of things   1000
In love, find these the growth of common day?°
I, long before the blesséd hour arrives,
Would sing in solitude the spousal verse
Of this great consummation, would proclaim—
Speaking of nothing more than what we are—
How exquisitely the individual Mind
(And the progressive powers perhaps no less
Of the whole species) to the external world
Is fitted; and how exquisitely too—
Theme this but little heard of among men—   1010
The external world is fitted to the mind;
And the creation (by no lower name
Can it be called) which they with blended might
Accomplish: this is my great argument.
Such [   ] foregoing, if I oft
Must turn elsewhere, and travel near the tribes
And fellowships of men, and see ill sights
Of passions ravenous from each other's rage,
Must hear humanity in fields and groves
Pipe solitary anguish, or must hang   1020
Brooding above the fierce confederate Storm
Of Sorrow, barricadoed evermore
Within the walls of Cities—may these sounds
Have their authentic comment, that even these
Hearing, I be not heartless or forlorn!

Come, thou prophetic Spirit, Soul of Man,
Thou human Soul of the wide earth that hast
Thy metropolitan Temple in the hearts
Of mighty Poets: unto me vouchsafe
Thy guidance, teach me to discern and part   1030
Inherent things from casual, what is fixed
From fleeting, that my verse may live, and be
Even as a light hung up in heaven to chear
Mankind in times to come! And if with this
I blend more lowly matter—with the thing
Contemplated describe the mind and man
Contemplating, and who and what he was,
The transitory Being that beheld
This vision, when and where and how he lived,
His joys and sorrows and his hopes and fears,   1040
With all his little realities of life—
Be not this labour useless. If such theme
With highest things may [   ], then Great God,
Thou who art breath and being, way and guide,
And power and understanding, may my life
Express the image of a better time,
More wise desires and simple manners; nurse
My heart in genuine freedom; all pure thoughts
Be with me and uphold me to the end!

Poems on the Naming of Places

I

'It was an April Morning: fresh and clear'

It was an April Morning: fresh and clear
The Rivulet, delighting in its strength,
Ran with a young man's speed, and yet the voice
Of waters which the winter had supplied
Was softened down into a vernal tone,
The spirit of enjoyment and desire,
And hopes and wishes, from all living things
Went circling, like a multitude of sounds.
The budding groves appeared as if in haste

To spur the steps of June; as if their shades   10
Of *various* green were hindrances that stood°
Between them and their object: yet, meanwhile,
There was such deep contentment in the air
That every naked ash, and tardy tree
Yet leafless, seemed as though the countenance
With which it looked on this delightful day
Were native to the summer.—Up the brook
I roamed in the confusion of my heart,
Alive to all things and forgetting all.
At length I to a sudden turning came   20
In this continuous glen, where down a rock
The stream, so ardent in its course before,
Sent forth such sallies of glad sound, that all
Which I till then had heard, appeared the voice
Of common pleasure: beast and bird, the lamb,
The Shepherd's dog, the linnet and the thrush
Vied with this waterfall, and made a song
Which, while I listened, seemed like the wild growth
Or like some natural produce of the air
That could not cease to be. Green leaves were here,   30
But 'twas the foliage of the rocks, the birch,
The yew, the holly, and the bright green thorn,
With hanging islands of resplendent furze:
And on a summit, distant a short space,
By any who should look beyond the dell,
A single mountain Cottage might be seen.
I gazed and gazed, and to myself I said,
'Our thoughts at least are ours; and this wild nook,
My EMMA, I will dedicate to thee.'°
——Soon did the spot become my other home,   40
My dwelling, and my out-of-doors abode.
And, of the Shepherds who have seen me there,
To whom I sometimes in our idle talk
Have told this fancy, two or three, perhaps,
Years after we are gone and in our graves,
When they have cause to speak of this wild place,
May call it by the name of EMMA'S DELL.

II

To Joanna

Amid the smoke of cities did you pass
Your time of early youth, and there you learned,
From years of quiet industry, to love
The living Beings by your own fire-side,
With such a strong devotion, that your heart
Is slow towards the sympathies of them
Who look upon the hills with tenderness,
And made dear friendships with the streams and groves.
Yet we who are transgressors in this kind,
Dwelling retired in our simplicity   10
Among the woods and fields, we love you well,
Joanna! and I guess, since you have been
So distant from us now for two long years,
That you will gladly listen to discourse
However trivial, if you thence are taught
That they, with whom you once were happy, talk
Familiarly of you and of old times.
While I was seated, now some ten days past,
Beneath those lofty firs, that overtop
Their ancient neighbour, the old Steeple tower,   20
The Vicar from his gloomy house hard by
Came forth to greet me, and when he had asked,
'How fares Joanna, that wild-hearted Maid!
And when will she return to us?' he paused,
And after short exchange of village news,
He with grave looks demanded, for what cause,
Reviving obsolcte Idolatry,
I like a Runic Priest, in characters
Of formidable size, had chiseled out
Some uncouth name upon the native rock,   30
Above the Rotha, by the forest side.
—Now, by those dear immunities of heart
Engendered betwixt malice and true love,
I was not loth to be so catechized,
And this was my reply.—'As it bcfcl,
One summer morning we had walked abroad
At break of day, Joanna and myself.
—'Twas that delightful season, when the broom,

Full flowered, and visible on every steep,
Along the copses runs in veins of gold.   40
Our pathway led us on to Rotha's banks,
And when we came in front of that tall rock
Which looks towards the East, I there stopped short,
And traced the lofty barrier with my eye
From base to summit; such delight I found
To note in shrub and tree, in stone and flower,
That intermixture of delicious hues,
Along so vast a surface, all at once,
In one impression, by connecting force
Of their own beauty, imaged in the heart.   50
—When I had gazed perhaps two minutes' space,
Joanna, looking in my eyes, beheld
That ravishment of mine, and laughed aloud.
The rock, like something starting from a sleep,
Took up the Lady's voice, and laughed again:
That ancient Woman seated on Helm-crag
Was ready with her cavern; Hammar-Scar,
And the tall Steep of Silver-How sent forth
A noise of laughter; southern Loughrigg heard,
And Fairfield answered with a mountain tone: 60
Helvellyn far into the clear blue sky
Carried the Lady's voice,—old Skiddaw blew
His speaking trumpet;—back out of the clouds
Of Glaramara southward came the voice;
And Kirkstone tossed it from his misty head.
Now whether, (said I to our cordial Friend
Who in the hey-day of astonishment
Smiled in my face) this were in simple truth
A work accomplished by the brotherhood
Of ancient mountains, or my ear was touched   70
With dreams and visionary impulses,
Is not for me to tell; but sure I am
That there was a loud uproar in the hills.
And, while we both were listening, to my side
The fair Joanna drew, is if she wished
To shelter from some object of her fear.
—And hence, long afterwards, when eighteen moons
Were wasted, as I chanced to walk alone
Beneath this rock, at sun-rise, on a calm

And silent morning, I sate down, and there,   80
In memory of affections old and true,
I chiseled out in those rude characters
Joanna's name upon the living stone.
And I, and all who dwell by my fire-side
Have called the lovely rock, Joanna's Rock.'

III

'There is an Eminence,—of these our hills'

There is an Eminence,—of these our hills
The last that parleys with the setting sun.
We can behold it from our Orchard seat,
And, when at evening we pursue our walk
Along the public way, this Cliff, so high
Above us, and so distant in its height,
Is visible, and often seems to send
Its own deep quiet to restore our hearts.
The meteors make of it a favorite haunt:
The star of Jove, so beautiful and large   10
In the mid heav'ns, is never half so fair
As when he shines above it. 'Tis in truth
The loneliest place we have among the clouds.
And She who dwells with me, whom I have loved°
With such communion, that no place on earth
Can ever be a solitude to me,
Hath said, this lonesome Peak shall bear my Name.

IV

'A narrow girdle of rough stones and crags'

A narrow girdle of rough stones and crags,
A rude and natural causeway, interposed
Between the water and a winding slope
Of copse and thicket, leaves the eastern shore
Of Grasmere safe in its own privacy.
And there, myself and two beloved Friends,
One calm September morning, ere the mist
Had altogether yielded to the sun,
Sauntered on this retired and difficult way.
——Ill suits the road with one in haste, but we   10

Played with our time; and, as we strolled along,
It was our occupation to observe
Such objects as the waves had tossed ashore,
Feather, or leaf, or weed, or withered bough,
Each on the other heaped along the line
Of the dry wreck. And in our vacant mood,°
Not seldom did we stop to watch some tuft
Of dandelion seed or thistle's beard,
Which, seeming lifeless half, and half impelled
By some internal feeling, skimmed along   20
Close to the surface of the lake that lay
Asleep in a dead calm, ran closely on
Along the dead calm lake, now here, now there,
In all its sportive wanderings all the while
Making report of an invisible breeze
That was its wings, its chariot, and its horse,
Its very playmate, and its moving soul.
——And often, trifling with a privilege
Alike indulged to all, we paused, one now,
And now the other, to point out, perchance   30
To pluck, some flower or water-weed, too fair
Either to be divided from the place
On which it grew, or to be left alone
To its own beauty. Many such there are,
Fair ferns and flowers, and chiefly that tall plant
So stately, of the Queen Osmunda named,°
Plant lovelier in its own retired abode
On Grasmere's beach, than Naiad by the side°
Of Grecian brook, or Lady of the Mere
Sole-sitting by the shores of old Romance.   40
——So fared we that sweet morning: from the fields
Meanwhile, a noise was heard, the busy mirth
Of Reapers, Men and Women, Boys and Girls.
Delighted much to listen to those sounds,
And in the fashion which I have described,
Feeding unthinking fancies, we advanced
Along the indented shore; when suddenly,
Through a thin veil of glittering haze, we saw
Before us on a point of jutting land
The tall and upright figure of a Man   50
Attired in peasant's garb, who stood alone

Angling beside the margin of the lake.
That way we turned our steps; nor was it long,
Ere making ready comments on the sight
Which then we saw, with one and the same voice
We all cried out, that he must be indeed
An idle man, who thus could lose a day
Of the mid harvest, when the labourer's hire
Is ample, and some little might be stored
Wherewith to chear him in the winter time.   60
Thus talking of that Peasant we approached
Close to the spot where with his rod and line
He stood alone; whereat he turned his head
To greet us—and we saw a man worn down
By sickness, gaunt and lean, with sunken cheeks
And wasted limbs, his legs so long and lean
That for my single self I looked at them,
Forgetful of the body they sustained.—
Too weak to labour in the harvest field,
The man was using his best skill to gain   70
A pittance from the dead unfeeling lake
That knew not of his wants. I will not say
What thoughts immediately were ours, nor how
The happy idleness of that sweet morn,
With all its lovely images, was changed
To serious musing and to self-reproach.
Nor did we fail to see within ourselves
What need there is to be reserved in speech,
And temper all our thoughts with charity.
—Therefore, unwilling to forget that day,   80
My Friend, Myself, and She who then received
The same admonishment, have called the place
By a memorial name, uncouth indeed
As e'er by Mariner was giv'n to Bay
Or Foreland on a new-discovered coast,
And, POINT RASH-JUDGMENT is the Name it bears.

V

To M.H.

Our walk was far among the ancient trees:
There was no road, nor any wood-man's path,

But the thick umbrage, checking the wild growth
Of weed and sapling, on the soft green turf
Beneath the branches of itself had made
A track which brought us to a slip of lawn,
And a small bed of water in the woods.
All round this pool both flocks and herds might drink
On its firm margin, even as from a well
Or some stone-bason which the Herdsman's hand   10
Had shaped for their refreshment, nor did sun
Or wind from any quarter ever come
But as a blessing to this calm recess,
This glade of water and this one green field.
The spot was made by Nature for herself:
The travellers know it not, and 'twill remain
Unknown to them; but it is beautiful,
And if a man should plant his cottage near,
Should sleep beneath the shelter of its trees,
And blend its waters with his daily meal,   20
He would so love it that in his death-hour
Its image would survive among his thoughts,
And, therefore, my sweet MARY, this still nook
With all its beeches we have named from You.

Rural Architecture

There's George Fisher, Charles Fleming, and Reginald Shore,
Three rosy-cheeked School-boys, the highest not more
Than the height of a Counsellor's bag;
To the top of Great How did it please them to climb,
And there they built up without mortar or lime
A Man on the peak of the crag.

They built him of stones gathered up as they lay,
They built him and christened him all in one day,
An Urchin both vigorous and hale;
And so without scruple they called him Ralph Jones.   10
Now Ralph is renowned for the length of his bones;
The Magog of Legberthwaite dale.°

Just half a week after the Wind sallied forth,
And, in anger or merriment, out of the North
Coming on with a terrible pother,
From the peak of the crag blew the Giant away.
And what did these School-boys?—The very next day
They went and they built up another.

—Some little I've seen of blind boisterous works
In Paris and London, 'mong Christians or Turks,   20
Spirits busy to do and undo:
At remembrance whereof my blood sometimes will flag.
—Then, light-hearted Boys, to the top of the Crag!
And I'll build up a Giant with you.

The Childless Father

Up, Timothy, up with your Staff and away!
Not a soul in the village this morning will stay;
The Hare has just started from Hamilton's grounds,
And Skiddaw is glad with the cry of the hounds.

—Of coats and of jackets grey, scarlet, and green,
On the slopes of the pastures all colours were seen,
With their comely blue aprons and caps white as snow,
The girls on the hills made a holiday show.

The bason of box-wood, just six months before,°
Had stood on the table at Timothy's door,   10
A Coffin through Timothy's threshold had passed,
One Child did it bear and that Child was his last.

Now fast up the dell came the noise and the fray,
The horse and the horn, and the hark! hark away!
Old Timothy took up his Staff, and he shut
With a leisurely motion the door of his hut.

Perhaps to himself at that moment he said,
'The key I must take, for my Ellen is dead';
But of this in my ears not a word did he speak,
And he went to the chase with a tear on his cheek.   20

Inscription

FOR THE SPOT WHERE THE HERMITAGE STOOD ON ST. HERBERT'S
ISLAND, DERWENT-WATER

If thou in the dear love of some one friend
Hast been so happy, that thou know'st what thoughts
Will, sometimes, in the happiness of love
Make the heart sink, then wilt thou reverence
This quiet spot.——St. Herbert hither came
And here, for many seasons, from the world
Removed, and the affections of the world
He dwelt in solitude. He living here,
This island's sole inhabitant! had left
A Fellow-labourer, whom the good Man loved   10
As his own soul; and when within his cave
Alone he knelt before the crucifix
While o'er the lake the cataract of Lodore
Pealed to his orisons, and when he paced
Along the beach of this small isle and thought
Of his Companion, he had prayed that both
Might die in the same moment. Nor in vain
So prayed he:—as our Chronicles report,
Though here the Hermit numbered his last days,
Far from St. Cuthbert his beloved friend,   20
Those holy men both died in the same hour.

' *'Tis said, that some have died for love'*

'Tis said, that some have died for love:
And here and there a church-yard grave is found
In the cold North's unhallowed ground,
Because the wretched man himself had slain,
His love was such a grievous pain.
And there is one whom I five years have known;
He dwells alone
Upon Helvellyn's side.
He loved——The pretty Barbara died,
And thus he makes his moan: 10

Three years had Barbara in her grave been laid
When thus his moan he made.

'Oh! move thou Cottage from behind that oak
Or let the aged tree uprooted lie,
That in some other way yon smoke
May mount into the sky!
The clouds pass on; they from the Heavens depart:
I look—the sky is empty space;
I know not what I trace;
But when I cease to look, my hand is on my heart.   20

O! what a weight is in these shades! Ye leaves,
When will that dying murmur be suppressed?
Your sound my heart of peace bereaves,
It robs my heart of rest.
Thou Thrush, that singest loud and loud and free,
Into yon row of willows flit,
Upon that alder sit;
Or sing another song, or chuse another tree.

Roll back, sweet rill! back to thy mountain bounds,
And there for ever be thy waters chained!   30
For thou dost haunt the air with sounds
That cannot be sustained;
If still beneath that pine-tree's ragged bough
Headlong yon waterfall must come,
Oh let it then be dumb!—
Be any thing, sweet rill, but that which thou art now.

Thou Eglantine whose arch so proudly towers
(Even like a rainbow spanning half the vale)
Thou one fair shrub, oh! shed thy flowers,
And stir not in the gale.   40
For thus to see thee nodding in the air,
To see thy arch thus stretch and bend,
Thus rise and thus descend,
Disturbs me, till the sight is more than I can bear.'

The man who makes this feverish complaint
Is one of giant stature, who could dance

Equipped from head to foot in iron mail.
Ah gentle Love! if ever thought was thine
To store up kindred hours for me, thy face
Turn from me, gentle Love, nor let me walk   50
Within the sound of Emma's voice, or know
Such happiness as I have known to-day.

Lines

WRITTEN WITH A SLATE-PENCIL UPON A STONE, THE LARGEST OF A HEAP
LYING NEAR A DESERTED QUARRY, UPON ONE OF THE ISLANDS AT RYDALE.

Stranger! this hillock of misshapen stones
Is not a ruin of the ancient time,
Nor, as perchance thou rashly deem'st, the Cairn
Of some old British Chief: 'tis nothing more
Than the rude embryo of a little dome
Or pleasure-house, which was to have been built
Among the birch-trees of this rocky isle.
But, as it chanced, Sir William having learned°   10
That from the shore a full-grown man might wade,
And make himself a freeman of this spot
At any hour he chose, the Knight forthwith
Desisted, and the quarry and the mound
Are monuments of his unfinished task.——
The block on which these lines are traced, perhaps,
Was once selected as the corner-stone
Of the intended pile, which would have been
Some quaint odd play-thing of elaborate skill,
So that, I guess, the linnet and the thrush,   20
And other little builders who dwell here,
Had wondered at the work. But blame him not,
For old Sir William was a gentle Knight
Bred in this vale to which he appertained
With all his ancestry. Then peace to him
And for the outrage which he had devised
Entire forgiveness.——But if thou art one
On fire with thy impatience to become
An Inmate of these mountains, if disturbed

By beautiful conceptions, thou hast hewn
Out of the quiet rock the elements
Of thy trim mansion destined soon to blaze   30
In snow-white splendour, think again, and taught°
By old Sir William and his quarry, leave
Thy fragments to the bramble and the rose,
There let the vernal slow-worm sun himself,
And let the red-breast hop from stone to stone.

The Oak and the Broom

A PASTORAL

His simple truths did Andrew glean
Beside the babbling rills;
A careful student he had been
Among the woods and hills.
One winter's night when through the Trees
The wind was thundering, on his knees
His youngest born did Andrew hold:
And while the rest, a ruddy quire
Were seated round their blazing fire,
This Tale the Shepherd told.   10

I saw a crag, a lofty stone
As ever tempest beat!
Out of its head an Oak had grown,
A Broom out of its feet.
The time was March, a chearful noon—
The thaw-wind with the breath of June
Breathed gently from the warm South-west;
When in a voice sedate with age
This Oak, half giant and half sage,
His neighbour thus addressed.   20

'Eight weary weeks, thro' rock and clay,
Along this mountain's edge
The Frost hath wrought both night and day,
Wedge driving after wedge.

Look up, and think, above your head
What trouble surely will be bred;
Last night I heard a crash—'tis true,
The splinters took another road—
I see them yonder—what a load
For such a Thing as you!   30

You are preparing as before
To deck your slender shape;
And yet, just three years back—no more—
You had a strange escape.
Down from yon Cliff a fragment broke,
It came, you know, with fire and smoke
And hither did it bend its way.
This pond'rous block was caught by me,
And o'er your head, as you may see,
'Tis hanging to this day.   40

The Thing had better been asleep,
Whatever thing it were,
Or Breeze, or Bird, or fleece of Sheep,
That first did plant you there.
For you and your green twigs decoy
The little witless Shepherd-boy
To come and slumber in your bower;
And trust me, on some sultry noon,
Both you and he, Heaven knows how soon!
Will perish in one hour.   50

From me this friendly warning take'—
—The Broom began to doze,
And thus to keep herself awake
Did gently interpose.
'My thanks for your discourse are due;
That it is true, and more than true,
I know and I have known it long;
Frail is the bond, by which we hold
Our being, be we young or old,
Wise, foolish, weak or strong.   60

Disasters, do the best we can,
Will reach both great and small,
And he is oft the wisest man,
Who is not wise at all.
For me, why should I wish to roam?
This spot is my paternal home,
It is my pleasant Heritage;
My Father many a happy year
Here spread his careless blossoms, here
Attained a good old age.   70

Even such as his may be my lot.
What cause have I to haunt
My heart with terrors? Am I not
In truth a favored plant!
The Spring for me a garland weaves
Of yellow flowers and verdant leaves,
And, when the Frost is in the sky,
My branches are so fresh and gay
That You might look on me and say
This plant can never die.   80

The butterfly, all green and gold,
To me hath often flown,
Here in my Blossoms to behold
Wings lovely as his own.
When grass is chill with rain or dew,
Beneath my shade the mother ewe
Lies with her infant lamb; I see
The love they to each other make,
And the sweet joy, which they partake,
It is a joy to me.'   90

Her voice was blithe, her heart was light;
The Broom might have pursued
Her speech, until the stars of night
Their journey had renewed.
But in the branches of the Oak
Two Ravens now began to croak

Their nuptial song, a gladsome air;
And to her own green bower the breeze
That instant brought two stripling Bees
To feed and murmur there.   100

One night the Wind came from the North
And blew a furious blast,
At break of day I ventured forth
And near the Cliff I passed.
The storm had fall'n upon the Oak
And struck him with a mighty stroke,
And whirled and whirled him far away;
And in one hospitable Cleft
The little careless Broom was left
To live for many a day.   110

The Waterfall and the Eglantine

'Begone, thou fond presumptuous Elf,'
Exclaimed a thundering Voice,
'Nor dare to thrust thy foolish self
Between me and my choice!'
A falling Water swoln with snows
Thus spake to a poor Briar-rose,
That all bespattered with his foam,
And dancing high, and dancing low,
Was living, as a child might know,
In an unhappy home.   10

'Dost thou presume my course to block?
Off, off! or, puny Thing!
I'll hurl thee headlong with the rock
To which thy fibres cling.'
The Flood was tyrannous and strong;
The patient Briar suffered long,
Nor did he utter groan or sigh,
Hoping the danger would be passed:
But seeing no relief, at last
He ventured to reply.   20

'Ah!' said the Briar, 'Blame me not!
Why should we dwell in strife?
We who in this, our natal spot,
Once lived a happy life!
Your stirred me on my rocky bed—
What pleasure thro' my veins you spread!
The Summer long from day to day
My leaves you freshened and bedewed;
Nor was it common gratitude
That did your cares repay.   30

When Spring came on with bud and bell,
Among these rocks did I
Before you hang my wreath to tell
That gentle days were nigh!
And in the sultry summer hours
I sheltered you with leaves and flowers;
And in my leaves now shed and gone
The linnet lodged and for us two
Chaunted his pretty songs when you
Had little voice or none.   40

But now proud thoughts are in your breast—
What grief is mine you see.
Ah! would you think, ev'n yet how blest
Together we might be!
Though of both leaf and flower bereft,
Some ornaments to me are left—
Rich store of scarlet hips is mine,
With which I in my humble way
Would deck you many a Winter's day,
A happy Eglantine!'   50

What more he said, I cannot tell.
The stream came thundering down the dell
And galloped loud and fast;
I listened, nor aught else could hear,
The Briar quaked and much I fear,
Those accents were his last.

The Two Thieves

OR THE LAST STAGE OF AVARICE

O now that the genius of Bewick were mine,°
And the skill which he learned on the banks of the Tyne!
Then the Muses might deal with me just as they chose,
For I'd take my last leave both of verse and of prose.

What feats would I work with my magical hand!
Book-learning and books should be banished the land;
And for hunger and thirst and such troublesome calls,
Every ale-house should then have a feast on its walls.

The Traveller would hang his wet clothes on a chair;
Let them smoke, let them burn, not a straw would he care: 10
For the Prodigal Son, Joseph's Dream and his Sheaves,°
Oh, what would they be to my tale of two Thieves?

Little Dan is unbreeched, he is three birthdays old;
His Grandsire, that age more than thirty times told;
There are ninety good seasons of fair and foul weather
Between them, and both go a-stealing together.

With chips is the Carpenter strewing his floor?
Is cartload of peats at an old Woman's door?
Old Daniel his hand to the treasure will slide;
And his Grandson's as busy at work by his side.   20

Old Daniel begins, he stops short—and his eye
Through the lost look of dotage is cunning and sly.
'Tis a look which at this time is hardly his own,
But tells a plain tale of the days that are flown.

Dan once had a heart that was moved by the wires
Of manifold pleasures and many desires:
And what if he cherished his purse? 'Twas no more
Than treading a path trod by thousands before.

'Twas a path trod by thousands; but Daniel is one
Who went something further than others have gone;   30
And now with old Daniel you see how it fares;
You see to what end he has brought his grey hairs.

The pair sally forth hand in hand; ere the sun
Has peered o'er the beeches their work is begun:
And yet, into whatever sin they may fall,
This Child but half knows it, and that not at all.

They hunt through the street with deliberate tread,
And each in his turn is both leader and led;
And, wherever they carry their plots and their wiles,
Every face in the village is dimpled with smiles.   40

Neither checked by the rich nor the needy they roam;
For grey-headed Dan has a daughter at home,
Who will gladly repair all the damage that's done;
And three, were it asked, would be rendered for one.

Old Man! whom so oft I with pity have eyed,
I love thee, and love the sweet boy at thy side:
Long yet mayst thou live! for a teacher we see
That lifts up the veil of our nature in thee.

The Idle Shepherd-Boys

OR DUNGEON-GILL FORCE, A PASTORAL

I

The valley rings with mirth and joy.
Among the hills the Echoes play
A never, never ending song
To welcome in the May.
The Magpie chatters with delight;

The mountain Raven's youngling Brood
Have left the Mother and the Nest,
And they go rambling east and west
In search of their own food,
Or thro' the glittering Vapors dart   10
In very wantonness of Heart.

II

Beneath a rock, upon the grass,
Two Boys are sitting in the sun;
It seems they have no work to do
Or that their work is done.
On pipes of sycamore they play
The fragments of a Christmas Hymn,
Or with that plant which in our dale
We call Stag-horn, or Fox's Tail,
Their rusty Hats they trim: 20
And thus as happy as the Day,
Those Shepherds wear the time away.

III

Along the river's stony marge
The sand-lark chaunts a joyous song;
The thrush is busy in the Wood,
And carols loud and strong.
A thousand lambs are on the rocks,
All newly born! both earth and sky
Keep jubilee, and more than all,
Those Boys with their green Coronal,   30
They never hear the cry,
That plaintive cry! which up the hill
Comes from the depth of Dungeon-Gill.

IV

Said Walter, leaping from the ground,
'Down to the stump of yon old yew
I'll run with you a race.'—No more—
Away the Shepherds flew.
They leapt, they ran, and when they came

Right opposite to Dungeon-Gill,
Seeing, that he should lose the prize,   40
'Stop!' to his comrade Walter cries—
James stopped with no good will:
Said Walter then, 'Your task is here,
'Twill keep you working half a year.

V

Till you have crossed where I shall cross,
Say that you'll neither sleep nor eat.'
James proudly took him at his word,
But did not like the feat.
It was a spot, which you may see
If ever you to Langdale go: 50
Into a chasm a mighty Block
Hath fallen, and made a bridge of rock;
The gulph is deep below,
And in a bason black and small
Receives a lofty Waterfall.

VI

With staff in hand across the cleft
The Challenger began his march;
And now, all eyes and feet, hath gained
The middle of the arch.
When list! he hears a piteous moan—   60
Again! his heart within him dies—
His pulse is stopped, his breath is lost,
He totters, pale as any ghost,
And looking down, he spies
A Lamb, that in the pool is pent
Within that black and frightful rent.

VII

The Lamb had slipped into the stream,
And safe without a bruise or wound
The Cataract had borne him down
Into the gulph profound.   70
His dam had seen him when he fell,

She saw him down the torrent borne;
And while with all a mother's love
She from the lofty rocks above
Sent forth a cry forlorn,
The Lamb, still swimming round and round
Made answer to that plaintive sound.

VIII

When he had learnt, what thing it was,
That sent this rueful cry; I ween,
The Boy recovered heart, and told   80
The sight which he had seen.
Both gladly now deferred their task;
Nor was there wanting other aid—
A Poet, one who loves the brooks
Far better than the sages' books,
By chance had thither strayed;
And there the helpless Lamb he found
By those huge rocks encompassed round.

IX

He drew it gently from the pool,
And brought it forth into the light: 90
The Shepherds met him with his charge
An unexpected sight!
Into their arms the Lamb they took,
Said they, 'He's neither maimed nor scarred'—
Then up the steep ascent they hied
And placed him at his Mother's side;
And gently did the Bard
Those idle Shepherd-boys upbraid,
And bade them better mind their trade.

'When first I journeyed hither'

When first I journeyed hither, to a home°
And dwelling of my own, it was a cold
And stormy season, and from week to week
The pathways and the publick roads were clogged

With frequent showers of snow. Upon a hill
At a short distance from my House there stands
A stately fir-grove, whither I was wont
To hasten, for within its shade I found
Commodious harbour, a sequestered nook
Or cloister with an unincumbered floor.   10
Here in safe covert on the shallow snow,
And sometimes on a speck of visible earth,
The red-breast near me hopped, nor was I loth
To sympathise with vulgar coppice birds
That hither came. A single beech tree grew
Within this grove of firs, and on the fork
Of that one beech there was a thrush's nest,
A last year's nest conspicuously built
At such small elevation from the ground
That even an unbreeched Boy might look into it: 20
Sure sign I thought that they who in that house
Of nature and of love had made their home
Among the fir-trees, all the summer long
Dwelt in a quiet place: and oftentimes
A few sheep, stragglers of a scattered flock,
Were my companions and would look at me
From the remotest outskirts of the grove,
Some nook where they had made their final stand
Huddling together from two fears, the fear
Of me and of the storm. Full many an hour   30
Here did I lose. But in this grove, the trees
Had by the planter been so crouded each
Upon on the other, and withal had thriven
In such perplexed array that I in vain
Between their stems endeavoured to find out
A length of open space where I might walk
Backwards and forwards long as I had liking
In easy and mechanic thoughtlessness.
And, for this cause, I loved the shady grove
Less than I wished to love a place so sweet.   40
   I have a Brother: many times the leaves°
Have faded, many times the spring has touched
The heart of bird and beast since from the shores
Of Windermere, from Esthwaite's chearful Lake
And her grey cottages, from all the life

And beauty of his native hills he went
To be a Sea-boy on the barren seas.
  When we had been divided fourteen years
At length he came to sojourn a short while
Beneath my roof, nor had the sun twice set   50
Before he made discov'ry of this grove
Whither from that time forward he repaired
With daily visitation. Other haunts
Meanwhile were mine but from the sultry heat
One morning chancing to betake myself
To this forsaken covert, there I found
A hoary pathway traced around the trees
And winding on with such an easy line
Along a natural opening that I stood
Much wondering at my own simplicity   60
That I myself had ever failed in search
Of what was now so obvious. With a sense
Of lively joy did I behold this path
Beneath the fir-trees, for at once I knew
That by my Brother's steps it had been traced.
My thoughts were pleased within me to perceive
That hither he had brought a finer eye,
A heart more wakeful: that more loth to part
From place so lovely he had worn the track,
One of his own deep paths! by pacing here   70
With that habitual restlessness of foot
Wherewith the Sailor measures o'er and o'er
His short domain upon the Vessel's deck
While she is travelling through the dreary seas.
  When thou hadst gone away from Esthwaite's shore
And taken thy first leave of these green hills
And rocks that were the play-ground of thy youth.
Year followed year my Brother! and we two
Conversing not knew little in what mold
Each other's minds were fashioned, and at length   80
When once again we met in Grasmere Vale
Between us there was little other bond
Than common feelings of fraternal love.
But thou a School-boy to the Sea hadst carried
Undying recollections, Nature there°
Was with thee, she who loved us both, she still

Was with thee, and even so thou didst become
A silent Poet! from the solitude
Of the vast Sea didst bring a watchful heart
Still couchant, an inevitable ear   90
And an eye practised like a blind man's touch.
Back to the joyless ocean thou art gone:
And now I call the path-way by thy name
And love the fir-grove with a perfect love.
Thither do I repair when cloudless suns
Shine hot or winds blow troublesome and strong;
And there I sit at evening when the steep
Of Silver-How, and Grasmere's silent Lake
And one green Island gleam between the stems
Of the close firs, a visionary scene!   100
And while I gaze upon this spectacle
Of clouded splendour, on this dream-like sight
Of solemn loveliness, I think on thee
My Brother, and on all which thou hast lost.
Nor seldom, if I rightly guess, when Thou,
Muttering the verses which I muttered first
Among the mountains, through the midnight watch
Art pacing to and fro' the Vessel's deck
In some far region, here, while o'er my head
At every impulse of the moving breeze   110
The fir-grove murmurs with a sea-like sound,
Alone I tread this path, for aught I know
Timing my steps to thine, and with a store
Of indistinguishable sympathies
Mingling most earnest wishes for the day
When We, and others whom we love shall meet
A second time in Grasmere's happy Vale.

A Character

IN THE ANTITHETICAL MANNER

I marvel how Nature could ever find space
For the weight and the levity seen in his face:
There's thought and no thought, and there's paleness and bloom,
And bustle and sluggishness, pleasure and gloom.

There's weakness, and strength both redundant and vain;
Such strength, as if ever affliction and pain
Could pierce through a temper that's soft to disease,
Would be rational peace—a philosopher's ease.

There's indifference, alike when he fails and succeeds,
And attention full ten times as much as there needs,　　　10
Pride where there's no envy, there's so much of joy;
And mildness, and spirit both forward and coy.

There's freedom, and sometimes a diffident stare
Of shame scarcely seeming to know that she's there.
There's virtue, the title it surely may claim,
Yet wants, heaven knows what, to be worthy the name.

What a picture! 'tis drawn without nature or art,
—Yet the Man would at once run away with your heart,
And I for five centuries right gladly would be
Such an odd, such a kind happy creature as he.　　　20

Michael

A PASTORAL POEM

If from the public way you turn your steps
Up the tumultuous brook of Green-head Gill,°
You will suppose that with an upright path
Your feet must struggle; in such bold ascent
The pastoral Mountains front you, face to face.
But, courage! for beside that boisterous Brook
The mountains have all opened out themselves,
And made a hidden valley of their own.
No habitation there is seen; but such
As journey thither find themselves alone　　　10
With a few sheep, with rocks and stones, and kites
That overhead are sailing in the sky.
It is in truth an utter solitude,
Nor should I have made mention of this Dell
But for one object which you might pass by,

Might see and notice not. Beside the brook
There is a straggling heap of unhewn stones!
And to that place a story appertains,
Which, though it be ungarnished with events,
Is not unfit, I deem, for the fire-side,   20
Or for the summer shade. It was the first,
The earliest of those tales that spake to me
Of Shepherds, dwellers in the vallies, men
Whom I already loved, not verily
For their own sakes, but for the fields and hills
Where was their occupation and abode.
And hence this Tale, while I was yet a boy
Careless of books, yet having felt the power
Of Nature, by the gentle agency
Of natural objects led me on to feel   30
For passions that were not my own, and think
At random and imperfectly indeed
On man; the heart of man and human life.
Therefore, although it be a history
Homely and rude, I will relate the same
For the delight of a few natural hearts,
And with yet fonder feeling, for the sake
Of youthful Poets, who among these Hills
Will be my second self when I am gone.

Upon the Forest-side in Grasmere Vale   40
There dwelt a Shepherd, Michael was his name,
An old man, stout of heart, and strong of limb.
His bodily frame had been from youth to age
Of an unusual strength: his mind was keen
Intense and frugal, apt for all affairs,
And in his Shepherd's calling he was prompt
And watchful more than ordinary men.
Hence he had learned the meaning of all winds,
Of blasts of every tone, and often-times
When others heeded not, He heard the South   50
Make subterraneous music, like the noise
Of Bagpipers on distant Highland hills;
The Shepherd, at such warning, of his flock
Bethought him, and he to himself would say
The winds are now devising work for me!

And truly at all times the storm, that drives
The Traveller to a shelter, summoned him
Up to the mountains: he had been alone
Amid the heart of many thousand mists
That came to him and left him on the heights.   60
So lived he till his eightieth year was passed.

And grossly that man errs, who should suppose
That the green Valleys, and the Streams and Rocks
Were things indifferent to the Shepherd's thoughts.
Fields, where with chearful spirits he had breathed
The common air; the hills, which he so oft
Had climbed with vigorous steps; which had impressed
So many incidents upon his mind
Of hardship, skill or courage, joy or fear;
Which like a book preserved the memory   70
Of the dumb animals, whom he had saved,
Had fed or sheltered, linking to such acts,
So grateful in themselves, the certainty
Of honorable gains; these fields, these hills
Which were his living Being, even more
Than his own Blood—what could they less? had laid
Strong hold on his affections, were to him
A pleasurable feeling of blind love,
The pleasure which there is in life itself.

He had not passed his days in singleness.   80
He had a Wife, a comely Matron, old
Though younger than himself full twenty years.
She was a woman of a stirring life
Whose heart was in her house: two wheels she had
Of antique form, this large for spining wool,
That small for flax, and if one wheel had rest,
It was because the other was at work.
The Pair had but one Inmate in their house,
An only Child, who had been born to them
When Michael telling o'er his years began   90
To deem that he was old, in Shepherd's phrase,
With one foot in the grave. This only son,
With two brave sheep dogs tried in many a storm,
The one of an inestimable worth,

Made all their Household. I may truly say,
That they were as a proverb in the vale
For endless industry. When day was gone,
And from their occupations out of doors
The Son and Father were come home, even then
Their labour did not cease, unless when all   100
Turned to their cleanly supper-board, and there
Each with a mess of pottage and skimmed milk,
Sate round their basket piled with oaten cakes,
And their plain home-made cheese. Yet when their meal
Was ended, Luke (for so the Son was named)
And his old Father, both betook themselves
To such convenient work, as might employ
Their hands by the fire-side; perhaps to card
Wool for the House-wife's spindle, or repair
Some injury done to sickle, flail, or scythe,   110
Or other implement of house or field.

Down from the cieling by the chimney's edge,
Which in our ancient uncouth country style
Did with a huge projection overbrow
Large space beneath, as duly as the light
Of day grew dim, the House-wife hung a lamp;
An aged utensil, which had performed
Service beyond all others of its kind.
Early at evening did it burn and late,
Surviving Comrade of uncounted Hours   120
Which going by from year to year had found
And left the Couple neither gay perhaps
Nor chearful, yet with objects and with hopes
Living a life of eager industry.
And now, when Luke was in his eighteenth year,
There by the light of this old lamp they sate,
Father and Son, while late into the night
The House-wife plied her own peculiar work,
Making the cottage thro' the silent hours
Murmur as with the sound of summer flies.   130
Not with a waste of words, but for the sake
Of pleasure, which I know that I shall give
To many living now, I of this Lamp
Speak thus minutely: for there are no few

Whose memories will bear witness to my tale.
The Light was famous in its neighbourhood,
And was a public Symbol of the life,
The thrifty Pair had lived. For, as it chanced,
Their Cottage on a plot of rising ground
Stood single, with large prospect North and South,   140
High into Easedale, up to Dunmal-Raise,
And Westward to the village near the Lake.
And from this constant light so regular
And so far seen, the House itself by all
Who dwelt within the limits of the vale,
Both old and young, was named the Evening Star.

Thus living on through such a length of years,
The Shepherd, if he loved himself, must needs
Have loved his Help-mate; but to Michael's heart
This Son of his old age was yet more dear—   150
Effect which might perhaps have been produced
By that instinctive tenderness, the same
Blind Spirit, which is in the blood of all,
Or that a child, more than all other gifts,
Brings hope with it, and forward-looking thoughts,
And stirrings of inquietude, when they
By tendency of nature needs must fail.
From such, and other causes, to the thoughts
Of the old Man his only Son was now
The dearest object that he knew on earth.   160
Exceeding was the love he bare to him,
His Heart and his Heart's joy! For oftentimes
Old Michael, while he was a babe in arms,
Had done him female service, not alone
For dalliance and delight, as is the use
Of Fathers, but with patient mind enforced
To acts of tenderness; and he had rocked
His cradle with a woman's gentle hand.

And in a later time, ere yet the Boy
Had put on Boy's attire, did Michael love,   170
Albeit of a stern unbending mind,
To have the young one in his sight, when he
Had work by his own door, or when he sate

With sheep before him on his Shepherd's stool,
Beneath that large old Oak, which near their door
Stood, and from its enormous breadth of shade
Chosen for the Shearer's covert from the sun,
Thence in our rustic dialect was called
The CLIPPING TREE, a name which yet it bears.°
There, while they two were sitting in the shade,   180
With others round them, earnest all and blithe,
Would Michael exercise his heart with looks
Of fond correction and reproof bestowed
Upon the child, if he disturbed the sheep
By catching at their legs, or with his shouts
Scared them, while they lay still beneath the shears.

And when by Heaven's good grace the Boy grew up
A healthy Lad, and carried in his cheek
Two steady roses that were five years old,
Then Michael from a winter coppice cut   190
With his own hand a sapling, which he hooped
With iron, making it throughout in all
Due requisites a perfect Shepherd's Staff,
And gave it to the Boy; wherewith equipped
He as a Watchman oftentimes was placed
At gate or gap, to stem or turn the flock,
And to his office prematurely called
There stood the urchin, as you will divine,
Something between a hindrance and a help,
And for this cause not always, I believe,   200
Receiving from his Father hire of praise.
Though nought was left undone, which staff or voice,
Or looks, or threatening gestures could perform.
    But soon as Luke, full ten years old, could stand
Against the mountain blasts, and to the heights,
Not fearing toil, nor length of weary ways,
He with his Father daily went, and they
Were as companions, why should I relate
That objects which the Shepherd loved before
Were dearer now? that from the Boy there came   210
Feelings and emanations, things which were
Light to the sun and music to the wind;
And that the Old Man's heart seemed born again.

Thus in his Father's sight the Boy grew up:
And now when he had reached his eighteenth year,
He was his comfort and his daily hope.

While this good household thus were living on
From day to day, to Michael's ear there came
Distressful tidings. Long before the time
Of which I speak, the Shepherd had been bound   220
In surety for his Brother's Son, a man
Of an industrious life, and ample means,
But unforeseen misfortunes suddenly
Had pressed upon him, and old Michael now
Was summoned to discharge the forfeiture,
A grievous penalty, but little less
Than half his substance. This un-looked for claim
At the first hearing, for a moment took
More hope out of his life than he supposed
That any old man ever could have lost.   230
As soon as he had gathered so much strength
That he could look his trouble in the face,
It seemed that his sole refuge was to sell
A portion of his patrimonial fields.
Such was his first resolve; he thought again,
And his heart failed him. 'Isabel,' said he,
Two evenings after he had heard the news,
'I have been toiling more than seventy years,
And in the open sun-shine of God's love
Have we all lived, yet if these fields of ours   240
Should pass into a Stranger's hand, I think
That I could not lie quiet in my grave.
Our lot is a hard lot; the Sun itself
Has scarcely been more diligent than I,
And I have lived to be a fool at last
To my own family. An evil Man
That was, and made an evil choice, if he
Were false to us; and if he were not false,
There are ten thousand to whom loss like this
Had been no sorrow. I forgive him—but   250
'Twere better to be dumb than to talk thus.
When I began, my purpose was to speak
Of remedies and of a chearful hope.

Our Luke shall leave us, Isabel; the land
Shall not go from us, and it shall be free,
He shall possess it, free as is the wind
That passes over it. We have, thou knowest,
Another Kinsman, he will be our friend
In this distress. He is a prosperous man,
Thriving in trade, and Luke to him shall go,   260
And with his Kinsman's help and his own thrift,
He quickly will repair this loss, and then
May come again to us. If here he stay,
What can be done? Where every one is poor
What can be gained?' At this, the old man paused,
And Isabel sate silent, for her mind
Was busy, looking back into past times.
There's Richard Bateman, thought she to herself,°
He was a parish-boy—at the church-door
They made a gathering for him, shillings, pence,   270
And halfpennies, wherewith the Neighbours bought
A Basket, which they filled with Pedlar's wares,
And with this Basket on his arm, the Lad
Went up to London, found a Master there,
Who out of many chose the trusty Boy
To go and overlook his merchandise
Beyond the seas, where he grew wond'rous rich,
And left estates and monies to the poor,
And at his birth-place built a Chapel, floored
With Marble, which he sent from foreign lands.   280
These thoughts, and many others of like sort,
Passed quickly thro' the mind of Isabel,
And her face brightened. The Old Man was glad,
And thus resumed. 'Well! Isabel, this scheme
These two days has been meat and drink to me.
Far more than we have lost is left us yet.
—We have enough—I wish indeed that I
Were younger, but this hope is a good hope.
—Make ready Luke's best garments, of the best
Buy for him more, and let us send him forth   290
To-morrow, or the next day, or to-night:
—If he could go, the Boy should go to-night.'
Here Michael ceased, and to the fields went forth
With a light heart. The House-wife for five days

Was restless morn and night, and all day long
Wrought on with her best fingers to prepare
Things needful for the journey of her Son.
But Isabel was glad when Sunday came
To stop her in her work; for, when she lay
By Michael's side, she for the two last nights   300
Heard him, how he was troubled in his sleep:
And when they rose at morning she could see
That all his hopes were gone. That day at noon
She said to Luke, while they two by themselves
Were sitting at the door, 'Thou must not go,
We have no other Child but thee to lose,
None to remember—do not go away,
For if thou leave thy Father he will die.'
The Lad made answer with a jocund voice,
And Isabel, when she had told her fears,   310
Recovered heart. That evening her best fare
Did she bring forth, and all together sate
Like happy people round a Christmas fire

Next morning Isabel resumed her work,
And all the ensuing week the house appeared
As cheerful as a grove in Spring: at length
The expected letter from their Kinsman came,
With kind assurances that he would do
His utmost for the welfare of the Boy,
To which requests were added that forthwith   320
He might be sent to him. Ten times or more
The letter was read over; Isabel
Went forth to shew it to the neighbours round:
Nor was there at that time on English Land
A prouder heart than Luke's. When Isabel
Had to her house returned, the Old Man said
'He shall depart to-morrow.' To this word
The House-wife answered, talking much of things
Which, if at such short notice he should go,
Would surely be forgotten. But at length   330
She gave consent, and Michael was at ease.

Near the tumultuous brook of Green-head Gill,
In that deep Valley, Michael had designed

To build a Sheep-fold, and, before he heard°
The tidings of his melancholy loss,
For this same purpose he had gathered up
A heap of stones, which close to the brook side
Lay thrown together, ready for the work.
With Luke that evening thitherward he walked;
And soon as they had reached the place he stopped   340
And thus the Old Man spake to him. 'My Son,
To-morrow thou wilt leave me; with full heart
I look upon thee, for thou art the same
That wert a promise to me ere thy birth,
And all thy life hast been my daily joy.
I will relate to thee some little part
Of our two histories; 'twill do thee good
When thou art from me, even if I should speak
Of things thou canst not know of.—After thou
First cam'st into the world, as it befalls   350
To new-born infants, thou didst sleep away
Two days, and blessings from thy Father's tongue
Then fell upon thee. Day by day passed on,
And still I loved thee with encreasing love.
Never to living ear came sweeter sounds
Than when I heard thee by our own fire-side
First uttering without words a natural tune,
When thou, a feeding babe, didst in thy joy
Sing at thy Mother's breast. Month followed month,
And in the open fields my life was passed   360
And in the mountains, else I think that thou
Hadst been brought up upon thy father's knees.
—But we were playmates, Luke; among these hills,
As well thou know'st, in us the old and young
Have played together, nor with me didst thou
Lack any pleasure which a boy can know.'
Luke had a manly heart; but at these words
He sobbed aloud; the Old Man grasped his hand,
And said, 'Nay do not take it so—I see
That these are things of which I need not speak.   370
—Even to the utmost I have been to thee
A kind and a good Father: and herein
I but repay a gift which I myself
Received at others hands, for, though now old

Beyond the common life of man, I still
Remember them who loved me in my youth.
Both of them sleep together: here they lived
As all their Forefathers had done, and when
At length their time was come, they were not loth
To give their bodies to the family mold.   380
I wished that thou should'st live the life they lived.
But 'tis a long time to look back, my Son,
And see so little gain from sixty years.
These fields were burthened when they came to me;
'Till I was forty years of age, not more
Than half of my inheritance was mine.
I toiled and toiled; God blessed me in my work,
And 'till these three weeks past the land was free.
—It looks as if it never could endure
Another Master. Heaven forgive me, Luke,   390
If I judge ill for thee, but it seems good
That thou should'st go.' At this the Old Man paused,
Then, pointing to the Stones near which they stood,
Thus, after a short silence, he resumed:
'This was a work for us, and now, my Son,
It is a work for me. But, lay one Stone—
Here, lay it for me, Luke, with thine own hands.
I for the purpose brought thee to this place.
Nay, Boy, be of good hope:—we both may live
To see a better day. At eighty-four   400
I still am strong and stout;—do thou thy part,
I will do mine.—I will begin again
With many tasks that were resigned to thee;
Up to the heights, and in among the storms,
Will I without thee go again, and do
All works which I was wont to do alone,
Before I knew thy face.—Heaven bless thee, Boy!
Thy heart these two weeks has been beating fast
With many hopes—it should be so—yes—yes—
I knew that thou could'st never have a wish   410
To leave me, Luke, thou hast been bound to me
Only by links of love, when thou art gone
What will be left to us!—But, I forget
My purposes. Lay now the corner-stone,
As I requested, and hereafter, Luke,

When thou art gone away, should evil men
Be thy companions, let this Sheep-fold be
Thy anchor and thy shield; amid all fear
And all temptation, let it be to thee
An emblem of the life thy Fathers lived,   420
Who, being innocent, did for that cause
Bestir them in good deeds. Now, fare thee well—
When thou return'st, thou in this place wilt see
A work which is not here, a covenant
'Twill be between us—but whatever fate
Befall thee, I shall love thee to the last,
And bear thy memory with me to the grave.'

The Shepherd ended here; and Luke stooped down,
And as his Father had requested, laid
The first stone of the Sheep-fold; at the sight   430
The Old Man's grief broke from him, to his heart
He pressed his Son, he kissed him and wept;
And to the House together they returned.

Next morning, as had been resolved, the Boy
Began his journey, and when he had reached
The public Way, he put on a bold face;
And all the Neighbours as he passed their doors
Came forth, with wishes and with farewell prayers,
That followed him 'till he was out of sight.
A good report did from their Kinsman come,   440
Of Luke and his well-doing; and the Boy
Wrote loving letters, full of wond'rous news,
Which, as the House-wife phrased it, were throughout
The prettiest letters that were ever seen.
Both parents read them with rejoicing hearts.
So, many months passed on: and once again
The Shepherd went about his daily work
With confident and cheerful thoughts; and now
Sometimes when he could find a leisure hour
He to that valley took his way, and there   450
Wrought at the Sheep-fold. Meantime Luke began
To slacken in his duty, and at length
He in the dissolute city gave himself
To evil courses: ignominy and shame

Fell on him, so that he was driven at last
To seek a hiding-place beyond the seas.

There is a comfort in the strength of love;
'Twill make a thing endurable, which else
Would break the heart:—Old Michael found it so.
I have conversed with more than one who well   460
Remember the Old Man, and what he was
Years after he had heard this heavy news.
His bodily frame had been from youth to age
Of an unusual strength. Among the rocks
He went, and still looked up upon the sun,
And listened to the wind; and as before
Performed all kinds of labour for his Sheep,
And for the land his small inheritance.
And to that hollow Dell from time to time
Did he repair, to build the Fold of which   470
His flock had need. 'Tis not forgotten yet
The pity which was then in every heart
For the Old Man—and 'tis believed by all
That many and many a day he thither went,
And never lifted up a single stone.
There, by the Sheep-fold, sometimes was he seen
Sitting alone, with that his faithful Dog,
Then old, beside him, lying at his feet.
The length of full seven years from time to time
He at the building of this Sheep-fold wrought,   480
And left the work unfinished when he died.

Three years, or little more, did Isabel,
Survive her Husband: at her death the estate
Was sold, and went into a Stranger's hand.
The Cottage which was named The Evening Star
Is gone, the ploughshare has been through the ground
On which it stood; great changes have been wrought
In all the neighbourhood, yet the Oak is left
That grew beside their Door; and the remains
Of the unfinished Sheep-fold may be seen   490
Beside the boisterous brook of Green-head Gill.

'I travelled among unknown Men'

I travelled among unknown Men,
  In Lands beyond the Sea;
Nor England! did I know till then
  What love I bore to thee.

'Tis past, that melancholy dream!
  Nor will I quit thy shore
A second time; for still I seem
  To love thee more and more.

Among thy mountains did I feel
  The joy of my desire;   10
And She I cherished turned her wheel
  Beside an English fire.

Thy mornings shewed—thy nights concealed
  The bowers where Lucy played;
And thine is, too, the last green field
  Which Lucy's eyes surveyed!

Louisa

I met Louisa in the shade;
And, having seen that lovely Maid,
Why should I fear to say
That she is ruddy, fleet, and strong;
And down the rocks can leap along,
Like rivulets in May?

And she hath smiles to earth unknown;
Smiles, that with motion of their own
Do spread, and sink, and rise;
That come and go with endless play,   10
And ever, as they pass away,
Are hidden in her eyes.

She loves her fire, her Cottage-home;
Yet o'er the moorland will she roam
In weather rough and bleak;
And when against the wind she strains,
Oh! might I kiss the mountain rains.
That sparkle on her cheek.

Take all that's mine 'beneath the moon,'°
If I with her but half a noon   20
May sit beneath the walls
Of some old cave, or mossy nook,
When up she winds along the brook,
To hunt the waterfalls.

To a Sky-Lark

Up with me! up with me into the clouds!
    For thy song, Lark, is strong;
Up with me, up with me into the clouds!
    Singing, singing,
With all the heav'ns about thee ringing,
    Lift me, guide me, till I find
That spot which seems so to thy mind!

I have walked through wildernesses dreary,
    And today my heart is weary;
    Had I now the soul of a Faery,   10
    Up to thee would I fly.
There is madness about thee, and joy divine
    In that song of thine;
Up with me, up with me, high and high,
To thy banqueting-place in the sky!
    Joyous as Morning,
    Thou art laughing and scorning;
Thou hast a nest, for thy love and thy rest:
And, though little troubled with sloth,
Drunken Lark! thou wouldn'st be loth   20
To be such a Traveller as I.
    Happy, happy Liver!
With a soul as strong as a mountain River,

Pouring out praise to the Almighty Giver,
Joy and jollity be with us both!
Hearing thee, or else some other,
  As merry a Brother,
I on the earth will go plodding on,
By myself, chearfully, till the day is done.

The Sparrow's Nest

Look, five blue eggs are gleaming there!
Few visions have I seen more fair,
Nor many prospects of delight
More pleasing than that simple sight!
I started, seeming to espy
The home and sheltered bed,
The Sparrow's dwelling, which, hard by
My Father's House, in wet or dry,
My Sister Emmeline and I
  Together visited.   10

She looked at it as if she feared it;
Still wishing, dreading to be near it:
Such heart was in her, being then
A little Prattler among men.
The Blessing of my later years
Was with me when a Boy;
She gave me eyes, she gave me ears;
And humble cares, and delicate fears;
A heart, the fountain of sweet tears;
  And love, and thought, and joy.   20

The Sailor's Mother

One morning (raw it was and wet,
A foggy day in winter time)
A Woman in the road I met,
Not old, though something past her prime:
Majestic in her person, tall and straight;
And like a Roman matron's was her mien and gait.

The ancient Spirit is not dead;
Old times, thought I, are breathing there;
Proud was I that my country bred
Such strength, a dignity so fair: 10
She begged an alms, like one in poor estate;
I looked at her again, nor did my pride abate.

When from these lofty thoughts I woke,
With the first word I had to spare
I said to her, 'Beneath your Cloak
What's that which on your arm you bear?'
She answered soon as she the question heard,
'A simple burthen, Sir, a little Singing-bird.'

And, thus continuing, she said,
'I had a Son, who many a day   20
Sailed on the seas; but he is dead;
In Denmark he was cast away;
And I have been as far as Hull, to see
What clothes he might have left, or other property.

The Bird and Cage they both were his;
'Twas my Son's Bird; and neat and trim
He kept it: many voyages
This Singing-bird hath gone with him;
When last he sailed he left the Bird behind;
As it might be, perhaps, from bodings of his mind.   30

He to a Fellow-lodger's care
Had left it, to be watched and fed,
Till he came back again; and there
I found it when my Son was dead;
And now, God help me for my little wit!
I trail it with me, Sir! he took so much delight in it.'

Alice Fell

The Post-boy drove with fierce career,
For threat'ning clouds the moon had drowned;
When suddenly I seemed to hear
A moan, a lamentable sound.

As if the wind blew many ways
I heard the sound, and more and more:
It seemed to follow with the Chaise,
And still I heard it as before.

At length I to the Boy called out,
He stopped his horses at the word;   10
But neither cry, nor voice, nor shout,
Nor aught else like it could be heard.

The Boy then smacked his whip, and fast
The horses scampered through the rain;
And soon I heard upon the blast
The voice, and bade him halt again.

Said I, alighting on the ground,
'What can it be, this piteous moan?'
And there a little Girl I found,
Sitting behind the Chaise, alone.   20

'My Cloak!' the word was last and first,
And loud and bitterly she wept,
As if her very heart would burst;
And down from off the Chaise she leapt.

'What ails you, Child?' She sobbed, 'Look here!'
I saw it in the wheel entangled,
A weather beaten Rag as e'er
From any garden scare-crow dangled.

'Twas twisted betwixt nave and spoke;
Her help she lent, and with good heed   30
Together we released the Cloak;
A wretched, wretched rag indeed!

'And whither are you going, Child,
Tonight along these lonesome ways?'
'To Durham' answered she half wild—
'Then come with me into the chaise.'

She sate like one past all relief;
Sob after sob she forth did send
In wretchedness, as if her grief
Could never, never, have an end.   40

'My Child, in Durham do you dwell?'
She checked herself in her distress,
And said, 'My name is Alice Fell;
I'm fatherless and motherless.

And I to Durham, Sir, belong.'
And then, as if the thought would choke
Her very heart, her grief grew strong;
And all was for her tattered Cloak.

The chaise drove on; our journey's end
Was nigh; and, sitting by my side,   50
As if she'd lost her only friend
She wept, nor would be pacified.

Up to the Tavern-door we post;
Of Alice and her grief I told;
And I gave money to the Host,
To buy a new Cloak for the old.

'And let it be a duffil grey,
As warm a cloak as man can sell!'
Proud Creature was she the next day,
The little Orphan, Alice Fell!   60

Beggars

She had a tall Man's height, or more;
No bonnet screened her from the heat;
A long drab-coloured Cloak she wore,
A Mantle reaching to her feet:
What other dress she had I could not know;
Only she wore a Cap that was as white as snow.

In all my walks, through field or town,
Such Figure had I never seen:
Her face was of Egyptian brown:
Fit person was she for a Queen,   10
To head those ancient Amazonian files:
Or ruling Bandit's Wife, among the Grecian Isles.

Before me begging did she stand,
Pouring out sorrows like a sea;
Grief after grief:—on English Land
Such woes I knew could never be;
And yet a boon I gave her; for the Creature
Was beautiful to see; a Weed of glorious feature!°

I left her, and pursued my way;
And soon before me did espy   20
A pair of little Boys at play,
Chasing a crimson butterfly;
The Taller followed with his hat in hand,
Wreathed round with yellow flow'rs, the gayest of the land.

The Other wore a rimless crown,
With leaves of laurel stuck about:
And they both followed up and down,
Each whooping with a merry shout;
Two Brothers seemed they, eight and ten years old;
And like that Woman's face as gold is like to gold.   30

They bolted on me thus, and lo!
Each ready with a plaintive whine;
Said I, 'Not half an hour ago
Your Mother has had alms of mine.'
'That cannot be,' one answered, 'She is dead.'
'Nay but I gave her pence, and she will buy you bread.'

'She has been dead, Sir, many a day.'
'Sweet Boys, you're telling me a lie;
It was your Mother, as I say—'
And in the twinkling of an eye,   40
'Come, come!' cried one; and, without more ado,
Off to some other play they both together flew.

To a Butterfly

Stay near me—do not take thy flight!
A little longer stay in sight!
Much converse do I find in Thee,
Historian of my Infancy!
Float near me; do not yet depart!
Dead times revive in thee:
Thou bring'st, gay Creature as thou art!
A solemn image to my heart,
My Father's Family!

Oh! pleasant, pleasant were the days,   10
The time, when in our childish plays
My sister Emmeline and I
Together chaced the Butterfly!
A very hunter did I rush
Upon the prey:—with leaps and springs
I followed on from brake to bush;
But She, God love her! feared to brush
The dust from off its wings.

To the Cuckoo

O blithe New-comer! I have heard,
I hear thee and rejoice:
O Cuckoo! shall I call thee Bird,
Or but a wandering Voice?

While I am lying on the grass,
I hear thy restless shout:
From hill to hill it seems to pass,
About, and all about!

To me, no Babbler with a tale
Of sunshine and of flowers,   10
Thou tellest, Cuckoo! in the vale
Of visionary hours.

Thrice welcome, Darling of the Spring!
Even yet thou art to me
No Bird; but an invisible Thing,
A voice, a mystery.

The same whom in my School-boy days
I listened to; that Cry
Which made me look a thousand ways;
In bush, and tree, and sky.   20

To seek thee did I often rove
Through woods and on the green;
And thou wert still a hope, a love;
Still longed for, never seen!

And I can listen to thee yet;
Can lie upon the plain
And listen, till I do beget
That golden time again.

O blessed Bird! the earth we pacc
Again appears to be   30
An unsubstantial, faery place;
That is fit home for Thee!

'My heart leaps up when I behold'

My heart leaps up when I behold
    A Rainbow in the sky:
So was it when my life began;
So is it now I am a Man;
So be it when I shall grow old,
    Or let me die!
The Child is Father of the Man;
And I could wish my days to be
Bound each to each by natural piety.

To H.C., Six Years Old

O Thou! whose fancies from afar are brought;
Who of thy words dost make a mock apparel,
And fittest to unutterable thought
The breeze-like motion and the self-born carol;
Thou Faery Voyager! that dost float
In such clear water, that thy Boat°
May rather seem
To brood on air than on an earthly stream;
Suspended in a stream as clear as sky,
Where earth and heaven do make one imagery;   10
O blessed Vision! happy Child!
That art so exquisitely wild,
I think of thee with many fears
For what may be thy lot in future years.

I thought of times when Pain might be thy guest,
Lord of thy house and hospitality;
And grief, uneasy Lover! never rest
But when she sate within the touch of thee.
Oh! too industrious folly!
Oh! vain and causeless melancholy!   20
Nature will either end thee quite;
Or, lengthening out thy season of delight,
Preserve for thee, by individual right,

A young Lamb's heart among the full-grown flocks.
What hast Thou to do with sorrow,
Or the injuries of tomorrow?
Thou art a Dew-drop, which the morn brings forth,
Not doomed to jostle with unkindly shocks;
Or to be trailed along the soiling earth;
A Gem that glitters while it lives,   30
And no forewarning gives;
But, at the touch of wrong, without a strife,
Slips in a moment out of life.

'Among all lovely things my Love had been'

Among all lovely things my Love had been;
Had noted well the stars, all flowers that grew
About her home; but she had never seen
A Glow-worm, never one, and this I knew.

While riding near her home one stormy night
A single Glow-worm did I chance to espy;
I gave a fervent welcome to the sight,
And from my Horse I leapt; great joy had I.

Upon a leaf the Glow-worm did I lay,
To bear it with me through the stormy night: 10
And, as before, it shone without dismay;
Albeit putting forth a fainter light.

When to the Dwelling of my Love I came,
I went into the Orchard quietly;
And left the Glow-worm, blessing it by name,
Laid safely by itself, beneath a Tree.

The whole next day, I hoped, and hoped with fear;
At night the Glow-worm shone beneath the Tree:
I led my Lucy to the spot, 'Look here!'
Oh! joy it was for her, and joy for me!   20

Written in March

WHILE RESTING ON THE BRIDGE AT THE FOOT OF BROTHER'S WATER

The cock is crowing,
The stream is flowing,
The small birds twitter,
The lake doth glitter,
The green field sleeps in the sun;
The oldest and youngest
Are at work with the strongest;
The cattle are grazing,
Their heads never raising;
There are forty feeding like one!   10

Like an army defeated
The Snow hath retreated,
And now doth fare ill
On the top of the bare hill;
The Plough-boy is whooping—anon—anon:
There's joy in the mountains;
There's life in the fountains;
Small clouds are sailing,
Blue sky prevailing;
The rain is over and gone!   20

The Green Linnet

The May is come again:—how sweet
To sit upon my Orchard-seat!
And Birds and Flowers once more to greet,
        My last year's Friends together:
My thoughts they all by turns employ;
A whispering Leaf is now my joy,
And then a Bird will be the toy
        That doth my fancy tether.

One have I marked, the happiest Guest
In all this covert of the blest: 10
Hail to Thee, far above the rest
          In joy of voice and pinion,
Thou, Linnet! in thy green array,
Presiding Spirit here to-day,
Dost lead the revels of the May,
          And this is thy dominion.

While Birds, and Butterflies, and Flowers
Make all one Band of Paramours,
Thou, ranging up and down the bowers,
          Art sole in thy employment;   20
A Life, a Presence like the Air,
Scattering thy gladness without care,
Too blessed with any one to pair,
          Thyself thy own enjoyment.

Upon yon tuft of hazel trees,
That twinkle to the gusty breeze,
Behold him perched in ecstasies,
          Yet seeming still to hover;
There! where the flutter of his wings
Upon his back and body flings   30
Shadows and sunny glimmerings,
          That cover him all over.

While thus before my eyes he gleams,
A Brother of the Leaves he seems;
When in a moment forth he teems
          His little song in gushes:
As if it pleased him to disdain
And mock the Form which he did feign,
While he was dancing with the train
          Of Leaves among the bushes.   40

To the Daisy

In youth from rock to rock I went,
From hill to hill, in discontent
Of pleasure high and turbulent,
  Most pleased when most uneasy;
But now my own delights I make,
My thirst at every rill can slake,
And gladly Nature's love partake
  Of thee, sweet Daisy!

When soothed a while by milder airs,
Thee Winter in the garland wears   10
That thinly shades his few grey hairs;
  Spring cannot shun thee;
Whole summer fields are thine by right;
And Autumn, melancholy Wight!
Doth in thy crimson head delight
  When rains are on thee.

In shoals and bands, a morrice train,
Thou greet'st the Traveller in the lane;
If welcome once thou count'st it gain;
  Thou art not daunted,   20
Nor car'st if thou be set at naught;
And oft alone in nooks remote
We meet thee, like a pleasant thought,
  When such are wanted.

Be Violets in their secret mews
The flowers the wanton Zephyrs chuse;
Proud be the Rose, with rains and dews
  Her head impearling;
Thou liv'st with less ambitious aim,
Yet hast not gone without thy fame;   30
Thou art indeed by many a claim
  The Poet's darling.

If to a rock from rains he fly,
Or, some bright day of April sky,
Imprisoned by hot sunshine lie

Near the green holly,
And wearily at length should fare;
He need but look about, and there
Thou art! a Friend at hand, to scare
  His melancholy.   40

A hundred times, by rock or bower,
Ere thus I have lain couched an hour,
Have I derived from thy sweet power
  Some apprehension;
Some steady love; some brief delight;
Some memory that had taken flight;
Some chime of fancy wrong or right;
  Or stray invention.

If stately passions in me burn,
And one chance look to Thee should turn, 50
I drink out of an humbler urn
  A lowlier pleasure;
The homely sympathy that heeds
The common life, our nature breeds
A wisdom fitted to the needs
  Of hearts at leisure.

When, smitten by the morning ray,
I see thee rise alert and gay,
Then, chearful Flower! my spirits play
  With kindred motion: 60
At dusk, I've seldom marked thee press
The ground, as if in thankfulness
Without some feeling, more or less,
  Of true devotion.

And all day long I number yet,
All seasons through another debt,
Which I wherever thou art met,
  To thee am owing;
An instinct call it, a blind sense;
A happy, genial influence,   70
Coming one knows not how nor whence,
  Nor whither going.

Child of the Year! that round dost run
Thy course, bold lover of the sun,
And chearful when the day's begun
    As morning Leveret,
Thou long the Poet's praise shalt gain;
Thou wilt be more beloved by men
In times to come; thou not in vain
    Art Nature's Favorite.   80

To the Daisy

With little here to do or see
Of things that in the great world be,
Sweet Daisy! oft I talk to thee,
    For thou art worthy,
Thou unassuming Common-place
Of Nature, with that homely face,
And yet with something of a grace,
    Which Love makes for thee!

Oft do I sit by thee at ease,
And weave a web of similies,   10
Loose types of Things through all degrees,
    Thoughts of thy raising:
And many a fond and idle name
I give to thee, for praise or blame,
As is the humour of the game,
    While I am gazing.

A Nun demure of lowly port,
Or sprightly Maiden of Love's Court,
In thy simplicity the sport
    Of all temptations;   20
A Queen in crown of rubies drest,
A Starveling in a scanty vest,
Are all, as seem to suit thee best,
    Thy appellations.

A little Cyclops, with one eye°
Staring to threaten and defy,
That thought comes next—and instantly
        The freak is over,
The shape will vanish, and behold!
A silver Shield with boss of gold,   30
That spreads itself, some Faery bold
        In fight to cover.

I see thee glittering from afar;—
And then thou art a pretty Star,
Not quite so fair as many are
        In heaven above thee!
Yet like a star, with glittering crest,
Self-poised in air thou seem'st to rest;—
May peace come never to his nest,
        Who shall reprove thee!   40

Sweet Flower! for by that name at last,
When all my reveries are past,
I call thee, and to that cleave fast,
        Sweet silent Creature!
That breath'st with me in sun and air,
Do thou, as thou art wont, repair
My heart with gladness, and a share
        Of thy meek nature!

To the Same Flower

Bright Flower, whose home is every where!
A Pilgrim bold in Nature's care,
And all the long year through the heir
        Of joy or sorrow,
Methinks that there abides in thee
Some concord with humanity,
Given to no other Flower I see
        The forest thorough!

Is it that Man is soon deprest?
A thoughtless Thing! who, once unblest,   10
Does little on his memory rest,
          Or on his reason,
And Thou would'st teach him how to find
A shelter under every wind,
A hope for times that are unkind
          And every season?

Thou wander'st the wide world about,
Unchecked by pride or scrupulous doubt,
With friends to greet thee, or without,
          Yet pleased and willing;   20
Meek, yielding to the occasion's call,
And all things suffering from all,
Thy function apostolical
          In peace fulfilling.

To a Butterfly

I've watched you now a full half hour,
Self-poised upon that yellow flower;
And, little Butterfly! indeed
I know not if you sleep, or feed.
How motionless! not frozen seas
More motionless! and then
What joy awaits you, when the breeze
Hath found you out among the trees,
And calls you forth again!

This plot of Orchard-ground is ours;   10
My trees they are, my Sister's flowers;
Stop here whenever you are weary,
And rest as in a sanctuary!
Come often to us, fear no wrong;
Sit near us on the bough!
We'll talk of sunshine and of song;
And summer days, when we were young,
Sweet childish days, that were as long
          As twenty days are now!

'These chairs they have no words to utter'

These chairs they have no words to utter,
No fire is in the grate to stir or flutter,
The ceiling and floor are mute as a stone,
My chamber is hushed and still,
    And I am alone,
    Happy and alone.

Oh! who would be afraid of life?
  The passion the sorrow and the strife,
    When he may lie
    Sheltered so easily?   10
May lie in peace on his bed,
Happy as they who are dead.

Half an hour afterwards

I have thoughts that are fed by the sun;
  The things which I see
  Are welcome to me,
  Welcome every one;
  I do not wish to lie
    Dead, dead,
Dead without any company°
  Here alone on my bed,   20
With thoughts that are fed by the sun
And hopes that are welcome everyone,
  Happy am I.

O life there is about thee
A deep delicious peace;
I would not be without thee,
  Stay, oh stay!
Yet be thou ever as now,
Sweetness and breath with the quiet of death,
  Peace, peace, peace.

The Tinker

Who leads a happy life
If it's not the merry Tinker?
Not too old to have a Wife;
Not too much a thinker.
Through the meadows, over stiles,
Where there are no measured miles,
Day by day he finds his way
Among the lonely houses:
Right before the Farmer's door
Down he sits; his brows he knits;   10
Then his hammer he rouzes;
Batter! batter! batter!
He begins to clatter;
And while the work is going on
Right good ale he bowses;
And, when it is done, away he is gone;
And, in his scarlet coat,
With a merry note,
He sings the sun to bed;
And, without making a pother,   20
Finds some place or other
For his own careless head.
    When in the woods the little fowls
Begin their merry-making,
Again the jolly Tinker bowls
Forth with small leave-taking:
Through the valley, up the hill;
He can't go wrong, go where he will:
Tricks he has twenty,
And pastimes in plenty;   30
He's the terror of boys in the midst of their noise;
When the market Maiden,
Bringing home her lading,
Hath passed him in a nook,
With his outlandish look,
And visage grim and sooty,
Bumming, bumming, bumming,
What is that that's coming?

Silly Maid as ever was!
She thinks that she and all she has   40
Will be the Tinker's booty;
At the pretty Maiden's dread
The Tinker shakes his head,
Laughing, laughing, laughing,
As if he would laugh himself dead.
And thus, with work or none,
The Tinker lives in fun,
With a light soul to cover him;
And sorrow and care blow over him,
Whether he's up or a-bed.   50

To the Small Celandine

Pansies, Lilies, Kingcups, Daisies,
Let them live upon their praises;
Long as there's a sun that sets
Primroses will have their glory;
Long as there are Violets,
They will have a place in story:
There's a flower that shall be mine,
'Tis the little Celandine.

Eyes of some men travel far
For the finding of a star;   10
Up and down the heavens they go,
Men that keep a mighty rout!
I'm as great as they, I trow,
Since the day I found thee out,
Little flower!—I'll make a stir
Like a great Astronomer.

Modest, yet withal an Elf
Bold, and lavish of thyself,
Since we needs must first have met
I have seen thee, high and low,   20
Thirty years or more, and yet
'Twas a face I did not know;

Thou hast now, go where I may,
Fifty greetings in a day.

Ere a leaf is on a bush,
In the time before the Thrush
Has a thought about its nest,
Thou wilt come with half a call,
Spreading out thy glossy breast
Like a careless Prodigal;   30
Telling tales about the sun,
When we've little warmth, or none.

Poets, vain men in their mood!
Travel with the multitude;
Never heed them; I aver
That they all are wanton Wooers;
But the thrifty Cottager,
Who stirs little out of doors,
Joys to spy thee near her home,
Spring is coming, Thou art come!   40

Comfort have thou of thy merit,
Kindly, unassuming Spirit!
Careless of thy neighbourhood,
Thou dost shew thy pleasant face
On the moor, and in the wood,
In the lane—there's not a place,
Howsoever mean it be,
But 'tis good enough for thee.

Ill befal the yellow Flowers,
Children of the flaring hours!   50
Buttercups, that will be seen,
Whether we will see or no;
Others, too, of lofty mien;
They have done as worldlings do,
Taken praise that should be thine,
Little, humble Celandine!

Prophet of delight and mirth,
Scorned and slighted upon earth!

Herald of a mighty band,
Of a joyous train ensuing,   60
Singing at my heart's command,
In the lanes my thoughts pursuing,
I will sing, as doth behove,
Hymns in praise of what I love!

To the Same Flower

Pleasures newly found are sweet
When they lie about our feet:
February last my heart
First at sight of thee was glad;
All unheard of as thou art,
Thou must needs, I think, have had,
Celandine! and long ago,
Praise of which I nothing know.

I have not a doubt but he,
Whosoe'er the man might be,   10
Who the first with pointed rays,
(Workman worthy to be sainted)
Set the Sign-board in a blaze,
When the risen sun he painted,
Took the fancy from a glance
At thy glittering countenance.

Soon as gentle breezes bring
News of winter's vanishing,
And the children build their bowers,
Sticking 'kerchief-plots of mold   20
All about with full-blown flowers,
Thick as sheep in shepherd's fold!
With the proudest Thou art there,
Mantling in the tiny square.

Often have I sighed to measure
By myself a lonely pleasure,
Sighed to think, I read a book
Only read perhaps by me;
Yet I long could overlook
Thy bright coronet and Thee,   30
And thy arch and wily ways,
And thy store of other praise.

Blithe of heart, from week to week
Thou dost play at hide-and-seek;
While the patient Primrose sits
Like a Beggar in the cold,
Thou, a Flower of wiser wits,
Slipp'st into thy sheltered hold;
Bright as any of the train
When ye all are out again.   40

Thou art not beyond the moon,
But a thing 'beneath our shoon;'
Let, as old Magellen did,
Others roam about the sea;
Build who will a pyramid;
Praise it is enough for me,
If there be but three or four
Who will love my little Flower.

Resolution and Independence

There was a roaring in the wind all night;
The rain came heavily and fell in floods;
But now the sun is rising calm and bright;
The birds are singing in the distant woods;
Over his own sweet voice the Stock-dove broods;
The Jay makes answer as the Magpie chatters;
And all the air is filled with pleasant noise of waters.

All things that love the sun are out of doors;
The sky rejoices in the morning's birth;
The grass is bright with rain-drops; on the moors   10
The Hare is running races in her mirth;
And with her feet she from the plashy earth
Raises a mist; which, glittering in the sun,
Runs with her all the way, wherever she doth run.

I was a Traveller then upon the moor;
I saw the Hare that raced about with joy;
I heard the woods, and distant waters, roar;
Or heard them not, as happy as a Boy:
The pleasant season did my heart employ:
My old remembrances went from me wholly;   20
And all the ways of men, so vain and melancholy.

But, as it sometimes chanceth, from the might
Of joy in minds that can no farther go,
As high as we have mounted in delight
In our dejection do we sink as low,
To me that morning did it happen so;
And fears, and fancies, thick upon me came;
Dim sadness, and blind thoughts I knew not nor could name.

I heard the Sky-lark singing in the sky;
And I bethought me of the playful Hare: 30
Even such a happy Child of earth am I;
Even as these blissful Creatures do I fare;
Far from the world I walk, and from all care;
But there may come another day to me,
Solitude, pain of heart, distress, and poverty.

My whole life I have lived in pleasant thought,
As if life's business were a summer mood;
As if all needful things would come unsought
To genial faith, still rich in genial good;
But how can He expect that others should   40
Build for him, sow for him, and at his call
Love him, who for himself will take no heed at all?

I thought of Chatterton, the marvellous Boy,°
The sleepless Soul that perished in its pride;
Of Him who walked in glory and in joy°
Behind his plough, upon the mountain-side:
By our own spirits are we deified;
We Poets in our youth begin in gladness;
But thereof comes in the end despondency and madness.

Now, whether it were by peculiar grace,   50
A leading from above, a something given,
Yet it befel, that, in this lonely place,
When up and down my fancy thus was driven,
And I with these untoward thoughts had striven,
I saw a Man before me unawares:
The oldest Man he seemed that ever wore grey hairs.

My course I stopped as soon as I espied
The Old Man in that naked wilderness:
Close by a Pond, upon the further side,
He stood alone: a minute's space I guess   60
I watched him, he continuing motionless:
To the Pool's further margin then I drew;
He being all the while before me full in view.

As a huge Stone is sometimes seen to lie°
Couched on the bald top of an eminence;
Wonder to all who do the same espy
By what means it could thither come, and whence;
So that it seems a thing endued with sense:
Like a Sea-beast crawled forth, which on a shelf
Of rock or sand reposeth, there to sun itself.   70

Such seemed this Man, not all alive nor dead,
Nor all asleep; in his extreme old age:
His body was bent double, feet and head
Coming together in their pilgrimage;
As if some dire constraint of pain, or rage
Of sickness felt by him in times long past,
A more than human weight upon his frame had cast.

Himself he propped, his body, limbs, and face,
Upon a long grey Staff of shaven wood:
And, still as I drew near with gentle pace,   80
Beside the little pond or moorish flood
Motionless as a Cloud the Old Man stood;
That heareth not the loud winds when they call;
And moveth altogether, if it move at all.

At length, himself unsettling, he the Pond
Stirred with his Staff, and fixedly did look
Upon the muddy water, which he conned,
As if he had been reading in a book:
And now such freedom as I could I took;
And, drawing to his side, to him did say,   90
'This morning gives us promise of a glorious day.'

A gentle answer did the Old Man make,
In courteous speech which forth he slowly drew:
And him with further words I thus bespake,
'What kind of work is that which you pursue?
This is a lonesome place for one like you.'
He answered me with pleasure and surprize;
And there was, while he spake, a fire about his eyes.

His words came feebly, from a feeble chest,
Yet each in solemn order followed each,   100
With something of a lofty utterance drest;
Choice word, and measured phrase; above the reach
Of ordinary men; a stately speech!
Such as grave Livers do in Scotland use,
Religious men, who give to God and Man their dues.

He told me that he to this pond had come
To gather Leeches, being old and poor:
Employment hazardous and wearisome!
And he had many hardships to endure:
From Pond to Pond he roamed, from moor to moor,   110
Housing, with God's good help, by choice or chance:
And in this way he gained an honest maintenance.

The Old Man still stood talking by my side;
But now his voice to me was like a stream
Scarce heard; nor word from word could I divide;
And the whole Body of the man did seem
Like one whom I had met with in a dream;
Or like a Man from some far region sent;
To give me human strength, and strong admonishment.°

My former thoughts returned: the fear that kills;   120
The hope that is unwilling to be fed;
Cold, pain, and labour, and all fleshly ills;
And mighty Poets in their misery dead.
And now, not knowing what the Old Man had said,
My question eagerly did I renew,
'How is it that you live, and what is it you do?'

He with a smile did then his words repeat;
And said, that, gathering Leeches, far and wide
He travelled; sitrring thus about his feet
The waters of the Ponds where they abide.   130
'Once I could meet with them on every side;
But they have dwindled long by slow decay;
Yet still I persevere, and find them where I may.'

While he was talking thus, the lonely place,
The Old Man's shape, and speech, all troubled me:
In my mind's eye I seemed to see him pace
About the weary moors continually,
Wandering about alone and silently.
While I these thoughts within myself pursued,
He, having made a pause, the same discourse renewed.   140

And soon with this he other matter blended,
Chearfully uttered, with demeanour kind,
But stately in the main; and, when he ended,
I could have laughed myself to scorn, to find
In that decrepit Man so firm a mind.
'God,' said I, 'be my help and stay secure;
I'll think of the Leech-gatherer on the lonely moor.'

Travelling

This is the spot:—how mildly does the sun
Shine in between these fading leaves! the air
In the habitual silence of this wood
Is more than silent: and this bed of heath,
Where shall we find so sweet a resting place?
Come!—let me see thee sink into a dream
Of quiet thoughts,—protracted till thine eye
Be calm as water, when the winds are gone
And no one can tell whither.—my sweet friend!
We two have had such happy hours together   10
That my heart melts in me to think of it.

'Within our happy Castle there dwelt one'

Within our happy Castle there dwelt one
Whom without blame I may not overlook:
For never sun on living creature shone
Who more devout enjoyment with us took.
Here on his hours he hung as on a book;
On his own time he here would float away;
As doth a fly upon a summer brook:
But, go tomorrow, or belike, today,
Seek for him, he is fled; and whither none could say.

Thus often would he leave our peaceful home,   10
And find elsewhere his business or delight.
Out of our Valley's limits did he roam:
Full many a time, upon a stormy night,
His voice came to us from the neighbouring height:
Oft did we see him driving full in view
At mid-day, when the sun was shining bright:
What ill was on him, what he had to do,
A mighty wonder bred among our quiet crew.

Ah! piteous sight it was to see this Man.
When he came back to us a withered flower;   20
Or like a sinful creature pale and wan:
Down would he lie, and without strength or power
Look at the common grass from hour to hour:
And oftentimes, how long I fear to say,
Where apple-trees in blossom made a bower,
Retired in that sunshiny shade he lay.
And, like a naked Indian, slept himself away.

Great wonder to our gentle tribe it was
Whenever from our Valley he withdrew;
For happier soul no living creature has   30
Than he had, being here the long day through.
Some thought he was a lover and did woo;
Some thought far worse of him, and did him wrong;
But Verse was what he had been wedded to:
And his own mind did, like a tempest strong,
Come to him thus; and drove the weary Man along.

With him there often walked in friendly wise,
Or lay upon the moss, by brook or tree,
A noticeable Man, with large dark eyes,
And a pale face, that seemed undoubtedly   40
As if a *blooming* face it *ought* to be:
Heavy his low-hung lip did oft appear,
A face divine of heaven-born ideotcy!
Profound his forehead was, though not severe;
Yet some did think that he had little business here.

Ah! God forefend! his was a lawful right.
Noisy he was, and gamesome as a boy:
His limbs would toss about him with delight,
Like branches when strong winds the trees annoy.
He lacked not implement, device, or toy,   50
To cheat away the hours that silent were:
He would have taught you how you might employ
Yourself; and many did to him repair,
And, certes, not in vain:—he had inventions rare.

Instruments had he, playthings for the ear,
Long blades of grass plucked round him as he lay;
These served to catch the wind as it came near;
Glasses he had with many colours gay;
Others that did all little things display;
The beetle with his radiance manifold,   60
A mailed angel on a battle day.
And leaves and flowers, and herbage green and gold,
And all the glorious sights which fairies do behold.

He would entice that other man to hear
His music, and to view his imagery:
And sooth, these two did love each other dear,
As far as love in such a place could be:
There did they lie from earthly labour free,
Most happy livers as were ever seen!
If but a bird, to keep them company,   70
Or butterfly sate down, they were, I ween,
As pleas'd as if the same had been a Maiden Queen.

'I grieved for Buonaparte'

I grieved for Buonaparte, with a vain
And an unthinking grief! the vital blood
Of that Man's mind what can it be? What food
Fed his first hopes? What knowledge could *He* gain?
'Tis not in battles that from youth we train
The Governor who must be wise and good,
And temper with the sternness of the brain
Thoughts motherly, and meek as womanhood.
Wisdom doth live with children round her knees:
Books, leisure, perfect freedom, and the talk   10
Man holds with week-day man in the hourly walk
Of the mind's business: these are the degrees
By which true Sway doth mount; this is the stalk
True Power doth grow on; and her rights are these.

On the Extinction of the Venetian Republic

Once did She hold the gorgeous East in fee;
And was the safeguard of the West: the worth
Of Venice did not fall below her birth,
Venice, the eldest Child of Liberty.
She was a Maiden City, bright and free;
No guile seduced, no force could violate;
And when She took unto herself a Mate°
She must espouse the everlasting Sea.
And what if she had seen those glories fade,
Those titles vanish, and that strength decay,   10
Yet shall some tribute of regret be paid
When her long life hath reached its final day:
Men are we, and must grieve when even the Shade
Of that which once was great is passed away.

'How sweet it is, when mother Fancy rocks'

How sweet it is, when mother Fancy rocks
The wayward brain, to saunter through a wood!
An old place, full of many a lovely brood,
Tall trees, green arbours, and ground flowers in flocks;
And Wild rose tip-toe upon hawthorn stocks,
Like to a bonny Lass, who plays her pranks
At Wakes and Fairs with wandering Mountebanks,
When she stands cresting the Clown's head, and mocks
The crowd beneath her. Verily I think,
Such place to me is sometimes like a dream   10
Or map of the whole world: thoughts, link by link,
Enter through ears and eyesight, with such gleam
Of all things, that at last in fear I shrink,
And leap at once from the delicious stream.

'I am not One who much or oft delight'

I am not One who much or oft delight
To season my fireside with personal talk,
About Friends, who live within an easy walk,
Or Neighbours, daily, weekly, in my sight:
And, for my chance-acquaintance, Ladies bright,
Sons, Mothers, Maidens withering on the stalk,°
These all wear out of me, like Forms, with chalk
Painted on rich men's floors, for one feast-night.
Better than such discourse doth silence long,
Long, barren silence, square with my desire;   10
To sit without emotion, hope, or aim,
By my half-kitchen my half-parlour fire,
And listen to the flapping of the flame,
Or kettle, whispering it's faint undersong.

'Yet life,' you say, 'is life; we have seen and see,
And with a living pleasure we describe;
And fits of sprightly malice do but bribe
The languid mind into activity.
Sound sense, and love itself, and mirth and glee,
Are fostered by the comment and the gibe.'   20
Even be it so: yet still among your tribe,
Our daily world's true Worldlings, rank not me!
Children are blest, and powerful; their world lies
More justly balanced; partly at their feet,
And part far from them:—sweetest melodies°
Are those that are by distance made more sweet;
Whose mind is but the mind of his own eyes
He is a Slave; the meanest we can meet!

Wings have we, and as far as we can go
We may find pleasure: wilderness and wood,   30
Blank ocean and mere sky, support that mood
Which with the lofty sanctifies the low:
Dreams, books, are each a world; and books, we know,
Are a substantial world, both pure and good:
Round these, with tendrils strong as flesh and blood,
Our pastime and our happiness will grow.

There do I find a never-failing store
Of personal themes, and such as I love best;
Matter wherein right voluble I am:
Two will I mention, dearer than the rest; 40
The gentle Lady, married to the Moor;°
And heavenly Una with her milk-white Lamb.

Nor can I not believe but that hereby
Great gains are mine: for thus I live remote
From evil-speaking; rancour, never sought,
Comes to me not; malignant truth, or lie.
Hence have I genial seasons, hence have I
Smooth passions, smooth discourse, and joyous thought:
And thus from day to day my little Boat
Rocks in its harbour, lodging peaceably. 50
Blessings be with them, and eternal praise,
Who gave us nobler loves, and nobler cares,
The Poets, who on earth have made us Heirs
Of truth and pure delight by heavenly lays!
Oh! might my name be numbered among theirs,
Then gladly would I end my mortal days.

'The world is too much with us'

The world is too much with us; late and soon,
Getting and spending, we lay waste our powers:
Little we see in nature that is ours;
We have given our hearts away, a sordid boon!
This Sea that bares her bosom to the moon;
The Winds that will be howling at all hours
And are up-gathered now like sleeping flowers;
For this, for every thing, we are out of tune;
It moves us not—Great God! I'd rather be
A Pagan suckled in a creed outworn; 10
So might I, standing on this pleasant lea,
Have glimpses that would make me less forlorn;
Have sight of Proteus coming from the sea;
Or hear old Triton blow his wreathed horn.

To the Memory of Raisley Calvert

Calvert! it must not be unheard by them
Who may respect my name that I to thee
Owed many years of early liberty.
This care was thine when sickness did condemn
Thy youth to hopeless wasting, root and stem:
That I, if frugal and severe, might stray
Where'er I liked; and finally array
My temples with the Muse's diadem.
Hence, if in freedom I have loved the truth,
If there be aught of pure, or good, or great,   10
In my past verse; or shall be, in the lays
Of higher mood, which now I meditate,
It gladdens me, O worthy, short-lived Youth!
To think how much of this will be thy praise.

'Where lies the Land to which yon Ship must go?'

Where lies the Land to which yon Ship must go?
Festively she puts forth in trim array;
As vigorous as a Lark at break of day:
Is she for tropic suns, or polar snow?
What boots the enquiry? Neither friend nor foe
She cares for; let her travel where she may,
She finds familiar names, a beaten way
Ever before her, and a wind to blow.
Yet still I ask, what Haven is her mark?
And, almost as it was when ships were rare,   10
From time to time, like Pilgrims, here and there
Crossing the waters; doubt, and something dark,
Of the old Sea some reverential fear,
Is with me at thy farewell, joyous Bark!

'With Ships the sea was sprinkled far and nigh'

With Ships the sea was sprinkled far and nigh,
Like stars in heaven, and joyously it showed;
Some lying fast at anchor in the road,
Some veering up and down, one knew not why.
A goodly Vessel did I then espy
Come like a Giant from a haven broad;
And lustily along the Bay she strode,
Her tackling rich, and of apparel high.
This Ship was nought to me, nor I to her,
Yet I pursued her with a Lover's look;   10
This Ship to all the rest did I prefer:
When will she turn, and whither? She will brook
No tarrying; where she comes the winds must stir:
On went She, and due north her journey took.

'It is no Spirit who from Heaven hath flown'

It is no Spirit who from Heaven hath flown,
And is descending on his embassy;
Nor Traveller gone from Earth the Heavens to espy!
'Tis Hesperus—there he stands with glittering crown,
First admonition that the sun is down!
For yet it is broad day-light: clouds pass by;
A few are near him still—and now the sky,
He hath it to himself—'tis all his own.
O most ambitious Star! an inquest wrought
Within me when I recognised thy light;   10
A moment I was startled at the sight:
And, while I gazed, there came to me a thought
That I might step beyond my natural race
As thou seem'st now to do; might one day trace
Some ground not mine; and, strong her strength above,
My Soul, an Apparition in the place,
Tread there, with steps that no one shall reprove!

'Methought I saw the footsteps of a throne'

Methought I saw the footsteps of a throne
Which mists and vapours from mine eyes did shroud,
Nor view of him who sate thereon allowed;
But all the steps and ground about were strown
With sights the ruefullest that flesh and bone
Ever put on; a miserable crowd,
Sick, hale, old, young, who cried before that cloud,
'Thou art our king, O Death! to thee we groan.'
I seemed to mount those steps; the vapours gave
Smooth way; and I beheld the face of one   10
Sleeping alone within a mossy cave,
With her face up to heaven; that seemed to have
Pleasing remembrance of a thought foregone;
A lovely Beauty in a summer grave!

'Are souls then nothing?'

Are souls then nothing? Must at length the die
Be cast by weight of multitudes? Shall hoardes
Of Slaves triumphant over noble words
And noble thoughts and antient liberty
Deal with us as they would with sheep and tie
Our hands behind our backs with felon cords?
Yields every thing to outnumbering of swords?
Is man as good as man? none low, none high?
This was not once the doctrine of our Land;
Then would we say great storms there are that nurse   10
Themselves in little clouds, a petty Band
Of gallant hearts to be an enemy's curse
Hath might beyond the might of Moses' wand;
God helps the brave to scatter man and horse.

' "*Beloved Vale!*" *I said, "when I shall con*" '

'Beloved Vale!' I said, 'when I shall con
Those many records of my childish years,
Remembrance of myself and of my peers
Will press me down: to think of what is gone
Will be an awful thought, if life have one.'
But, when into the Vale I came, no fears
Distressed me; I looked round, I shed no tears;
Deep thought, or awful vision, I had none.
By thousand petty fancies I was crossed,
To see the Trees, which I had thought so tall,   10
Mere dwarfs; the Brooks so narrow, Fields so small.
A Juggler's Balls old Time about him tossed;
I looked, I stared, I smiled, I laughed; and all
The weight of sadness was in wonder lost.

'*Brook, that hast been my solace days and weeks*'

Brook, that hast been my solace days and weeks
And months, and let me add, the long year through,
I come to thee, thou dost my heart renew;
O happy Thing! among thy flowery creeks,
And happy, dancing down thy water-breaks.
If I some type of thee did wish to view,
Thee, and not thee thyself, I would not do
Like Grecian Poets, give thee human cheeks,
Channels for tears! no Naiad shouldst thou be;°
Have neither wings, feet, feathers, joints, nor hairs;   10
It seems, the Eternal Soul is clothed in thee
With purer robes than those of flesh and blood;
And hath bestowed on thee a better good;
The joy of fleshly life, without its cares.

'Dear Native Brooks your ways have I pursued'

Dear Native Brooks your ways have I pursued
How fondly! whether you delight in screen
Of shady woods to rest yourselves unseen,
Or from your lofty dwellings scarcely viewed
But by the mountain eagle, your bold brood
Pure as the morning, angry, boisterous, keen,
Green as sea water, foaming white and green,
Comes roaring like a joyous multitude.
Nor have I been your follower in vain;
For not to speak of life and its first joys   10
Bound to your goings by a tender chain
Of flowers and delicate dreams that entertain
Loose minds when Men are growing into Boys,
My manly heart has owed to your rough noise
Triumph and thoughts no bondage could restrain.

'England! the time is come when thou shouldst wean'

England! the time is come when thou shouldst wean
Thy heart from its emasculating food;
The truth should now be better understood;
Old things have been unsettled; we have seen
Fair seed-time, better harvest might have been
But for thy trespasses; and, at this day,
If for Greece, Egypt, India, Africa,
Aught good were destined, Thou wouldst step between.
England! all nations in this charge agree:
But worse, more ignorant in love and hate,   10
Far, far more abject is thine Enemy:
Therefore the wise pray for thee, though the freight
Of thy offences be a heavy weight:
Oh grief! that Earth's best hopes rest all with Thee!

'Great Men have been among us'

Great Men have been among us; hands that penned
And tongues that uttered wisdom, better none:
The later Sydney, Marvel, Harrington,
Young Vane, and others who called Milton Friend.
These Moralists could act and comprehend:
They knew how genuine glory was put on;
Taught us how rightfully a nation shone
In splendor: what strength was, that would not bend
But in magnanimous meekness. France, 'tis strange,
Hath brought forth no such souls as we had then.   10
Perpetual emptiness! unceasing change!
No single Volume paramount, no code,
No master spirit, no determined road;
But equally a want of Books and Men!

'It is not to be thought of that the Flood'

It is not to be thought of that the Flood
Of British freedom, which to the open Sea
Of the world's praise from dark antiquity
Hath flowed, 'with pomp of waters, unwithstood,'°
Road by which all might come and go that would,
And bear out freights of worth to foreign lands;
That this most famous Stream in Bogs and Sands
Should perish; and to evil and to good
Be lost for ever. In our Halls is hung
Armoury of the invincible Knights of old: 10
We must be free or die, who speak the tongue
That Shakespeare spake; the faith and morals hold
Which Milton held. In every thing we are sprung
Of Earth's first blood, have titles manifold.

'There is a bondage which is worse to bear'

There is a bondage which is worse to bear
Than his who breathes, by roof, and floor, and wall,
Pent in, a Tyrant's solitary Thrall:
'Tis his who walks about in the open air,
One of a Nation who, henceforth, must wear
Their fetters in their Souls. For who could be,
Who, even the best, in such condition, free
From self-reproach, reproach which he must share
With Human Nature? Never be it ours
To see the Sun how brightly it will shine,   10
And know that noble Feelings, manly Powers,
Instead of gathering strength must droop and pine,
And Earth with all her pleasant fruits and flowers
Fade, and participate in Man's decline.

'When I have borne in memory what has tamed'

When I have borne in memory what has tamed
Great Nations, how ennobling thoughts depart
When Men change Swords for Ledgers, and desert
The Student's bower for gold, some fears unnamed
I had, my Country! am I to be blamed?
But, when I think of Thee, and what Thou art,
Verily, in the bottom of my heart,
Of those unfilial fears I am ashamed.
But dearly must we prize thee; we who find
In thee a bulwark of the cause of men;   10
And I by my affection was beguiled.
What wonder, if a Poet, now and then,
Among the many movements of his mind,
Felt for thee as a Lover or a Child.

'Farewell, thou little Nook of mountain ground'

Farewell, thou little Nook of mountain ground,
Thou rocky corner in the lowest stair
Of Fairfield's mighty Temple that doth bound°
One side of our whole vale with grandeur rare,
Sweet Garden-orchard! of all spots that are
The loveliest surely man hath ever found.
Farewell! we leave thee to heaven's peaceful care.
Thee and the Cottage which thou dost surround.

Our Boat is safely anchored by the Shore:°
And safely she will ride when we are gone: 10
And ye few things that lie about our door
Shall have our best protection, every one;
Fields, goods, and distant chattels we have none;
This is the place which holds our private store
Of things earth makes and sun doth shine upon;
Here are they in our sight: we have no more.

Sunshine and showers be with you, bud and bell!
For two months now in vain we shall be sought:
We leave you here in solitude to dwell
With these our latest gifts of tender thought,   20
Thou like the morning in thy saffron coat
Bright Gowan! and marsh-marygold, farewell!
Whom from the borders of the Lake we brought
And placed together near our rocky well.

We go for one to whom ye will be dear;
And she will love this Bower, this Indian shed,
Our own contrivance, building without peer:
A gentle maid! whose heart is lowly bred,
Her pleasures are in wild fields gathered;
With joyousness, and with a thoughtful cheer   30
She'll come to you; to you herself will wed;
And love the blessed life which we lead here.

Dear Spot! whom we have watched with tender heed,
Bringing thee chosen plants and blossoms blown
Among the distant mountains, flower and weed
Which thou hast taken to thee as thy own,
Making all kindness registered and known;
Thou for our sakes, though Nature's Child indeed,
Fair in thyself and beautiful alone,
Hast taken gifts which thou dost little need;   40

And, O most constant and most fickle place!
That hath a wayward heart, as thou dost shew
To them who look not daily on thy face,
Who being loved in love no bounds dost know,
And say'st when we forsake thee, 'Let them go!'
Thou easy-hearted thing! with thy wild race
Of weeds and flowers till we return be slow
And travel with the year at a soft pace:

Help us to tell her tales of years gone by
And this sweet spring the best-beloved and best.   50
Joy will be gone in its mortality,
Something must stay to tell us of the rest,
Here with its primroses the steep rock's breast
Glittered at evening like a starry sky;
And in this bush our sparrow built its nest,
Of which I sung one song that will not die.

O happy Garden! loved for hours of sleep,
O quiet Garden! loved for waking hours.
For soft half-slumbers that did gently steep
Our spirits, carrying with them dreams of flowers,   60
Beloved for days of rest in fruit-tree bowers!
Two burning months let summer overleap,
And, coming back with her who will be ours,
Into thy bosom we again shall creep.

'The Sun has long been set'

The Sun has long been set:
The Stars are out by twos and threes;
The little Birds are piping yet
Among the bushes and trees;
There's a Cuckoo, and one or two thrushes;
And a noise of wind that rushes,
With a noise of water that gushes;
And the Cuckoo's sovereign cry
Fills all the hollow of the sky!

Who would go 'parading'°   10
In London, and 'masquerading,'
On such a night of June?
With that beautiful soft half-moon,
And all these innocent blisses,
On such a night as this is!

Calais

AUGUST, 1802

Is it a Reed that's shaken by the wind,
Or what is it that ye go forth to see?
Lords, Lawyers, Statesmen, Squires of low degree,
Men known, and men unknown, Sick, Lame, and Blind,
Post forward all, like Creatures of one kind,
With first-fruit offerings crowd to bend the knee
In France, before the new-born Majesty.
'Tis ever thus. Ye Men of prostrate mind!
A seemly reverence may be paid to power;
But that's a loyal virtue, never sown   10
In haste, nor springing with a transient shower:
When truth, when sense, when liberty were flown
What hardship had it been to wait an hour?
Shame on you, feeble Heads, to slavery prone!

Composed by the Sea-Side, near Calais

AUGUST, 1802

Fair Star of Evening, Splendor of the West,
Star of my Country! on the horizon's brink
Thou hangest, stooping, as might seem, to sink
On England's bosom; yet well pleased to rest,
Meanwhile, and be to her a glorious crest
Conspicuous to the Nations. Thou, I think,
Should'st be my Country's emblem; and should'st wink,
Bright Star! with laughter on her banners, drest
In thy fresh beauty. There! that dusky spot
Beneath thee, it is England; there it lies.   10
Blessings be on you both! one hope, one lot,
One life, one glory! I, with many a fear
For my dear Country, many heartfelt sighs,
Among Men who do not love her linger here.

'It is a beauteous Evening, calm and free'

It is a beauteous Evening, calm and free;
The holy time is quiet as a Nun
Breathless with adoration; the broad sun
Is sinking down in its tranquillity;
The gentleness of heaven is on the Sea:
Listen! the mighty Being is awake
And doth with his eternal motion make
A sound like thunder—everlastingly.
Dear Child! dear Girl! that walkest with me here,
If thou appear'st untouched by solemn thought,   10
Thy nature is not therefore less divine:
Thou liest in Abraham's bosom all the year;
And worshipp'st at the Temple's inner shrine,
God being with thee when we know it not.

To Toussaint L'Ouverture

Toussaint, the most unhappy Man of Men!
Whether the rural Milk-maid by her Cow
Sing in thy hearing, or thou liest now
Alone in some deep dungeon's earless den,
O miserable Chieftain! where and when
Wilt thou find patience? Yet die not; do thou
Wear rather in thy bonds a chearful brow:
Though fallen Thyself, never to rise again,
Live, and take comfort. Thou hast left behind
Powers that will work for thee; air, earth, and skies;　　10
There's not a breathing of the common wind
That will forget thee; thou hast great allies;
Thy friends are exultations, agonies,
And love, and Man's unconquerable mind.°

To a Friend, Composed near Calais

ON THE ROAD LEADING TO ARDRES, AUGUST 7TH, 1802

Jones! when from Calais southward you and I
Travelled on foot together; then this Way,
Which I am pacing now, was like the May
With festivals of new-born Liberty:
A homeless sound of joy was in the Sky;
The antiquated Earth, as one might say,
Beat like the heart of Man: songs, garlands, play,
Banners, and happy faces, far and nigh!
And now, sole register that these things were,
Two solitary greetings have I heard,　　10
'*Good morrow, Citizen!*' a hollow word,
As if a dead Man spake it! Yet despair
I feel not: happy am I as a Bird:
Fair seasons yet will come, and hopes as fair.

Calais

Festivals have I seen that were not names:
This is young Buonaparte's natal day;
And his is henceforth an established sway,
Consul for life. With worship France proclaims
Her approbation, and with pomps and games.
Heaven grant that other Cities may be gay!
Calais is not: and I have bent my way
To the Sea-coast, noting that each man frames
His business as he likes. Another time
That was, when I was here long years ago: 10
The senselessness of joy was then sublime!
Happy is he, who, caring not for Pope,
Consul, or King, can sound himself to know
The destiny of Man, and live in hope.

September 1st, 1802

We had a fellow-Passenger who came
From Calais with us, gaudy in array,
A Negro Woman like a Lady gay,
Yet silent as a woman fearing blame;
Dejected, meek, yea pitiably tame,
She sate, from notice turning not away,
But on our proffered kindness still did lay
A weight of languid speech, or at the same
Was silent, motionless in eyes and face.
She was a Negro Woman driv'n from France,   10
Rejected like all others of that race,
Not one of whom may now find footing there;
This the poor Out-cast did to us declare,
Nor murmured at the unfeeling Ordinance.

Composed in the Valley, near Dover

ON THE DAY OF LANDING

Dear fellow Traveller! here we are once more.
The Cock that crows, the Smoke that curls, that sound
Of Bells, those Boys that in yon meadow-ground
In white sleeved shirts are playing by the score,
And even this little River's gentle roar,
All, all are English. Oft have I looked round
With joy in Kent's green vales; but never found
Myself so satisfied in heart before.
Europe is yet in Bonds; but let that pass,
Thought for another moment. Thou art free   10
My Country! and 'tis joy enough and pride
For one hour's perfect bliss, to tread the grass
Of England once again, and hear and see,
With such a dear Companion at my side.

September, 1802

Inland, within a hollow Vale, I stood,
And saw, while sea was calm and air was clear,
The Coast of France, the Coast of France how near!
Drawn almost into frightful neighbourhood.
I shrunk, for verily the barrier flood
Was like a Lake, or River bright and fair,
A span of waters; yet what power is there!
What mightiness for evil and for good!
Even so doth God protect us if we be
Virtuous and wise; Winds blow, and Waters roll,   10
Strength to the brave, and Power, and Deity,
Yet in themselves are nothing! One decree
Spake laws to *them*, and said that by the Soul
Only the Nations shall be great and free.

Composed Upon Westminster Bridge

SEPT. 2, 1802

Earth has not any thing to shew more fair:
Dull would he be of soul who could pass by
A sight so touching in its majesty:
This City now doth like a garment wear
The beauty of the morning; silent, bare,
Ships, towers, domes, theatres, and temples lie
Open unto the fields, and to the sky;
All bright and glittering in the smokeless air.
Never did sun more beautifully steep
In his first splendor valley, rock, or hill;   10
Ne'er saw I, never felt, a calm so deep!
The river glideth at his own sweet will:
Dear God! the very houses seem asleep;
And all that mighty heart is lying still!

Written in London

SEPTEMBER, 1802

O Friend! I know not which way I must look
For comfort, being, as I am, opprest,
To think that now our Life is only drest
For shew; mean handywork of craftsman, cook,
Or groom! We must run glittering like a Brook
In the open sunshine, or we are unblest:
The wealthiest man among us is the best:
No grandeur now in nature or in book
Delights us. Rapine, avarice, expence,°
This is idolatry; and these we adore: 10
Plain living and high thinking are no more:
The homely beauty of the good old cause
Is gone; our peace, our fearful innocence,
And pure religion breathing household laws.

London

1802

Milton! thou should'st be living at this hour:
England hath need of thee: she is a fen
Of stagnant waters: altar, sword and pen,
Fireside, the heroic wealth of hall and bower,
Have forfeited their ancient English dower
Of inward happiness. We are selfish men;
Oh! raise us up, return to us again;
And give us manners, virtue, freedom, power.
Thy soul was like a Star and dwelt apart:
Thou hadst a voice whose sound was like the sea;   10
Pure as the naked heavens, majestic, free,
So didst thou travel on life's common way,
In chearful godliness; and yet thy heart
The lowliest duties on itself did lay.

'Nuns fret not at their Convent's narrow room'

Nuns fret not at their Convent's narrow room;
And Hermits are contented with their Cells;
And Students with their pensive Citadels:
Maids at the Wheel, the Weaver at his Loom,
Sit blithe and happy; Bees that soar for bloom,
High as the highest Peak of Furness Fells,
Will murmur by the hour in Foxglove bells:
In truth, the prison, unto which we doom
Ourselves, no prison is: and hence to me,
In sundry moods, 'twas pastime to be bound   10
Within the Sonnet's scanty plot of ground:
Pleased if some Souls (for such there needs must be)
Who have felt the weight of too much liberty,
Should find short solace there, as I have found.

Composed after a Journey across the Hamilton Hills, Yorkshire

Ere we had reached the wished-for place, night fell:
We were too late at least by one dark hour,
And nothing could we see of all that power
Of prospect, whereof many thousands tell.
The western sky did recompence us well
With Grecian Temple, Minaret, and Bower;
And, in one part, a Minster with its Tower
Substantially distinct, a place for Bell
Or Clock to toll from. Many a glorious pile
Did we behold, sights that might well repay   10
All disappointment! and, as such, the eye
Delighted in them; but we felt, the while,
We should forget them: they are of the sky,
And from our earthly memory fade away.

'These words were uttered in a pensive mood'

. . . they are of the sky,
And from our earthly memory fade away.

These words were uttered in a pensive mood,
Even while mine eyes were on that solemn sight:
A contrast and reproach to gross delight,
And life's unspiritual pleasures daily wooed!
But now upon this thought I cannot brood:
It is unstable, and deserts me quite;
Nor will I praise a Cloud, however bright,
Disparaging Man's gifts, and proper food.
The Grove, the sky-built Temple, and the Dome,
Though clad in colours beautiful and pure,   10
Find in the heart of man no natural home:
The immortal Mind craves objects that endure:
These cleave to it; from these it cannot roam,
Nor they from it: their fellowship is secure.

The Small Celandine

There is a Flower, the Lesser Celandine,
That shrinks, like many more, from cold and rain;
And, the first moment that the sun may shine,
Bright as the sun itself, 'tis out again!

When hailstones have been falling swarm on swarm,
Or blasts the green field and the trees distressed,
Oft have I seen it muffled up from harm,
In close self-shelter, like a Thing at rest.

But lately, one rough day, this Flower I passed,
And recognized it, though an altered Form,   10
Now standing forth an offering to the Blast,
And buffetted at will by Rain and Storm.

I stopped, and said with inly muttered voice,
'It doth not love the shower, nor seek the cold:
This neither is its courage nor its choice,
But its necessity in being old.

The sunshine may not bless it, nor the dew;
It cannot help itself in its decay;
Stiff in its members, withered, changed of hue.'
And, in my spleen, I smiled that it was grey.   20

To be a Prodigal's Favorite—then, worse truth,
A Miser's Pensioner—behold our lot!
O Man! that from thy fair and shining youth
Age might but take the things Youth needed not!

Sonnet

SEPTEMBER 25TH, 1803

Fly, some kind Spirit, fly to Grasmere Vale!
Say that we come, and come by this day's light.
Glad tidings! spread them over field and height.
But, chiefly, let one Cottage hear the tale!
There let a mystery of joy prevail,
The Kitten frolic with a gusty might,
And *Ranger* whine as at a second sight
Of near-approaching good, that will not fail.
And from that Infant's face let joy appear,
Yea, let our Mary's one Companion child,   10
That hath her six weeks' solitude beguiled
With intimations manifold and dear,
While we have wandered over wood and wild,
Smile on its Mother now with bolder chear!

To the Men of Kent

OCTOBER, 1803

Vanguard of Liberty, ye Men of Kent,
Ye Children of a Soil that doth advance
Its haughty brow against the coast of France,
Now is the time to prove your hardiment!
To France be words of invitation sent!
They from their Fields can see the countenance
Of your fierce war, may ken the glittering lance,
And hear you shouting forth your brave intent.
Left single, in bold parley, Ye, of yore,
Did from the Norman win a gallant wreath;   10
Confirmed the charters that were yours before;—
No parleying now! In Britain is one breath;
We all are with you now from Shore to Shore:—
Ye Men of Kent, 'tis Victory or Death!

Anticipation

OCTOBER, 1803

Shout, for a mighty Victory is won!
On British ground the Invaders are laid low;
The breath of Heaven has drifted them like snow,
And left them lying in the silent sun,
Never to rise again!—the work is done.
Come forth, ye Old Men, now in peaceful show
And greet your Sons! drums beat, and trumpets blow!
Make merry, Wives! ye little Children stun
Your Grandame's ears with pleasure of your noise!
Clap, Infants, clap your hands! Divine must be   10
That triumph, when the very worst, the pain,
And even the prospect of our Brethren slain,
Hath something in it which the heart enjoys:—
In glory will they sleep and endless sanctity.

Yarrow Unvisited

(See the various Poems the scene of which is laid upon the Banks of the Yarrow;
in particular, the exquisite Ballad of Hamilton, beginning

> 'Busk ye, busk ye my bonny, bonny Bride,
> Busk ye, busk ye my winsome Marrow!'—)

From Stirling Castle we had seen
The mazy Forth unravelled;
Had trod the banks of Clyde, and Tay,
And with the Tweed had travelled;
And, when we came to Clovenford,
Then said my '*winsome Marrow*,'°
'Whate'er betide, we'll turn aside,
And see the Braes of Yarrow.'

'Let Yarrow Folk, *frae* Selkirk Town,
Who have been buying, selling,   10
Go back to Yarrow, 'tis their own,
Each Maiden to her Dwelling!

On Yarrow's Banks let herons feed,
Hares couch, and rabbits burrow!
But we will downwards with the Tweed,
Nor turn aside to Yarrow.

There's Galla water, Leader Haughs,
Both lying right before us;
And Dryborough, where with chiming Tweed
The Lintwhites sing in chorus;°   20
There's pleasant Tiviot Dale, a land
Made blithe with plough and harrow;
Why throw away a needful day
To go in search of Yarrow?

What's Yarrow but a River bare
That glides the dark hills under?
There are a thousand such elsewhere
As worthy of your wonder.'
—Strange words they seemed of slight and scorn;
My True-love sighed for sorrow;   30
And looked me in the face, to think
I thus could speak of Yarrow!

'Oh! green,' said I, 'are Yarrow's Holms,
And sweet is Yarrow flowing!
Fair hangs the apple frae the rock,
But we will leave it growing.
O'er hilly path, and open Strath,°
We'll wander Scotland thorough;
But, though so near, we will not turn
Into the Dale of Yarrow.   40

Let Beeves and home-bred Kine partake
The sweets of Burn-mill meadow;°
The Swan on still St. Mary's Lake
Float double, Swan and Shadow!
We will not see them; will not go,
Today, nor yet tomorrow;
Enough if in our hearts we know,
There's such a place as Yarrow.

Be Yarrow Stream unseen, unknown!
It must, or we shall rue it: 50
We have a vision of our own;
Ah! why should we undo it?
The treasured dreams of times long past
We'll keep them, winsome Marrow!
For when we're there although 'tis fair
'Twill be another Yarrow!

If Care with freezing years should come,
And wandering seem but folly,
Should we be loth to stir from home,
And yet be melancholy;   60
Should life be dull, and spirits low,
'Twill soothe us in our sorrow
That earth has something yet to show,
The bonny Holms of Yarrow!'

'She was a Phantom of delight'

She was a Phantom of delight
When first she gleamed upon my sight;
A lovely Apparition, sent
To be a moment's ornament;
Her eyes as stars of Twilight fair;
Like Twilight's, too, her dusky hair;
But all things else about her drawn
From May-time and the chearful Dawn;
A dancing Shape, an Image gay,
To haunt, to startle, and way-lay.   10

I saw her upon nearer view,
A Spirit, yet a Woman too!
Her household motions light and free,
And steps of virgin liberty;
A countenance in which did meet
Sweet records, promises as sweet;

A Creature not too bright or good
For human nature's daily food;
For transient sorrows, simple wiles,
Praise, blame, love, kisses, tears, and smiles.   20

And now I see with eye serene
The very pulse of the machine;
A Being breathing thoughtful breath;
A Traveller betwixt life and death;
The reason firm, the temperate will,
Endurance, foresight, strength and skill;
A perfect Woman; nobly planned,
To warn, to comfort, and command;
And yet a Spirit still, and bright
With something of an angel light.   30

October, 1803

One might believe that natural miseries
Had blasted France, and made of it a land
Unfit for Men; and that in one great Band
Her Sons were bursting forth, to dwell at ease.
But 'tis a chosen soil, where sun and breeze
Shed gentle favors; rural works are there;
And ordinary business without care;
Spot rich in all things that can soothe and please!
How piteous then that there should be such dearth
Of knowledge; that whole myriads should unite   10
To work against themselves such fell despite:
Should come in phrenzy and in drunken mirth,
Impatient to put out the only light
Of Liberty that yet remains on Earth!

October, 1803

When, looking on the present face of things,
I see one Man, of Men the meanest too!
Raised up to sway the World, to do, undo,
With mighty Nations for his Underlings,
The great events with which old story rings
Seem vain and hollow; I find nothing great;
Nothing is left which I can venerate;
So that almost a doubt within me springs
Of Providence, such emptiness at length
Seems at the heart of all things. But, great God!   10
I measure back the steps which I have trod,
And tremble, seeing, as I do, the strength
Of such poor Instruments, with thoughts sublime
I tremble at the sorrow of the time.

October, 1803

These times touch moneyed Worldlings with dismay:
Even rich men, brave by nature, taint the air
With words of apprehension and despair:
While tens of thousands, thinking on the affray,
Men unto whom sufficient for the day
And minds not stinted or untilled are given,
Sound, healthy Children of the God of Heaven,
Are cheerful as the rising Sun in May.
What do we gather hence but firmer faith
That every gift of noble origin   10
Is breathed upon by Hope's perpetual breath;
That virtue and the faculties within
Are vital, and that riches are akin
To fear, to change, to cowardice, and death!

October, 1803

Six thousand Veterans practised in War's game,
Tried Men, at Killicranky were arrayed
Against an equal Host that wore the Plaid,
Shepherds and Herdsmen.—Like a whirlwind came
The Highlanders, the slaughter spread like flame;
And Garry thundering down his mountain-road
Was stopped, and could not breathe beneath the load
Of the dead bodies. 'Twas a day of shame
For them whom precept and the pedantry
Of cold mechanic battle do enslave.   10
Oh! for a single hour of that Dundee
Who on that day the word of onset gave!
Like conquest would the Men of England see;
And her Foes find a like inglorious Grave.

Ode to Duty

Stern Daughter of the Voice of God!°
O Duty! if that name thou love
Who art a Light to guide, a Rod
To check the erring, and reprove;
Thou who art victory and law
When empty terrors overawe;
From vain temptations dost set free;
From strife and from despair; a glorious ministry.

There are who ask not if thine eye
Be on them; who, in love and truth,   10
Where no misgiving is, rely
Upon the genial sense of youth:
Glad Hearts! without reproach or blot;
Who do thy work, and know it not:
May joy be theirs while life shall last!
And Thou, if they should totter, teach them to stand fast!

Serene will be our days and bright,
And happy will our nature be,
When love is an unerring light,
And joy its own security.   20
And blessed are they who in the main
This faith, even now, do entertain:
Live in the spirit of this creed;
Yet find that other strength, according to their need.

I, loving freedom, and untried;
No sport of every random gust,
Yet being to myself a guide,
Too blindly have reposed my trust:
Resolved that nothing e'er should press
Upon my present happiness,   30
I shoved unwelcome tasks away;
But thee I now would serve more strictly, if I may.

Through no disturbance of my soul,
Or strong compunction in me wrought,
I supplicate for thy controul;
But in the quietness of thought:
Me this unchartered freedom tires;
I feel the weight of chance desires:
My hopes no more must change their name,
I long for a repose which ever is the same.   40

Yet not the less would I throughout°
Still act according to the voice
Of my own wish; and feel past doubt
That my submissiveness was choice:
Not seeking in the school of pride
For 'precepts over dignified,'°
Denial and restraint I prize
No farther than they breed a second Will more wise.

Stern Lawgiver! yet thou dost wear°
The Godhead's most benignant grace;   50
Nor know we any thing so fair
As is the smile upon thy face;

Flowers laugh before thee on their beds;
And Fragrance in thy footing treads;
Thou dost preserve the Stars from wrong;
And the most ancient Heavens through Thee are fresh and strong.

To humbler functions, awful Power!°
I call thee: I myself commend
Unto thy guidance from this hour;
Oh! let my weakness have an end!   60
Give unto me, made lowly wise,
The spirit of self-sacrifice;
The confidence of reason give;
And in the light of truth thy Bondman let me live!

Ode

Paulò majora canamus.

There was a time when meadow, grove, and stream,
The earth, and every common sight,
                    To me did seem
                    Apparelled in celestial light,
The glory and the freshness of a dream.
It is not now as it has been of yore;—
                    Turn wheresoe'er I may,
                    By night or day,
The things which I have seen I now can see no more.

                    The Rainbow comes and goes,   10
                    And lovely is the Rose,
                    The Moon doth with delight
Look round her when the heavens are bare;
                    Waters on a starry night
                    Are beautiful and fair;
                    The sunshine is a glorious birth;
                    But yet I know, where'er I go,
That there hath passed away a glory from the earth.

Now, while the Birds thus sing a joyous song,
    And while the young Lambs bound   20
        As to the tabor's sound,
To me alone there came a thought of grief:
A timely utterance gave that thought relief,
        And I again am strong.
The Cataracts blow their trumpets from the steep,
No more shall grief of mine the season wrong;
I hear the Echoes through the mountains throng,
The Winds come to me from the fields of sleep,
        And all the earth is gay,
            Land and sea   30
    Give themselves up to jollity,
        And with the heart of May
    Doth every Beast keep holiday,
        Thou Child of Joy
Shout round me, let me hear thy shouts, thou happy
  Shepherd Boy!

Ye blessed Creatures, I have heard the call
    Ye to each other make; I see
The heavens laugh with you in your jubilee;
    My heart is at your festival,
        My head hath its coronal,   40
The fullness of your bliss, I feel—I feel it all.
        Oh evil day! if I were sullen
        While the Earth herself is adorning,
           This sweet May-morning,
        And the Children are pulling,
           On every side,
        In a thousand vallies far and wide,
        Fresh flowers; while the sun shines warm,
And the Babe leaps up on his mother's arm:—
        I hear, I hear, with joy I hear!   50
        —But there's a Tree, of many one,
A single Field which I have looked upon,
Both of them speak of something that is gone:
        The Pansy at my feet
        Doth the same tale repeat:
Whither is fled the visionary gleam?
Where is it now, the glory and the dream?

Our birth is but a sleep and a forgetting:°
The Soul that rises with us, our life's Star,
  Hath had elsewhere its setting,   60
  And cometh from afar:
  Not in entire forgetfulness,
  And not in utter nakedness,
But trailing clouds of glory do we come
   From God, who is our home:
Heaven lies about us in our infancy!
Shades of the prison-house begin to close
   Upon the growing Boy,
But He beholds the light, and whence it flows,
   He sees it in his joy;   70
The Youth, who daily farther from the East
  Must travel, still is Nature's Priest,
   And by the vision splendid
   Is on his way attended;
At length the Man perceives it die away,
And fade into the light of common day.

Earth fills her lap with pleasures of her own;
Yearnings she hath in her own natural kind,
And, even with something of a Mother's mind,
   And no unworthy aim,   80
  The homely Nurse doth all she can
To make her Foster-child, her Inmate Man,
  Forget the glories he hath known,
And that imperial palace whence he came.

Behold the Child among his new-born blisses,
A four year's Darling of a pigmy size!
See, where 'mid work of his own hand he lies,
Fretted by sallies of his Mother's kisses,
With light upon him from his Father's eyes!
See, at his feet, some little plan or chart,   90
Some fragment from his dream of human life,
Shaped by himself with newly-learned art;
   A wedding or a festival,
   A mourning or a funeral;
   And this hath now his heart,

And unto this he frames his song:
    Then will he fit his tongue
To dialogues of business, love, or strife;
    But it will not be long
    Ere this be thrown aside,   100
    And with new joy and pride
The little Actor cons another part,
Filling from time to time his 'humorous stage'°
With all the Persons, down to palsied Age,
That Life brings with her in her Equipage;
    As if his whole vocation
    Were endless imitation.

Thou, whose exterior semblance doth belie
    Thy Soul's immensity;
Thou best Philosopher, who yet dost keep   110
Thy heritage, thou Eye among the blind,
That, deaf and silent, read'st the eternal deep,
Haunted for ever by the eternal mind,—
    Mighty Prophet! Seer blest!
    On whom those truths do rest,
Which we are toiling all our lives to find;
Thou, over whom thy Immortality°
Broods like the Day, a Master o'er a Slave,
A Presence which is not to be put by;
    To whom the grave   120
Is but a lonely bed without the sense or sight
    Of day or the warm light,
A place of thought where we in waiting lie;
Thou little Child, yet glorious in the might
Of untamed pleasures, on thy Being's height,
Why with such earnest pains dost thou provoke
The Years to bring the inevitable yoke,
Thus blindly with thy blessedness at strife?
Full soon thy Soul shall have her earthly freight,
And custom lie upon thee with a weight,   130
Heavy as frost, and deep almost as life!

    O joy! that in our embers
    Is something that doth live,
    That nature yet remembers
    What was so fugitive!

The thought of our past years in me doth breed
Perpetual benedictions: not indeed
For that which is most worthy to be blest;
Delight and liberty, the simple creed
Of Childhood, whether fluttering or at rest,   140
With new-born hope for ever in his breast:—
     Not for these I raise
    The song of thanks and praise;
   But for those obstinate questionings°
   Of sense and outward things,
   Fallings from us, vanishings;
   Blank misgivings of a Creature
Moving about in worlds not realized,
High instincts, before which our mortal Nature
Did tremble like a guilty Thing surprized: 150
   But for those first affections,
   Those shadowy recollections,
    Which, be they what they may,
Are yet the fountain light of all our day,
Are yet a master light of all our seeing;
    Uphold us, cherish us, and make°
Our noisy years seem moments in the being
Of the eternal Silence: truths that wake,
    To perish never;
Which neither listlessness, nor mad endeavour,   160
    Nor Man nor Boy,
Nor all that is at enmity with joy,
Can utterly abolish or destroy!
   Hence, in a season of calm weather,
    Though inland far we be,
Our Souls have sight of that immortal sea
    Which brought us hither,
    Can in a moment travel thither,
And see the Children sport upon the shore,
And hear the mighty waters rolling evermore.   170

Then, sing ye Birds, sing, sing a joyous song!
    And let the young Lambs bound
    As to the tabor's sound!
We in thought will join your throng,

> Ye that pipe and ye that play,
> Ye that through your hearts today
> Feel the gladness of the May!
> What though the radiance which was once so bright
> Be now for ever taken from my sight,
> > Though nothing can bring back the hour   180
> Of splendour in the grass, of glory in the flower;
> > We will grieve not, rather find
> > Strength in what remains behind,
> > In the primal sympathy
> > Which having been must ever be,
> > In the soothing thoughts that spring
> > Out of human suffering,
> > In the faith that looks through death,
> In years that bring the philosophic mind.

> And oh ye Fountains, Meadows, Hills, and Groves,   190
> Think not of any severing of our loves!
> Yet in my heart of hearts I feel your might;
> I only have relinquished one delight
> To live beneath your more habitual sway.
> I love the Brooks which down their channels fret,
> Even more than when I tripped lightly as they;
> The innocent brightness of a new-born Day
> > Is lovely yet;
> The Clouds that gather round the setting sun
> Do take a sober colouring from an eye   200
> That hath kept watch o'er man's mortality;
> Another race hath been, and other palms are won.
> Thanks to the human heart by which we live,
> Thanks to its tenderness, its joys, and fears,
> To me the meanest flower that blows can give
> Thoughts that do often lie too deep for tears.

'Who fancied what a pretty sight'

Who fancied what a pretty sight
This Rock would be if edged around
With living Snowdrops? circlet bright!
How glorious to this Orchard ground!
Who loved the little Rock, and set
Upon its Head this Coronet?

Was it the humour of a Child?
Or rather of some love-sick Maid,
Whose brows, the day that she was styled
The Shepherd Queen were thus arrayed?   10
Of Man mature, or Matron sage?
Or old Man toying with his age?

I asked—'twas whispered, The device
To each or all might well belong.
It is the Spirit of Paradise
That prompts such work, a Spirit strong,
That gives to all the self-same bent
Where life is wise and innocent.

'I wandered lonely as a Cloud'

I wandered lonely as a Cloud
That floats on high o'er Vales and Hills,
When all at once I saw a crowd
A host of dancing Daffodils;
Along the Lake, beneath the trees,
Ten thousand dancing in the breeze.

The waves beside them danced, but they
Outdid the sparkling waves in glee:—
A Poet could not but be gay
In such a laughing company: 10
I gazed—and gazed—but little thought
What wealth the shew to me had brought:

For oft when on my couch I lie
In vacant or in pensive mood.
They flash upon that inward eye
Which is the bliss of solitude,
And then my heart with pleasure fills,
And dances with the Daffodils.

The Matron of Jedborough and Her Husband

At Jedborough we went into private Lodgings for a few days; and the following
Verses were called forth by the character, and domestic situation, of our Hostess.

Age! twine thy brows with fresh spring flowers!
And call a train of laughing Hours;
And bid them dance, and bid them sing;
And Thou, too, mingle in the Ring!
Take to thy heart a new delight;
If not, make merry in despite!
For there is one who scorns thy power.
—But dance! for under Jedborough Tower
There liveth in the prime of glee,
A Woman, whose years are seventy-three,   10
And She will dance and sing with thee!

Nay! start not at that Figure—there!
Him who is rooted to his chair!
Look at him—look again! for He
Hath long been of thy Family.
With legs that move not, if they can,
And useless arms, a Trunk of Man,
He sits, and with a vacant eye;
A Sight to make a Stranger sigh!
Deaf, drooping, that is now his doom: 20
His world is in this single room:
Is this a place for mirth and cheer?
Can merry-making enter here?

The joyous Woman is the Mate
Of Him in that forlorn estate!
He breathes a subterraneous damp,
But bright as Vesper shines her lamp:
He is as mute as Jedborough Tower;
She jocund as it was of yore,
With all its bravery on; in times,   30
When, all alive with merry chimes,
Upon a sun-bright morn of May,
It rouzed the Vale to Holiday.

I praise thee, Matron! and thy due
Is praise; heroic praise, and true!
With admiration I behold
Thy gladness unsubdued and bold:
Thy looks, thy gestures, all present
The picture of a life well-spent:
This do I see; and something more;   40
A strength unthought of heretofore!
Delighted am I for thy sake;
And yet a higher joy partake.
Our Human-nature throws away
Its second Twilight, and looks gay:
A Land of promise and of pride
Unfolding, wide as life is wide.

Ah! see her helpless Charge! enclosed
Within himself, as seems; composed;
To fear of loss, and hope of gain,   50
The strife of happiness and pain,
Utterly dead! yet, in the guise
Of little Infants, when their eyes
Begin to follow to and fro
The persons that before them go,
He tracks her motions, quick or slow.
Her buoyant Spirit can prevail
Where common cheerfulness would fail:
She strikes upon him with the heat
Of July Suns; he feels it sweet;   60
An animal delight though dim!
'Tis all that now remains for him!

I looked, I scanned her o'er and o'er;
The more I looked I wondered more:
When suddenly I seemed to espy
A trouble in her strong black eye;
A remnant of uneasy light,
A flash of something over-bright!
And soon she made this matter plain;
And told me, in a thoughtful strain,   70
That she had borne a heavy yoke,
Been stricken by a twofold stroke;
Ill health of body; and had pined
Beneath worse ailments of the mind.

So be it! but let praise ascend
To Him who is our Lord and Friend!
Who from disease and suffering
Hath called for thee a second Spring;
Repaid thee for that sore distress
By no untimely joyousness;   80
Which makes of thine a blissful state;
And cheers thy melancholy Mate!

To the River Duddon

O mountain Stream! the Shepherd and his Cot
Are privileged Inmates of deep solitude:
Nor would the nicest Anchorite exclude
A Field or two of brighter green, or Plot
Of tillage-ground, that seemeth like a spot
Of stationary sunshine: thou hast viewed
These only, Duddon! with their paths renewed
By fits and starts, yet this contents thee not.
Thee hath some awful Spirit impelled to leave,
Utterly to desert, the haunts of men,   10
Though simple thy Companions were and few;
And through this wilderness a passage cleave
Attended but by thy own Voice, save when
The Clouds and Fowls of the air thy way pursue.

To the Daisy

Sweet Flower! belike one day to have
A place upon thy Poet's grave.
I welcome thee once more;
But He, who was, on land, at sea,
My Brother, too, in loving thee
Although he loved more silently,
Sleeps by his native shore.

Ah! hopeful, hopeful was the day
When to that Ship he went his way,
To govern and to guide: 10
His wish was gained; a little time
Would bring him back in manhood's prime,
And free for life, these hills to climb
With all his wants supplied.

And hopeful, hopeful was the day°
When that stout Ship at anchor lay
Beside the shores of Wight:
The May had then made all things green;
And goodly, also, to be seen
Was that proud Ship, of Ships the Queen,   20
His hope and his delight.

Yet then, when called ashore (I know
The truth of this, he told me so)
In more than happy mood
To your abodes, Sweet Daisy Flowers!
He oft would steal at leisure hours;
And loved you glittering in the bowers,
A starry multitude.

But hark the Word! the Ship is gone;
Returns from her long course: anon   30
Sets sail: in season due
Once more on English earth they stand:
But, when a third time from the land
They parted, sorrow was at hand
For Him and for his Crew.

Six weeks beneath the moving Sea°
He lay in slumber quietly,
Unforced by wind or wave
To quit the Ship for which he died,
All claims of duty satisfied.   40
And there they found him at her side
And bore him to the grave.

Vain service! yet not vainly done
For this, if other end were none,
That he, who had been cast
Upon a way of life unmeet
For such a gentle Soul and sweet,
Should find an undisturbed retreat
Near what he loved, at last:

That neighbourhood of Wood and Field   50
To him a resting-place should yield,
A meek Man and a brave!
The Birds shall sing, and Ocean make
A mournful murmur for *his* sake;
And Thou sweet Flower! shalt sleep and wake
Upon his senseless Grave.

'I only looked for pain and grief'

I only looked for pain and grief
And trembled as I drew more near;
But God's unbounded love is here,
And I have found relief.
The precious Spot is all my own,
Save only that this Plant unknown,°
A little one and lowly sweet,
Not surely now without Heaven's grace,
First seen, and seen, too, in this place,
Is flowering at my feet.   10

The Shepherd Boy hath disappeared;
The Buzzard, too, hath soared away;

And undisturbed I now may pay
My debt to what I feared.
Sad register! but this is sure:
Peace built on suffering will endure.
But such the peace that will be ours.
Though many suns, alas! must shine
Ere tears shall cease from me and mine
To fall in bitter show'rs.   20

The Sheep-boy whistled loud, and lo!
Thereafter, having felt the shock,
The Buzzard mounted from the rock
Deliberate and slow:
Lord of the air, he took his flight;
Oh could he on that woeful night
Have lent his wing, my Brother dear!
For one poor moment's space to Thee
And all who struggle with the Sea
When safety is so near.   30

Thus in the weakness of my heart
I said (but let that pang be still)
When rising from the rock at will,
I saw the Bird depart.
And let me calmly bless the Power
That meets me in this unknown Flower,
Affecting type of Him I mourn!
With calmness suffer and believe,
And grieve, and know that I must grieve,
Not cheerless, though forlorn.   40

Here did we stop, and here looked round°
While each into himself descends
For that last thought of parting Friends
That is not to be found.
Our Grasmere vale was out of sight,
Our home and his, his heart's delight,
His quiet heart's delicious home.
But time before him melts away,
And he hath feeling of a day
Of blessedness to come.   50

Here did we part, and halted here
With One he loved, I saw him bound
Downwards along the rocky ground
As if with eager cheer.
A lovely sight as on he went,
For he was bold and innocent,
Had lived a life of self-command.
Heaven, did it seem to me and her,
Had laid on such a Mariner
A consecrating hand.   60

And therefore also do we weep
To find that such a faith was dust,
With sorrow, but for higher trust,
How miserably deep!
All vanished in a single word,
A breath, a sound, and scarcely heard.
Sea, Ship, drowned, shipwreck—so it came,
The meek, the brave, the good was gone;
He who had been our living John
Was nothing but a name.   70

That was indeed a parting! oh,
Glad am I, glad that it is past;
For there were some on whom it cast
Unutterable woe.
But they as well as I have gains,
The worthiest and the best; to pains
Like these, there comes a mild release;
Even here I feel it, even this Plant
So peaceful is ministrant
Of comfort and of peace.   80

He would have loved thy modest grace,
Meek flower! to Him I would have said,
'It grows upon its native bed
Beside our Parting-place;
Close to the ground like dew it lies
With multitude of purple eyes
Spangling a cushion green like moss;
But we will see it, joyful tide!

Some day to see it in its pride
The mountain we will cross.'   90

Well, well, if ever verse of mine
Have power to make his merits known,
Then let a monumental Stone
Stand here—a sacred Shrine;
And to the few who come this way,
Traveller or Shepherd, let it say,
Long as these mighty rocks endure,
Oh do not Thou too fondly brood,
Although deserving of all good,
On any earthly hope, however pure!   100

'Distressful gift! this Book receives'

Distressful gift! this Book receives
Upon its melancholy leaves,
This poor ill-fated Book:
I wrote, and when I reached the end
Started to think that thou, my Friend,
Upon the words which I had penned
Must never, never look.

Alas, alas, it is a Tale
Of Thee thyself: fond heart and frail!
The sadly-tuneful line,   10
The written words that seem to throng
The dismal page, the sound, the song,
The murmur, all to thee belong:
Too surely they are thine.

And so I write what neither Thou
Must look upon, nor others now.
Their tears would flow too fast;
Some solace thus I strive to gain,
Making a kind of secret chain,
If so I may, betwixt us twain   20
In memory of the past.

Oft have I handled, often eyed,
This book with boyish glee and pride,
The written page and white:
How have I turned them o'er and o'er,
One after one and score by score,
All filled or to be filled with store
Of verse for his delight.

He framed the Book which now I see,
This very Book upon my knee   30
He framed with dear intent
To travel with him night and day,
And in his private hearing say
Refreshing things whatever way
His weary Vessel went.

But now upon the written leaf
I look indeed with pain and grief,
I do, but gracious God,°
Oh grant that I may never find
Worse matter or a heavier mind;   40
For those which yet remain behind
Grant this, and let me be resigned
Beneath thy chast'ning rod.

Glen-Almain

OR THE NARROW GLEN

In this still place, remote from men,
Sleeps Ossian, in the NARROW GLEN;°
In this still place, where murmurs on
But one meek Streamlet, only one:
He sang of battles, and the breath
Of stormy war, and violent death;
And should, methinks, when all was past,
Have rightfully been laid at last
Where rocks were rudely heaped, and rent
As by a spirit turbulent;   10

Where sights were rough, and sounds were wild,
And everything unreconciled;
In some complaining, dim retreat,
For fear and melancholy meet;
But this is calm; there cannot be
A more entire tranquillity.

Does then the Bard sleep here indeed?
Or is it but a groundless creed?
What matters it? I blame them not
Whose Fancy in this lonely Spot   20
Was moved; and in this way expressed
Their notion of its perfect rest.
A Convent, even a hermit's Cell
Would break the silence of this Dell:
It is not quiet, is not ease;
But something deeper far than these:
The separation that is here
Is of the grave; and of austere
And happy feelings of the dead:
And, therefore, was it rightly said   30
That Ossian, last of all his race!
Lies buried in this lonely place.

Stepping Westward

While my Fellow-traveller and I were walking by the side of Loch Ketterine, one
fine evening after sun-set, in our road to a Hut where in the course of our Tour
we had been hospitably entertained some weeks before, we met, in one of the
loneliest parts of that solitary region, two well-dressed Women, one of whom said
to us, by way of greeting, 'What you are stepping westward?'

'*What you are stepping westward?*'—'*Yea*'
—'Twould be a wildish destiny,
If we, who thus together roam
In a strange Land, and far from home,
Were in this place the guests of Chance:
Yet who would stop, or fear to advance,
Though home or shelter he had none,
With such a Sky to lead him on?

The dewy ground was dark and cold;
Behind, all gloomy to behold;   10
And stepping westward seemed to be
A kind of *heavenly* destiny;
I liked the greeting; 'twas a sound
Of something without place or bound;
And seemed to give me spiritual right
To travel through that region bright.

The voice was soft, and she who spake
Was walking by her native Lake:
The salutation had to me
The very sound of courtesy: 20
Its power was felt; and while my eye
Was fixed upon the glowing sky,
The echo of the voice enwrought
A human sweetness with the thought
Of travelling through the world that lay
Before me in my endless way.

Rob Roy's Grave

The History of Rob Roy is sufficiently known; his Grave is near the head of Loch
Ketterine, in one of those small Pin-fold-like Burial-grounds, of neglected and
desolate appearance, which the Traveller meets with in the Highlands of
Scotland.

A famous Man is Robin Hood,°
The English Ballad-singer's joy!
And Scotland has a Thief as good,
An Outlaw of as daring mood,
She has her brave ROB ROY!°
Then clear the weeds from off his Grave,
And let us chaunt a passing Stave
In honour of that Hero brave!

Heaven gave Rob Roy a dauntless heart,
And wondrous length and strength of arm   10
Nor craved he more to quell his Foes,
    Or keep his Friends from harm.

Yet was Rob Roy as *wise* as brave;
Forgive me if the phrase be strong;—
A Poet worthy of Rob Roy
    Must scorn a timid song.

Say, then, that he was wise as brave
As wise in thought as bold in deed:
For in the principles of things
    He sought his moral creed.   20

Said generous Rob, 'What need of Books?
Burn all the Statutes and their shelves:
They stir us up against our Kind;
    And worse, against Ourselves.

We have a passion, make a law,
Too false to guide us or controul!
And for the law itself we fight
    In bitterness of soul.

And, puzzled, blinded thus, we lose
Distinctions that are plain and few: 30
These find I graven on my heart:
    That tells me what to do.

The Creatures see of flood and field,
And those that travel on the wind!
With them no strife can last; they live
    In peace, and peace of mind.

For why?—because the good old Rule
Sufficeth them, the simple Plan,
That they should take who have the power,
    And they should keep who can.   40

A lesson which is quickly learned,
A signal this which all can see!
Thus nothing here provokes the Strong
    To wanton cruelty.

All freakishness of mind is checked;
He tamed, who foolishly aspires;
While to the measure of his might
    Each fashions his desires.

All Kinds, and Creatures, stand and fall
By strength of prowess or of wit: 50
'Tis God's appointment who must sway,
    And who is to submit.

Since then,' said Robin, 'right is plain,
And longest life is but a day;
To have my ends, maintain my rights,
    I'll take the shortest way.'

And thus among these rocks he lived,
Through summer's heat and winter's snow:
The Eagle, he was Lord above,
    And Rob was Lord below.   60

So was it—*would*, at least, have been
But through untowardness of fate:
For Polity was then too strong;
    He came an age too late.

Or shall we say an age too soon?
For, were the bold Man living *now*,
How might he flourish in his pride,
    With buds on every bough!

Then rents and Factors, rights of chace,
Sheriffs, and Lairds and their domains,   70
Would all have seemed but paltry things,
    Not worth a moment's pains.

Rob Roy had never lingered here,
To these few meagre Vales confined;
But thought how wide the world, the times
    How fairly to his mind!

And to his Sword he would have said,
'Do Thou my sovereign will enact
From land to land through half the earth!
    Judge thou of law and fact!   80

'Tis fit that we should do our part;
Becoming, that mankind should learn
That we are not to be surpassed
    In fatherly concern.

Of old things all are over old,
Of good things none are good enough:—
We'll shew that we can help to frame
    A world of other stuff.

I, too, will have my Kings that take
From me the sign of life and death: 90
Kingdoms shall shift about, like clouds,
    Obedient to my breath.'

And, if the word had been fulfilled,
As *might* have been, then, thought of joy!
France would have had her present Boast;°
    And we our brave Rob Roy!

Oh! say not so; compare them not;
I would not wrong thee, Champion brave!
Would wrong thee no where; least of all
    Here standing by thy Grave.   100

For Thou, although with some wild thoughts,
Wild Chieftain of a Savage Clan!
Hadst this to boast of; thou didst love
    The *liberty* of Man.

And, had it been thy lot to live
With us who now behold the light,
Thou would'st have nobly stirred thyself,
    And battled for the Right.

For Robin was the poor Man's stay
The poor man's heart, the poor man's hand;   110
And all the oppressed, who wanted strength,
    Had Robin's to command.

Bear witness many a pensive sigh
Of thoughtful Herdsman when he strays
Alone upon Loch Veol's Heights,
    And by Loch Lomond's Braes!

And, far and near, through vale and hill,
Are faces that attest the same;
And kindle, like a fire new stirred,
    At sound of ROB ROY's name.   120

Address to the Sons of Burns

AFTER VISITING THEIR FATHER'S GRAVE (AUGUST 14TH, 1803)

Ye now are panting up life's hill!
'Tis twilight time of good and ill,
And more than common strength and skill
    Must ye display
If ye would give the better will
    Its lawful sway.

Strong bodied if ye be to bear
Intemperance with less harm, beware!
But if your Father's wit ye share,
    Then, then indeed,   10
Ye Sons of Burns! for watchful care
    There will be need.

For honest men delight will take
To shew you favor for his sake,
Will flatter you; and Fool and Rake
    Your steps pursue:
And of your Father's name will make
    A snare for you.

Let no mean hope your souls enslave;
Be independent, generous, brave!   20
Your Father such example gave,
        And such revere!
But be admonished by his Grave,
        And think, and fear!

The Solitary Reaper

Behold her, single in the field,
Yon solitary Highland Lass!
Reaping and singing by herself;
Stop here, or gently pass!
Alone she cuts, and binds the grain,
And sings a melancholy strain;
O listen! for the Vale profound
Is overflowing with the sound.

No Nightingale did ever chaunt
So sweetly to reposing bands   10
Of Travellers in some shady haunt,
Among Arabian Sands:
No sweeter voice was ever heard
In spring-time from the Cuckoo-bird,
Breaking the silence of the seas
Among the farthest Hebrides.

Will no one tell me what she sings?
Perhaps the plaintive numbers flow
For old, unhappy, far-off things,
And battles long ago: 20
Or is it some more humble lay,
Familiar matter of today?
Some natural sorrow, loss, or pain,
That has been, and may be again!

Whate'er the theme, the Maiden sang
As if her song could have no ending;
I saw her singing at her work,
And o'er the sickle bending;

I listened till I had my fill:
And, as I mounted up the hill,   30
The music in my heart I bore,
Long after it was heard no more.

Character of the Happy Warrior

Who is the happy Warrior? Who is he
Whom every Man in arms should wish to be?
—It is the generous Spirit, who, when brought
Among the tasks of real life, hath wrought
Upon the plan that pleased his childish thought:
Whose high endeavours are an inward light
That make the path before him always bright:
Who, with a natural instinct to discern
What knowledge can perform, is diligent to learn;
Abides by this resolve, and stops not there,   10
But makes his moral being his prime care;
Who, doomed to go in company with Pain,
And Fear, and Bloodshed, miserable train!
Turns his necessity to glorious gain;
In face of these doth exercise a power
Which is our human-nature's highest dower;
Controls them and subdues, transmutes, bereaves
Of their bad influence, and their good receives;
By objects, which might force the soul to abate
Her feeling, rendered more compassionate;   20
Is placable because occasions rise
So often that demand such sacrifice;
More skilful in self-knowledge, even more pure,
As tempted more; more able to endure,
As more exposed to suffering and distress;
Thence, also, more alive to tenderness.
'Tis he whose law is reason; who depends
Upon that law as on the best of friends;
Whence, in a state where men are tempted still
To evil for a guard against worse ill,   30
And what in quality or act is best
Doth seldom on a right foundation rest,

He fixes good on good alone, and owes
To virtue every triumph that he knows:
—Who, if he rise to station of command,
Rises by open means; and there will stand
On honourable terms, or else retire,
And in himself possess his own desire;
Who comprehends his trust, and to the same
Keeps faithful with a singleness of aim; 40
And therefore does not stoop, nor lie in wait
For wealth, or honors, or for worldly state;
Whom they must follow; on whose head must fall,
Like showers of manna, if they come at all:
Whose powers shed round him in the common strife,
Or mild concerns of ordinary life,
A constant influence, a peculiar grace;
But who, if he be called upon to face
Some awful moment to which heaven has joined
Great issues, good or bad for human-kind, 50
Is happy as a Lover; and attired
With sudden brightness like a Man inspired;
And through the heat of conflict keeps the law
In calmness made, and sees what he foresaw;
Or if an unexpected call succeed,
Come when it will, is equal to the need:
—He who, though thus endued as with a sense
And faculty for storm and turbulence,
Is yet a Soul whose master bias leans
To home-felt pleasures and to gentle scenes; 60
Sweet images! which, wheresoe'er he be,
Are at his heart; and such fidelity
It is his darling passion to approve;
More brave for this, that he hath much to love:
'Tis, finally, the Man, who, lifted high,
Conspicuous object in a Nation's eye,
Or left unthought-of in obscurity,
Who, with a toward or untoward lot,
Prosperous or adverse, to his wish or not,
Plays, in the many games of life, that one 70
Where what he most doth value must be won;
Whom neither shape of danger can dismay,
Nor thought of tender happiness betray;

Who, not content that former worth stand fast,
Looks forward, persevering to the last,
From well to better, daily self-surpast:
Who, whether praise of him must walk the earth
For ever, and to noble deeds give birth,
Or He must go to dust without his fame,
And leave a dead unprofitable name,   80
Finds comfort in himself and in his cause;
And, while the mortal mist is gathering, draws
His breath in confidence of Heaven's applause;
This is the happy Warrior; this is He
Whom every Man in arms should wish to be.

Star Gazers

What crowd is this? what have we here! we must not pass it by;
A Telescope upon its frame, and pointed to the sky:
Long is it as a Barber's Poll, or Mast of little Boat,
Some little Pleasure-Skiff, that doth on Thames's waters float.

The Show-man chuses well his place, 'tis Leicester's busy Square;
And he's as happy in his night, for the heavens are blue and fair;
Calm, though impatient is the Crowd; each is ready with the fee,
And envies him that's looking—what an insight must it be!

Yet, Show-man, where can lie the cause? Shall thy Implement have
   blame,
A Boaster, that when he is tried, fails, and is put to shame?   10
Or is it good as others are, and be their eyes in fault?
Their eyes, or minds? or, finally, is this resplendent Vault?

Is nothing of that radiant pomp so good as we have here?
Or gives a thing but small delight that never can be dear?
The silver Moon with all her Vales, and Hills of mightiest fame,
Do they betray us when they're seen? and are they but a name?

Or is it rather that Conceit rapacious is and strong,
And bounty never yields so much but it seems to do her wrong?
Or is it, that when human Souls a journey long have had,
And are returned into themselves, they cannot but be sad?   20

Or must we be constrained to think that these Spectators rude,
Poor in estate, of manners base, men of the multitude,
Have souls which never yet have ris'n, and therefore prostrate lie?
No, no, this cannot be—Men thirst for power and majesty!

Does, then, a deep and earnest thought the blissful mind employ
Of him who gazes, or has gazed? a grave and steady joy,
That doth reject all shew of pride, admits no outward sign,
Because not of this noisy world, but silent and divine!

Whatever be the cause, 'tis sure that they who pry and pore
Seem to meet with little gain, seem less happy than before: 30
One after One they take their turns, nor have I one espied
That doth not slackly go away, as if dissatisfied.

Power of Music

An Orpheus! An Orpheus!—yes, Faith may grow bold,
And take to herself all the wonders of old;—
Near the stately Pantheon you'll meet with the same,
In the street that from Oxford hath borrowed its name.

His station is there;—and he works on the crowd,
He sways them with harmony merry and loud;
He fills with his power all their hearts to the brim—
Was aught ever heard like his fiddle and him!

What an eager assembly! what an empire is this!
The weary have life and the hungry have bliss;   10
The mourner is cheared, and the anxious have rest;
And the guilt-burthened Soul is no longer opprest.

As the Moon brightens round her the clouds of the night
So he where he stands is a centre of light;
It gleams on the face, there, of dusky-faced Jack,
And the pale-visaged Baker's, with basket on back.

That errand-bound 'Prentice was passing in haste—
What matter! he's caught—and his time runs to waste—
The News-man is stopped, though he stops on the fret,
And the half-breathless Lamp-lighter he's in the net!   20

The Porter sits down on the weight which he bore;
The Lass with her barrow wheels hither her store;—
If a Thief could be here he might pilfer at ease;
She sees the Musician, 'tis all that she sees!

He stands, backed by the Wall;—he abates not his din;
His hat gives him vigour, with boons dropping in,
From the Old and the Young, from the Poorest; and there!
The one-pennied Boy has his penny to spare.

O blest are the Hearers and proud be the Hand
Of the pleasure it spreads through so thankful a Band;   30
I am glad for him, blind as he is!—all the while
If they speak 'tis to praise, and they praise with a smile.

That tall Man, a Giant in bulk and in height,
Not an inch of his body is free from delight;
Can he keep himself still, if he would? oh, not he!
The music stirs in him like wind through a tree.

There's a Cripple who leans on his Crutch; like a Tower
That long has leaned forward, leans hour after hour!—
A Mother, whose Spirit in fetters is bound,
While she dandles the babe in her arms to the sound.   40

Now, Coaches and Chariots, roar on like a stream;
Here are twenty souls happy as Souls in a dream:
They are deaf to your murmurs—they care not for you,
Nor what ye are flying, or what ye pursue!

'By their floating Mill'

'—Pleasure is spread through the earth
In stray gifts to be claimed by whoever shall find.'

By their floating Mill,
    Which lies dead and still,
Behold yon Prisoners three!
The Miller with two Dames, on the breast of the Thames;
The Platform is small, but there's room for them all;
And they're dancing merrily.

    From the shore come the notes
    To their Mill where it floats,
To their House and their Mill tethered fast!
To the small wooden isle where their work to beguile   10
They from morning to even take whatever is given:—
And many a blithe day they have past.

    In sight of the Spires
    All alive with the fires
Of the Sun going down to his rest,
In the broad open eye of the solitary sky,
They dance,—there are three, as jocund as free,
While they dance on the calm river's breast.

    Man and Maidens wheel,
    They themselves make the Reel,   20
And their Music's a prey which they seize;
It plays not for them,—what matter! 'tis their's;
And if they had care it has scattered their cares,
While they dance, crying, 'Long as ye please!'

    They dance not for me,
    Yet mine is their glee!
Thus pleasure is spread through the earth
In stray gifts to be claimed by whoever shall find;
Thus a rich loving-kindness, redundantly kind,
Moves all nature to gladness and mirth.   30

The Showers of the Spring
Rouze the Birds and they sing;
If the Wind do but stir for his proper delight,°
Each Leaf, that and this, his neighbour will kiss,
Each Wave, one and t'other, speeds after his Brother;
They are happy, for that is their right!

Elegiac Stanzas

SUGGESTED BY A PICTURE OF PEELE CASTLE, IN A STORM, PAINTED BY
SIR GEORGE BEAUMONT

I was thy Neighbour once, thou rugged Pile!
Four summer weeks I dwelt in sight of thee:
I saw thee every day; and all the while
Thy Form was sleeping on a glassy sea.

So pure the sky, so quiet was the air!
So like, so very like, was day to day!
Whene'er I looked, thy Image still was there;
It trembled, but it never passed away.

How perfect was the calm! it seemed no sleep;
No mood, which season takes away, or brings: 10
I could have fancied that the mighty Deep
Was even the gentlest of all gentle Things.

Ah! THEN, if mine had been the Painter's hand,
To express what then I saw; and add the gleam,
The light that never was, on sea or land,
The consecration, and the Poet's dream;

I would have planted thee, thou hoary Pile!
Amid a world how different from this!
Beside a sea that could not cease to smile;
On tranquil land, beneath a sky of bliss: 20

Thou shouldst have seemed a treasure-house, a mine
Of peaceful years; a chronicle of heaven:—
Of all the sunbeams that did ever shine
The very sweetest had to thee been given.

A Picture had it been of lasting ease,
Elysian quiet, without toil or strife;
No motion but the moving tide, a breeze,
Or merely silent Nature's breathing life.

Such, in the fond delusion of my heart,
Such Picture would I at that time have made: 30
And seen the soul of truth in every part;
A faith, a trust, that could not be betrayed.

So once it would have been,—'tis so no more;
I have submitted to a new controul:
A power is gone, which nothing can restore;
A deep distress hath humanized my Soul.

Not for a moment could I now behold
A smiling sea and be what I have been:
The feeling of my loss will ne'er be old;
This, which I know, I speak with mind serene.   40

Then, Beaumont, Friend! who would have been the Friend,
If he had lived, of Him whom I deplore,
This Work of thine I blame not, but commend;
This sea in anger, and the dismal shore.

Oh 'tis a passionate Work!—yet wise and well;
Well chosen is the spirit that is here;
That Hulk which labours in the deadly swell,
This rueful sky, this pageantry of fear!

And this huge Castle, standing here sublime,
I love to see the look with which it braves,   50
Cased in the unfeeling armour of old time,
The light'ning, the fierce wind, and trampling waves.

Farewell, farewell the Heart that lives alone,
Housed in a dream, at distance from the Kind!
Such happiness, wherever it be known,
Is to be pitied; for 'tis surely blind.

But welcome fortitude, and patient chear,
And frequent sights of what is to be borne!
Such sights, or worse, as are before me here.—
Not without hope we suffer and we mourn.   60

'Yes! full surely 'twas the Echo'

Yes! full surely 'twas the Echo,
Solitary, clear, profound,
Answering to Thee, shouting Cuckoo!
Giving to thee Sound for Sound.

Whence the Voice? from air or earth?
This the Cuckoo cannot tell;
But a startling sound had birth,
As the Bird must know full well;

Like the voice through earth and sky
By the restless Cuckoo sent;   10
Like her ordinary cry,
Like—but oh how different!

Hears not also mortal Life?
Hear not we, unthinking Creatures!
Slaves of Folly, Love, or Strife,
Voices of two different Natures?

Have not We too? Yes we have
Answers, and we know not whence;
Echoes from beyond the grave,
Recognized intelligence?   20

Such within ourselves we hear
Oft-times, ours though sent from far;
Listen, ponder, hold them dear;
For of God, of God they are!

Lines

COMPOSED AT GRASMERE, DURING A WALK, ONE EVENING, AFTER A
STORMY DAY, THE AUTHOR HAVING JUST READ IN A NEWSPAPER THAT THE
DISSOLUTION OF MR. FOX WAS HOURLY EXPECTED.

Loud is the Vale! the Voice is up
With which she speaks when storms are gone,
A mighty Unison of streams!
Of all her Voices, One!

Loud is the Vale;—this inland Depth
In peace is roaring like the Sea;
Yon Star upon the mountain-top
Is listening quietly.

Sad was I, ev'n to pain depressed,
Importunate and heavy load!°   10
The Comforter hath found me here,
Upon this lonely road;

And many thousands now are sad,
Wait the fulfilment of their fear;
For He must die who is their Stay,
Their Glory disappear.

A Power is passing from the earth
To breathless Nature's dark abyss;
But when the Mighty pass away
What is it more than this,   20

That Man, who is from God sent forth,
Doth yet again to God return?—
Such ebb and flow must ever be,
Then wherefore should we mourn?

A Complaint

There is a change—and I am poor;
Your Love hath been, nor long ago,
A Fountain at my fond Heart's door,
Whose only business was to flow;
And flow it did; not taking heed
Of its own bounty, or my need.

What happy moments did I count!
Blessed was I then all bliss above!
Now, for this consecrated Fount
Of murmuring, sparkling, living love,   10
What have I? Shall I dare to tell?
A comfortless, and hidden WELL.

A Well of love—it may be deep—
I trust it is, and never dry:
What matter? if the Waters sleep
In silence and obscurity.
—Such change, and at the very door
Of my fond Heart, hath made me poor.

Thought of a Briton on the Subjugation of Switzerland

Two Voices are there; one is of the Sea,
One of the Mountains; each a mighty Voice:
In both from age to age Thou didst rejoice,
They were thy chosen Music, Liberty!
There came a Tyrant, and with holy glee
Thou fought'st against Him; but hast vainly striven;
Thou from thy Alpine Holds at length art driven,
Where not a torrent murmurs heard by thee.
Of one deep bliss thine ear hath been bereft:
Then cleave, O cleave to that which still is left!   10
For, high-souled Maid, what sorrow would it be
That mountain Floods should thunder as before,
And Ocean bellow from his rocky shore,
And neither awful Voice be heard by thee!

November, 1806

Another year!—another deadly blow!
Another mighty Empire overthrown!°
And we are left, or shall be left, alone;
The last that dares to struggle with the Foe.
'Tis well! from this day forward we shall know
That in ourselves our safety must be sought;
That by our own right hands it must be wrought,
That we must stand unpropped, or be laid low.
O Dastard whom such foretaste doth not chear!
We shall exult, if They who rule the land°   10
Be Men who hold its many blessings dear,
Wise, upright, valiant; not a venal Band,
Who are to judge of danger which they fear,°
And honour which they do not understand.

'O Nightingale! thou surely art'

O Nightingale! thou surely art
A Creature of a fiery heart—°
These notes of thine they pierce, and pierce;
Tumultuous harmony and fierce!
Thou sing'st as if the God of wine
Had helped thee to a Valentine;
A song in mockery and despite
Of shades, and dews, and silent Night,
And steady bliss, and all the Loves
Now sleeping in these peaceful groves!   10

I heard a Stockdove sing or say
His homely tale, this very day.
His voice was buried among trees,°
Yet to be come at by the breeze:
He did not cease; but cooed—and cooed;
And somewhat pensively he wooed:
He sang of love with quiet blending,
Slow to begin, and never ending;
Of serious faith, and inward glee;
That was the Song, the Song for me!   20

Gipsies

Yet are they here?—the same unbroken knot
Of human Beings, in the self-same spot!
 Men, Women, Children, yea the frame
 Of the whole Spectacle the same!
Only their fire seems bolder, yielding light:
Now deep and red, the colouring of night;
 That on their Gipsy-faces falls,
 Their bed of straw and blanket-walls.
—Twelve hours, twelve bounteous hours, are gone while I
Have been a Traveller under open sky,   10
 Much witnessing of change and chear,
 Yet as I left I find them here!

The weary Sun betook himself to rest.
—Then issued Vesper from the fulgent West,
 Outshining like a visible God
 The glorious path in which he trod.
And now, ascending, after one dark hour,
And one night's diminution of her power,
 Behold the mighty Moon! this way
 She looks as if at them—but they   20
Regard not her:—oh better wrong and strife
Better vain deeds or evil than such life!
 The silent Heavens have goings on;
 The stars have tasks—but these have none.

St Paul's

 Pressed with conflicting thoughts of love and fear
I parted from thee, Friend! and took my way
Through the great City, pacing with an eye
Downcast, ear sleeping, and feet masterless
That were sufficient guide unto themselves,
And step by step went pensively. Now, mark!
Not how my trouble was entirely hushed,
(That might not be) but how by sudden gift,
Gift of Imagination's holy power,

My soul in her uneasiness received   10
An anchor of stability. It chanced
That while I thus was pacing I raised up
My heavy eyes and instantly beheld,
Saw at a glance in that familiar spot,
A visionary scene—a length of street
Laid open in its morning quietness,
Deep, hollow, unobstructed, vacant, smooth,
And white with winter's purest white, as fair,
As fresh and spotless as he ever sheds
On field or mountain. Moving Form was none   20
Save here and there a shadowy Passenger,
Slow, shadowy, silent, dusky, and beyond
And high above this winding length of street,
This noiseless and unpeopled avenue,
Pure, silent, solemn, beautiful, was seen
The huge majestic Temple of St Paul
In awful sequestration, through a veil,
Through its own sacred veil of falling snow.

Characteristics of a Child three Years old

Loving she is, and tractable, though wild;
And Innocence hath privilege in her
To dignify arch looks and laughing eyes;
And feats of cunning; and the pretty round
Of trespasses, affected to provoke
Mock-chastisement and partnership in play.
And, as a faggot sparkles on the hearth,
Not less if unattended and alone
Than when both young and old sit gathered round
And take delight in its activity,   10
Even so this happy Creature of herself
Is all sufficient: solitude to her°
Is blithe society, who fills the air
With gladness and involuntary songs.
Light are her sallies as the tripping Fawn's
Forth-startled from the fern where she lay couched;
Unthought-of, unexpected as the stir

Of the soft breeze ruffling the meadow flowers;
Or from before it chasing wantonly
The many-coloured images impressed   20
Upon the bosom of a placid lake.

'Surprized by joy—impatient as the Wind'

Surprized by joy—impatient as the Wind
I wished to share the transport—Oh! with whom
But Thee, long buried in the silent Tomb,
That spot which no vicissitude can find?
Love, faithful love recalled thee to my mind—
But how could I forget thee!—Through what power
Even for the least division of an hour,
Have I been so beguiled as to be blind
To my most grievous loss?—That thought's return
Was the worst pang that sorrow ever bore,   10
Save one, one only, when I stood forlorn,
Knowing my heart's best treasure was no more;
That neither present time, nor years unborn
Could to my sight that heavenly face restore.

Yew-Trees

There is a Yew-tree, pride of Lorton Vale,
Which to this day stands single, in the midst
Of its own darkness, as it stood of yore,
Not loth to furnish weapons for the Bands
Of Umfraville or Percy ere they marched
To Scotland's Heaths; or Those that crossed the Sea
And drew their sounding bows at Azincour,
Perhaps at earlier Crecy, or Poictiers.
Of vast circumference and gloom profound
This solitary Tree!—a living thing   10
Produced too slowly ever to decay;
Of form and aspect too magnificent
To be destroyed. But worthier still of note

Are those fraternal Four of Borrowdale,
Joined in one solemn and capacious grove;
Huge trunks!—and each particular trunk a growth
Of intertwisted fibres serpentine
Up-coiling, and inveterately convolved,—
Nor uninformed with Phantasy, and looks
That threaten the prophane;—a pillared shade,   20
Upon whose grassless floor of red-brown hue,
By sheddings from the pining umbrage tinged
Perennially—beneath whose sable roof
Of boughs, as if for festal purpose, decked
With unrejoicing berries, ghostly Shapes
May meet at noontide—Fear and trembling Hope,
Silence and Foresight—Death the Skeleton
And Time the Shadow,—there to celebrate,
As in a natural temple scattered o'er
With altars undisturbed of mossy stone,   30
United worship; or in mute repose
To lie, and listen to the mountain flood
Murmuring from Glaramara's inmost caves.

Yarrow Visited

SEPTEMBER, 1814

And is this—Yarrow?—*This* the Stream
Of which my fancy cherished,
So faithfully, a waking dream?
An image that hath perished!
O that some Minstrel's harp were near,
To utter notes of gladness,
And chase this silence from the air,
That fills my heart with sadness!

Yet why?—a silvery current flows
With uncontrolled meanderings;   10
Nor have these eyes by greener hills
Been soothed, in all my wanderings.

And, through her depths, Saint Mary's Lake
Is visibly delighted;
For not a feature of those hills
Is in the mirror slighted.

A blue sky bends o'er Yarrow vale,
Save where that pearly whiteness
Is round the rising sun diffused,
A tender, hazy brightness;   20
Mild dawn of promise! that excludes
All profitless dejection;
Though not unwilling here to admit
A pensive recollection.

Where was it that the famous Flower
Of Yarrow Vale lay bleeding?
His bed perchance was yon smooth mound
On which the herd is feeding:
And haply from this crystal pool,
Now peaceful as the morning,   30
The Water-wraith ascended thrice—
And gave his doleful warning.

Delicious is the Lay that sings
The haunts of happy Lovers,
The path that leads them to the grove,
The leafy grove that covers:
And Pity sanctifies the Verse
That paints, by strength of sorrow,
The unconquerable strength of love;
Bear witness, rueful Yarrow!   40

But thou, that didst appear so fair
To fond imagination,
Dost rival in the light of day
Her delicate creation:
Meek loveliness is round thee spread,
A softness still and holy;
The grace of forest charms decayed,
And pastoral melancholy.

That Region left, the Vale unfolds
Rich groves of lofty stature,   50
With Yarrow winding through the pomp
Of cultivated nature;
And, rising from those lofty groves,
Behold a Ruin hoary!
The shattered front of Newark's Towers,°
Renowned in Border story.

Fair scenes for childhood's opening bloom,
For sportive youth to stray in;
For manhood to enjoy his strength;
And age to wear away in!   60
Yon Cottage seems a bower of bliss;
It promises protection
To studious ease, and generous cares,
And every chaste affection!

How sweet, on this autumnal day,
The wild wood's fruits to gather,
And on my True-love's forehead plant
A crest of blooming heather!
And what if I enwreathed my own!
'Twere no offence to reason;   70
The sober Hills thus deck their brows
To meet the wintry season.

I see—but not by sight alone,
Loved Yarrow, have I won thee;
A ray of Fancy still survives—
Her sunshine plays upon thee!
Thy ever-youthful waters keep
A course of lively pleasure;
And gladsome notes my lips can breathe,
Accordant to the measure.   80

The vapours linger round the Heights,
They melt, and soon must vanish;
One hour is theirs, not more is mine—
Sad thought, which I would banish,

But that I know, where'er I go
Thy genuine image, Yarrow!
Will dwell with me—to heighten joy,
And cheer my mind in sorrow.

Composed at Cora Linn

IN SIGHT OF WALLACE'S TOWER

'—How Wallace fought for Scotland, left the name
Of Wallace to be found, like a wild flower,
All over his dear Country; left the deeds
Of Wallace, like a family of ghosts,
To people the steep rocks and river banks
Her Natural sanctuaries, with a local soul
Of independence and stern liberty.'

Lord of the Vale! astounding Flood!
The dullest leaf, in this thick wood,
Quakes—conscious of thy power;
The caves reply with hollow moan;
And vibrates, to its central stone,
Yon time-cemented Tower!

And yet how fair the rural scene!
For thou, O Clyde, hast ever been
Beneficent as strong;
Pleased in refreshing dews to steep   10
The little trembling flowers that peep
Thy shelving rocks among.

Hence all who love their country, love
To look on thee—delight to rove
Where they thy voice can hear;
And, to the patriot-warrior's Shade,
Lord of the vale! to Heroes laid
In dust, that voice is dear!

Along thy banks, at dead of night,
Sweeps visibly the Wallace Wight;° 20
Or stands, in warlike vest,
Aloft, beneath the moon's pale beam,
A Champion worthy of the Stream,
Yon grey tower's living crest!

But clouds and envious darkness hide
A Form not doubtfully descried:—
Their transient mission o'er,
O say to what blind regions flee
These Shapes of awful phantasy?
To what untrodden shore? 30

Less than divine command they spurn;
But this we from the mountains learn,
And this the valleys show,
That never will they deign to hold
Communion where the heart is cold
To human weal and woe.

The man of abject soul in vain
Shall walk the Marathonian Plain;
Or thrid the shadowy gloom,
That still invests the guardian Pass, 40
Where stood sublime Leonidas,°
Devoted to the tomb.°

Nor deem that it can aught avail
For such to glide with oar or sail
Beneath the piny wood,
Where Tell once drew, by Uri's lake,°
His vengeful shafts—prepared to slake
Their thirst in Tyrants' blood!

To B. R Haydon, Esq.

High is our calling, Friend!—Creative Art
(Whether the instrument of words she use,
Or pencil pregnant with etherial hues,)
Demands the service of a mind and heart,
Though sensitive, yet, in their weakest part,
Heroically fashioned—to infuse
Faith in the whispers of the lonely Muse,
While the whole world seems adverse to desert:
And, oh! when Nature sinks, as oft she may,
Through long-lived pressure of obscure distress,   10
Still to be strenuous for the bright reward,
And in the soul admit of no decay,—
Brook no continuance of weak-mindedness:
Great is the glory, for the strife is hard!

November 1, 1815

How clear, how keen, how marvellously bright
The effluence from yon distant mountain's head,
Which, strewn with snow as smooth as heaven can shed,
Shines like another Sun—on mortal sight
Uprisen, as if to check approaching night,
And all her twinkling stars. Who now would tread,
If so he might, yon mountain's glittering head—
Terrestrial—but a surface, by the flight
Of sad mortality's earth-sullying wing,
Unswept, unstained? Nor shall the aerial Powers   10
Dissolve that beauty—destined to endure,
White, radiant, spotless, exquisitely pure,
Through all vicissitudes—till genial spring
Have filled the laughing vales with welcome flowers.

'While not a leaf seems faded'

While not a leaf seems faded,—while the fields,
With ripening harvest prodigally fair,
In brightest sunshine bask,—this nipping air,
Sent from some distant clime where Winter wields
His icy scymetar, a foretaste yields
Of bitter change—and bids the Flowers beware;
And whispers to the silent Birds, 'Prepare
Against the threatening Foe your trustiest shields.'
For me, who under kindlier laws belong
To Nature's tuneful quire, this rustling dry   10
Through the green leaves, and yon crystalline sky,
Announce a season potent to renew,
'Mid frost and snow, the instinctive joys of song,—
And nobler cares than listless summer knew.

Ode.—1817

Beneath the concave of an April sky,
When all the fields with freshest green were dight,
Appeared, in presence of that spiritual eye
That aids or supersedes our grosser sight,
The form and rich habiliments of One
Whose countenance bore resemblance to the sun,
When it reveals, in evening majesty,
Features half lost amid their own pure light.
Poised in the middle region of the air
He hung,—then floated with angelic ease,   10
Softening that bright effulgence by degrees,
Until he reached a rock, of summit bare,
Where oft the vent'rous Heifer drinks the summer breeze.
Upon the apex of that lofty cone
Alighted, there the Stranger stood alone;
Fair as a gorgeous Fabric of the East
Suddenly raised by some Enchanter's power,
Where nothing was; and firm as some old Tower

Of Britain's realm, whose leafy crest
Waves high, embellished by a gleaming shower!   20

II

Beneath the shadow of his purple wings
Rested a golden Harp;—he touched the strings;
And, after prelude of unearthly sound
Poured through the echoing hills around,
He sang, 'No wintry desolations,
Scorching blight, or noxious dew,
Affect my native habitations;
Buried in glory, far beyond the scope
Of man's enquiring gaze, and imaged to his hope
(Alas, how faintly!) in the hue   30
Profound of night's ethereal blue;
And in the aspect of each radiant orb;—
Some fixed, some wandering with no timid curb;
But wandering orb and fixed, to mortal eye,
Blended in absolute serenity,
And free from semblance of decline;—
So wills eternal Love with Power divine.

III

And what if his presiding breath
Impart a sympathetic motion
Unto the gates of life and death,   40
Throughout the bounds of earth and ocean;
Though all that feeds on nether air,
Howe'er magnificent or fair,
Grows but to perish, and entrust
Its ruins to their kindred dust;
Yet, by the Almighty's ever-during care,
Her procreant vigils Nature keeps
Amid the unfathomable deeps;
And saves the peopled fields of earth
From dread of emptiness or dearth.   50
Thus, in their stations, lifting tow'rd the sky
The foliaged head in cloud-like majesty,
The shadow-casting race of Trees survive:
Thus, in the train of Spring, arrive

Sweet Flowers;—what living eye hath viewed
Their myriads?—endlessly renewed,
Wherever strikes the sun's glad ray:
Where'er the joyous water stray;
Wherever sportive zephyrs bend
Their course, or genial showers descend!   60
Rejoice, O men! the very Angels quit
Their mansions unsusceptible of change,
Amid your pleasant bowers to sit,
And through your sweet vicissitudes to range!'

IV

O, nursed at happy distance from the cares
Of a too-anxious world, mild pastoral Muse!
That, to the sparkling crown Urania wears,°
And to her sister Clio's laurel wreath,
Prefer'st a garland culled from purple heath,
Or blooming thicket moist with morning dews;   70
Was such bright Spectacle vouchsafed to me?
And was it granted to the simple ear
Of thy contented Votary
Such melody to hear!
Him rather suits it, side by side with thee,
Wrapped in a fit of pleasing indolence,
While thy tired lute hangs on the hawthorn tree,
To lie and listen, till o'er-drowsed sense
Sinks, hardly conscious of the influence,
To the soft murmur of the vagrant Bee.   80
—A slender sound! yet hoary Time
Doth, to the *Soul* exalt it with the chime
Of all his years;—a company
Of ages coming, ages gone;
Nations from before them sweeping—
Regions in destruction steeping;—
But every awful note in unison
With that faint utterance, which tells
Of treasure sucked from buds and bells,
For the pure keeping of those waxen cells;   90
Where She, a statist prudent to confer
Upon the public weal; a warrior bold,—

Radiant all over with unburnished gold,
And armed with living spear for mortal fight;
   A cunning forager
That spreads no waste;—a social builder, one
In whom all busy offices unite
With all fine functions that afford delight,
Safe through the winter storm in quiet dwells!

          V

And is She brought within the power   100
Of vision?—o'er this tempting flower
Hovering until the petals stay
Her flight, and take its voice away?
Observe each wing—a tiny van!—
The structure of her laden thigh;
How fragile!—yet of ancestry
Mysteriously remote and high;
High as the imperial front of man,
The roseate bloom on woman's cheek;
The soaring eagle's curved beak;   110
The white plumes of the floating swan;
Old as the tyger's paws, the lion's mane
Ere shaken by that mood of stern disdain
At which the desart trembles.—Humming Bee!
Thy sting was needless then, perchance unknown;
The seeds of malice were not sown;
All creatures met in peace, from fierceness free,
And no pride blended with their dignity.
—Tears had not broken from their source;
Nor anguish strayed from her Tartarian den:°   120
The golden years maintained a course
Not undiversified, though smooth and even;
We were not mocked with glimpse and shadow then;
Bright Seraphs mixed familiarly with men;
And earth and stars composed a universal heaven!

Ode

I

Within the mind strong fancies work,
A deep delight the bosom thrills,
Oft as I pass along the fork
Of these fraternal hills:
Where, save the rugged road, we find
No appanage of human kind;
Nor hint of man, if stone or rock
Seem not his handy-work to mock
By something cognizably shaped;
Mockery—or model—roughly hewn,   10
And left as if by earthquake strewn,
Or from the Flood escaped:—
Altars for Druid service fit;
(But where no fire was ever lit
Unless the glow-worm to the skies
Thence offer nightly sacrifice;)
Wrinkled Egyptian monument;
Green moss-grown tower; or hoary tent;
Tents of a camp that never shall be raised;
On which four thousand years have gazed!   20

II

Ye plowshares sparkling on the slopes!
Ye snow-white lambs that trip
Imprisoned 'mid the formal props
Of restless ownership!
Ye trees that may to-morrow fall,
To feed the instatiate Prodigal!
Lawns, houses, chattels, groves, and fields,
All that the fertile valley shields;
Wages of folly—baits of crime;—
Of life's uneasy game the stake,—   30
Playthings that keep the eyes awake
Of drowsy, dotard Time;—

O care! O guilt!—O vales and plains,
Here, 'mid his own unvexed domains,
A Genius dwells, that can subdue
At once all memory of You,—
Most potent when mists veil the sky,
Mists that distort and magnify;
While the coarse rushes, to the sweeping breeze,
Sigh forth their ancient melodies!   40

                              III

List to those shriller notes!—*that* march
Perchance was on the blast,
When through this Height's inverted arch
Rome's earliest legion passed!
—They saw, adventurously impelled,
And older eyes than theirs beheld,
This block—and yon whose Church-like frame
Gives to the savage Pass its name.
Aspiring Road! that lov'st to hide
Thy daring in a vapoury bourn,   50
Not seldom may the hour return
When thou shalt be my Guide;
And I (as often we find cause,
When life is at a weary pause,
And we have panted up the hill
Of duty with reluctant will)
Be thankful, even though tired and faint,
For the rich bounties of Constraint;
Whence oft invigorating transports flow
That Choice lacked courage to bestow!   60

                              IV

My soul was grateful for delight
That wore a threatening brow;
A veil is lifted—can she slight
The scene that opens now?
Though habitation none appear,
The greenness tells, man must be there;
The shelter—that the perspective
Is of the clime in which we live;

Where Toil pursues his daily round;
Where Pity sheds sweet tears, and Love,   70
In woodbine bower or birchen grove,
Inflicts his tender wound.
—Who comes not hither ne'er shall know
How beautiful the world below;
Nor can he guess how lightly leaps
The brook adown the rocky steeps.
Farewell thou desolate Domain!
Hope, pointing to the cultured Plain,
Carols like a shepherd boy;
And who is she?—can that be Joy?   80
Who, with a sun-beam for her guide,
Smoothly skims the meadows wide;
While Faith, from yonder opening cloud,
To hill and vale proclaims aloud,
'Whate'er the weak may dread the wicked dare,
Thy lot, O man, is good, thy portion fair!'

Ode

COMPOSED UPON AN EVENING OF EXTRAORDINARY
SPLENDOR AND BEAUTY

I

Had this effulgence disappeared
With flying haste, I might have sent
Among the speechless clouds a look
Of blank astonishment;
But 'tis endued with power to stay,
And sanctify one closing day,
That frail Mortality may see,
What is?—ah no, but what *can* be!
Time was when field and watery cove
With modulated echoes rang,   10
While choirs of fervent Angels sang
Their vespers in the grove;
Or, ranged like stars along some sovereign height,
Warbled, for heaven above and earth below,

Strains suitable to both.—Such holy rite,
Methinks, if audibly repeated now
From hill or valley, could not move
Sublimer transport, purer love,
Than doth this silent spectacle—the gleam—
The shadow—and the peace supreme!   20

II

No sound is uttered,—but a deep
And solemn harmony pervades
The hollow vale from steep to steep,
And penetrates the glades.
Far-distant images draw nigh,
Called forth by wond'rous potency
Of beamy radiance, that imbues
Whate'er it strikes, with gem-like hues!
In vision exquisitely clear,
Herds range along the mountain side;   30
And glistening antlers are descried;
And gilded flocks appear.
Thine is the tranquil hour, purpureal Eve!
But long as god-like wish, or hope divine,
Informs my spirit, ne'er can I believe
That this magnificence is wholly thine!
—From worlds not quickened by the sun
A portion of the gift is won;
An intermingling of Heaven's pomp is spread
On ground which British shepherds tread!   40

III

And, if there be whom broken ties
Afflict, or injuries assail,
Yon hazy ridges to their eyes,
Present a glorious scale,
Climbing suffused with sunny air,
To stop—no record hath told where!
And tempting fancy to ascend,
And with immortal spirits blend!
—Wings at my shoulder seem to play;
But, rooted here, I stand and gaze   50

On those bright steps that heaven-ward raise
Their practicable way.
Come forth, ye drooping old men, look abroad
And see to what fair countries ye are bound!
And if some Traveller, weary of his road,
Hath slept since noon-tide on the grassy ground,
Ye Genii! to his covert speed;
And wake him with such gentle heed
As may attune his soul to meet the dow'r
Bestowed on this transcendent hour!   60

IV

Such hues from their celestial Urn
Were wont to stream before my eye,
Where'er it wandered in the morn
Of blissful infancy.
This glimpse of glory, why renewed?
Nay, rather speak with gratitude;
For, if a vestige of those gleams
Survived, 'twas only in my dreams.
Dread Power! whom peace and calmness serve
No less than Nature's threatening voice,   70
If aught unworthy be my choice,
From THEE if I would swerve,
O, let thy grace remind me of the light,
Full early lost and fruitlessly deplored;
Which, at this moment, on my waking sight
Appears to shine, by miracle restored!
My soul, though yet confined to earth,
Rejoices in a second birth;
—'Tis past, the visionary splendour fades,
And Night approaches with her shades.   80

Sequel to [Beggars]

COMPOSED MANY YEARS AFTER

Where are they now, those wanton Boys?°
For whose free range the dædal earth°
Was filled with animated toys,
And implements of frolic mirth;
With tools for ready wit to guide;
And ornaments of seemlier pride,
More fresh, more bright, than Princes wear;
For what one moment flung aside,
Another could repair;
What good or evil have they seen   10
Since I their pastime witnessed here,
Their daring wiles, their sportive cheer?
I ask—but all is dark between!

Spirits of beauty and of grace!
Associates in that eager chase;
Ye, by a course to nature true,
The sterner judgment can subdue;
And waken a relenting smile
When she encounters fraud or guile;
And sometimes ye can charm away   20
The inward mischief, or allay,
Ye, who within the blameless mind
Your favourite seat of empire find!

They met me in a genial hour,
When universal nature breathed
As with the breath of one sweet flower,—
A time to overrule the power
Of discontent, and check the birth
Of thoughts with better thoughts at strife,
The most familiar bane of life   30
Since parting Innocence bequeathed
Mortality to Earth!
Soft clouds, the whitest of the year,
Sailed through the sky—the brooks ran clear;

The lambs from rock to rock were bounding;
With songs the budded groves resounding;
And to my heart is still endeared
The faith with which it then was cheered;
The faith which saw that gladsome pair
Walk through the fire with unsinged hair.   40
Or, if such thoughts must needs deceive,
Kind Spirits! may we not believe
That they, so happy and so fair,
Through your sweet influence, and the care
Of pitying Heaven, at least were free
From touch of *deadly* injury?
Destined, whate'er their earthly doom,
For mercy and immortal bloom!

The River Duddon

CONCLUSION

I thought of Thee, my partner and my guide,
As being past away.—Vain sympathies!
For, *backward*, Duddon! as I cast my eyes,
I see what was, and is, and will abide;
Still glides the Stream, and shall for ever glide;°
The Form remains, the Function never dies;
While *we*, the brave, the mighty, and the wise,
We Men, who in our morn of youth defied
The elements, must vanish;—be it so!
Enough, if something from our hands have power   10
To live, and act, and serve the future hour;
And if, as tow'rd the silent tomb we go,
Thro' love, thro' hope, and faith's transcendent dower,
We feel that we are greater than we know.

Bruges

Bruges I saw attired with golden light
(Streamed from the west) as with a robe of power:
'Tis passed away;—and now the sunless hour,
That slowly introducing peaceful night
Best suits with fallen grandeur, to my sight
Offers her beauty, her magnificence,
And all the graces left her for defence
Against the injuries of time, the spite
Of Fortune, and the desolating storms
Of future War. Advance not—spare to hide,　10
O gentle Power of Darkness! these mild hues;
Obscure not yet these silent avenues
Of stateliest Architecture, where the forms
Of Nun-like Females, with soft motion, glide!

Bruges

The Spirit of Antiquity, enshrined
In sumptuous Buildings, vocal in sweet Song
And Tales transmitted through the popular tongue,
And with devout solemnities entwined,
Strikes at the seat of grace within the mind:
Hence Forms that slide with swan-like ease along;
Hence motions, even amid the vulgar throng,
To an harmonious decency confined:
As if the Streets were consecrated ground,
The City one vast Temple—dedicate　10
To mutual respect in thought and deed;
To leisure, to forbearances sedate;
To social cares from jarring passions freed;
A nobler peace than that in desarts found!

Mutability

From low to high doth dissolution climb,
And sinks from high to low, along a scale
Of awful notes, whose concord shall not fail;
A musical but melancholy chime,
Which they can hear who meddle not with crime,
Nor avarice, nor over-anxious care.
Truth fails not; but her outward forms that bear
The longest date do melt like frosty rime,
That in the morning whitened hill and plain
And is no more; drop like the tower sublime   10
Of yesterday, which royally did wear
Its crown of weeds, but could not even sustain
Some casual shout that broke the silent air,
Or the unimaginable touch of Time.

To the Torrent at the Devil's Bridge, North Wales

How art thou named? In search of what strange land
From what huge height, descending? Can such force
Of waters issue from a British source,
Or hath not Pindus fed Thee, where the band°
Of Patriots scoop their freedom out, with hand
Desperate as thine? Or come the incessant shocks
From that young Stream, that smites the throbbing rocks°
Of Viamala? There I seem to stand,
As in Life's Morn; permitted to behold,
From the dread chasm, woods climbing above woods   10
In pomp that fades not, everlasting snows,
And skies that ne'er relinquish their repose;
Such power possess the Family of floods
Over the minds of Poets, young or old!

Composed Among the Ruins of a Castle in North Wales

Through shattered galleries, 'mid roofless halls,
Wandering with timid footstep oft betrayed,

The Stranger sighs, nor scruples to upbraid
Old Time, though He, gentlest among the Thralls
Of Destiny, upon these wounds hath laid
His lenient touches, soft as light that falls,
From the wan Moon, upon the Towers and Walls,
Light deepening the profoundest sleep of shade.
Relic of Kings! Wreck of forgotten Wars,
To winds abandoned and the prying Stars,   10
Time *loves* Thee! at his call the Seasons twine
Luxuriant wreaths around thy forehead hoar;
And, though past pomp no changes can restore,
A soothing recompense, his gift, is Thine!

To ——

O dearer far than light and life are dear,
Full oft our human foresight I deplore;
Trembling, through my unworthiness, with fear
That friends, by death disjoined, may meet no more!

Misgivings, hard to vanquish or control,
Mix with the day, and cross the hour of rest;
While all the future, for thy purer soul,
With 'sober certainties' of love is blest.°

If a faint sigh, not meant for human ear,
Tell that these words thy humbleness offend,   10
Cherish me still—else faltering in the rear
Of a steep march; uphold me to the end.

Peace settles where the Intellect is meek,
And Love is dutiful in thought and deed;
Through Thee communion with that Love I seek;
The faith Heaven strengthens where *he* moulds the creed.

To ——

Let other Bards of Angels sing,
    Bright Suns without a spot;
But thou art no such perfect Thing;
    Rejoice that thou art not!

Such if thou wert in all men's view,
   A universal show,
What would my Fancy have to do,
   My Feelings to bestow?

The world denies that Thou art fair;
   So, Mary, let it be   10
If nought in loveliness compare
   With what thou art to me.

True beauty dwells in deep retreats,
   Whose veil is unremoved
Till heart with heart in concord beats,
   And the Lover is beloved.

'Once I could hail (howe'er serene the sky)'

'Late, late yestreen I saw the new moone
Wi' the auld moone in hir arme.'
        Ballad of Sir Patrick Spence,
        Percy's Reliques

Once I could hail (howe'er serene the sky)
The Moon re-entering her monthly round,
No faculty yet given me to espy
The dusky Shape within her arms imbound,
That thin memento of effulgence lost
Which some have named her Predecessor's Ghost.

Young, like the Crescent that above me shone,
Nought I perceived within it dull or dim;
All that appeared was suitable to One
Whose fancy had a thousand fields to skim;   10
To expectations spreading with wild growth,
And hope that kept with me her plighted troth.

I saw (ambition quickening at the view)
A silver boat launched on a boundless flood;
A pearly crest, like Dian's when it threw°
Its brightest splendour round a leafy wood;

But not a hint from under-ground, no sign
Fit for the glimmering brow of Proserpine.°

Or was it Dian's self that seemed to move
Before me? nothing blemished the fair sight;   20
On her I looked whom jocund Fairies love,
Cynthia, who puts the *little* stars to flight,
And by that thinning magnifies the great,
For exaltation of her sovereign state.

And when I learned to mark the spectral Shape
As each new Moon obeyed the call of Time,
If gloom fell on me, swift was my escape;
Such happy privilege hath Life's gay Prime,
To see or not to see, as best may please
A buoyant Spirit, and a heart at ease.   30

Now, dazzling Stranger! when thou meet'st my glance,
Thy dark Associate ever I discern;
Emblem of thoughts too eager to advance
While I salute my joys, thoughts sad or stern;
Shades of past bliss, or phantoms that to gain
Their fill of promised lustre wait in vain.

So changes mortal Life with fleeting years;
A mournful change, should Reason fail to bring
The timely insight that can temper fears,
And from vicissitude remove its sting;   40
While Faith aspires to seats in that Domain
Where joys are perfect, neither wax nor wane.

'Scorn not the Sonnet'

Scorn not the Sonnet; Critic, you have frowned,
Mindless of its just honours;—with this Key
Shakespeare unlocked his heart; the melody
Of this small Lute gave ease to Petrarch's wound;

A thousand times this Pipe did Tasso sound;
Camöens soothed with it an Exile's grief;
The Sonnet glittered a gay myrtle Leaf
Amid the cypress with which Dante crowned
His visionary brow: a glow-worm Lamp,
It cheered mild Spenser, called from Faery-land   10
To struggle through dark ways; and when a damp
Fell round the path of Milton, in his hand
The Thing became a Trumpet, whence he blew
Soul-animating strains—alas, too few!

Incident at Bruges

In Brugès town is many a street
   Whence busy life hath fled;
Where, without hurry, noiseless feet,
   The grass-grown pavement tread.
There heard we, halting in the shade
   Flung from a Convent-tower,
A harp that tuneful prelude made
   To a voice of thrilling power.

The measure, simple truth to tell,
   Was fit for some gay throng;   10
Though from the same grim turret fell
   The shadow and the song.
When silent were both voice and chords
   The strain seemed doubly dear,
Yet sad as sweet, for *English* words
   Had fallen upon the ear.

It was a breezy hour of eve;
   And pinnacle and spire
Quivered and seemed almost to heave,
   Clothed with innocuous fire;   20
But where we stood, the setting sun
   Showed little of his state;
And, if the glory reached the Nun,
   'Twas through an iron grate.

Not always is the heart unwise,
    Nor pity idly born,
If even a passing Stranger sighs
    For them who do not mourn.
Sad is thy doom, self-solaced dove,
    Captive, whoe'er thou be!   30
Oh! what is beauty, what is love,
    And opening life to thee?

Such feeling pressed upon my soul,
    A feeling sanctified
By one soft trickling tear that stole
    From the Maiden at my side;
Less tribute could she pay than this,
    Borne gaily o'er the sea,
Fresh from the beauty and the bliss
    Of English liberty?   40

On the Power of Sound

ARGUMENT

The Ear addressed, as occupied by a spiritual functionary, in communion with
sounds, individual, or combined in studied harmony.—Sources and effects of
those sounds (to the close of 6th Stanza).—The power of music, whence
proceeding, exemplified in the idiot.—Origin of music, and its effect in early
ages—how produced (to the middle of 10th Stanza).—The mind recalled to
sounds acting casually and severally.—Wish uttered (11th Stanza) that these
could be united into a scheme or system for moral interests and intellectual
contemplation.—(Stanza 12th). The Pythagorean theory of numbers and music,
with their supposed power over the motions of the universe—imaginations
consonant with such a theory.—Wish expressed (in 11th Stanza) realised, in
some degree, by the representation of all sounds under the form of thanksgiving
to the Creator.—(Last Stanza) the destruction of earth and the planetary
system—the survival of audible harmony, and its support in the Divine Nature, as
revealed in Holy Writ.

I

Thy functions are etherial,
As if within thee dwelt a glancing Mind,
Organ of Vision! And a Spirit aerial
Informs the cell of hearing, dark and blind;

Intricate labyrinth, more dread for thought
To enter than oracular cave;
Strict passage, through which sighs are brought,
And whispers, for the heart, their slave;
And shrieks, that revel in abuse
Of shivering flesh; and warbled air,   10
Whose piercing sweetness can unloose
The chains of frenzy, or entice a smile
Into the ambush of despair;
Hosannas pealing down the long-drawn aisle,°
And requiems answered by the pulse that beats
Devoutly, in life's last retreats!

II

The headlong Streams and Fountains
Serve Thee, Invisible Spirit, with untired powers;
Cheering the wakeful Tent on Syrian mountains,
They lull perchance ten thousand thousand flowers.   20
That roar, the prowling Lion's *Here I am*,
How fearful to the desert wide!
That bleat, how tender! of the Dam
Calling a straggler to her side.
Shout, Cuckoo! let the vernal soul
Go with thee to the frozen zone;
Toll from thy loftiest perch, lone Bell-bird, toll!
At the still hour to Mercy dear,
Mercy from her twilight throne
Listening to Nun's faint sob of holy fear,   30
To Sailor's prayer breathed from a darkening sea,
Or Widow's cottage lullaby.

III

Ye Voices, and ye Shadows,
And Images of voice—to hound and horn
From rocky steep and rock-bestudded meadows
Flung back, and, in the sky's blue caves, reborn,
On with your pastime! till the church-tower bells
A greeting give of *measured* glee;
And milder echoes from their cells
Repeat the bridal symphony.   40

Then, or far earlier, let us rove
Where mists are breaking up or gone,
And from aloft look down into a cove
Besprinkled with a careless quire,
Happy Milk-maids, one by one
Scattering a ditty each to her desire,
A liquid concert matchless by nice Art,
A stream as if from one full heart.

IV

Blest be the song that brightens
The blind Man's gloom, exalts the Veteran's mirth: 50
Unscorned the Peasant's whistling breath, that lightens
His duteous toil of furrowing the green earth.
For the tired Slave, Song lifts the languid oar,
And bids it aptly fall, with chime
That beautifies the fairest shore,
And mitigates the harshest clime.
Yon Pilgrims see—in lagging file
They move; but soon the appointed way
A choral *Ave Marie* shall beguile,
And to their hope the distant shrine   60
Glisten with a livelier ray:
Nor friendless He, the Prisoner of the Mine,
Who from the well-spring of his own clear breast
Can draw, and sing his griefs to rest.

V

When civic renovation
Dawns on a kingdom, and for needful haste
Best eloquence avails not, Inspiration
Mounts with a tune, that travels like a blast
Piping through cave and battlemented tower;
Then starts the Sluggard, pleased to meet   70
That voice of Freedom, in its power
Of promises, shrill, wild, and sweet!
Who, from a martial *pageant*, spreads
Incitements of a battle-day,
Thrilling the unweaponed crowd with plumeless heads;
Even She whose Lydian airs inspire°

Peaceful striving, gentle play
Of timid hope and innocent desire
Shot from the dancing Graces, as they move
Fanned by the plausive wings of Love.   80

VI

How oft along thy mazes,
Regent of Sound, have dangerous Passions trod!
O Thou, through whom the Temple rings with praises,
And blackening clouds in thunder speak of God,
Betray not by the cozenage of sense
Thy Votaries, wooingly resigned
To a voluptuous influence
That taints the purer, better mind;
But lead sick Fancy to a harp
That hath in noble tasks been tried;   90
And, if the Virtuous feel a pang too sharp,
Soothe it into patience,—stay
The uplifted arm of Suicide;
And let some mood of thine in firm array
Knit every thought the impending issue needs,
Ere Martyr burns, or Patriot bleeds!

VII

As Conscience, to the centre
Of Being, smites with irrestible pain,
So shall a solemn cadence, if it enter
The mouldy vaults of the dull Idiot's brain,   100
Transmute him to a wretch from quiet hurled—
Convulsed as by a jarring din;
And then aghast, as at the world
Of reason partially let in
By concords winding with a sway
Terrible for sense and soul!
Or, awed he weeps, struggling to quell dismay.
Point not these mysteries to an Art
Lodged above the starry pole;
Pure modulations flowing from the heart   110
Of divine Love, where Wisdom, Beauty, Truth
With Order dwell, in endless youth?

VIII

Oblivion may not cover
All treasures hoarded by the Miser, Time.
Orphean Insight! Truth's undaunted Lover,
To the first leagues of tutored passion climb,
When Music delighted within this grosser sphere
Her subtle essence to enfold,
And Voice and Shell drew forth a tear
Softer than Nature's self could mould.   120
Yet *strenuous* was the infant Age:
Art, daring because souls could feel,
Stirred nowhere but an urgent equipage
Of rapt imagination sped her march
Through the realms of woe and weal:
Hell to the lyre bowed low; the upper arch°
Rejoiced that clamorous spell and magic verse
Her wan disasters could disperse.

IX

The GIFT to King Amphion°
That walled a city with its melody   130
Was for belief no dream; thy skill, Arion!°
Could humanise the creatures of the sea,
Where men were monsters. A last grace he craves,
Leave for one chant;—the dulcet sound°
Steals from the deck o'er willing waves,
And listening Dolphins gather round.
Self-cast, as with a desperate course,
'Mid that strange audience, he bestrides
A proud One docile as a managed horse;
And singing, while the accordant hand   140
Sweeps his harp, the Master rides;
So shall he touch at length a friendly strand,
And he, with his Preserver, shine star-bright
In memory, through silent night.

X

The pipe of Pan, to Shepherds
Couched in the shadow of Menalian Pines,°
Was passing sweet; the eyeballs of the Leopards,

That in high triumph drew the Lord of vines,
How did they sparkle to the cymbal's clang!
While Fauns and Satyrs beat the ground°   150
In cadence,—and Silenus swang
This way and that, with wild-flowers crowned.
To life, to *life* give back thine Ear:
Ye who are longing to be rid
Of Fable, though to truth subservient, hear
The little sprinkling of cold earth that fell
Echoed from the coffin lid;
The Convict's summons in the steeple knell.
'The vain distress-gun,' from a leeward shore,
Repeated—heard, and heard no more!   160

XI

For terror, joy, or pity,
Vast is the compass, and the swell of notes:
From the Babe's first cry to voice of regal City,
Rolling a solemn sea-like bass, that floats
Far as the woodlands—with the trill to blend
Of that shy Songstress, whose love-tale
Might tempt an Angel to descend,
While hovering o'er the moonlight vale.
O for some soul-affecting scheme
Of *moral* music, to unite   170
Wanderers whose portion is the faintest dream
Of memory!—O that they might stoop to bear
Chains, such precious chains of sight
As laboured minstrelsies through ages wear!
O for a balance fit the truth to tell
Of the Unsubstantial, pondered well!

XII

By one pervading Spirit
Of tones and numbers all things are controlled,
As Sages taught, where faith was found to merit
Initiation in that mystery old.   180
The Heavens, whose aspect makes our minds as still
As they themselves *appear* to be,
Innumerable voices fill

With everlasting harmony;
The towering Headlands, crowned with mist,
Their feet among the billows, know
That Ocean is a mighty harmonist;
Thy pinions, universal Air,
Ever waving to and fro,
Are delegates of harmony, and bear   190
Strains that support the Seasons in their round;
Stern Winter loves a dirge-like sound.

XIII

Break forth into thanksgiving,
Ye banded Instruments of wind and chords;
Unite, to magnify the Ever-living,
Your inarticulate notes with the voice of words!
Nor hushed be service from the lowing mead,
Nor mute the forest hum of noon;
Thou too be heard, lone Eagle! freed°
From snowy peak and cloud, attune   200
Thy hungry barkings to the hymn
Of joy, that from her utmost walls
The six-days' Work, by flaming Seraphim,
Transmits to Heaven! As Deep to Deep
Shouting through one valley calls,
All worlds, all natures, mood and measure keep
For praise and ceaseless gratulation, poured
Into the ear of God, their Lord!

XIV

A Voice to Light gave Being;
To Time, and Man his earth-born Chronicler;   210
A Voice shall finish doubt and dim foreseeing,
And sweep away life's visionary stir;
The Trumpet (we, intoxicate with pride,
Arm at its blast for deadly wars)
To archangelic lips applied,
The grave shall open, quench the stars.
O Silence! are Man's noisy years°
No more than moments of thy life?
Is Harmony, blest Queen of smiles and tears,

With her smooth tones and discords just,   220
Tempered into rapturous strife,
Thy destined Bond-slave? No! though Earth be dust
And vanish, though the Heavens dissolve, her stay
Is in the WORD, that shall not pass away.

Yarrow Revisited

[The following Stanzas are a memorial of a day passed with Sir Walter Scott, and
other Friends visiting the Banks of the Yarrow under his guidance, immediately
before his departure from Abbotsford, for Naples.

The title *Yarrow Revisited* will stand in no need of explanation, for Readers
acquainted with the Author's previous poems suggested by that celebrated
Stream.]

The gallant Youth, who may have gained,
    Or seeks, a 'Winsome Marrow,'°
Was but an Infant in the lap
    When first I looked on Yarrow;
Once more, by Newark's Castle-gate
    Long left without a Warder,
I stood, looked, listened, and with Thee,
    Great Minstrel of the Border!°

Grave thoughts ruled wide on that sweet day,
    Their dignity installing   10
In gentle bosoms, while sere leaves
    Were on the bough, or falling;
But breezes played, and sunshine gleamed—
    The forest to embolden;
Reddened the fiery hues, and shot
    Transparence through the golden.

For busy thoughts the Stream flowed on
    In foamy agitation;
And slept in many a crystal pool
    For quiet contemplation: 20
No public and no private care
    The freeborn mind enthralling,
We made a day of happy hours,
    Our happy days recalling.

Brisk Youth appeared, the Morn of youth,
  With freaks of graceful folly,—
Life's temperate Noon, her sober Eve,
  Her Night not melancholy,
Past, present, future, all appeared
  In harmony united   30
Like guests that meet, and some from far,
  By cordial love invited.

And if, as Yarrow, through the woods
  And down the meadow ranging,
Did meet us with unaltered face,
  Though we were changed and changing;
If, *then*, some natural shadows spread
  Our inward prospect over,
The soul's deep valley was not slow
  Its brightness to recover.   40

Eternal blessings on the Muse,
  And her divine employment!
The blameless Muse, who trains her Sons
  For hope and calm enjoyment;
Albeit sickness lingering yet
  Has o'er their pillow brooded;
And Care waylay their steps—a Sprite
  Not easily eluded.

For thee, O SCOTT! compelled to change°
  Green Eildon-hill and Cheviot   50
For warm Vesuvio's vine-clad slopes;
  And leave thy Tweed and Teviot
For mild Sorento's breezy waves;
  May classic Fancy, linking
With native Fancy her fresh aid,
  Preserve thy heart from sinking!

O! while they minister to thee,
  Each vying with the other,
May Health return to mellow Age,
  With Strength, her venturous brother;   60

And Tiber, and each brook and rill
　　Renowned in song and story,
With unimagined beauty shine,
　　Nor lose one ray of glory!

For Thou, upon a hundred streams,
　　By tales of love and sorrow,
Of faithful love, undaunted truth,
　　Hast shed the power of Yarrow;
And streams unknown, hills yet unseen,
　　Where'er thy path invite thee,   70
At parent Nature's grateful call,
　　With gladness must requite Thee.

A gracious welcome shall be thine,
　　Such looks of love and honour
As thy own Yarrow gave to me
　　When first I gazed upon her;
Beheld what I had feared to see,
　　Unwilling to surrender
Dreams treasured up from early days,
　　The holy and the tender.   80

And what, for this frail world, were all
　　That mortals do or suffer,
Did no responsive harp, no pen,
　　Memorial tribute offer?
Yea, what were mighty Nature's self?
　　Her features, could they win us,
Unhelped by the poetic voice
　　That hourly speaks within us?

Nor deem that localised Romance
　　Plays false with our affections;   90
Unsanctifies our tears—made sport
　　For fanciful dejections:
Ah, no! the visions of the past
　　Sustain the heart in feeling
Life as she is—our changeful Life,
　　With friends and kindred dealing.

Bear witness, Ye, whose thoughts that day
   In Yarrow's groves were centered;
Who through the silent portal arch
   Of mouldering Newark entered,   100
And clomb the winding stair that once
   Too timidly was mounted
By the 'last Minstrel,' (not the last)
   Ere he his Tale recounted!

Flow on for ever, Yarrow Stream!
   Fulfil thy pensive duty,
Well pleased that future Bards should chant
   For simple hearts thy beauty,
To dream-light dear while yet unseen,
   Dear to the common sunshine,   110
And dearer still, as now I feel,
   To memory's shadowy moonshine!

On the Departure of Sir Walter Scott from Abbotsford, for Naples

A trouble, not of clouds, or weeping rain,
Nor of the setting sun's pathetic light
Engendered, hangs o'er Eildon's triple height:
Spirits of Power, assembled there, complain
For kindred Power departing from their sight;
While Tweed, best pleased in chanting a blithe strain,
Saddens his voice again, and yet again.
Lift up your hearts, ye Mourners! for the might
Of the whole world's good wishes with him goes;
Blessings and prayers in nobler retinue   10
Than sceptred King or laurelled Conqueror knows,
Follow this wondrous Potentate. Be true,
Ye winds of ocean, and the midland sea,
Wafting your Charge to soft Parthenope!°

'Calm is the fragrant air, and loth to lose'

Calm is the fragrant air, and loth to lose
Day's grateful warmth, tho' moist with falling dews.
Look for the stars, you'll say that there are none;
Look up a second time, and, one by one,
You mark them twinkling out with silvery light,
And wonder how they could elude the sight.
The birds, of late so noisy in their bowers,
Warbled a while with faint and fainter powers,
But now are silent as the dim-seen flowers:
Nor does the Village Church-clock's iron tone   10
The time's and season's influence disown;
Nine beats distinctly to each other bound
In drowsy sequence; how unlike the sound
That, in rough winter, oft inflicts a fear
On fireside Listeners, doubting what they hear!
The Shepherd, bent on rising with the sun,
Had closed his door before the day was done,
And now with thankful heart to bed doth creep,
And join his little Children in their sleep.
The Bat, lured forth where trees the lane o'ershade,   20
Flits and reflits along the close arcade;
Far-heard the Dor-hawk chases the white Moth
With burring note, which Industry and Sloth
Might both be pleased with, for it suits them both.
Wheels and the tread of hoofs are heard no more;
One Boat there was, but it will touch the shore
With the next dipping of its slackened oar;
Faint sound, that, for the gayest of the gay,
Might give to serious thought a moment's sway,
As a last token of Man's toilsome day!   30

Airey-Force Valley

——Not a breath of air
Ruffles the bosom of this leafy glen.
From the brook's margin, wide around, the trees
Are stedfast as the rocks; the brook itself,

Old as the hills that feed it from afar,
Doth rather deepen than disturb the calm
Where all things else are still and motionless.
And yet, even now, a little breeze, perchance
Escaped from boisterous winds that rage without,
Has entered, by the sturdy oaks unfelt,   10
But to its gentle touch how sensitive
Is the light ash! that, pendent from the brow
Of yon dim cave, in seeming silence makes
A soft eye-music of slow-waving boughs,
Powerful almost as vocal harmony
To stay the wanderer's steps and soothe his thoughts.

Extempore Effusion Upon the Death of James Hogg

When first, descending from the moorlands,°
I saw the Stream of Yarrow glide
Along a bare and open valley,
The Ettrick Shepherd was my guide.

When last along its banks I wandered,
Through groves that had begun to shed
Their golden leaves upon the pathways,
My steps the border minstrel led.

The mighty Minstrel breathes no longer,
'Mid mouldering ruins low he lies;°   10
And death upon the braes of Yarrow,
Has closed the Shepherd-poet's eyes:°

Nor has the rolling year twice measured,
From sign to sign, its stedfast course,
Since every mortal power of Coleridge
Was frozen at its marvellous source;

The rapt One, of the godlike forehead,
The heaven-eyed creature sleeps in earth:
And Lamb, the frolic and the gentle,°
Has vanished from his lonely hearth.   20

Like clouds that rake the mountain-summits,
Or waves that own no curbing hand,
How fast has brother followed brother,
From sunshine to the sunless land!

Yet I, whose lids from infant slumbers
Were earlier raised, remain to hear
A timid voice, that asks in whispers,
'Who next will drop and disappear?'

Our haughty life is crowned with darkness,
Like London with its own black wreath,   30
On which with thee, O Crabbe! forth-looking,
I gazed from Hampstead's breezy heath.

As if but yesterday departed,
Thou too art gone before; but why,
O'er ripe fruit, seasonably gathered,
Should frail survivors heave a sigh?

Mourn rather for that holy Spirit,
Sweet as the spring, as ocean deep;
For Her who, ere her summer faded,
Has sunk into a breathless sleep.   40

No more of old romantic sorrows,
For slaughtered Youth or love-lorn Maid!
With sharper grief is Yarrow smitten,
And Ettrick mourns with her their Poet dead.

November, 1836

Even so for me a Vision sanctified
The sway of Death; long ere mine eyes had seen
Thy countenance—the still rapture of thy mien—
When thou, dear Sister! wert become Death's Bride:
No trace of pain or languor could abide
That change:—age on thy brow was smoothed—thy cold
Wan cheek at once was privileged to unfold
A loveliness to living youth denied.

Oh! if within me hope should ere decline,
The lamp of faith, lost Friend! too faintly burn;　　　10
Then may that heaven-revealing smile of thine,
The bright assurance, visibly return:
And let my spirit in that power divine
Rejoice, as, through that power, it ceased to mourn.

'I know an aged Man constrained to dwell'

I know an aged Man constrained to dwell
In a large house of public charity,
Where he abides, as in a Prisoner's cell,
With numbers near, alas! no company.

When he could creep about, at will, though poor
And forced to live on alms, this old Man fed
A Redbreast, one that to his cottage door
Came not, but in a lane partook his bread.

There, at the root of one particular tree,
An easy seat this worn-out Labourer found　　　　10
While Robin pecked the crumbs upon his knee
Laid one by one, or scattered on the ground.

Dear intercourse was theirs, day after day;
What signs of mutual gladness when they met!
Think of their common peace, their simple play,
The parting moment and its fond regret.

Months passed in love that failed not to fulfil,
In spite of season's change, its own demand,
By fluttering pinions here and busy bill;
There by caresses from a tremulous hand.　　　　　20

Thus in the chosen spot a tie so strong
Was formed between the solitary pair,
That when his fate had housed him 'mid a throng
The Captive shunned all converse proffered there.

Wife, children, kindred, they were dead and gone;
But, if no evil hap his wishes crossed,
One living Stay was left, and in that one
Some recompense for all that he had lost.

O that the good old Man had power to prove,
By message sent through air or visible token,   30
That still he loves the Bird, and still must love;
That friendship lasts though fellowship is broken!

THE PRELUDE

BOOK ONE

Introduction—Childhood and School-Time

Oh there is blessing in this gentle breeze°
That blows from the green fields and from the clouds
And from the sky: it beats against my cheek,
And seems half-conscious of the joy it gives.
O welcome Messenger! O welcome Friend!
A captive greets thee, coming from a house
Of bondage, from yon City's walls set free,
A prison where he hath been long immured.
Now I am free, enfranchised and at large,
May fix my habitation where I will.   10
What dwelling shall receive me? In what Vale
Shall be my harbour? Underneath what grove
Shall I take up my home, and what sweet stream
Shall with its murmurs lull me to my rest?
The earth is all before me: with a heart
Joyous, nor scared at its own liberty,
I look about, and should the guide I chuse
Be nothing better than a wandering cloud,
I cannot miss my way. I breathe again;
Trances of thought and mountings of the mind   20
Come fast upon me: it is shaken off,
As by miraculous gift 'tis shaken off,
That burthen of my own unnatural self,
The heavy weight of many a weary day
Not mine, and such as were not made for me.
Long months of peace (if such bold word accord
With any promises of human life),
Long months of ease and undisturbed delight
Are mine in prospect; whither shall I turn
By road or pathway or through open field,   30
Or shall a twig or any floating thing
Upon the river, point me out my course?

   Enough that I am free; for months to come
May dedicate myself to chosen tasks;

May quit the tiresome sea and dwell on shore,
If not a Settler on the soil, at least
To drink wild water, and to pluck green herbs,
And gather fruits fresh from their native bough.
Nay more, if I may trust myself, this hour
Hath brought a gift that consecrates my joy;   40
For I, methought, while the sweet breath of Heaven
Was blowing on my body, felt within
A corresponding mild creative breeze,
A vital breeze which travelled gently on
O'er things which it had made, and is become
A tempest, a redundant energy°
Vexing its own creation. 'Tis a power
That does not come unrecognized, a storm,
Which, breaking up a long-continued frost
Brings with it vernal promises, the hope   50
Of active days, of dignity and thought,
Of prowess in an honorable field,
Pure passions, virtue, knowledge, and delight,
The holy life of music and of verse.

    Thus far, O Friend! did I, not used to make
A present joy the matter of my Song,
Pour out, that day, my soul in measured strains,
Even in the very words which I have here
Recorded: to the open fields I told
A prophecy: poetic numbers came   60
Spontaneously, and clothed in priestly robe
My spirit, thus singled out, as it might seem,
For holy services: great hopes were mine;
My own voice cheared me, and, far more, the mind's
Internal echo of the imperfect sound;
To both I listened, drawing from them both
A chearful confidence in things to come.

    Whereat, being not unwilling now to give
A respite to this passion, I paced on
Gently, with careless steps, and came, erelong,   70
To a green shady place where down I sate
Beneath a tree, slackening my thoughts by choice,

And settling into gentler happiness.
'Twas Autumn, and a calm and placid day,
With warmth as much as needed from a sun
Two hours declined towards the west, a day
With silver clouds, and sunshine on the grass,
And, in the sheltered grove where I was couched
A perfect stillness. On the ground I lay
Passing through many thoughts, yet mainly such   80
As to myself pertained. I made a choice
Of one sweet Vale whither my steps should turn,°
And saw, methought, the very house and fields
Present before my eyes: nor did I fail
To add, meanwhile, assurance of some work
Of glory, there forthwith to be begun,
Perhaps, too, there performed. Thus long I lay
Cheared by the genial pillow of the earth
Beneath my head, soothed by a sense of touch
From the warm ground, that balanced me, else lost   90
Entirely, seeing nought, nought hearing, save
When here and there, about the grove of Oaks
Where was my bed, an acorn from the trees
Fell audibly, and with a startling sound.

   Thus occupied in mind, I lingered here
Contented, nor rose up until the sun
Had almost touched the horizon; bidding then
A farewell to the City left behind,
Even with the chance equipment of that hour
I journeyed towards the Vale that I had chosen.   100
It was a splendid evening, and my soul
Did once again make trial of the strength
Restored to her afresh; nor did she want
Eolian visitations; but the harp°
Was soon defrauded, and the banded host
Of harmony dispersed in straggling sounds
And, lastly, utter silence. 'Be it so,
It is an injury,' said I, 'to this day
To think of any thing but present joy.'
So like a Peasant I pursued my road   110
Beneath the evening sun, nor had one wish
Again to bend the sabbath of that time

To a servile yoke. What need of many words?
A pleasant loitering journey, through two days
Continued, brought me to my hermitage.

  I spare to speak, my Friend, of what ensued—
The admiration and the love, the life
In common things; the endless store of things
Rare, or at least so seeming, every day
Found all about me in one neighbourhood,   120
The self-congratulation, the complete°
Composure, and the happiness entire.
But speedily a longing in me rose
To brace myself to some determined aim,
Reading or thinking, either to lay up
New stores, or rescue from decay the old
By timely interference. I had hopes
Still higher, that with a frame of outward life,
I might endue, might fix in a visible home
Some portion of those phantoms of conceit   130
That had been floating loose about so long,
And to such Beings temperately deal forth
The many feelings that oppressed my heart.
But I have been discouraged; gleams of light
Flash often from the East, then disappear
And mock me with a sky that ripens not
Into a steady morning: if my mind,
Remembering the sweet promise of the past,
Would gladly grapple with some noble theme,
Vain is her wish; where'er she turns she finds   140
Impediments from day to day renewed.

  And now it would content me to yield up
Those lofty hopes awhile for present gifts
Of humbler industry. But, O dear Friend!
The Poet, gentle creature as he is,
Hath, like the Lover, his unruly times,
His fits when he is neither sick nor well,
Though no distress be near him but his own
Unmanageable thoughts. The mind itself,
The meditative mind, best pleased, perhaps,   150
While she, as duteous as the Mother Dove,°

Sits brooding, lives not always to that end,
But hath less quiet instincts, goadings on
That drive her as in trouble through the groves.
With me is now such passion, which I blame
No otherwise than as it lasts too long.

  When, as becomes a man who would prepare
For such a glorious work, I through myself
Make rigorous inquisition, the report
Is often chearing; for I neither seem   160
To lack, that first great gift! the vital soul,
Nor general truths which are themselves a sort
Of Elements and Agents, Under-Powers,
Subordinate helpers of the living mind.
Nor am I naked in external things,
Forms, images; nor numerous other aids
Of less regard, though won perhaps with toil,
And needful to build up a Poet's praise.
Time, place, and manners; these I seek, and these
I find in plenteous store; but nowhere such   170
As may be singled out with steady choice;
No little Band of yet remembered names
Whom I, in perfect confidence, might hope
To summon back from lonesome banishment
And make them inmates in the hearts of men
Now living, or to live in times to come.
Sometimes, mistaking vainly, as I fear,
Proud spring-tide swellings for a regular sea,
I settle on some British theme, some old
Romantic tale, by Milton left unsung;°   180
More often resting at some gentle place
Within the groves of Chivalry, I pipe
Among the Shepherds, with reposing Knights
Sit by a Fountain-side, and hear their tales.
Sometimes, more sternly moved, I would relate
How vanquished Mithridates northward passed,°
And, hidden in the cloud of years, became
That Odin, Father of a Race, by whom
Perished the Roman Empire: how the Friends
And Followers of Sertorius, out of Spain°   190
Flying, found shelter in the Fortunate Isles;

And left their usages, their arts, and laws,
To disappear by a slow gradual death;
To dwindle and to perish one by one
Starved in those narrow bounds: but not the Soul
Of Liberty, which fifteen hundred years
Survived, and, when the European came,
With skill and power that could not be withstood,
Did, like a pestilence, maintain its hold,
And wasted down by glorious death that Race   200
Of natural Heroes: or I would record
How in tyrannic times some unknown man,
Unheard of in the Chronicles of Kings,
Suffered in silence for the love of truth;
How that one Frenchman, through continued force°
Of meditation on the inhuman deeds
Of the first Conquerors of the Indian Isles,
Went single in his ministry across
The Ocean, not to comfort the Oppressed,
But, like a thirsty wind, to roam about,   210
Withering the Oppressor: how Gustavus found°
Help at his need in Dalecarlia's Mines:
How Wallace fought for Scotland, left the name°
Of Wallace to be found like a wild flower,
All over his dear Country, left the deeds
Of Wallace, like a family of Ghosts,
To people the steep rocks and river banks,
Her natural sanctuaries, with a local soul
Of independence and stern liberty.
Sometimes it suits me better to shape out   220
Some Tale from my own heart, more near akin
To my own passions and habitual thoughts,
Some variegated story, in the main
Lofty, with interchange of gentler things.
But deadening admonitions will succeed
And the whole beauteous Fabric seems to lack
Foundation, and, withal, appears throughout
Shadowy and unsubstantial. Then, last wish,
My last and favourite aspiration! then
I yearn towards some philosophic Song   230
Of Truth that cherishes our daily life;
With meditations passionate from deep

Recesses in man's heart, immortal verse
Thoughtfully fitted to the Orphean lyre;°
But from this awful burthen I full soon
Take refuge, and beguile myself with trust
That mellower years will bring a riper mind
And clearer insight. Thus from day to day
I live, a mockery of the brotherhood
Of vice and virtue, with no skill to part   240
Vague longing that is bred by want of power,
From paramount impulse not to be withstood,
A timorous capacity, from prudence;
From circumspection, infinite delay.
Humility and modest awe themselves
Betray me, serving often for a cloak
To a more subtle selfishness, that now
Doth lock my functions up in blank reserve,
Now dupes me by an over-anxious eye
That with a false activity beats off   250
Simplicity and self-presented truth.
—Ah! better far than this, to stray about
Voluptuously through fields and rural walks,
And ask no record of the hours, given up
To vacant musing, unreproved neglect
Of all things, and deliberate holiday;
Far better never to have heard the name
Of zeal and just ambition than to live
Thus baffled by a mind that every hour
Turns recreant to her task, takes heart again,   260
Then feels immediately some hollow thought
Hang like an interdict upon her hopes.
This is my lot; for either still I find
Some imperfection in the chosen theme,
Or see of absolute accomplishment
Much wanting, so much wanting, in myself,
That I recoil and droop, and seek repose
In listlessness from vain perplexity,
Unprofitably travelling towards the grave,
Like a false steward who hath much received°   270
And renders nothing back.
                              —Was it for this°
That one, the fairest of all Rivers, loved

To blend his murmurs with my Nurse's song,
And from his alder shades and rocky falls,
And from his fords and shallows, sent a voice
That flowed along my dreams? For this, didst Thou,
O Derwent, travelling over the green Plains
Near my 'sweet Birthplace', didst thou, beauteous Stream,°
Make ceaseless music through the night and day
Which with its steady cadence, tempering   280
Our human waywardness, composed my thoughts
To more than infant softness, giving me,
Among the fretful dwellings of mankind,
A knowledge, a dim earnest, of the calm
Which Nature breathes among the hills and groves.
When, having left his Mountains, to the Towers
Of Cockermouth that beauteous River came,
Behind my Father's House he passed, close by,
Along the margin of our Terrace Walk.
He was a Playmate whom we dearly loved.   290
Oh! many a time have I, a five years' Child,
A naked Boy, in one delightful Rill,
A little Mill-race severed from his stream,
Made one long bathing of a summer's day,
Basked in the sun, and plunged, and basked again
Alternate all a summer's day, or coursed
Over the sandy fields, leaping through groves
Of yellow grunsel, or when crag and hill,
The woods, and distant Skiddaw's lofty height,
Were bronzed with a deep radiance, stood alone   300
Beneath the sky, as if I had been born
On Indian Plains, and from my Mother's hut
Had run abroad in wantonness, to sport,
A naked Savage, in the thunder shower.

    Fair seed-time had my soul, and I grew up
Fostered alike by beauty and by fear;
Much favored in my birthplace, and no less
In that beloved Vale to which, erelong,
I was transplanted. Well I call to mind°
('Twas at an early age, ere I had seen   310
Nine summers) when upon the mountain slope
The frost and breath of frosty wind had snapped

The last autumnal crocus, 'twas my joy
To wander half the night among the Cliffs
And the smooth Hollows, where the woodcocks ran
Along the open turf. In thought and wish
That time, my shoulder all with springes hung,°
I was a fell destroyer. On the heights
Scudding away from snare to snare, I plied
My anxious visitation, hurrying on,   320
Still hurrying, hurrying onward; moon and stars
Were shining o'er my head; I was alone,
And seemed to be a trouble to the peace
That was among them. Sometimes it befel
In these night-wanderings, that a strong desire
O'erpowered my better reason, and the bird
Which was the captive of another's toils
Became my prey; and, when the deed was done
I heard among the solitary hills
Low breathings coming after me, and sounds   330
Of undistinguishable motion, steps
Almost as silent as the turf they trod.

Nor less in springtime when on southern banks
The shining sun had from his knot of leaves
Decoyed the primrose flower, and when the Vales
And woods were warm, was I a plunderer then
In the high places, on the lonesome peaks
Where'er, among the mountains and the winds,
The Mother Bird had built her lodge. Though mean
My object, and inglorious, yet the end   340
Was not ignoble. Oh! when I have hung
Above the raven's nest, by knots of grass
And half-inch fissures in the slippery rock
But ill sustained, and almost, as it seemed,
Suspended by the blast which blew amain,
Shouldering the naked crag; Oh! at that time,
While on the perilous ridge I hung alone,
With what strange utterance did the loud dry wind
Blow through my ears! the sky seemed not a sky
Of earth, and with what motion moved the clouds!   350

The mind of Man is framed even like the breath
And harmony of music. There is a dark

Invisible workmanship that reconciles
Discordant elements, and makes them move
In one society. Ah me! that all
The terrors, all the early miseries,
Regrets, vexations, lassitudes, that all
The thoughts and feelings which have been infused
Into my mind, should ever have made up
The calm existence that is mine when I   360
Am worthy of myself! Praise to the end!
Thanks likewise for the means! But I believe
That Nature, oftentimes, when she would frame
A favored Being, from his earliest dawn
Of infancy doth open out the clouds,
As at the touch of lightning, seeking him
With gentlest visitation; not the less,
Though haply aiming at the self-same end,
Does it delight her sometimes to employ
Severer interventions, ministry   370
More palpable, and so she dealt with me.

    One evening (surely I was led by her)
I went alone into a Shepherd's Boat,
A Skiff that to a Willow tree was tied
Within a rocky Cave, its usual home.
'Twas by the shores of Patterdale, a Vale°
Wherein I was a Stranger, thither come
A School-boy Traveller, at the Holidays.
Forth rambled from the Village Inn alone,
No sooner had I sight of this small Skiff,   380
Discovered thus by unexpected chance,
Than I unloosed her tether and embarked.
The moon was up, the Lake was shining clear
Among the hoary mountains; from the Shore
I pushed, and struck the oars and struck again
In cadence, and my little Boat moved on
Even like a Man who walks with stately step
Though bent on speed. It was an act of stealth
And troubled pleasure; not without the voice
Of mountain-echoes did my Boat move on,   390
Leaving behind her still on either side
Small circles glittering idly in the moon,

Until they melted all into one track
Of sparkling light. A rocky Steep uprose
Above the Cavern of the Willow tree
And now, as suited one who proudly rowed
With his best skill, I fixed a steady view
Upon the top of that same craggy ridge,
The bound of the horizon, for behind
Was nothing but the stars and the grey sky.   400
She was an elfin Pinnace; lustily
I dipped my oars into the silent Lake,
And, as I rose upon the stroke, my Boat
Went heaving through the water, like a Swan;
When from behind that craggy Steep, till then
The bound of the horizon, a huge Cliff,
As if with voluntary power instinct,
Upreared its head. I struck, and struck again,
And, growing still in stature, the huge Cliff
Rose up between me and the stars, and still,   410
With measured motion, like a living thing,
Strode after me. With trembling hands I turned,
And through the silent water stole my way
Back to the Cavern of the Willow tree.
There, in her mooring-place, I left my Bark,
And, through the meadows homeward went, with grave
And serious thoughts; and after I had seen
That spectacle, for many days, my brain
Worked with a dim and undetermined sense
Of unknown modes of being; in my thoughts   420
There was a darkness, call it solitude,
Or blank desertion, no familiar shapes
Of hourly objects, images of trees,
Of sea or sky, no colours of green fields;
But huge and mighty Forms that do not live
Like living men moved slowly through my mind
By day and were the trouble of my dreams.

Wisdom and Spirit of the universe!
Thou Soul that art the Eternity of Thought!
That giv'st to forms and images a breath   430
And everlasting motion! not in vain,
By day or star-light thus from my first dawn

Of Childhood didst Thou intertwine for me
The passions that build up our human Soul,
Not with the mean and vulgar works of Man,
But with high objects, with enduring things,
With life and nature, purifying thus
The elements of feeling and of thought,
And sanctifying, by such discipline,
Both pain and fear, until we recognize   440
A grandeur in the beatings of the heart.

    Nor was this fellowship vouchsafed to me
With stinted kindness. In November days,
When vapours rolling down the valleys made
A lonely scene more lonesome; among woods
At noon, and 'mid the calm of summer nights,
When, by the margin of the trembling Lake,
Beneath the gloomy hills I homeward went
In solitude, such intercourse was mine;
'Twas mine among the fields both day and night,   450
And by the waters all the summer long.

    And in the frosty season, when the sun
Was set, and visible for many a mile
The cottage windows through the twilight blazed,
I heeded not the summons:—happy time
It was, indeed, for all of us; to me
It was a time of rapture: clear and loud
The village clock tolled six; I wheeled about,
Proud and exulting, like an untired horse,
That cares not for its home.—All shod with steel,   460
We hissed along the polished ice in games
Confederate, imitative of the chace
And woodland pleasures, the resounding horn,
The Pack loud bellowing, and the hunted hare.
So through the darkness and the cold we flew,
And not a voice was idle; with the din,
Meanwhile, the precipices rang aloud;
The leafless trees, and every icy crag
Tinkled like iron; while the distant hills
Into the tumult sent an alien sound   470

Of melancholy, not unnoticed; while the stars,
Eastward, were sparkling clear, and in the west
The orange sky of evening died away.

   Not seldom from the uproar I retired
Into a silent bay, or sportively
Glanced sideway, leaving the tumultuous throng,
To cut across the image of a star
That gleamed upon the ice. And oftentimes
When we had given our bodies to the wind,
And all the shadowy banks, on either side,   480
Came sweeping through the darkness, spinning still
The rapid line of motion; then at once
Have I, reclining back upon my heels,
Stopped short, yet still the solitary Cliffs
Wheeled by me, even as if the earth had rolled
With visible motion her diurnal round.
Behind me did they stretch in solemn train
Feebler and feebler, and I stood and watched
Till all was tranquil as a dreamless sleep.

   Ye Presences of Nature, in the sky   490
Or on the earth! Ye Visions of the hills!
And Souls of lonely places! can I think
A vulgar hope was yours when Ye employed
Such ministry, when Ye through many a year
Haunting me thus among my boyish sports,
On caves and trees, upon the woods and hills,
Impressed upon all forms the characters°
Of danger or desire, and thus did make
The surface of the universal earth
With triumph, and delight, and hope, and fear,   500
Work like a sea?

             Not uselessly employed,
I might pursue this theme through every change
Of exercise and play, to which the year
Did summon us in its delightful round.
We were a noisy crew, the sun in heaven
Beheld not vales more beautiful than ours,
Nor saw a race in happiness and joy

More worthy of the fields where they were sown.
I would record with no reluctant voice
The woods of autumn and their hazel bowers   510
With milk-white clusters hung; the rod and line,
True symbol of the foolishness of hope,
Which with its strong enchantment led us on
By rocks and pools, shut out from every star
All the green summer, to forlorn cascades
Among the windings of the mountain brooks.
—Unfading recollections! at this hour
The heart is almost mine with which I felt
From some hill-top, on sunny afternoons
The Kite high up among the fleecy clouds   520
Pull at its rein, like an impatient Courser,
Or, from the meadows sent on gusty days,
Beheld her breast the wind, then suddenly
Dashed headlong; and rejected by the storm.

        Ye lowly Cottages in which we dwelt,
A ministration of your own was yours,
A sanctity, a safeguard, and a love!
Can I forget you, being as ye were
So beautiful among the pleasant fields
In which ye stood? Or can I here forget   530
The plain and seemly countenance with which
Ye dealt out your plain comforts? Yet had ye
Delights and exultations of your own.
Eager and never weary we pursued
Our home amusements by the warm peat-fire
At evening, when with pencil and with slate,
In square divisions parcelled out, and all
With crosses and with cyphers scribbled o'er,
We schemed and puzzled, head opposed to head
In strife too humble to be named in Verse.   540
Or round the naked table, snow-white deal,
Cherry or maple, sate in close array,
And to the combat, Lu or Whist, led on
A thick-ribbed Army; not as in the world
Neglected and ungratefully thrown by
Even for the very service they had wrought,
But husbanded through many a long campaign.

Uncouth assemblage was it, where no few
Had changed their functions, some, plebeian cards,
Which Fate beyond the promise of their birth   550
Had glorified, and called to represent
The persons of departed Potentates.
Oh! with what echoes on the Board they fell!
Ironic Diamonds, Clubs, Hearts, Diamonds, Spades,
A congregation piteously akin.
Cheap matter did they give to boyish wit,
Those sooty knaves, precipitated down
With scoffs and taunts, like Vulcan out of Heaven;
The paramount Ace, a moon in her eclipse;
Queens, gleaming through their splendour's last decay;   560
And Monarchs, surly at the wrongs sustained
By royal visages. Meanwhile, abroad
The heavy rain was falling, or the frost
Raged bitterly, with keen and silent tooth,
And, interrupting oft the impassioned game,
From Esthwaite's neighbouring Lake the splitting ice,
While it sank down towards the water, sent,
Among the meadows and the hills, its long
And dismal yellings, like the noise of wolves
When they are howling round the Bothnic Main.°   570

   Nor, sedulous as I have been to trace
How Nature by extrinsic passion first
Peopled my mind with beauteous forms or grand
And made me love them, may I well forget
How other pleasures have been mine, and joys
Of subtler origin; how I have felt,
Not seldom, even in that tempestuous time,
Those hallowed and pure motions of the sense
Which seem, in their simplicity, to own
An intellectual charm, that calm delight   580
Which, if I err not, surely must belong
To those first-born affinities that fit
Our new existence to existing things,
And, in our dawn of being, constitute
The bond of union betwixt life and joy.

Yes, I remember, when the changeful earth,
And twice five seasons on my mind had stamped

The faces of the moving year, even then,
A Child, I held unconscious intercourse
With the eternal Beauty, drinking in   590
A pure organic pleasure from the lines
Of curling mist, or from the level plain
Of waters coloured by the steady clouds.
The Sands of Westmoreland, the Creeks and Bays
Of Cumbria's rocky limits, they can tell
How when the Sea threw off his evening shade
And to the Shepherd's huts beneath the crags
Did send sweet notice of the rising moon,
How I have stood, to fancies such as these,
Engrafted in the tenderness of thought,   600
A stranger, linking with the spectacle
No conscious memory of a kindred sight,
And bringing with me no peculiar sense
Of quietness or peace, yet I have stood,
Even while mine eye has moved o'er three long leagues
Of shining water, gathering, as it seemed,
Through every hair-breadth of that field of light,
New pleasure, like a bee among the flowers.

      Thus, often in those fits of vulgar joy
Which, through all seasons, on a child's pursuits   610
Are prompt attendants, 'mid that giddy bliss
Which, like a tempest, works along the blood
And is forgotten; even then I felt
Gleams like the flashing of a shield. The earth
And common face of Nature spake to me
Rememberable things; sometimes, 'tis true,
By chance collisions and quaint accidents
Like those ill-sorted unions, work supposed
Of evil-minded fairies, yet not vain,
Nor profitless, if haply they impressed   620
Collateral objects and appearances,
Albeit lifeless then, and doomed to sleep
Until maturer seasons called them forth
To impregnate and to elevate the mind.
—And if the vulgar joy by its own weight
Wearied itself out of the memory,
The scenes which were a witness of that joy

Remained, in their substantial lineaments
Depicted on the brain, and to the eye
Were visible, a daily sight. And thus 630
By the impressive discipline of fear,
By pleasure and repeated happiness,
So frequently repeated, and by force
Of obscure feelings representative
Of joys that were forgotten, these same scenes,
So beauteous and majestic in themselves,
Though yet the day was distant, did at length
Become habitually dear, and all
Their hues and forms were by invisible links
Allied to the affections. 640

I began
My story early, feeling, as I fear,
The weakness of a human love, for days
Disowned by memory, ere the birth of spring
Planting my snowdrops among winter snows.
Nor will it seem to thee, my Friend! so prompt°
In sympathy, that I have lengthened out,
With fond and feeble tongue, a tedious tale.
Meanwhile, my hope has been that I might fetch
Invigorating thoughts from former years,
Might fix the wavering balance of my mind, 650
And haply meet reproaches, too, whose power
May spur me on, in manhood now mature,
To honorable toil. Yet should these hopes°
Be vain, and thus should neither I be taught
To understand myself, nor thou to know
With better knowledge how the heart was framed
Of him thou lovest, need I dread from thee
Harsh judgments, if I am so loth to quit
Those recollected hours that have the charm
Of visionary things, and lovely forms 660
And sweet sensations, that throw back our life
And almost make our Infancy itself
A visible scene, on which the sun is shining?

One end hereby at least hath been attained,
My mind hath been revived, and if this mood

Desert me not, I will forthwith bring down,
Through later years, the story of my life.
The road lies plain before me; 'tis a theme
Single and of determined bounds; and hence
I chuse it rather at this time, than work   670
Of ampler or more varied argument,
Where I might be discomfited and lost,
And certain hopes are with me, that to thee
This labour will be welcome, honored Friend.

BOOK TWO

School-Time (*continued*)

Thus far, O Friend! have we, though leaving much
Unvisited, endeavoured to retrace
My life through its first years, and measured back
The way I travelled when I first began
To love the woods and fields. The passion yet
Was in its birth, sustained, as might befal,
By nourishment that came unsought; for still,
From week to week, from month to month, we lived
A round of tumult. Duly were our games
Prolonged in summer till the day-light failed;   10
No chair remained before the doors, the bench
And threshold steps were empty; fast asleep
The Labourer, and the Old Man who had sate,
A later lingerer, yet the revelry
Continued, and the loud uproar: at last,
When all the ground was dark, and the huge clouds
Were edged with twinkling stars, to bed we went,
With weary joints, and with a beating mind.
Ah! is there one who ever has been young,
And needs a monitory voice to tame   20
The pride of virtue, and of intellect?
And is there one, the wisest and the best
Of all mankind, who does not sometimes wish
For things which cannot be, who would not give,
If so he might, to duty and to truth

The eagerness of infantine desire?
A tranquillizing spirit presses now
On my corporeal frame: so wide appears
The vacancy between me and those days,
Which yet have such self-presence in my mind   30
That, sometimes, when I think of them, I seem
Two consciousnesses, conscious of myself
And of some other Being. A grey Stone
Of native rock, left midway in the Square
Of our small market Village, was the home
And centre of these joys, and when returned
After long absence, thither I repaired,
I found that it was split, and gone to build
A smart Assembly-room that perked and flared°
With wash and rough-cast, elbowing the ground   40
Which had been ours. But let the fiddle scream,
And be ye happy! yet, my Friends! I know
That more than one of you will think with me
Of those soft starry nights, and that old Dame
From whom the stone was named, who there had sate
And watched her Table with its huxter's wares,
Assiduous thro' the length of sixty years.

We ran a boisterous race; the year span round
With giddy motion. But the time approached
That brought with it a regular desire   50
For calmer pleasures, when the beauteous forms
Of Nature were collaterally attached
To every scheme of holiday delight,
And every boyish sport, less grateful else,
And languidly pursued.
                              When summer came
It was the pastime of our afternoons
To beat along the plain of Windermere
With rival oars, and the selected bourne
Was now an Island musical with birds
That sang for ever; now a Sister Isle   60
Beneath the oaks' umbrageous covert, sown
With lillies of the valley like a field;
And now a third small Island where remained
An old stone Table, and a mouldered Cave,

A Hermit's history. In such a race,
So ended, disappointment could be none,
Uneasiness, or pain, or jealousy:
We rested in the shade, all pleased alike,
Conquered and Conqueror. Thus the pride of strength,
And the vain-glory of superior skill   70
Were interfused with objects which subdued
And tempered them, and gradually produced
A quiet independence of the heart.
And to my Friend, who knows me, I may add,
Unapprehensive of reproof, that hence
Ensued a diffidence and modesty,
And I was taught to feel, perhaps too much,
The self-sufficing power of solitude.

      No delicate viands sapped our bodily strength;
More than we wished we knew the blessing then   80
Of vigorous hunger, for our daily meals
Were frugal, Sabine fare! and then, exclude°
A little weekly stipend, and we lived
Through three divisions of the quartered year
In pennyless poverty. But now, to School
Returned, from the half-yearly holidays,
We came with purses more profusely filled,
Allowance which abundantly sufficed
To gratify the palate with repasts
More costly than the Dame of whom I spake,   90
That ancient Woman, and her board supplied.
Hence inroads into distant Vales, and long
Excursions far away among the hills,
Hence rustic dinners on the cool green ground,
Or in the woods, or near a river side,
Or by some shady fountain, while soft airs°
Among the leaves were stirring, and the sun
Unfelt, shone sweetly round us in our joy.

      Nor is my aim neglected, if I tell
How twice in the long length of those half-years   100
We from our funds, perhaps, with bolder hand
Drew largely, anxious for one day, at least,

To feel the motion of the galloping Steed;
And with the good old Inn-keeper, in truth,
On such occasion sometimes we employed
Sly subterfuge; for the intended bound
Of the day's journey was too distant far
For any cautious man, a Structure famed°
Beyond its neighbourhood, the antique Walls
Of that large Abbey which within the Vale   110
Of Nightshade, to St. Mary's honour built,
Stands yet, a mouldering Pile, with fractured Arch,
Belfry, and Images, and living Trees,
A holy Scene! Along the smooth green turf
Our Horses grazed: to more than inland peace
Left by the sea wind passing overhead
(Though wind of roughest temper) trees and towers
May in that Valley oftentimes be seen,
Both silent and both motionless alike;
Such is the shelter that is there, and such   120
The safeguard for repose and quietness.

   Our steeds remounted, and the summons given,
With whip and spur we by the Chauntry flew
In uncouth race, and left the cross-legged Knight,
And the stone-Abbot, and that single Wren
Which one day sang so sweetly in the Nave
Of the old Church, that, though from recent showers
The earth was comfortless, and, touched by faint
Internal breezes, sobbings of the place,
And respirations, from the roofless walls   130
The shuddering ivy dripped large drops, yet still,
So sweetly 'mid the gloom the invisible Bird
Sang to itself, that there I could have made
My dwelling-place, and lived for ever there
To hear such music. Through the Walls we flew
And down the valley, and a circuit made
In wantonness of heart, through rough and smooth
We scampered homeward. Oh! ye Rocks and Streams,
And that still Spirit of the evening air!
Even in this joyous time I sometimes felt   140
Your presence, when with slackened step we breathed°
Along the sides of the steep hills, or when,

Lighted by gleams of moonlight from the sea,
We beat with thundering hoofs the level sand.

Upon the Eastern Shore of Windermere,
Above the crescent of a pleasant Bay,
There stood an Inn, no homely-featured Shed,
Brother of the surrounding Cottages,
But 'twas a splendid place, the door beset
With Chaises, Grooms, and Liveries, and within   150
Decanters, Glasses, and the blood-red Wine.°
In ancient times, or ere the Hall was built
On the large Island, had this Dwelling been
More worthy of a Poet's love, a Hut,
Proud of its one bright fire, and sycamore shade.
But though the rhymes were gone which once inscribed
The threshold, and large golden characters
On the blue-frosted Signboard had usurped
The place of the old Lion, in contempt
And mockery of the rustic painter's hand,   160
Yet to this hour the spot to me is dear
With all its foolish pomp. The garden lay
Upon a slope surmounted by the plain
Of a small Bowling-green; beneath us stood
A grove, with gleams of water through the trees
And over the tree-tops; nor did we want
Refreshment, strawberries and mellow cream.
And there, through half an afternoon, we played
On the smooth platform, and the shouts we sent
Made all the mountains ring. But ere the fall   170
Of night, when in our pinnace we returned
Over the dusky Lake, and to the beach
Of some small Island steered our course with one,
The Minstrel of our troop, and left him there,°
And rowed off gently, while he blew his flute
Alone upon the rock, Oh! then the calm
And dead still water lay upon my mind
Even with a weight of pleasure, and the sky
Never before so beautiful, sank down
Into my heart, and held me like a dream.   180

Thus daily were my sympathies enlarged,
And thus the common range of visible things

Grew dear to me: already I began
To love the sun, a Boy I loved the sun,
Not as I since have loved him, as a pledge
And surety of our earthly life, a light
Which while we view we feel we are alive,
But, for this cause, that I had seen him lay
His beauty on the morning hills, had seen
The western mountain touch his setting orb   190
In many a thoughtless hour, when, from excess
Of happiness, my blood appeared to flow
With its own pleasure, and I breathed with joy.
And from like feelings, humble though intense,
To patriotic and domestic love
Analogous, the moon to me was dear;
For I would dream away my purposes,
Standing to look upon her while she hung
Midway between the hills, as if she knew
No other region but belonged to thee,   200
Yea, appertained by a peculiar right
To thee and thy grey huts, my darling Vale!

    Those incidental charms which first attached
My heart to rural objects, day by day
Grew weaker, and I hasten on to tell
How Nature, intervenient till this time,
And secondary, now at length was sought
For her own sake. But who shall parcel out
His intellect, by geometric rules,
Split, like a province, into round and square?   210
Who knows the individual hour in which
His habits were first sown, even as a seed,
Who that shall point, as with a wand, and say,
'This portion of the river of my mind
Came from yon fountain?' Thou, my Friend! art one
More deeply read in thy own thoughts; to thee
Science appears but, what in truth she is,
Not as our glory and our absolute boast,
But as a succedaneum, and a prop
To our infirmity. Thou art no slave   220
Of that false secondary power, by which
In weakness we create distinctions, then

Deem that our puny boundaries are things
Which we perceive, and not which we have made.
To thee, unblinded by these outward shows,
The unity of all has been revealed,
And thou wilt doubt with me, less aptly skilled
Than many are to class the cabinet°
Of their sensations, and, in voluble phrase,
Run through the history and birth of each   230
As of a single independent thing.
Hard task to analyse a soul, in which,
Not only general habits and desires,
But each most obvious and particular thought,
Not in a mystical and idle sense,
But in the words of reason deeply weighed,
Hath no beginning.
                    Blessed the infant Babe,
(For with my best conjectures I would trace
The progress of our being) blest the Babe,
Nursed in his Mother's arms, the Babe who sleeps   240
Upon his Mother's breast, who, when his soul
Claims manifest kindred with an earthly soul,
Doth gather passion from his Mother's eye!
Such feelings pass into his torpid life
Like an awakening breeze, and hence his mind,
Even in the first trial of its powers,
Is prompt and watchful, eager to combine
In one appearance, all the elements
And parts of the same object, else detached
And loth to coalesce. Thus, day by day,   250
Subjected to the discipline of love,
His organs and recipient faculties
Are quickened, are more vigorous, his mind spreads,
Tenacious of the forms which it receives.
In one beloved presence, nay and more,
In that most apprehensive habitude
And those sensations which have been derived
From this beloved Presence, there exists
A virtue which irradiates and exalts
All objects through all intercourse of sense.   260
No outcast he, bewildered and depressed;
Along his infant veins are interfused

The gravitation and the filial bond
Of nature, that connect him with the world.
Emphatically such a Being lives,
An inmate of this *active* universe;
From nature largely he receives; nor so
Is satisfied, but largely gives again,
For feeling has to him imparted strength,
And powerful in all sentiments of grief,   270
Of exultation, fear, and joy, his mind,
Even as an agent of the one great mind,
Creates, creator and receiver both,
Working but in alliance with the works
Which it beholds.—Such, verily, is the first
Poetic spirit of our human life;
By uniform controul of after years
In most abated or suppressed, in some,
Through every change of growth or of decay,
Pre-eminent till death.   280
               From early days,
Beginning not long after that first time
In which, a Babe, by intercourse of touch
I held mute dialogues with my Mother's heart,
I have endeavoured to display the means
Whereby the infant sensibility,
Great birthright of our Being, was in me
Augmented and sustained. Yet is a path
More difficult before me, and I fear
That in its broken windings we shall need
The chamois' sinews, and the eagle's wing: 290
For now a trouble came into my mind
From unknown causes. I was left alone,
Seeking the visible world, nor knowing why.
The props of my affections were removed,
And yet the building stood, as if sustained
By its own spirit! All that I beheld
Was dear to me, and from this cause it came,
That now to Nature's finer influxes
My mind lay open, to that more exact
And intimate communion which our hearts   300
Maintain with the minuter properties
Of objects which already are beloved,

And of those only. Many are the joys
Of youth; but oh! what happiness to live
When every hour brings palpable access
Of knowledge, when all knowledge is delight,
And sorrow is not there. The seasons came,
And every season to my notice brought
A store of transitory qualities
Which, but for this most watchful power of love   310
Had been neglected, left a register
Of permanent relations, else unknown.
Hence life, and change, and beauty, solitude
More active, even, than 'best society',°
Society made sweet as solitude
By silent inobtrusive sympathies,
And gentle agitations of the mind
From manifold distinctions, difference
Perceived in things, where to the common eye,
No difference is; and hence, from the same source   320
Sublimer joy. For I would walk alone,
In storm and tempest, or in starlight nights
Beneath the quiet Heavens; and, at that time,
Have felt whate'er there is of power in sound
To breathe an elevated mood, by form
Or image unprofaned; and I would stand,
Beneath some rock, listening to sounds that are
The ghostly language of the ancient earth,
Or make their dim abode in distant winds.
Thence did I drink the visionary power.   330
I deem not profitless those fleeting moods
Of shadowy exultation: not for this,
That they are kindred to our purer mind
And intellectual life; but that the soul,
Remembering how she felt, but what she felt
Remembering not, retains an obscure sense
Of possible sublimity, to which,
With growing faculties she doth aspire,
With faculties still growing, feeling still
That whatsoever point they gain, they still   340
Have something to pursue.
                              And not alone
In grandeur and in tumult, but no less

In tranquil scenes, that universal power
And fitness in the latent qualities
And essences of things, by which the mind
Is moved by feelings of delight, to me
Came strengthened with a superadded soul,
A virtue not its own. My morning walks
Were early; oft, before the hours of School°
I travelled round our little Lake, five miles   350
Of pleasant wandering, happy time! more dear
For this, that one was by my side, a Friend
Then passionately loved; with heart how full
Will he peruse these lines, this page, perhaps
A blank to other men! for many years
Have since flowed in between us; and our minds,
Both silent to each other, at this time
We live as if those hours had never been.
Nor seldom did I lift our cottage latch
Far earlier, and before the vernal thrush   360
Was audible, among the hills I sate
Alone, upon some jutting eminence
At the first hour of morning, when the Vale
Lay quiet in an utter solitude.
How shall I trace the history, where seek
The origin of what I then have felt?
Oft in those moments such a holy calm
Did overspread my soul, that I forgot
That I had bodily eyes, and what I saw
Appeared like something in myself, a dream,   370
A prospect in my mind.
                          'Twere long to tell
What spring and autumn, what the winter snows,
And what the summer shade, what day and night,
The evening and the morning, what my dreams
And what my waking thoughts supplied, to nurse
That spirit of religious love in which
I walked with Nature. But let this at least
Be not forgotten, that I still retained
My first creative sensibility,
That by the regular action of the world   380
My soul was unsubdued. A plastic power°
Abode with me, a forming hand, at times

Rebellious, acting in a devious mood,
A local spirit of its own, at war
With general tendency, but for the most
Subservient strictly to the external things
With which it communed. An auxiliar light
Came from my mind which on the setting sun
Bestowed new splendor; the melodious birds,
The gentle breezes, fountains that ran on,   390
Murmuring so sweetly in themselves, obeyed
A like dominion; and the midnight storm
Grew darker in the presence of my eye.
Hence my obeisance, my devotion hence,
And hence my transport.
                              Nor should this, perchance,
Pass unrecorded, that I still had loved
The exercise and produce of a toil
Than analytic industry to me
More pleasing, and whose character I deem
Is more poetic, as resembling more   400
Creative agency. I mean to speak
Of that interminable building reared
By observation of affinities
In objects where no brotherhood exists
To common minds. My seventeenth year was come,
And, whether from this habit rooted now
So deeply in my mind, or from excess
Of the great social principle of life,
Coercing all things into sympathy,
To unorganic natures I transferred   410
My own enjoyments, or, the power of truth
Coming in revelation, I conversed
With things that really are, I at this time
Saw blessings spread around me like a sea.
Thus did my days pass on, and now at length
From Nature and her overflowing soul
I had received so much that all my thoughts
Were steeped in feeling. I was only then
Contented when with bliss ineffable
I felt the sentiment of Being spread   420
O'er all that moves, and all that seemeth still,
O'er all, that, lost beyond the reach of thought

And human knowledge, to the human eye
Invisible, yet liveth to the heart,
O'er all that leaps, and runs, and shouts, and sings,
Or beats the gladsome air, o'er all that glides
Beneath the wave, yea, in the wave itself
And mighty depth of waters. Wonder not
If such my transports were, for in all things
I saw one life, and felt that it was joy.   430
One song they sang, and it was audible,
Most audible then when the fleshly ear,
O'ercome by grosser prelude of that strain,
Forgot its functions, and slept undisturbed.

    If this be error, and another faith
Find easier access to the pious mind,
Yet were I grossly destitute of all
Those human sentiments which make this earth
So dear, if I should fail, with grateful voice
To speak of you, Ye Mountains and Ye Lakes,   440
And sounding Cataracts! Ye Mists and Winds
That dwell among the hills where I was born.
If, in my youth, I have been pure in heart,
If, mingling with the world, I am content
With my own modest pleasures, and have lived,
With God and Nature communing, removed
From little enmities and low desires,
The gift is yours; if in these times of fear,°
This melancholy waste of hopes o'erthrown,
If, 'mid indifference and apathy   450
And wicked exultation, when good men,
On every side fall off we know not how,
To selfishness, disguised in gentle names
Of peace, and quiet, and domestic love,
Yet mingled, not unwillingly, with sneers
On visionary minds; if in this time
Of dereliction and dismay, I yet
Despair not of our nature; but retain
A more than Roman confidence, a faith
That fails not, in all sorrow my support,   460
The blessing of my life, the gift is yours,
Ye mountains! thine, O Nature! Thou hast fed

My lofty speculations; and in thee
For this uneasy heart of ours I find
A never-failing principle of joy,
And purest passion.
                        Thou, my Friend! wert reared
In the great City, 'mid far other scenes;
But we, by different roads at length have gained
The self-same bourne. And for this cause to Thee
I speak, unapprehensive of contempt,   470
The insinuated scoff of coward tongues,
And all that silent language which so oft
In conversation betwixt man and man
Blots from the human countenance all trace
Of beauty and of love. For Thou hast sought
The truth in solitude, and Thou art one,
The most intense of Nature's worshippers
In many things my Brother, chiefly here
In this my deep devotion.
                        Fare Thee well!
Health, and the quiet of a healthful mind   480
Attend thee! seeking oft the haunts of men,
And yet more often living with Thyself,
And for Thyself, so haply shall thy days
Be many, and a blessing to mankind.

BOOK THREE

Residence at Cambridge

It was a dreary morning when the Chaise°
Rolled over the flat Plains of Huntingdon
And, through the open windows, first I saw
The long-backed Chapel of King's College rear
His pinnacles above the dusky groves.
Soon afterwards, we espied upon the road,
A student clothed in Gown and tasselled Cap;
He passed; nor was I master of my eyes
Till he was left a hundred yards behind.
The Place, as we approached, seemed more and more   10

To have an eddy's force, and sucked us in
More eagerly at every step we took.
Onward we drove beneath the Castle, down
By Magdalene Bridge we went and crossed the Cam,
And at the *Hoop* we landed, famous Inn.

My spirit was up, my thoughts were full of hope;
Some Friends I had, acquaintances who there
Seemed Friends, poor simple Schoolboys, now hung round
With honour and importance; in a world
Of welcome faces up and down I roved;   20
Questions, directions, counsel and advice
Flowed in upon me from all sides, fresh day
Of pride and pleasure! to myself I seemed
A man of business and expence, and went
From shop to shop about my own affairs,
To Tutors or to Tailors, as befel,
From street to street with loose and careless heart.

I was the Dreamer, they the Dream; I roamed
Delighted, through the motley spectacle;
Gowns grave or gaudy, Doctors, Students, Streets,   30
Lamps, Gateways, Flocks of Churches, Courts and Towers:
Strange transformation for a mountain Youth,
A northern Villager. As if by word
Of magic or some Fairy's power, at once
Behold me rich in monies, and attired
In splendid clothes, with hose of silk, and hair
Glittering like rimy trees when frost is keen.°
My lordly Dressing-gown I pass it by,
With other signs of manhood which supplied
The lack of beard.—The weeks went roundly on,   40
With invitations, suppers, wine, and fruit,
Smooth housekeeping within, and all without
Liberal and suiting Gentleman's array!

The Evangelist St. John my Patron was,
Three gloomy Courts are his; and in the first
Was my abiding-place, a nook obscure!
Right underneath, the College kitchens made
A humming sound, less tuneable than bees,
But hardly less industrious; with shrill notes

Of sharp command and scolding intermixed.   50
Near me was Trinity's loquacious Clock,
Who never let the Quarters, night or day,
Slip by him unproclaimed, and told the hours
Twice over with a male and female voice.
Her pealing organ was my neighbour too;
And, from my Bedroom, I in moonlight nights
Could see, right opposite, a few yards off,
The Antechapel, where the Statue stood
Of Newton, with his Prism and silent Face.

    Of College labours, of the Lecturer's Room,   60
All studded round, as thick as chairs could stand,
With loyal Students, faithful to their books,
Half-and-half Idlers, hardy Recusants,°
And honest Dunces;—of important Days,
Examinations, when the Man was weighed
As in the balance,—of excessive hopes,
Tremblings withal, and commendable fears,
Small jealousies, and triumphs good or bad
I make short mention; things they were which then
I did not love, nor do I love them now.   70
Such glory was but little sought by me,
And little won. But it is right to say
That even so early, from the first crude days
Of settling-time in this my new abode,
Not seldom I had melancholy thoughts,
From personal and family regards,
Wishing to hope without a hope; some fears
About my future worldly maintenance,
And, more than all, a strangeness in my mind,
A feeling that I was not for that hour,   80
Nor for that place. But wherefore be cast down?
Why should I grieve? I was a chosen Son.
For hither I had come with holy powers
And faculties, whether to work or feel:
To apprehend all passions and all moods
Which time, and place, and season do impress
Upon the visible universe, and work
Like changes there by force of my own mind.
I was a Freeman; in the purest sense

Was free, and to majestic ends was strong.   90
I do not speak of learning, moral truth,
Or understanding; 'twas enough for me
To know that I was otherwise endowed.
When the first glitter of the show was passed,
And the first dazzle of the taper light,
As if with a rebound my mind returned
Into its former self. Oft did I leave
My Comrades, and the Crowd, Buildings and Groves,
And walked along the fields, the level fields,
With Heaven's blue concave reared above my head;   100
And now it was, that, thro' such change entire,
And this first absence from those shapes sublime
Wherewith I had been conversant, my mind
Seemed busier in itself than heretofore;
At least, I more directly recognised
My powers and habits: let me dare to speak
A higher language, say that now I felt
The strength and consolation which were mine.
As if awakened, summoned, rouzed, constrained,
I looked for universal things; perused   110
The common countenance of earth and heaven;
And, turning the mind in upon itself,
Pored, watched, expected, listened; spread my thoughts
And spread them with a wider creeping; felt
Incumbences more awful, visitings
Of the Upholder, of the tranquil Soul,
Which underneath all passion lives secure
A steadfast life. But peace! it is enough
To notice that I was ascending now
To such community with highest truth.   120

    A track pursuing not untrod before,
From deep analogies by thought supplied,
Or consciousnesses not to be subdued,
To every natural form, rock, fruit or flower,
Even the loose stones that cover the high-way,
I gave a moral life, I saw them feel,
Or linked them to some feeling: the great mass
Lay bedded in a quickening soul, and all
That I beheld respired with inward meaning.

Thus much for the one Presence, and the Life   130
Of the great whole; suffice it here to add
That whatsoe'er of Terror or of Love,
Or Beauty, Nature's daily face put on
From transitory passion, unto this
I was as wakeful, even, as waters are
To the sky's motion; in a kindred sense
Of passion was obedient as a lute
That waits upon the touches of the wind.
So was it with me in my solitude;
So often among multitudes of men.   140
Unknown, unthought of, yet I was most rich,
I had a world about me; 'twas my own,
I made it; for it only lived to me,
And to the God who looked into my mind.
Such sympathies would sometimes shew themselves
By outward gestures and by visible looks.
Some called it madness: such, indeed, it was,
If child-like fruitfulness in passing joy,
If steady moods of thoughtfulness, matured
To inspiration, sort with such a name;   150
If prophesy be madness; if things viewed
By Poets in old time, and higher up
By the first men, earth's first inhabitants,
May in these tutored days no more be seen
With undisordered sight: but leaving this
It was no madness: for I had an eye
Which in my strongest workings, evermore
Was looking for the shades of difference
As they lie hid in all exterior forms,
Near or remote, minute or vast, an eye   160
Which from a stone, a tree, a withered leaf,
To the broad ocean and the azure heavens,
Spangled with kindred multitudes of stars,
Could find no surface where its power might sleep,
Which spake perpetual logic to my soul,
And by an unrelenting agency
Did bind my feelings, even as in a chain.

    And here, O Friend! have I retraced my life
Up to an eminence, and told a tale

Of matters which, not falsely, I may call   170
The glory of my youth. Of Genius, Power,
Creation and Divinity itself
I have been speaking, for my theme has been
What passed within me. Not of outward things
Done visibly for other minds, words, signs,
Symbols or actions; but of my own heart
Have I been speaking, and my youthful mind.
O Heavens! how awful is the might of Souls,
And what they do within themselves, while yet
The yoke of earth is new to them, the world   180
Nothing but a wild field where they were sown.
This is, in truth, heroic argument,°
And genuine prowess, which I wished to touch
With hand however weak; but in the main
It lies far hidden from the reach of words.
Points have we all of us within our souls,
Where all stand single; this I feel, and make
Breathings for incommunicable powers.
Yet each man is a memory to himself,
And, therefore, now that I must quit this theme,   190
I am not heartless; for there's not a man
That lives who hath not had his godlike hours,
And knows not what majestic sway we have,
As natural beings in the strength of Nature.

   Enough: for now into a populous Plain
We must descend.—A Traveller I am,
And all my Tale is of myself; even so,
So be it, if the pure in heart delight
To follow me; and Thou, O honored Friend!
Who in my thoughts art ever at my side,   200
Uphold, as heretofore, my fainting steps.

   It hath been told already, how my sight
Was dazzled by the novel show, and how,
Erelong, I did into myself return.
So did it seem, and so, in truth, it was.
Yet this was but short lived: thereafter came
Observance less devout. I had made a change

In climate; and my nature's outward coat
Changed also, slowly and insensibly.
To the deep quiet and majestic thoughts   210
Of loneliness succeeded empty noise
And superficial pastimes; now and then
Forced labour, and, more frequently, forced hopes;
And, worse than all, a treasonable growth
Of indecisive judgements that impaired
And shook the mind's simplicity. And yet
This was a gladsome time. Could I behold,
Who less insensible than sodden clay
On a sea River's bed at ebb of tide,
Could have beheld with undelighted heart,   220
So many happy Youths, so wide and fair
A congregation, in its budding-time
Of health, and hope, and beauty; all at once
So many divers samples of the growth
Of life's sweet season, could have seen unmoved
That miscellaneous garland of wild flowers
Upon the matron temples of a Place
So famous through the world? To me, at least,
It was a goodly prospect: for, through youth,
Though I had been trained up to stand unpropped,   230
And independent musings pleased me so
That spells seemed on me when I was alone,
Yet could I only cleave to solitude
In lonesome places; if a throng was near
That way I leaned by nature; for my heart
Was social, and loved idleness and joy.

Not seeking those who might participate
My deeper pleasures (nay I had not once,
Though not unused to mutter lonesome songs,
Even with myself divided such delight,   240
Or looked that way for aught that might be cloathed
In human language), easily I passed
From the remembrances of better things,
And slipped into the weekday works of youth,
Unburthened, unalarmed, and unprofaned.
Caverns there were within my mind, which sun
Could never penetrate, yet did there not

Want store of leafy arbours where the light
Might enter in at will. Companionships,
Friendships, acquaintances, were welcome all;   250
We sauntered, played, we rioted, we talked
Unprofitable talk at morning hours,
Drifted about along the streets and walks,
Read lazily in lazy books, went forth
To gallop through the country in blind zeal
Of senseless horsemanship, or on the breast
Of Cam sailed boisterously, and let the stars
Come out, perhaps without one quiet thought.

    Such was the tenor of the opening act
In this new life. Imagination slept,   260
And yet not utterly. I could not print
Ground where the grass had yielded to the steps
Of generations of illustrious Men,
Unmoved; I could not always lightly pass
Through the same Gateways; sleep where they had slept,
Wake where they waked, range that enclosure old,
That garden of great intellects, undisturbed.
Place also by the side of this dark sense
Of nobler feeling, that those spiritual Men,
Even the great Newton's own etherial Self,   270
Seemed humbled in these precincts, thence to be
The more beloved, invested here with tasks
Of life's plain business, as a daily garb;
Dictators at the plough, a change that left°
All genuine admiration unimpaired.

    Beside the pleasant Mills of Trompington°
I laughed with Chaucer; in the hawthorn shade
Heard him (while birds were warbling) tell his tales
Of amorous passion. And that gentle Bard,
Chosen by the Muses for their Page of State,   280
Sweet Spenser, moving through his clouded heaven
With the moon's beauty and the moon's soft pace,
I called him Brother, Englishman, and Friend.
Yea, our blind Poet, who, in his later day,
Stood almost single, uttering odious truth,
Darkness before, and danger's voice behind;°

Soul awful! if the earth has ever lodged
An awful Soul, I seemed to see him here
Familiarly, and in his Scholar's dress
Bounding before me, yet a stripling Youth,   290
A Boy, no better, with his rosy cheeks
Angelical, keen eye, courageous look,
And conscious step of purity and pride.

Among the Band of my Compeers was one,
My class-fellow at School, whose chance it was
To lodge in the Apartments which had been,
Time out of mind, honored by Milton's name;
The very shell reputed of the abode
Which he had tenanted. O temperate Bard!
One afternoon, the first time I set foot   300
In this thy innocent Nest and Oratory,
Seated with others in a festive ring
Of common-place convention, I to thee
Poured out libations, to thy memory drank,
Within my private thoughts, till my brain reeled,
Never so clouded by the fumes of wine
Before that hour, or since. Thence forth I ran
From that assembly, through a length of streets,
Ran, Ostrich-like, to reach our Chapel Door
In not a desperate or opprobrious time,   310
Albeit long after the importunate Bell
Had stopped, with wearisome Cassandra voice°
No longer haunting the dark winter night.
Call back, O Friend! a moment to thy mind,
The place itself and fashion of the rites.
Upshouldering in a dislocated lump,
With shallow ostentatious carelessness,
My Surplice, gloried in, and yet despised,
I clove in pride through the inferior throng
Of the plain Burghers, who in audience stood   320
On the last skirts of their permitted ground,
Beneath the pealing Organ. Empty thoughts!
I am ashamed of them; and that great Bard,
And thou, O Friend! who in thy ample mind
Hast stationed me for reverence and love,
Ye will forgive the weakness of that hour

In some of its unworthy vanities,
Brother of many more.
                              In this mixed sort
The months passed on, remissly, not given up
To wilful alienation from the right,   330
Or walks of open scandal; but in vague
And loose indifference, easy likings, aims
Of a low pitch; duty and zeal dismissed,
Yet Nature, or a happy course of things
Not doing in their stead the needful work.
The memory languidly revolved, the heart
Reposed in noontide rest; the inner pulse
Of contemplation almost failed to beat.
Rotted as by a charm, my life became
A floating island, an amphibious thing,   340
Unsound, of spungy texture, yet withal,
Not wanting a fair face of water-weeds
And pleasant flowers.—The thirst of living praise,
A reverence for the glorious Dead, the sight
Of those long Vistos, Catacombs in which
Perennial minds lie visibly entombed,
Have often stirred the heart of youth, and bred
A fervent love of rigorous discipline.
Alas! such high commotion touched not me;
No look was in these walls to put to shame   350
My easy spirits, and discountenance
Their light composure, far less to instil
A calm resolve of mind, firmly addressed
To puissant efforts. Nor was this the blame
Of others, but my own; I should, in truth,
As far as doth concern my single self
Misdeem most widely, lodging it elsewhere.
For I, bred up in Nature's lap, was even
As a spoiled Child; and rambling like the wind
As I had done in daily intercourse   360
With those delicious rivers, solemn heights,
And mountains; ranging like a fowl of the air,
I was ill tutored for captivity,
To quit my pleasure, and from month to month,
Take up a station calmly on the perch
Of sedentary peace. Those lovely forms

Had also left less space within my mind,
Which, wrought upon instinctively, had found
A freshness in those objects of its love,
A winning power, beyond all other power.   370
Not that I slighted Books; that were to lack
All sense; but other passions had been mine,
More fervent, making me less prompt, perhaps,
To in-door study than was wise or well,
Or suited to my years. Yet I could shape
The image of a Place which, soothed and lulled
As I had been, trained up in paradise
Among sweet garlands and delightful sounds,
Accustomed in my loneliness to walk
With Nature magisterially, yet I,   380
Methinks, could shape the image of a Place
Which with its aspect should have bent me down
To instantaneous service, should at once
Have made me pay to science and to arts
And written lore, acknowledged my liege Lord,
A homage, frankly offered up, like that
Which I had paid to Nature. Toil and pains
In this recess which I have bodied forth
Should spread from heart to heart; and stately groves,
Majestic edifices, should not want   390
A corresponding dignity within.
The congregating temper, which pervades
Our unripe years, not wasted, should be made
To minister to works of high attempt,
Which the enthusiast would perform with love;
Youth should be awed, possessed, as with a sense
Religious, of what holy joy there is
In knowledge, if it be sincerely sought
For its own sake, in glory, and in praise,
If but by labour won, and to endure.   400
The passing Day should learn to put aside
Her trappings here, should strip them off, abashed
Before antiquity, and stedfast truth,
And strong book-mindedness; and over all
Should be a healthy, sound simplicity,
A seemly plainness, name it as you will,
Republican or pious.

                  If these thoughts
Be a gratuitous emblazonry
That does but mock this recreant age, at least
Let Folly and False-seeming, we might say,   410
Be free to affect whatever formal gait
Of moral or scholastic discipline
Shall raise them highest in their own esteem;
Let them parade, among the Schools at will;
But spare the House of God. Was ever known
The witless Shepherd who would drive his Flock
With serious repetition to a pool
Of which 'tis plain to sight they never taste?
A weight must surely hang on days begun
And ended with worst mockery. Be wise,   420
Ye Presidents and Deans, and to your Bells
Give seasonable rest; for 'tis a sound
Hollow as ever vexed the tranquil air;
And your officious doings bring disgrace
On the plain Steeples of our English Church,
Whose worship 'mid remotest village trees
Suffers for this. Even Science, too, at hand°
In daily sight of such irreverence,
Is smitten thence with an unnatural taint,
Loses her just authority, falls beneath   430
Collateral suspicion, else unknown.
This obvious truth did not escape me then,
Unthinking as I was, and I confess
That, having in my native hills given loose
To a Schoolboy's dreaming, I had raised a pile
Upon the basis of the coming time,
Which now before me melted fast away,
Which could not live, scarcely had life enough
To mock the Builder. Oh! what joy it were
To see a Sanctuary for our Country's Youth,   440
With such a spirit in it as might be
Protection for itself, a Virgin grove,
Primaeval in its purity and depth;
Where, though the shades were filled with chearfulness,
Nor indigent of songs, warbled from crowds
In under-coverts, yet the countenance
Of the whole place should wear a stamp of awe;

A habitation sober and demure
For ruminating creatures, a domain
For quiet things to wander in, a haunt   450
In which the Heron might delight to feed
By the shy rivers, and the Pelican°
Upon the cypress spire in lonely thought
Might sit and sun himself. Alas! alas!
In vain for such solemnity we look;
Our eyes are crossed by Butterflies, our ears
Hear chattering Popinjays; the inner heart
Is trivial, and the impresses without
Are of a gaudy region.
                        Different sight
Those venerable Doctors saw of old   460
When all who dwelt within these famous Walls
Led in abstemiousness a studious life,
When, in forlorn and naked chambers cooped
And crowded, o'er their ponderous Books they sate
Like caterpillars eating out their way
In silence, or with keen devouring noise
Not to be tracked or fathered. Princes then
At matins froze, and couched at curfew-time,
Trained up, through piety and zeal, to prize
Spare diet, patient labour, and plain weeds.   470
O Seat of Arts! renowned throughout the world,
Far different service in those homely days
The Nurslings of the Muses underwent
From their first childhood. In that glorious time,
When Learning, like a Stranger come from far,
Sounding through Christian Lands her Trumpet, rouzed
The Peasant and the King; when Boys and Youths,
The growth of ragged villages and huts,
Forsook their homes, and, errant in the quest
Of Patron, famous School or friendly Nook,   480
Where, pensioned, they in shelter might sit down,
From Town to Town and through wide-scattered Realms
Journeyed with their huge folios in their hands;
And often, starting from some covert place,
Saluted the chance-comer on the road,
Crying, 'an obolus, a penny give°
To a poor Scholar'; when illustrious Men,

Lovers of truth, by penury constrained,°
Bucer, Erasmus, or Melancthon, read
Before the doors or windows of their Cells 490
By moonshine, through mere lack of taper light.

But peace to vain regrets! We see but darkly
Even when we look behind us; and best things
Are not so pure by nature that they needs
Must keep to all, as fondly all believe,
Their highest promise. If the Mariner,
When at reluctant distance he hath passed
Some fair enticing Island, did but know
What fate might have been his, could he have brought
His Bark to land upon the wished-for spot, 500
Good cause full often would he have to bless
The belt of churlish Surf that scared him thence,
Or haste of the inexorable wind.
For me, I grieve not; happy is the man,
Who only misses what I missed, who falls
No lower than I fell.
                    I did not love,
As hath been noticed heretofore, the guise
Of our scholastic studies; could have wished
The river to have had an ampler range,
And freer pace; but this I tax not; far, 510
Far more I grieved to see among the Band
Of those who in the field of contest stood
As combatants, passions that did to me
Seem low and mean; from ignorance of mine,
In part, and want of just forbearance, yet
My wiser mind grieves now for what I saw.
Willingly did I part from these, and turn
Out of their track, to travel with the shoal
Of more unthinking Natures; easy Minds
And pillowy, and not wanting love that makes 520
The day pass lightly on, when foresight sleeps,
And wisdom, and the pledges interchanged
With our own inner being are forgot.

To Books, our daily fare prescribed, I turned
With sickly appetite, and when I went,

At other times, in quest of my own food,
I chaced not steadily the manly deer,
But laid me down to any casual feast
Of wild wood-honey; or, with truant eyes
Unruly, peeped about for vagrant fruit.   530
And, as for what pertains to human life,
The deeper passions working round me here,
Whether of envy, jealousy, pride, shame,
Ambition, emulation, fear, or hope,
Or those of dissolute pleasure, were by me
Unshared, and only now and then observed,
So little was their hold upon my being,
As outward things that might administer
To knowledge or instruction. Hushed, meanwhile,
Was the under soul, locked up in such a calm,   540
That not a leaf of the great nature stirred.

　　Yet was this deep vacation not given up
To utter waste. Hitherto I had stood
In my own mind remote from human life,
At least from what we commonly so name,
Even as a shepherd on a promontory,
Who, lacking occupation, looks far forth
Into the endless sea, and rather makes
Than finds what he beholds. And sure it is,
That this first transit from the smooth delights   550
And wild outlandish walks of simple youth,
To something that resembled an approach
Towards mortal business, to a privileged world
Within a world, a midway residence
With all its intervenient imagery,
Did better suit my visionary mind,
Far better, than to have been bolted forth,
Thrust out abruptly into Fortune's way
Among the conflicts of substantial life;
By a more just gradation did lead on   560
To higher things, more naturally matured,
For permanent possession, better fruits
Whether of truth or virtue, to ensue.

　　In playful zest of fancy did we note,
(How could we less?) the manners and the ways

Of those who in the livery were arrayed
Of good or evil fame; of those with whom
By frame of academic discipline
Perforce we were connected, men whose sway
And whose authority of Office served   570
To set our minds on edge, and did no more.
Nor wanted we rich pastime of this kind,
Found everywhere, but chiefly, in the ring
Of the grave Elders, Men unscoured, grotesque
In character, tricked out like aged trees
Which, through the lapse of their infirmity,
Give ready place to any random seed
That chuses to be reared upon their trunks.

　　Here on my view, confronting as it were
Those Shepherd Swains whom I had lately left,   580
Did flash a different image of old age;
How different! yet both withal alike,
A Book of rudiments for the unpractised sight,
Objects embossed! and which with sedulous care
Nature holds up before the eye of Youth
In her great School; with further view, perhaps,
To enter early on her tender scheme
Of teaching comprehension with delight,
And mingling playful with pathetic thoughts.

                                                        590
　　The surfaces of artificial life
And manners finely spun, the delicate race
Of colours, lurking, gleaming up and down
Through that state arras woven with silk and gold;
This wily interchange of snaky hues,
Willingly and unwillingly revealed
I had not learned to watch, and at this time
Perhaps, had such been in my daily sight
I might have been indifferent thereto,
As Hermits are to tales of distant things.
Hence for these rarities elaborate   600
Having no relish yet, I was content
With the more homely produce, rudely piled
In this our coarser warehouse. At this day
I smile in many a mountain solitude
At passages and fragments that remain

Of that inferior exhibition, played
By wooden images, a theatre
For Wake or Fair. And oftentimes do flit
Remembrances before me of old Men,
Old Humourists who have been long in their graves,   610
And having almost in my mind put off
Their human names, have into Phantoms passed
Of texture midway betwixt life and books.

  I play the Loiterer: 'tis enough to note
That here, in dwarf proportions, were expressed
The limbs of the great world, its goings-on
Collaterally pourtrayed, as in mock fight,
A Tournament of blows, some hardly dealt,
Though short of mortal combat; and whate'er
Might of this pageant be supposed to hit   620
A simple Rustic's notice, this way less,
More that way, was not wasted upon me.
—And yet this spectacle may well demand
A more substantial name, no mimic shew,
Itself a living part of a live whole,
A creek of the vast sea. For all Degrees
And Shapes of spurious fame and short-lived praise
Here sate in state, and fed with daily alms,
Retainers won away from solid good.
And here was Labour, his own Bond-slave; Hope   630
That never set the pains against the prize;
Idleness, halting with his weary clog;
And poor misguided Shame, and witless Fear,
And simple Pleasure, foraging for Death,
Honour misplaced, and Dignity astray;
Feuds, Factions, Flatteries, Enmity, and Guile,
Murmuring Submission, and bald Government;
The Idol weak as the Idolater;
And Decency and Custom starving Truth;
And blind Authority, beating with his Staff   640
The Child that might have led him; Emptiness
Followed, as of good omen; and meek Worth
Left to itself unheard of, and unknown.

  Of these and other kindred notices
I cannot say what portion is in truth

The naked recollection of that time,
And what may rather have been called to life
By after-meditation. But delight,
That, in an easy temper lulled asleep,
Is still with innocence its own reward,   650
This surely was not wanting. Carelessly
I gazed, roving as through a Cabinet
Or wide Museum (thronged with fishes, gems,
Birds, crocodiles, shells) where little can be seen,
Well understood, or naturally endeared,
Yet still does every step bring something forth
That quickens, pleases, stings; and here and there
A casual rarity is singled out
And has its brief perusal, then gives way
To others, all supplanted in their turn.   660
Meanwhile, amid this gaudy Congress, framed
Of things by nature most unneighbourly,
The head turns round, and cannot right itself;
And, though an aching and a barren sense
Of gay confusion still be uppermost,
With few wise longings and but little love,
Yet something to the memory sticks at last,
Whence profit may be drawn in times to come.

     Thus in submissive idleness, my Friend,
The labouring time of Autumn, Winter, Spring,   670
Nine months, rolled pleasingly away; the tenth
Returned me to my native hills again.

BOOK FOUR

Summer Vacation

A pleasant sight it was when, having clomb
The Heights of Kendal, and that dreary Moor
Was crossed, at length, as from a rampart's edge,
I overlooked the bed of Windermere.
I bounded down the hill, shouting amain

A lusty summons to the farther shore
For the old Ferryman; and when he came
I did not step into the well-known Boat
Without a cordial welcome. Thence right forth
I took my way, now drawing towards home,   10
To that sweet Valley where I had been reared;°
'Twas but a short hour's walk ere, veering round,
I saw the snow-white Church upon its hill
Sit like a thronèd Lady, sending out
A gracious look all over its domain.
Glad greetings had I, and some tears, perhaps,
From my old Dame, so motherly and good,
While she perused me with a Parent's pride.
The thoughts of gratitude shall fall like dew
Upon thy grave, good Creature! While my heart   20
Can beat I never will forget thy name.
Heaven's blessing be upon thee where thou liest,
After thy innocent and busy stir
In narrow cares, thy little daily growth
Of calm enjoyments, after eighty years,
And more than eighty, of untroubled life,
Childless, yet by the strangers to thy blood
Honoured with little less than filial love.
Great joy was mine to see thee once again,
Thee and thy dwelling, and a throng of things   30
About its narrow precincts all beloved,
And many of them seeming yet my own.
Why should I speak of what a thousand hearts
Have felt, and every man alive can guess?
The rooms, the court, the garden were not left
Long unsaluted, and the spreading Pine
And broad stone Table underneath its boughs,
Our summer seat in many a festive hour;
And that unruly Child of mountain birth,
The froward Brook, which soon as he was boxed   40
Within our Garden, found himself at once,
As if by trick insidious and unkind,
Stripped of his voice, and left to dimple down
Without an effort and without a will,
A channel paved by the hand of man.
I looked at him, and smiled, and smiled again,

And in the press of twenty thousand thoughts,
'Ha,' quoth I, 'pretty Prisoner, are you there!'
And now, reviewing soberly that hour,
I marvel that a fancy did not flash   50
Upon me, and a strong desire, straitway,
At sight of such an emblem that shewed forth
So aptly my late course of even days
And all their smooth enthralment, to pen down
A satire on myself. My aged Dame
Was with me, at my side: She guided me;
I willing, nay—nay—wishing to be led.
The face of every neighbour whom I met
Was as a volume to me; some I hailed
Far off, upon the road, or at their work,   60
Unceremonious greetings, interchanged
With half the length of a long field between.
Among my Schoolfellows I scattered round
A salutation that was more constrained,
Though earnest, doubtless with a little pride,
But with more shame, for my habiliments,
The transformation, and the gay attire.

Delighted did I take my place again
At our domestic Table: and, dear Friend!
Relating simply as my wish hath been   70
A Poet's history, can I leave untold
The joy with which I laid me down at night
In my accustomed bed, more welcome now,
Perhaps, than if it had been more desired
Or been more often thought of with regret?
That bed whence I had heard the roaring wind
And clamorous rain, that Bed where I, so oft,
Had lain awake, on breezy nights, to watch
The moon in splendour couched among the leaves
Of a tall Ash, that near our Cottage stood,   80
And watched her with fixed eyes, while to and fro
In the dark summit of the moving Tree
She rocked with every impulse of the wind.

Among the faces which it pleased me well
To see again, was one by ancient right

Our Inmate, a rough Terrier of the hills,
By birth and call of Nature pre-ordained
To hunt the badger and unearth the fox
Among the impervious crags; but, having been
From youth our own adopted, he had passed   90
Into a gentler service. And when first
The boyish spirit flagged, and day by day
Along my veins I kindled with the stir,
The fermentation and the vernal heat
Of Poesy, affecting private shades
Like a sick lover, then this Dog was used
To watch me, an attendant and a friend
Obsequious to my steps, early and late,
Though often of such dilatory walk
Tired, and uneasy at the halts I made.   100
A hundred times when, in these wanderings,
I have been busy with the toil of verse,
Great pains and little progress, and at once
Some fair enchanting image in my mind
Rose up, full-formed like Venus from the sea,
Have I sprung forth towards him, and let loose
My hand upon his back with stormy joy,
Caressing him again, and yet again.
And when, in the public roads at eventide
I sauntered, like a river murmuring   110
And talking to itself, at such a season
It was his custom to jog on before;
But, duly, whensoever he had met
A passenger approaching, would he turn
To give me timely notice, and straitway,
Punctual to such admonishment, I hushed
My voice, composed my gait, and shaped myself
To give and take a greeting that might save
My name from piteous rumours, such as wait
On men suspected to be crazed in brain.   120

   Those walks, well worthy to be prized and loved—
Regretted! that word, too, was on my tongue,
But they were richly laden with all good,
And cannot be remembered but with thanks
And gratitude, and perfect joy of heart—

Those walks did now, like a returning spring,
Come back on me again. When first I made
Once more the circuit of our little Lake
If ever happiness hath lodged with man,
That day consummate happiness was mine,   130
Wide-spreading, steady, calm, contemplative.
The sun was set, or setting, when I left
Our cottage door, and evening soon brought on
A sober hour, not winning or serene,
For cold and raw the air was, and untuned:
But, as a face we love is sweetest then
When sorrow damps it, or, whatever look
It chance to wear is sweetest if the heart
Have fulness in itself, even so with me
It fared that evening. Gently did my soul   140
Put off her veil, and, self-transmuted, stood
Naked as in the presence of her God.
As on I walked, a comfort seemed to touch
A heart that had not been disconsolate,
Strength came where weakness was not known to be,
At least not felt; and restoration came,
Like an intruder, knocking at the door
Of unacknowledged weariness. I took
The balance in my hand and weighed myself.
I saw but little, and thereat was pleased;   150
Little did I remember, and even this
Still pleased me more; but I had hopes and peace
And swellings of the spirits, was rapt and soothed,
Conversed with promises, had glimmering views
How Life pervades the undecaying mind,
How the immortal Soul with God-like power
Informs, creates, and thaws the deepest sleep
That time can lay upon her; how on earth,
Man, if he do but live within the light
Of high endeavours, daily spreads abroad   160
His being with a strength that cannot fail.
Nor was there want of milder thoughts, of love,
Of innocence, and holiday repose,
And more than pastoral quiet, in the heart
Of amplest projects, and a peaceful end
At last, or glorious, by endurance won.

Thus musing, in a wood I sate me down,
Alone, continuing there to muse: meanwhile
The mountain heights were slowly overspread
With darkness, and before a rippling breeze   170
The long Lake lengthened out its hoary line;
And in the sheltered coppice where I sate,
Around me, from among the hazel leaves,
Now here, now there, stirred by the straggling wind,
Came intermittingly a breath-like sound,
A respiration short and quick, which oft,
Yea, might I say, again and yet again,
Mistaking for the panting of my Dog,
The off-and-on Companion of my walk,
I turned my head, to look if he were there.   180

    A freshness also found I at this time
In human Life, the life I mean of those
Whose occupations really I loved.
The prospect often touched me with surprize,
Crowded and full, and changed, as seemed to me,
Even as a garden in the heat of Spring,
After an eight-days' absence. For (to omit
The things which were the same and yet appeared
So different) amid this solitude,
The little Vale where was my chief abode,   190
'Twas not indifferent to a youthful mind
To note, perhaps, some sheltered Seat in which
An old Man had been used to sun himself,
Now empty; pale-faced Babes whom I had left
In arms, known children of the neighbourhood,
Now rosy prattlers, tottering up and down;
And growing Girls whose beauty, filched away
With all its pleasant promises, was gone
To deck some slighted Playmate's homely cheek.

    Yes, I had something of another eye,   200
And often, looking round, was moved to smiles,
Such as a delicate work of humour breeds.
I read, without design, the opinions, thoughts,
Of those plain-living people, in a sense

Of love and knowledge; with another eye
I saw the quiet Woodman in the Woods,
The Shepherd on the Hills. With new delight,
This chiefly, did I view my grey-haired Dame,
Saw her go forth to Church, or other work
Of state, equipped in monumental trim,   210
Short Velvet Cloak (her Bonnet of the like)
A Mantle such as Spanish Cavaliers
Wore in old time. Her smooth domestic life,
Affectionate without uneasiness,
Her talk, her business pleased me, and no less
Her clear though shallow stream of piety,
That ran on Sabbath days a fresher course.
With thoughts unfelt till now, I saw her read
Her Bible on the Sunday afternoons;
And loved the book, when she had dropped asleep,   220
And made of it a pillow for her head.

   Nor less do I remember to have felt
Distinctly manifested at this time
A dawning, even as of another sense,
A human-heartedness about my love
For objects hitherto the gladsome air
Of my own private being, and no more;
Which I had loved, even as a blessed Spirit
Or Angel, if he were to dwell on earth,
Might love, in individual happiness.   230
But now there opened on me other thoughts,
Of change, congratulation, and regret,
A new-born feeling. It spread far and wide;
The trees, the mountains shared it, and the brooks,
The stars of Heaven, now seen in their old haunts,
White Sirius, glittering over the southern crags,
Orion with his belt, and those fair Seven,°
Acquaintances of every little child,
And Jupiter, my own beloved Star.
Whatever shadings of mortality   240
Had fallen upon these objects heretofore
Were different in kind; not tender: strong,
Deep, gloomy were they and severe, the scatterings
Of Childhood; and, moreover, had given way,

In later youth, to beauty, and to love
Enthusiastic, to delight and joy.

        As one who hangs down-bending from the side
Of a slow-moving Boat, upon the breast
Of a still water, solacing himself
With such discoveries as his eye can make,   250
Beneath him, in the bottom of the deeps,
Sees many beauteous sights, weeds, fishes, flowers,
Grots, pebbles, roots of trees, and fancies more,
Yet often is perplexed, and cannot part
The shadow from the substance, rocks and sky,
Mountains and clouds, from that which is indeed
The region, and the things which there abide
In their true dwelling; now is crossed by gleam
Of his own image, by a sunbeam now,
And motions that are sent he knows not whence,   260
Impediments that make his task more sweet;
—Such pleasant office have we long pursued
Incumbent o'er the surface of past time
With like success; nor have we often looked
On more alluring shows (to me, at least,)
More soft, or less ambiguously descried,
Than those which now we have been passing by,
And where we still are lingering. Yet, in spite
Of all these new employments of the mind,
There was an inner falling-off. I loved,   270
Loved deeply, all that I had loved before,
More deeply even than ever; but a swarm
Of heady thoughts jostling each other, gawds,
And feast, and dance, and public revelry,
And sports and games (less pleasing in themselves,
Than as they were a badge glossy and fresh
Of manliness and freedom) these did now
Seduce me from the firm habitual quest
Of feeding pleasures, from that eager zeal,
Those yearnings which had every day been mine,   280
A wild, unworldly-minded Youth, given up
To Nature and to Books, or, at the most,
From time to time, by inclination shipped,
One among many, in societies,

That were, or seemed, as simple as myself.
But now was come a change; it would demand
Some skill, and longer time than may be spared,
To paint, even to myself, these vanities,
And how they wrought. But, sure it is that now
Contagious air did oft environ me,   290
Unknown among these haunts in former days.
The very garments that I wore appeared
To prey upon my strength, and stopped the course
And quiet stream of self-forgetfulness.
Something there was about me that perplexed
The authentic sight of reason, pressed too closely
On that religious dignity of mind,
That is the very faculty of truth;
Which wanting, either, from the very first,
A function never lighted up, or else   300
Extinguished, Man, a creature great and good,
Seems but a pageant plaything with wild claws,
And this great frame of breathing elements
A senseless Idol.
                        That vague heartless chace
Of trivial pleasures was a poor exchange
For Books and Nature at that early age.
'Tis true, some casual knowledge might be gained
Of character or life; but at that time,
Of manners put to school I took small note,
And all my deeper passions lay elsewhere.   310
Far better had it been to exalt the mind
By solitary study, to uphold
Intense desire by thought and quietness.
And yet, in chastisement of these regrets,
The memory of one particular hour
Doth here rise up against me. In a throng,
A festal company of Maids and Youths,
Old Men, and Matrons staid, promiscuous rout,°
A medley of all tempers, I had passed
The night in dancing, gaiety and mirth;   320
With din of instruments, and shuffling feet,
And glancing forms, and tapers glittering,
And unaimed prattle flying up and down,
Spirits upon the stretch, and here and there

Slight shocks of young love-liking interspersed,
That mounted up like joy into the head,
And tingled through the veins. Ere we retired,
The cock had crowed, the sky was bright with day.
Two miles I had to walk along the fields
Before I reached my home. Magnificent   330
The morning was, a memorable pomp,
More glorious than I ever had beheld.
The Sea was laughing at a distance; all
The solid Mountains were as bright as clouds,
Grain-tinctured, drenched in empyrean light;°
And, in the meadows and the lower grounds,
Was all the sweetness of a common dawn,
Dews, vapours, and the melody of birds,
And Labourers going forth into the fields.
—Ah! need I say, dear Friend, that to the brim   340
My heart was full? I made no vows, but vows
Were then made for me; bond unknown to me
Was given, that I should be, else sinning greatly,
A dedicated Spirit. On I walked
In blessedness, which even yet remains.

   Strange rendezvous my mind was at that time,
A party-coloured shew of grave and gay,
Solid and light, short-sighted and profound,
Of inconsiderate habits and sedate,
Consorting in one mansion unreproved.   350
I knew the worth of that which I possessed,
Though slighted and misused. Besides, in truth,
That Summer, swarming as it did with thoughts
Transient and loose, yet wanted not a store
Of primitive hours, when, by these hindrances
Unthwarted, I experienced in myself
Conformity as just as that of old
To the end and written spirit of God's works,
Whether held forth in Nature or in Man.

   From many wanderings that have left behind   360
Remembrances not lifeless, I will here°
Single out one, then pass to other themes.
   A favorite pleasure hath it been with me,
From time of earliest youth, to walk alone

Along the public Way, when, for the night
Deserted, in its silence it assumes
A character of deeper quietness
Than pathless solitudes. At such an hour
Once, ere these summer months were passed away,
I slowly mounted up a steep ascent   370
Where the road's wat'ry surface, to the ridge
Of that sharp rising, glittered in the moon
And seemed before my eyes another stream
Creeping with silent lapse to join the brook
That murmured in the valley. On I went
Tranquil, receiving in my own despite
Amusement, as I slowly passed along,
From such near objects as from time to time
Perforce intruded on the listless sense
Quiescent, and disposed to sympathy,   380
With an exhausted mind, worn out by toil,
And all unworthy of the deeper joy
Which waits on distant prospect, cliff, or sea,
The dark blue vault, and universe of stars.
Thus did I steal along that silent road,
My body from the stillness drinking in
A restoration like the calm of sleep,
But sweeter far. Above, before, behind,
Around me, all was peace and solitude;
I looked not round, nor did the solitude   390
Speak to my eye; but it was heard and felt.
O happy state! what beauteous pictures now
Rose in harmonious imagery—they rose
As from some distant region of my soul
And came along like dreams; yet such as left
Obscurely mingled with their passing forms
A consciousness of animal delight,
A self-possession felt in every pause
And every gentle movement of my frame.
     While thus I wandered, step by step led on,   400
It chanced a sudden turning of the road
Presented to my view an uncouth shape,
So near, that, slipping back into the shade
Of a thick hawthorn, I could mark him well,
Myself unseen. He was of stature tall,

A foot above man's common measure tall,
Stiff in his form, and upright, lank and lean;
A man more meagre, as it seemed to me,
Was never seen abroad by night or day.
His arms were long, and bare his hands; his mouth   410
Shewed ghastly in the moonlight; from behind
A milestone propped him, and his figure seemed
Half-sitting, and half-standing. I could mark
That he was clad in military garb,
Though faded, yet entire. He was alone,
Had no attendant, neither Dog, nor Staff,
Nor knapsack; in his very dress appeared
A desolation, a simplicity
That seemed akin to solitude. Long time
Did I peruse him with a mingled sense   420
Of fear and sorrow. From his lips, meanwhile,
There issued murmuring sounds, as if of pain
Or of uneasy thought; yet still his form
Kept the same steadiness, and at his feet
His shadow lay, and moved not. In a Glen
Hard by, a Village stood, whose roofs and doors
Were visible among the scattered trees,
Scarce distant from the spot an arrow's flight.
I wished to see him move, but he remained
Fixed to his place, and still from time to time   430
Sent forth a murmuring voice of dead complaint,
Groans scarcely audible. Without self-blame
I had not thus prolonged my watch; and now,
Subduing my heart's specious cowardise,
I left the shady nook where I had stood,
And hailed him. Slowly from his resting-place
He rose, and with a lean and wasted arm
In measured gesture lifted to his head,
Returned my salutation, then resumed
His station as before. And when, erelong,   440
I asked his history, he in reply
Was neither slow nor eager, but unmoved,
And with a quiet, uncomplaining voice,
A stately air of mild indifference,
He told, in simple words, a Soldier's tale.
That in the Tropic Islands he had served,

Whence he had landed scarcely ten days past,
That on his landing he had been dismissed,
And now was travelling to his native home.
At this, I turned and looked towards the Village   450
But all were gone to rest; the fires all out;
And every silent window to the Moon
Shone with a yellow glitter. 'No one there,'
Said I, 'is waking, we must measure back
The way which we have come: behind yon wood
A Labourer dwells, and, take it on my word
He will not murmur should we break his rest,
And with a ready heart will give you food
And lodging for the night.' At this he stooped,
And from the ground took up an oaken Staff,   460
By me yet unobserved, a Traveller's Staff,
Which, I suppose, from his slack hand had dropped,
And lain till now neglected in the grass.

  Towards the Cottage without more delay
We shaped our course. As it appeared to me,
He travelled without pain, and I beheld
With ill-suppressed astonishment his tall
And ghastly figure moving at my side;
Nor, while we journeyed thus could I forbear
To question him of what he had endured   470
From hardship, battle, or the pestilence.
He, all the while, was in demeanour calm,
Concise in answer; solemn and sublime
He might have seemed, but that in all he said
There was a strange half-absence, and a tone
Of weakness and indifference, as of one
Remembering the importance of his theme
But feeling it no longer. We advanced
Slowly, and, ere we to the wood were come
Discourse had ceased. Together on we passed,   480
In silence, through the shades, gloomy and dark;
Then, turning up along an open field
We gained the Cottage. At the door I knocked,
Calling aloud, 'my Friend, here is a Man
By sickness overcome; beneath your roof
This night let him find rest, and give him food,

If food he need, for he is faint and tired.'
Assured that now my Comrade would repose
In comfort, I entreated that henceforth
He would not linger in the public ways   490
But ask for timely furtherance and help
Such as his state required. At this reproof,
With the same ghastly mildness in his look
He said, 'My trust is in the God of Heaven
And in the eye of him that passes me.'
The Cottage door was speedily unlocked,
And now the Soldier touched his hat again
With his lean hand, and in a voice that seemed
To speak with a reviving interest,
Till then unfelt, he thanked me; I returned   500
The blessing of the poor unhappy Man;
And so we parted. Back I cast a look,
And lingered near the door a little space;
Then sought with quiet heart my distant home.

BOOK FIVE
Books

Even in the steadiest mood of reason, when
All sorrow for thy transitory pains
Goes out, it grieves me for thy state, O Man,
Thou paramount Creature! and thy race, while ye
Shall sojourn on this planet; not for woes
Which thou endurest; that weight, albeit huge,
I charm away; but for those palms atchieved
Through length of time, by study and hard thought,
The honours of thy high endowments; there
My sadness finds its fuel. Hitherto,   10
In progress through this Verse, my mind hath looked
Upon the speaking face of earth and heaven
As her prime Teacher, intercourse with man
Established by the sovereign Intellect,
Who through that bodily Image hath diffused
A soul divine which we participate,
A deathless spirit. Thou also, Man, hast wrought,

For commerce of thy nature with itself,
Things worthy of unconquerable life;
And yet we feel, we cannot chuse but feel,   20
That these must perish. Tremblings of the heart
It gives, to think that the immortal being
No more shall need such garments; and yet Man,
As long as he shall be the Child of Earth,
Might almost 'weep to have' what he may lose,°
Nor be himself extinguished, but survive
Abject, depressed, forlorn, disconsolate.
A thought is with me sometimes, and I say,
'Should earth by inward throes be wrenched throughout,
Or fire be sent from far to wither all   30
Her pleasant habitations, and dry up
Old Ocean in his bed left singed and bare,
Yet would the living Presence still subsist
Victorious; and composure would ensue,
And kindlings like the morning; presage sure,
Though slow, perhaps, of a returning day.'
But all the meditations of mankind,
Yea, all the adamantine holds of truth,
By reason built, or passion, which itself
Is highest reason in a soul sublime;   40
The consecrated works of Bard and Sage,
Sensuous or intellectual, wrought by men,
Twin labourers and heirs of the same hopes,
Where would they be? Oh! why hath not the mind
Some element to stamp her image on
In nature somewhat nearer to her own?
Why, gifted with such powers to send abroad
Her spirit, must it lodge in shrines so frail?

    One day, when in the hearing of a Friend,
I had given utterance to thoughts like these,   50
He answered with a smile that, in plain truth,
'Twas going far to seek disquietude;
But on the front of his reproof, confessed
That he, at sundry seasons, had himself
Yielded to kindred hauntings. And forthwith
Added, that once upon a summer's noon,
While he was sitting in a rocky cave

By the sea-side, perusing, as it chanced,
The famous History of the Errant Knight
Recorded by Cervantes, these same thoughts°   60
Came to him; and to height unusual rose
While listlessly he sate, and having closed
The Book, had turned his eyes towards the Sea.
On Poetry and geometric Truth,
The knowledge that endures, upon these two,
And their high privilege of lasting life,
Exempt from all internal injury,
He mused: upon these chiefly: and at length,
His senses yielding to the sultry air,
Sleep seized him, and he passed into a dream.   70
He saw before him an Arabian Waste,°
A Desart, and he fancied that himself
Was sitting there in the wide wilderness,
Alone, upon the sands. Distress of mind
Was growing in him when, behold! at once
To his great joy a Man was at his side,
Upon a dromedary mounted high.
He seemed an Arab of the Bedouin Tribes;
A Lance he bore, and underneath one arm
A Stone, and, in the opposite hand, a Shell   80
Of a surpassing brightness. Much rejoiced
The dreaming Man that he should have a Guide
To lead him through the Desart; and he thought,
While questioning himself what this strange freight
Which the Newcomer carried through the Waste
Could mean, the Arab told him that the Stone,
To give it in the language of the Dream,
Was Euclid's Elements; 'and this,' said he,
'This other,' pointing to the Shell, 'this Book
Is something of more worth.' 'And, at the word,   90
The Stranger', said my Friend continuing,
'Stretched forth the Shell towards me, with command
That I should hold it to my ear. I did so,
And heard that instant in an unknown Tongue,
Which yet I understood, articulate sounds,
A loud prophetic blast of harmony,
An Ode, in passion uttered, which foretold
Destruction to the Children of the Earth

By deluge now at hand. No sooner ceased
The Song, but with calm look, the Arab said   100
That all was true; that it was even so
As had been spoken; and that he himself
Was going then to bury those two Books:
The one that held acquaintance with the stars,
And wedded man to man by purest bond
Of nature, undisturbed by space or time;
The other that was a God, yea many Gods,
Had voices more than all the winds, and was
A joy, a consolation, and a hope.'
My friend continued, 'Strange as it may seem,   110
I wondered not, although I plainly saw
The one to be a Stone, the other a Shell,
Nor doubted once but that they both were Books,
Having a perfect faith in all that passed.
A wish was now ingendered in my fear
To cleave unto this Man, and I begged leave
To share his errand with him. On he passed
Not heeding me; I followed, and took note
That he looked often backward with wild look,
Grasping his twofold treasure to his side.   120
Upon a Dromedary, Lance in rest,
He rode, I keeping pace with him, and now
I fancied that he was the very Knight
Whose Tale Cervantes tells, yet not the Knight,
But was an Arab of the Desart too;
Of these was neither, and was both at once.
His countenance, meanwhile, grew more disturbed,
And, looking backwards when he looked, I saw
A glittering light, and asked him whence it came.
"It is," said he, "the waters of the deep   130
Gathering upon us," quickening then his pace
He left me: I called after him aloud;
He heeded not; but with his twofold charge
Beneath his arm, before me full in view
I saw him riding o'er the Desart Sands,
With the fleet waters of the drowning world
In chace of him; whereat I waked in terror,
And saw the Sea before me, and the Book,
In which I had been reading at my side.'

Full often, taking from the world of sleep   140
This Arab Phantom, which my Friend beheld,
This Semi-Quixote, I to him have given
A substance, fancied him a living man,
A gentle Dweller in the Desert, crazed
By love and feeling and internal thought,
Protracted among endless solitudes;
Have shaped him, in the oppression of his brain,
Wandering upon this quest, and thus equipped.
And I have scarcely pitied him; have felt
A reverence for a Being thus employed,   150
And thought that in the blind and awful lair
Of such a madness, reason did lie couched.
Enow there are on earth to take in charge
Their Wives, their Children, and their virgin Loves,
Or whatsoever else the heart holds dear;
Enow to think of these; yea, will I say,
In sober contemplation of the approach
Of such great overthrow, made manifest
By certain evidence, that I, methinks,
Could share that Maniac's anxiousness, could go   160
Upon like errand. Oftentimes, at least,
Me hath such deep entrancement half-possessed,
When I have held a volume in my hand
Poor earthly casket of immortal Verse!
Shakespeare, or Milton, Labourers divine!

Mighty, indeed supreme, must be the power
Of living Nature, which could thus so long
Detain me from the best of other thoughts.
Even in the lisping time of Infancy,
And later down, in prattling Childhood, even   170
While I was travelling back among those days,
How could I ever play an ingrate's part?°
Once more should I have made those bowers resound,
And intermingled strains of thankfulness
With their own thoughtless melodies. At least,
It might have well beseemed me to repeat
Some simply fashioned tale; to tell again,
In slender accents of sweet Verse, some tale
That did bewitch me then, and soothes me now.

O Friend! O Poet! Brother of my soul,   180
Think not that I could ever pass along
Untouched by these remembrances; no, no,
But I was hurried forward by a stream,
And could not stop. Yet wherefore should I speak,
Why call upon a few weak words to say
What is already written in the hearts
Of all that breathe? what in the path of all
Drops daily from the tongue of every child,
Wherever Man is found. The trickling tear
Upon the cheek of listening Infancy   190
Tells it, and the insuperable look
That drinks as if it never could be full.

   That portion of my story I shall leave
There registered: whatever else there be
Of power or pleasure, sown or fostered thus,
Peculiar to myself, let that remain
Where it lies hidden in its endless home
Among the depths of time. And yet it seems
That here, in memory of all books which lay
Their sure foundations in the heart of Man,   200
Whether by native prose or numerous verse,°
That in the name of all inspired Souls,
From Homer, the great Thunderer; from the voice
Which roars along the bed of Jewish Song;
And that, more varied and elaborate,
Those trumpet-tones of harmony that shake
Our Shores in England; from those loftiest notes
Down to the low and wren-like warblings, made
For Cottagers and Spinners at the wheel,
And weary Travellers when they rest themselves   210
By the highways and hedges; ballad tunes,
Food for the hungry ears of little Ones,
And of old Men who have survived their joy;
It seemeth, in behalf of these, the works
And of the Men who framed them, whether known,
Or sleeping nameless in their scattered graves,
That I should here assert their rights, attest
Their honours, and should, once for all, pronounce
Their benediction; speak of them as Powers

For ever to be hallowed; only less,   220
For what we may become, and what we need,
Than Nature's self, which is the breath of God.

    Rarely, and with reluctance, would I stoop
To transitory themes; yet I rejoice,
And, by these thoughts admonished, must speak out
Thanksgivings from my heart, that I was reared
Safe from an evil which these days have laid
Upon the Children of the Land, a pest
That might have dried me up, body and soul.
This Verse is dedicate to Nature's self,   230
And things that teach as Nature teaches, then
Oh where had been the Man, the Poet where?
Where had we been, we two, beloved Friend,
If we, in lieu of wandering, as we did,
Through heights and hollows, and bye-spots of tales
Rich with indigenous produce, open ground
Of Fancy, happy pastures ranged at will!
Had been attended, followed, watched, and noosed,°
Each in his several melancholy walk,
Stringed like a poor man's Heifer at its feed,   240
Led through the lanes in forlorn servitude;
Or rather like a stallèd ox shut out
From touch of growing grass; that may not taste
A flower till it have yielded up its sweets.
A prelibation to the mower's scythe.

    Behold the Parent Hen amid her Brood,
Though fledged and feathered, and well pleased to part
And straggle from her presence, still a Brood,
And she herself from the maternal bond
Still undischarged; yet doth she little more   250
Than move with them in tenderness and love,
A centre of the circle which they make;
And, now and then, alike from need of theirs,
And call of her own natural appetites,
She scratches, ransacks up the earth for food
Which they partake at pleasure. Early died°
My honoured Mother; she who was the heart
And hinge of all our learnings and our loves:

She left us destitute, and as we might
Trooping together. Little suits it me   260
To break upon the sabbath of her rest
With any thought that looks at others' blame,
Nor would I praise her but in perfect love.
Hence am I checked: but I will boldly say,
In gratitude, and for the sake of truth,
Unheard by her, that she, not falsely taught,
Fetching her goodness rather from time past
Than shaping novelties from those to come,
Had no presumption, no such jealousy;
Nor did by habit of her thoughts mistrust   270
Our Nature, but had virtual faith that he,°
Who fills the Mother's breasts with innocent milk,
Doth also for our nobler part provide,
Under his great correction and controul,
As innocent instincts, and as innocent food.
This was her creed, and therefore she was pure
From feverish dread of error or mishap
And evil, overweeningly so called;
Was not puffed up by false unnatural hopes;
Nor selfish with unnecessary cares;   280
Nor with impatience from the season asked
More than its timely produce; rather loved
The hours for what they are than from regards
Glanced on their promises in restless pride.
Such was she; not from faculties more strong
Than others have, but from the times, perhaps,
And spot in which she lived, and through a grace
Of modest meekness, simple-mindedness,
A heart that found benignity and hope,
Being itself benign.   290
                          My drift hath scarcely,
I fear, been obvious; for I have recoiled
From showing as it is the monster birth
Engendered by these too industrious times.
Let few words paint it: 'tis a Child, no Child,
But a dwarf Man; in knowledge, virtue, skill;
In what he is not, and in what he is,
The noontide shadow of a man complete;
A worshipper of worldly seemliness,

Not quarrelsome; for that were far beneath
His dignity; with gifts he bubbles o'er   300
As generous as a fountain; selfishness
May not come near him, gluttony or pride;
The wandering Beggars propagate his name,
Dumb creatures find him tender as a nun.
Yet deem him not for this a naked dish
Of goodness merely; he is garnished out.
Arch are his notices, and nice his sense°
Of the ridiculous; deceit and guile,
Meanness and falsehood, he detects, can treat
With apt and graceful laughter; nor is blind   310
To the broad follies of the licensed world;
Though shrewd, yet innocent himself withal
And can read lectures upon innocence.
He is fenced round, nay armed, for aught we know
In panoply complete; and fear itself,
Natural or supernatural alike,
Unless it leap upon him in a dream,
Touches him not. Briefly, the moral part
Is perfect, and in learning and in books
He is a prodigy. His discourse moves slow,   320
Massy and ponderous as a prison door,
Tremendously embossed with terms of art;°
Rank growth of propositions overruns
The Stripling's brain; the path in which he treads
Is choked with grammars; cushion of Divine
Was never such a type of thought profound
As is the pillow where he rests his head.
The Ensigns of the Empire which he holds,
The globe and sceptre of his royalties,
Are telescopes, and crucibles, and maps.   330
Ships he can guide across the pathless sea,
And tell you all their cunning; he can read°
The inside of the earth, and spell the stars;
He knows the policies of foreign Lands;
Can string you names of districts, cities, towns,
The whole world over, tight as beads of dew
Upon a gossamer thread; he sifts, he weighs;
Takes nothing upon trust: his Teachers stare,
The Country People pray for God's good grace,

And tremble at his deep experiments.   340
All things are put to question; he must live
Knowing that he grows wiser every day,
Or else not live at all; and seeing, too,
Each little drop of wisdom as it falls
Into the dimpling cistern of his heart.
Meanwhile old Grandame Earth is grieved to find
The playthings, which her love designed for him,
Unthought of: in their woodland beds the flowers
Weep, and the river sides are all forlorn.

Now this is hollow, 'tis a life of lies   350
From the beginning, and in lies must end.
Forth bring him to the air of common sense,
And, fresh and shewy as it is, the Corps
Slips from us into powder. Vanity
That is his soul, there lives he, and there moves;
It is the soul of every thing he seeks;
That gone, nothing is left which he can love.
Nay, if a thought of purer birth should rise
To carry him towards a better clime,
Some busy helper still is on the watch   360
To drive him back and pound him like a Stray
Within the pinfold of his own conceit,°
Which is his home, his natural dwelling place.
Oh! give us once again the Wishing-Cap°
Of Fortunatus, and the invisible Coat
Of Jack the Giant-killer, Robin Hood,
And Sabra in the forest with St. George!
The child, whose love is here, at least, doth reap
One precious gain, that he forgets himself.

These mighty workmen of our late age   370
Who with a broad highway have overbridged
The froward chaos of futurity,
Tamed to their bidding; they who have the art
To manage books, and things, and make them work
Gently on infant minds, as does the sun
Upon a flower; the Tutors of our Youth
The Guides, the Wardens of our faculties,
And Stewards of our labour, watchful men

And skilful in the usury of time,
Sages, who in their prescience would controul   380
All accidents, and to the very road
Which they have fashioned would confine us down,
Like engines, when will they be taught°
That in the unreasoning progress of the world
A wiser Spirit is at work for us,
A better eye than theirs, most prodigal
Of blessings, and most studious of our good,
Even in what seem our most unfruitful hours?

    There was a Boy, ye knew him well, ye Cliffs°
And Islands of Winander! many a time   390
At evening, when the stars had just begun
To move along the edges of the hills,
Rising or setting, would he stand alone
Beneath the trees, or by the glimmering Lake,
And there, with fingers interwoven, both hands
Pressed closely, palm to palm, and to his mouth
Uplifted, he, as through an instrument,
Blew mimic hootings to the silent owls
That they might answer him.—And they would shout
Across the wat'ry Vale, and shout again,   400
Responsive to his call, with quivering peals,
And long halloos, and screams, and echoes loud
Redoubled and redoubled; concourse wild
Of mirth and jocund din! And when it chanced
That pauses of deep silence mocked his skill,
Then sometimes, in that silence, while he hung
Listening, a gentle shock of mild surprize
Has carried far into his heart the voice
Of mountain torrents; or the visible scene
Would enter unawares into his mind   410
With all its solemn imagery, its rocks,
Its woods, and that uncertain Heaven, received
Into the oosom of the steady Lake.

    This Boy was taken from his Mates, and died
In childhood, ere he was full ten years old.
—Fair are the woods, and beauteous is the spot,
The Vale where he was born; the Churchyard hangs

Upon a Slope above the Village School,
And there, along that bank, when I have passed
At evening, I believe that oftentimes   420
A full half-hour together I have stood
Mute—looking at the Grave in which he lies.
Even now, methinks, before my sight I have
That self-same Village Church; I see her sit,
The throned Lady spoken of erewhile,
On her green hill; forgetful of this Boy
Who slumbers at her feet; forgetful, too,
Of all her silent neighbourhood of graves,
And listening only to the gladsome sounds
That, from the rural School ascending, play   430
Beneath her and about her. May she long
Behold a race of young Ones like to those
With whom I herded! (easily, indeed,
We might have fed upon a fatter soil
Of Arts and Letters, but be that forgiven)
A race of real children, not too wise,
Too learned, or too good; but wanton, fresh,
And bandied up and down by love and hate;
Fierce, moody, patient, venturous, modest, shy;
Mad at their sports like withered leaves in winds;   440
Though doing wrong, and suffering, and full oft
Bending beneath our life's mysterious weight
Of pain and fear; yet still in happiness
Not yielding to the happiest upon earth.
Simplicity in habit, truth in speech,
Be these the daily strengtheners of their minds!
May books and nature be their early joy!
And knowledge, rightly honored with that name,
Knowledge not purchased with the loss of power!

    Well do I call to mind the very week   450
When I was first entrusted to the care
Of that sweet Valley; when its paths, its shores,
And brooks, were like a dream of novelty
To my half-infant thoughts; that very week
While I was roving up and down alone,
Seeking I knew not what, I chanced to cross
One of those open fields, which, shaped like ears,

Make green peninsulas on Esthwaite's Lake:
Twilight was coming on; yet through the gloom,
I saw distinctly on the opposite Shore   460
A heap of garments, left, as I supposed,
By one who there was bathing; long I watched,
But no one owned them; meanwhile the calm Lake
Grew dark, with all the shadows on its breast,
And, now and then, a fish up-leaping, snapped
The breathless stillness. The succeeding day,
(Those unclaimed garments telling a plain Tale)
Went there a Company, and, in their Boat
Sounded with grappling irons, and long poles.
At length, the dead Man, 'mid that beauteous scene°   470
Of trees, and hills and water, bolt upright
Rose with his ghastly face; a spectre shape
Of terror even! and yet no vulgar fear,
Young as I was, a Child not nine years old,
Possessed me, for my inner eye had seen
Such sights before, among the shining streams
Of Fairy Land, the Forests of Romance:
Thence came a spirit hallowing what I saw
With decoration and ideal grace;
A dignity, a smoothness, like the works   480
Of Grecian Art, and purest Poesy.

    I had a precious treasure at that time
A little, yellow canvass-covered Book,
A slender abstract of the Arabian Tales;
And when I learned, as now I first did learn,
From my Companions in this new abode,
That this dear prize of mine was but a block
Hewn from a mighty quarry—in a word,
That there were four large Volumes, laden all
With kindred matter—'twas, in truth, to me   490
A promise scarcely earthly. Instantly
I made a league, a covenant with a Friend
Of my own age, that we should lay aside
The monies we possessed, and hoard up more,
Till our joint savings had amassed enough
To make this Book our own. Through several months
Religiously did we preserve that vow,

And spite of all temptation hoarded up
And hoarded up; but firmness failed at length
Nor were we ever masters of our wish.   500

    And afterwards, when to my Father's House
Returning at the holidays, I found
That golden store of books which I had left
Open to my enjoyment once again
What heart was mine! Full often through the course
Of those glad respites in the summer-time
When, armed with rod and line we went abroad
For a whole day together, I have lain
Down by thy side, O Derwent! murmuring Stream,
On the hot stones and in the glaring sun,   510
And there have read, devouring as I read,
Defrauding the day's glory, desperate!
Till, with a sudden bound of smart reproach,
Such as an Idler deals with in his shame,
I to my sport betook myself again.

    A gracious Spirit o'er this earth presides,
And o'er the heart of man: invisibly
It comes, directing those to works of love
Who care not, know not, think not what they do.
The Tales that charm away the wakeful night   520
In Araby, Romances, Legends, penned
For solace, by the light of monkish Lamps;
Fictions for Ladies, of their Love, devised
By youthful Squires; adventures endless, spun
By the dismantled Warrior in old age,
Out of the bowels of those very thoughts
In which his youth did first extravagate,
These spread like day, and something in the shape
Of these, will live till man shall be no more.
Dumb yearnings, hidden appetites are ours,   530
And they must have their food: our childhood sits,
Our simple childhood sits upon a throne
That hath more power than all the elements.
I guess not what this tells of Being past,
Nor what it augurs of the life to come;
But so it is; and in that dubious hour,

That twilight when we first begin to see
This dawning earth, to recognise, expect;
And in the long probation that ensues,
The time of trial, ere we learn to live   540
In reconcilement with our stinted powers,
To endure this state of meagre vassalage;
Unwilling to forego, confess, submit,
Uneasy and unsettled, yoke-fellows
To custom, mettlesome, and not yet tamed
And humbled down, oh! then we feel, we feel,
We know when we have Friends. Ye dreamers, then,
Forgers of lawless tales! we bless you then,
Impostors, drivellers, dotards, as the ape
Philosophy will call you: then we feel   550
With what, and how great might ye are in league,
Who make our wish our power, our thought a deed,
An empire, a possession; Ye whom Time
And Seasons serve; all Faculties; to whom
Earth crouches, the elements are potter's clay,
Space like a Heaven filled up with Northern lights;
Here, nowhere, there, and everywhere at once.

    It might demand a more impassioned strain
To tell of later pleasures, linked to these,
A tract of the same isthmus which we cross   560
In progress from our native continent
To earth and human life; I mean to speak
Of that delightful time of growing youth
When cravings for the marvellous relent,
And we begin to love what we have seen;
And sober truth, experience, sympathy,
Take stronger hold of us; and words themselves
Move us with conscious pleasure.
                                    I am sad
At thought of raptures now for ever flown,
Even unto tears I sometimes could be sad   570
To think of, to read over, many a page,
Poems withal of name, which at that time
Did never fail to entrance me, and are now
Dead in my eyes as is a theatre
Fresh emptied of spectators. Thirteen years

Or haply less, I might have seen, when first
My ears began to open to the charm
Of words in tuneful order, found them sweet
For *their own sakes*, a passion and a power;
And phrases pleased me, chosen for delight,   580
For pomp, or love. Oft in the public roads,
Yet unfrequented, while the morning light
Was yellowing the hill-tops, with that dear Friend,
The same whom I have mentioned heretofore,°
I went abroad, and for the better part
Of two delightful hours we strolled along
By the still borders of the misty Lake,
Repeating favorite verses with one voice,
Or conning more, as happy as the birds
That round us chaunted. Well might we be glad,   590
Lifted above the ground by airy fancies
More bright than madness or the dreams of wine,
And, though full oft the objects of our love
Were false, and in their splendour overwrought,
Yet, surely, at such time no vulgar power
Was working in us, nothing less, in truth,
Than that most noble attribute of man,
Though yet untutored and inordinate,°
That wish for something loftier, more adorned,
Than is the common aspect, daily garb   600
Of human life. What wonder then if sounds
Of exultation echoed through the groves!
For images, and sentiments, and words,
And everything with which we had to do
In that delicious world of poesy,
Kept holiday; a never-ending show,
With music, incense, festival, and flowers!
    Here must I pause: this only will I add,
From heart-experience, and in the humblest sense
Of modesty, that he, who, in his youth   610
A wanderer among the woods and fields,
With living Nature hath been intimate,
Not only in that raw unpractised time
Is stirred to ecstasy, as others are,
By glittering verse; but, he doth furthermore,
In measure only dealt out to himself,

Receive enduring touches of deep joy
From the great Nature that exists in works
Of mighty Poets. Visionary Power
Attends upon the motions of the winds   620
Embodied in the mystery of words;
There darkness makes abode, and all the host
Of shadowy things do work their changes there,
As in a mansion like their proper home;
Even forms and substances are circumfused
By that transparent veil with light divine;
And through the turnings intricate of Verse,
Present themselves as objects recognised,
In flashes, and with a glory scarce their own.

    Thus far a scanty record is deduced   630
Of what I owed to Books in early life;
Their later influence yet remains untold;
But as this work was taking in my thoughts
Proportions that seemed larger than had first
Been meditated, I was indisposed
To any further progress at a time
When these acknowledgements were left unpaid.

BOOK SIX

Cambridge and the Alps

The leaves were yellow when to Furness Fells,°
The haunt of Shepherds, and to cottage life
I bade adieu, and, one among the Flock
Who by that season are convened, like birds
Trooping together at the Fowler's lure,
Went back to Granta's cloisters; not so fond,°
Or eager, though as gay and undepressed
In spirit, as when I thence had taken flight
A few short months before. I turned my face
Without repining from the mountain pomp   10
Of Autumn, and its beauty entered in

With calmer Lakes, and louder Streams; and You,
Frank-hearted Maids of rocky Cumberland,
You and your not unwelcome days of mirth
I quitted, and your nights of revelry,
And in my own unlovely Cell sate down
In lightsome mood; such privilege has Youth,
That cannot take long leave of pleasant thoughts.

We need not linger o'er the ensuing time,
But let me add at once that now, the bonds   20
Of indolent and vague society
Relaxing in their hold, I lived henceforth
More to myself, read more, reflected more,
Felt more, and settled daily into habits
More promising. Two winters may be passed°
Without a separate notice; many books
Were read in process of this time, devoured,
Tasted or skimmed, or studiously perused,
Yet with no settled plan. I was detached
Internally from academic cares,   30
From every hope of prowess and reward,
And wished to be a lodger in that house
Of Letters, and no more: and should have been
Even such, but for some personal concerns
That hung about me in my own despite
Perpetually, no heavy weight, but still
A baffling and a hindrance, a controul
Which made the thought of planning for myself
A course of independent study seem
An act of disobedience towards them   40
Who loved me, proud rebellion and unkind.
This bastard virtue, rather let it have
A name it more deserves, this cowardise,
Gave treacherous sanction to that overlove
Of freedom planted in me from the very first
And indolence, by force of which I turned
From regulations even of my own,
As from restraints and bonds. And who can tell,
Who knows what thus may have been gained, both then
And at a later season, or preserved;   50
What love of nature, what original strength

Of contemplation, what intuitive truths
The deepest and the best, and what research
Unbiassed, unbewildered, and unawed?

   The Poet's soul was with me at that time,
Sweet meditations, the still overflow
Of happiness and truth. A thousand hopes
Were mine, a thousand tender dreams, of which
No few have since been realized, and some
Do yet remain, hopes for my future life.°   60
Four years and thirty, told this very week,
Have I been now a sojourner on earth,
And yet the morning gladness is not gone
Which then was in my mind. Those were the days
Which also first encouraged me to trust
With firmness, hitherto but lightly touched
With such a daring thought, that I might leave
Some monument behind me which pure hearts
Should reverence. The instinctive humbleness,
Upheld even by the very name and thought   70
Of printed books and authorship, began
To melt away, and further, the dread awe
Of mighty names was softened down, and seemed
Approachable, admitting fellowship
Of modest sympathy. Such aspect now,
Though not familiarly, my mind put on;
I loved, and I enjoyed, that was my chief
And ruling business, happy in the strength
And loveliness of imagery and thought.
All winter long, whenever free to take   80
My choice, did I at night frequent our Groves
And tributary walks, the last, and oft
The only one, who had been lingering there
Through hours of silence, till the Porter's Bell,
A punctual follower on the stroke of nine,
Rang with its blunt unceremonious voice,
Inexorable summons. Lofty Elms,
Inviting shades of opportune recess,
Did give composure to a neighbourhood
Unpeaceful in itself. A single Tree   90
There was, no doubt yet standing there, an Ash,

With sinuous trunk, boughs exquisitely wreathed;
Up from the ground and almost to the top
The trunk and master branches everywhere
Were green with ivy; and the lightsome twigs
And outer spray profusely tipped with seeds
That hung in yellow tassels and festoons,
Moving or still, a Favorite trimmed out
By Winter for himself, as if in pride,
And with outlandish grace. Oft have I stood   100
Foot-bound, uplooking at this lovely Tree
Beneath a frosty moon. The hemisphere
Of magic fiction, verse of mine perhaps
May never tread; but scarcely Spenser's self
Could have more tranquil visions in his youth,
More bright appearances could scarcely see
Of human Forms and superhuman Powers,
Than I beheld, standing on winter nights
Alone, beneath this fairy work of earth.
'Twould be a waste of labour to detail   110
The rambling studies of a truant Youth,
Which further may be easily divined,
What, and what kind they were. My inner knowledge,
(This barely will I note) was oft in depth
And delicacy like another mind
Sequestered from my outward taste in books,
And yet the books which then I loved the most
Are dearest to me now; for, being versed
In living Nature, I had there a guide
Which opened frequently my eyes, else shut,   120
A standard which was usefully applied,
Even when unconsciously, to other things
Which less I understood. In general terms,
I was a better judge of thoughts than words,
Misled as to these latter, not alone
By common inexperience of youth,
But by the trade in classic niceties,
Delusion to young Scholars incident
And old ones also, by that overprized
And dangerous craft of picking phrases out°   130
From languages that want the living voice
To make of them a nature to the heart,

To tell us what is passion, what is truth,
What reason, what simplicity and sense.

    Yet must I not entirely overlook
The pleasure gathered from the elements
Of geometric science. I had stepped
In these inquiries but a little way,
No farther than the threshold; with regret
Sincere I mention this; but there I found   140
Enough to exalt, to chear me and compose.
With Indian awe and wonder, ignorance
Which even was cherished, did I meditate
Upon the alliance of those simple, pure
Proportions and relations with the frame
And laws of Nature, how they could become
Herein a leader to the human mind,
And made endeavours frequent to detect
The process by dark guesses of my own.
Yet from this source more frequently I drew   150
A pleasure calm and deeper, a still sense
Of permanent and universal sway
And paramount endowment in the mind,
An image not unworthy of the one
Surpassing Life, which out of space and time,
Nor touched by welterings of passion, is
And hath the name of God. Transcendent peace
And silence did await upon these thoughts
That were a frequent comfort to my youth.

    And as I have read of one by shipwreck thrown°   160
With fellow Sufferers whom the waves had spared
Upon a region uninhabited,
An island of the Deep, who having brought
To land a single Volume and no more,
A treatise of Geometry, was used,
Although of food and clothing destitute,
And beyond common wretchedness depressed,
To part from company and take this book,
Then first a self-taught pupil in those truths,
To spots remote and corners of the Isle   170
By the sea side, and draw his diagrams
With a long stick upon the sand, and thus

Did oft beguile his sorrow, and almost
Forget his feeling; even so, if things
Producing like effect, from outward cause
So different, may rightly be compared,
So was it with me then, and so will be
With Poets ever. Mighty is the charm
Of those abstractions to a mind beset
With images, and haunted by itself;   180
And specially delightful unto me
Was that clear Synthesis built up aloft
So gracefully, even then when it appeared
No more than as a plaything, or a toy
Embodied to the sense, not what it is
In verity, an independent world
Created out of pure Intelligence.

Such dispositions then were mine, almost
Through grace of Heaven and inborn tenderness.
And not to leave the picture of that time   190
Imperfect, with these habits I must rank
A melancholy, from humours of the blood
In part, and partly taken up, that loved
A pensive sky, sad days, and piping winds,
The twilight more than dawn, Autumn than Spring;
A treasured and luxurious gloom, of choice
And inclination mainly, and the mere
Redundancy of youth's contentedness.
Add unto this a multitude of hours
Pilfered away by what the Bard who sang°   200
Of the Enchanter Indolence hath called
'Good-natured lounging,' and behold a map
Of my Collegiate life, far less intense
Than Duty called for, or without regard
To Duty, might have sprung up of itself
By change of accidents, or even, to speak
Without unkindness, in another place.

In summer among distant nooks I roved,
Dovedale, or Yorkshire Dales, or through bye-tracts
Of my own native region, and was blest   210
Between these sundry wanderings with a joy
Above all joys, that seemed another morn

Risen on mid noon, the presence, Friend, I mean
Of that sole Sister, she who hath been long
Thy Treasure also, thy true friend and mine,
Now, after separation desolate°
Restored to me, such absence that she seemed
A gift then first bestowed. The gentle Banks
Of Emont, hitherto unnamed in Song,
And that monastic Castle, on a Flat°   220
Low-standing by the margin of the Stream,
A Mansion not unvisited of old
By Sidney, where, in sight of our Helvellyn,
Some snatches he might pen, for aught we know,
Of his Arcadia, by fraternal love
Inspired; that River and that mouldering Dome
Have seen us sit in many a summer hour,
My sister and myself, when having climbed
In danger through some window's open space,
We looked abroad, or on the Turret's head   230
Lay listening to the wild flowers and the grass,
As they gave out their whispers to the wind.
Another Maid there was, who also breathed°
A gladness o'er that season, then to me
By her exulting outside look of youth
And placid under-countenance, first endeared,
That other Spirit, Coleridge, who is now
So near to us, that meek confiding heart,
So reverenced by us both. O'er paths and fields
In all that neighbourhood, through narrow lanes   240
Of eglantine, and through the shady woods,
And o'er the Border Beacon and the Waste°
Of naked Pools and common Crags that lay
Exposed on the bare Fell, was scattered love,
A spirit of pleasure and youth's golden gleam.
O Friend! we had not seen thee at that time;
And yet a power is on me and a strong
Confusion, and I seem to plant thee there.
Far art Thou wandered now in search of health,°
And milder breezes, melancholy lot!   250
But Thou art with us, with us in the past,
The present, with us in the times to come:
There is no grief, no sorrow, no despair,

No languor, no dejection, no dismay,
No absence scarcely can there be for those
Who love as we do. Speed thee well! divide
Thy pleasure with us, thy returning strength
Receive it daily as a joy of ours;
Share with us thy fresh spirits, whether gift
Of gales Etesian, or of loving thoughts.°   260

    I, too, have been a Wanderer; but, alas!
How different is the fate of different men
Though Twins almost in genius and in mind!
Unknown unto each other, yea, and breathing
As if in different elements, we were framed
To bend at last to the same discipline,
Predestined, if two Beings ever were,
To seek the same delights, and have one health,
One happiness. Throughout this narrative,
Else sooner ended, I have known full well   270
For whom I thus record the birth and growth
Of gentleness, simplicity, and truth,
And joyous loves that hallow innocent days
Of peace and self-command. Of Rivers, Fields,
And Groves, I speak to thee, my Friend; to thee,
Who, yet a liveried School-Boy, in the depths°
Of the huge City, on the leaded Roof
Of that wide Edifice, thy home and School,
Wast used to lie and gaze upon the clouds
Moving in Heaven; or haply, tired of this,   280
To shut thine eyes, and by internal light
See trees, and meadows, and thy native Stream°
Far distant, thus beheld from year to year
Of thy long exile. Nor could I forget
In this late portion of my argument
That scarcely had I finally resigned
My rights among those academic Bowers
When Thou wert thither guided. From the heart
Of London, and from Cloisters there, Thou camest,
And didst sit down in temperance and peace,   290
A rigorous Student. What a stormy course
Then followed. Oh! it is a pang that calls°
For utterance, to think how small a change

Of circumstances might to Thee have spared
A world of pain, ripened ten thousand hopes
For ever withered. Through this retrospect
Of my own College life I still have had
Thy after sojourn in the self-same place
Present before my eyes; have played with times,
(I speak of private business of the thought)   300
And accidents as children do with cards,
Or as a man, who, when his house is built,
A frame locked up in wood and stone, doth still,
In impotence of mind, by his fireside
Rebuild it to his liking. I have thought
Of Thee, thy learning, gorgeous eloquence,
And all the strength and plumage of thy Youth,
Thy subtle speculations, toils abstruse
Among the Schoolmen, and platonic forms°
Of wild ideal pageantry, shaped out   310
From things well-matched, or ill, and words for things,
The self-created sustenance of a mind
Debarred from Nature's living images,
Compelled to be a life unto itself,
And unrelentingly possessed by thirst
Of greatness, love, and beauty. Not alone,
Ah! surely not in a singleness of heart
Should I have seen the light of evening fade
Upon the silent Cam, if we had met,
Even at that early time; I needs must hope,   320
Must feel, must trust, that my maturer age,
And temperature less willing to be moved,
My calmer habits and more steady voice,
Would with an influence benign have soothed
Or chased away the airy wretchedness
That battened on thy youth. But thou hast trod,
In watchful meditation thou hast trod
A march of glory, which doth put to shame
These vain regrets; health suffers in thee; else
Such grief for thee would be the weakest thought   330
That ever harboured in the breast of man.

A passing word erewhile did lightly touch
On wanderings of my own; and now to these

My Poem leads me with an easier mind.
The employments of three winters when I wore
A student's gown have been already told,
Or shadowed forth, as far as there is need.
When the third Summer brought its liberty
A Fellow Student and myself, he too°
A Mountaineer, together sallied forth   340
And, Staff in hand, on foot pursued our way
Towards the distant Alps. An open slight
Of College cares and study was the scheme,
Nor entertained without concern for those
To whom my worldly interests were dear:
But Nature then was sovereign in my heart,
And mighty forms seizing a youthful Fancy
Had given a charter to irregular hopes.
In any age, without an impulse sent
From work of Nations, and their goings-on,   350
I should have been possessed by like desire:
But 'twas a time when Europe was rejoiced,
France standing on the top of golden hours,
And human nature seeming born again.
Bound, as I said, to the Alps, it was our lot
To land at Calais on the very eve
Of that great federal Day; and there we saw,°
In a mean City, and among a few,
How bright a face is worn when joy of one
Is joy of tens of millions. Southward thence   360
We took our way direct through Hamlets, Towns,
Gaudy with reliques of that Festival,
Flowers left to wither on triumphal Arcs,
And window-Garlands. On the public roads,
And once three days successively through paths
By which our toilsome journey was abridged,
Among sequestered villages we walked,
And found benevolence and blessedness
Spread like a fragrance everywhere, like Spring
That leaves no corner of the Land untouched.   370
Where Elms, for many and many a league, in files,
With their thin umbrage, on the stately roads
Of that great Kingdom, rustled o'er our heads,
For ever near us as we paced along,

'Twas sweet at such a time, with such delights
On every side, in prime of youthful strength,
To feed a Poet's tender melancholy
And fond conceit of sadness, to the noise
And gentle undulations which they made.
Unhoused, beneath the Evening Star we saw   380
Dances of Liberty, and, in late hours
Of darkness, dances in the open air.
Among the vine-clad Hills of Burgundy,
Upon the bosom of the gentle Soane
We glided forward with the flowing stream:
Swift Rhone, thou wert the wings on which we cut
Between thy lofty rocks! Enchanting show
Those woods, and farms, and orchards did present,
And single Cottages, and lurking Towns,
Reach after reach, procession without end   390
Of deep and stately Vales. A lonely Pair
Of Englishmen we were, and sailed along
Clustered together with a merry crowd
Of those emancipated, with a host
Of Travellers, chiefly Delegates, returning
From the great Spousals newly solemnized
At their chief City, in the sight of Heaven.
Like bees they swarmed, gaudy and gay as bees;
Some vapoured in the unruliness of joy
And flourished with their swords, as if to fight   400
The saucy air. In this blithe Company
We landed, took with them our evening Meal,
Guests welcome almost as the Angels were
To Abraham of old. The Supper done,°
With flowing cups elate and happy thoughts,
We rose at signal given, and formed a ring,
And hand in hand danced round and round the Board;
All hearts were open, every tongue was loud
With amity and glee. We bore a name
Honoured in France, the name of Englishmen,   410
And hospitably did they give us Hail
As their forerunners in a glorious course,°
And round and round the board they danced again.
With this same Throng our voyage we pursued
At early dawn; the Monastery Bells

Made a sweet jingling in our youthful ears;
The rapid River flowing without noise,
And every Spire we saw among the rocks
Spake with a sense of peace, at intervals
Touching the heart amid the boisterous Crew   420
With which we were environed. Having parted
From this glad Rout, the Convent of Chartreuse
Received us two days afterwards, and there
We rested in an awful Solitude;
Thence onward to the Country of the Swiss.

　　'Tis not my present purpose to retrace
That variegated journey step by step:
A march it was of military speed,
And earth did change her images and forms
Before us, fast as clouds are changed in Heaven.   430
Day after day, up early and down late,
From vale to vale, from hill to hill we went,
From Province on to Province did we pass,
Keen Hunters in a chace of fourteen weeks,
Eager as birds of prey, or as a Ship
Upon the stretch when winds are blowing fair.
Sweet coverts did we cross of pastoral life,
Enticing Vallies, greeted them, and left
Too soon, while yet the very flash and gleam
Of salutation were not passed away.   440
Oh! sorrow for the Youth who could have seen
Unchastened, unsubdued, unawed, unraised
To patriarchal dignity of mind
And pure simplicity of wish and will,
Those sanctified abodes of peaceful Man.
My heart leaped up when first I did look down
On that which was first seen of these deep haunts,
A green recess, an aboriginal vale
Quiet, and lorded over and possessed
By naked huts, wood-built, and sown like tents   450
Or Indian cabins over the fresh lawns,
And by the river side. That day we first
Beheld the summit of Mont Blanc, and grieved
To have a soulless image on the eye
Which had usurped upon a living thought

That never more could be: the wondrous Vale
Of Chamouny did, on the following dawn,
With its dumb cataracts and streams of ice,
A motionless array of mighty waves,
Five rivers broad and vast, make rich amends,   460
And reconciled us to realities.
There small birds warble from the leafy trees,
The Eagle soareth in the element;
There doth the Reaper bind the yellow sheaf,
The Maiden spread the haycock in the sun,
While Winter like a tamed Lion walks
Descending from the mountain to make sport
Among the cottages by beds of flowers.

Whate'er in this wide circuit we beheld,
Or heard, was fitted to our unripe state   470
Of intellect and heart. By simple strains
Of feeling, the pure breath of real life,
We were not left untouched. With such a book
Before our eyes, we could not chuse but read
A frequent lesson of sound tenderness,
The universal reason of mankind,
The truth of Young and Old. Nor, side by side
Pacing, two brother Pilgrims, or alone
Each with his humour, could we fail to abound
(Craft this which hath been hinted at before)   480
In dreams and fictions pensively composed,
Dejection taken up for pleasure's sake,
And gilded sympathies; the willow wreath,
Even among those solitudes sublime,
And sober posies of funereal flowers,
Culled from the gardens of the Lady Sorrow,
Did sweeten many a meditative hour.

Yet still in me, mingling with these delights
Was something of stern mood, an under-thirst
Of vigour, never utterly asleep.   490
Far different dejection once was mine,
A deep and genuine sadness then I felt;
The circumstances I will here relate
Even as they were. Upturning with a Band
Of Travellers, from the Valais we had clomb

Along the road that leads to Italy;
A length of hours, making of these our Guides,
Did we advance, and having reached an Inn
Among the mountains, we together ate
Our noon's repast, from which the Travellers rose,   500
Leaving us at the Board. Ere long we followed,
Descending by the beaten road that led
Right to a rivulet's edge, and there broke off.
The only track now visible was one
Upon the further side, right opposite,
And up a lofty Mountain. This we took
After a little scruple, and short pause,
And climbed with eagerness, though not, at length,
Without surprise and some anxiety
On finding that we did not overtake   510
Our Comrades gone before. By fortunate chance,
While every moment now encreased our doubts,
A Peasant met us, and from him we learned
That to the place which had perplexed us first
We must descend, and there should find the road
Which in the stony channel of the Stream
Lay a few steps, and then along its Banks;
And further, that thenceforward all our course
Was downwards, with the current of that Stream.
Hard of belief, we questioned him again,   520
And all the answers which the Man returned
To our inquiries, in their sense and substance,
Translated by the feelings which we had,
Ended in this; that we had crossed the Alps.

Imagination! lifting up itself
Before the eye and progress of my Song
Like an unfathered vapour; here that Power,
In all the might of its endowments, came
Athwart me; I was lost as in a cloud,
Halted, without a struggle to break through.   530
And now recovering, to my Soul I say
'I recognise thy glory'. In such strength
Of usurpation, in such visitings
Of awful promise, when the light of sense
Goes out in flashes that have shewn to us

The invisible world, doth Greatness make abode,
There harbours whether we be young or old.
Our destiny, our nature, and our home,
Is with infinitude, and only there;
With hope it is, hope that can never die,   540
Effort, and expectation, and desire,
And something evermore about to be.
The mind beneath such banners militant
Thinks not of spoils or trophies, nor of aught
That may attest its prowess, blest in thoughts
That are their own perfection and reward,
Strong in itself, and in the access of joy
Which hides it like the overflowing Nile.

The dull and heavy slackening that ensued
Upon those tidings by the Peasant given   550
Was soon dislodged; downwards we hurried fast,
And entered with the road which we had missed
Into a narrow chasm. The brook and road
Were fellow-travellers in this gloomy Pass,
And with them did we journey several hours
At a slow step. The immeasurable height
Of woods decaying, never to be decayed,
The stationary blasts of water-falls,
And every where along the hollow rent
Winds thwarting winds, bewildered and forlorn,   560
The torrents shooting from the clear blue sky,
The rocks that muttered close upon our ears,
Black drizzling crags that spake by the way-side
As if a voice were in them, the sick sight
And giddy prospect of the raving stream,
The unfettered clouds and region of the heavens,
Tumult and peace, the darkness and the light
Were all like workings of one mind, the features
Of the same face, blossoms upon one tree,
Characters of the great Apocalypse,   570
The types and symbols of Eternity,
Of first and last, and midst, and without end.°

That night our lodging was an Alpine House,
An Inn, or Hospital, as they are named,

Standing in that same valley by itself,
And close upon the confluence of two Streams;
A dreary Mansion, large beyond all need,
With high and spacious rooms, deafened and stunned
By noise of waters, making innocent Sleep
Lie melancholy among weary bones.   580

   Uprisen betimes, our journey we renewed,
Led by the Stream, ere noon-day magnified
Into a lordly River, broad and deep,
Dimpling along in silent majesty,
With mountains for its neighbours, and in view
Of distant mountains and their snowy tops,
And thus proceeding to Locarno's Lake,°
Fit resting-place for such a Visitant.
—Locarno, spreading out in width like Heaven,
And Como, thou, a treasure by the earth   590
Kept to itself, a darling bosomed up
In Abyssinian privacy, I spake
Of thee, thy chestnut woods, and garden plots
Of Indian corn tended by dark-eyed Maids,
Thy lofty steeps, and pathways roofed with vines
Winding from house to house, from town to town,
Sole link that binds them to each other, walks
League after league, and cloistral avenues
Where silence is, if music be not there:
While yet a Youth, undisciplined in Verse,   600
Through fond ambition of my heart, I told°
Your praises; nor can I approach you now
Ungreeted by a more melodious Song,
Where tones of learned Art and Nature mixed
May frame enduring language. Like a breeze
Or sunbeam over your domain I passed
In motion without pause; but Ye have left
Your beauty with me, an impassioned sight
Of colours and of forms, whose power is sweet
And gracious, almost might I dare to say,   610
As virtue is, or goodness, sweet as love,
Or the remembrance of a noble deed,
Or gentlest visitations of pure thought
When God, the Giver of all joy, is thanked

Religiously, in silent blessedness,
Sweet as this last herself, for such it is.

Through those delightful pathways we advanced
Two days, and still in presence of the Lake,
Which, winding up among the Alps, now changed
Slowly its lovely countenance, and put on   620
A sterner character. The second night
(In eagerness, and by report misled
Of those Italian Clocks that speak the time
In fashion different from ours) we rose
By moonshine, doubting not that day was near,
And that, meanwhile, coasting the Water's edge
As hitherto, and with as plain a track
To be our guide, we might behold the scene
In its most deep repose.—We left the Town
Of Gravedona with this hope, but soon   630
Were lost, bewildered among woods immense,
Where, having wandered for a while, we stopped
And on a rock sate down, to wait for day.
An open place it was, and overlooked
From high, the sullen water underneath,
On which a dull red image of the moon
Lay bedded, changing oftentimes its form
Like an uneasy snake: long time we sate,
For scarcely more than one hour of the night,
Such was our error, had been gone, when we   640
Renewed our journey. On the rock we lay
And wished to sleep but could not, for the stings
Of insects, which with noise like that of noon
Filled all the woods. The cry of unknown birds,
The mountains, more by darkness visible
And their own size, than any outward light,
The breathless wilderness of clouds, the clock
That told with unintelligible voice
The widely-parted hours, the noise of streams
And sometimes rustling motions nigh at hand   650
Which did not leave us free from personal fear,
And lastly the withdrawing Moon, that set
Before us while she still was high in heaven,
These were our food, and such a summer's night

Did to that pair of golden days succeed,
With now and then a doze and snatch of sleep,
On Como's Banks, the same delicious Lake.

But here I must break off, and quit at once,
Though loth, the record of these wanderings,
A theme which may seduce me else beyond   660
All reasonable bounds. Let this alone
Be mentioned as a parting word, that not
In hollow exultation, dealing forth
Hyperboles of praise comparative,
Not rich one moment to be poor for ever,
Not prostrate, overborn, as if the mind
Itself were nothing, a mean pensioner
On outward forms, did we in presence stand
Of that magnificent region. On the front
Of this whole Song is written that my heart   670
Must in such temple needs have offered up
A different worship. Finally, whate'er
I saw, or heard, or felt, was but a stream
That flowed into a kindred stream, a gale
That helped me forwards, did administer
To grandeur and to tenderness, to the one
Directly, but to tender thoughts by means
Less often instantaneous in effect;
Conducted me to these along a path
Which in the main was more circuitous.   680

Oh! most beloved Friend, a glorious time,
A happy time that was. Triumphant looks
Were then the common language of all eyes:
As if awaked from sleep, the Nations hailed
Their great expectancy: the fife of War
Was then a spirit-stirring sound indeed,
A blackbird's whistle in a vernal grove.
We left the Swiss exulting in the fate
Of their near Neighbours, and when shortening fast
Our pilgrimage, nor distant far from home,   690
We crossed the Brabant Armies on the fret°
For battle in the cause of Liberty.
A Stripling, scarcely of the household then

Of social life, I looked upon these things
As from a distance, heard, and saw, and felt,
Was touched, but with no intimate concern;
I seemed to move among them as a bird
Moves through the air, or as a fish pursues
Its business, in its proper element.
I needed not that joy, I did not need   700
Such help; the ever-living Universe,
And independent spirit of pure youth
Were with me at that season, and delight
Was in all places spread around my steps
As constant as the grass upon the fields.

BOOK SEVEN

Residence in London

Five years are vanished since I first poured out,
Saluted by that animating breeze
Which met me issuing from the City's Walls,
A glad preamble to this Verse: I sang°
Aloud, in Dythyrambic fervour, deep
But short-lived uproar, like a torrent sent
Out of the bowels of a bursting cloud
Down Scawfell or Blencathara's rugged sides,°
A water-spout from Heaven. But 'twas not long
Ere the interrupted stream broke forth once more,   10
And flowed awhile in strength, then stopped for years;
Not heard again until a little space
Before last primrose-time. Beloved Friend,°
The assurances then given unto myself,
Which did beguile me of some heavy thoughts
At thy departure to a foreign Land,
Have failed; for slowly doth this work advance.
Through the whole summer have I been at rest,
Partly from voluntary holiday
And part through outward hindrance. But I heard,   20
After the hour of sunset yester even,
Sitting within doors betwixt light and dark,
A voice that stirred me. 'Twas a little Band,

A Quire of Redbreasts gathered somewhere near
My threshold, Minstrels from the distant woods
And dells, sent in by Winter to bespeak
For the Old Man a welcome, to announce,
With preparation artful and benign,
Yea the most gentle music of the year,
That their rough Lord had left the surly North   30
And hath begun his journey. A delight
At this unthought of greeting unawares
Smote me, a sweetness of the coming time,
And listening, I half whispered, 'We will be
Ye heartsome Choristers, ye and I will be
Brethren, and in the hearing of bleak winds
Will chaunt together.' And, thereafter, walking
By later twilight on the hills, I saw
A Glow-worm from beneath a dusky shade
Or canopy of the yet unwithered fern   40
Clear-shining, like a Hermit's taper seen
Through a thick forest. Silence touched me here
No less than sound had done before; the Child
Of Summer, lingering, shining by itself,
The voiceless Worm on the unfrequented hills,
Seemed sent on the same errand with the Quire
Of Winter that had warbled at my door,
And the whole year seemed tenderness and love.

    The last Night's genial feeling overflowed
Upon this morning, and my favorite Grove,°   50
Now tossing its dark boughs in sun and wind,
Spreads through me a commotion like its own,
Something that fits me for the Poet's task,
Which we will now resume with chearful hope,
Nor checked by aught of tamer argument
That lies before us, needful to be told.

    Returned from that excursion, soon I bade
Farewell for ever to the private Bowers°
Of gownèd Students, quitted these, no more
To enter them, and pitched my vagrant tent,   60
A casual dweller and at large, among
The unfenced regions of society.

Yet undetermined to what plan of life
I should adhere, and seeming thence to have
A little space of intermediate time
Loose and at full command, to London first
I turned, if not in calmness, nevertheless
In no disturbance of excessive hope,
At ease from all ambition personal,
Frugal as there was need, and though self-willed,   70
Yet temperate and reserved, and wholly free
From dangerous passions. 'Twas at least two years
Before this season when I first beheld
That mighty place, a transient visitant;
And now it pleased me my abode to fix
Single in the wide waste, to have a house
It was enough (what matter for a home?)
That owned me, living chearfully abroad,
With fancy on the stir from day to day,
And all my young affections out of doors.   80

There was a time when whatsoe'er is feigned
Of airy Palaces, and Gardens built
By Genii of Romance, or hath in grave
Authentic History been set forth of Rome,
Alcairo, Babylon, or Persepolis,
Or given upon report by Pilgrim-Friars
Of golden Cities ten months' journey deep
Among Tartarean Wilds, fell short, far short,
Of that which I in simpleness believed
And thought of London; held me by a chain   90
Less strong of wonder and obscure delight.
I know not that herein I shot beyond
The common mark of childhood; but I well
Remember that among our flock of Boys
Was one, a Cripple from the birth, whom chance°
Summoned from School to London, fortunate
And envied Traveller! and when he returned,
After short absence, and I first set eyes
Upon his person, verily, though strange
The thing may seem, I was not wholly free   100
From disappointment to behold the same
Appearance, the same body, not to find

Some change, some beams of glory brought away
From that new region. Much I questioned him,
And every word he uttered, on my ears
Fell flatter than a cagèd Parrot's note,
That answers unexpectedly awry,
And mocks the Prompter's listening. Marvellous things
My fancy had shaped forth, of sights and shows,
Processions, Equipages, Lords and Dukes,   110
The King, and the King's Palace, and not last
Or least, heaven bless him! the renowned Lord Mayor:
Dreams hardly less intense than those which wrought
A change of purpose in young Whittington,
When he in friendlessness, a drooping Boy,
Sate on a Stone, and heard the Bells speak out
Articulate music. Above all, one thought°
Baffled my understanding, how men lived
Even next-door neighbours, as we say, yet still
Strangers, and knowing not each other's names.   120

    Oh wond'rous power of words, how sweet they are
According to the meaning which they bring!
Vauxhall and Ranelagh, I then had heard°
Of your green groves, and wilderness of lamps,
Your gorgeous Ladies, fairy cataracts,
And pageant fireworks; nor must we forget
Those other wonders different in kind,
Though scarcely less illustrious in degree,
The River proudly bridged, the giddy Top
And whispering Gallery of St. Paul's, the Tombs   130
Of Westminster, the Giants of Guildhall,°
Bedlam, and the two figures at its Gates,°
Streets without end, and Churches numberless,
Statues, with flowery gardens in vast Squares,
The Monument, and Armoury of the Tower.°
These fond imaginations of themselves
Had long before given way in season due,
Leaving a throng of others in their stead;
And now I looked upon the real scene,
Familiarly perused it day by day   140
With keen and lively pleasure even there
Where disappointment was the strongest, pleased

Through courteous self-submission, as a tax
Paid to the object by prescriptive right,
A thing that ought to be. Shall I give way,
Copying the impression of the memory,
Though things remembered idly do half seem
The work of Fancy, shall I, as the mood
Inclines me, here describe, for pastime's sake
Some portion of that motley imagery,   150
A vivid pleasure of my youth, and now
Among the lonely places that I love
A frequent day-dream for my riper mind?
—And first the look and aspect of the place,
The broad high-way appearance, as it strikes
On Strangers of all ages, the quick dance
Of colours, lights and forms, the Babel din
The endless stream of men, and moving things,
From hour to hour the illimitable walk
Still among streets with clouds and sky above,   160
The wealth, the bustle and the eagerness,
The glittering Chariots with their pampered Steeds,
Stalls, Barrows, Porters; midway in the Street
The Scavenger, who begs with hat in hand,
The labouring Hackney Coaches, the rash speed
Of Coaches travelling far, whirled on with horn
Loud blowing, and the sturdy Drayman's Team,
Ascending from some Alley of the Thames
And striking right across the crowded Strand
Till the fore Horse veer round with punctual skill: 170
Here, there, and everywhere, a weary throng,
The Comers and the Goers face to face,
Face after face; the string of dazzling Wares,
Shop after shop, with Symbols, blazoned Names,
And all the Tradesman's honours overhead;
Here, fronts of houses, like a title-page
With letters huge inscribed from top to toe;
Stationed above the door, like guardian Saints,
There, allegoric shapes, female or male,
Or physiognomies of real men,   180
Land-Warriors, Kings, or Admirals of the Sea,
Boyle, Shakspear, Newton, or the attractive head
Of some Scotch doctor, famous in his day.°

   Meanwhile the roar continues, till at length,
Escaped as from an enemy, we turn
Abruptly into some sequestered nook
Still as a sheltered place when winds blow loud.
At leisure thence, through tracts of thin resort,
And sights and sounds that come at intervals,
We take our way: a raree-show is here°   190
With Children gathered round, another Street
Presents a company of dancing Dogs,
Or Dromedary, with an antic pair
Of Monkies on his back, a minstrel Band
Of Savoyards, or, single and alone,
An English Ballad-singer. Private Courts,
Gloomy as Coffins, and unsightly Lanes
Thrilled by some female Vendor's scream, belike
The very shrillest of all London Cries,
May then entangle us awhile,   200
Conducted through those labyrinths unawares
To privileged Regions and inviolate,
Where from their airy lodges studious Lawyers
Look out on waters, walks, and gardens green.

   Thence back into the throng, until we reach,
Following the tide that slackens by degrees,
Some half-frequented scene where wider Streets
Bring straggling breezes of suburban air.
Here files of ballads dangle from dead walls,
Advertisements of giant-size, from high   210
Press forward in all colours on the sight;
These, bold in conscious merit; lower down
That, fronted with a most imposing word,
Is, peradventure, one in masquerade.
As on the broadening Causeway we advance,
Behold a Face turned up toward us, strong
In lineaments, and red with over-toil;
'Tis one perhaps, already met elsewhere,
A travelling Cripple, by the trunk cut short,
And stumping with his arms: in Sailor's garb°   220
Another lies at length beside a range
Of written characters, with chalk inscribed
Upon the smooth flat stones: the Nurse is here,

The Bachelor that loves to sun himself,
The military Idler, and the Dame,
That field-ward takes her walk in decency.

   Now homeward through the thickening hubbub, where
See, among less distinguishable shapes,
The Italian, with his Frame of Images
Upon his head; with Basket at his waist   230
The Jew; the stately and slow-moving Turk
With freight of slippers piled beneath his arm.
Briefly, we find, if tired of random sights
And haply to that search our thoughts should turn,
Among the crowd, conspicuous less or more,
As we proceed, all specimens of man
Through all the colours which the sun bestows,
And every character of form and face;
The Swede, the Russian; from the genial South,
The Frenchman and the Spaniard; from remote   240
America, the Hunter-Indian; Moors,
Malays, Lascars, the Tartar and Chinese,
And Negro Ladies in white muslin gowns.

   At leisure let us view, from day to day,
As they present themselves, the Spectacles
Within doors: troops of wild Beasts, birds and beasts
Of every nature, from all climes convened;
And, next to these, those mimic sights that ape
The absolute presence of reality,
Expressing, as in mirror, sea and land,   250
And what earth is, and what she has to shew;
I do not here allude to subtlest craft,
By means refined attaining purest ends,
But imitations fondly made in plain
Confession of man's weakness and his loves.°
Whether the Painter fashioning a work
To Nature's circumambient scenery,
And with his greedy pencil taking in
A whole horizon on all sides, with power,
Like that of Angels or commissioned Spirits,   260
Plant us upon some lofty Pinnacle,

Or in a Ship on Waters, with a world
Of life, and life-like mockery, to East,
To West, beneath, behind us, and before:
Or more mechanic Artist represent
By scale exact, in Model, wood or clay,
From shading colours also borrowing help,
Some miniature of famous spots and things
Domestic, or the boast of foreign Realms;
The Firth of Forth, and Edinburgh throned   270
On crags, fit empress of that mountain Land;
St. Peter's Church; or, more aspiring aim,
In microscopic vision, Rome itself;
Or, else perhaps, some rural haunt, the Falls
Of Tivoli, and dim Frescati's bowers,
And high upon the steep, that mouldering Fane
The Temple of the Sibyl, every tree
Through all the landscape, tuft, stone, scratch minute,
And every Cottage, lurking in the rocks,
All that the Traveller sees when he is there.   280

   Add to these exhibitions mute and still
Others of wider scope, where living men,
Music, and shifting pantomimic scenes,
Together joined their multifarious aid
To heighten the allurement. Need I fear
To mention by its name, as in degree
Lowest of these, and humblest in attempt,
Though richly graced with honours of its own,
Half-rural Sadler's Wells? Though at that time.°
Intolerant, as is the way of Youth   290
Unless itself be pleased, I more than once
Here took my seat, and, maugre frequent fits
Of irksomeness, with ample recompense
Saw Singers, Rope-dancers, Giants and Dwarfs,
Clowns, Conjurors, Posture-masters, Harlequins,
Amid the uproar of the rabblement,
Perform their feats. Nor was it mean delight
To watch crude nature work in untaught minds,
To note the laws and progress of belief;
Though obstinate on this way, yet on that   300
How willingly we travel, and how far!

To have, for instance, brought upon the scene
The Champion Jack the Giant-killer, Lo!
He dons his Coat of Darkness; on the Stage
Walks, and atchieves his wonders from the eye
Of living mortal safe as is the moon
'Hid in her vacant interlunar cave'.
Delusion bold! and faith must needs be coy;
How is it wrought? His garb is black, the word
INVISIBLE flames forth upon his chest.   310

   Nor was it unamusing here to view
Those samplers as of ancient Comedy
And Thespian times, dramas of living Men,°
And recent things, yet warm with life; a Sea-fight,
Shipwreck, or some domestic incident
The fame of which is scattered through the Land,
Such as this daring brotherhood of late
Set forth, too holy theme for such a place,
And doubtless treated with irreverence
Albeit with their very best of skill,   320
I mean, O distant Friend! a Story drawn
From our own ground, the Maid of Buttermere,°
And how the Spoiler came, 'a bold bad Man'
To God unfaithful, Children, Wife, and Home,
And wooed the artless Daughter of the hills,
And wedded her, in cruel mockery
Of love and marriage bonds. O Friend! I speak
With tender recollection of that time
When first we saw the Maiden, then a name
By us unheard of; in her cottage Inn   330
Were welcomed, and attended on by her,
Both stricken with one feeling of delight,
An admiration of her modest mien,
And carriage, marked by unexampled grace.
Not unfamiliarly we since that time
Have seen her; her discretion have observed,
Her just opinions, female modesty,
Her patience, and retiredness of mind
Unsoiled by commendation, and the excess
Of public notice. This memorial Verse   340
Comes from the Poet's heart, and is her due.

For we were nursed, as almost might be said,
On the same mountains, Children at one time,
Must haply often on the self-same day
Have from our several dwellings gone abroad
To gather daffodils on Coker's Stream.°

      These last words uttered, to my argument
I was returning, when, with sundry Forms
Mingled, that in the way which I must tread
Before me stand, thy image rose again,   350
Mary of Buttermere! She lives in peace
Upon the spot where she was born and reared;
Without contamination does she live
In quietness, without anxiety:
Beside the mountain-Chapel sleeps in earth
Her new-born Infant, fearless as a lamb
That thither comes, from some unsheltered place,
To rest beneath the little rock-like Pile
When storms are blowing. Happy are they both
Mother and Child! These feelings, in themselves   360
Trite, do yet scarcely seem so when I think
Of those ingenuous moments of our youth,
Ere yet by use we have learned to slight the crimes
And sorrows of the world. Those days are now
My theme; and, 'mid the numerous scenes which they
Have left behind them, foremost I am crossed
Here by remembrance of two figures: One
A rosy Babe, who, for a twelvemonth's space
Perhaps, had been of age to deal about
Articulate prattle, Child as beautiful   370
As ever sate upon a Mother's knee;
The other was the Parent of that Babe;
But on the Mother's cheek the tints were false,
A painted bloom. 'Twas at a Theatre
That I beheld this Pair; the Boy had been
The pride and pleasure of all lookers-on
In whatsoever place, but seemed in this
A sort of Alien scattered from the clouds.
Of lusty vigour, more than infantine,
He was in limbs, in face a Cottage rose   380
Just three parts blown; a Cottage Child, but ne'er

Saw I, by Cottage or elsewhere, a Babe
By Nature's gifts so honored. Upon a Board
Whence an attendant of the Theatre
Served out refreshments, had this Child been placed,
And there he sate, environed with a Ring
Of chance Spectators, chiefly dissolute men
And shameless women; treated and caressed,
Ate, drank, and with the fruit and glasses played,
While oaths, indecent speech, and ribaldry   390
Were rife about him as are songs of birds
In spring-time after showers. The Mother, too,
Was present! but of her I know no more
Than hath been said, and scarcely at this time
Do I remember her. But I behold
The lovely Boy as I beheld him then,
Among the wretched and the falsely gay,
Like one of those who walked with hair unsinged
Amid the fiery furnace. He hath since°
Appeared to me oft times as if embalmed   400
By Nature; through some special privilege,
Stopped at the growth he had; destined to live,
To be, to have been, come and go, a Child
And nothing more, no partner in the years
That bear us forward to distress and guilt,
Pain and abasement, beauty in such excess
Adorned him in that miserable place.
So have I thought of him a thousand times,
And seldom otherwise. But he perhaps
Mary! may now have lived till he could look   410
With envy on thy nameless Babe that sleeps
Beside the mountain Chapel, undisturbed!

   It was but little more than three short years
Before the season which I speak of now
When first, a Traveller from our pastoral hills,
Southward two hundred miles I had advanced,°
And for the first time in my life did hear
The voice of Woman utter blasphemy;
Saw Woman as she is to open shame
Abandoned, and the pride of public vice.   420
Full surely from the bottom of my heart

I shuddered; but the pain was almost lost,
Absorbed and buried in the immensity
Of the effect: a barrier seemed at once
Thrown in, that from humanity divorced
The human Form, splitting the race of Man
In twain, yet leaving the same outward shape.
Distress of mind ensued upon this sight
And ardent meditation; afterwards
A milder sadness of such spectacles   430
Attended; thought, commiseration, grief
For the individual, and the overthrow
Of her soul's beauty; farther at that time
Than this I was but seldom led; in truth
The sorrow of the passion stopped me here.

    I quit this painful theme; enough is said
To shew what thoughts must often have been mine
At theatres, which then were my delight,
A yearning made more strong by obstacles
Which slender funds imposed. Life then was new,   440
The senses easily pleased; the lustres, lights,°
The carving and the gilding, paint and glare,
And all the mean upholstery of the place,
Wanted not animation in my sight:
Far less the living Figures on the Stage,
Solemn or gay: whether some beauteous Dame
Advanced in radiance through a deep recess
Of thick-entangled forest, like the Moon
Opening the clouds; or sovereign King, announced
With flourishing Trumpets, came in full-blown State   450
Of the world's greatness, winding round with Train
Of Courtiers, Banners, and a length of Guards;
Or Captive led in abject weeds, and jingling
His slender manacles; or romping Girl
Bounced, leapt, and pawed the air; or mumbling Sire,
A scare-crow pattern of old Age, patched up
Of all the tatters of infirmity,
All loosely put together, hobbled in,
Stumping upon a Cane, with which he smites,
From time to time, the solid boards, and makes them   460
Prate somewhat loudly of the whereabout

Of one so overloaded with his years.
But what of this! the laugh, the grin, grimace,
And all the antics and buffoonery,
The least of them not lost, were all received
With charitable pleasure. Through the night,
Between the show, and many-headed mass
Of the Spectators, and each little nook
That had its fray or brawl, how eagerly,
And with what flashes, as it were, the mind   470
Turned this way, that way! sportive and alert
And watchful, as a kitten when at play,
While winds are blowing round her, among grass
And rustling leaves. Enchanting age and sweet!
Romantic almost, looked at through a space,
How small of intervening years! For then,
Though surely no mean progress had been made
In meditations holy and sublime,
Yet something of a girlish child-like gloss
Of novelty survived for scenes like these;   480
Pleasure that had been handed down from times
When, at a Country-Playhouse, having caught,
In summer, through the fractured wall, a glimpse
Of daylight, at the thought of where I was
I gladdened more than if I had beheld
Before me some bright cavern of Romance,
Or than we do, when on our beds we lie
At night, in warmth, when rains are beating hard.

      The matter that detains me now will seem
To many neither dignified enough   490
Nor arduous; and is, doubtless, in itself
Humble and low; yet not to be despised
By those who have observed the curious props
By which the perishable hours of life
Rest on each other, and the world of thought
Exists and is sustained. More lofty Themes,
Such as, at least, do wear a prouder face,
Might here be spoken of; but when I think
Of these, I feel the imaginative Power
Languish within me. Even then it slept   500
When, wrought upon by tragic sufferings,

The heart was full; amid my sobs and tears
It slept, even in the season of my youth:
For though I was most passionately moved
And yielded to the changes of the scene
With most obsequious feeling, yet all this
Passed not beyond the suburbs of the mind:
If aught there were of real grandeur here
'Twas only then when gross realities,
The incarnation of the Spirits that moved   510
Amid the Poet's beauteous world, called forth,
With that distinctness which a contrast gives
Or opposition, made me recognize
As by a glimpse, the things which I had shaped
And yet not shaped, had seen, and scarcely seen,
Had felt, and thought of in my solitude.

    Pass we from entertainments that are such
Professedly, to others titled higher,
Yet in the estimate of Youth at least,
More near akin to those than names imply,   520
I mean the brawls of Lawyers in their Courts
Before the ermined Judge, or that great Stage
Where Senators, tongue-favored Men, perform,
Admired and envied. Oh! the beating heart!
When one among the prime of these rose up,
One, of whose name from Childhood we had heard
Familiarly, a household term, like those,
The Bedfords, Glocesters, Salisburys of old,°
Which the fifth Harry talks of. Silence! hush!
This is no trifler, no short-flighted Wit,   530
No stammerer of a minute, painfully
Delivered. No! the Orator hath yoked
The hours, like young Aurora, to his Car;°
O Presence of delight, can patience e'er
Grow weary of attending on a track
That kindles with such glory? Marvellous!
The enchantment spreads and rises; all are rapt
Astonished; like a Hero in Romance
He winds away his never-ending horn;
Words follow words, sense seems to follow sense;   540
What memory and what logic! till the Strain

Transcendent, superhuman as it is,
Grows tedious even in a young man's ear.

   These are grave follies: other public Shows
The capital City teems with, of a kind
More light, and where but in the holy Church?
There have I seen a comely Bachelor,
Fresh from a toilette of two hours, ascend
The Pulpit, with seraphic glance look up,
And, in a tone elaborately low   550
Beginning, lead his voice through many a maze
A minuet course, and winding up his mouth,
From time to time into an orifice
Most delicate, a lurking eyelet, small
And only not invisible, again
Open it out, diffusing thence a smile
Of rapt irradiation exquisite.
Meanwhile the Evangelists, Isaiah, Job,
Moses, and he who penned the other day
The Death of Abel, Shakespear, Doctor Young,°   560
And Ossian, (doubt not, 'tis the naked truth)
Summoned from streamy Morven, each and all
Must in their turn lend ornament and flowers
To entwine the Crook of eloquence with which
This pretty Shepherd, pride of all the Plains,
Leads up and down his captivated Flock.

   I glance but at a few conspicuous marks,
Leaving ten thousand others, that do each,
In Hall or Court, Conventicle, or Shop,
In public Room or private, Park or Street,   570
With fondness reared on his own Pedestal,
Look out for admiration. Folly, vice,
Extravagance in gesture, mien, and dress,
And all the strife of singularity,
Lies to the ear, and lies to every sense,
Of these, and of the living shapes they wear,
There is no end. Such Candidates for regard,
Although well pleased to be where they were found,
I did not hunt after, or greatly prize,
Nor made unto myself a secret boast   580
Of reading them with quick and curious eye;

But as a common produce, things that are
To-day, to-morrow will be, took of them
Such willing note as, on some errand bound
Of pleasure or of Love, some Traveller might,
Among a thousand other images,
Of sea-shells that bestud the sandy beach,
Or daisies swarming through the fields in June.

But foolishness, and madness in parade,
Though most at home in this their dear domain,   590
Are scattered everywhere, no rarities,
Even to the rudest novice of the Schools.
O Friend! one feeling was there which belonged
To this great City, by exclusive right;
How often in the overflowing Streets,
Have I gone forward with the Crowd, and said
Unto myself, the face of every one
That passes by me is a mystery.
Thus have I looked, nor ceased to look, oppressed
By thoughts of what, and whither, when and how,   600
Until the shapes before my eyes became
A second-sight procession, such as glides
Over still mountains, or appears in dreams;°
And all the ballast of familiar life,
The present, and the past; hope, fear; all stays,
All laws of acting, thinking, speaking man
Went from me, neither knowing me, nor known.
And once, far-travelled in such mood, beyond
The reach of common indications, lost
Amid the moving pageant, 'twas my chance   610
Abruptly to be smitten with the view
Of a blind Beggar, who, with upright face,
Stood propped against a Wall, upon his Chest
Wearing a written paper, to explain
The story of the Man, and who he was.
My mind did at this spectacle turn round
As with the might of waters, and it seemed
To me that in this Label was a type,
Or emblem, of the utmost that we know,
Both of ourselves and of the universe;   620
And, on the shape of the unmoving man,

His fixèd face and sightless eyes, I looked
As if admonished from another world.

    Though reared upon the base of outward things,
These, chiefly, are such structures as the mind
Builds for itself. Scenes different there are,
Full-formed, which take, with small internal help,
Possession of the faculties; the peace
Of night, for instance, the solemnity
Of nature's intermediate hours of rest,   630
When the great tide of human life stands still,
The business of the day to come unborn,
Of that gone by, locked up as in the grave;
The calmness, beauty, of the spectacle,
Sky, stillness, moonshine, empty streets, and sounds
Unfrequent as in desarts; at late hours
Of winter evenings when unwholesome rains
Are falling hard, with people yet astir,
The feeble salutation from the voice
Of some unhappy Woman, now and then   640
Heard as we pass; when no one looks about,
Nothing is listened to. But these, I fear,
Are falsely catalogued, things that are, are not,
Even as we give them welcome, or assist,
Are prompt, or are remiss. What say you then,
To times, when half the City shall break out
Full of one passion, vengeance, rage, or fear,
To executions, to a Street on fire,
Mobs, riots, or rejoicings? From these sights
Take one, an annual Festival, the Fair   650
Holden where Martyrs suffered in past time,°
And named of Saint Bartholomew; there see
A work that's finished to our hands, that lays,
If any spectacle on earth can do,
The whole creative powers of man asleep!
For once the Muse's help will we implore,
And she shall lodge us, wafted on her wings,
Above the press and danger of the Crowd,
Upon some Showman's platform: what a hell
For eyes and ears! what anarchy and din   660
Barbarian and infernal! 'tis a dream,

Monstrous in colour, motion, shape, sight, sound.
Below, the open space, through every nook
Of the wide area, twinkles, is alive
With heads; the midway region and above
Is thronged with staring pictures, and huge scrolls,
Dumb proclamations of the prodigies;
And chattering monkeys dangling from their poles,
And children whirling in their roundabouts;
With those that stretch the neck, and strain the eyes,   670
And crack the voice in rivalship, the crowd
Inviting; with buffoons against buffoons
Grimacing, writhing, screaming; him who grinds
The hurdy-gurdy, at the fiddle weaves;
Rattles the salt-box, thumps the kettle-drum,°
And him who at the trumpet puffs his cheeks,
The silver-collared Negro with his timbrel,
Equestrians, Tumblers, Women, Girls, and Boys,
Blue-breeched, pink-vested, and with towering plumes.
—All moveables of wonder from all parts,   680
Are here, Albinos, painted Indians, Dwarfs,
The Horse of Knowledge, and the learned Pig,
The Stone-eater, the Man that swallows fire,
Giants, Ventriloquists, the Invisible Girl,
The Bust that speaks, and moves its goggling eyes,
The Wax-work, Clock-work, all the marvellous craft°
Of modern Merlins, wild Beasts, Puppet-shows,
All out-o'-th'-way, far-fetched, perverted things,
All freaks of Nature, all Promethean thoughts°
Of man; his dulness, madness, and their feats,   690
All jumbled up together to make up
This Parliament of Monsters. Tents and Booths
Meanwhile, as if the whole were one vast Mill,
Are vomiting, receiving, on all sides,
Men, Women, three-years' Children, Babes in arms.

Oh, blank confusion! and a type not false
Of what the mighty City is itself
To all except a Straggler here and there,
To the whole swarm of its inhabitants;
An undistinguishable world to men,   700
The slaves unrespited of low pursuits,

Living amid the same perpetual flow
Of trivial objects, melted and reduced
To one identity, by differences
That have no law, no meaning, and no end;
Oppression under which even highest minds
Must labour, whence the strongest are not free.
But though the picture weary out the eye,
By nature an unmanageable sight,
It is not wholly so to him who looks   710
In steadiness, who hath among least things
An under-sense of greatest; sees the parts
As parts, but with a feeling of the whole.
This, of all acquisitions first, awaits
On sundry and most widely different modes
Of education; nor with least delight
On that through which I passed. Attention comes,
And comprehensiveness and memory,
From early converse with the works of God
Among all regions; chiefly where appear   720
Most obviously simplicity and power.
By influence habitual to the mind
The mountain's outline and its steady form
Gives a pure grandeur, and its presence shapes
The measure and the prospect of the soul
To majesty; such virtue have the forms
Perennial of the ancient hills; nor less
The changeful language of their countenances
Gives movement to the thoughts, and multitude,
With order and relation. This, if still,   730
As hitherto, with freedom I may speak,
And the same perfect openness of mind,
Not violating any just restraint,
As I would hope, of real modesty,
This did I feel in that vast receptacle.
The Spirit of Nature was upon me here;
The Soul of Beauty and enduring life
Was present as a habit, and diffused,
Through meagre lines and colours, and the press
Of self-destroying, transitory things,   740
Composure and ennobling harmony.

BOOK EIGHT

Retrospect.—Love of Nature Leading to Love of Mankind

What sounds are those, Helvellyn, which are heard°
Up to thy summit? Through the depth of air
Ascending, as if distance had the power
To make the sounds more audible: what Crowd
Is yon, assembled in the gay green Field?
Crowd seems it, solitary Hill! to thee,
Though but a little Family of Men,
Twice twenty, with their Children and their Wives,
And here and there a Stranger interspersed.
It is a summer festival, a Fair,   10
Such as, on this side now, and now on that,
Repeated through his tributary Vales,
Helvellyn, in the silence of his rest,
Sees annually, if storms be not abroad,
And mists have left him an unshrouded head.
Delightful day it is for all who dwell
In this secluded Glen, and eagerly
They give it welcome. Long ere heat of noon
Behold the cattle are driven down; the sheep
That have for traffic been culled out are penned   20
In cotes that stand together on the Plain
Ranged side by side; the chaffering is begun.
The Heifer lows uneasy at the voice
Of a new Master, bleat the Flocks aloud;
Booths are there none; a Stall or two is here,
A lame Man, or a blind, the one to beg,
The other to make music; hither, too,
From far, with Basket, slung upon her arm,
Of Hawker's Wares, books, pictures, combs, and pins,
Some aged Woman finds her way again,   30
Year after year a punctual visitant!
The Showman with his Freight upon his Back,
And once, perchance, in lapse of many years
Prouder Itinerant, Mountebank, or He
Whose Wonders in a covered Wain lie hid.
But One is here, the loveliest of them all,

Some sweet Lass of the Valley, looking out
For gains, and who that sees her would not buy?
Fruits of her Father's Orchard, apples, pears,
(On that day only to such office stooping)   40
She carries in her Basket, and walks round
Among the crowd, half pleased with, half ashamed
Of her new calling, blushing restlessly.
The Children now are rich, the Old Man now
Is generous; so gaiety prevails
Which all partake of, Young and Old. Immense
Is the Recess, the circumambient World
Magnificent, by which they are embraced.
They move about upon the soft green field:
How little They, they and their doings seem,   50
Their herds and flocks about them, they themselves,
And all that they can further or obstruct!
Through utter weakness pitiably dear
As tender Infants are: and yet how great!
For all things serve them; them the Morning light
Loves as it glistens on the silent rocks,
And them the silent Rocks, which now from high
Look down upon them; the reposing Clouds,
The lurking Brooks from their invisible haunts,
And Old Helvellyn, conscious of the stir,   60
And the blue Sky that roofs their calm abode.

    With deep devotion, Nature, did I feel
In that great City what I owed to thee,
High thoughts of God and Man, and love of Man,
Triumphant over all those loathsome sights
Of wretchedness and vice; a watchful eye,
Which with the outside of our human life
Not satisfied, must read the inner mind.
For I already had been taught to love
My Fellow-beings, to such habits trained   70
Among the woods and mountains, where I found
In thee a gracious Guide, to lead me forth
Beyond the bosom of my Family,
My Friends and youthful Playmates. 'Twas thy power
That raised the first complacency in me,°
And noticeable kindliness of heart,

Love human to the Creature in himself
As he appeared, a Stranger in my path,
Before my eyes a Brother of this world;
Thou first didst with those motions of delight   80
Inspire me.—I remember, far from home
Once having strayed, while yet a very Child,
I saw a sight, and with what joy and love!
It was a day of exhalations, spread
Upon the mountains, mists and steam-like fogs
Redounding everywhere, not vehement,°
But calm and mild, gentle and beautiful,
With gleams of sunshine on the eyelet spots
And loop-holes of the hills, wherever seen,
Hidden by quiet process, and as soon   90
Unfolded, to be huddled up again:
Along a narrow Valley and profound
I journeyed, when, aloft above my head,
Emerging from the silvery vapours, lo!
A Shepherd and his Dog! in open day:
Girt round with mists they stood and looked about
From that enclosure small, inhabitants
Of an aerial Island floating on,
As seemed, with that Abode in which they were,
A little pendant area of grey rocks,   100
By the soft wind breathed forward. With delight
As bland almost, one Evening I beheld,
And at as early age (the spectacle
Is common, but by me was then first seen)
A Shepherd in the bottom of a Vale
Towards the centre standing, who with voice,
And hand waved to and fro as need required
Gave signal to his Dog, thus teaching him
To chace along the mazes of steep crags
The Flock he could not see: and so the Brute   110
Dear Creature! with a Man's intelligence
Advancing, or retreating on his steps,
Through every pervious strait, to right or left,
Thridded a way unbaffled; while the Flock
Fled upwards from the terror of his Bark
Through rocks and seams of turf with liquid gold
Irradiate, that deep farewell light by which

The setting sun proclaims the love he bears
To mountain regions.
                        Beauteous the domain
Where to the sense of beauty first my heart   120
Was opened, tract more exquisitely fair
Than is that Paradise of ten thousand Trees,
Or Gehol's famous Gardens, in a Clime°
Chosen from widest Empire, for delight
Of the Tartarian Dynasty composed;
(Beyond that mighty Wall, not fabulous,
China's stupendous mound!) by patient skill
Of myriads, and boon Nature's lavish help;
Scene linked to scene, an evergrowing change,
Soft, grand, or gay! with Palaces and Domes   130
Of Pleasure spangled over, shady Dells
For Eastern Monasteries, sunny Mounds
With Temples crested, Bridges, Gondolas,
Rocks, Dens, and Groves of foliage taught to melt
Into each other their obsequious hues,
Going and gone again, in subtile chace,
Too fine to be pursued; or standing forth
In no discordant opposition, strong
And gorgeous as the colours side by side
Bedded among the plumes of Tropic Birds: 140
And mountains over all embracing all;
And all the landscape endlessly enriched
With waters running, falling, or asleep.

   But lovelier far than this the Paradise
Where I was reared; in Nature's primitive gifts
Favored no less, and more to every sense
Delicious, seeing that the sun and sky,
The elements and seasons in their change
Do find their dearest Fellow-labourer there,
The heart of Man; a district on all sides   150
The fragrance breathing of humanity,
Man free, man working for himself, with choice
Of time, and place, and object; by his wants,
His comforts, native occupations, cares,
Conducted on to individual ends
Or social, and still followed by a train

Unwooed, unthought-of even, simplicity,
And beauty, and inevitable grace.

    Yea, doubtless, at an age when but a glimpse
Of those resplendent Gardens, with their frame   160
Imperial, and elaborate ornaments,
Would to a Child be transport over-great,
When but a half-hour's roam through such a place
Would leave behind a dance of images
That shall break in upon his sleep for weeks,
Even then the common haunts of the green earth,
With the ordinary human interests
Which they embosom, all without regard
As both may seem, are fastening on the heart
Insensibly, each with the other's help,   170
So that we love, not knowing that we love,
And feel, not knowing whence our feeling comes.

    Such league have these two principles of joy
In our affections. I have singled out
Some moments, the earliest that I could, in which
Their several currents blended into one,
Weak yet, and gathering imperceptibly,
Flowed in by gushes. My first human love,
As hath been mentioned, did incline to those
Whose occupations and concerns were most   180
Illustrated by Nature and adorned,
And Shepherds were the men who pleased me first.
Not such as in Arcadian Fastnesses°
Sequestered, handed down among themselves,
So ancient Poets sing, the golden Age;
Nor such, a second Race, allied to these,
As Shakespeare in the Wood of Arden placed
Where Phoebe sighed for the false Ganymede,
Or there where Florizel and Perdita
Together danced, Queen of the Feast and King;   190
Nor such as Spenser fabled. True it is,
That I had heard, what he perhaps had seen,
Of maids at sunrise bringing in from far
Their Maybush, and along the Streets, in flocks,
Parading with a Song of taunting Rhymes,

Aimed at the Laggards slumbering within doors;
Had also heard, from those who yet remembered,
Tales of the May-pole Dance, and flowers that decked
The Posts and the Kirk-pillars, and of Youths,
That each one with his Maid, at break of day,   200
By annual custom issued forth in troops,
To drink the waters of some favorite Well,
And hang it round with Garlands. This, alas,
Was but a dream; the times had scattered all
These lighter graces, and the rural custom
And manners which it was my chance to see
In childhood were severe and unadorned,
The unluxuriant produce of a life
Intent on little but substantial needs,
Yet beautiful, and beauty that was felt.   210
But images of danger, and distress,
And suffering, these took deepest hold of me,
Man suffering among awful Powers, and Forms;
Of this I heard and saw enough to make
The imagination restless; nor was free
Myself from frequent perils; nor were tales
Wanting, the tragedies of former times,
Or hazards and escapes, which in my walks
I carried with me among crags and woods
And mountains; and of these may here be told   220
One, as recorded by my Household Dame.°

     'At the first falling of autumnal snow
A Shepherd and his Son one day went forth'
(Thus did the Matron's Tale begin) 'to seek
A Straggler of their Flock. They both had ranged
Upon this service the preceding day
All over their own pastures and beyond,
And now, at sun-rise sallying out again,
Renewed their search begun, where from Dove Crag,°
Ill home for bird so gentle, they looked down   230
On Deep-dale Head, and Brothers-water, named
From those two Brothers that were drowned therein.
Thence, northward, having passed by Arthur's Seat,
To Fairfield's highest summit; on the right
Leaving St. Sunday's Pike, to Grisedale Tarn

They shot, and over that cloud-loving Hill,
Seat Sandal, a fond lover of the clouds;
Thence up Helvellyn, a superior Mount
With prospect underneath of Striding-Edge,
And Grisedale's houseless Vale, along the brink   240
Of Russet Cove, and those two other Coves,
Huge skeletons of crags, which from the trunk
Of old Helvellyn spread their arms abroad,
And make a stormy harbour for the winds.
Far went those Shepherds in their devious quest.
From mountain ridges peeping as they passed
Down into every Glen: at length the Boy
Said, 'Father, with your leave I will go back,
And range the ground which we have seached before.'
So speaking, southward down the hill the Lad   250
Sprang like a gust of wind, crying aloud
"I know where I shall find him." 'For take note,'
Said here my grey-haired Dame, 'that tho' the storm
Drive one of these poor Creatures miles and miles,
If he can crawl he will return again
To his own hills, the spots where, when a Lamb,
He learned to pasture at his Mother's side.
After so long a labour, suddenly
Bethinking him of this, the Boy
Pursued his way towards a brook whose course   260
Was through that unfenced tract of mountain-ground
Which to his Father's little Farm belonged,
The home and ancient Birth-right of their Flock.
Down the deep channel of the Stream he went,
Prying through every nook. Meanwhile the rain
Began to fall upon the mountain tops,
Thick storm and heavy which for three hours' space
Abated not; and all that time the Boy
Was busy in his search, until at length
He spied the Sheep upon a plot of grass,   270
An Island in the Brook. It was a place
Remote and deep, piled round with rocks where foot
Of man or beast was seldom used to tread;
But now, when everywhere the summer grass
Had failed, this one Adventurer, hunger-pressed,
Had left his Fellows, and made his way alone

To the green plot of pasture in the Brook.
Before the Boy knew well what he had seen
He leapt upon the Island with proud heart
And with a Prophet's joy. Immediately   280
The Sheep sprang forward to the further Shore
And was borne headlong by the roaring flood.
At this the Boy looked round him, and his heart
Fainted with fear; thrice did he turn his face
To either brink; nor could he summon up
The courage that was needful to leap back
Cross the tempestuous torrent; so he stood,
A prisoner on the Island, not without
More than one thought of death and his last hour:
Meanwhile the Father had returned alone   290
To his own house; and now at the approach
Of evening he went forth to meet his Son,
Conjecturing vainly for what cause the Boy
Had stayed so long. The Shepherd took his way
Up his own mountain grounds, where, as he walked
Along the Steep that overhung the Brook,
He seemed to hear a voice, which was again
Repeated, like the whistling of a kite.
At this, not knowing why, as oftentimes
Long afterwards he has been heard to say,   300
Down to the Brook he went, and tracked its course
Upwards among the o'erhanging rocks; nor thus
Had he gone far, ere he espied the Boy
Where on that little plot of ground he stood
Right in the middle of the roaring Stream,
Now stronger every moment and more fierce.
The sight was such as no one could have seen
Without distress and fear. The Shepherd heard
The outcry of his Son, he stretched his Staff
Towards him, bade him leap, which word scarce said 310
The Boy was safe within his Father's arms.'

  Smooth life had Flock and Shepherd in old time,
Long Springs and tepid Winters on the Banks
Of delicate Galesus; and no less°
Those scattered along Adria's myrtle Shores:
Smooth life the Herdsman and his snow-white Herd

To Triumphs and to sacrificial Rites
Devoted, on the inviolable Stream
Of rich Clitumnus; and the Goatherd lived
As sweetly, underneath the pleasant brows   320
Of cool Lucretilis, where the Pipe was heard
Of Pan, the invisible God, thrilling the rocks
With tutelary muscic, from all harm
The Fold protecting. I myself, mature
In manhood then, have seen a pastoral Tract
Like one of these, where Fancy might run wild,
Though under skies less generous and serene;
Yet there, as for herself, had Nature framed
A Pleasure-ground, diffused a fair expanse
Of level Pasture, islanded with Groves   330
And banked with woody Risings; but the Plain
Endless, here opening widely out, and there
Shut up in lesser lakes or beds of lawn
And intricate recesses, creek or bay
Sheltered within a shelter, where at large
The Shepherd strays, a rolling hut his home:
Thither he comes with spring-time, there abides
All summer, and at sunrise ye may hear
His flute or flagelet resounding far.°
There's not a Nook or Hold of that vast space,   340
Nor Strait where passage is, but it shall have
In turn its Visitant, telling there his hours
In unlaborious pleasure, with no task
More toilsome than to carve a beechen bowl
For Spring or Fountain, which the Traveller finds
When through the region he pursues at will
His devious course. A glimpse of such sweet life
I saw when, from the melancholy Walls
Of Goslar, one Imperial! I renewed°
My daily walk along that chearful Plain,   350
Which, reaching to her Gates, spreads East and West
And Northwards, from beneath the mountainous verge
Of the Hercynian forest. Yet hail to You,
Your rocks and precipices, Ye that seize
The heart with firmer grasp! your snows and streams
Ungovernable, and your terrifying winds,
That howled so dismally when I have been

Companionless, among your solitudes.
There 'tis the Shepherd's task the winter long
To wait upon the storms: of their approach   360
Sagacious, from the height he drives his Flock
Down into sheltering coves, and feeds them there
Through the hard time, long as the storm is locked,
(So do they phrase it) bearing from the stalls
A toilsome burden up the craggy ways,
To strew it on the snow. And when the Spring°
Looks out, and all the mountains dance with lambs,
He through the enclosures won from the steep Waste,
And through the lower Heights hath gone his rounds;
And when the Flock with warmer weather climbs   370
Higher and higher, him his office leads
To range among them, through the hills dispersed,
And watch their goings, whatsoever track
Each Wanderer chuses for itself; a work
That lasts the summer through. He quits his home
At day-spring, and no sooner doth the sun
Begin to strike him with a fire-like heat
Than he lies down upon some shining place
And breakfasts with his Dog; when he hath stayed,
As for the most he doth, beyond his time,   380
He springs up with a bound, and then away!
Ascending fast with his long Pole in hand,
Or winding in and out among the crags.
What need to follow him through what he does
Or sees in his day's march? He feels himself
In those vast regions where his service is
A Freeman; wedded to his life of hope
And hazard, and hard labour interchanged
With that majestic indolence so dear
To native Man. A rambling school-boy, thus   390
Have I beheld him; without knowing why,
Have felt his presence in his own domain
As of a Lord and Master; or a Power
Or Genius, under Nature, under God,
Presiding; and severest solitude
Seemed more commanding oft when he was there.
Seeking the Raven's Nest, and suddenly
Surprized with vapours, or on rainy days

When I have angled up the lonely brooks
Mine eyes have glanced upon him, few steps off,   400
In size a Giant, stalking through the fog,
His Sheep like Greenland Bears. At other times
When round some shady promontory turning,
His Form hath flashed upon me, glorified
By the deep radiance of the setting sun:
Or him have I descried in distant sky,
A solitary object and sublime,
Above all height! like an aerial Cross,
As it is stationed on some spiry Rock
Of the Chartreuse, for worship. Thus was Man   410
Ennobled outwardly before mine eyes,
And thus my heart at first was introduced
To an unconscious love and reverence
Of human nature; hence the human form
To me was like an index of delight,
Of grace and honour, power and worthiness.
Meanwhile, this Creature, spiritual almost
As those of Books; but more exalted far,
Far more of an imaginative form,
Was not a Corin of the groves, who lives°   420
For his own fancies, or to dance by the hour
In coronal, with Phillis in the midst,
But, for the purposes of kind, a Man
With the most common; Husband, Father; learned,
Could teach, admonish, suffered with the rest
From vice and folly, wretchedness and fear;
Of this I little saw, cared less for it,
But something must have felt.
                      Call ye these appearances
Which I beheld of Shepherds in my youth,
This sanctity of nature given to man   430
A shadow, a delusion, ye who are fed
By the dead letter, not the spirit of things,
Whose truth is not a motion or a shape
Instinct with vital functions, but a Block
Or waxen Image which yourselves have made,
And ye adore. But blessed be the God
Of Nature and of Man that this was so,
That Men did at the first present themselves

Before my untaught eyes thus purified,
Removed, and at a distance that was fit.   440
And so we all of us in some degree
Are led to knowledge, whencesoever led,
And howsoever; were it otherwise,
And we found evil fast as we find good
In our first years, or think that it is found,
How could the innocent heart bear up and live!
But doubly fortunate my lot; not here
Alone, that something of a better life
Perhaps was round me than it is the privilege
Of most to move in, but that first I looked   450
At Man through objects that were great and fair,
First communed with him by their help. And thus
Was founded a sure safeguard and defence
Against the weight of meanness, selfish cares,
Coarse manners, vulgar passions, that beat in
On all sides from the ordinary world
In which we traffic. Starting from this point,
I had my face towards the truth, began
With an advantage; furnished with that kind
Of prepossession without which the soul   460
Receives no knowledge that can bring forth good,
No genuine insight ever comes to her:
Happy in this, that I with nature walked,
Not having a too early intercourse
With the deformities of crowded life,
And those ensuing laughters and contempts
Self-pleasing, which if we would wish to think
With admiration and respect of man
Will not permit us; but pursue the mind
That to devotion willingly would be raised   470
Into the Temple and the Temple's heart.

       Yet do not deem, my Friend, though thus I speak
Of Man as having taken in my mind
A place thus early which might also seem
Preeminent, that this was really so.
Nature herself was at this unripe time,
But secondary to my own pursuits
And animal activities, and all

Their trivial pleasures; and long afterwards
When these had died away, and Nature did   480
For her own sake become my joy, even then
And upwards through late youth, until not less
Than three and twenty summers had been told
Was man in my affections and regards
Subordinate to her; her awful forms
And viewless agencies: a passion, she!
A rapture often, and immediate joy,
Ever at hand; he distant, but a grace
Occasional, an accidental thought,
His hour being not yet come. Far less had then   490
The inferior Creatures, beast or bird, attuned
My spirit to that gentleness of love,
Won from me those minute obeisances
Of tenderness, which I may number now
With my first blessings. Nevertheless, on these
The light of beauty did not fall in vain,
Or grandeur circumfuse them to no end.

     Why should I speak of Tillers of the soil?
The Ploughman and his Team; or Men and Boys
In festive summer busy with the rake,   500
Old Men and ruddy Maids, and Little Ones
All out together, and in sun and shade
Dispersed among the hay-grounds alder-fringed,
The Quarry-man, far heard! that blasts the rock,
The Fishermen in pairs, the one to row,
And one to drop the Net, plying their trade
"Mid tossing lakes and tumbling boats' and winds°
Whistling; the Miner, melancholy Man!
That works by taper light, while all the hills
Are shining with the glory of the day.   510

     But when that first poetic Faculty
Of plain imagination and severe,
No longer a mute Influence of the soul,
An Element of the nature's inner self,
Began to have some promptings to put on
A visible shape, and to the works of art,
The notions and the images of books,

Did knowingly conform itself, by these
Enflamed, and proud of that her new delight,
There came among those shapes of human life   520
A wilfulness of fancy and conceit
Which gave them new importance to the mind;
And Nature and her objects beautified
These fictions, as in some sort, in their turn,
They burnished her. From touch of this new power
Nothing was safe: the Elder-tree that grew
Beside the well-known Charnel-house had then
A dismal look; the Yew-tree had its Ghost,
That took its station there for ornament.
Then common death was none, common mishap,   530
But matter for this humour everywhere,
The tragic super-tragic, else left short.
Then, if a Widow, staggering with the blow
Of her distress, was known to have made her way
To the cold grave in which her Husband slept,
One night, or haply more than one, through pain
Or half-insensate impotence of mind,
The fact was caught at greedily, and there
She was a Visitant the whole year through,
Wetting the turf with never-ending tears,   540
And all the storms of Heaven must beat on her.

Through wild obliquities could I pursue
Among all objects of the fields and groves
These cravings; when the Fox-glove, one by one,
Upwards through every stage of its tall stem,
Had shed its bells, and stood by the wayside
Dismantled, with a single one, perhaps,
Left at the ladder's top, with which the Plant
Appeared to stoop, as slender blades of grass
Tipped with a bead of rain or dew, behold!   550
If such sight were seen, would Fancy bring
Some Vagrant thither with her Babes, and seat her
Upon the Turf beneath the stately Flower
Drooping in sympathy, and making so
A melancholy Crest above the head
Of the lorn Creature, while her Little-Ones,
All unconcerned with her unhappy plight,

Were sporting with the purple cups that lay
Scattered upon the ground.
                              There was a Copse
An upright bank of wood and woody rock   560
That opposite our rural Dwelling stood,
In which a sparkling patch of diamond light
Was in bright weather duly to be seen
On summer afternoons, within the wood
At the same place. 'Twas doubtless nothing more
Than a black rock, which, wet with constant springs,
Glistered far seen from out its lurking-place
As soon as ever the declining sun
Had smitten it. Beside our cottage hearth,
Sitting with open door, a hundred times   570
Upon this lustre have I gazed, that seemed
To have some meaning which I could not find:
And now it was a burnished shield, I fancied,
Suspended over a Knight's Tomb, who lay
Inglorious, buried in the dusky wood;
An entrance now into some magic cave
Or Palace for a Fairy of the rock;
Nor would I, though not certain whence the cause
Of the effulgence, thither have repaired
Without a precious bribe, and day by day   580
And month by month I saw the spectacle,
Nor ever once have visited the spot
Unto this hour. Thus sometimes were the shapes
Of wilful fancy grafted upon feelings
Of the imagination, and they rose
In worth accordingly.
                          My present Theme
Is to retrace the way that led me on
Through nature to the love of human Kind;
Nor could I with such object overlook
The Influence of this Power which turned itself   590
Instinctively to human passions, things
Least understood; of this adulterate Power,
For so it may be called, and without wrong,
When with that first compared. Yet in the midst
Of these vagaries, with an eye so rich
As mine was, through the chance, on me not wasted

Of having been brought up in such a grand
And lovely region, I had forms distinct
To steady me. These thoughts did oft revolve
About some centre palpable, which at once   600
Incited them to motion, and controlled,
And whatsoever shape the fit might take,
And whencesoever it might come, I still
At all times had a real solid world
Of images about me; did not pine
As one in cities bred might do; as Thou,
Beloved Friend! hast told me that thou didst,
Great Spirit as thou art, in endless dreams
Of sickliness, disjoining, joining things
Without the light of knowledge. Where the harm,   610
If, when the Woodman languished with disease
From sleeping night by night among the woods
Within his sod-built Cabin, Indian-wise,
I called the pangs of disappointed love
And all the long Etcetera of such thought
To help him to his grave? Meanwhile the Man,
If not already from the woods retired
To die at home, was haply, as I knew,
Pining alone among the gentle airs,
Birds, running streams, and hills so beautiful   620
On golden evenings, while the charcoal Pile
Breathed up its smoke, an image of his ghost
Or spirit that was soon to take its flight.

     There came a time of greater dignity
Which had been gradually prepared, and now
Rushed in as if on wings, the time in which
The pulse of Being everywhere was felt,
When all the several frames of things, like stars
Through every magnitude distinguishable,
Were half confounded in each other's blaze,   630
One galaxy of life and joy. Then rose
Man, inwardly contemplated, and present
In my own being, to a loftier height;
As of all visible natures crown; and first
In capability of feeling what
Was to be felt; in being rapt away

By the divine effect of power and love,
As, more than anything we know, instinct
With Godhead, and by reason and by will
Acknowledging dependency sublime.   640

　　Erelong transported hence as in a dream
I found myself begirt with temporal shapes
Of vice and folly thrust upon my view,
Objects of sport, and ridicule, and scorn,
Manners and characters discriminate,
And little busy passions that eclipsed,
As well they might, the impersonated thought,
The idea of abstraction of the Kind.
An Idler among academic Bowers,
Such was my new condition, as at large   650
Hath been set forth; yet here the vulgar light
Of present actual superficial life,
Gleaming through colouring of other times,
Old usages and local privilege,
Thereby was softened, almost solemnized,
And rendered apt and pleasing to the view.
This notwithstanding, being brought more near
As I was now, to guilt and wretchedness,
I trembled, thought of human life at times
With an indefinite terror and dismay,   660
Such as the storms and angry elements
Had bred in me, but gloomier far, a dim
Analogy to uproar and misrule,
Disquiet, danger, and obscurity.

　　It might be told (but wherefore speak of things
Common to all?) that seeing, I essayed
To give relief, began to deem myself
A moral agent, judging between good
And evil, not as for the mind's delight
But for her safety, one who was to *act*,   670
As sometimes, to the best of my weak means,
I did, by human sympathy impelled,
And through dislike and most offensive pain
Was to the truth conducted; of this faith
Never forsaken, that by acting well

And understanding, I should learn to love
The end of life and every thing we know.

     Preceptress stern, that didst instruct me next,
London! to thee I willingly return.
Erewhile my Verse played only with the flowers   680
Enwrought upon thy mantle, satisfied°
With this amusement, and a simple look
Of child-like inquisition, now and then
Cast upwards on thine eye to puzzle out
Some inner meanings, which might harbour there.
Yet did I not give way to this light mood
Wholly beguiled, as one incapable
Of higher things, and ignorant that high things
Were round me. Never shall I forget the hour
The moment rather say when having thridded   690
The labyrinth of suburban Villages,
At length I did unto myself first seem
To enter the great City. On the Roof
Of an itinerant Vehicle I sate,
With vulgar men about me, vulgar forms
Of houses, pavement, streets, of men and things,
Mean shapes on every side: but, at the time,
When to myself it fairly might be said,
The very moment that I seemed to know
The threshold now is overpassed, Great God!   700
That aught *external* to the living mind
Should have such mighty sway! yet so it was
A weight of Ages did at once descend
Upon my heart; no thought embodied, no
Distinct remembrances; but weight and power,
Power growing with the weight: alas! I feel
That I am trifling: 'twas a moment's pause.
All that took place within me, came and went
As in a moment, and I only now
Remember that it was a thing divine.   710

     As when a traveller hath from open day
With torches passed into some Vault of Earth,
The Grotto of Antiparos, or the Den°
Of Yordas among Craven's mountain tracts;

He looks and sees the Cavern spread and grow,
Widening itself on all sides, sees, or thinks
He sees, erelong, the roof above his head,
Which instantly unsettles and recedes
Substance and shadow, light and darkness, all
Commingled, making up a Canopy   720
Of Shapes and Forms and Tendencies to Shape,
That shift and vanish, change and interchange
Like Spectres, ferment quiet and sublime,
Which, after a short space, works less and less,
Till every effort, every motion gone,
The scene before him lies in perfect view,
Exposed and lifeless, as a written book.
But let him pause awhile, and look again
And a new quickening shall succeed, at first
Beginning timidly, then creeping fast   730
Through all which he beholds; the senseless mass,
In its projections, wrinkles, cavities,
Through all its surface, with all colours streaming,
Like a magician's airy pageant, parts
Unites, embodying everywhere some pressure
Or image, recognised or new, some type
Or picture of the world; forests and lakes,
Ships, rivers, towers, the Warrior clad in Mail,
The prancing Steed, the Pilgrim with his Staff,
The mitred Bishop and the throned King,   740
A Spectacle to which there is no end.

    No otherwise had I at first been moved
With such a swell of feeling, followed soon
By a blank sense of greatness passed away,
And afterwards continued to be moved
In presence of that vast Metropolis,
The Fountain of my Country's destiny
And of the destiny of Earth itself,
That great Emporium, Chronicle at once
And Burial-place of passions and their home   750
Imperial, and chief living residence.

    With strong Sensations, teeming as it did
Of past and present, such a place must needs

Have pleased me, in those times; I sought not then
Knowledge; but craved for power, and power I found
In all things. Nothing had a circumscribed
And narrow influence; but all objects, being
Themselves capacious, also found in me
Capaciousness and amplitude of mind;
Such is the strength and glory of our Youth.   760
The Human nature unto which I felt
That I belonged, and which I loved and reverenced,
Was not a punctual Presence, but a Spirit°
Living in time and space, and far diffused.
In this my joy, in this my dignity
Consisted; the external universe,
By striking upon what is found within,
Had given me this conception, with the help
Of Books, and what they picture and record.

    'Tis true the History of my native Land,   770
With those of Greece compared and popular Rome,°
Events not lovely nor magnanimous,
But harsh and unaffecting in themselves,
And in our high-wrought modern narratives
Stript of their harmonising soul, the life
Of manners and familiar incidents,
Had never much delighted me. And less
Than other minds I had been used to owe
The pleasure which I found in place or thing
To extrinsic transitory accidents,   780
To records or traditions; but a sense
Of what had been here done, and suffered here
Through ages, and was doing, suffering, still,
Weighed with me, could support the test of thought,
Was like the enduring majesty and power
Of independent nature; and not seldom
Even individual remembrances,
By working on the Shapes before my eyes,
Became like vital functions of the soul;
And out of what had been, what was, the place   790
Was thronged with impregnations, like those wilds
In which my early feelings had been nursed,
And naked valleys, full of caverns, rocks,

And audible seclusions, dashing lakes,
Echoes and Waterfalls, and pointed crags
That into music touch the passing wind.

    Thus here imagination also found
An element that pleased her, tried her strength
Among new objects simplified, arranged,
Impregnated my knowledge, made it live,   800
And the result was elevating thoughts
Of human Nature. Neither guilt nor vice,
Debasement of the body or the mind,
Nor all the misery forced upon my sight,
Which was not lightly passed, but often scanned
Most feelingly, could overthrow my trust
In what we may become, induce belief
That I was ignorant, had been falsely taught,
A Solitary, who with vain conceits
Had been inspired, and walked about in dreams.   810
When from that awful prospect, overcast
And in eclipse, my meditations turned,
Lo! everything that was indeed divine
Retained its purity inviolate
And unencroached upon, nay, seemed brighter far
For this deep shade in counterview, that gloom
Of opposition, such as shewed itself
To the eyes of Adam, yet in Paradise,
Though fallen from bliss, when in the East he saw°
Darkness ere day's mid course, and morning light   820
More orient in the western cloud, that drew
'O'er the blue firmament a radiant white,
Descending slow with something heavenly fraught.'

    Add also, that among the multitudes
Of that great City, oftentimes was seen
Affectingly set forth, more than elsewhere
Is possible, the unity of man,
One spirit over ignorance and vice
Predominant, in good and evil hearts
One sense for moral judgements, as one eye   830
For the sun's light. When strongly breathed upon
By this sensation, whencesoe'er it comes

Of union or communion, doth the soul
Rejoice as in her highest joy: for there,
There chiefly, hath she feeling whence she is,
And passing through all Nature rests with God.

And is not, too, that vast Abiding-place
Of human Creatures, turn where'er we may,
Profusely sown with individual sights
Of courage, and integrity, and truth,   840
And tenderness, which, here set off by foil,
Appears more touching. In the tender scenes
Chiefly was my delight, and one of these
Never will be forgotten. 'Twas a Man,
Whom I saw sitting in an open Square
Close to an iron paling that fenced in
The spacious Grass-plot; on the corner stone
Of the low wall in which the pales were fixed
Sate this one Man, and with a sickly Babe
Upon his knee, whom he had thither brought   850
For sunshine, and to breathe the fresher air.
Of those who passed, and me who looked at him,
He took no note; but in his brawny Arms
(The Artificer was to the elbow bare,
And from his work this moment had been stolen)
He held the Child, and, bending over it
As if he were afraid both of the sun
And of the air which he had come to seek,
He eyed it with unutterable love.

    Thus were my thoughts attracted more and more   860
By slow gradations towards human Kind
And to the good and ill of human life;
Nature had led me on, and now I seemed
To travel independent of her help,
As if I had forgotten her; but no,
My Fellow beings still were unto me
Far less than she was; though the scale of love
Were filling fast, 'twas light, as yet, compared
With that in which her mighty objects lay.

BOOK NINE
Residence in France

As oftentimes a River, it might seem,
Yielding in part to old remembrances,
Part swayed by fear to tread an onward road
That leads direct to the devouring sea,
Turns, and will measure back his course, far back,
Towards the very regions which he crossed
In his first outset; so have we long time
Made motions retrograde, in like pursuit
Detained. But now we start afresh; I feel
An impulse to precipitate my Verse.   10
Fair greetings to this shapeless eagerness,
Whene'er it comes, needful in work so long,
Thrice needful to the argument which now
Awaits us; Oh! how much unlike the past!
One which though bright the promise, will be found
Ere far we shall advance, ungenial, hard
To treat of, and forbidding in itself.

    Free as a colt at pasture on the hills,
I ranged at large, through the Metropolis
Month after month. Obscurely did I live,   20
Not courting the society of Men
By literature, or elegance, or rank
Distinguished; in the midst of things, it seemed,
Looking as from a distance on the world
That moved about me. Yet insensibly
False preconceptions were corrected thus
And errors of the fancy rectified,
Alike with reference to men and things,
And sometimes from each quarter were poured in
Novel imaginations and profound.   30
A year thus spent, this field (with small regret°
Save only for the Book-stalls in the streets,
Wild produce, hedge-row fruit, on all sides hung
To lure the sauntering traveller from his track)
I quitted, and betook myself to France,
Led thither chiefly by a personal wish

To speak the language more familiarly,
With which intent I chose for my abode
A City on the Borders of the Loire.°

    Through Paris lay my readiest path, and there   40
I sojourned a few days, and visited
In haste each spot of old and recent fame,
The latter chiefly, from the Field of Mars°
Down to the Suburbs of St. Anthony,
And from Mont Martyr southward, to the Dome
Of Geneviève. In both her clamorous Halls,
The National Synod and the Jacobins,
I saw the revolutionary Power
Toss like a Ship at anchor, rocked by storms;
The Arcades I traversed in the Palace huge   50
Of Orleans, coasted round and round the line
Of Tavern, Brothel, Gaming-house, and Shop,
Great rendezvous of worst and best, the walk
Of all who had a purpose, or had not;
I stared and listened with a stranger's ears
To Hawkers and Haranguers, hubbub wild!
And hissing Factionists with ardent eyes,
In knots, or pairs, or single, ant-like swarms
Of Builders and Subverters, every face
That hope or apprehension could put on,   60
Joy, anger, and vexation in the midst
Of gaiety and dissolute idleness.

    Where silent zephyrs sported with the dust
Of the Bastille I sate in the open sun,
And from the rubbish gathered up a stone
And pocketed the relick in the guise
Of an Enthusiast, yet, in honest truth
Though not without some strong incumbences,
And glad, (could living man be otherwise?)
I looked for something that I could not find,   70
Affecting more emotion than I felt,
For 'tis most certain that the utmost force
Of all these various objects which may shew
The temper of my mind as then it was
Seemed less to recompense the Traveller's pains,
Less moved me, gave me less delight, than did

A single picture merely, hunted out
Among other sights, the Magdalene of le Brun,°
A Beauty exquisitely wrought, fair face
And rueful, with its ever-flowing tears.   80

   But hence to my more permanent residence
I hasten; there, by novelties in speech,
Domestic manners, customs, gestures, looks,
And all the attire of ordinary life,
Attention was at first engrossed; and thus,
Amused and satisfied, I scarcely felt
The shock of these concussions, unconcerned,
Tranquil almost, and careless as a flower
Glassed in a Green-house, or a Parlour shrub,
When every bush and tree, the country through,   90
Is shaking to the roots; indifference this
Which may seem strange, but I was unprepared
With needful knowledge, had abruptly passed
Into a theatre, of which the stage
Was busy with an action far advanced.
Like others I had read, and eagerly
Sometimes, the master Pamphlets of the day;
Nor wanted such half-insight as grew wild
Upon that meagre soil, helped out by Talk
And public News; but having never chanced   100
To see a regular Chronicle which might shew,
(If any such indeed existed then)
Whence the main Organs of the public Power
Had sprung, their transmigrations when and how
Accomplished, giving thus unto events
A form and body, all things were to me
Loose and disjointed, and the affections left
Without a vital interest. At that time,
Moreover, the first storm was overblown,
And the strong hand of outward violence   110
Locked up in quiet. For myself—I fear
Now in connection with so great a Theme
To speak (as I must be compelled to do)
Of one so unimportant—a short time
I loitered, and frequented night by night
Routs, card-tables, the formal haunts of Men,

Whom in the City privilege of birth
Sequestered from the rest, societies
Where, through punctilios of elegance
And deeper causes, all discourse, alike   120
Of good and evil in the time, was shunned
With studious care; but 'twas not long ere this
Proved tedious, and I gradually withdrew
Into a noisier world; and thus did soon
Become a Patriot, and my heart was all
Given to the People, and my love was theirs.

    A knot of military Officers,
That to a Regiment appertained which then
Was stationed in the City, were the chief
Of my associates: some of these wore Swords   130
Which had been seasoned in the Wars, and all
Were men well-born, at least laid claim to such
Distinction, as the Chivalry of France.
In age and temper differing, they had yet
One spirit ruling in them all, alike
(Save only one, hereafter to be named)
Were bent upon undoing what was done:
This was their rest, and only hope, therewith
No fear had they of bad becoming worse,
For worst to them was come, nor would have stirred,   140
Or deemed it worth a moment's while to stir,
In anything, save only as the act
Looked thitherward. One, reckoning by years,
Was in the prime of manhood, and erewhile
He had sate Lord in many tender hearts,
Though heedless of such honours now, and changed:
His temper was quite mastered by the times,
And they had blighted him, had eat away
The beauty of his person, doing wrong
Alike to body and to mind: his port,   150
Which once had been erect and open, now
Was stooping and contracted, and a face,
By nature lovely in itself, expressed,
As much as any that was ever seen,
A ravage out of season, made by thoughts
Unhealthy and vexatious. At the hour,

The most important of each day, in which
The public News was read, the fever came,
A punctual visitant, to shake this Man,
Disarmed his voice, and fanned his yellow cheek   160
Into a thousand colours; while he read,
Or mused, his sword was haunted by his touch
Continually, like an uneasy place
In his own body. 'Twas in truth an hour
Of universal ferment; mildest men
Were agitated; and commotions, strife
Of passion and opinion filled the walls
Of peaceful houses with unquiet sounds.
The soil of common life was at that time
Too hot to tread upon; oft said I then,   170
And not then only, 'what a mockery this
Of history, the past and that to come!
Now do I feel how I have been deceived,
Reading of Nations and their works, in faith,
Faith given to vanity and emptiness;
Oh! laughter for the Page that would reflect
To future times the face of what now is!'
The land all swarmed with passion, like a Plain
Devoured by locusts, Carra, Gorsas, add°
A hundred other names, forgotten now,   180
Nor to be heard of more, yet were they Powers,
Like earthquakes, shocks repeated day by day,
And felt through every nook of town and field.

    The Men already spoken of as chief
Of my Associates were prepared for flight
To augment the band of Emigrants in Arms
Upon the borders of the Rhine, and leagued
With foreign Foes mustered for instant war.
This was their undisguised intent, and they
Were waiting with the whole of their desires   190
The moment to depart.
                    An Englishman,
Born in a Land, the name of which appeared
To license some unruliness of mind,
A Stranger, with Youth's further privilege,
And that indulgence which a half-learned speech

Wins from the courteous, I, who had been else
Shunned and not tolerated, freely lived
With these Defenders of the Crown, and talked
And heard their notions, nor did they disdain
The wish to bring me over to their cause.   200
But though untaught by thinking or by books
To reason well of polity or law
And nice distinctions, then on every tongue,
Of natural rights and civil, and to acts
Of Nations, and their passing interests,
(I speak comparing these with other things)
Almost indifferent, even the Historian's Tale
Prizing but little otherwise than I prized
Tales of the Poets, as it made my heart
Beat high and filled my fancy with fair forms,   210
Old Heroes and their sufferings and their deeds;
Yet in the regal Sceptre, and the pomp
Of Orders and Degrees, I nothing found
Then, or had ever, even in crudest youth,
That dazzled me; but rather what my soul
Mourned for, or loathed, beholding that the best
Ruled not, and feeling that they ought to rule.

For, born in a poor District, and which yet
Retaineth more of ancient homeliness,
Manners erect, and frank simplicity,   220
Than any other nook of English Land,
It was my fortune scarcely to have seen
Through the whole tenor of my School-day time
The face of one, who, whether Boy or Man,
Was vested with attention or respect
Through claims of wealth or blood. Nor was it least
Of many debts which afterwards I owed
To Cambridge and an academic life,
That something there was holden up to view
Of a Republic, where all stood thus far   230
Upon equal ground, that they were brothers all
In honour, as in one community,
Scholars and Gentlemen, where, furthermore,
Distinction lay open to all that came,
And wealth and titles were in less esteem

Than talents and successful industry.
Add unto this, subservience from the first
To God and Nature's single sovereignty,
Familiar presences of awful Power,
And fellowship with venerable books   240
To sanction the proud workings of the soul,
And mountain liberty. It could not be
But that one tutored thus, who had been formed
To thought and moral feelings in the way
This story hath described, should look with awe
Upon the faculties of Man, receive
Gladly the highest promises, and hail
As best the government of equal rights
And individual worth. And hence, O Friend!
If at the first great outbreak I rejoiced   250
Less than might well befit my youth, the cause
In part lay here, that unto me the events
Seemed nothing out of nature's certain course,
A gift that rather was come late than soon.
No wonder, then, if advocates like these
Whom I have mentioned, at this riper day
Were impotent to make my hopes put on
The shape of theirs, my understanding bend
In honour to their honour. Zeal which yet
Had slumbered, now in opposition burst   260
Forth like a polar summer; every word
They uttered was a dart, by counter-winds
Blown back upon themselves, their reason seemed
Confusion-stricken by a higher power
Than human understanding, their discourse
Maimed, spiritless, and in their weakness strong
I triumphed.
                    Meantime, day by day, the roads
(While I consorted with these Royalists)
Were crowded with the bravest Youth of France,
And all the promptest of her Spirits, linked   270
In gallant Soldiership, and posting on
To meet the War upon her Frontier Bounds.
Yet at this very moment do tears start
Into mine eyes; I do not say I weep,
I wept not then, but tears have dimmed my sight,

In memory of the farewells of that time,
Domestic severings, female fortitude
At dearest separation, patriot love
And self-devotion, and terrestrial hope
Encouraged with a martyr's confidence.   280
Even files of Strangers merely, seen but once,
And for a moment, men from far, with sound
Of music, martial tunes, and banners spread,
Entering the City, here and there a face
Or person singled out among the rest,
Yet still a stranger and beloved as such,
Even by these passing spectacles my heart
Was oftentimes uplifted, and they seemed
Like arguments from Heaven, that 'twas a cause
Good, and which no one could stand up against   290
Who was not lost, abandoned, selfish, proud,
Mean, miserable, wilfully depraved,
Hater perverse of equity and truth.

    Among that band of Officers was one,°
Already hinted at, of other mold,
A Patriot, thence rejected by the rest
And with an oriental loathing spurned,
As of a different Cast. A meeker Man
Than this lived never, or a more benign,
Meek, though enthusiastic to the height   300
Of highest expectation. Injuries
Made him more gracious, and his nature then
Did breathe its sweetness out most sensibly
As aromatic flowers on alpine turf
When foot hath crushed them. He through events
Of that great change wandered in perfect faith,
As through a Book, an old Romance or Tale
Of Fairy, or some dream of actions wrought
Behind the summer clouds. By birth he ranked
With the most noble, but unto the poor   310
Among mankind he was in service bound
As by some tie invisible, oaths professed
To a religious Order. Man he loved
As Man, and to the mean and the obscure,
And all the homely in their homely works,

Transferred a courtesy which had no air
Of condescension, but did rather seem
A passion and a gallantry, like that
Which he, a Soldier, in his idler day
Had payed to Woman. Somewhat vain he was,   320
Or seemed so, yet it was not vanity
But fondness, and a kind of radiant joy
That covered him about when he was bent
On works of love or freedom, or revolved
Complacently the progress of a cause
Whereof he was a part; yet this was meek
And placid, and took nothing from the Man
That was delightful. Oft in solitude
With him did I discourse about the end
Of civil government, and its wisest forms,   330
Of ancient prejudice, and chartered rights,
Allegiance, faith, and laws by time matured,
Custom and habit, novelty and change,
Of self-respect, and virtue in the Few
For patrimonial honour set apart,
And ignorance in the labouring Multitude.
For he, an upright Man and tolerant,
Balanced these contemplations in his mind
And I, who at that time was scarcely dipped
Into the turmoil, had a sounder judgment   340
Than afterwards, carried about me yet
With less alloy to its integrity
The experience of past ages, as through help
Of Books and common life it finds its way
To youthful minds, by objects over near
Not pressed upon, nor dazzled or misled
By struggling with the crowd for present ends.

But though not deaf and obstinate to find
Error without apology on the side
Of those who were against us, more delight   350
We took, and let this freely be confessed,
In painting to ourselves the miseries
Of royal Courts, and that voluptuous life
Unfeeling, where the Man who is of soul
The meanest thrives the most, where dignity,

True personal dignity, abideth not,
A light and cruel world, cut off from all
The natural inlets of just sentiment,
From lowly sympathy, and chastening truth,
Where good and evil never have that name,   360
That which they ought to have, but wrong prevails,
And vice at home. We added dearest themes,
Man and his noble nature, as it is
The gift of God and lies in his own power,
His blind desires and steady faculties
Capable of clear truth, the one to break
Bondage, the other to build liberty
On firm foundations, making social life,°
Through knowledge spreading and imperishable,
As just in regulation, and as pure   370
As individual in the wise and good.
We summoned up the honorable deeds
Of ancient Story, thought of each bright spot
That could be found in all recorded time
Of truth preserved and error passed away,
Of single Spirits that catch the flame from Heaven,
And how the multitude of men will feed
And fan each other, thought of Sects, how keen
They are to put the appropriate nature on,
Triumphant over every obstacle   380
Of custom, language, Country, love and hate,
And what they do and suffer for their creed,
How far they travel, and how long endure,
How quickly mighty Nations have been formed
From least beginnings, how, together locked
By new opinions, scattered tribes have made
One body spreading wide as clouds in heaven.
To aspirations then of our own minds
Did we appeal; and, finally, beheld
A living confirmation of the whole   390
Before us in a People risen up
Fresh as the morning Star. Elate we looked
Upon their virtues, saw in rudest men
Self-sacrifice the firmest, generous love
And continence of mind, and sense of right
Uppermost in the midst of fiercest strife.

Oh! sweet it is, in academic Groves,
Or such retirement, Friend! as we have known
Among the mountains, by our Rotha's Stream,°
Greta or Derwent, or some nameless Rill,   400
To ruminate with interchange of talk
On rational liberty, and hope in man,
Justice and peace; but far more sweet such toil,
Toil say I, for it leads to thoughts abstruse,
If Nature then be standing on the brink
Of some great trial, and we hear the voice
Of One devoted, one whom circumstance
Hath called upon to embody his deep sense
In action, give it outwardly a shape,
And that of benediction to the world.   410
Then doubt is not, and truth is more than truth,
A hope it is and a desire, a creed
Of zeal by an authority divine
Sanctioned, of danger, difficulty or death.
Such conversation under Attic shades°
Did Dion hold with Plato, ripened thus
For a Deliverer's glorious task, and such,
He, on that ministry already bound,
Held with Eudemus and Timonides,
Surrounded by Adventurers in Arms,   420
When those two Vessels with their daring Freight
For the Sicilian Tyrant's overthrow
Sailed from Zacynthus, philosophic war
Led by Philosophers. With harder fate,
Though like ambition, such was he, O Friend!
Of whom I speak, so Beaupuis (let the Name
Stand near the worthiest of Antiquity)
Fashioned his life, and many a long discourse
With like persuasion honored we maintained,
He on his part accoutred for the worst.   430
He perished fighting in supreme command
Upon the Borders of the unhappy Loire
For Liberty against deluded Men,
His Fellow-countrymen, and yet most blessed
In this, that he the fate of later times
Lived not to see, nor what we now behold
Who have as ardent hearts as he had then.

Along that very Loire, with Festivals
Resounding at all hours, and innocent yet
Of civil slaughter, was our frequent walk   440
Or in wide Forests of the neighbourhood,
High woods and over-arched, with open space
On every side, and footing many a mile,
Inwoven roots and moss smooth as the sea,
A solemn region. Often in such place
From earnest dialogues I slipped in thought,
And let remembrance steal to other times
When Hermits, from their sheds and caves forth strayed,
Walked by themselves, so met in shades like these,
And if a devious Traveller was heard   450
Approaching from a distance, as might chance,
With speed and echoes loud of trampling hoofs
From the hard floor reverberated, then
It was Angelica thundering through the woods°
Upon her Palfrey, or that gentler Maid
Erminia, fugitive as fair as She.
Sometimes I saw, methought, a pair of Knights
Joust underneath the trees, that, as in storm,
Did rock above their heads; anon the din
Of boisterous merriment and music's roar,   460
With sudden Proclamation, burst from haunt
Of Satyrs in some viewless glade, with dance
Rejoicing o'er a Female in the midst,
A mortal Beauty, their unhappy Thrall.
The width of those huge Forests, unto me
A novel scene, did often in this way
Master my fancy, while I wandered on
With that revered Companion. And sometimes
When to a Convent in a meadow green
By a brook-side we came, a roofless Pile,   470
And not by reverential touch of Time
Dismantled, but by violence abrupt,
In spite of those heart-bracing colloquies,
In spite of real fervour, and of that
Less genuine and wrought up within myself,
I could not but bewail a wrong so harsh,
And for the matin Bell to sound no more
Grieved, and the evening Taper, and the Cross

High on the topmost Pinnacle, a sign
Admonitory by the Traveller   480
First seen above the woods.
                                        And when my Friend
Pointed upon occasion to the Site
Of Romorentin, home of ancient Kings,°
To the imperial Edifice of Blois,
Or to that rural Castle, name now slipped
From my remembrance, where a Lady lodged
By the first Francis wooed, and bound to him
In chains of mutual passion; from the Tower,
As a tradition of the Country tells,
Practised to commune with her Royal Knight   490
By cressets and love-beacons, intercourse
'Twixt her high-seated Residence and his
Far off at Chambord on the Plain beneath:°
Even here, though less than with the peaceful House
Religious, 'mid these frequent monuments
Of Kings, their vices and their better deeds,
Imagination, potent to enflame
At times with virtuous wrath and noble scorn,
Did also often mitigate the force
Of civic prejudice, the bigotry,   500
So call it, of a youthful Patriot's mind,
And on these spots with many gleams I looked
Of chivalrous delight. Yet not the less,
Hatred of absolute rule, where will of One
Is law for all, and of that barren pride
In them who, by immunities unjust,
Betwixt the Sovereign and the People stand,
His helper and not theirs, laid stronger hold
Daily upon me, mixed with pity too
And love; for where hope is there love will be   510
For the abject multitude. And when we chanced
One day to meet a hunger-bitten Girl,
Who crept along, fitting her languid self
Unto a Heifer's motion, by a cord
Tied to her arm, and picking thus from the lane
Its sustenance, while the Girl with her two hands
Was busy knitting, in a heartless mood
Of solitude, and at the sight my Friend

In agitation said, ''Tis against *that*
Which we are fighting,' I with him believed   520
Devoutly that a spirit was abroad
Which could not be withstood, that poverty
At least like this, would in a little time
Be found no more, that we should see the earth
Unthwarted in her wish to recompense
The industrious, and the lowly Child of Toil,
All institutes for ever blotted out
That legalised exclusion, empty pomp
Abolished, sensual state and cruel power
Whether by edict of the one or few,   530
And finally, as sum and crown of all,
Should see the People having a strong hand
In making their own Laws, whence better days
To all mankind. But, these things set apart,
Was not the single confidence enough
To animate the mind that ever turned
A thought to human welfare, that henceforth
Captivity by mandate without law
Should cease, and open accusation lead
To sentence in the hearing of the world,   540
And open punishment, if not the air
Be free to breathe in, and the heart of Man
Dread nothing. Having touched this argument
I shall not, as my purpose was, take note
Of other matters which detained us oft
In thought or conversation, public acts,
And public persons, and the emotions wrought
Within our minds by the ever-varying wind
Of Record and Report which day by day
Swept over us; but I will here instead   550
Draw from obscurity a tragic Tale,
Not in its spirit singular indeed,
But haply worth memorial, as I heard
The events related by my patriot Friend
And others who had borne a part therein.°

Oh! happy time of youthful Lovers! thus
My Story may begin, Oh! balmy time

In which a Love-knot on a Lady's brow
Is fairer than the fairest Star in heaven!
To such inheritance of blessedness   560
Young Vaudracour was brought by years that had
A little overstepped his stripling prime.
A Town of small repute in the heart of France
Was the Youth's Birth-place; there he vowed his love
To Julia, a bright Maid, from Parents sprung
Not mean in their condition, but with rights
Unhonoured of Nobility, and hence
The Father of the young Man, who had place
Among that order, spurned the very thought
Of such alliance. From their cradles up,   570
With but a step between their several homes
The Pair had thriven together year by year,
Friends, Playmates, Twins in pleasure, after strife
And petty quarrels had grown fond again,
Each other's advocate, each other's help,
Nor ever happy if they were apart.
A basis this for deep and solid love,
And endless constancy, and placid truth;
But whatsoever of such treasures might,
Beneath the outside of their youth, have lain°   580
Reserved for mellower years, his present mind
Was under fascination; he beheld
A vision, and he loved the thing he saw.
Arabian Fiction never filled the world
With half the wonders that were wrought for him.
Earth lived in one great presence of the spring,
Life turned the meanest of her implements
Before his eyes to price above all gold,
The house she dwelt in was a sainted shrine,
Her chamber-window did surpass in glory   590
The portals of the East, all paradise
Could by the simple opening of a door
Let itself in upon him, pathways, walks,
Swarmed with enchantment, till his spirit sank
Beneath the burthen, overblessed for life.
This state was theirs, till whether through effect
Of some delirious hour, or that the Youth,
Seeing so many bars betwixt himself

And the dear haven where he wished to be
In honourable wedlock with his love,   600
Without a certain knowledge of his own
Was inwardly prepared to turn aside
From law and custom, and entrust himself
To Nature for a happy end of all,
And thus abated of that pure reserve
Congenial to his loyal heart, with which
It would have pleased him to attend the steps
Of Maiden so divinely beautiful,
I know not, but reluctantly must add
That Julia, yet without the name of Wife,   610
Carried about her for a secret grief
The promise of a Mother.
                              To conceal
The threatened shame the Parents of the Maid
Found means to hurry her away by night
And unforewarned, that in a distant Town
She might remain shrouded in privacy,
Until the Babe was born. When morning came
The Lover thus bereft, stung with his loss
And all uncertain whither he should turn,
Chafed like a wild beast in the toils. At length,   620
Following as his suspicions led, he found
O joy! sure traces of the fugitives,
Pursued them to the Town where they had stopped,
And lastly to the very house itself
Which had been chosen for the Maid's retreat.
The sequel may be easily divined:
Walks backwards, forwards, morning, noon and night,
When decency and caution would allow,
And Julia, who, whenever to herself
She happened to be left a moment's space,   630
Was busy at her casement, as a swallow
About its nest, ere long did thus espy
Her Lover, thence a stolen interview
By night accomplished, with a ladder's help.

    I pass the raptures of the Pair; such theme
Hath by a hundred Poets been set forth
In more delightful verse than skill of mine

Could fashion, chiefly by that darling Bard°
Who told of Juliet and her Romeo,
And of the lark's note heard before its time, 640
And of the streaks that laced the severing clouds
In the unrelenting East. 'Tis mine to tread
The humbler province of plain history,
And, without choice of circumstance, submissively
Relate what I have heard. The Lovers came
To this resolve, with which they parted, pleased
And confident, that Vaudracour should hie
Back to his Father's house, and there employ
Means aptest to obtain a sum of gold,
A final portion even, if that might be, 650
Which done, together they could then take flight
To some remote and solitary place
Where they might live with no one to behold
Their happiness, or to disturb their love.
Immediately, and with this mission charged,
Home to his Father's House did he return
And there remained a time without hint given
Of his design; but if a word were dropped
Touching the matter of his passion, still
In hearing of his Father, Vaudracour 660
Persisted openly that nothing less
Than death should make him yield up hope to be
A blessed Husband of the Maid he loved.

Incensed at such obduracy and slight
Of exhortations and remonstrances,
The Father threw out threats that by a mandate
Bearing the private signet of the State°
He should be baffled in his mad intent,
And that should cure him. From this time the Youth
Conceived a terror, and by night or day 670
Stirred nowhere without Arms. Soon afterwards
His Parents to their Country Seat withdrew
Upon some feigned occasion, and the Son
Was left with one Attendant in the house.
Retiring to his Chamber for the night,
While he was entering at the door, attempts
Were made to seize him by three armed Men,

The instruments of ruffian power. The Youth
In the first impulse of his rage, laid one
Dead at his feet, and to the second gave   680
A perilous wound, which done, at sight
Of the dead Man, he peacefully resigned
His Person to the Law, was lodged in prison,
And wore the fetters of a Criminal.

    Through three weeks' space, by means which love devised,
The Maid in her seclusion had received
Tidings of Vaudracour, and how he sped
Upon his enterprize. Thereafter came
A silence, half a circle did the moon
Complete, and then a whole, and still the same   690
Silence; a thousand thousand fears and hopes
Stirred in her mind; thoughts waking, thoughts of sleep,
Entangled in each other, and at last
Self-slaughter seemed her only resting-place.
So did she fare in her uncertainty.

    At length, by interference of a Friend,
One who had sway at court, the Youth regained
His liberty, on promise to sit down
Quietly in his Father's House, nor take
One step to reunite himself with her   700
Of whom his Parents disapproved: hard law
To which he gave consent only because
His freedom else could nowise be procured.
Back to his Father's house he went, remained
Eight days, and then his resolution failed:
He fled to Julia, and the words with which
He greeted her were these. 'All right is gone,
Gone from me. Thou no longer now art mine,
I thine. A Murderer, Julia, cannot love
An innocent Woman. I behold thy face,   710
I see thee and my misery is complete.'
She could not give him answer; afterwards
She coupled with his Father's name some words
Of vehement indignation, but the Youth

Checked her, nor would he hear of this, for thought
Unfilial, or unkind, had never once
Found harbour in his breast. The Lovers thus
United once again together lived
For a few days, which were to Vaudracour
Days of dejection, sorrow and remorse   720
For that ill deed of violence which his hand
Had hastily committed; for the Youth
Was of a loyal spirit, a conscience nice
And over tender for the trial which
His fate had called him to. The Father's mind,
Meanwhile, remained unchanged, and Vaudracour
Learned that a mandate had been newly issued
To arrest him on the spot. Oh pain it was
To part! he could not—and he lingered still
To the last moment of his time, and then,   730
At dead of night with snow upon the ground,
He left the City, and in Villages
The most sequestered of the neighbourhood
Lay hidden for the space of several days,
Until the horseman bringing back report
That he was nowhere to be found, the search
Was ended. Back returned the ill-fated Youth,
And from the House where Julia lodged (to which
He now found open ingress, having gained
The affection of the family, who loved him   740
Both for his own, and for the Maiden's sake)
One night retiring, he was seized—But here
A portion of the Tale may well be left
In silence, though my memory could add
Much how the Youth, and in short space of time,
Was traversed from without, much, too, of thoughts
By which he was employed in solitude
Under privation and restraint, and what
Through dark and shapeless fear of things to come,
And what through strong compunction for the past,   750
He suffered, breaking down in heart and mind.
Such grace, if grace it were, had been vouchsafed,
Or such effect had through the Father's want
Of power, or through his negligence ensued,
That Vaudracour was suffered to remain,

Though under guard and without liberty,
In the same City with the unhappy Maid
From whom he was divided. So they fared
Objects of general concern, till, moved
With pity for their wrongs, the Magistrate,   760
The same who had placed the Youth in custody,
By application to the Minister
Obtained his liberty upon condition
That to his Father's House he should return.

He left his Prison almost on the eve
Of Julia's travail. She had likewise been
As from the time, indeed, when she had first
Been brought for secresy to this abode,
Though treated with consoling tenderness,
Herself a Prisoner, a dejected one,   770
Filled with a lover's and a Woman's fears,
And whensoe'er the Mistress of the House
Entered the Room for the last time at night,
And Julia with a low and plaintive voice
Said 'You are coming then to lock me up'
The Housewife when these words, always the same,
Were by her Captive languidly pronounced,
Could never hear them uttered without tears.

A day or two before her child-bed time
Was Vaudracour restored to her, and soon   780
As he might be permitted to return
Into her Chamber after the Child's birth,
The Master of the Family begged that all
The household might be summoned, doubting not
But that they might receive impressions then
Friendly to human kindness. Vaudracour
(This heard I from one present at the time)
Held up the new-born Infant in his arms
And kissed, and blessed, and covered it with tears,
Uttering a prayer that he might never be   790
As wretched as his Father. Then he gave
The Child to her who bare it, and she too
Repeated the same prayer, took it again
And muttering something faintly afterwards,

He gave the Infant to the Standers-by,
And wept in silence upon Julia's neck.

   Two months did he continue in the House,
And often yielded up himself to plans
Of future happiness. 'You shall return,
Julia,' said he, 'and to your Father's House   800
Go with your Child; you have been wretched, yet
It is a town where both of us were born,
None will reproach you, for our loves are known.
With ornaments the prettiest you shall dress
Your Boy, as soon as he can run about,
And when he thus is at his play my Father
Will see him from the window, and the Child
Will by his beauty move his Grandsire's heart,
So that it will be softened, and our loves
End happily, as they began.' These gleams   810
Appeared but seldom, oftener he was seen
Propping a pale and melancholy face
Upon the Mother's bosom, resting thus
His head upon one breast, while from the other
The Babe was drawing in its quiet food.
At other times, when he, in silence, long
And fixedly had looked upon her face,
He would exclaim, 'Julia, how much thine eyes
Have cost me!' During day-time, when the child
Lay in its cradle, by its side he sate,   820
Not quitting it an instant. The whole Town
In his unmerited misfortunes now
Took part, and if he either at the door
Or window for a moment with his Child
Appeared, immediately the Street was thronged,
While others frequently without reserve
Passed and repassed before the house to steal
A look at him. Oft at this time he wrote
Requesting, since he knew that the consent
Of Julia's Parents never could be gained   830
To a clandestine marriage, that his Father
Would from the birthright of an eldest Son
Exclude him, giving but, when this was done,
A sanction to his nuptials: vain request,

To which no answer was returned. And now
From her own home the Mother of his Love
Arrived to apprise the Daughter of her fixed
And last resolve, that, since all hope to move
The old Man's heart proved vain, she must retire
Into a Convent and be there immured.   840
Julia was thunderstricken by these words,
And she insisted on a Mother's rights
To take her Child along with her, a grant
Impossible, as she at last perceived.
The Persons of the house no sooner heard
Of this decision upon Julia's fate
Than everyone was overwhelmed with grief,
Nor could they frame a manner soft enough
To impart the tidings to the Youth; but great
Was their astonishment when they beheld him   850
Receive the news in calm despondency,
Composed and silent, without outward sign
Of even the last emotion. Seeing this,
When Julia scattered some upbraiding words
Upon his slackness, he thereto returned
No answer, only took the Mother's hand
Who loved him scarcely less than her own Child,
And kissed it, without seeming to be pressed
By any pain that 'twas the hand of one
Whose errand was to part him from his Love   860
For ever. In the City he remained
A season after Julia had retired
And in the Convent taken up her home,
To the end that he might place his infant Babe
With a fit Nurse, which done, beneath the roof
Where now his little One was lodged, he passed
The day entire, and scarcely could at length
Tear himself from the cradle to return
Home to his Father's House, in which he dwelt
Awhile, and then came back that he might see   870
Whether the Babe had gained sufficient strength
To bear removal. He quitted this same Town
For the last time, attendant by the side
Of a close chair, a Litter or Sedan,
In which the Child was carried. To a hill,

Which rose at a League's distance from the Town,
The Family of the house where he had lodged
Attended him, and parted from him there,
Watching below till he had disappeared
On the hill top. His eyes he scarcely took   880
Through all that journey from the Chair in which
The Babe was carried, and at every Inn
Or place at which they halted or reposed
Laid him upon his knees, nor would permit
The hands of any but himself to dress
The Infant or undress. By one of those
Who bore the Chair these facts, at his return,
Were told, and in relating them he wept.

        This was the manner in which Vaudracour
Departed with his Infant, and thus reached   890
His Father's House, where to the innocent Child
Admittance was denied. The young Man spake
No words of indignation or reproof,
But of his Father begged, a last request,
That a retreat might be assigned to him,
A house where in the Country he might dwell
With such allowance as his wants required,
And the more lonely that the Mansion was
'Twould be more welcome. To a lodge that stood
Deep in a Forest, with leave given, at the age   900
Of four and twenty summers he retired;
And thither took with him his Infant Babe,
And one Domestic for their common needs,
An aged woman. It consoled him here
To attend upon the Orphan and perform
The office of a Nurse to his young Child,
Which, after a short time, by some mistake
Or indiscretion of the Father, died.
The Tale I follow to its last recess
Of suffering or of peace, I know not which;   910
Theirs be the blame who caused the woe, not mine.

        From that time forth he never uttered word
To any living. An Inhabitant
Of that same Town in which the Pair had left

So lively a remembrance of their griefs,
By chance of business coming within reach
Of his retirement, to the spot repaired
With the intent to visit him: he reached
The house and only found the Matron there,
Who told him that his pains were thrown away,   920
For that her Master never uttered word
To living soul—not even to her. Behold,
While they were speaking, Vaudracour approached;
But, seeing some one there, just as his hand
Was stretched towards the garden-gate, he shrunk,
And like a shadow glided out of view.
Shocked at his savage outside, from the place
The Visitor retired.
                    Thus lived the Youth
Cut off from all intelligence with Man,
And shunning even the light of common day;   930
Nor could the voice of Freedom, which through France
Soon afterwards resounded, public hope,
Or personal memory of his own deep wrongs,
Rouze him; but in those solitary shades
His days he wasted, an imbecile mind.

BOOK TEN

Residence in France and French Revolution

It was a beautiful and silent day
That overspread the countenance of earth,
Then fading, with unusual quietness,
When from the Loire I parted, and through scenes°
Of vineyard, orchard, meadow-ground and tilth,
Calm waters, gleams of sun, and breathless trees,
Towards the fierce Metropolis turned my steps
Their homeward way to England. From his Throne
The King had fallen; the congregated Host,°
Dire cloud upon the front of which was written   10
The tender mercies of the dismal wind
That bore it, on the Plains of Liberty
Had burst innocuously, say more, the swarm

That came elate and jocund, like a Band
Of Eastern Hunters, to enfold in ring
Narrowing itself by moments and reduce
To the last punctual spot of their despair
A race of victims, so they seemed, *themselves*
Had shrunk from sight of their own task, and fled
In terror. Desolation and dismay   20
Remained for them whose fancies had grown rank
With evil expectations, confidence
And perfect triumph to the better cause.
The State, as if to stamp the final seal
On her security, and to the world
Shew what she was, a high and fearless soul,
Or rather in a spirit of thanks to those
Who had stirred up her slackening faculties
To a new transition, had assumed with joy
The body and the venerable name   30
Of a Republic. Lamentable crimes,°
'Tis true, had gone before this hour, the work
Of massacre, in which the senseless sword
Was prayed to as a judge; but these were past,
Earth free from them for ever, as was thought,
Ephemeral monsters, to be seen but once;
Things that could only shew themselves and die.

     This was the time in which enflamed with hope,
To Paris I returned. Again I ranged,
More eagerly than I had done before,   40
Through the wide City, and in progress passed
The Prison where the unhappy Monarch lay,
Associate with his Children and his Wife
In bondage, and the Palace lately stormed
With roar of cannon, and a numerous Host.
I crossed (a blank and empty area then)°
The Square of the Carousel, few weeks back
Heaped up with dead and dying, upon these
And other sights looking as doth a man
Upon a volume whose contents he knows   50
Are memorable, but from him locked up,
Being written in a tongue he cannot read,
So that he questions the mute leaves with pain

And half upbraids their silence. But that night
When on my bed I lay, I was most moved
And felt most deeply in what world I was;
My room was high and lonely, near the roof
Of a large Mansion or Hotel, a spot
That would have pleased me in more quiet times,
Nor was it wholly without pleasure then.   60
With unextinguished taper I kept watch,
Reading at intervals. The fear gone by
Pressed on me almost like a fear to come.
I thought of those September Massacres,
Divided from me by a little month,°
And felt and touched them, a substantial dread;
The rest was conjured up from tragic fictions,
And mournful Calendars of true history,
Remembrances and dim admonishments.
'The horse is taught his manage, and the wind°   70
Of heaven wheels round and treads in his own steps,
Year follows year, the tide returns again,
Day follows day, all things have second birth;
The earthquake is not satisfied at once.'
And in such way I wrought upon myself,
Until I seemed to hear a voice that cried,
To the whole City, 'Sleep no more.' To this
Add comments of a calmer mind, from which
I could not gather full security,
But at the best it seemed a place of fear,   80
Unfit for the repose of night,
Defenceless as a wood where tigers roam.

   Betimes next morning to the Palace Walk
Of Orleans I repaired and entering there
Was greeted, among divers other notes,
By voices of the Hawkers in the crowd
Bawling, *Denunciation of the crimes*
Of Maximilian Robespierre. The speech
Which in their hands they carried was the same
Which had been recently pronounced, the day   90
When Robespierre, well knowing for what mark
Some words of indirect reproof had been
Intended, rose in hardihood, and dared

The Man who had an ill surmise of him
To bring his charge in openness; whereat
When a dead pause ensued, and no one stirred,
In silence of all present, from his seat
Louvet walked singly through the avenue
And took his station in the 'Tribune, saying,
'I, Robespierre, accuse thee!' 'Tis well known   100
What was the issue of that charge, and how
Louvet was left alone without support
Of his irresolute Friends; but these are things°
Of which I speak, only as they were storm
Or sunshine to my individual mind,
No further. Let me then relate that now,
In some sort seeing with my proper eyes
That Liberty, and Life, and Death, would soon
To the remotest corners of the land
Lie in the arbitrement of those who ruled   110
The capital City, what was struggled for,
And by what combatants victory must be won;
The indecision on their part whose aim
Seemed best, and the straightforward path of those
Who in attack or in defence alike
Were strong through their impiety, greatly I
Was agitated; yea I could almost
Have prayed that throughout earth upon all souls
Worthy of liberty, upon every soul
Matured to live in plainness and in truth,   120
The gift of tongues might fall, and men arrive
From the four quarters of the winds to do
For France what without help she could not do,
A work of honour; think not that to this
I added, work of safety; from such thought,
And the least fear about the end of things,
I was as far as Angels are from guilt.

    Yet did I grieve, nor only grieved, but thought
Of opposition and of remedies:
An insignificant Stranger, and obscure,   130
Mean as I was, and little graced with power
Of eloquence even in my native speech,
And all unfit for tumult and intrigue,

Yet would I willingly have taken up
A service at this time for cause so great,
However dangerous. Inly I revolved
How much the destiny of man had still
Hung upon single persons, that there was,
Transcendent to all local patrimony,
One Nature as there is one Sun in heaven;   140
That objects, even as they are great, thereby
Do come within the reach of humblest eyes;
That Man was only weak through his mistrust
And want of hope, where evidence divine
Proclaimed to him that hope should be most sure;
That, with desires heroic and firm sense,
A Spirit thoroughly faithful to itself,
Unquenchable, unsleeping, undismayed,
Was as an instinct among men, a stream
That gathered up each petty straggling rill   150
And vein of water, glad to be rolled on
In safe obedience; that a mind whose rest
Was where it ought to be, in self-restraint,
In circumspection and simplicity,
Fell rarely in entire discomfiture
Below its aim, or met with from without
A treachery that defeated it or foiled.

On the other side, I called to mind those truths
Which are the common-places of the Schools,
A theme for Boys, too trite even to be felt,   160
Yet, with a revelation's liveliness,
In all their comprehensive bearings known
And visible to Philosophers of old,
Men who, to business of the world untrained,
Lived in the Shade; and to Harmodius known°
And his Compeer Aristogiton; known
To Brutus; that tyrannic Power is weak,
Hath neither gratitude, nor faith, nor love,
Nor the support of good or evil men
To trust in, that the Godhead which is ours   170
Can never utterly be charmed or stilled,
That nothing hath a natural right to last
But equity and reason, that all else

Meets foes irreconcilable, and at best
Doth live but by variety of disease.

    Well might my wishes be intense, my thoughts
Strong and perturbed, not doubting at that time,
Creed which ten shameful years have not annulled,
But that the virtue of one paramount mind
Would have abashed those impious crests, have quelled   180
Outrage and bloody power, and in despite
Of what the People were through ignorance
And immaturity, and in the teeth
Of desperate opposition from without,
Have cleared a passage for just government,
And left a solid birthright to the State,
Redeemed according to example given
By ancient Lawgivers.
                        In this frame of mind,
Reluctantly to England I returned,
Compelled by nothing less than absolute want   190
Of funds for my support; else, well assured
That I both was and must be of small worth,
No better than an alien in the Land,
I doubtless should have made a common cause
With some who perished, haply perished too,
A poor mistaken and bewildered offering,
Should to the breast of Nature have gone back
With all my resolutions, all my hopes,
A Poet only to myself, to Men
Useless, and even, beloved Friend! a soul   200
To thee unknown.
                    When to my native Land
(After a whole year's absence) I returned
I found the air yet busy with the stir
Of a contention which had been raised up
Against the Traffickers in Negro blood,°
An effort, which though baffled, nevertheless
Had called back old forgotten principles
Dismissed from service, had diffused some truths
And more of virtuous feeling through the heart
Of the English People. And no few of those   210
So numerous (little less in verity

Than a whole Nation crying with one voice)
Who had been crossed in their just intent
And righteous hope, thereby were well prepared
To let that journey sleep awhile, and join
Whatever other Caravan appeared
To travel forward towards Liberty
With more success. For me that strife had ne'er
Fastened on my affections, nor did now
Its unsuccessful issue much excite   220
My sorrow, having laid this faith to heart,
That if France prospered good Men would not long
Pay fruitless worship to humanity,
And this most rotten branch of human shame,
Object, as seemed, of a superfluous pains
Would fall together with its parent tree.

    Such was my then belief, that there was one,
And only one solicitude for all.
And now the strength of Britain was put forth
In league with the confederated Host;°   230
Not in my single self alone I found,
But in the minds of all ingenuous Youth,
Change and subversion from this hour. No shock
Given to my moral nature had I known
Down to that very moment; neither lapse
Nor turn of sentiment that might be named
A revolution, save at this one time;
All else was progress on the self-same path
On which with a diversity of pace
I had been travelling; this a stride at once   240
Into another region. True it is,
'Twas not concealed with what ungracious eyes
Our native Rulers from the very first
Had looked upon regenerated France;
Nor had I doubted that this day would come.
But in such contemplation I had thought
Of general interests only, beyond this
Had never once foretasted the event.
Now had I other business, for I felt
The ravage of this most unnatural strife   250
In my own heart; there lay it like a weight

At enmity with all the tenderest springs
Of my enjoyments. I, who with the breeze
Had played, a green leaf on the blessed tree
Of my beloved Country—nor had wished
For happier fortune than to wither there—
Now from my pleasant station was cut off,
And tossed about in whirlwinds. I rejoiced,
Yea, afterwards, truth painful to record!
Exulted in the triumph of my soul   260
When Englishmen by thousands were o'erthrown,
Left without glory on the Field, or driven,
Brave hearts, to shameful flight. It was a grief,
Grief call it not, 'twas anything but that,
A conflict of sensations without name,
Of which he only who may love the sight
Of a Village Steeple as I do can judge,
When in the Congregation, bending all
To their great Father, prayers were offered up
Or praises for our Country's Victories,   270
And 'mid the simple worshippers, perchance,
I only, like an uninvited Guest
Whom no one owned sate silent, shall I add,
Fed on the day of vengeance yet to come!

Oh! much have they to account for, who would tear
By violence at one decisive rent
From the best Youth in England their dear pride,
Their joy, in England; this, too, at a time
In which worst losses easily might wear
The best of names, when patriotic love   280
Did of itself in modesty give away
Like the Precursor when the Deity
Is come, whose Harbinger he is, a time
In which apostacy from ancient faith
Seemed but conversion to a higher creed,
Withal a season dangerous and wild,
A time in which Experience would have plucked
Flowers out of any hedge to make thereof
A Chaplet, in contempt of his grey locks.

Ere yet the Fleet of Britain had gone forth   290
On this unworthy service, whereunto

The unhappy counsel of a few weak men
Had doomed it, I beheld the Vessels lie,
A brood of gallant creatures, on the Deep
I saw them in their rest, a sojourner
Through a whole month of calm and glassy days
In that delightful Island which protects°
Their place of convocation; there I heard
Each evening, walking by the still sea-shore,
A monitory sound that never failed,   300
The sunset cannon. While the Orb went down
In the tranquillity of Nature, came
That voice, ill requiem! seldom heard by me
Without a spirit overcast, a deep
Imagination, thought of woes to come,
And sorrow for mankind, and pain of heart.

    In France, the Men who for their desperate ends
Had plucked up mercy by the roots were glad
Of this new enemy. Tyrants, strong before
In devilish pleas were ten times stronger now,°   310
And thus beset with Foes on every side
The goaded Land waxed mad; the crimes of few
Spread into madness of the many; blasts
From hell came sanctified like airs from heaven;
The sternness of the Just, the faith of those
Who doubted not that Providence had times
Of anger and of vengeance,—theirs who throned
The human understanding paramount°
And made of that their God, the hopes of those
Who were content to barter short-lived pangs   320
For a paradise of ages, the blind rage
Of insolent tempers, the light vanity
Of intermeddlers, steady purposes
Of the suspicious, slips of the indiscreet,
And all the accidents of life, were pressed
Into one service, busy with one work.
The Senate was heart-stricken, not a voice
Uplifted, none to oppose or mitigate.
Domestic carnage now filled all the year
With Feast-days; the Old Man from the chimney-nook, 330

The Maiden from the bosom of her Love,
The Mother from the Cradle of her Babe,
The Warrior from the Field, all perished, all,
Friends, enemies, of all parties, ages, ranks,
Head after head, and never heads enough
For those who bade them fall. They found their joy,
They made it, ever thirsty, as a Child,
If light desires of innocent little Ones
May with such heinous appetites be matched,
Having a toy, a wind-mill, though the air   340
Do of itself blow fresh, and makes the vane
Spin in his eyesight, he is not content,
But with the play-thing at arm's length he sets
His front against the blast, and runs amain,
To make it whirl the faster.
                              In the depth
Of those enormities, even thinking minds
Forgot at seasons whence they had their being,
Forgot that such a sound was ever heard
As Liberty upon earth: yet all beneath
Her innocent authority was wrought,   350
Nor could have been, without her blessed name.
The illustrious Wife of Roland, in the hour°
Of her composure, felt that agony
And gave it vent in her last words. O Friend,
It was a lamentable time for man
Whether a hope had e'er been his or not,
A woeful time for them whose hopes did still
Outlast the shock; most woeful for those few,
They had the deepest feeling of the grief,
Who still were flattered, and had trust in man.   360
Meanwhile, the Invaders fared as they deserved;
The Herculean Commonwealth had put forth her arms°
And throttled with an infant Godhead's might
The snakes about her cradle; that was well
And as it should be, yet no cure for those
Whose souls were sick with pain of what would be
Hereafter brought in charge against mankind.
Most melancholy at that time, O Friend!
Were my day-thoughts, my dreams were miserable;
Through months, through years, long after the last beat 370

Of those atrocities (I speak bare truth,
As if to thee alone in private talk)
I scarcely had one night of quiet sleep,
Such ghastly visions had I of despair
And tyranny, and implements of death,
And long orations which in dreams I pleaded
Before unjust Tribunals, with a voice
Labouring, a brain confounded, and a sense,
Of treachery and desertion in the place
The holiest that I knew of, my own soul.   380

When I began at first, in early youth,
To yield myself to Nature, when that strong
And holy passion overcame me first,
Neither day nor night, evening or morn
Were free from the oppression; but, Great God!
Who send'st thyself into this breathing world
Through Nature and through every kind of life,
And mak'st Man what he is, Creature divine,
In single or in social eminence,
Above all these raised infinite ascents   390
When reason, which enables him to be,
Is not sequestered, what a change is here!
How different ritual for this after worship,
What countenance to promote this second love.
That first was service but to things which lie
At rest, within the bosom of thy will:
Therefore to serve was high beatitude;
The tumult was a gladness, and the fear
Ennobling, venerable; sleep secure,
And waking thoughts more rich than happiest dreams. 400

But as the ancient Prophets were enflamed
Nor wanted consolations of their own
And majesty of mind, when they denounced
On Towns and Cities, wallowing in the abyss
Of their offences, punishment to come;
Or saw like other men with bodily eyes
Before them in some desolated place
The consummation of the wrath of Heaven;
So did some portion of that spirit fall

On me, to uphold me through those evil times,   410
And in their rage and dog-day heat I found
Something to glory in, as just and fit,
And in the order of sublimest laws.
And even if that were not, amid the awe
Of unintelligible chastisement
I felt a kind of sympathy with power,
Motions raised up within me, nevertheless,
Which had relationship to highest things.
Wild blasts of music thus did find their way
Into the midst of terrible events,   420
So that worst tempests might be listened to:
Then was the truth received into my heart,
That under heaviest sorrow earth can bring,
Griefs bitterest of ourselves or of our Kind,
If from the affliction somewhere do not grow
Honour which could not else have been, a faith,
An elevation, and a sanctity,
If new strength be not given, or old restored,
The blame is ours not Nature's. When a taunt
Was taken up by scoffers in their pride,   430
Saying, 'Behold the harvest which we reap
From popular Government and Equality,'
I saw that it was neither these, nor aught
Of wild belief engrafted on their names
By false philosophy, that caused the woe,
But that it was a reservoir of guilt
And ignorance, filled up from age to age,
That could no longer hold its loathsome charge,
But burst and spread in deluge through the Land.

    And as the desert hath green spots, the sea   440
Small islands in the midst of stormy waves,
So that disastrous period did not want
Such sprinklings of all human excellence,
As were a joy to hear of. Yet (nor less
For those bright spots, those fair examples given
Of fortitude, and energy, and love,
And human nature faithful to itself
Under worst trials) was I impelled to think
Of the glad time when first I traversed France,

A youthful pilgrim, above all remembered   450
That day when through an Arch that spanned the street,
A rainbow made of garish ornaments,
Triumphal pomp for Liberty confirmed,
We walked, a pair of weary Travellers,
Along the Town of Arras, place from which°
Issued that Robespierre, who afterwards
Wielded the sceptre of the atheist crew.
When the calamity spread far and wide,
And this same City, which had even appeared
To outrun the rest in exultation, groaned   460
Under the vengeance of her cruel Son,
As Lear reproached the winds, I could almost
Have quarreled with that blameless spectacle
For being yet an image in my mind
To mock me under such a strange reverse.

    O Friend! few happier moments have been mine
Through my whole life than that when first I heard
That this foul Tribe of Moloch was o'erthrown,°
And their chief Regent levelled with the dust.
The day was one which haply may deserve   470
A separate chronicle. Having gone abroad°
From a small Village where I tarried then,
To the same far-secluded privacy
I was returning. Over the smooth Sands
Of Leven's ample Æstuary lay
My journey, and beneath a genial sun;
With distant prospect among gleams of sky
And clouds, and intermingled mountain tops,
In one inseparable glory clad,
Creatures of one ethereal substance, met   480
In Consistory, like a diadem
Or crown of burning Seraphs, as they sit
In the Empyrean. Underneath this show
Lay, as I knew, the nest of pastoral vales
Among whose happy fields I had grown up
From childhood. On the fulgent spectacle
Which neither changed, nor stirred, nor passed away,
I gazed, and with a fancy more alive
On this account, that I had chanced to find

That morning, ranging through the churchyard graves 490
Of Cartmell's rural Town, the place in which
An honored Teacher of my youth was laid.°
While we were Schoolboys he had died among us,
And was born hither, as I knew, to rest
With his own Family. A plain Stone, inscribed
With name, date, office, pointed out the spot,
To which a slip of verses was subjoined,
(By his desire, as afterwards I learned)
A fragment from the Elegy of Gray.
A week, or little less, before his death 500
He had said to me, 'my head will soon lie low;'
And when I saw the turf that covered him,
After the lapse of full eight years, those words,
With sound of voice, and countenance of the Man,
Came back upon me, so that some few tears
Fell from me in my own despite. And now,
Thus travelling smoothly o'er the level Sands,
I thought with pleasure of the Verses graven
Upon his Tombstone, saying to myself
He loved the Poets, and if now alive, 510
Would have loved me, as one not destitute
Of promise, nor belying the kind hope
Which he had formed, when I at his commmand,
Began to spin, at first, my toilsome Songs.

Without me and within, as I advanced,
All that I saw, or felt, or communed with
Was gentleness and peace. Upon a small
And rocky Island near, a fragment stood
(Itself like a sea rock) of what had been
A Romish Chapel, where in ancient times 520
Masses were said at the hour which suited those
Who crossed the Sands with ebb of morning tide.
Not far from this still Ruin all the Plain
Was spotted with a variegated crowd
Of Coaches, Wains, and Travellers, horse and foot,
Wading, beneath the conduct of their Guide
In loose procession through the shallow Stream
Of inland water; the great Sea meanwhile
Was at safe distance, far retired. I paused,

Unwilling to proceed, the scene appeared   530
So gay and chearful; when a Traveller
Chancing to pass, I carelessly inquired
If any news were stirring; he replied
In the familiar language of the day
That, *Robespierre was dead*. Nor was a doubt,°
On further question, left within my mind
But that the tidings were substantial truth;
That he and his supporters all were fallen.

    Great was my glee of spirit, great my joy
In vengeance, and eternal justice, thus   540
Made manifest. 'Come now ye golden times,'
Said I, forth-breathing on those open Sands
A Hymn of triumph, 'as the morning comes
Out of the bosom of the night, come Ye:
Thus far our trust is verified; behold!
They who with clumsy desperation brought
Rivers of Blood, and preached that nothing else
Could cleanse the Augean Stable, by the might°
Of their own helper have been swept away;°
Their madness is declared and visible,   550
Elsewhere will safety now be sought, and Earth
March firmly towards righteousness and peace.'
Then schemes I framed more calmly, when and how
The madding Factions might be tranquillised,
And, though through hardships manifold and long,
The mighty renovation would proceed;
Thus, interrupted by uneasy bursts
Of exultation, I pursued my way
Along that very Shore which I had skimmed°
In former times, when, spurring from the Vale   560
Of Nightshade, and St. Mary's mouldering Fane,
And the Stone Abbot, after circuit made
In wantonness of heart, a joyous Crew
Of School-boys, hastening to their distant home,
Along the margin of the moonlight Sea,
We beat with thundering hoofs the level Sand.

    From this time forth, in France, as is well known,
Authority put on a milder face,
Yet everything was wanting that might give

Courage to those who looked for good by light   570
Of rational experience, good I mean
At hand, and in the spirit of past aims.
The same belief I, nevertheless, retained;
The language of the Senate and the acts
And public measures of the Government,
Though both of heartless omen, had not power
To daunt me. In the People was my trust
And in the vertues which mine eyes had seen,
And to the ultimate repose of things
I looked with unabated confidence.   580
I knew that wound external could not take
Life from the young Republic, that new foes
Would only follow in the path of shame
Their brethren, and her triumphs be in the end
Great, universal, irresistible.
This faith, which was an object in my mind
Of passionate intuition, had effect
Not small in dazzling me; for thus, through zeal,
Such victory I confounded in my thoughts
With one far higher and more difficult,   590
Triumphs of unambitious peace at home,
And noiseless fortitude. Beholding still
Resistance strong as heretofore, I thought
That what was in degree the same was likewise
The same in quality, that as the worse
Of the two spirits then at strife remained
Untired, the better surely would preserve
The heart that first had rouzed him, never dreamt
That transmigration could be undergone,
A fall of being suffered, and of hope°   600
By creature that appeared to have received
Entire conviction what a great ascent
Had been accomplished, what high faculties
It had been called to. Youth maintains, I knew,
In all conditions of society,
Communion more direct and intimate
With Nature, and the inner strength she has,
And hence, oft-times, no less, with Reason too,
Than Age or Manhood, even. To Nature then,
Power had reverted: habit, custom, law,   610

Had left an interregnum's open space
For her to stir about in, uncontroled.
The warmest judgments, and the most untaught,
Found in events which every day brought forth
Enough to sanction them, and far, far more
To shake the authority of canons drawn
From ordinary practice. I could see
How Babel-like the employment was of those°
Who, by the recent Deluge stupefied,
With their whole souls went culling from the day   620
Its petty promises to build a tower
For their own safety; laughed at gravest heads,
Who, watching in their hate of France for signs
Of her disasters, if the stream of rumour
Brought with it one green branch, conceited thence
That not a single tree was left alive
In all her forests. How could I believe
That wisdom could in any shape come near
Men clinging to delusions so insane?
And thus, experience proving that no few   630
Of my opinions had been just, I took
Like credit to myself where less was due,
And thought that other notions were as sound,
Yea, could not but be right, because I saw
That foolish men opposed them.
                                        To a strain
More animated I might here give way,
And tell, since juvenile errors are my theme,
What in those days through Britain was performed
To turn *all* judgments out of their right course;
But this is passion over-near ourselves,   640
Reality too close and too intense,
And mingled up with something, in my mind,
Of scorn and condemnation personal
That would profane the sanctity of verse.
Our Shepherds (this say merely) at that time°
Thirsted to make the guardian Crook of Law
A tool of Murder. They who ruled the State,
Though with such awful proof before their eyes
That he who would sow death, reaps death, or worse,
And can reap nothing better, child-like longed   650

To imitate, not wise enough to avoid,
Giants in their impiety alone,
But, in their weapons and their warfare base
As vermin working out of reach, they leagued
Their strength perfidiously, to undermine
Justice, and make an end of Liberty.

But from these bitter truths I must return
To my own History. It hath been told
That I was led to take an eager part
In arguments of civil polity   660
Abruptly, and indeed before my time:
I had approached, like other Youth, the Shield
Of human nature from the golden side,
And would have fought, even to the death, to attest
The quality of the metal which I saw.
What there is best in individual Man,
Of wise in passion, and sublime in power,
What there is strong and pure in household love,
Benevolent in small societies,
And great in large ones also, when called forth   670
By great occasions, these were things of which
I something knew, yet even these themselves,
Felt deeply, were not thoroughly understood
By Reason; nay, far from it, they were yet,
As cause was given me afterwards to learn,
Not proof against the injuries of the day,
Lodged only at the Sanctuary's door,
Not safe within its bosom. Thus prepared,
And with such general insight into evil,
And of the bounds which sever it from good,   680
As books and common intercourse with life
Must needs have given (to the noviciate mind,
When the world travels in a beaten road,
Guide faithful as is needed), I began
To think with fervour upon management
Of Nations, what it is and ought to be,
And how their worth depended on their Laws
And on the Constitution of the State.

    O pleasant exercise of hope and joy!
For great were the auxiliars which then stood   690

Upon our side, we who were strong in love.
Bliss was it in that dawn to be alive,
But to be young was very heaven! O times,
In which the meagre, stale, forbidding ways
Of custom, law, and statute took at once
The attraction of a Country in Romance;
When Reason seemed the most to assert her rights
When most intent on making of herself
A prime Enchanter to assist the work
Which then was going forwards in her name.   700
Not favored spots alone, but the whole earth
The beauty wore of promise, that which sets,
To take an image which was felt, no doubt,
Among the bowers of paradise itself,
The budding rose above the rose full blown.
What temper at the prospect did not wake
To happiness unthought of? The inert
Were rouzed, and lively natures rapt away:
They who had fed their childhood upon dreams,
The Play-fellows of Fancy, who had made   710
All powers of swiftness, subtlety, and strength
Their ministers, used to stir in lordly wise
Among the grandest objects of the sense,
And deal with whatsoever they found there
As if they had within some lurking right
To wield it; they too, who, of gentle mood
Had watched all gentle motions, and to these
Had fitted their own thoughts, schemers more mild,
And in the region of their peaceful selves,
Did now find helpers to their hearts' desire,   720
And stuff at hand, plastic as they could wish,
Were called upon to exercise their skill
Not in Utopia, subterraneous Fields,
Or some secreted Island, Heaven knows where,
But in the very world which is the world
Of all of us, the place in which, in the end,
We find our happiness, or not at all.

  Why should I not confess that earth was then
To me what an inheritance new-fallen
Seems, when the first time visited, to one   730

Who thither comes to find in it his home?
He walks about and looks upon the place
With cordial transport, moulds it, and remoulds,
And is half pleased with things that are amiss,
'Twill be such joy to see them disappear.

    An active partisan, I thus convoked
From every object pleasant circumstance
To suit my ends. I moved among mankind
With genial feelings still predominant;
When erring, erring on the better part,   740
And in the kinder spirit; placable,
Indulgent oft-times to the worst desires,
As, on one side, not uninformed that men
See as it hath been taught them, and that time
Gives rights to error; on the other hand,
That throwing off oppression must be work
As well of license as of liberty;
And above all, for this was more than all,
Not caring if the wind did now and then
Blow keen upon an eminence that gave   750
Prospect so large into futurity;
In brief, a child of Nature, as at first,
Diffusing only those affections wider
That from the cradle had grown up with me,
And losing, in no other way than light
Is lost in light, the weak in the more strong.

    In the main outline, such, it might be said,
Was my condition, till with open war
Britain opposed the Liberties of France.
This threw me first out of the pale of love,   760
Soured and corrupted upwards to the source
My sentiments, was not, as hitherto,
A swallowing up of lesser things in great,
But change of them into their opposites,
And thus a way was opened for mistakes
And false conclusions of the intellect,
As gross in their degree and in their kind
Far, far more dangerous. What had been a pride

Was now a shame; my likings and my loves
Ran in new channels, leaving old ones dry;   770
And thus a blow which, in maturer age,
Would but have touched the judgment, struck more deep
Into sensations near the heart: meantime,
As from the first, wild theories were afloat,
Unto the subtleties of which, at least,
I had but lent a careless ear, assured
Of this, that time would soon set all things right,
Prove that the multitude had been oppressed,
And would be so no more.
                              But when events
Brought less encouragement, and unto these   780
The immediate proof of principles no more
Could be entrusted, while the events themselves,
Worn out in greatness, and in novelty,
Less occupied the mind, and sentiments
Could through my understanding's natural growth
No longer justify themselves through faith
Of inward consciousness, and hope that laid
Its hand upon its object, evidence
Safer, of universal application, such
As could not be impeached, was sought elsewhere.   790

    And now, become oppressors in their turn,
Frenchmen had changed a war of self-defence
For one of conquest, losing sight of all
Which they had struggled for; and mounted up,
Openly, in the view of earth and heaven,
The scale of Liberty. I read her doom,
Vexed inly somewhat, it is true, and sore,
But not dismayed, nor taking to the shame
Of a false Prophet; but, rouzed up I stuck
More firmly to old tenets, and to prove   800
Their temper, strained them more, and thus in heat
Of contest did opinions every day
Grow into consequence, till round my mind
They clung, as if they were the life of it.

    This was the time when, all things tending fast
To depravation, the Philosophy

That promised to abstract the hopes of man
Out of his feelings, to be fixed thenceforth
For ever in a purer element
Found ready welcome. Tempting region that° 810
For Zeal to enter and refresh herself,
Where passions had the privilege to work,
And never hear the sound of their own names;
But, speaking more in charity, the dream
Was flattering to the young ingenuous mind
Pleased with extremes, and not the least with that
Which makes the human Reason's naked self
The object of its fervour. What delight!
How glorious! in self-knowledge and self-rule,
To look through all the frailties of the world, 820
And, with a resolute mastery shaking off
The accidents of nature, time, and place,
That make up the weak being of the past,
Build social freedom on its only basis:
The freedom of the individual mind,
Which, to the blind restraint of general laws
Superior, magisterially adopts
One guide, the light of circumstances, flashed
Upon an independent intellect.

    For howsoe'er unsettled, never once 830
Had I thought ill of human kind, or been
Indifferent to its welfare, but, enflamed
With thirst of a secure intelligence,
And sick of other passion, I pursued
A higher nature, wished that Man should start
Out of the worm-like state in which he is,
And spread abroad the wings of Liberty,
Lord of himself, in undisturbed delight—
A noble aspiration, yet I feel
The aspiration, but with other thoughts 840
And happier; for I was perplexed and sought
To accomplish the transition by such means
As did not lie in nature, sacrificed
The exactness of a comprehensive mind
To scrupulous and microscopic views

That furnished out materials for a work
Of false imagination, placed beyond
The limits of experience and of truth.

Enough, no doubt, the advocates themselves
Of ancient institutions had performed   850
To bring disgrace upon their very names;
Disgrace of which custom and written law,
And sundry moral sentiments, as props
And emanations of these institutes
Too justly bore a part. A veil had been
Uplifted; why deceive ourselves? 'Twas so,
'Twas even so; and sorrow for the Man
Who either had not eyes wherewith to see,
Or seeing hath forgotten. Let this pass,
Suffice it that a shock had then been given   860
To old opinions, and the minds of all men
Had felt it; that my mind was both let loose,
Let loose and goaded. After what hath been
Already said of patriotic love,
And hinted at in other sentiments,
We need not linger long upon this theme.
This only may be said, that from the first
Having two natures in me, joy the one
The other melancholy, and withal
A happy man, and therefore bold to look   870
On painful things, slow, somewhat, too, and stern
In temperament, I took the knife in hand
And, stopping not at parts less sensitive,
Endeavoured with my best of skill to probe
The living body of society
Even to the heart. I pushed without remorse
My speculations forward; yea, set foot
On Nature's holiest places. Time may come
When some dramatic Story may afford
Shapes livelier to convey to thee, my Friend,   880
What then I learned, or think I learned, of truth,
And the errors into which I was betrayed
By present objects, and by reasonings false
From the beginning, inasmuch as drawn
Out of a heart which had been turned aside

From Nature by external accidents,
And which was thus confounded more and more,
Misguiding and misguided. Thus I fared,
Dragging all passions, notions, shapes of faith,
Like culprits to the bar, suspiciously   890
Calling the mind to establish in plain day
Her titles and her honours, now believing,
Now disbelieving, endlessly perplexed
With impulse, motive, right and wrong, the ground
Of moral obligation, what the rule
And what the sanction, till, demanding *proof*,
And seeking it in everything, I lost
All feeling of conviction, and, in fine,
Sick, wearied out with contrarieties,
Yielded up moral questions in despair,   900
And for my future studies, as the sole
Employment of the enquiring faculty,
Turned towards mathematics, and their clear
And solid evidence—Ah! then it was
That Thou, most precious Friend! about this time°
First known to me, didst lend a living help
To regulate my Soul, and then it was
That the belovèd Woman in whose sight°
Those days were passed, now speaking in a voice
Of sudden admonition, like a brook   910
That does but cross a lonely road, and now
Seen, heard and felt, and caught at every turn,
Companion never lost through many a league,
Maintained for me a saving intercourse
With my true self; for, though impaired and changed
Much, as it seemed, I was no further changed
Than as a clouded, not a waning moon:
She, in the midst of all, preserved me still
A Poet, made me seek beneath that name
My office upon earth, and nowhere else;   920
And lastly, Nature's self, by human love
Assisted, through the weary labyrinth
Conducted me again to open day,
Revived the feelings of my earlier life,
Gave me that strength and knowledge full of peace,
Enlarged, and never more to be disturbed,

Which through the steps of our degeneracy,
All degradation of this age, hath still
Upheld me, and upholds me at this day
In the catastrophe (for so they dream,   930
And nothing less), when, finally, to close
And rivet up the gains of France, a Pope
Is summoned in to crown an Emperor;
This last opprobrium, when we see the dog
Returning to his vomit, when the sun
That rose in splendour, was alive, and moved
In exultation among living clouds,
Hath put his function and his glory off,
And, turned into gewgaw, a machine,
Sets like an opera phantom.   940
                    Thus, O Friend!°
Through times of honour, and through times of shame,
Have I descended, tracing faithfully
The workings of a youthful mind, beneath
The breath of great events, its hopes no less
Than universal, and its boundless love;
A Story destined for thy ear, who now,
Among the basest and the lowest fallen
Of all the race of men, dost make abode
Where Etna looketh down on Syracuse,
The city of Timoleon! Living God!°   950
How are the Mighty prostrated! they first,
They first of all that breathe should have awaked
When the great voice was heard out of the tombs
Of ancient Heroes. If for France I have grieved
Who, in the judgment of no few, hath been
A trifler only, in her proudest day,
Have been distressed to think of what she once
Promised, now is, a far more sober cause
Thine eyes must see of sorrow in a Land
Strewed with the wreck of loftiest years, a Land   960
Glorious indeed, substantially renowned
Of simple vertue once, and manly praise,
Now without one memorial hope, not even
A hope to be deferred; for that would serve
To chear the heart in such entire decay.

But indignation works where hope is not,
And thou, O Friend! wilt be refreshed. There is
One great Society alone on earth
The noble Living and the noble Dead:
Thy consolation shall be there, and Time   970
And Nature shall before thee spread in store
Imperishable thoughts, the Place itself
Be conscious of thy presence, and the dull
Sirocco air of its degeneracy
Turn as thou mov'st into a healthful breeze
To cherish and invigorate thy frame.

Thine be those motions strong and sanative,
A ladder for thy Spirit to reascend
To health and joy and pure contentedness;
To me the grief confined that Thou art gone   980
From this last spot of earth where Freedom now
Stands single in her only sanctuary;°
A lonely wanderer, art gone, by pain
Compelled and sickness, at this latter day,
This heavy time of change for all mankind;
I feel for Thee, must utter what I feel:
The sympathies, erewhile, in part discharged,
Gather afresh, and will have vent again.
My own delights do scarcely seem to me
My own delights; the lordly Alps themselves,   990
Those rosy Peaks, from which the Morning looks
Abroad on many Nations, are not now
Since thy migration and departure, Friend,
The gladsome image in my memory
Which they were used to be. To kindred scenes,
On errand, at a time how different!
Thou tak'st thy way, carrying a heart more ripe
For all divine enjoyment, with the soul
Which Nature gives to Poets, now by thought
Matured, and in the summer of its strength.   1000
Oh! wrap him in your Shades, ye Giant Woods,
On Etna's side, and thou, O flowery Vale
Of Enna! is there not some nook of thine°
From the first playtime of the infant earth
Kept sacred to restorative delight?

Child of the mountains, among Shepherds reared,
Even from my earliest school-day time, I loved
To dream of Sicily; and now a sweet
And vital promise wafted from that Land
Comes o'er my heart; there's not a single name   1010
Of note belonging to that honored isle,
Philosopher or Bard, Empedocles,°
Or Archimedes, deep and tranquil Soul!
That is not like a comfort to my grief.
And, O Theocritus, so far have some°
Prevailed among the Powers of heaven and earth,
By force of graces which were their's, that they
Have had, as thou reportest, miracles
Wrought for them in old time: yea, not unmoved,
When thinking of my own beloved Friend,   1020
I hear thee tell how bees with honey fed
Divine Comates, by his tyrant lord
Within a chest imprisoned impiously,
How with their honey from the fields they came
And fed him there, alive, from month to month,
Because the Goatherd, blessed Man! had lips
Wet with the Muses' Nectar.
                           Thus I soothe
The pensive moments by this calm fire side,
And find a thousand fancied images
That chear the thoughts of those I love, and mine.   1030
Our prayers have been accepted; Thou wilt stand
Not as an Exile but a Visitant
On Etna's top; by pastoral Arethuse°
Or, if that fountain be indeed no more,
Then near some other Spring, which by the name
Thou gratulatest, willingly deceived;°
Shalt linger as a gladsome Votary,°
And not a Captive, pining for his home.

BOOK ELEVEN

Imagination, How Impaired and Restored

Long time hath Man's unhappiness and guilt
Detained us; with what dismal sights beset
For the outward view, and inwardly oppressed
With sorrow, disappointment, vexing thoughts,
Confusion of opinion, zeal decayed,
And lastly, utter loss of hope itself,
And things to hope for. Not with these began
Our Song, and not with these our Song must end.
Ye motions of delight, that through the fields
Stir gently, breezes and soft airs that breathe   10
The breath of paradise, and find your way
To the recesses of the soul! Ye Brooks
Muttering along the stones, a busy noise
By day, a quiet one in silent night,
And you, ye Groves, whose ministry it is
To interpose the covert of your shades,
Even as a sleep, betwixt the heart of man
And the uneasy world, 'twixt man himself
Not seldom, and his own unquiet heart,
Oh! that I had a music and a voice,   20
Harmonious as your own, that I might tell
What ye have done for me. The morning shines,
Nor heedeth Man's perverseness; Spring returns,
I saw the Spring return, when I was dead
To deeper hope, yet had I joy for her,
And welcomed her benevolence, rejoiced
In common with the Children of her Love,
Plants, insects, beasts in field, and birds in bower.
So neither were complacency, nor peace,
Nor tender yearnings wanting for my good.   30
Through those distracted times; in Nature still°
Glorying, I found a counterpoise in her,
Which, when the spirit of evil was at height,
Maintained for me a secret happiness.
Her I resorted to, and loved so much
I seemed to love as much as heretofore;
And yet this passion, fervent as it was,

Had suffered change; how could there fail to be
Some change, if merely hence, that years of life
Were going on, and with them loss or gain   40
Inevitable, sure alternative.

   This History, my Friend, hath chiefly told
Of intellectual power, from stage to stage
Advancing, hand in hand with love and joy,
And of imagination teaching truth
Until that natural graciousness of mind
Gave way to over-pressure of the times
And their disastrous issues. What availed,
When Spells forbade the Voyager to land,
The fragrance which did ever and anon   50
Give notice of the Shore, from arbours breathed
Of blessed sentiment and fearless love?
What did such sweet remembrances avail,
Perfidious then, as seemed, what served they then?
My business was upon the barren seas,
My errand was to sail to other coasts.
Shall I avow that I had hope to see,
I mean that future times would surely see,
The man to come parted as by a gulph
From him who had been, that I could no more   60
Trust the elevation which had made me one
With the great Family that here and there
Is scattered through the abyss of ages past,
Sage, Patriot, Lover, Hero; for it seemed
That their best virtues were not free from taint
Of something false and weak, which could not stand
The open eye of Reason. Then I said,
Go to the Poets; they will speak to thee
More perfectly of purer creatures, yet
If Reason be nobility in man,   70
Can aught be more ignoble than the man
Whom they describe, would fasten if they may
Upon our love by sympathies of truth.

   Thus strangely did I war against myself;
A Bigot to a new Idolatry,
Did like a Monk who hath forsworn the world

Zealously labour to cut off my heart
From all the sources of her former strength;
And, as by simple waving of a wand
The wizard instantaneously dissolves   80
Palace or grove, even so did I unsoul
As readily by syllogistic words,
Some Charm of Logic, ever within reach,
Those mysteries of passion which have made,
And shall continue evermore to make,
(In spite of all that Reason hath performed
And shall perform to exalt and to refine)
One brotherhood of all the human race,
Through all the habitations of past years,
And those to come; and hence an emptiness   90
Fell on the Historian's Page, and even on that
Of Poets, pregnant with more absolute truth.
The works of both withered in my esteem,
Their sentence was, I thought, pronounced; their rights
Seemed mortal, and their empire passed away.

What then remained in such eclipse? what light
To guide or chear? The laws of things which lie
Beyond the reach of human will or power;
The life of nature, by the God of love
Inspired, celestial presence ever pure;   100
These left, the soul of Youth must needs be rich,
Whatever else be lost, and these were mine.
Not a deaf echo, merely, of the thought
Bewildered recollections, solitary,
But living sounds. Yet in despite of this,
This feeling, which howe'er impaired or damped,
Yet having been once born can never die,
'Tis true that Earth with all her appanage°
Of elements and organs, storm and sunshine,
With its pure forms and colours, pomp of clouds,   110
Rivers and mountains, objects among which
It might be thought that no dislike or blame,
No sense of weakness or infirmity
Or aught amiss could possibly have come,
Yea, even the visible universe was scanned
With something of a kindred spirit, fell

Beneath the domination of a taste
Less elevated, which did in my mind
With its more noble influence interfere,
Its animation and its deeper sway.   120

There comes (if need be now to speak of this
After such long detail of our mistakes),
There comes a time when Reason, not the grand
And simple Reason, but that humbler power
Which carries on its no inglorious work
By logic and minute analysis
Is of all Idols that which pleases most
The growing mind. A Trifler would he be
Who on the obvious benefits should dwell
That rise out of this process; but to speak   130
Of all the narrow estimates of things
Which hence originate were a worthy theme
For philosophic Verse. Suffice it here
To hint that danger cannot but attend
Upon a Function rather proud to be
The enemy of falsehood, than the friend
Of truth, to sit in judgment than to feel.

Oh! soul of Nature, excellent and fair,
That didst rejoice with me, with whom I too
Rejoiced, through early youth, before the winds   140
And powerful waters, and in lights and shades
That marched and countermarched about the hills
In glorious apparition, now all eye
And now all ear, but ever with the heart
Employed, and the majestic intellect;
Oh! Soul of Nature! that dost overflow
With passion and with life, what feeble men
Walk on this earth! how feeble have I been
When thou wert in thy strength! Nor this through stroke
Of human suffering, such as justifies   150
Remissness and inaptitude of mind,
But through presumption, even in pleasure pleased
Unworthily, disliking here, and there
Liking, by rules of mimic art transferred
To things above all art. But more, for this,°
Although a strong infection of the age,

Was never much my habit, giving way
To a comparison of scene with scene,
Bent overmuch on superficial things,
Pampering myself with meagre novelties   160
Of colour and proportion, to the moods
Of time or season, to the moral power,
The affections, and the spirit of the place,
Less sensible. Nor only did the love
Of sitting thus in judgment interrupt
My deeper feelings, but another cause
More subtle and less easily explained
That almost seems inherent in the Creature,
Sensuous and intellectual as he is,
A twofold Frame of body and of mind: 170
The state to which I now allude was one
In which the eye was master of the heart,
When that which is in every state of life
The most despotic of our senses gained
Such strength in me as often held my mind
In absolute dominion. Gladly here,
Entering upon abstruser argument,
Would I endeavour to unfold the means
Which Nature studiously employs to thwart
This tyranny, summons all the senses each   180
To counteract the other and themselves,
And makes them all, and the objects with which all
Are conversant, subservient in their turn
To the great ends of Liberty and Power.
But this is matter for another Song;
Here only let me add that my delights,
Such as they were, were sought insatiably.°
Though 'twas a transport of the outward sense,
Not of the mind, vivid but not profound:
Yet was I often greedy in the chace,   190
And roamed from hill to hill, from rock to rock,
Still craving combinations of new forms,
New pleasure, wider empire for the sight,
Proud of its own endowments, and rejoiced
To lay the inner faculties asleep.
Amid the turns and counterturns, the strife
And various trials of our complex being

As we grow up, such thraldom of that sense
Seems hard to shun; and yet I knew a Maid,°
Who, young as I was then, conversed with things   200
In higher style; from appetites like these
She, gentle Visitant, as well she might
Was wholly free; far less did critic rules
Or barren intermeddling subtleties
Perplex her mind; but, wise as Women are
When genial circumstance hath favored them,
She welcomed what was given, and craved no more.
Whatever scene was present to her eyes,
That was the best, to that she was attuned
Through her humility and lowliness,   210
And through a perfect happiness of soul,
Whose variegated feelings were in this
Sisters, that they were each some new delight:
For she was Nature's inmate. Her the birds
And every flower she met with, could they but
Have known her, would have loved. Methought such charm
Of sweetness did her presence breathe around
That all the trees, and all the silent hills,
And every thing she looked on, should have had
An intimation how she bore herself   220
Towards them and to all creatures. God delights
In such a being; for her common thoughts
Are piety, her life is blessedness.

Even like this Maid, before I was called forth
From the retirement of my native hills
I loved whate'er I saw; nor lightly loved,
But fervently, did never dream of aught
More grand, more fair, more exquisitely framed
Than those few nooks to which my happy feet
Were limited. I had not at that time   230
Lived long enough, nor in the least survived
The first diviner influence of this world
As it appears to unaccustomed eyes;
I worshipped then among the depths of things
As my soul bade me; could I then take part
In aught but admiration, or be pleased
With any thing but humbleness and love?

I felt, and nothing else; I did not judge,
I never thought of judging, with the gift
Of all this glory filled and satisfied.   240
And afterwards, when through the gorgeous Alps
Roaming, I carried with me the same heart.
In truth, this degradation, howsoe'er
Induced, effect in whatsoe'er degree
Of custom, that prepares such wantonness
As makes the greatest things give way to least,
Or any other cause which hath been named;
Or lastly, aggravated by the times,
Which with their passionate sounds might often make
The milder minstrelsies of rural scenes   250
Inaudible, was transient. I had felt
Too forcibly, too early in my life,
Visitings of imaginative power
For this to last: I shook the habit off
Entirely and for ever, and again
In Nature's presence stood, as I stand now,
A sensitive, and a creative soul.

    There are in our existence spots of time,°
Which with distinct pre-eminence retain
A renovating Virtue, whence, depressed   260
By false opinion and contentious thought,
Or aught of heavier and more deadly weight
In trivial occupations, and the round
Of ordinary intercourse, our minds
Are nourished and invisibly repaired;
A virtue by which pleasure is enhanced,
That penetrates, enables us to mount
When high, more high, and lifts us up when fallen.
This efficacious spirit chiefly lurks
Among those passages of life in which   270
We have had deepest feeling that the mind
Is lord and master, and that outward sense
Is but the obedient servant of her will.
Such moments worthy of all gratitude,
Are scattered everywhere, taking their date
From our first childhood: in our childhood even
Perhaps are most conspicuous. Life with me,

As far as memory can look back, is full
Of this beneficent influence.
                              At a time
When scarcely (I was then not six years old)   290
My hand could hold a bridle, with proud hopes
I mounted, and we rode towards the hills:
We were a pair of Horsemen; honest James
Was with me, my encourager and guide.
We had not travelled long ere some mischance
Disjoined me from my Comrade, and, through fear
Dismounting, down the rough and stony Moor
I led my Horse, and stumbling on, at length
Came to a bottom, where in former times
A Murderer had been hung in iron chains.   290
The Gibbet-mast was mouldered down, the bones
And iron case were gone, but on the turf,
Hard by, soon after that fell deed was wrought,
Some unknown hand had carved the Murderer's name.
The monumental writing was engraven
In times long past, and still from year to year
By superstition of the neighbourhood
The grass is cleared away; and to this hour
The letters are all fresh and visible.
Faltering, and ignorant where I was, at length   300
I chanced to espy those characters inscribed
On the green sod: forthwith I left the spot
And, reascending the bare Common, saw
A naked Pool that lay beneath the hills,
The Beacon on the summit, and more near,°
A Girl who bore a Pitcher on her head
And seemed with difficult steps to force her way
Against the blowing wind. It was, in truth,
An ordinary sight; but I should need
Colours and words that are unknown to man   310
To paint the visionary dreariness
Which, while I looked all round for my lost guide,
Did at that time invest the naked Pool,
The Beacon on the lonely Eminence,
The Woman, and her garments vexed and tossed
By the strong wind. When, in a blessed season
With those two dear Ones, to my heart so dear,°

When in the blessed time of early love,
Long afterwards, I roamed about
In daily presence of this very scene,   320
Upon the naked pool and dreary crags,
And on the melancholy Beacon, fell
The spirit of pleasure and youth's golden gleam;
And think ye not with radiance more divine
From these remembrances, and from the power
They left behind? So feeling comes in aid
Of feeling, and diversity of strength
Attends us, if but once we have been strong.
Oh! mystery of Man, from what a depth
Proceed thy honours! I am lost, but see   330
In simple childhood something of the base
On which thy greatness stands; but this I feel,
That from thyself it is that thou must give,
Else never canst receive. The days gone by
Come back upon me from the dawn almost
Of life: the hiding-places of my power
Seem open; I approach, and then they close;
I see by glimpses now; when age comes on,
May scarcely see at all, and I would give,
While yet we may, as far as words can give,   340
A substance and a life to what I feel:
I would enshrine the spirit of the past
For future restoration. Yet another
Of these to me affecting incidents
With which we will conclude.
                              One Christmas-time,
The day before the Holidays began,
Feverish, and tired, and restless, I went forth
Into the fields, impatient for the sight
Of those two Horses which should bear us home,
My Brothers and myself. There was a crag,   350
An Eminence, which from the meeting-point
Of two highways ascending, overlooked
At least a long half-mile of those two roads,
By each of which the expected Steeds might come,
The choice uncertain. Thither I repaired
Up to the highest summit. 'Twas a day
Stormy, and rough, and wild, and on the grass

I sate, half-sheltered by a naked wall;
Upon my right hand was a single sheep,
A whistling hawthorn on my left, and there,   360
With those companions at my side, I watched,
Straining my eyes intensely, as the mist
Gave intermitting prospect of the wood
And plain beneath. Ere I to School returned
That dreary time, ere I had been ten days
A dweller in my Father's House, he died,°
And I and my two Brothers, Orphans then,°
Followed his Body to the Grave. The event
With all the sorrow which it brought appeared
A chastisement; and when I called to mind   370
That day so lately passed, when from the crag
I looked in such anxiety of hope,
With trite reflections of morality,
Yet in the deepest passion, I bowed low
To God, who thus corrected my desires;
And afterwards, the wind and sleety rain,
And all the business of the elements,
The single sheep, and the one blasted tree,
And the bleak music of that old stone wall,
The noise of wood and water, and the mist   380
Which on the line of each of those two Roads
Advanced in such indisputable shapes,
All these were spectacles and sounds to which
I often would repair and thence would drink,
As at a fountain; and I do not doubt
That in this later time, when storm and rain
Beat on my roof at midnight, or by day
When I am in the woods, unknown to me
The workings of my spirit thence are brought.

Thou wilt not languish here, O Friend, for whom   390
I travel in these dim uncertain ways;
Thou wilt assist me as a pilgrim gone
In quest of highest truth. Behold me then
Once more in Nature's presence, thus restored
Or otherwise, and strengthened once again
(With memory left of what had been escaped)
To habits of devoutest sympathy.

BOOK TWELVE

Same Subject (continued)

From Nature doth emotion come, and moods
Of calmness equally are Nature's gift,
This is her glory; these two attributes
Are sister horns that constitute her strength;
This twofold influence is the sun and shower
Of all her bounties, both in origin
And end alike benignant. Hence it is,
That Genius, which exists by interchange
Of peace and excitation, finds in her
His best and purest Friend, from her receives   10
That energy by which he seeks the truth,
Is rouzed, aspires, grasps, struggles, wishes, craves,
From her that happy stillness of the mind
Which fits him to receive it, when unsought.

  Such benefit may souls of humblest frame
Partake of, each in their degree; 'tis mine
To speak of what myself have known and felt;
Sweet task! for words find easy way, inspired
By gratitude and confidence in truth.
Long time in search of knowledge desperate,   20
I was benighted heart and mind, but now
On all sides day began to reappear,
And it was proved indeed that not in vain
I had been taught to reverence a Power
That is the very quality and shape
And image of right reason, that matures
Her processes by steady laws, gives birth
To no impatient or fallacious hopes,
No heat of passion or excessive zeal,
No vain conceits, provokes to no quick turns   30
Of self-applauding intellect, but lifts
The Being into magnanimity,
Holds up before the mind, intoxicate
With present objects and the busy dance
Of things that pass away, a temperate shew
Of objects that endure, and by this course

Disposes her, when over-fondly set
On leaving her incumbrances behind,
To seek in Man, and in the frame of life,
Social and individual, what there is   40
Desireable, affecting, good or fair,
Of kindred permanence, the gifts divine
And universal, the pervading grace
That hath been, is, and shall be. Above all
Did Nature bring again that wiser mood,
More deeply re-established in my soul,
Which, seeing little worthy or sublime
In what we blazon with the pompous names
Of power and action, early tutored me
To look with feelings of fraternal love   50
Upon those unassuming things, that hold
A silent station in this beauteous world.

Thus moderated, thus composed, I found
Once more in Man an object of delight,
Of pure imagination, and of love;
And, as the horizon of my mind enlarged,
Again I took the intellectual eye
For my instructor, studious more to see
Great Truths, than touch and handle little ones.
Knowledge was given accordingly; my trust   60
Was firmer in the feelings which had stood
The test of such a trial; clearer far
My sense of what was excellent and right;
The promise of the present time retired
Into its true proportion; sanguine schemes,
Ambitious virtues pleased me less; I sought
For good in the familiar face of life
And built thereon my hopes of good to come.

With settling judgments now of what would last
And what would disappear; prepared to find   70
Ambition, folly, madness in the men
Who thrust themselves upon this passive world
As Rulers of the world, to see in these,
Even when the public welfare is their aim,
Plans without thought, or bottomed on false thought
And false philosophy; having brought to test

Of solid life and true result the Books
Of modern Statists, and thereby perceived°
The utter hollowness of what we name
The wealth of Nations, where alone that wealth   80
Is lodged, and how encreased; and having gained
A more judicious knowledge of what makes
The dignity of individual Man,
Of Man, no composition of the thought,
Abstraction, shadow, image, but the man
Of whom we read, the man whom we behold
With our own eyes; I could not but inquire,
Not with less interest than heretofore,
But greater, though in spirit more subdued,
Why is this glorious Creature to be found   90
One only in ten thousand? What one is,
Why may not many be? What bars are thrown
By Nature in the way of such a hope?
Our animal wants and the necessities
Which they impose, are these the obstacles?
If not, then others vanish into air.
Such meditations bred an anxious wish
To ascertain how much of real worth
And genuine knowledge, and true power of mind,
Did at this day exist in those who lived   100
By bodily labour, labour far exceeding
Their due proportion, under all the weight
Of that injustice which upon ourselves
By composition of society
Ourselves entail. To frame such estimate
I chiefly looked (what need to look beyond?)
Among the natural abodes of men,
Fields with their rural works, recalled to mind
My earliest notices, with these compared
The observations of my later youth,   110
Continued downwards to that very day.

    For time had never been in which the throes
And mighty hopes of Nations, and the stir
And tumult of the world, to me could yield,
How far soe'er transported and possessed,
Full measure of content, but still I craved

An intermixture of distinct regards
And truths of individual sympathy
Nearer ourselves. Such often might be gleaned
From that great City, else it must have been   120
A heart-depressing wilderness indeed,
Full soon to me a wearisome abode;
But much was wanting; therefore did I turn
To you, ye Pathways and ye lonely Roads,
Sought you enriched with everything I prized,
With human kindness and with Nature's joy.

   Oh! next to one dear state of bliss, vouchsafed
Alas! to few in this untoward world,
The bliss of walking daily in Life's prime
Through field or forest with the Maid we love,   130
While yet our hearts are young, while yet we breathe
Nothing but happiness, living in some place,
Deep Vale, or anywhere, the home of both,
From which it would be misery to stir;
Oh! next to such enjoyment of our youth,
In my esteem, next to such dear delight,
Was that of wandering on from day to day
Where I could meditate in peace, and find
The knowledge which I love, and teach the sound
Of Poet's music to strange fields and groves,   140
Converse with men, where if we meet a face
We almost meet a friend, on naked Moors
With long, long ways before, by Cottage Bench
Or Well-spring where the weary Traveller rests.

   I love a public road: few sights there are
That please me more; such object hath had power
O'er my imagination since the dawn
Of childhood, when its disappearing line,
Seen daily afar off, on one bare steep
Beyond the limits which my feet had trod,   150
Was like a guide into eternity,
At least to things unknown and without bound.
Even something of the grandeur which invests
The Mariner who sails the roaring sea
Through storm and darkness, early in my mind
Surrounded, too, the Wanderers of the Earth,

Grandeur as much, and loveliness far more.
Awed have I been by strolling Bedlamites;
From many other uncouth Vagrants passed
In fear, have walked with quicker step; but why   160
Take note of this? When I began to inquire,
To watch and question those I met, and held
Familiar talk with them, the lonely roads
Were schools to me in which I daily read
With most delight the passions of mankind,
There saw into the depth of human souls,
Souls that appear to have no depth at all
To vulgar eyes. And now convinced at heart°
How little that to which alone we give
The name of education hath to do   170
With real feeling and just sense, how vain
A correspondence with the talking world
Proves to the most, and called to make good search
If man's estate, by doom of Nature yoked
With toil, is therefore yoked with ignorance,
If virtue be indeed so hard to rear,
And intellectual strength so rare a boon,
I prized such walks still more; for there I found
Hope to my hope, and to my pleasure peace
And steadiness; and healing and repose   180
To every angry passion. There I heard,
From mouths of lowly men and of obscure
A tale of honour; sounds in unison
With loftiest promises of good and fair.

    There are who think that strong affections, love
Known by whatever name, is falsely deemed
A gift, to use a term which they would use,
Of vulgar Nature, that its growth requires
Retirement, leisure, language purified
By manners thoughtful and elaborate,   190
That whoso feels such passion in excess
Must live within the very light and air
Of elegances that are made by man.
True is it, where oppression worse than death
Salutes the Being at his birth, where grace
Of culture hath been utterly unknown,

And labour in excess and poverty
From day to day pre-occupy the ground
Of the affections, and to Nature's self
Oppose a deeper nature, there indeed,   200
Love cannot be; nor does it easily thrive
In cities, where the human heart is sick,
And the eye feeds it not, and cannot feed:
Thus far, no further, is that inference good.

    Yes, in those wanderings deeply did I feel
How we mislead each other, above all
How Books mislead us, looking for their fame
To judgments of the wealthy Few, who see
By artificial lights, how they debase
The Many for the pleasure of those few,   210
Effeminately level down the truth
To certain general notions for the sake
Of being understood at once, or else
Through want of better knowledge in the men
Who frame them, flattering thus our self-conceit
With pictures that ambitiously set forth
The differences, the outside marks by which
Society has parted man from man,
Neglectful of the universal heart.

    Here calling up to mind what then I saw   220
A youthful Traveller, and see daily now
Before me in my rural neighbourhood,
Here might I pause, and bend in reverence
To Nature, and the power of human minds,
To men as they are men within themselves.
How oft high service is performed within
When all the external man is rude in shew,
Not like a temple rich with pomp and gold,
But a mere mountain-Chapel such as shields
Its simple worshippers from sun and shower.   230
Of these, said I, shall be my Song; of these,
If future years mature me for the task,
Will I record the praises, making Verse
Deal boldly with substantial things, in truth
And sanctity of passion, speak of these
That justice may be done, obeisance paid

Where it is due. Thus haply shall I teach,
Inspire, through unadulterated ears
Pour rapture, tenderness, and hope, my theme
No other than the very heart of man   240
As found among the best of those who live
Not unexalted by religious hope,
Nor uninformed by books, good books though few,
In Nature's presence: thence may I select
Sorrow that is not sorrow, but delight,
And miserable love that is not pain
To hear of, for the glory that redounds
Therefrom to human kind and what we are.
Be mine to follow with no timid step
Where knowledge leads me; it shall be my pride   250
That I have dared to tread this holy ground,
Speaking no dream but things oracular,
Matter not lightly to be heard by those
Who to the letter of the outward promise
Do read the invisible soul, by men adroit
In speech and for communion with the world
Accomplished, minds whose faculties are then
Most active when they are most eloquent,
And elevated most when most admired.
Men may be found of other mold than these,   260
Who are their own upholders, to themselves
Encouragement, and energy and will,
Expressing liveliest thoughts in lively words
As native passion dictates. Others, too,
There are among the walks of homely life
Still higher, men for contemplation framed,
Shy, and unpractised in the strife of phrase,
Meek men, whose very souls perhaps would sink
Beneath them, summoned to such intercourse:
Theirs is the language of the heavens, the power,   270
The thought, the image, and the silent joy;
Words are but under-agents in their souls;
When they are grasping with their greatest strength
They do not breathe among them: this I speak
In gratitude to God, who feeds our hearts
For his own service, knoweth, loveth us
When we are unregarded by the world.

Also about this time did I receive
Convictions still more strong than heretofore
Not only that the inner frame is good,   280
And graciously composed, but that no less
Nature through all conditions hath a power
To consecrate, if we have eyes to see,
The outside of her creatures, and to breathe
Grandeur upon the very humblest face
Of human life. I felt that the array
Of outward circumstance and visible form
Is to the pleasure of the human mind
What passion makes it, that meanwhile the forms
Of Nature have a passion in themselves   290
That intermingles with those works of man
To which she summons him, although the works
Be mean, have nothing lofty of their own;
And that the genius of the Poet hence
May boldly take his way among mankind
Wherever Nature leads, that he hath stood
By Nature's side among the men of old,
And so shall stand for ever. Dearest Friend,
Forgive me if I say that I, who long
Had harboured reverentially a thought   300
That Poets, even as Prophets, each with each
Connected in a mighty scheme of truth,
Have each for his peculiar dower, a sense
By which he is enabled to perceive
Something unseen before; forgive me, Friend,
If I, the meanest of this Band, had hope
That unto me had also been vouchsafed
An influx, that in some sort I possessed
A privilege, and that a work of mine,
Proceeding from the depth of untaught things,   310
Enduring and creative, might become
A power like one of Nature's.
                              To such mood,
Once above all, a Traveller at that time
Upon the Plain of Sarum was I raised;°
There on the pastoral Downs without a track
To guide me, or along the bare white roads
Lengthening in solitude their dreary line,

While through those vestiges of ancient times
I ranged, and by the solitude o'ercome,
I had a reverie and saw the past,   320
Saw multitudes of men, and here and there,
A single Briton in his wolf-skin vest
With shield and stone-axe, stride across the Wold;
The voice of spears was heard, the rattling spear
Shaken by arms of mighty bone, in strength
Long mouldered of barbaric majesty.
I called upon the darkness; and it took,
A midnight darkness seemed to come and take
All objects from my sight; and lo! again
The desert visible by dismal flames!   330
It is the sacrificial Altar, fed
With living men; how deep the groans; the voice
Of those in the gigantic wicker thrills
Throughout the region far and near, pervades
The monumental hillocks; and the pomp
Is for both worlds, the living and the dead.
At other moments, for through that wide waste
Three summer days I roamed, when 'twas my chance
To have before me on the downy Plain
Lines, circles, mounts, a mystery of shapes   340
Such as in many quarters yet survive,
With intricate profusion figuring o'er
The untilled ground, the work, as some divine,
Of infant science, imitative forms
By which the Druids covertly expressed
Their knowledge of the heavens, and imaged forth
The constellations, I was gently charmed,
Albeit with an antiquarian's dream;
I saw the bearded Teachers, with white wands
Uplifted, pointing to the starry sky   350
Alternately, and Plain below, while breath
Of music seemed to guide them, and the Waste
Was cheared with stillness and a pleasant sound.

      This for the past, and things that may be viewed
Or fancied, in the obscurities of time.
Nor is it, Friend, unknown to thee; at least

Thyself delighted, Thou for my delight
Hast said, perusing some imperfect verse
Which in that lonesome journey was composed,
That also then I must have exercised   360
Upon the vulgar forms of present things
And actual world of our familiar days,
A higher power, have caught from them a tone,
An image, and a character, by books
Not hitherto reflected. Call we this°
But a persuasion taken up by thee
In friendship, yet the mind is to herself
Witness and judge, and I remember well
That in life's every-day appearances
I seemed about this period to have sight   370
Of a new world, a world, too, that was fit
To be transmitted and made visible
To other eyes, as having for its base
That whence our dignity originates,
That which both gives it being and maintains
A balance, an ennobling interchange
Of action from within and from without:
The excellence, pure spirit, and best power
Both of the object seen, and eye that sees.

BOOK THIRTEEN

Conclusion

In one of these excursions, travelling then
Through Wales on foot, and with a youthful Friend,
I left Bethkelet's huts at couching-time,
And westward took my way to see the sun
Rise from the top of Snowdon. Having reached°
The Cottage at the Mountain's foot, we there
Rouzed up the Shepherd, who by ancient right
Of office is the Stranger's usual Guide,
And after short refreshment sallied forth.

            It was a Summer's night, a close warm night,   10
Wan, dull and glaring, with a dripping mist°
Low-hung and thick that covered all the sky,
Half threatening storm and rain; but on we went
Unchecked, being full of heart and having faith
In our tried Pilot. Little could we see,
Hemmed round on every side with fog and damp,
And, after ordinary travellers' chat
With our Conductor, silently we sank
Each into commerce with his private thoughts.
Thus did we breast the ascent, and by myself   20
Was nothing either seen or heard the while
Which took me from my musings, save that once
The Shepherd's Cur did to his own great joy
Unearth a hedgehog in the mountain crags
Round which he made a barking turbulent.
This small adventure, for even such it seemed
In that wild place and at the dead of night,
Being over and forgotten, on we wound
In silence as before. With forehead bent
Earthward, as if in opposition set   30
Against an enemy, I panted up
With eager pace, and no less eager thoughts.
Thus might we wear perhaps an hour away,
Ascending at loose distance each from each,
And I, as chanced, the foremost of the Band;
When at my feet the ground appeared to brighten,
And with a step or two seemed brighter still;
Nor had I time to ask the cause of this,
For instantly a Light upon the turf
Fell like a flash: I looked about, and lo!   40
The Moon stood naked in the Heavens, at height
Immense above my head, and on the shore
I found myself of a huge sea of mist,
Which, meek and silent, rested at my feet.
A hundred hills their dusky backs upheaved
All over this still Ocean, and beyond,
Far, far beyond, the vapours shot themselves,
In headlands, tongues, and promontory shapes,
Into the Sea, the real Sea, that seemed
To dwindle and give up its majesty,   50

Usurped upon as far as sight could reach.
Meanwhile, the Moon looked down upon this shew
In single glory, and we stood, the mist
Touching our very feet; and from the shore
At distance not the third part of a mile
Was a blue chasm; a fracture in the vapour,
A deep and gloomy breathing-place, through which
Mounted the roar of waters, torrents, streams
Innumerable, roaring with one voice.
The universal spectacle throughout   60
Was shaped for admiration and delight,
Grand in itself alone, but in that breach
Through which the homeless voice of waters rose,
That dark deep thoroughfare, had Nature lodged
The Soul, the Imagination of the whole.

     A meditation rose in me that night
Upon the lonely Mountain when the scene
Had passed away, and it appeared to me
The perfect image of a mighty Mind,
Of one that feeds upon infinity,   70
That is exalted by an underpresence,
The sense of God, or whatso'er is dim
Or vast in its own being; above all
One function of such mind had Nature there
Exhibited by putting forth, and that
With circumstance most awful and sublime,
That domination which she oftentimes
Exerts upon the outward face of things,
So moulds them, and endues, abstracts, combines,
Or by abrupt and unhabitual influence   80
Doth make one object so impress itself
Upon all others, and pervade them so,
That even the grossest minds must see and hear
And cannot chuse but feel. The Power which these
Acknowledge when thus moved, which Nature thus
Thrusts forth upon the senses, is the express
Resemblance, in the fulness of its strength
Made visible, a genuine Counterpart
And Brother of the glorious faculty
Which higher minds bear with them as their own.   90

This is the very spirit in which they deal
With all the objects of the universe;
They from their native selves can send abroad
Like transformations, for themselves create
A like existence, and, whene'er it is
Created for them, catch it by an instinct;
Them the enduring and the transient both
Serve to exalt; they build up greatest things
From least suggestions, ever on the watch,
Willing to work and to be wrought upon.   100
They need not extraordinary calls
To rouze them, in a world of life they live,
By sensible impressions not enthralled,
But quickened, rouzed, and made thereby more fit
To hold communion with the invisible world.
Such minds are truly from the Deity,
For they are Powers; and hence the highest bliss
That can be known is theirs, the consciousness
Of whom they are, habitually infused
Through every image, and through every thought,   110
And all impressions; hence religion, faith,
And endless occupation for the soul
Whether discursive or intuitive;°
Hence sovereignty within and peace at will,
Emotion which best foresight need not fear,
Most worthy then of trust when most intense;
Hence chearfulness in every act of life;
Hence truth in moral judgements and delight
That fails not, in the external universe.

  Oh! who is he that hath his whole life long   120
Preserved, enlarged this freedom in himself?
For this alone is genuine Liberty.
Witness, ye Solitudes! where I received
My earliest visitations, careless then
Of what was given me, and where now I roam,
A meditative, oft a suffering Man,
And yet, I trust, with undiminished powers;
Witness, whatever falls my better mind,
Revolving with the accidents of life,
May have sustained, that, howsoe'er misled,   130

I never, in the quest of right and wrong,
Did tamper with myself from private aims;
Nor was in any of my hopes the dupe
Of selfish passions; nor did wilfully
Yield ever to mean cares and low pursuits;
But rather did with jealousy shrink back
From every combination that might aid
The tendency, too potent in itself,
Of habit to enslave the mind, I mean
Oppress it by the laws of vulgar sense,   140
And substitute a universe of death,
The falsest of all worlds, in place of that
Which is divine and true. To fear and love,
To love as first and chief, for there fear ends,
Be this ascribed; to early intercourse,
In presence of sublime and lovely forms,
With the adverse principles of pain and joy,
Evil as one is rashly named by those
Who know not what they say. From love, for here
Do we begin and end, all grandeur comes,   150
All truth and beauty, from pervading love,
That gone, we are as dust. Behold the fields
In balmy spring-time, full of rising flowers
And happy creatures; see that Pair, the Lamb
And the Lamb's Mother, and their tender ways
Shall touch thee to the heart; in some green bower
Rest, and be not alone, but have thou there
The One who is thy choice of all the world,
There linger, lulled and lost, and rapt away,
Be happy to thy fill; thou call'st this love   160
And so it is, but there is higher love
Than this, a love that comes into the heart
With awe and a diffusive sentiment;
Thy love is human merely; this proceeds
More from the brooding Soul, and is divine.

    This love more intellectual cannot be
Without Imagination, which, in truth,
Is but another name for absolute strength
And clearest insight, amplitude of mind,

And reason in her most exalted mood. 170
This faculty hath been the moving soul
Of our long labour: we have traced the stream
From darkness, and the very place of birth
In its blind cavern, whence is faintly heard
The sound of waters; followed it to light
And open day, accompanied its course
Among the ways of Nature, afterwards
Lost sight of it bewildered and engulphed,
Then given it greeting, as it rose once more
With strength, reflecting in its solemn breast 180
The works of man and face of human life;
And lastly, from its progress have we drawn
The feeling of life endless, the one thought
By which we live, Infinity and God.
Imagination having been our theme,
So also hath that intellectual love,
For they are each in each, and cannot stand
Dividually.—Here must thou be, O Man!
Strength to thyself; no Helper hast thou here;
Here keepest thou thy individual state: 190
No other can divide with thee this work,
No secondary hand can intervene
To fashion this ability. 'Tis thine,
The prime and vital principle is thine
In the recesses of thy nature, far
From any reach of outward fellowship,
Else 'tis not thine at all. But joy to him,
Oh, joy to him who here hath sown, hath laid
Here the foundations of his future years!
For all that friendship, all that love can do, 200
All that a darling countenance can look
Or dear voice utter, to complete the man,
Perfect him, made imperfect in himself,
All shall be his: and he whose soul hath risen
Up to the height of feeling intellect
Shall want no humbler tenderness, his heart
Be tender as a nursing Mother's heart;
Of female softness shall his life be full,
Of little loves and delicate desires,
Mild interests and gentlest sympathies. 210

Child of my Parents! Sister of my Soul!
Elsewhere have strains of gratitude been breathed
To thee for all the early tenderness
Which I from thee imbibed. And true it is
That later seasons owed to thee no less;
For, spite of thy sweet influence and the touch
Of other kindred hands that opened out
The springs of tender thought in infancy,
And spite of all which singly I had watched
Of elegance, and each minuter charm   220
In Nature and in life, still to the last,
Even to the very going out of youth,
The period which our Story now hath reached,
I too exclusively esteemed that love,
And sought that beauty, which, as Milton sings,
Hath terror in it. Thou didst soften down
This over-sternness; but for thee, sweet Friend,
My soul, too reckless of mild grace, had been
Far longer what by Nature it was framed,
Longer retained its countenance severe,   230
A rock with torrents roaring, with the clouds
Familiar, and a favorite of the Stars;
But thou didst plant its crevices with flowers,
Hang it with shrubs that twinkle in the breeze,
And teach the little birds to build their nests
And warble in its chambers. At a time
When Nature, destined to remain so long
Foremost in my affections, had fallen back
Into a second place, well pleased to be
A handmaid to a nobler than herself,   240
When every day brought with it some new sense
Of exquisite regard for common things,
And all the earth was budding with these gifts
Of more refined humanity, thy breath,
Dear Sister, was a kind of gentler spring
That went before my steps.
                              With such a theme,
Coleridge! with this my argument, of thee
Shall I be silent? O most loving Soul!
Placed on this earth to love and understand,
And from thy presence shed the light of love,   250

Shall I be mute ere thou be spoken of?
Thy gentle Spirit to my heart of hearts
Did also find its way; and thus the life
Of all things and the mighty unity
In all which we behold, and feel, and are,
Admitted more habitually a mild
Interposition, and closelier gathering thoughts
Of man and his concerns, such as become
A human Creature, be he who he may!
Poet, or destined for a humbler name;   260
And so the deep enthusiastic joy,
The rapture of the Hallelujah sent
From all that breathes and is, was chastened, stemmed,
And balanced, by a Reason which indeed
Is reason; duty and pathetic truth;
And God and Man divided, as they ought,
Between them the great system of the world,
Where Man is sphered, and which God animates.

    And now, O Friend! this History is brought
To its appointed close: the discipline   270
And consummation of the Poet's mind,
In everything that stood most prominent,
Have faithfully been pictured; we have reached
The time (which was our object from the first)
When we may, not presumptuously, I hope,
Suppose my powers so far confirmed, and such
My knowledge, as to make me capable
Of building up a work that should endure.
Yet much hath been omitted, as need was;
Of Books how much! and even of the other wealth   280
Which is collected among woods and fields,
Far more: for Nature's secondary grace,
That outward illustration which is hers,
Hath hitherto been barely touched upon,
The charm more superficial, and yet sweet,
Which from her works finds way, contemplated
As they hold forth a genuine counterpart
And softening mirror of the moral world.

    Yes, having tracked the main essential Power,
Imagination, up her way sublime,   290

In turn might Fancy also be pursued
Through all her transmigrations, till she too
Was purified, had learned to ply her craft
By judgment steadied. Then might we return
And in the Rivers and the Groves behold
Another face, might hear them from all sides
Calling upon the more instructed mind
To link their images, with subtle skill
Sometimes, and by elaborate research,
With forms and definite appearances   300
Of human life, presenting them sometimes
To the involuntary sympathy
Of our internal being, satisfied
And soothed with a conception of delight
Where meditation cannot come, which thought
Could never heighten. Above all, how much
Still nearer to ourselves is overlooked
In human nature and that marvellous world
As studied first in my own heart, and then
In life, among the passions of mankind   310
And qualities commixed and modified
By the infinite varieties and shades
Of individual character. Herein
It was for me (this justice bids me say)
No useless preparation to have been
The pupil of a public School, and forced
In hardy independence to stand up
Among conflicting passions and the shock
Of various tempers, to endure and note
What was not understood though known to be;   320
Among the mysteries of love and hate,
Honour and shame, looking to right and left,
Unchecked by innocence too delicate
And moral notions too intolerant,
Sympathies too contracted. Hence, when called
To take a station among Men, the step
Was easier, the transition more secure,
More profitable also; for the mind
Learns from such timely exercise to keep
In wholesome separation the two natures,   330
The one that feels, the other that observes.

   Let one word more of personal circumstance,
Not needless, as it seems, be added here.
Since I withdrew unwillingly from France,
The Story hath demanded less regard
To time and place; and where I lived, and how,
Hath been no longer scrupulously marked.
Three years, until a permanent abode
Received me with that Sister of my heart
Who ought by rights the dearest to have been   340
Conspicuous through this biographic Verse,
Star seldom utterly concealed from view,
I led an undomestic Wanderer's life.
In London chiefly was my home, and thence
Excursively, as personal friendships, chance
Or inclination led, or slender means
Gave leave, I roamed about from place to place
Tarrying in pleasant nooks, wherever found
Through England or through Wales. A Youth (he bore°
The name of Calvert; it shall live, if words°   350
Of mine can give it life,) without respect
To prejudice or custom, having hope
That I had some endowments by which good
Might be promoted, in his last decay
From his own Family withdrawing part
Of no redundant Patrimony, did
By a Bequest sufficient for my needs
Enable me to pause for choice, and walk
At large and unrestrained, nor damped too soon
By mortal cares. Himself no Poet, yet   360
Far less a common Spirit of the world,
He deemed that my pursuits and labours lay
Apart from all that leads to wealth, or even
Perhaps to necessary maintenance,
Without some hazard to the finer sense;
He cleared a passage for me, and the stream
Flowed in the bent of Nature.
                         Having now
Told what best merits mention, further pains
Our present labour seems not to require,
And I have other tasks. Call back to mind   370
The mood in which this Poem was begun,

O Friend! the termination of my course
Is nearer now, much nearer; yet even then
In that distraction and intense desire
I said unto the life which I had lived,
Where art thou? Hear I not a voice from thee
Which 'tis reproach to hear? Anon I rose
As if on wings, and saw beneath me stretched
Vast prospect of the world which I had been
And was; and hence this Song, which like a lark   380
I have protracted, in the unwearied Heavens
Singing, and often with more plaintive voice
Attempered to the sorrows of the earth;
Yet centring all in love, and in the end
All gratulant if rightly understood.

      Whether to me shall be allotted life,°
And with life power to accomplish aught of worth
Sufficient to excuse me in men's sight
For having given this Record of myself,
Is all uncertain: but, beloved Friend,   390
When, looking back thou seest, in clearer view
Than any sweetest sight of yesterday,
That summer when on Quantock's grassy Hills°
Far ranging, and among the sylvan Coombs,
Thou in delicious words, with happy heart,
Didst speak the Vision of that Ancient Man,
The bright-eyed Mariner, and rueful woes
Didst utter of the Lady Christabel;
And I, associate in such labour, walked
Murmuring of him who, joyous hap! was found,   400
After the perils of his moonlight ride
Near the loud Waterfall; or her who sate
In misery near the miserable Thorn;
When thou dost to that summer turn thy thoughts,
And hast before thee all which then we were,
To thee, in memory of that happiness
It will be known, by thee at least, my Friend,
Felt, that the history of a Poet's mind
Is labour not unworthy of regard:
To thee the work shall justify itself.   410

The last and later portions of this Gift
Which I for Thee design, have been prepared
In times which have from those wherein we first
Together wantoned in wild Poesy,
Differed thus far, that they have been, my Friend,
Times of such sorrow, of a private grief°
Keen and enduring, which the frame of mind
That in this meditative History
Hath been described, more deeply makes me feel,
Yet likewise hath enabled me to bear   420
More firmly; and a comfort now, a hope,
One of the dearest which this life can give,
Is mine; that Thou art near, and will be soon
Restored to us in renovated health;
When, after the first mingling of our tears,
'Mong other consolations we may find
Some pleasure from this Offering of my love.

        Oh! yet a few short years of useful life,
And all will be complete, thy race be run,
Thy monument of glory will be raised.   430
Then, though, too weak to tread the ways of truth,
This Age fall back to old idolatry,
Though men return to servitude as fast
As the tide ebbs, to ignominy and shame
By Nations sink together, we shall still
Find solace in the knowledge which we have,
Blessed with true happiness if we may be
United helpers forward of a day
Of firmer trust, joint-labourers in the work
(Should Providence such grace to us vouchsafe)   440
Of their redemption, surely yet to come.
Prophets of Nature, we to them will speak
A lasting inspiration, sanctified
By reason and by truth; what we have loved
Others will love; and we may teach them how;
Instruct them how the mind of man becomes
A thousand times more beautiful than the earth
On which he dwells, above this Frame of things
(Which, 'mid all revolutions in the hopes

And fears of men, doth still remain unchanged)   450
In beauty exalted, as it is itself
Of substance and of fabric more divine.

Advertisement to Lyrical Ballads (*1798*)

It is the honourable characteristic of Poetry that its materials are to be found in every subject which can interest the human mind. The evidence of this fact is to be sought, not in the writings of Critics, but in those of Poets themselves.

The majority of the following poems are to be considered as experiments. They were written chiefly with a view to ascertain how far the language of conversation in the middle and lower classes of society is adapted to the purposes of poetic pleasure. Readers accustomed to the gaudiness and inane phraseology of many modern writers, if they persist in reading this book to its conclusion, will perhaps frequently have to struggle with feelings of strangeness and aukwardness: they will look round for poetry, and will be induced to enquire by what species of courtesy these attempts can be permitted to assume that title. It is desirable that such readers, for their own sakes, should not suffer the solitary word Poetry, a word of very disputed meaning, to stand in the way of their gratification; but that, while they are perusing this book, they should ask themselves if it contains a natural delineation of human passions, human characters, and human incidents; and if the answer be favorable to the author's wishes, that they should consent to be pleased in spite of that most dreadful enemy to our pleasures, our own pre-established codes of decision.

Readers of superior judgment may disapprove of the style in which many of these pieces are executed: it must be expected that many lines and phrases will not exactly suit their taste. It will perhaps appear to them, that wishing to avoid the prevalent fault of the day, the author has sometimes descended too low, and that many of his expressions are too familiar, and not of sufficient dignity. It is apprehended, that the more conversant the reader is with our elder writers, and with those in modern times who have been the most successful in painting manners and passions, the fewer complaints of this kind will he have to make.

An accurate taste in poetry, and in all the other arts, Sir Joshua Reynolds has observed, is an acquired talent, which can only be produced by severe thought, and a long continued intercourse with the best models of composition. This is mentioned not with so ridiculous a purpose as to prevent the most inexperienced reader from judging for himself; but merely to temper the rashness of decision, and to suggest that if poetry be a subject on which much time has not been bestowed, the judgment may be erroneous, and that in many cases it necessarily will be so.

The tale of Goody Blake and Harry Gill is founded on a well-authenticated fact which happened in Warwickshire. Of the other poems in the collection, it may be proper to say that they are either absolute inventions of the author, or facts which took place within his personal observation or that of his friends. The poem of the Thorn, as the reader will soon discover, is not supposed to be spoken in the author's own person: the character of the loquacious narrator will sufficiently shew itself in the course of the story. The Rime of the Ancyent Marinere was professedly written in imitation of the *style*, as well as of the spirit of the elder poets; but with a few exceptions, the Author believes that the language adopted in it has been equally intelligible for these three last centuries. The lines entitled Expostulation and Reply, and those which follow, arose out of conversation with a friend who was somewhat unreasonably attached to modern books of moral philosophy.

Note to The Thorn *(1800)*

This Poem ought to have been preceded by an introductory Poem, which I have been prevented from writing by never having felt myself in a mood when it was probable that I should write it well.—The character which I have here introduced speaking is sufficiently common. The Reader will perhaps have a general notion of it, if he has ever known a man, a Captain of a small trading vessel for example, who being past the middle age of life, had retired upon an annuity or small independent income to some village or country town of which he was not a native, or in which he had not been accustomed to live. Such men having little to do become credulous and talkative from indolence; and from the same cause, and other predisposing causes by which it is probable that such men may have been affected, they are prone to superstition. On which account it appeared to me proper to select a character like this to exhibit some of the general laws by which superstition acts upon the mind. Superstitious men are almost always men of slow faculties and deep feelings; their minds are not loose but adhesive; they have a reasonable share of imagination, by which word I mean the faculty which produces impressive effects out of simple elements; but they are utterly destitute of fancy, the power by which pleasure and surprize are excited by sudden varieties of situation and by accumulated imagery.

It was my wish in this poem to shew the manner in which such men cleave to the same ideas; and to follow the turns of passion, always different, yet not palpably different, by which their conversation is swayed. I had two objects to attain; first, to represent a picture which should not be unimpressive yet consistent with the character that should describe it, secondly, while I adhered to the style in which such persons describe, to take care that words, which in their minds are impregnated with passion, should likewise convey passion to Readers who are not accustomed to sympathize with men feeling in that manner or using such language. It seemed to me that this might be done by calling in the assistance of Lyrical and rapid Metre. It was necessary that the Poem, to be natural, should in reality move slowly; yet I hoped, that, by the aid of the metre, to those who should at all enter into the spirit of the Poem, it would appear to move quickly. The Reader will have the kindness to excuse this note as I am sensible that an introductory Poem is necessary to give this Poem its full effect.

Upon this occasion I will request permission to add a few words closely connected with THE THORN and many other Poems in these Volumes.

There is a numerous class of readers who imagine that the same words cannot be repeated without tautology: this is a great error: virtual tautology is much oftener produced by using different words when the meaning is exactly the same. Words, a Poet's words more particularly, ought to be weighed in the balance of feeling and not measured by the space which they occupy upon paper. For the Reader cannot be too often reminded that Poetry is passion: it is the history or science of feelings: now every man must know that an attempt is rarely made to communicate impassioned feelings without something of an accompanying conscious-ness of the inadequateness of our own powers, or the deficiencies of language. During such efforts there will be a craving in the mind, and as long as it is unsatisfied the Speaker will cling to the same words, or words of the same character. There are also various other reasons why repetition and apparent tautology are frequently beauties of the highest kind. Among the chief of these reasons is the interest which the mind attaches to words, not only as symbols of the passion, but as *things*, active and efficient, which are of themselves part of the passion. And further, from a spirit of fondness, exultation, and gratitude, the mind luxuriates in the repetition of words which appear successfully to communicate its feelings. The truth of these remarks might be shewn by innumerable passages from the Bible and from the impassioned poetry of every nation.

'Awake, awake Deborah: awake, awake, utter a song:
Arise Barak, and lead thy captivity captive, thou Son of Abinoam.
At her feet he bowed, he fell, he lay down: at her feet he bowed, he fell; where he
    bowed there he fell down dead.
Why is his Chariot so long in coming? Why tarry the Wheels of his Chariot?'

Judges, Chap. 5th. Verses 12th, 27th, and part of 28th.

See also the whole of that tumultuous and wonderful Poem.

Preface to Lyrical Ballads, with Pastoral and Other Poems (*1802*)

The first Volume of these Poems has already been submitted to general perusal. It was published, as an experiment, which, I hoped, might be of some use to ascertain, how far, by fitting to metrical arrangement a selection of the real language of men in a state of vivid sensation, that sort of pleasure and that quantity of pleasure may be imparted, which a Poet may rationally endeavour to impart.

I had formed no very inaccurate estimate of the probable effect of those Poems: I flattered myself that they who should be pleased with them would read them with more than common pleasure: and, on the other hand, I was well aware, that by those who should dislike them they would be read with more than common dislike. The result has differed from my expectation in this only, that I have pleased a greater number, than I ventured to hope I should please.

For the sake of variety, and from a consciousness of my own weakness, I was induced to request the assistance of a Friend, who furnished me with the Poems of the ANCIENT MARINER, the FOSTER-MOTHER'S TALE, the NIGHTINGALE, and the Poem entitled LOVE. I should not, however, have requested this assistance, had I not believed that the Poems of my Friend would in a great measure have the same tendency as my own, and that, though there would be found a difference, there would be found no discordance in the colours of our style; as our opinions on the subject of poetry do almost entirely coincide.

Several of my Friends are anxious for the success of these Poems from a belief, that, if the views with which they were composed were indeed realized, a class of Poetry would be produced, well adapted to interest mankind permanently, and not unimportant in the multiplicity, and in the quality of its moral relations: and on this account they have advised me to prefix a systematic defence of the theory, upon which the poems were written. But I was unwilling to undertake the task, because I knew that on this occasion the Reader would look coldly upon my arguments, since I might be suspected of having been principally influenced by the selfish and foolish hope of *reasoning* him into an approbation of these particular Poems: and I was still more unwilling to undertake the task, because, adequately to display my opinions, and fully to enforce my arguments, would require a space wholly disproportionate to the nature of a preface. For to treat the subject with the clearness and coherence, of which I believe it susceptible, it would be necessary to give a full account of the present state of the public taste in this country, and to determine how far this taste is healthy or depraved; which, again, would not be determined, without pointing out, in what manner language and the human mind act and re-act on each other, and without retracing the revolutions, not of literature alone, but likewise of society itself. I have therefore altogether declined to enter regularly upon this defence; yet I am sensible, that there would be some impropriety in abruptly obtruding upon the Public, without a few words of introduction, Poems so materially different from those, upon which general approbation is at present bestowed.

It is supposed, that by the act of writing in verse an Author makes a formal engagement that he will gratify certain known habits of association; that he not only thus apprizes the Reader that certain classes of ideas and expressions will be found in his book, but that others will be carefully excluded. This exponent or symbol held forth by metrical language must in different æras of literature have excited very different expectations: for example, in the age of Catullus, Terence and Lucretius, and that of Statius or Claudian; and in our own country, in the age of Shakespeare and Beaumont and Fletcher, and that of Donne and Cowley, or Dryden, or Pope. I will not take upon me to determine the exact import of the promise which by the act of writing in verse an Author, in the present day, makes to his Reader; but I am certain, it will appear to many persons that I have not fulfilled the terms of an engagement thus voluntarily contracted. [They who have been accustomed to the gaudiness and inane phraseology of many modern writers, if they persist in reading this book to its conclusion, will, no doubt, frequently have to struggle with feelings of strangeness and aukwardness: they will look round for poetry, and will be induced to inquire by what species of courtesy these attempts can be permitted to assume that title.] I hope therefore the Reader will not censure me, if I attempt to state what I have proposed to myself to perform; and also, (as far as the limits of a preface will permit) to explain some of the chief reasons which have determined me in the choice of my purpose: that at least he may be spared any unpleasant feeling of disappointment, and that I myself may be protected from the most dishonourable accusation which can be brought against an Author, namely, that of an indolence which prevents him from endeavouring to ascertain what is his duty, or, when his duty is ascertained, prevents him from performing it.

The principal object, then, which I proposed to myself in these Poems was to [chuse incidents and situations from common life, and to relate or describe them, throughout, as far as was possible, in a selection of language really used by men; and, at the same time, to throw over them a certain colouring of imagination, whereby ordinary things should be presented to the mind in an unusual way; and, further, and above all, to make these incidents and situations interesting] by tracing in them, truly though not ostentatiously, the primary laws of our nature: chiefly, as far as regards the manner in which we associate ideas in a state of excitement. Low and rustic life was generally chosen, because in that condition, the essential passions of the heart find a better soil in which they can attain their maturity, are less under restraint, and speak a plainer and more emphatic language; because in that condition of life our elementary feelings co-exist in a state of greater simplicity, and, consequently, may be more accurately contemplated, and more forcibly communicated; because the manners of rural life germinate from those elementary feelings; and, from the necessary character of rural occupations, are more easily comprehended; and are more durable; and lastly, because in that condition the passions of men are incorporated with the beautiful and permanent forms of nature. The language, too, of these men is adopted (purified indeed from what appear to be its real defects, from all lasting and rational causes of dislike or disgust) because such men hourly communicate with the best objects from which the best part of language is originally derived; and because, from their rank in society and the sameness and narrow circle of their intercourse, being less under the influence of social vanity they convey their feelings and notions in simple and unelaborated expressions. Accordingly, such a language, arising out of repeated experience and regular feelings, is a more permanent, and a far more philosophical language, than that which is frequently substituted for it by Poets, who think that they are conferring honour upon themselves and their art, in proportion as they separate themselves from the sympathies of men, and indulge in arbitrary and capricious habits of expression, in order to furnish food for fickle tastes, and fickle appetites, of their own creation.*

I cannot, however, be insensible of the present outcry against the triviality and meanness both of thought and language, which some of my contemporaries have occasionally introduced into their metrical compositions; and I acknowledge that this defect, where it exists, is more dishonourable to the Writer's own character than false refinement or arbitrary innovation, though I should contend at the same time that it is far less pernicious in the sum of its consequences. From such verses the Poems in these volumes will be found distinguished at least by one mark

---

* It is worth while here to observe that the affecting parts of Chaucer are almost always expressed in language pure and universally intelligible even to this day.

of difference, that each of them has a worthy *purpose*. Not that I mean to say, that I always began to write with a distinct purpose formally conceived; but I believe that my habits of meditation have so formed my feelings, as that my descriptions of such objects as strongly excite those feelings, will be found to carry along with them a *purpose*. If in this opinion I am mistaken, I can have little right to the name of a Poet. For all good poetry is the spontaneous overflow of powerful feelings: but though this be true, Poems to which any value can be attached, were never produced on any variety of subjects but by a man, who being possessed of more than usual organic sensibility, had also thought long and deeply. For our continued influxes of feeling are modified and directed by our thoughts, which are indeed the representatives of all our past feelings; and, as by contemplating the relation of these general representatives to each other we discover what is really important to men, so, by the repetition and continuance of this act, our feelings will be connected with important subjects, till at length, if we be originally possessed of much sensibility, such habits of mind will be produced, that, by obeying blindly and mechanically the impulses of those habits, we shall describe objects, and utter sentiments, of such a nature and in such connection with each other, that the understanding of the being to whom we address ourselves, if he be in a healthful state of association, must necessarily be in some degree enlightened, and his affections ameliorated.

I have said that each of these poems has a purpose. I have also informed my Reader what this purpose will be found principally to be: namely, to illustrate the manner in which our feelings and ideas are associated in a state of excitement. But, speaking in language somewhat more appropriate, it is to follow the fluxes and refluxes of the mind when agitated by the great and simple affections of our nature. This object I have endeavoured in these short essays to attain by various means; by tracing the maternal passion through many of its more subtle windings, as in the poems of the IDIOT BOY and the MAD MOTHER; by accompanying the last struggles of a human being, at the approach of death, cleaving in solitude to life and society, as in the Poem of the FORSAKEN INDIAN; by showing, as in the Stanzas entitled WE ARE SEVEN, the perplexity and obscurity which in childhood attend our notion of death, or rather our utter inability to admit that notion; or by displaying the strength of fraternal, or to speak more philosophically, of moral attachment when early associated with the great and beautiful objects of nature, as in THE BROTHERS; or, as in the Incident of SIMON LEE, by placing my Reader in the way of receiving from ordinary moral sensations another and more salutary impression than we are accustomed to receive from them. It has also been part of my general purpose to attempt to sketch characters under the influence of less impassioned feelings, as in the TWO APRIL MORNINGS, THE FOUNTAIN, THE OLD MAN TRAVELLING, THE TWO THIEVES, &c. characters of which the elements are simple, belonging rather to nature than to manners, such as exist now, and will probably always exist, and which from their constitution may be distinctly and profitably contemplated. I will not abuse the indulgence of my Reader by dwelling longer upon this subject; but it is proper that I should mention one other circumstance which distinguishes these Poems from the popular Poetry of the day; it is this, that the feeling therein developed gives importance to the action and situation, and not the action and situation to the feeling. My meaning will be rendered perfectly intelligible by referring my Reader to the Poems entitled POOR SUSAN and the CHILDLESS FATHER, particularly to the last Stanza of the latter Poem.

I will not suffer a sense of false modesty to prevent me from asserting, that I point my Reader's attention to this mark of distinction, far less for the sake of these particular Poems than from the general importance of the subject. The subject is indeed important! For the human mind is capable of being excited without the application of gross and violent stimulants; and he must have a very faint perception of its beauty and dignity who does not know this, and who does not further know, that one being is elevated above another, in proportion as he possesses this capability. It has therefore appeared to me, that to endeavour to produce or enlarge this capability is one of the best services in which, at any period, a Writer can be engaged; but this service, excellent at all times, is especially so at the present day. For a multitude of causes, unknown to former times, are now acting with a combined force to blunt the discriminating powers of the mind, and unfitting it for all voluntary exertion to reduce it to a state of almost savage torpor. The most effective of these causes are the great national events which are daily taking place, and the encreasing accumulation of men in cities, where the uniformity of their occupations produces a craving for extraordinary incident, which the rapid communication of intelligence hourly gratifies. To this tendency of life and manners the literature and theatrical exhibitions of the country have conformed themselves. The invaluable works of our elder writers, I had almost said the works of Shakespear and Milton, are driven into neglect by frantic novels, sickly and stupid German Tragedies, and deluges of idle and extravagant stories in verse.—When I think upon this degrading thirst after outrageous stimulation, I am

almost ashamed to have spoken of the feeble effort with which I have
endeavoured to counteract it; and, reflecting upon the magnitude of the
general evil, I should be oppressed with no dishonorable melancholy,
had I not a deep impression of certain inherent and indestructible
qualities of the human mind, and likewise of certain powers in the great
and permanent objects that act upon it, which are equally inherent and
indestructible; and did I not further add to this impression a belief, that
the time is approaching when the evil will be systematically opposed, by
men of greater powers, and with far more distinguished success.

Having dwelt thus long on the subjects and aim of these Poems, I shall
request the Reader's permission to apprize him of a few circumstances
relating to their *style*, in order, among other reasons, that I may not be
censured for not having performed what I never attempted. [The Reader
will find that personifications of abstract ideas rarely occur in these
volumes; and, I hope, are utterly rejected as an ordinary device to elevate
the style, and raise it above prose. I have proposed to myself to imitate,
and, as far as is possible, to adopt the very language of men; and assuredly
such personifications do not make any natural or regular part of that
language. They are, indeed, a figure of speech occasionally prompted by
passion, and I have made use of them as such; but I have endeavoured
utterly to reject them as a mechanical device of style, or as a family
language which Writers in metre seem to lay claim to by prescription.] I
have wished to keep my Reader in the company of flesh and blood,
persuaded that by so doing I shall interest him. I am, however, well aware
that others who pursue a different track may interest him likewise; I do
not interfere with their claim, I only wish to prefer a different claim of my
own. There will also be found in these volumes little of what is usually
called poetic diction; I have taken as much pains to avoid it as others
ordinarily take to produce it; this I have done for the reason already
alleged, to bring my language near to the language of men, and further,
because the pleasure which I have proposed to myself to impart is of a
kind very different from that which is supposed by many persons to be
the proper object of poetry. I do not know how, without being culpably
particular, I can give my Reader a more exact notion of the style in which
I wished these poems to be written than by informing him that I have at all
times endeavoured to look steadily at my subject, consequently, I hope
that there is in these Poems little falsehood of description, and that my
ideas are expressed in language fitted to their respective importance.
Something I must have gained by this practice, as it is friendly to one
property of all good poetry, namely good sense; but it has necessarily cut
me off from a large portion of phrases and figures of speech which from

father to son have long been regarded as the common inheritance of Poets. I have also thought it expedient to restrict myself still further, having abstained from the use of many expressions, in themselves proper and beautiful, but which have been foolishly repeated by bad Poets, till such feelings of disgust are connected with them as it is scarcely possible by any art of association to overpower.

If in a Poem there should be found a series of lines, or even a single line, in which the language, though naturally arranged, and according to the strict laws of metre, does not differ from that of prose, there is a numerous class of critics, who, when they stumble upon these prosaisms, as they call them, imagine that they have made a notable discovery, and exult over the Poet as over a man ignorant of his own profession. Now these men would establish a canon of criticism which the Reader will conclude he must utterly reject, if he wishes to be pleased with these volumes. And it would be a most easy task to prove to him, that not only the language of a large portion of every good poem, even of the most elevated character, must necessarily, except with reference to the metre, in no respect differ from that of good prose, but likewise that some of the most interesting parts of the best poems will be found to be strictly the language of prose, when prose is well written. The truth of this assertion might be demonstrated by innumerable passages from almost all the poetical writings, even of Milton himself. I have not space for much quotation; but, to illustrate the subject in a general manner, I will here adduce a short composition of Gray, who was at the head of those who, by their reasonings, have attempted to widen the space of separation betwixt Prose and Metrical composition, and was more than any other man curiously elaborate in the structure of his own poetic diction.

> In vain to me the smiling mornings shine,
> And reddening Phoebus lifts his golden fire:
> The birds in vain their amorous descant join,
> Or chearful fields resume their green attire.
> These ears, alas! for other notes repine;
> *A different object do these eyes require;*
> *My lonely anguish melts no heart but mine;*
> *And in my breast the imperfect joys expire;*
> Yet morning smiles the busy race to cheer,
> And new-born pleasure brings to happier men;
> The fields to all their wonted tribute bear;
> To warm their little loves the birds complain.
> *I fruitless mourn to him that cannot hear,*
> *And weep the more because I weep in vain.*

It will easily be perceived that the only part of this Sonnet which is of any value is the lines printed in Italics: it is equally obvious, that, except in the rhyme, and in the use of the single word 'fruitless' for fruitlessly, which is so far a defect, the language of these lines does in no respect differ from that of prose.

[By the foregoing quotation I have shewn that the language of Prose may yet be well adapted to Poetry; and I have previously asserted that a large portion of the language of every good poem can in no respect differ from that of good Prose. I will go further. I do not doubt that it may be safely affirmed, that there neither is, nor can be, any essential difference between the language of prose and metrical composition.] We are fond of tracing the resemblance between Poetry and Painting, and, accordingly, we call them Sisters: but where shall we find bonds of connection sufficiently strict to typify the affinity betwixt metrical and prose composition? They both speak by and to the same organs; the bodies in which both of them are clothed may be said to be of the same substance, their affections are kindred, and almost identical, not necessarily differing even in degree; Poetry* sheds no tears 'such as Angels weep,' but natural and human tears; she can boast of no celestial Ichor that distinguishes her vital juices from those of prose; the same human blood circulates through the veins of them both.

If it be affirmed that rhyme and metrical arrangement of themselves constitute a distinction which overturns what I have been saying on the strict affinity of metrical language with that of prose, and paves the way for other artificial distinctions which the mind voluntarily admits, [I answer that the language of such Poetry as I am recommending is, as far as is possible, a selection of the language really spoken by men; that this selection, wherever it is made with true taste and feeling, will of itself form a distinction far greater than would at first be imagined, and will entirely separate the composition from the vulgarity and meanness of ordinary life; and, if metre be superadded thereto, I believe that a dissimilitude will be produced altogether sufficient for the gratification of a rational mind. What other distinction would we have? Whence is it to come? And where is it to exist? Not, surely, where the Poet speaks through the mouths of his characters: it cannot be necessary here, either

---

* I here use the word 'Poetry' (though against my own judgment) as opposed to the word Prose, and synonymous with metrical composition. But much confusion has been introduced into criticism by this contradistinction of Poetry and Prose, instead of the more philosophical one of Poetry and Matter of Fact, or Science. The only strict antithesis to Prose is Metre; nor is this, in truth, a *strict* antithesis; because lines and passages of metre so naturally occur in writing prose, that it would be scarcely possible to avoid them, even were it desirable.

for elevation of style, or any of its supposed ornaments; for, if the Poet's subject be judiciously chosen, it will naturally, and upon fit occasion, lead him to passions the language of which, if selected truly and judiciously, must necessarily be dignified and variegated, and alive with metaphors and figures. I forbear to speak of an incongruity which would shock the intelligent Reader, should the Poet interweave any foreign splendour of his own with that which the passion naturally suggests: it is sufficient to say that such addition is unnecessary. And, surely, it is more probable that those passages, which with propriety abound with metaphors and figures, will have their due effect, if, upon other occasions where the passions are of a milder character, the style also be subdued and temperate.

But, as the pleasure which I hope to give by the Poems I now present to the Reader must depend entirely on just notions upon this subject, and, as it is in itself of the highest importance to our taste and moral feelings, I cannot content myself with these detached remarks. And if, in what I am about to say, it shall appear to some that my labour is unnecessary, and that I am like a man fighting a battle without enemies, I would remind such persons that, whatever may be the language outwardly holden by men, a practical faith in the opinions which I am wishing to establish is almost unknown. If my conclusions are admitted, and carried as far as they must be carried if admitted at all, our judgments concerning the works of the greatest Poets both ancient and modern will be far different from what they are at present, both when we praise, and when we censure: and our moral feelings influencing, and influenced by these judgments will, I believe, be corrected and purified.

Taking up the subject, then, upon general grounds, I ask what is meant by the word Poet? What is a Poet? To whom does he address himself? And what language is to be expected from him? He is a man speaking to men: a man, it is true, endued with more lively sensibility, more enthusiasm and tenderness, who has a greater knowledge of human nature, and a more comprehensive soul, than are supposed to be common among mankind; a man pleased with his own passions and volitions, and who rejoices more than other men in the spirit of life that is in him; delighting to contemplate similar volitions and passions as manifested in the goings-on of the Universe, and habitually impelled to create them where he does not find them. To these qualities he has added a disposition to be affected more than other men by absent things as if they were present; an ability of conjuring up in himself passions, which are indeed far from being the same as those produced by real events, yet (especially in those parts of the general sympathy which are pleasing and delightful) do more nearly resemble the passions produced by real events, than any thing which, from the motions of their own minds merely, other men are accustomed to feel in themselves; whence, and from practice, he has acquired a greater readiness and power in expressing what he thinks and feels, and especially those thoughts and feelings which, by his own choice, or from the structure of his own mind, arise in him without immediate external excitement.

But, whatever portion of this faculty we may suppose even the greatest Poet to possess, there cannot be a doubt but that the language which it will suggest to him, must, in liveliness and truth, fall far short of that which is uttered by men in real life, under the actual pressure of those passions, certain shadows of which the Poet thus produces, or feels to be produced, in himself. However exalted a notion we would wish to cherish of the character of a Poet, it is obvious, that, while he describes and imitates passions, his situation is altogether slavish and mechanical, compared with the freedom and power of real and substantial action and suffering. So that it will be the wish of the Poet to bring his feelings near to those of the persons whose feelings he describes, nay, for short spaces of time perhaps, to let himself slip into an entire delusion, and even confound and identify his own feelings with theirs; modifying only the language which is thus suggested to him, by a consideration that he describes for a particular purpose, that of giving pleasure. Here, then, he will apply the principle on which I have so much insisted, namely, that of selection; on this he will depend for removing what would otherwise be painful or disgusting in the passion; he will feel that there is no necessity to trick out or elevate nature: and, the more industriously he applies this principle, the deeper will be his faith that no words, which his fancy or imagination can suggest, will be to be compared with those which are in the emanations of reality and truth.

But it may be said by those who do not object to the general spirit of these remarks, that, as it is impossible for the Poet to produce upon all occasions language as exquisitely fitted for the passion as that which the real passion itself suggests, it is proper that he should consider himself as in the situation of a translator, who deems himself justified when he substitutes excellences of another kind for those which are unattainable by him; and endeavours occasionally to surpass his original, in order to make some amends for the general inferiority to which he feels that he must submit. But this would be to encourage idleness and unmanly despair. Further, it is the language of men who speak of what they do not understand; who talk of Poetry as of a matter of amusement and idle pleasure; who will converse with us as gravely about a *taste* for Poetry, as they express it, as if it were a thing as indifferent as a taste for Rope-dancing, or Frontiniac or Sherry. Aristotle, I have been told, hath said, that Poetry is the most philosophic of all writing: it is so: its object is truth, not individual and local, but general, and operative; not standing upon external testimony, but carried alive into the heart by passion; truth which is its own testimony, which gives strength and divinity to the tribunal to which it appeals, and receives them from the same tribunal. Poetry is the image of man and nature. The obstacles which stand in the way of the fidelity of the Biographer and Historian, and of their consequent utility, are incalculably greater than those which are to be encountered by the Poet who has an adequate notion of the dignity of his art. The Poet writes under one restriction only, namely, that of the necessity of giving immediate pleasure to a human Being possessed of that information which may be expected from him, not as a lawyer, a physician, a mariner, an astronomer or a natural philosopher, but as a Man. Except this one restriction, there is no object standing between the Poet and the image of things; between this, and the Biographer and Historian there are a thousand.

Nor let this necessity of producing immediate pleasure be considered as a degradation of the Poet's art. It is far otherwise. It is an acknowledgment of the beauty of the universe, an acknowledgment the more sincere, because it is not formal, but indirect; it is a task light and easy to him who looks at the world in the spirit of love: further, it is a homage paid to the native and naked dignity of man, to the grand elementary principle of pleasure, by which he knows, and feels, and lives, and moves. We have no sympathy but what is propagated by pleasure: I would not be misunderstood; but wherever we sympathize with pain it will be found that the sympathy is produced and carried on by subtle combinations with pleasure. We have no knowledge, that is, no general principles drawn from the contemplation of particular facts, but what has been built up by pleasure, and exists in us by pleasure alone. The Man of Science, the Chemist and Mathematician, whatever difficulties and disgusts they may have had to struggle with, know and feel this. However painful may be the objects with which the Anatomist's knowledge is connected, he feels that his knowledge is pleasure; and where he has no pleasure he has no knowledge. What then does the Poet? He considers man and the objects that surround him as acting and re-acting upon each other, so as to produce an infinite complexity of pain and pleasure; he considers man in his own nature and in his ordinary life as contemplating this with a certain quantity of immediate knowledge, with certain convictions, intuitions, and deductions which by habit become of the nature of intuitions; he considers him as looking upon this complex scene of ideas and sensations, and finding every where objects that immediately excite in him sympathies which, from the necessities of his nature, are accompanied by an overbalance of enjoyment.

To this knowledge which all men carry about with them, and to these sympathies in which without any other discipline than that of our daily life we are fitted to take delight, the Poet principally directs his attention. He considers man and nature as essentially adapted to each other, and the mind of man as naturally the mirror of the fairest and most interesting qualities of nature. And thus the Poet, prompted by this feeling of pleasure with accompanies him through the whole course of his studies, converses with general nature with affections akin to those, which, through labour and length of time, the Man of Science has raised up in himself, by conversing with those particular parts of nature which are the objects of his studies. The knowledge both of the Poet and the Man of Science is pleasure; but the knowledge of the one cleaves to us as a necessary part of our existence, our natural and unalienable inheritance; the other is a personal and individual acquisition, slow to come to us, and by no habitual and direct sympathy connecting us with our fellow-beings. The Man of Science seeks truth as a remote and unknown benefactor; he cherishes and loves it in his solitude: the Poet, singing a song in which all human beings join with him, rejoices in the presence of truth as our visible friend and hourly companion. Poetry is the breath and finer spirit of all knowledge; it is the impassioned expression which is in the countenance of all Science. Emphatically may it be said of the Poet, as Shakespeare hath said of man, 'that he looks before and after.' He is the rock of defence of human nature; an upholder and preserver, carrying every where with him relationship and love. In spite of difference of soil and climate, of language and manners, of laws and customs, in spite of things silently gone out of mind and things violently destroyed, the Poet binds together by passion and knowledge the vast empire of human society, as it is spread over the whole earth, and over all time. The objects of the Poet's thoughts are every where; though the eyes and senses of man are, it is true, his favorite guides, yet he will follow wheresoever he can find an atmosphere of sensation in which to move his wings. Poetry is the first and last of all knowledge—it is as immortal as the heart of man. If the labours of Men of Science should ever create any material revolution, direct or indirect, in our condition, and in the impressions which we habitually receive, the Poet will sleep then no more than at present, but he will be ready to follow the steps of the Man of Science, not only in those general indirect effects, but he will be at his side, carrying sensation into the midst of the objects of the Science itself. The remotest discoveries of the Chemist, the Botanist, or Mincralogist, will be as proper objects of the Poet's art as any upon which it can be employed, if the time should ever come when these things shall be familiar to us, and the relations under which they are contemplated by the followers of these respective Sciences shall be manifestly and palpably material to us as enjoying and suffering beings. If the time should ever come when what is now called Science, thus familiarized to men, shall be ready to put on, as it were, a form of flesh and blood, the Poet will lend his divine spirit to aid the transfiguration, and will welcome the Being thus produced, as a dear and genuine inmate of the household of man.—It is not, then, to be supposed that any one, who holds that sublime notion of Poetry which I have attempted to convey, will break in upon the sanctity and truth of his pictures by transitory and accidental ornaments, and endeavour to excite admiration of himself by arts, the necessity of which must manifestly depend upon the assumed meanness of his subject.

What I have thus far said applies to Poetry in general; but especially to those parts of composition where the Poet speaks through the mouths of his characters; and upon this point it appears to have such weight that I will conclude, there are few persons of good sense, who would not allow that the dramatic parts of composition are defective, in proportion as they deviate from the real language of nature, and are coloured by a diction of the Poet's own, either peculiar to him as an individual Poet, or belonging simply to Poets in general, to a body of men who, from the circumstance of their compositions being in metre, it is expected will employ a particular language.

It is not, then, in the dramatic parts of composition that we look for this distinction of language; but still it may be proper and necessary where the Poet speaks to us in his own person and character. To this I answer by referring my Reader to the description which I have before given of a Poet. Among the qualities which I have enumerated as principally conducing to form a Poet, is implied nothing differing in kind from other men, but only in degree. The sum of what I have there said is, that the Poet is chiefly distinguished from other men by a greater promptness to think and feel without immediate external excitement, and a greater power in expressing such thoughts and feelings as are produced in him in that manner. But these passions and thoughts and feelings are the general passions and thoughts and feelings of men. And with what are they connected? Undoubtedly with our moral sentiments and animal sensations, and with the causes which excite these; with the operations of the elements and the appearances of the visible universe; with storm and sun-shine, with the revolutions of the seasons, with cold and heat, with loss of friends and kindred, with injuries and resentments, gratitude and hope, with fear and sorrow. These, and the like, are the sensations and objects which the Poet describes, as they are the sensations of other men, and the objects which interest them. The Poet thinks and feels in the spirit of the passions of men. How, then, can his language differ in any material degree from that of all other men who feel vividly and see clearly? It might be *proved* that it is impossible. But supposing that this were not the case, the Poet might then be allowed to use a peculiar language when expressing his feelings for his own gratification, or that of men like himself. But Poets do not write for Poets alone, but for men. Unless therefore we are advocates for that admiration which depends upon ignorance, and that pleasure which arises from hearing what we do not understand, the Poet must descend from this supposed height, and, in order to excite rational sympathy, he must express himself as other men express themselves. To this it may be added, that while he is only selecting from the real language of men, or, which amounts to the same thing, composing accurately in the spirit of such selection, he is treading upon safe ground, and we know what we are to expect from him. Our feelings are the same with respect to metre; for, as it may be proper to remind the Reader,] the distinction of metre is regular and uniform, and not like that which is produced by what is usually called poetic diction, arbitrary, and subject to infinite caprices upon which no calculation whatever can be made. In the one case, the Reader is utterly at the mercy of the Poet respecting what imagery or diction he may choose to connect with the passion, whereas, in the other, the metre obeys certain laws, to which the Poet and Reader both willingly submit because they are certain, and because no interference is made by them with the passion but such as the concurring testimony of ages has shown to heighten and improve the pleasure which co-exists with it.

It will now be proper to answer an obvious question, namely, Why, professing these opinions, have I written in verse? To this, in addition to such answer as is included in what I have already said, I reply in the first place, because, however I may have restricted myself, there is still left open to me what confessedly constitutes the most valuable object of all writing, whether in prose or verse, the great and universal passions of men, the most general and interesting of their occupations, and the entire world of nature, from which I am at liberty to supply myself with endless combinations of forms and imagery. Now, supposing for a moment that whatever is interesting in these objects may be as vividly described in prose, why am I to be condemned, if to such description I have endeavoured to superadd the charm which, by the consent of all nations, is acknowledged to exist in metrical language? To this, by such as are unconvinced by what I have already said, it may be answered, that a very small part of the pleasure given by Poetry depends upon the metre, and that it is injudicious to write in metre, unless it be accompanied with the other artificial distinctions of style with which metre is usually accompanied, and that by such deviation more will be lost from the shock which will be thereby given to the Reader's associations, than will be counterbalanced by any pleasure which he can derive from the general power of numbers. In answer to those who still contend for the necessity of accompanying metre with certain appropriate colours of style in order to the accomplishment of its appropriate end, and who also, in my opinion, greatly under-rate the power of metre in itself, it might perhaps, as far as relates to these Poems, have been almost sufficient to observe, that poems are extant, written upon more humble subjects, and in a more naked and simple style than I have aimed at, which poems have continued to give pleasure from generation to generation. Now, if nakedness and simplicity be a defect, the fact here mentioned affords a strong presumption that poems somewhat less naked and simple are capable of affording pleasure at the present day; and, what I wished *chiefly* to attempt, at present, was to justify myself for having written under the impression of this belief.

But I might point out various causes why, when the style is manly, and the subject of some importance, words metrically arranged will long continue to impart such a pleasure to mankind as he who is sensible of the extent of that pleasure will be desirous to impart. The end of Poetry is to produce excitement in co-existence with an over-balance of pleasure. Now, by the supposition, excitement is an unusual and irregular state of the mind; ideas and feelings do not in that state succeed each other in accustomed order. But, if the words by which this excitement is produced are in themselves powerful, or the images and feelings have an undue proportion of pain connected with them, there is some danger that the excitement may be carried beyond its proper bounds. Now the co-presence of something regular, something to which the mind has been accustomed in various moods and in a less excited state, cannot but have great efficacy in tempering and restraining the passion by an intertexture of ordinary feeling, [and of feeling not strictly and necessarily connected with the passion. This is unquestionably true, and hence, though the opinion will at first appear paradoxical, from the tendency of metre to divest language in a certain degree of its reality, and thus to throw a sort of half consciousness of unsubstantial existence over the whole composition, there can be little doubt but that more pathetic situations and sentiments, that is, those which have a greater proportion of pain connected with them, may be endured in metrical composition, especially in rhyme, than in prose. The metre of the old Ballads is very artless; yet they contain many passages which would illustrate this opinion, and, I hope, if the following Poems be attentively perused, similar instances will be found in them.] This opinion may be further illustrated by appealing to the Reader's own experience of the reluctance with which he comes to the re-perusal of the distressful parts of Clarissa Harlowe, or the Gamester. While Shakespeare's writings, in the most pathetic scenes, never act upon us as pathetic beyond the bounds of pleasure—an effect which, in a much greater degree than might at first be imagined, is to be ascribed to small, but continual and regular impulses of pleasurable surprise from the metrical arrangement.—On the other hand (what it must be allowed will much more frequently happen) if the Poet's words should be incommensurate with the passion, and inadequate to raise the Reader to a height of desirable excitement, then, (unless the Poet's choice of his metre has been grossly injudicious) in the feelings of pleasure which the Reader has been accustomed to connect with metre in general, and in the feeling, whether chearful or melancholy, which he has been accustomed to connect with that particular movement of metre, there will be found something which will greatly contribute to impart passion to the words, and to effect the complex end which the Poet proposes to himself.

If I had undertaken a systematic defence of the theory upon which these poems are written, it would have been my duty to develope the various causes upon which the pleasure received from metrical language depends. Among the chief of these causes is to be reckoned a principle which must be well known to those who have made any of the Arts the object of accurate reflection; I mean the pleasure which the mind derives from the perception of similitude in dissimilitude. This principle is the great spring of the activity of our minds, and their chief feeder. From this principle the direction of the sexual appetite, and all the passions connected with it, take their origin: it is the life of our ordinary conversation; and upon the accuracy with which similitude in dissimilitude, and dissimilitude in similitude are perceived, depend our taste and our moral feelings. It would not have been a useless employment to have applied this principle to the consideration of metre, and to have shown that metre is hence enabled to afford much pleasure, and to have pointed out in what manner that pleasure is produced. But my limits will not permit me to enter upon this subject, and I must content myself with a general summary.

I have said that Poetry is the spontaneous overflow of powerful feelings: it takes its origin from emotion recollected in tranquillity: the emotion is contemplated till by a species of reaction the tranquillity disappears, and an emotion, kindred to that which was before the subject of contemplation, is gradually produced, and does itself actually exist in the mind. In this mood successful composition generally begins, and in a mood similar to this it is carried on; but the emotion, of whatever kind and in whatever degree, from various causes is qualified by various pleasures, so that in describing any passions whatsoever, which are voluntarily described, the mind will upon the whole be in a state of enjoyment. Now, if Nature be thus cautious in preserving in a state of enjoyment a being thus employed, the Poet ought to profit by the lesson thus held forth to him, and ought especially to take care, that whatever passions he communicates to his Reader, those passions, if his Reader's mind be sound and vigorous, should always be accompanied with an overbalance of pleasure. Now the music of harmonious metrical language, the sense of difficulty overcome, and the blind association of pleasure which has been previously received from works of rhyme or metre of the same or similar construction, an indistinct perception perpetually renewed of language closely resembling that of real life, and yet, in the circumstance of metre, differing from it so widely, all these imperceptibly make up a complex feeling of delight, which is of the most important use in tempering the painful feeling which will always be found intermingled with powerful descriptions of the deeper passions. This effect is always produced in pathetic and impassioned poetry; while, in lighter compositions, the ease and gracefulness with which the Poet manages his numbers are themselves confessedly a principal source of the gratification of the Reader. I might perhaps include all which it is *necessary* to say upon this subject by affirming, what few persons will deny, that, of two descriptions, either of passions, manners, or characters, each of them equally well executed, the one in prose and the other in verse, the verse will be read a hundred times where the prose is read once. We see that Pope, by the power of verse alone, has contrived to render the plainest common sense interesting, and even frequently to invest it with the appearance of passion. In consequence of these convictions I related in metre the Tale of GOODY BLAKE AND HARRY GILL, which is one of the rudest of this collection. I wished to draw attention to the truth, that the power of the human imagination is sufficient to produce such changes even in our physical nature as might almost appear miraculous. The truth is an important one; the fact (for it is a *fact*) is a valuable illustration of it. And I have the satisfaction of knowing that it has been communicated to many hundreds of people who would never have heard of it, had it not been narrated as a Ballad, and in a more impressive metre than is usual in Ballads.

Having thus explained a few of the reasons why I have written in verse, and why I have chosen subjects from common life, and endeavoured to bring my language near to the real language of men, if I have been too minute in pleading my own cause, I have at the same time been treating a subject of general interest; and it is for this reason that I request the Reader's permission to add a few words with reference solely to these particular poems, and to some defects which will probably be found in them. I am sensible that my associations must have sometimes been particular instead of general, and that, consequently, giving to things a false importance, sometimes from diseased impulses I may have written upon unworthy subjects; but I am less apprehensive on this account, than that my language may frequently have suffered from those arbitrary connections of feelings and ideas with particular words and phrases, from which no man can altogether protect himself. Hence I have no doubt, that, in some instances, feelings even of the ludicrous may be given to my Readers by expressions which appeared to me tender and pathetic. Such faulty expressions, were I convinced they were faulty at present, and that they must necessarily continue to be so, I would willingly take all reasonable pains to correct. But it is dangerous to make these alterations on the simple authority of a few individuals, or even of certain classes of men; for where the understanding of an Author is not convinced, or his feelings altered, this cannot be done without great injury to himself: for his own feelings are his stay and support, and, if he sets them aside in one instance, he may be induced to repeat this act till his mind loses all confidence in itself, and becomes utterly debilitated. To this it may be added, that the Reader ought never to forget that he is himself exposed to the same errors as the Poet, and perhaps in a much greater degree: for there can be no presumption in saying, that it is not probable he will be so well acquainted with the various stages of meaning through which words have passed, or with the fickleness or stability of the relations of particular ideas to each other; and above all, since he is so much less interested in the subject, he may decide lightly and carelessly.

Long as I have detained my Reader, I hope he will permit me to caution him against a mode of false criticism which has been applied to Poetry in which the language closely resembles that of life and nature.

Such verses have been triumphed over in parodies of which Dr. Johnson's stanza is a fair specimen.

> 'I put my hat upon my head,
> And walk'd into the Strand,
> And there I met another man
> Whose hat was in his hand.'

Immediately under these lines I will place one of the most justly admired stanzas of the '*Babes* in the Wood.'

> 'These pretty Babes with hand in hand
> Went wandering up and down;
> But never more they saw the Man
> Approaching from the Town.'

In both these stanzas the words, and the order of the words, in no respect differ from the most unimpassioned conversation. There are words in both, for example, 'the Strand,' and 'the Town,' connected with none but the most familiar ideas; yet the one stanza we admit as admirable, and the other as a fair example of the superlatively contemptible. Whence arises this difference? Not from the metre, not from the language, not from the order of the words; but the *matter* expressed in Dr. Johnson's stanza is contemptible. The proper method of treating trivial and simple verses, to which Dr. Johnson's stanza would be a fair parallelism, is not to say, This is a bad kind of poetry, or This is not poetry; but This wants sense; it is neither interesting in itself, nor can *lead* to any thing interesting; the images neither originate in that sane state of feeling which arises out of thought, nor can excite thought or feeling in the Reader. This is the only sensible manner of dealing with such verses. Why trouble yourself about the species till you have previously decided upon the genus? Why take pains to prove that an ape is not a Newton, when it is self-evident that he is not a man?

I have one request to make of my Reader, which is, that in judging these Poems he would decide by his own feelings genuinely, and not by reflection upon what will probably be the judgment of others. How common is it to hear a person say, 'I myself do not object to this style of composition, or this or that expression, but to such and such classes of people it will appear mean or ludicrous.' This mode of criticism, so destructive of all sound unadulterated judgment, is almost universal: I have therefore to request, that the Reader would abide independently by his own feelings, and that if he finds himself affected he would not suffer such conjectures to interfere with his pleasure.

If an Author by any single composition has impressed us with respect for his talents, it is useful to consider this as affording a presumption, that, on other occasions where we have been displeased, he nevertheless may not have written ill or absurdly; and, further, to give him so much credit for this one composition as may induce us to review what has displeased us with more care than we should otherwise have bestowed upon it. This is not only an act of justice, but, in our decisions upon poetry especially, may conduce in a high degree to the improvement of our own taste: for an *accurate* taste in poetry, and in all the other arts, as Sir Joshua Reynolds has observed, is an *acquired* talent, which can only be produced by thought, and a long continued intercourse with the best models of composition. This is mentioned, not with so ridiculous a purpose as to prevent the most inexperienced Reader from judging for himself, (I have already said that I wish him to judge for himself;) but merely to temper the rashness of decision, and to suggest, that, if Poetry be a subject on which much time has not been bestowed, the judgment may be erroneous; and that in many cases it necessarily will be so.

I know that nothing would have so effectually contributed to further the end which I have in view, as to have shewn of what kind the pleasure is, and how that pleasure is produced, which is confessedly produced by metrical composition essentially different from that which I have here endeavoured to recommend: for the Reader will say that he has been pleased by such composition; and what can I do more for him? The power of any art is limited; and he will suspect, that, if I propose to furnish him with new friends, it is only upon condition of his abandoning his old friends. Besides, as I have said, the Reader is himself conscious of the pleasure which he has received from such composition, composition to which he has peculiarly attached the endearing name of Poetry; and all men feel an habitual gratitude, and something of an honorable bigotry for the objects which have long continued to please them; we not only wish to be pleased, but to be pleased in that particular way in which we have been accustomed to be pleased. There is a host of arguments in these feelings; and I should be the less able to combat them successfully, as I am willing to allow, that, in order entirely to enjoy the Poetry which I am recommending, it would be necessary to give up much of what is ordinarily enjoyed. But, would my limits have permitted me to point out how this pleasure is produced, I might have removed many obstacles, and assisted my Reader in perceiving that the powers of language are not so limited as he may suppose; and that it is possible that poetry may give other enjoyments, of a purer, more lasting, and more exquisite nature. This part of my subject I have not altogether neglected; but it has been less my present aim to prove, that the interest excited by some other kinds of poetry is less vivid, and less worthy of the nobler powers of the mind, than to offer reasons for presuming, that, if the object which I have proposed to myself were adequately attained, a species of poetry would be produced, which is genuine poetry; in its nature well adapted to interest mankind permanently, and likewise important in the multiplicity and quality of its moral relations.

From what has been said, and from a perusal of the Poems, the Reader will be able clearly to perceive the object which I have proposed to myself: he will determine how far I have attained this object; and, what is a much more important question, whether it be worth attaining: and upon the decision of these two questions will rest my claim to the approbation of the public.

Appendix to the Preface (1802)

[*See Preface, page 608—'by what is usually called poetic diction.'*]

As perhaps I have no right to expect from a Reader of an Introduction to a volume of Poems that attentive perusal without which it is impossible, imperfectly as I have been compelled to express my meaning, that what I have said in the Preface should throughout be fully understood, I am the more anxious to give an exact notion of the sense in which I use the phrase *poetic diction*; and for this purpose I will here add a few words concerning the origin of the phraseology which I have condemned under that name.—The earliest Poets of all nations generally wrote from passion excited by real events; they wrote naturally, and as men: feeling powerfully as they did, their language was daring, and figurative. In succeeding times, Poets, and men ambitious of the fame of Poets, perceiving the influence of such language, and desirous of producing the same effect, without having the same animating passion, set themselves to a mechanical adoption of those figures of speech, and made use of them, sometimes with propriety, but much more frequently applied them to feelings and ideas with which they had no natural connection whatsoever. A language was thus insensibly produced, differing materially from the real language of men in *any situation*. The Reader or Hearer of this distorted language found himself in a perturbed and unusual state of mind: when affected by the genuine language of passion he had been in a perturbed and unusual state of mind also: in both cases he was willing that his common judgment and understanding should be laid asleep, and he had no instinctive and infallible perception of the true to make him reject the false; the one served as a passport for the other. The agitation and confusion of mind were in both cases delightful, and no wonder if he confounded the one with the other, and believed them both to be produced by the same, or similar causes. Besides, the Poet spake to him in the character of a man to be looked up to, a man of genius and authority. Thus, and from a variety of other causes, this distorted language was received with admiration; and Poets, it is probable, who had before contented themselves for the most part with misapplying only expressions which at first had been dictated by real passion, carried the abuse still further, and introduced phrases composed apparently in the spirit of the original figurative language of passion, yet altogether of their own invention, and distinguished by various degrees of wanton deviation from good sense and nature.

It is indeed true that the language of the earliest Poets was felt to differ materially from ordinary language, because it was the language of extraordinary occasions; but it was really spoken by men, language which the Poet himself had uttered when he had been affected by the events which he described, or which he had heard uttered by those around him. To this language it is probable that metre of some sort or other was early superadded. This separated the genuine language of Poetry still further from common life, so that whoever read or heard the poems of these earliest Poets felt himself moved in a way in which he had not been accustomed to be moved in real life, and by causes manifestly different from those which acted upon him in real life. This was the great temptation to all the corruptions which have followed: under the protection of this feeling succeeding Poets constructed a phraseology which had one thing, it is true, in common with the genuine language of poetry, namely, that it was not heard in ordinary conversation; that it was unusual. But the first Poets, as I have said, spake a language which, though unusual, was still the language of men. This circumstance, however, was disregarded by their successors; they found that they could please by easier means: they became proud of a language which they themselves had invented, and which was uttered only by themselves; and, with the spirit of a fraternity, they arrogated it to themselves as their own. In process of time metre became a symbol or promise of this unusual language, and whoever took upon him to write in metre, according as he possessed more or less of true poetic genius, introduced less or more of this adulterated phraseology into his compositions, and the true and the false became so inseparably interwoven that the taste of men was gradually perverted; and this language was received as a natural language; and at length, by the influence of books upon men, did to a certain degree really become so. Abuses of this kind were imported from one nation to another, and with the progress of refinement this diction became daily more and more corrupt, thrusting out of sight the plain humanities of nature by a motley masquerade of tricks, quaintnesses, hieroglyphics, and enigmas.

It would be highly interesting to point out the causes of the pleasure given by this extravagant and absurd language: but this is not the place; it depends upon a great variety of causes, but upon none perhaps more than its influence in impressing a notion of the peculiarity and exaltation of the Poet's character, and in flattering the Reader's self-love by bringing him nearer to a sympathy with that character; an effect which is accomplished by unsettling ordinary habits of thinking, and thus assisting the Reader to approach to that perturbed and dizzy state of mind in which if he does not find himself, he imagines that he is *balked* of a peculiar enjoyment which poetry can, and ought to bestow.

The sonnet which I have quoted from Gray, in the Preface, except the lines printed in Italics, consists of little else but this diction, though not of the worst kind; and indeed, if I may be permitted to say so, it is far too common in the best writers, both antient and modern. Perhaps I can in no way, by positive example, more easily give my Reader a notion of what I mean by the phrase *poetic diction* than by referring him to a comparison between the metrical paraphrases which we have of passages in the old and new Testament, and those passages as they exist in our common Translation. See Pope's 'Messiah' throughout, Prior's 'Did sweeter sounds adorn my flowing tongue,' &c. &c. 'Though I speak with the tongues of men and of angels,' &c. &c. See 1st Corinthians, chapter 13th. By way of immediate example, take the following of Dr. Johnson:

> 'Turn on the prudent Ant thy heedless eyes,
> Observe her labours, Sluggard, and be wise;
> No stern command, no monitory voice,
> Prescribes her duties, or directs her choice;
> Yet, timely provident, she hastes away
> To snatch the blessings of a plenteous day;
> When fruitful Summer loads the teeming plain,
> She crops the harvest and she stores the grain.
> How long shall sloth usurp thy useless hours,
> Unnerve thy vigour, and enchain thy powers?
> While artful shades thy downy couch enclose,
> And soft solicitation courts repose,
> Amidst the drowsy charms of dull delight,
> Year chases year with unremitted flight,
> Till want now following, fraudulent and slow,
> Shall spring to seize thee, like an ambushed foe.'

From this hubbub of words pass to the original. 'Go to the Ant, thou Sluggard, consider her ways, and be wise: which having no guide, overseer, or ruler, provideth her meat in the summer, and gathereth her food in the harvest. How long wilt thou sleep, O Sluggard? when wilt thou arise out of thy sleep? Yet a little sleep, a little slumber, a little folding of the hands to sleep. So shall thy poverty come as one that travaileth, and thy want as an armed man.' Proverbs, chap. 6th.

One more quotation and I have done. It is from Cowper's verses supposed to be written by Alexander Selkirk:

> 'Religion! what treasure untold
> Resides in that heavenly word!

> More precious than silver and gold,
> Or all that this earth can afford.
> But the sound of the church-going bell
> These valleys and rocks never heard,
> Ne'er sighed at the sound of a knell,
> Or smiled when a sabbath appear'd.
>
> Ye winds, that have made me your sport,
> Convey to this desolate shore
> Some cordial endearing report
> Of a land I must visit no more.
> My Friends, do they now and then send
> A wish or a thought after me?
> O tell me I yet have a friend,
> Though a friend I am never to see.'

I have quoted this passage as an instance of three different styles of composition. The first four lines are poorly expressed; some Critics would call the language prosaic; the fact is, it would be bad prose, so bad, that it is scarcely worse in metre. The epithet 'church-going' applied to a bell, and that by so chaste a writer as Cowper, is an instance of the strange abuses which Poets have introduced into their language till they and their Readers take them as matters of course, if they do not single them out expressly as objects of admiration. The two lines 'Ne'er sighed at the sound,' &c. are, in my opinion, an instance of the language of passion wrested from its proper use, and, from the mere circumstance of the composition being in metre, applied upon an occasion that does not justify such violent expressions; and I should condemn the passage, though perhaps few Readers will agree with me, as vicious poetic diction. The last stanza is throughout admirably expressed: it would be equally good whether in prose or verse, except that the Reader has an exquisite pleasure in seeing such natural language so naturally connected with metre. The beauty of this stanza tempts me here to add a sentiment which ought to be the pervading spirit of a system, detached parts of which have been imperfectly explained in the Preface,—namely, that in proportion as ideas and feelings are valuable, whether the composition be in prose or in verse, they require and exact one and the same language.

Letter to John Wilson (7 June 1802)

My dear Sir,

Had it not been for a very amiable modesty you could not have imagined that your letter could give me any offence. It was on many accounts highly grateful to me. I was pleased to find that I had given so much pleasure to an ingenuous and able mind and I further considered the enjoyment which you had had from my poems as an earnest that others might be delighted with them in the same or a like manner. It is plain from your letter that the pleasure which I have given you has not been blind or unthinking you have studied the poems and prove that you have entered into the spirit of them. They have not given you a cheap or vulgar pleasure therefore I feel that you are entitled to my kindest thanks for having done some violence to your natural diffidence in the communication which you have made to me.

There is scarcely any part of your letter that does not deserve particular notice, but partly from a weakness in my stomach and digestion and partly from certain habits of mind I do not write any letters unless upon business not ev[en] to my dearest Friends. Except during absence from my own family I ha[ve] not written five letters of friendship during the last five years. I have mentioned this in order that I may retain your good opinion should my le[tter] be less minute than you are entitled to expect. You seem to be desirous [of] my opinion on the influence of natural objects in forming the character of nati[ons]. This cannot be understood without first considering their influence upon men in [general?] first with reference to such subjects as are common to all countries: and [next?] such as belong exclusively to any particular country or in a greater d[egree] to it than to another. Now it is manifest that no human being can be so besotted and debased by oppression, penury or any other evil which unhum[anizes] man as to be utterly insensible to the colours, forms, or smell of flowers, the [voices?] and motions of birds and beasts, the appearances of the sky and heavenly bodies, the [genial?] warmth of a fine day, the terror and uncomfortableness of a storm, &c &c. How dead soever many full-grown men may outwardly seem to these thi[ngs] they all are more or less affected by them, and in childhood, in the first practice and exercise of their senses, they must have been not the nourish[ers] merely, but often the fathers of their passions. There cannot be a doubt that in tracts of country where images of danger, melancholy, grandeur, or loveliness, softness, and ease prevail, that they will make themselves felt powerfully in forming the characters of the people, so as to produce a uniformity of national character, where the nation is small and is not made up of men who, inhabiting different soils, climates, &c by their civil usages, and relations materially interfere with each other. It was so formerly, no doubt, in the Highlands of Scotland but we cannot perhaps observe much of it in our own island at the present day, because, even in the most sequestered places, by manufactures, traffic, religion, Law, interchange of inhabitants &c distinctions are done away which would otherwise have been strong and obvious. This complex state of society does not, however, prevent the characters of individuals from frequently receiving a strong bias not merely from the impressions of general nature, but also from local objects and images. But it seems that to produce these effects in the degree in which we frequently find them to be produced there must be a peculiar sensibility of original organization combining with moral accidents, as is exhibited in *The Brothers* and in *Ruth*—I mean, to produce this in a marked degree not that I believe that any man was ever brought up in the country without loving it, especially in his better moments, or in a district of particular grandeur or beauty without feeling some stronger attachment to it on that account than he would otherwise have felt. I include, you will observe, in these considerations the influence of climate, changes in the atmosphere and elements and the labours and occupations which particular districts require.

You begin what you say upon the Idiot Boy with this observation, that nothing is a fit subject for poetry which does not please. But here follows a question, Does not please whom? Some have little knowledge of natural imagery of any kind, and, of course, little relish for it, some are disgusted with the very mention of the words pastoral poetry, sheep or shepherds, some cannot tolerate a poem with a ghost or any supernatural agency in it, others would shrink from an animated description of the pleasures of love, as from a thing carnal and libidinous some cannot bear to see delicate and refined feelings ascribed to men in low conditions of society, because their vanity and self-love tell them that these belong only to themselves and men like themselves in dress, station, and way of life: others are disgusted with the naked language of some of the most interesting passions of men, because either it is indelicate, or gross, or [vu]lgar, as many fine ladies could not bear certain expressions in The [Mad] Mother and the Thorn, and, as in the instance of Adam Smith, who, we [are] told, could not endure the Ballad of Clym of the Clough, because the [au]thor had not written like a gentleman; then there are professional[, loca]l and national prejudices forevermore some take no interest in the [descri]ption of a particular passion or quality, as love of solitariness, we will say, [gen]ial activity of fancy, love of nature, religion, and so forth, because they have [little or?] nothing of it in themselves, and so on without end. I return then to [the] question, please whom? or what? I answer, human nature, as it has been [and eve]r will be. But where are we to find the best measure of this? I answer, [from with]in; by stripping our own hearts naked, and by looking out of ourselves to[wards me]n who lead the simplest lives most according to nature men who [ha]ve never known false refinements, wayward and artificial desires, false criti[ci]sms, effeminate habits of thinking and feeling, or who, having known these [t]hings, have outgrown them. This latter class is the most to be depended upon, but it is very small in number. People in our rank in life are perpetually falling into one sad mistake, namely, that of supposing that human nature and the persons they associate with are one and the same thing. Whom do we generally associate with? Gentlemen, persons of fortune, professional men, ladies persons who can afford to buy or can easily procure books of half a guinea price, hot-pressed, and printed upon superfine paper. These persons are, it is true, a part of human nature, but we err lamentably if we suppose them to be fair representatives of the vast mass of human existence. And yet few ever consider books but with reference to their power of pleasing these persons and men of a higher rank few descend lower among cottages and fields and among children. A man must have done this habitually before his judgment upon the Idiot Boy would be in any way decisive with me. I *know* I have done this myself habitually; I wrote the poem with exceeding delight and pleasure, and whenever I read it I read it with pleasure. You have given me praise for having reflected faithfully in my poems the feelings of human nature I would fain hope that I have done so. But a great Poet ought to do more than this he ought to a certain degree to rectify men's feelings, to give them new compositions of feeling, to render their feelings more sane pure and permanent, in short, more consonant to nature, that is, to eternal nature, and the great moving spirit of things. He ought to travel before men occasionally as well as at their sides. I may illustrate this by a reference to natural objects. What false notions have prevailed from generation to generation as to the true character of the nightingale. As far as my Friend's Poem in the Lyrical Ballads, is read it will contribute greatly to rectify these. You will recollect a passage in Cowper where, speaking of rural sounds, he says—

> 'and *even* the boding Owl
> That hails the rising moon has charms for me.'

Cowper was passionately fond of natural objects yet you see he mentions it as a marvellous thing that he could connect pleasure with the cry of the owl. In the same poem he speaks in the same manner of that beautiful plant, the gorse; making in some degree an amiable boast of his loving it, '*unsightly* and unsmooth['] as it is. There are many aversions of this kind, which, though they have some foundation in nature, have yet so slight a one, that though they may have prevailed hundreds of years, a philosopher will look upon them as accidents. So with respect to many moral feelings, either of [lo]ve or dislike what excessive admiration was payed in former times to personal prowess and military success it is so with [the] latter even at the present day but surely not nearly so much as hereto[fore]. So with regard to birth, and innumerable other modes of sentiment, civil and religious. But you will be inclined to ask by this time how all this applies to the Idiot Boy. To this I can only say that the loathing and disgust which many people have at the sight of an Idiot, is a feeling which, though having som[e] foundation in human nature is not necessarily attached to it in any vi[rtuous?] degree, but is owing, in a great measure to a false delicacy, and, if I [may] say it without rudeness, a certain want of comprehensiveness of think[ing] and feeling. Persons in the lower classes of society have little or nothing [of] this: if an Idiot is born in a poor man's house, it must be taken car[e of] and cannot be boarded out, as it would be by gentlefolks, or sent [to a] public or private receptacle for such unfortunate beings. [Poor people] seeing frequently among their neighbours such objects, easily [forget what]ever there is of natural disgust about them, and have t[herefore] a sane state, so that without pain or suffering they [perform] their duties towards them. I could with pleasure pursue this subj[ect, but] I must now strictly adopt the plan which I proposed [to my]self when I began to write this letter, namely, that of setting down a few hints or memorandums, which you will think of for my sake.

I have often applied to Idiots, in my own mind, that sublime expression of scripture that, '*their life is hidden' with God.*' They are worshipped, probably from a feeling of this sort, in several parts of the East. Among the Alps where they are numerous, they are considered, I believe, as a blessing to the family to which they belong I have indeed often looked upon the conduct of fathers and mothers of the lower classes of society towards Idiots as the great triumph of the human heart. It is there that we see the strength, disinterestedness, and grandeur of love, nor have I ever been able to contemplate an object that calls out so many excellent and virtuous sentiments without finding it hallowed thereby and having something in me which bears down before it, like a deluge, every feeble sensation of disgust and aversion.

There are in my opinion, several important mistakes in the latter part of your letter which I could have wished to notice; but I find myself much fatigued. These refer both to the Boy and the Mother. I must content myself simply with observing that it is probable that the principle cause of your dislike to this particular poem lies in the *word* Idiot. If there had been any such word in our language, *to which we had attached passion*, as lack-wit, half-wit, witless &c I should have certainly employed it in preference but there is no such word. Observe, (this is entirely in reference to this particular poem) my Idiot is not one of those who cannot articulate and such as are usually disgusting in their persons—

> 'Whether in cunning or in joy'
> 'And then his words were not a few' &c

and the last speech at the end of the poem. The Boy whom I had in my mind was, by no means disgusting in his appearance quite the contrary and I have known several with imperfect faculties who are handsome in their persons and features. There is one, at present, within a mile of my own house remarkably so, though there is something of a stare and vacancy in his countenance. A Friend of mine, knowing that some persons had a dislike to the poem such as you have expressed advised me to add a stanza describing the person of the Boy [so a]s entirely to separate him in the imaginations of my Readers from [that] class of idiots who are disgusting in their persons, but the narration [in] the poem is so rapid and impassioned that I could not find a place [in] which to insert the stanza without checking the progress of it, and [so lea]ving a deadness upon the feeling. This poem has, I know, frequently produced [the s]ame effect as it did upon you and your Friends but there are many [peo]ple also to whom it affords exquisite delight, and who indeed, prefer [it] to any other of my Poems. This proves that the feelings there delineated [are] such as all men *may* sympathize with. This is enough for my purpose. [It] is not enough for me as a poet, to delineate merely such feelings as all men *do* sympathize with but, it is also highly desirable to add to these others, such as all men *may* sympathise with, and such as there is reason to believe they would be better and more moral beings if they did sympathize with.

I conclude with regret, because I have not said one half of [what I inten]ded to say: but I am sure you will deem my excuse suf[ficient when I] inform you that my head aches violently, and I am, in [other respect]s, unwell. I must, however, again give you my warmest [thanks] for your kind letter. I shall be happy to hear from you again [and] do not think it unreasonable that I should request a letter from you when I feel that the answer which I may make to it will not perhaps, be above three or four lines. This I mention to you with frankness, and you will not take it ill after what I have before said of my remissness in writing letters.

> I am, dear Sir
> With great Respect,
> Yours sincerely W Wordsworth.

Preface to Poems (*1815*)

The observations prefixed to that portion of these Volumes, which was published many years ago, under the title of 'Lyrical Ballads,' have so little of a special application to the greater part, perhaps, of this collection, as subsequently enlarged and diversified, that they could not with any propriety stand as an Introduction to it. Not deeming it, however, expedient to suppress that exposition, slight and imperfect as it is, of the feelings which had determined the choice of the subjects, and the principles which had regulated the composition of those Pieces, I have transferred it to the end of the second Volume, to be attended to, or not, at the pleasure of the Reader.

In the Preface to that part of 'The Recluse,' lately published under the title of 'The Excursion,' I have alluded to a meditated arrangement of my minor Poems, which should assist the attentive Reader in perceiving their connection with each other, and also their subordination to that Work. I shall here say a few words explanatory of this arrangement, as carried into effect in the present Volumes.

The powers requisite for the production of poetry are, first, those of observation and description, i.e. the ability to observe with accuracy things as they are in themselves, and with fidelity to describe them, unmodified by any passion or feeling existing in the mind of the Describer: whether the things depicted be actually present to the senses, or have a place only in the memory. This power, though indispensable to a Poet, is one which he employs only in submission to necessity, and never for a continuance of time; as its exercise supposes all the higher qualities of the mind to be passive, and in a state of subjection to external objects, much in the same way as the Translator or Engraver ought to be to his Original. 2dly, Sensibility,—which, the more exquisite it is, the wider will be the range of a Poet's perceptions; and the more will he be incited to observe objects, both as they exist in themselves and as re-acted upon by his own mind. (The distinction between poetic and human sensibility has been marked in the character of the Poet delineated in the original preface, before-mentioned). 3rdly, Reflection,—which makes the Poet acquainted with the value of actions, images, thoughts, and feelings; and assists the sensibility in perceiving their connection with each other. 4thly, Imagination and Fancy,—to modify, to create, and to associate. 5thly, Invention,—by which characters are composed out of materials supplied by observation;

whether of the Poet's own heart and mind, or of external life and nature; and such incidents and situations produced as are most impressive to the imagination, and most fitted to do justice to the characters, sentiments, and passions, which the Poet undertakes to illustrate. And, lastly, Judgment,—to decide how and where, and in what degree, each of these faculties ought to be exerted; so that the less shall not be sacrificed to the greater; nor the greater, slighting the less, arrogate, to its own injury, more than its due. By judgment, also, is determined what are the laws and appropriate graces of every species of composition.

The materials of Poetry, by these powers collected and produced, are cast, by means of various moulds, into divers forms. The moulds may be enumerated, and the forms specified, in the following order. 1st, the Narrative,—including the Epopoeia, the Historic Poem, the Tale, the Romance, the Mock-heroic, and, if the spirit of Homer will tolerate such neighbourhood, that dear production of our days, the metrical Novel. Of this Class, the distinguishing mark, is, that the Narrator, however liberally his speaking agents be introduced, is himself the source from which every thing primarily flows. Epic Poets, in order that their mode of composition may accord with the elevation of their subject, represent themselves as *singing* from the inspiration of the Muse, Arma virumque *cano*; but this is a fiction, in modern times, of slight value: The Iliad or the Paradise Lost would gain little in our estimation by being chaunted. The other poets who belong to this class are commonly content to *tell* their tale;—so that of the whole it may be affirmed that they neither require nor reject the accompaniment of music.

2ndly, The Dramatic,—consisting of Tragedy, Historic Drama, Comedy, and Masque; in which the poet does not appear at all in his own person, and where the whole action is carried on by speech and dialogue of the agents; music being admitted only incidentally and rarely. The Opera may be placed here, in as much as it proceeds by dialogue; though depending, to the degree that it does, upon music, it has a strong claim to be ranked with the Lyrical. The characteristic and impassioned Epistle, of which Ovid and Pope have given examples, considered as a species of monodrama, may, without impropriety, be placed in this class.

3rdly, The Lyrical,—containing the Hymn, the Ode, the Elegy, the Song, and the Ballad; in all which, for the production of their *full* effect, an accompaniment of music is indispensable.

4thly, The Idyllium,—descriptive chiefly either of the processes and appearances of external nature, as the 'Seasons' of Thomson; or of characters, manners, and sentiments, as are Shenstone's School-mistress, The Cotter's Saturday Night of Burns, The Twa Dogs of the same Author; or of these in conjunction with the appearances of Nature, as most of the pieces of Theocritus, the Allegro and Penseroso of Milton, Beattie's Minstrel, Goldsmith's 'Deserted Village.' The Epitaph, the Inscription, the Sonnet, most of the epistles of poets writing in their own persons, and all loco-descriptive poetry, belong to this class.

5thly, Didactic,—the principal object of which is direct instruction; as the Poem of Lucretius, the Georgics of Virgil, 'the Fleece' of Dyer, Mason's 'English Garden,' &c.

And, lastly, philosophical satire, like that of Horace and Juvenal; personal and occasional Satire rarely comprehending sufficient of the general in the individual to be dignified with the name of Poetry.

Out of the three last classes has been constructed a composite species, of which Young's Night Thoughts and Cowper's Task are excellent examples.

It is deducible from the above, that poems, apparently miscellaneous, may with propriety be arranged with reference to the powers of mind *predominant* in the production of them; or to the mould in which they are cast; or, lastly, to the subjects to which they relate. From each of these considerations, the following Poems have been divided into classes; which, that the work may more obviously correspond with the course of human life, for the sake of exhibiting in it the three requisites of a legitimate whole, a beginning, a middle, and an end, have been also arranged, as far as it was possible, according to an order of time, commencing with Childhood, and terminating with Old Age, Death, and Immortality. My guiding wish was, that the small pieces of which these volumes consist, thus discriminated, might be regarded under a two-fold view; as composing an entire work within themselves, and as adjuncts to the philosophical Poem, 'The Recluse.' This arrangement has long presented itself habitually to my own mind. Nevertheless, I should have preferred to scatter the contents of these volumes at random, if I had been persuaded that, by the plan adopted, any thing material would be taken from the natural effect of the pieces, individually, on the mind of the unreflecting Reader. I trust there is a sufficient variety in each class to prevent this; while, for him who reads with reflection, the arrangement will serve as a commentary unostentatiously directing his attention to my purposes, both particular and general. But, as I wish to guard against the possibility of misleading by this classification, it is proper first to remind the Reader, that certain poems are placed according to the powers of mind, in the Author's conception, predominant in the production of them; *predominant*, which implies the exertion of other faculties in less degree. Where there is more imagination than fancy in a poem it is placed under the head of imagination, and vice versa. Both the above Classes might without impropriety have been enlarged from that consisting of 'Poems founded on the Affections'; as might this latter from those, and from the class 'Proceeding from Sentiment and Reflection'. The most striking characteristics of each piece, mutual illustration, variety, and proportion, have governed me throughout.

It may be proper in this place to state, that the Extracts in the 2nd Class entitled 'Juvenile Pieces,' are in many places altered from the printed copy, chiefly by omission and compression. The slight alterations of another kind were for the most part made not long after the publication of the Poems from which the Extracts are taken. These Extracts seem to have a title to be placed here as they were the productions of youth, and represent implicitly some of the features of a youthful mind, at a time when images of nature supplied to it the place of thought, sentiment, and almost of action; or, as it will be found expressed, of a state of mind when

> 'the sounding cataract
> Haunted me like a passion: the tall rock,
> The mountain, and the deep and gloomy wood,
> Their colours and their forms were then to me
> An appetite, a feeling and a love,
> That had no need of a remoter charm,
> By thought supplied, or any interest
> Unborrowed from the eye'—

I will own that I was much at a loss what to select of these descriptions; and perhaps it would have been better either to have reprinted the whole, or suppressed what I have given.

None of the other Classes, except those of Fancy and Imagination, require any particular notice. But a remark of general application may be made. All Poets, except the dramatic, have been in the practice of feigning that their works were composed to the music of the harp or lyre: with what degree of affectation this has been done in modern times, I leave to the judicious to determine. For my own part, I have not been disposed to violate probability so far, or to make such a large demand upon the Reader's charity. Some of these pieces are essentially lyrical; and, therefore, cannot have their due force without a supposed musical accompaniment; but, in much the greatest part, as a substitute for the classic lyre or romantic harp, I require nothing more than an animated or impassioned recitation, adapted to the subject. Poems, however humble in their kind, if they be good in that kind, cannot read themselves: the law of long syllable and short must not be so inflexible—the letter of metre must not be so impassive to the spirit of versification—as to deprive the Reader of a voluntary power to modulate, in subordination to the sense, the music of the poem;—in the same manner as his mind is left at liberty, and even summoned, to act upon its thoughts and images. But, though the accompaniment of a musical instrument be frequently dispensed with, the true Poet does not therefore abandon his privilege distinct from that of the mere Proseman;

> 'He murmurs near the running brooks
> A music sweeter than their own.'

I come now to the consideration of the words Fancy and Imagination, as employed in the classification of the following Poems. 'A man,' says an intelligent Author, 'has "imagination," in proportion as he can distinctly copy in idea the impressions of sense: it is the faculty which *images* within the mind the phenomena of sensation. A man has fancy in proportion as he can call up, connect, or associate, at pleasure, those internal images (φαντάζειν is to cause to appear) so as to complete ideal representations of absent objects. Imagination is the power of depicting, and fancy of evoking and combining. The imagination is formed by patient observation; the fancy by a voluntary activity in shifting the scenery of the mind. The more accurate the imagination, the more safely may a painter, or a poet, undertake a delineation, or a description, without the presence of the objects to be characterized. The more versatile the fancy, the more original and striking will be the decorations produced.'—*British Synonyms discriminated, by W. Taylor.*

Is not this as if a man should undertake to supply an account of a building, and be so intent upon what he had discovered of the foundation as to conclude his task without once looking up at the superstructure? Here, as in other instances throughout the volume, the judicious Author's mind is enthralled by Etymology; he takes up the original word as his guide, his conductor, his escort, and too often does not perceive how soon he becomes its prisoner, without liberty to tread in any path but that to which it confines him. It is not easy to find out how imagination, thus explained, differs from distinct remembrance of images; or fancy from quick and vivid recollection of them: each is nothing more than a mode of memory. If the two words bear the above meaning, and no other, what term is left to designate that Faculty of which the Poet is 'all compact'; he whose eye glances from earth to heaven, whose spiritual attributes body-forth what his pen is prompt in turning to shape; or what is left to characterise fancy, as insinuating herself into the heart of objects with creative activity?—Imagination, in the sense of the word as giving title to a Class of the following Poems, has no reference to images that are merely a faithful copy, existing in the mind, of absent external objects; but is a word of higher import, denoting operations of the mind upon those objects, and processes of creation or of composition, governed by certain fixed laws. I proceed to illustrate my meaning by instances. A parrot *hangs* from the wires of his cage by his beak or by his claws; or a monkey from the bough of a tree by his paws or his tail. Each creature does so literally and actually. In the first Eclogue of Virgil, the Shepherd, thinking of the time when he is to take leave of his Farm, thus addresses his Goats;

> 'Non ego vos posthac viridi projectus in antro
> Dumosa *pendere* procul de rupe videbo,'

> —'half way up
> *Hangs* one who gathers samphire,'

is the well-known expression of Shakespear, delineating an ordinary image upon the Cliffs of Dover. In these two instances is a slight exertion of the faculty which I denominate imagination, in the use of one word: neither the goats nor the samphire-gatherer do literally hang, as does the parrot or the monkey; but, presenting to the senses something of such an appearance, the mind in its activity, for its own gratification, contemplates them as hanging.

> 'As when far off at Sea a Fleet descried
> *Hangs* in the clouds, by equinoxial winds
> Close sailing from Bengala or the Isles
> Of Ternate or Tydore, whence Merchants bring
> Their spicy drugs; they on the trading flood
> Through the wide Ethiopian to the Cape
> Ply, stemming nightly toward the Pole: so seemed
> Far off the flying Fiend.'

Here is the full strength of the imagination involved in the word, *hangs*, and exerted upon the whole image: First, the Fleet, an aggregate of many Ships, is represented as one mighty Person, whose track, we know and feel, is upon the waters; but, taking advantage of its appearance of the senses, the Poet dares to represent it as *hanging in the clouds*, both for the gratification of the mind in contemplating the image itself, and in reference to the motion and appearance of the sublime object to which it is compared.

From images of sight we will pass to those of sound:

> 'Over his own sweet voice the Stock-dove *broods*';

of the same bird,

> 'His voice was *buried* among trees,
> Yet to be come at by the breeze';

> 'Oh, Cuckoo! shall I call thee *Bird*,
> Or but a wandering *Voice*?'

The Stock-dove is said to *coo*, a sound well imitating the note of the bird; but, by the intervention of the metaphor *broods*, the affections are called in by the imagination to assist in marking the manner in which the Bird reiterates and prolongs her soft note, as if herself delighting to listen to it, and participating of a still and quiet satisfaction, like that which may be supposed inseparable from the continuous process of incubation. 'His voice was buried among trees,' a metaphor expressing the love of *seclusion* by which this Bird is marked; and characterising its note as not partaking of the shrill and the piercing, and therefore more easily deadened by the intervening shade; yet a note so peculiar, and withal so pleasing, that the breeze, gifted with that love of the sound which the Poet feels, penetrates the shade in which it is entombed, and conveys it to the ear of the listener.

> Shall I call thee Bird
> Or but a wandering Voice?

This concise interrogation characterises the seeming ubiquity of the voice of the Cuckoo, and dispossesses the creature almost of a corporeal existence; the imagination being tempted to this exertion of her power by a consciousness in the memory that the Cuckoo is almost perpetually heard throughout the season of Spring, but seldom becomes an object of sight.

Thus far of images independent of each other, and immediately endowed by the mind with properties that do not inhere in them, upon an incitement from properties and qualities the existence of which is inherent and obvious. These processes of imagination are carried on either by conferring additional properties upon an object, or abstracting from it some of those which it actually possesses, and thus enabling it to react upon the mind which hath performed the process, like a new existence.

I pass from the Imagination acting upon an individual image to a consideration of the same faculty employed upon images in a conjunction by which they modify each other. The Reader has already had a fine instance before him in the passage quoted from Virgil, where the apparently perilous situation of the Goat, hanging upon the shaggy precipice, is contrasted with that of the Shepherd, contemplating it from the seclusion of the Cavern in which he lies stretched at ease and in security. Take these images separately, and how unaffecting the picture compared with that produced by their being thus connected with, and opposed to, each other!

> 'As a huge Stone is sometimes seen to lie
> Couched on the bald top of an eminence,
> Wonder to all who do the same espy
> By what means it could thither come, and whence;
> So that it seems a thing endued with sense,
> Like a Sea-beast crawled forth, which on a shelf
> Of rock or sand reposeth, there to sun himself.
>
> Such seemed this Man; not all alive or dead,
> Nor all asleep, in his extreme old age.
> Motionless as a cloud the old Man stood,
> That heareth not the loud winds when they call,
> And moveth altogether if it move at all.'

In these images, the conferring, the abstracting, and the modifying powers of the Imagination, immediately and mediately acting, are all brought into conjunction. The Stone is endowed with something of the power of life to approximate it to the Sea-beast; and the Sea-beast stripped of some of its vital qualities to assimilate it to the stone; which intermediate image is thus treated for the purpose of bringing the original image, that of the stone, to a nearer resemblance to the figure and condition of the aged Man; who is divested of so much of the indications of life and motion as to bring him to the point where the two objects unite and coalesce in just comparison. After what has been said, the image of the Cloud need not be commented upon.

Thus far of an endowing or modifying power: but the Imagination also shapes and *creates*; and how? By innumerable processes; and in none does it more delight than in that of consolidating numbers into unity, and dissolving and separating unity into number,—alternations proceeding from, and governed by, a sublime consciousness of the soul in her own mighty and almost divine powers. Recur to the passage already cited from Milton. When the compact Fleet, as one Person, has been introduced 'Sailing from Bengala,' 'They,' i.e. the 'Merchants,' representing the Fleet resolved into a Multitude of Ships, 'ply' their voyage towards the extremities of the earth: 'So' (referring to the word 'As' in the commencement) 'seemed the flying Fiend'; the image of his Person acting to recombine the multitude of Ships into one body,—the point from which the comparison set out. 'So seemed,' and to whom seemed? To the heavenly Muse who dictates the poem, to the eye of the Poet's mind, and to that of the Reader, present at one moment in the wide Ethiopian, and the next in the solitudes, then first broken in upon, of the infernal regions!

> Modo me Thebis, modo ponit Athenis.

Hear again this mighty Poet,—speaking of the Messiah going forth to expel from Heaven the rebellious Angels,

> Attended by ten thousand, thousand Saints
> He onward came: far off his coming shone,—

the retinue of Saints, and the Person of the Messiah himself, lost almost and merged in the splendour of that indefinite abstraction, 'His coming!'

As I do not mean here to treat this subject further than to throw some light upon the present Volumes, and especially upon one division of them, I shall spare myself and the Reader the trouble of considering the Imagination as it deals with thoughts and sentiments, as it regulates the composition of characters, and determines the course of actions: I will not consider it (more than I have already done by implication) as that power which, in the language of one of my most esteemed Friends, 'draws all things to one, which makes things animate or inanimate, beings with their attributes, subjects with their accessaries, take one colour and serve to one effect.'* The grand store-house of enthusiastic and meditative Imagination, of poetical, as contradistinguished from human and dramatic Imagination, is the prophetic and lyrical parts of the holy Scriptures, and the works of Milton, to which I cannot forbear to add those of Spenser. I select these writers in preference to those of ancient Greece and Rome because the anthropomorphitism of the Pagan religion subjected the minds of the greatest poets in those countries too much to the bondage of definite form; from which the Hebrews were preserved by their abhorrence of idolatry. This abhorrence was almost as strong in our great epic Poet, both from circumstances of his life, and from the constitution of his mind. However imbued the surface might be with classical literature, he was a Hebrew in soul; and all things tended in him towards the sublime. Spenser, of a gentler nature, maintained his freedom by aid of his allegorical spirit, at one time inciting him to create persons out of abstractions; and at another, by a superior effort of genius, to give the universality and permanence of abstractions to his human beings, by means of attributes and emblems that belong to the highest

---

* Charles Lamb upon the genius of Hogarth.

moral truths and the purest sensations,—of which his character of Una is a glorious example. Of the human and dramatic Imagination the works of Shakespear are an inexhaustible source.

> 'I tax not you, ye Elements, with unkindness,
> I never gave you Kingdoms, called you Daughters.'

And if, bearing in mind the many Poets distinguished by this prime quality, whose names I omit to mention; yet justified by a recollection of the insults which the Ignorant, the Incapable, and the Presumptuous have heaped upon these and my other writings, I may be permitted to anticipate the judgment of posterity upon myself; I shall declare (censurable, I grant, if the notoriety of the fact above stated does not justify me) that I have given, in these unfavourable times, evidence of exertions of this faculty upon its worthiest objects, the external universe, the moral and religious sentiments of Man, his natural affections, and his acquired passions; which have the same ennobling tendency as the productions of men, in this kind, worthy to be holden in undying remembrance.

I dismiss this subject with observing—that, in the series of Poems placed under the head of Imagination, I have begun with one of the earliest processes of Nature in the development of this faculty. Guided by one of my own primary consciousnesses, I have represented a commutation and transfer of internal feelings, co-operating with external accidents to plant, for immortality, images of sound and sight, in the celestial soil of the Imagination. The Boy, there introduced, is listening, with something of a feverish and restless anxiety, for the recurrence of the riotous sounds which he had previously excited; and, at the moment when the intenseness of his mind is beginning to remit, he is surprised into a perception of the solemn and tranquillizing images which the Poem describes.—The Poems next in succession exhibit the faculty exerting itself upon various objects of the external universe; then follow others, where it is employed upon feelings, characters, and actions; and the Class is concluded with imaginative pictures of moral, political, and religious sentiments.

To the mode in which Fancy has already been characterized as the Power of evoking and combining, or, as my friend Mr. Coleridge has styled it, 'the aggregative and associative Power,' my objection is only that the definition is too general. To aggregate and to associate, to evoke and to combine, belong as well to the Imagination as to the Fancy; but either the materials evoked and combined are different; or they are brought together under a different law, and for a different purpose. Fancy does not require that the materials which she makes use of should be susceptible of change in their constitution, from her touch; and, where they admit of modification, it is enough for her purpose if it be slight, limited, and evanescent. Directly the reverse of these, are the desires and demands of the Imagination. She recoils from every thing but the plastic, the pliant, and the indefinite. She leaves it to Fancy to describe Queen Mab as coming,

> 'In shape no bigger than an agate stone
> On the fore-finger of an Alderman.'

Having to speak of stature, she does not tell you that her gigantic Angel was as tall as Pompey's pillar; much less that he was twelve cubits, or twelve hundred cubits high; or that his dimensions equalled those of Teneriffe or Atlas;—because these, and if they were a million times as high, it would be the same, are bounded: The expression is, 'His stature reached the sky!' the illimitable firmament!—When the Imagination frames a comparison, if it does not strike on the first presentation, a sense of the truth of the likeness, from the moment that it is perceived, grows—and continues to grow—upon the mind; the resemblance depending less upon outline of form and feature than upon expression and effect, less upon casual and outstanding, than upon inherent and internal, properties:—moreover, the images invariably modify each other.—The law under which the processes of Fancy are carried on is as capricious as the accidents of things, and the effects are surprizing, playful, ludicrous, amusing, tender, or pathetic, as the objects happen to be appositely produced or fortunately combined. Fancy depends upon the rapidity and profusion with which she scatters her thoughts and images, trusting that their number, and the felicity with which they are linked together, will make amends for the want of individual value: or she prides herself upon the curious subtilty and the successful elaboration with which she can detect their lurking affinities. If she can win you over to her purpose, and impart to you her feelings, she cares not how unstable or transitory may be her influence, knowing that it will not be out of her power to resume it upon an apt occasion. But the Imagination is conscious of an indestructible dominion;—the Soul may fall away from it, not being able to sustain its grandeur, but, if once felt and acknowledged, by no act of any other faculty of the mind can it be relaxed, impaired, or diminished.—Fancy is given to quicken and to beguile the temporal part of our Nature, Imagination to incite and to support the eternal.—Yet is it not the less true that Fancy, as she is an active, is also, under her own laws and in her own spirit, a creative faculty.

In what manner Fancy ambitiously aims at a rivalship with the Imagination, and Imagination stoops to work with the materials of Fancy, might be illustrated from the compositions of all eloquent writers, whether in prose or verse; and chiefly from those of our own Country. Scarcely a page of the impassioned parts of Bishop Taylor's Works can be opened that shall not afford examples.—Referring the Reader to those inestimable Volumes, I will content myself with placing a conceit (ascribed to Lord Chesterfield) in contrast with a passage from the Paradise Lost;

> 'The dews of the evening most carefully shun,
> They are the tears of the sky for the loss of the Sun.'

After the transgression of Adam, Milton, with other appearances of sympathizing Nature, thus marks the immediate consequence,

> 'Sky lowered, and muttering thunder, some sad drops
> Wept at completion of the mortal sin.'

The associating link is the same in each instance;—dew or rain, not distinguishable from the liquid substance of tears, are employed as indications of sorrow. A flash of surprize is the effect in the former case, a flash of surprize and nothing more; for the nature of things does not sustain the combination. In the latter, the effects of the act, of which there is this immediate consequence and visible sign, are so momentous that the mind acknowledges the justice and reasonableness of the sympathy in Nature so manifested; and the sky weeps drops of water as if with human eyes, as 'Earth had, before, trembled from her entrails, and Nature given a second groan.'

Awe-stricken as I am by contemplating the operations of the mind of this truly divine Poet, I scarcely dare venture to add that 'An address to an Infant,' which the Reader will find under the Class of Fancy in the present Volumes, exhibits something of this communion and interchange of instruments and functions between the two powers; and is, accordingly, placed last in the class, as a preparation for that of Imagination which follows.

Finally, I will refer to Cotton's 'Ode upon Winter,' an admirable composition though stained with some peculiarities of the age in which he lived, for a general illustration of the characteristics of Fancy. The middle part of this ode contains a most lively description of the entrance of Winter, with his retinue, as 'A palsied King,' and yet a military Monarch,—advancing for conquest with his Army; the several bodies of which, and their arms and equipments, are described with a rapidity of detail, and a profusion of *fanciful* comparisons, which indicate on the part of the Poet extreme activity of intellect, and a correspondent hurry of delightful feeling. He retires from the Foe into his fortress, where

> 'a magazine
> Of sovereign juice is cellared in.
> Liquor that will the siege maintain
> Should Phoebus ne'er return again.'

Though myself a water-drinker, I cannot resist the pleasure of transcribing what follows, as an instance still more happy of Fancy employed in the treatment of feeling than, in its preceding passages, the Poem supplies of her management of forms.

> 'Tis that, that gives the Poet rage,
> And thaws the gelly'd blood of Age;
> Matures the Young, restores the Old,
> And makes the fainting Coward bold.

> It lays the careful head to rest,
> Calms palpitations in the breast,
> Renders our lives' misfortune sweet;

> .   .   .   .   .   .

> Then let the chill Scirocco blow,
> And gird us round with hills of snow,
> Or else go whistle to the shore,
> And make the hollow mountains roar.

> Whilst we together jovial sit
> Careless, and crown'd with mirth and wit;
> Where, though bleak winds confine us home,
> Our fancies round the world shall roam.

> We'll think of all the Friends we know,
> And drink to all worth drinking to;
> When having drunk all thine and mine,
> We rather shall want healths than wine.

> But where Friends fail us, we'll supply
> Our friendships with our charity;
> Men that remote in sorrows live,
> Shall by our lusty Brimmers thrive.

We'll drink the Wanting into Wealth,
And those that languish into health,
The Afflicted into joy; th' Opprest
Into security and rest.

The Worthy in disgrace shall find
Favour return again more kind,
And in restraint who stifled lie,
Shall taste the air of liberty.

The Brave shall triumph in success,
The Lovers shall have Mistresses,
Poor unregarded Virtue, praise,
And the neglected Poet, Bays.

Thus shall our healths do others good,
Whilst we ourselves do all we would;
For, freed from envy and from care,
What would we be but what we are?'

It remains that I should express my regret at the necessity of separating my compositions from some beautiful Poems of Mr. Coleridge, with which they have been long associated in publication. The feelings, with which that joint publication was made, have been gratified; its end is answered, and the time is come when considerations of general propriety dictate the separation. Three short pieces, (now first published) are the work of a Female Friend; and the Reader, to whom they may be acceptable, is indebted to me for his pleasure; if any one regard them with dislike, or be disposed to condemn them, let the censure fall upon him, who, trusting in his own sense of their merit and their fitness for the place which they occupy, *extorted* them from the Authoress.

When I sate down to write this preface it was my intention to have made it more comprehensive; but as all that I deem necessary is expressed, I will here detain the reader no longer:—what I have further to remark shall be inserted, by way of interlude, at the close of this Volume.

Essay, Supplementary to the Preface (1815)

By this time, I trust that the judicious Reader, who has now first become acquainted with these poems, is persuaded that a very senseless outcry has been raised against them and their Author.—Casually, and very rarely only, do I see any periodical publication, except a daily newspaper; but I am not wholly unacquainted with the spirit in which my most active and persevering Adversaries have maintained their hostility; nor with the impudent falsehoods and base artifices to which they have had recourse. These, as implying a consciousness on their parts that attacks honestly and fairly conducted would be unavailing, could not but have been regarded by me with triumph; had they been accompanied with such display of talents and information as might give weight to the opinions of the Writers, whether favourable or unfavourable. But the ignorance of those who have chosen to stand forth as my enemies, as far as I am acquainted with their enmity, has unfortunately been still more gross than their disingenuousness, and their incompetence more flagrant than their malice. The effect in the eyes of the discerning is indeed ludicrous; yet, contemptible as such men are, in return for the forced compliment paid me by their long-continued notice (which, as I have appeared so rarely before the public, no one can say has been solicited) I entreat them to spare themselves. The lash, which they are aiming at my productions, does, in fact, only fall on phantoms of their own brain; which, I grant, I am innocently instrumental in raising.—By what fatality the orb of my genius (for genius none of them seem to deny me) acts upon these men like the moon upon a certain description of patients, it would be irksome to inquire; nor would it consist with the respect which I owe myself to take further notice of opponents whom I internally despise.

With the young, of both sexes, Poetry is, like love, a passion; but, for much the greater part of those who have been proud of its power over their minds, a necessity soon arises of breaking the pleasing bondage; or it relaxes of itself;—the thoughts being occupied in domestic cares, or the time engrossed by business. Poetry then becomes only an occasional recreation; while to those whose existence passes away in a course of fashionable pleasure it is a species of luxurious amusement.—In middle and declining age, a scattered number of serious persons resort to poetry, as to religion, for a protection against the pressure of trivial employments, and as a consolation for the afflictions of life. And lastly, there are many, who, having been enamoured of this art, in their youth, have found leisure, after youth was spent, to cultivate general literature; in which poetry has continued to be comprehended *as a study*.

Into the above Classes the Readers of poetry may be divided; Critics abound in them all; but from the last only can opinions be collected of absolute value, and worthy to be depended upon, as prophetic of the destiny of a new work. The young, who in nothing can escape delusion, are especially subject to it in their intercourse with poetry. The cause, not so obvious as the fact is unquestionable, is the same as that from which erroneous judgments in this art, in the minds of men of all ages, chiefly proceed; but upon Youth it operates with peculiar force. The appropriate business of poetry (which, nevertheless, if genuine is as permanent as pure science) her appropriate employment, her privilege and her *duty*, is to treat of things not as they *are*, but as they *appear*; not as they exist in themselves, but as they *seem* to exist to the *senses* and to the *passions*. What a world of delusion does this acknowledged principle prepare for the inexperienced! what temptations to go astray are here held forth for those whose thoughts have been little disciplined by the understanding, and whose feelings revolt from the sway of reason!—When a juvenile Reader is in the height of his rapture with some vicious passage, should experience throw in doubts, or common-sense suggest suspicions, a lurking consciousness that the realities of the Muse are but shows, and that her liveliest excitements are raised by transient shocks of conflicting feeling and successive assemblages of contradictory thoughts—is ever at hand to justify extravagance, and to sanction absurdity. But, it may be asked, as these illusions are unavoidable, and no doubt eminently useful to the mind as a process, what good can be gained by making observations the tendency of which is to diminish the confidence of youth in its feelings, and thus to abridge its innocent and even profitable pleasures? The reproach implied in the question could not be warded off, if Youth were incapable of being delighted with what is truly excellent; or if these errors always terminated of themselves in due season. But, with the majority, though their force be abated, they continue through life. Moreover, the fire of youth is too vivacious an element to be extinguished or damped by a philosophical remark; and, while there is no danger that what has been said will be injurious or painful to the ardent and the confident, it may prove beneficial to those who, being enthusiastic, are, at the same time, modest and ingenuous. The intimation may unite with their own misgivings to regulate their sensibility, and to bring in, sooner than it would otherwise have arrived, a more discreet and sound judgment.

If it should excite wonder that men of ability, in later life, whose understandings have been rendered acute by practice in affairs, should be so easily and so far imposed upon when they happen to take up a new work in verse, this appears to be the cause;—that, having discontinued their attention to poetry, whatever progress may have been made in other departments of knowledge, they have not, as to this art, advanced in true discernment beyond the age of youth. If then a new poem falls in their way, whose attractions are of that kind which would have enraptured them during the heat of youth, the judgment not being improved to a degree that they shall be disgusted, they are dazzled; and prize and cherish the faults for having had power to make the present time vanish before them, and to throw the mind back, as by enchantment, into the happiest season of life. As they read, powers seem to be revived, passions are regenerated, and pleasures restored. The Book was probably taken up after an escape from the burthen of business, and with a wish to forget the world, and all its vexations and anxieties. Having obtained this wish, and so much more, it is natural that they should make report as they have felt.

If Men of mature age, through want of practice, be thus easily beguiled into admiration of absurdities, extravagances, and misplaced ornaments, thinking it proper that their understandings should enjoy a holiday, while they are unbending their minds with verse, it may be expected that such Readers will resemble their former selves also in strength of prejudice, and an inaptitude to be moved by the unostentatious beauties of a pure style. In the higher poetry, an enlightened Critic chiefly looks for a reflexion of the wisdom of the heart and the grandeur of the imagination. Wherever these appear, simplicity accompanies them; Magnificence herself, when legitimate, depending upon a simplicity of her own, to regulate her ornaments. But it is a well known property of human nature that our estimates are ever governed by comparisons, of which we are conscious with various degrees of distinctness. Is it not, then, inevitable (confining these observations to the effects of style merely) that an eye, accustomed to the glaring hues of diction by which such Readers are caught and excited, will for the most part be rather repelled than attracted by an original Work the coloring of which is disposed according to a pure and refined scheme of harmony? It is in the fine arts as in the affairs of life, no man can *serve* (i.e. obey with zeal and fidelity) two Masters.

As Poetry is most just to its own divine origin when it administers the comforts and breathes the spirit of religion, they who have learned to perceive this truth, and who betake themselves to reading verse for sacred purposes, must be preserved from numerous illusions to which the two Classes of Readers, whom we have been considering, are liable. But, as the mind grows serious from the weight of life, the range of its passions is contracted accordingly; and its sympathies become so exclusive that many species of high excellence wholly escape, or but languidly excite, its notice. Besides, Men who read from religious or moral inclinations, even when the subject is of that kind which they approve, are beset with misconceptions and mistakes peculiar to themselves. Attaching so much importance to the truths which interest them, they are prone to overrate the Authors by whom these truths are expressed and enforced. They come prepared to impart so much passion to the Poet's language, that they remain unconscious how little, in fact, they receive from it. And, on the other hand, religious faith is to him who holds it so momentous a thing, and error appears to be attended with such tremendous consequences, that, if opinions touching upon religion occur which the Reader condemns, he not only cannot sympathize with them however animated the expression, but there is, for the most part, an end put to all satisfaction and enjoyment. Love, if it before existed, is converted into dislike; and the heart of the Reader is set against the Author and his book.—To these excesses, they, who from their professions ought to be the most guarded against them, are perhaps the most liable; I mean those sects whose religion, being from the calculating understanding, is cold and formal. For when Christianity, the religion of humility, is founded upon the proudest quality of our nature, what can be expected but contradictions? Accordingly, believers of this cast are at one time contemptuous; at another, being troubled as they are and must be with inward misgivings, they are jealous and suspicious;—and at all seasons, they are under temptation to supply, by the heat with which they defend their tenets, the animation which is wanting to the constitution of the religion itself.

Faith was given to man that his affections, detached from the treasures of time, might be inclined to settle upon those of eternity:—the elevation of his nature, which this habit produces on earth, being to him a presumptive evidence of a future state of existence; and giving him a title to partake of its holiness. The religious man values what he sees chiefly as an 'imperfect shadowing forth' of what he is incapable of seeing. The concerns of religion refer to indefinite objects, and are too weighty for the mind to support them without relieving itself by resting a great part of the burthen upon words and symbols. The commerce between Man and his Maker cannot be carried on but by a process where much is represented in little, and the infinite Being accommodates himself to a finite capacity. In all this may be perceived the affinities between religion and poetry;—between religion—making up the deficiencies of reason by faith, and poetry—passionate for the instruction of reason; between religion—whose element is infinitude, and whose ultimate trust is the supreme of things, submitting herself to circumscription and reconciled to substitutions; and poetry—etherial and transcendant, yet incapable to sustain her existence without sensuous incarnation. In this community of nature may be perceived also the lurking incitements of kindred error;—so that we shall find that no poetry has been more subject to distortion, than that species the argument and scope of which is religious; and no lovers of the art have gone further astray than the pious and the devout.

Whither then shall we turn for that union of qualifications which must necessarily exist before the decisions of a critic can be of absolute value? For a mind at once poetical and philosophical; for a critic whose affections are as free and kindly as the spirit of society, and whose understanding is severe as that of dispassionate government? Where are we to look for that initiatory composure of mind which no selfishness can disturb? For a natural sensibility that has been tutored into correctness without losing any thing of its quickness; and for active faculties capable of answering the demands which an Author of original imagination shall make upon them,—associated with a judgment that cannot be duped into admiration by aught that is unworthy of it?—Among those and those only, who, never having suffered their youthful love of poetry to remit much of its force, have applied, to the consideration of the laws of this art, the best power of their understandings. At the same time it must be observed—that, as this Class comprehends the only judgments which are trust-worthy, so does it include the most erroneous and perverse. For to be mis-taught is worse than to be untaught; and no perverseness equals that which is supported by system, no errors are so difficult to root out as those which the understanding has pledged its credit to uphold. In this Class are contained Censors, who, if they be pleased with what is good, are pleased with it only by imperfect glimpses, and upon false principles; who, should they generalize rightly to a certain point, are sure to suffer for it in the end;—who, if they stumble upon a sound rule, are fettered by misapplying it, or by straining it too far; being incapable of perceiving when it ought to yield to one of higher order. In it are found Critics too petulant to be passive to a genuine Poet, and too feeble to grapple with him; Men, who take upon them to report of the course which *he* holds whom they are utterly unable to accompany,— confounded if he turn quick upon the wing, dismayed if he soar steadily into 'the region';—Men of palsied imaginations and indurated hearts;

in whose minds all healthy action is languid,—who, therefore, feed as the many direct them, or with the many, are greedy after vicious provocatives;—Judges, whose censure is auspicious, and whose praise ominous! In this Class meet together the two extremes of best and worst.

The observations presented in the foregoing series, are of too ungracious a nature to have been made without reluctance; and were it only on this account I would invite the Reader to try them by the test of comprehensive experience. If the number of judges who can be confidently relied upon be in reality so small, it ought to follow that partial notice only, or neglect, perhaps long continued, or attention wholly inadequate to their merits—must have been the fate of most works in the higher departments of poetry; and that, on the other hand, numerous productions have blazed into popularity, and have passed away, leaving scarcely a trace behind them:—it will be, further, found that when Authors have at length raised themselves into general admiration and maintained their ground, errors and prejudices have prevailed concerning their genius and their works, which the few who are conscious of those errors and prejudices would deplore; if they were not recompensed by perceiving that there are select Spirits for whom it is ordained that their fame shall be in the world an existence like that of Virtue, which owes its being to the struggles it makes, and its vigour to the enemies whom it provokes;—a vivacious quality ever doomed to meet with opposition, and still triumphing over it; and, from the nature of its dominion, incapable of being brought to the sad conclusion of Alexander, when he wept that there were no more worlds for him to conquer.

Let us take a hasty retrospect of the poetical literature of this Country for the greater part of the last two Centuries, and see if the facts correspond with these inferences.

Who is there that can now endure to read the 'Creation' of Dubartas? Yet all Europe once resounded with his praise; he was caressed by Kings; and, when his Poem was translated into our language, the Faery Queen faded before it. The name of Spenser, whose genius is of a higher order than even that of Ariosto, is at this day scarcely known beyond the limits of the British Isles. And, if the value of his works is to be estimated from the attention now paid to them by his Countrymen, compared with that which they bestow on those of other writers, it must be pronounced small indeed.

'The laurel, meed of mighty Conquerors
And Poets *sage*'—

are his own words; but his wisdom has, in this particular, been his worst enemy; while, its opposite, whether in the shape of folly or madness, has been their best friend. But he was a great power; and bears a high name: the laurel has been awarded to him.

A Dramatic Author, if he write for the Stage, must adapt himself to the taste of the Audience, or they will not endure him; accordingly the mighty genius of Shakespeare was listened to. The People were delighted; but I am not sufficiently versed in Stage antiquities to determine whether they did not flock as eagerly to the representation of many pieces of contemporary Authors, wholly undeserving to appear upon the same boards. Had there been a formal contest for superiority among dramatic Writers, that Shakespeare, like his predecessors Sophocles and Euripides, would have often been subject to the mortification of seeing the prize adjudged to sorry competitors, becomes too probable when we reflect that the Admirers of Settle and Shadwell were, in a later age, as numerous, and reckoned as respectable in point of talent as those of Dryden. At all events, that Shakespeare stooped to accommodate himself to the People, is sufficiently apparent; and one of the most striking proofs of his almost omnipotent genius, is, that he could turn to such glorious purpose those materials which the prepossessions of the age compelled him to make use of. Yet even this marvellous skill appears not to have been enough to prevent his rivals from having some advantage over him in public estimation; else how can we account for passages and scenes that exist in his works, unless upon a supposition that some of the grossest of them, a fact which in my own mind I have no doubt of, were foisted in by the Players, for the gratification of the many?

But that his Works, whatever might be their reception upon the stage, made little impression upon the ruling Intellects of the time, may be inferred from the fact that Lord Bacon, in his multifarious writings, no where either quotes or alludes to him.* His dramatic excellence enabled him to resume possession of the stage after the Restoration; but Dryden tells us that in his time two of Beaumont's and Fletcher's Plays was acted for one of Shakespeare's. And so faint and limited was the perception of the poetic beauties of his dramas in the time of Pope, that, in his Edition of the Plays, with a view of rendering to the general Reader a necessary service, he printed between inverted commas those passages which he thought most worthy of notice.

* The learned Hakewill (a 3d edition of whose book bears date 1635) writing to refute the error 'touching Nature's perpetual and universal decay', cites triumphantly the names of Ariosto, Tasso, Bartas, and Spenser, as instances that poetic genius had not degenerated; but he makes no mention of Shakespeare.

At this day, the French Critics have abated nothing of their aversion to this darling of our Nation: 'the English with their Buffon de Shakespeare' is as familiar an expression among them as in the time of Voltaire. Baron Grimm is the only French writer who seems to have perceived his infinite superiority to the first names of the French Theatre; an advantage which the Parisian Critic owed to his German blood and German education. The most enlightened Italians, though well acquainted with our language, are wholly incompetent to measure the proportions of Shakespeare. The Germans only, of foreign nations, are approaching towards a knowledge and feeling of what he is. In some respects they have acquired a superiority over the fellow-countrymen of the Poet; for among us it is a current, I might say, an established opinion that Shakespeare is justly praised when he is pronounced to be 'a wild irregular genius, in whom great faults are compensated by great beauties.' How long may it be before this misconception passes away, and it becomes universally acknowledged that the judgment of Shakespeare in the selection of his materials, and in the manner in which he has made them, heterogeneous as they often are, constitute a unity of their own, and contribute all to one great end, is not less admirable than his imagination, his invention, and his intuitive knowledge of human Nature!

There is extant a small Volume of miscellaneous Poems in which Shakespeare expresses his own feelings in his own Person. It is not difficult to conceive that the Editor, George Stevens, should have been insensible to the beauties of one portion of that Volume, the Sonnets; though there is not a part of the writings of this Poet where is found in an equal compass a greater number of exquisite feelings felicitously expressed. But, from regard to the Critic's own credit, he would not have ventured to talk of an* act of parliament not being strong enough to compel the perusal of these, or any production of Shakespeare, if he had not known that the people of England were ignorant of the treasures contained in those little pieces; and if he had not, moreover, shared the too common propensity of human nature to exult over a supposed fall into the mire of a genius whom he had been compelled to regard with admiration, as an inmate of the celestial regions,—'there sitting where he durst not soar.'

---

* This flippant insensibility was publicly reprehended by Mr. Coleridge in a course of Lectures upon Poetry given by him at the Royal Institution. For the various merits of thought and language in Shakespeare's Sonnets see Numbers 27, 29 , 30, 32, 33, 54, 64, 66, 68, 73, 76, 86, 91, 92, 93, 97, 98, 105, 107, 108, 109, 111, 113, 114, 116, 117, 129, and many others.

Nine years before the death of Shakespeare, Milton was born; and early in life he published several small poems, which, though on their first appearance they were praised by a few of the judicious, were afterwards neglected to that degree that Pope, in his youth, could pilfer from them without danger of detection.—Whether these poems are at this day justly appreciated I will not undertake to decide: nor would it imply a severe reflection upon the mass of Readers to suppose the contrary; seeing that a Man of the acknowledged genius of Voss, the German Poet, could suffer their spirit to evaporate; and could change their character, as is done in the translation made by him of the most popular of those pieces. At all events it is certain that these Poems of Milton are now much read, and loudly praised; yet were they little heard of till more than 150 years after their publication; and of the Sonnets, Dr. Johnson, as appears from Boswell's Life of him, was in the habit of thinking and speaking as contemptuously as Stevens wrote upon those of Shakespeare.

About the time when the Pindaric Odes of Cowley and his imitators, and the productions of that class of curious thinkers whom Dr. Johnson has strangely styled Metaphysical Poets, were beginning to lose something of that extravagant admiration which they had excited, the Paradise Lost made its appearance. 'Fit audience find though few,' was the petition addressed by the Poet to his inspiring Muse. I have said elsewhere that he gained more than he asked; this I believe to be true; but Dr. Johnson has fallen into a gross mistake when he attempts to prove, by the sale of the work, that Milton's Countrymen were '*just* to it' upon its first appearance. Thirteen hundred Copies were sold in two years; an uncommon example, he asserts, of the prevalence of genius in opposition to so much recent enmity as Milton's public conduct had excited. But be it remembered that, if Milton's political and religious opinions, and the manner in which he announced them, had raised him many enemies, they had procured him numerous friends; who, as all personal danger was passed away at the time of publication, would be eager to produce the master-work of a Man whom they revered, and whom they would be proud of praising. The demand did not immediately increase; 'for,' says Dr. Johnson, 'many more Readers' (he means Persons in the habit of reading poetry) 'than were supplied at first the Nation did not afford.' How careless must a writer be who can make this assertion in the face of so many existing title pages to belie it! Turning to my own shelves, I find the folio of Cowley, 7th Edition, 1681. A book near it is Flatman's Poems, 4th Edition, 1686; Waller, 5th Edition, same date. The poems of Norris of Bemerton not long after went, I believe, through nine Editions. What further demand there might be for these works I do not know, but I well remember, that 25 Years ago, the Booksellers' stalls in London swarmed with the folios of Cowley. This is not mentioned in disparagement of that able writer and amiable Man; but merely to shew—that, if Milton's work was not more read, it was not because readers did not exist at the time. Only 3000 copies of the Paradise Lost sold in 11 Years; and the Nation, says Dr. Johnson, had been satisfied from 1623 to 1644, that is 41 Years, with only two Editions of the Works of Shakespeare; which probably did not together make 1000 Copies; facts adduced by the critic to prove the 'paucity of Readers'—There were Readers in multitudes; but their money went for other purposes, as their admiration was fixed elsewhere. We are authorized, then, to affirm that the reception of the Paradise Lost, and the slow progress of its fame, are proofs as striking as can be desired that the positions which I am attempting to establish are not erroneous.—* How amusing to shape to one's self such a critique as a Wit of Charles's days, or a Lord of the Miscellanies, or trading Journalist, of King William's time, would have brought forth, if he had set his faculties industriously to work upon this Poem, everywhere impregnated with *original* excellence!

So strange indeed are the obliquities of admiration, that they whose opinions are much influenced by authority will often be tempted to think that there are no fixed principles in human nature for this art to rest upon.† I have been honoured by being permitted to peruse in MS. a tract composed between the period of the Revolution and the close of that Century. It is the Work of an English Peer of high accomplishments, its object to form the character and direct the studies of his Son. Perhaps no where does a more beautiful treatise of the kind exist. The good sense and wisdom of the thoughts, the delicacy of the feelings, and the charm of the style, are, throughout, equally conspicuous. Yet the Author, selecting among the Poets of his own Country those whom he deems most worthy of his son's perusal, particularizes only Lord Rochester, Sir John Denham, and Cowley. Writing about the same time, Shaftesbury, an Author at present unjustly depreciated, describes the English Muses as only yet lisping in their Cradles.

---

* Hughes is express upon this subject; in his dedication of Spenser's Works to Lord Somers he writes thus. 'It was your Lordship's encouraging a beautiful Edition of Paradise Lost that first brought that incomparable Poem to be generally known and esteemed.'

† This opinion seems actually to have been entertained by Adam Smith, the worst critic, David Hume not excepted, that Scotland, a soil to which this sort of weed seems natural, has produced.

The arts by which Pope, soon afterwards, contrived to procure to himself a more general and higher reputation than perhaps any English Poet ever attained during his life-time, are known to the judicious. And as well known is it to them, that the undue exertion of these arts, is the cause why Pope has for some time held a rank in literature, to which, if he had not been seduced by an over-love of immediate popularity, and had confided more in his native genius, he never could have descended. He bewitched the nation by his melody, and dazzled it by his polished style, and was himself blinded by his own success. Having wandered from humanity in his Eclogues with boyish inexperience, the praise, which these compositions obtained, tempted him into a belief that nature was not to be trusted, at least in pastoral Poetry. To prove this by example, he put his friend Gay upon writing those Eclogues which the Author intended to be burlesque. The Instigator of the work, and his Admirers, could perceive in them nothing but what was ridiculous. Nevertheless, though these Poems contain some odious and even detestable passages, the effect, as Dr. Johnson well observes, 'of reality and truth became conspicuous even when the intention was to shew them grovelling and degrading.' These Pastorals, ludicrous to those who prided themselves upon their refinement, in spite of those disgusting passages 'became popular, and were read with delight as just representations of rural manners and occupations.'

Something less than 60 years after the publication of the Paradise Lost appeared Thomson's Winter; which was speedily followed by his other Seasons. It is a work of inspiration; much of it is written from himself, and nobly from himself. How was it received? 'It was no sooner read,' says one of his contemporary Biographers, 'than universally admired: those only excepted who had not been used to feel, or to look for any thing in poetry, beyond a *point* of satirical or epigrammatic wit, a smart *antithesis* richly trimmed with rhyme, or the softness of an *elegiac* complaint. To such his manly classical spirit could not readily commend itself; till, after a more attentive perusal, they had got the better of their prejudices, and either acquired or affected a truer taste. A few others stood aloof, merely because they had long before fixed the articles of their poetical creed, and resigned themselves to an absolute despair of ever seeing any thing new and original. These were somewhat mortified to find their notions disturbed by the appearance of a poet, who seemed to owe nothing but to nature and his own genius. But, in a short time, the applause became unanimous; every one wondering how so many pictures, and pictures so familiar, should have moved them but faintly to what they felt in his descriptions. His digressions too, the overflow-ings of a tender benevolent heart, charmed the reader no less; leaving him in doubt, whether he should more admire the Poet or love the Man.'

This case appears to bear strongly against us:—but we must distinguish between wonder and legitimate admiration. The subject of the work is the changes produced in the appearances of nature by the revolution of the year: and, by undertaking to write in verse, Thomson pledged himself to treat his subject as became a Poet. Now it is remarkable that, excerpting a passage or two in the Windsor Forest of Pope, and some delightful pictures in the Poems of Lady Winchelsea, the Poetry of the period intervening between the publication of the Paradise Lost and the Seasons does not contain a single new image of external nature; and scarcely presents a familiar one from which it can be inferred that the eye of the Poet had been steadily fixed upon his object, much less that his feelings had urged him to work upon it in the spirit of genuine imagination. To what a low state knowledge of the most obvious and important phenomena had sunk, is evident from the style in which Dryden has executed a description of Night in one of his Tragedies, and Pope his translation of the celebrated moon-light scene in the Iliad. A blind man, in the habit of attending accurately to descriptions casually dropped from the lips of those around him, might easily depict these appearances with more truth. Dryden's lines are vague, bombastic, and senseless;* those of Pope, though he had Homer to guide him, are throughout false and contradictory. The verses of Dryden, once highly celebrated, are forgotten; those of Pope still retain their hold upon public estimation,—nay, there is not a passage of descriptive poetry, which at this day finds so many and such ardent admirers. Strange to think of an Enthusiast, as may have been the case with thousands, reciting those verses under the cope of a moon-light sky, without having his raptures in the least disturbed by a suspicion of their absurdity. —If these two distinguished Writers could habitually think that the visible universe was of so little consequence to a Poet, that it was

---

*   CORTES *alone, in a night-gown.*

All things are hush'd as Nature's self lay dead:
The mountains seem to nod their drowsy head:
The little Birds in dreams their songs repeat,
And sleeping Flowers beneath the Night-dew sweat:
Even Lust and Envy sleep; yet Love denies
Rest to my soul, and slumber to my eyes.

Dryden's Indian Emperor

scarcely necessary for him to cast his eyes upon it, we may be assured that those passages of the elder Poets which faithfully and poetically describe the phenomena of nature, were not at that time holden in much estimation, and that there was little accurate attention paid to these appearances.

Wonder is the natural produce of Ignorance; and as the soil was *in such good condition* at the time of the publication of the Seasons, the crop was doubtless abundant. Neither individuals nor nations become corrupt all at once, nor are they enlightened in a moment. Thomson was an inspired Poet, but he could not work miracles; in cases where the art of seeing had in some degree been learned, the teacher would further the proficiency of his pupils, but he could do little *more*, though so far does vanity assist men in acts of self-deception that many would often fancy they recognized a likeness when they knew nothing of the original. Having shewn that much of what his Biographer deemed genuine admiration must in fact have been blind wonderment,—how is the rest to be accounted for?—Thomson was fortunate in the very title of his Poem, which seemed to bring it home to the prepared sympathies of every one: in the next place, notwithstanding his high powers, he writes a vicious style; and his false ornaments are exactly of that kind which would be most likely to strike the undiscerning. He likewise abounds with sentimental common-places, that from the manner in which they were brought forward bore an imposing air of novelty. In any well-used Copy of the Seasons the Book generally opens of itself with the rhapsody on love, or with one of the stories, (perhaps Damon and Musidora); these also are prominent in our Collections of Extracts; and are the parts of his Works which, after all, were probably most efficient in first recommending the Author to general notice. Pope, repaying praises which he had received, and wishing to extol him to the highest, only styles him 'an elegant and philosophical Poet'; nor are we able to collect any unquestionable proofs that the true characteristics of Thomson's genius as an imaginative Poet were perceived, till the elder Warton, almost 40 Years after the publication of the Seasons, pointed them out by a note in his Essay on the life and writings of Pope. In the Castle of Indolence (of which Gray speaks so coldly) these characteristics were almost as conspicuously displayed, and in verse more harmonious and diction more pure. Yet that fine Poem was neglected on its appearance, and is at this day the delight only of a Few!

When Thomson died, Collins breathed his regrets into an Elegiac Poem, in which he pronounces a poetical curse upon *him* who should regard with insensibility the place where the Poet's remains were deposited. The Poems of the mourner himself have now passed through innumerable Editions, and are universally known; but if, when Collins died, the same kind of imprecation had been pronounced by a surviving admirer, small is the number whom it would not have comprehended. The notice which his poems attained during his life-time was so small, and of course the sale so insignificant, that not long before his death he deemed it right to repay to the Bookseller the sum which he had advanced for them, and threw the Edition into the fire.

Next in importance to the Seasons of Thomson, though at considerable distance from that work in order of time, come the Reliques of Ancient English Poetry; collected, new-modelled, and in many instances (if such a contradiction in terms may be used) composed, by the editor, Dr. Percy. This Work did not steal silently into the world, as is evident from the number of legendary tales, which appeared not long after its publication; and which were modelled, as the Authors persuaded themselves, after the old Ballad. The Compilation was however ill-suited to the then existing taste of City society; and Dr. Johnson, mid the little senate to which he gave laws, was not sparing in his exertions to make it an object of contempt. The Critic triumphed, the legendary imitators were deservedly disregarded, and, as undeservedly, their ill-imitated models sank, in this Country, into temporary neglect; while Burger, and other able Writers of Germany, were translating, or imitating, these Reliques, and composing, with the aid of inspiration thence derived, Poems, which are the delight of the German nation. Dr. Percy was so abashed by the ridicule flung upon his labours from the ignorance and insensibility of the Persons with whom he lived, that, though while he was writing under a mask he had not wanted resolution to follow his genius into the regions of true simplicity and genuine pathos, (as is evinced by the exquisite ballad of Sir Cauline and by many other pieces) yet, when he appeared in his own person and character as a poetical writer, he adopted, as in the tale of the Hermit of Warkworth, a diction scarcely in any one of its features distinguishable from the vague, the glossy, and unfeeling language of his day. I mention this remarkable fact with regret, esteeming the genius of Dr. Percy in this kind of writing superior to that of any other man by whom, in modern times, it has been cultivated. That even Burger, (to whom Klopstock gave, in my hearing, a commendation which he denied to Goethe and Schiller, pronouncing him to be a genuine Poet, and one of the few among the Germans whose works would last) had not the fine sensibility of Percy, might be shewn from many passages, in which he has deserted his original only to go astray.

For example,

> Now daye was gone, and night was come,
> And all were fast asleepe,
> All, save the Lady Emmeline,
> Who sate in her bowre to weepe:
>
> And soone shee heard her true Love's voice
> Low whispering at the walle,
> Awake, awake, my deare Ladye,
> 'Tis I thy true-love call.

Which is thus tricked out and dilated,

> Als nun die Nacht Gebirg' und Thal
> Vermummt in Rabenschatten,
> Und Hochburgs Lampen über-all
> Schon ausgeflimmert hatten,
> Und alles tief entschlafen war;
> Doch nur das Fraulein immerdar,
> Voll Fieberangst, noch wachte,
> Und seinen Ritter dachte:
> Da horch! Ein süsser Liebeston
> Kam leis empor geflogen.
> 'Ho, Trudchen, ho! Da bin ich schon!
> Frisch auf! Dich angezogen!'

But from humble ballads we must ascend to heroics.

All hail Macpherson! hail to thee, Sire of Ossian! The Phantom was begotten by the snug embrace of an impudent Highlander upon a cloud of tradition—it travelled southward, where it was greeted with acclamation, and the thin Consistence took its course through Europe, upon the breath of popular applause. The Editor of the 'Reliques' had indirectly preferred a claim to the praise of invention by not concealing that his supplementary labours were considerable: how selfish his conduct contrasted with that of the disinterested Gael, who, like Lear, gives his kingdom away, and is content to become a pensioner upon his own issue for a beggarly pittance!—Open this far-famed Book!—I have done so at random, and the beginning of the 'Epic Poem Temora,' in 8 Books, presents itself. 'The blue waves of Ullin roll in light. The green hills are covered with day. Trees shake their dusky heads in the breeze. Grey torrents pour their noisy streams. Two green hills with aged oak surround a narrow plain. The blue course of a stream is there. On its banks stood Cairbar of Atha. His spear supports the king; the red eyes of his fear are sad. Cormac rises on his soul with all his ghastly wounds.'

Precious memorandums from the pocket-book of the blind Ossian!

If it be unbecoming, as I acknowledge that for the most part it is, to speak disrespectfully of Works that have enjoyed for a length of time a widely spread reputation, without at the same time producing irrefragable proofs of their unworthiness, let me be forgiven upon this occasion.—Having had the good fortune to be born and reared in a mountainous Country, from my very childhood I have felt the falsehood that pervades the volumes imposed upon the World under the name of Ossian. From what I saw with my own eyes, I knew that the imagery was spurious. In nature every thing is distinct, yet nothing defined into absolute independent singleness. In Macpherson's work it is exactly the reverse; every thing (that is not stolen) is in this manner defined, insulated, dislocated, deadened,—yet nothing distinct. It will always be so when words are substituted for things. To say that the characters never could exist, that the manners are impossible, and that a dream has more substance than the whole state of society, as there depicted, is doing nothing more than pronouncing a censure which Macpherson defied; when, with the steeps of Morven before his eyes, he could talk so familiarly of his Car-borne heroes;—Of Morven, which, if one may judge from its appearance at the distance of a few miles, contains scarcely an acre of ground sufficiently accommodating for a sledge to be trailed along its surface.—Mr. Malcolm Laing has ably shewn that the diction of this pretended translation is a motley assembly from all quarters; but he is so fond of making out parallel passages as to call poor Macpherson to account for his very 'ands' and his 'buts!' and he has weakened his argument by conducting it as if he thought that every striking resemblance was a *conscious* plagiarism. It is enough that the coincidences are too remarkable for its being probable or possible that they could arise in different minds without communication between them. Now as the Translators of the Bible, Shakespeare, Milton, and Pope, could not be indebted to Macpherson, it follows that he must have owed his fine feathers to them; unless we are prepared gravely to assert, with Madame de Stael, that many of the characteristic beauties of our most celebrated English Poets, are derived from the ancient Fingallian; in which case the modern translator would have been but giving back to Ossian his own.—It is consistent that Lucien Buonaparte, who could censure Milton for having surrounded Satan in the infernal regions with courtly and regal splendour, should pronounce the modern Ossian to be the glory of Scotland;—a Country that has produced a Dunbar, a Buchanan, a Thomson, and a Burns! These opinions are of ill omen for the Epic ambition of him who has given them to the world.

Yet, much as these pretended treasures of antiquity have been admired, they have been wholly uninfluential upon the literature of the Country. No succeeding Writer appears to have caught from them a ray of inspiration; no Author in the least distinguished, has ventured formally to imitate them—except the Boy, Chatterton, on their first appearance. He had perceived, from the successful trials which he himself had made in literary forgery, how few critics were able to distinguish between a real ancient medal and a counterfeit of modern manufacture; and he set himself to the work of filling a Magazine with *Saxon poems*,—counterparts of those of Ossian, as like his as one of his misty stars is to another. This incapability to amalgamate with the literature of the Island, is, in my estimation, a decisive proof that the book is essentially unnatural; nor should I require any other to demonstrate it to be a forgery, audacious as worthless.—Contrast, in this respect, the effect of Macpherson's publication with the Reliques of Percy, so unassuming, so modest in their pretensions!—I have already stated how much Germany is indebted to this latter work; and for our own Country, its Poetry has been absolutely redeemed by it. I do not think that there is an able Writer in verse of the present day who would not be proud to acknowledge his obligations to the Reliques; I know that it is so with my friends; and, for myself, I am happy in this occasion to make a public avowal of my own.

Dr. Johnson, more fortunate in his contempt of the labours of Macpherson than those of his modest friend, was solicited not long after to furnish Prefaces biographical and critical for some of the most eminent English Poets. The Booksellers took upon themselves to make the collection; they referred probably to the most popular miscellanies, and, unquestionably, to their Books of accounts; and decided upon the claim of Authors to be admitted into a body of the most Eminent, from the familiarity of their names with the readers of that day, and by the profits, which, from the sale of his works, each had brought and was bringing to the Trade. The Editor was allowed a limited exercise of discretion, and the Authors whom he recommended are scarcely to be mentioned without a smile. We open the volume of Prefatory Lives, and to our astonishment the *first* name we find is that of Cowley!—What is become of the Morning-star of English Poetry? Where is the bright Elizabethan Constellation? Or, if Names are more acceptable than images, where is the ever-to-be-honoured Chaucer? where is Spenser? where is Sydney? and lastly where he, whose rights as a Poet, contradistinguished from those which he is universally allowed to possess as a Dramatist, we have vindicated, where Shakespeare?—

These, and a multitude of others not unworthy to be placed near them, their contemporaries and successors, we have *not*. But in their stead, we have (could better be expected when precedence was to be settled by an abstract of reputation at any given period made as in the case before us?) we have Roscommon, and Stepney, and Phillips, and Walsh, and Smith, and Duke, and King, and Spratt—Halifax, Granville, Sheffield, Congreve, Broome, and other reputed Magnates; Writers in metre utterly worthless and useless, except for occasions like the present, when their productions are referred to as evidence what a small quantity of brain is necessary to procure a considerable stock of admiration, provided the aspirant will accommodate himself to the likings and fashions of his day.

As I do not mean to bring down this retrospect to our own times, it may with propriety be closed at the era of this distinguished event. From the literature of other ages and countries, proofs equally cogent might have been adduced that the opinions announced in the former part of this Essay are founded upon truth. It was not an agreeable office, not a prudent undertaking, to declare them, but their importance seemed to render it a duty. It may still be asked, where lies the particular relation of what has been said to these Volumes?—The question will be easily answered by the discerning Reader who is old enough to remember the taste that was prevalent when some of these Poems were first published, 17 years ago; who has also observed to what degree the Poetry of this Island has since that period been coloured by them; and who is further aware of the unremitting hostility with which, upon some principle or other, they have each and all been opposed. A sketch of my own notion of the constitution of Fame, has been given; and, as far as concerns myself, I have cause to be satisfied. The love, the admiration, the indifference, the slight, the aversion, and even the contempt, with which these Poems have been received, knowing, as I do, the source within my own mind, from which they have proceeded, and the labour and pains, which, when labour and pains appeared needful, have been bestowed upon them,—must all, if I think consistently, be received as pledges and tokens, bearing the same general impression though widely different in value;—they are all proofs that for the present time I have not laboured in vain; and afford assurances, more or less authentic, that the products of my industry will endure.

If there be one conclusion more forcibly pressed upon us than another by the review which has been given of the fortunes and fate of Poetical Works, it is this,—that every Author, as far as he is great and at the same time *original*, has had the task of *creating* the taste by which he is to be enjoyed: so has it been, so will it continue to be. This remark was long since made to me by the philosophical Friend for the separation of whose Poems from my own I have previously expressed my regret. The predecessors of an original Genius of a high order will have smoothed the way for all that he has in common with them;—and much he will have in common; but, for what is peculiarly his own, he will be called upon to clear and often to shape his own road:—he will be in the condition of Hannibal among the Alps.

And where lies the real difficulty of creating that taste by which a truly original Poet is to be relished? Is it in breaking the bonds of custom, in overcoming the prejudices of false refinement, and displacing the aversions of inexperience? Or, if he labour for an object which here and elsewhere I have proposed to myself, does it consist in divesting the Reader of the pride that induces him to dwell upon those points wherein Men differ from each other, to the exclusion of those in which all Men are alike, or the same; and in making him ashamed of the vanity that renders him insensible of the appropriate excellence which civil arrangements, less unjust than might appear, and Nature illimitable in her bounty, have conferred on Men who stand below him in the scale of society? Finally, does it lie in establishing that dominion over the spirits of Readers by which they are to be humbled and humanized, in order that they may be purified and exalted?

If these ends are to be attained by the mere communication of *knowledge*, it does *not* lie here.—TASTE, I would remind the Reader, like IMAGINATION, is a word which has been forced to extend its services far beyond the point to which philosophy would have confined them. It is a metaphor, taken from a *passive* sense of the human body, and transferred to things which are in their essence *not* passive,—to intellectual *acts* and *operations*. The word, imagination, has been overstrained, from impulses honourable to mankind, to meet the demands of the faculty which is perhaps the noblest of our nature. In the instance of taste, the process has been reversed; and from the prevalence of dispositions at once injurious and discreditable,—being no other than that selfishness which is the child of apathy,—which, as Nations decline in productive and creative power, makes them value themselves upon a presumed refinement of judging. Povery of language is the primary cause of the use which we make of the word, imagination; but the word, Taste, has been stretched to the sense which it bears in modern Europe by habits of self-conceit, inducing that inversion in the order of things whereby a passive faculty is made paramount among the faculties conversant with the fine arts. Proportion and congruity, the requisite knowledge being supposed, are subjects upon which taste may be trusted; it is competent to this office;—for in its intercourse with these the mind is *passive*, and is affected painfully or pleasurably as by an instinct. But the profound and the exquisite in feeling, the lofty and universal in thought and imagination; or in ordinary language the pathetic and the sublime;—are neither of them, accurately speaking, objects of a faculty which could ever without a sinking in the spirit of Nations have been designated by the metaphor—*Taste*. And why? Because without the exertion of a co-operating *power* in the mind of the Reader, there can be no adequate sympathy with either of these emotions: without this auxiliar impulse elevated or profound passion cannot exist.

Passion, it must be observed, is derived from a word which signifies, *suffering*; but the connection which suffering has with effort, with exertion, and *action*, is immediate and inseparable. How strikingly is this property of human nature exhibited by the fact, that, in popular language, to be in a passion, is to be angry!—But,

> 'Anger in hasty *words* or *blows*
> Itself discharges on its foes.'

To be moved, then, by a passion, is to be excited, often to external, and always to internal, effort; whether for the continuance and strengthening of the passion, or for its suppression, accordingly as the course which it takes may be painful or pleasurable. If the latter, the soul must contribute to its support, or it never becomes vivid,—and soon languishes, and dies. And this brings us to the point. If every great Poet with whose writings men are familiar, in the highest exercise of his genius, before he can be thoroughly enjoyed, has to call forth and to communicate *power*, this service, in a still greater degree, falls upon an original Writer, at his first appearance in the world.—Of genius the only proof is, the act of doing well what is worthy to be done, and what was never done before: Of genius, in the fine arts, the only infallible sign is the widening the sphere of human sensibility, for the delight, honor, and benefit of human nature. Genius is the introduction of a new element into the intellectual universe: or, if that be not allowed, it is the application of powers to objects on which they had not before been exercised, or the employment of them in such a manner as to produce effects hitherto unknown. What is all this but an advance, or a conquest, made by the soul of the Poet? Is it to be supposed that the Reader can make progress of this kind, like an Indian Prince or General—stretched on his Palanquin, and borne by his Slaves? No, he is invigorated and inspirited by his Leader, in order that he may exert himself, for he cannot proceed in quiescence, he cannot be carried like a dead weight. Therefore to create taste is to call forth and bestow power, of which knowledge is the effect; and *there* lies the true difficulty.

As the pathetic participates of an *animal* sensation, it might seem—that, if the springs of this emotion were genuine, all men, possessed of competent knowledge of the facts and circumstances, would be instantaneously affected. And, doubtless, in the works of every true Poet will be found passages of that species of excellence, which is proved by effects immediate and universal. But there are emotions of the pathetic that are simple and direct, and others—that are complex and revolutionary; some—to which the heart yields with gentleness, others,—against which it struggles with pride: these varieties are infinite as the combinations of circumstance and the constitutions of character. Remember, also, that the medium through which, in poetry, the heart is to be affected—is language; a thing subject to endless fluctuations and arbitrary associations. The genius of the Poet melts these down for his purpose; but they retain their shape and quality to him who is not capable of exerting, within his own mind, a corresponding energy. There is also a meditative, as well as a human, pathos; an enthusiastic, as well as an ordinary, sorrow; a sadness that has its seat in the depths of reason, to which the mind cannot sink gently of itself—but to which it must descend by treading the steps of thought. And for the sublime,—if we consider what are the cares that occupy the passing day, and how remote is the practice and the course of life from the sources of sublimity, in the soul of Man, can it be wondered that there is little existing preparation for a Poet charged with a new mission to extend its kingdom, and to augment and spread its enjoyments?

Away, then, with the senseless iteration of the word, *popular*, applied to new works in Poetry, as if there were no test of excellence in this first of the fine arts but that all Men should run after its productions, as if urged by an appetite, or constrained by a spell!—The qualities of writing best fitted for eager reception are either such as startle the world into attention by their audacity and extravagance; or they are chiefly of a superficial kind, lying upon the surfaces of manners; or arising out of a selection and arrangement of incidents, by which the mind is kept upon the stretch of curiosity, and the fancy amused without the trouble of thought. But in every thing which is to send the soul into herself, to be admonished of her weakness or to be made conscious of her power;—wherever life and nature are described as operated upon by the creative or abstracting virtue of the imagination; wherever the instinctive wisdom of antiquity and her heroic passions uniting, in the heart of the

Poet, with the meditative wisdom of later ages, have produced that accord of sublimated humanity, which is at once a history of the remote past and a prophetic annunciation of the remotest future, *there*, the Poet must reconcile himself for a season to few and scattered hearers.— Grand thoughts, (and Shakespeare must often have sighed over this truth) as they are most naturally and most fitly conceived in solitude, so can they not be brought forth in the midst of plaudits without some violation of their sanctity. Go to a silent exhibition of the productions of the Sister Art, and be convinced that the qualities which dazzle at first sight, and kindle the admiration of the multitude, are essentially different from those by which permanent influence is secured. Let us not shrink from following up these principles as far as they will carry us, and conclude with observing—that there never has been a period, and perhaps never will be, in which vicious poetry, of some kind or other, has not excited more zealous admiration, and been far more generally read, than good; but this advantage attends the good, that the *individual*, as well as the species, survives from age to age: whereas, of the depraved, though the species be immortal the individual quickly *perishes*; the object of present admiration vanishes, being supplanted by some other as easily produced; which, though no better, brings with it at least the irritation of novelty,—with adaptation, more or less skilful, to the changing humours of the majority of those who are most at leisure to regard poetical works when they first solicit their attention.

Is it the result of the whole that, in the opinion of the Writer, the judgment of the People is not to be respected? The thought is most injurious; and could the charge be brought against him, he would repel it with indignation. The People have already been justified, and their eulogium pronounced by implication, when it was said, above—that, of *good* Poetry, the *individual*, as well as the species, *survives*. And how does it survive but through the People? what preserves it but their intellect and their wisdom?

> '—Past and future, are the wings
> On whose support, harmoniously conjoined,
> Moves the great Spirit of human knowledge—'
>
> *MS.*

The voice that issues from this Spirit, is that Vox populi which the Deity inspires. Foolish must he be who can mistake for this a local acclamation, or a transitory outcry—transitory though it be for years, local though from a Nation. Still more lamentable is his error, who can believe that there is any thing of divine infallibility in the clamour of that small though loud portion of the community, ever governed by factitious influence, which, under the name of the PUBLIC, passes itself, upon the unthinking, for the PEOPLE. Towards the Public, the Writer hopes that he feels as much deference as it is intitled to: but to the People, philosophically characterized, and to the embodied spirit of their knowledge, so far as it exists and moves, at the present, faithfully supported by its two wings, the past and the future, his devout respect, his reverence, is due. He offers it willingly and readily; and, this done, takes leave of his Readers, by assuring them—that, if he were not persuaded that the Contents of these Volumes, and the Work to which they are subsidiary, evinced something of the 'Vision and the Faculty divine'; and that, both in words and things, they will operate in their degree, to extend the domain of sensibility for the delight, the honor, and the benefit of human nature, notwithstanding the many happy hours which he has employed in their composition, and the manifold comforts and enjoyments they have procured to him, he would not, if a wish could do it, save them from immediate destruction;—from becoming at this moment, to the world, as a thing that had never been.

A Letter to a Friend of Robert Burns (*1816*)

TO JAMES GRAY, ESQ., EDINBURGH

Dear Sir,

I have carefully perused the Review of the Life of your friend Robert Burns*, which you kindly transmitted to me; the author has rendered a substantial service to the poet's memory; and the annexed letters are all important to the subject. After having expressed this opinion, I shall not trouble you by commenting upon the publication; but will confine myself to the request of Mr. Gilbert Burns, that I would furnish him with my notions upon the best mode of conducting the defence of his brother's injured reputation; a favourable opportunity being now afforded him to convey his sentiments to the world, along with a republication of Dr. Currie's book, which he is about to superintend. From the respect which I have long felt for the character of the person who has thus honoured me, and from the gratitude which, as a lover of poetry, I owe to the genius of his departed relative, I should most gladly comply with this wish; if I could hope that any suggestions of mine would be of service to the cause. But, really, I feel it is a thing of much delicacy, to give advice upon this occasion, as it appears to me, mainly, not a question of opinion, or of taste, but a matter of conscience. Mr. Gilbert Burns must know, if any man living does, what his brother was; and no one will deny that he, who possesses this knowledge, is a man of unimpeachable veracity. He has already spoken to the world in contradiction of the injurious assertions that have been made, and has told why he forbore to do this on their first appearance. If it be deemed adviseable to reprint Dr. Currie's narrative, without striking out such passages as the author, if he were now alive, would probably be happy to efface, let there be notes attached to the most obnoxious of them, in which the misrepresentations may be corrected, and the exaggerations exposed. I recommend this course, if Dr. Currie's Life is to be republished, as it now stands, in connexion with the poems and letters, and especially if prefixed to them; but, in my judgment, it would be best to copy the example which Mason has given in his second edition of Gray's works. There, inverting the order which had been properly adopted, when the Life and Letters were new matter, the poems are placed first; and the rest takes its place as subsidiary to them. If this

---

* A Review of the Life of Robert Burns, and of various criticisms on his character and writings, by Alexander Peterkin, 1814.

were done in the intended edition of Burns's works, I should strenuously recommend, that a concise life of the poet be prefixed, from the pen of Gilbert Burns, who has already given public proof how well qualified he is for the undertaking. I know no better model as to proportion, and the degree of detail required, nor, indeed, as to the general execution, than the life of Milton by Fenton, prefixed to many editions of the Paradise Lost. But a more copious narrative would be expected from a brother; and some allowance ought to be made, in this and other respects, for an expectation so natural.

In this prefatory memoir, when the author has prepared himself by reflecting, that fraternal partiality may have rendered him, in some points, not so trust-worthy as others less favoured by opportunity, it will be incumbent upon him to proceed candidly and openly, as far as such a procedure will tend to restore to his brother that portion of public estimation, of which he appears to have been unjustly deprived. Nay, when we recal to mind the black things which have been written of this great man, and the frightful ones that have been insinuated against him; and, as far as the public knew, till lately, without complaint, remonstrance, or disavowal, from his nearest relatives; I am not sure that it would not be best, at this day, explicitly to declare to what degree Robert Burns had given way to pernicious habits, and, as nearly as may be, to fix the point to which his moral character had been degraded. It is a disgraceful feature of the times that this measure should be necessary; most painful to think that a *brother* should have such an office to perform. But, if Gilbert Burns be conscious that the subject will bear to be so treated, he has no choice; the duty has been imposed upon him by the errors into which the former biographer has fallen, in respect to the very principles upon which his work ought to have been conducted.

I well remember the acute sorrow with which, by my own fire-side, I first perused Dr. Currie's Narrative, and some of the letters, particularly of those composed in the latter part of the poet's life. If my pity for Burns was extreme, this pity did not preclude a strong indignation, of which he was not the object. If, said I, it were in the power of a biographer to relate the truth, the *whole* truth, and nothing *but* the truth, the friends and surviving kindred of the deceased, for the sake of general benefit to mankind, might endure that such heart-rending communication should be made to the world. But in no case is this possible; and, in the present, the opportunities of directly acquiring other than superficial knowledge have been most scanty; for the writer has barely seen the person who is the subject of his tale; nor did his avocations allow him to take the pains necessary for ascertaining what portion of the information conveyed to him was authentic. So much for facts and actions; and to what purpose relate them even were they true, if the narrative cannot be heard without extreme pain; unless they are placed in such a light, and brought forward in such order, that they shall explain their own laws, and leave the reader in as little uncertainty as the mysteries of our nature will allow, respecting the spirit from which they derived their existence, and which governed the agent? But hear on this pathetic and awful subject, the poet himself, pleading for those who have transgressed!

> 'One point must still be greatly dark,
> The moving *why* they do it,
> And just as lamely can ye mark
> How far, perhaps, they rue it.
>
> Who made the heart, 'tis *he* alone
> Decidedly can try us;
> He knows each chord—its various tone,
> Each spring, its various bias.
>
> Then at the balance let's be mute,
> We never can adjust it;
> What's done we partly may compute,
> But know not what's *resisted*.'

How happened it that the recollection of this affecting passage did not check so amiable a man as Dr. Currie, while he was revealing to the world the infirmities of its author? He must have known enough of human nature to be assured that men would be eager to sit in judgment, and pronounce *decidedly* upon the guilt or innocence of Burns by his testimony; nay, that there were multitudes whose main interest in the allegations would be derived from the incitements which they found therein to undertake this presumptuous office. And where lies the collateral benefit, or what ultimate advantage can be expected, to counteract the injury that the many are thus tempted to do to their own minds; and to compensate the sorrow which must be fixed in the hearts of the considerate few, by language that proclaims so much, and provokes conjectures as unfavourable as imagination can furnish? Here, said I, being moved beyond what it would become me to express, here is a revolting account of a man of exquisite genius, and confessedly of many high moral qualities, sunk into the lower depths of vice and misery! But the painful story, notwithstanding its minuteness, is incomplete,—in essentials it is deficient; so that the most attentive and sagacious reader cannot explain how a mind, so well established by knowledge, fell—and continued to fall, without power to prevent or retard its own ruin.

Would a bosom friend of the author, his counsellor and confessor, have told such things, if true, as this book contains? and who, but one possessed of the intimate knowledge which none but a bosom friend can acquire, could have been justified in making these avowals? Such a one, himself a pure spirit, having accompanied, as it were, upon wings, the pilgrim along the sorrowful road which he trod on foot; such a one, neither hurried down by its slippery descents, nor entangled among its thorns, nor perplexed by its windings, nor discomfited by its founderous passages—for the instruction of others—might have delineated, almost as in a map, the way which the afflicted pilgrim had pursued till the sad close of his diversified journey. In this manner the venerable spirit of Isaac Walton was qualified to have retraced the unsteady course of a highly-gifted man, who, in this lamentable point, and in versatility of genius, bore no unobvious resemblance to the Scottish bard; I mean his friend COTTON—whom, notwithstanding all that the sage must have disapproved in his life, he honoured with the title of son. Nothing like this, however, has the biographer of Burns accomplished; and, with his means of information, copious as in some respects they were, it would have been absurd to attempt it. The only motive, therefore, which could authorize the writing and publishing matter so distressing to read—is wanting!

Nor is Dr. Currie's performance censurable from these considerations alone; for information, which would have been of absolute worth if in his capacity of biographer and editor he had known when to stop short, is rendered unsatisfactory and inefficacious through the absence of this reserve, and from being coupled with statements of improbable and irreconcileable facts. We have the author's letters discharged upon us in showers; but how few readers will take the trouble of comparing those letters with each other, and with the other documents of the publication, in order to come at a genuine knowledge of the writer's character!—The life of Johnson by Boswell had broken through many pre-existing delicacies, and afforded the British public an opportunity of acquiring experience, which before it had happily wanted; nevertheless, at the time when the ill-selected medley of Burns's correspondence first appeared, little progress had been made (nor is it likely that, by the mass of mankind, much ever will be made) in determining what portion of these confidential communications escapes the pen in courteous, yet often innocent, compliance—to gratify the several tastes of correspondents; and as little towards distinguishing opinions and sentiments uttered for the momentary amusement of the writer's own fancy, from those which his judgment deliberately approves, and his heart faithfully cherishes.

But the subject of this book was a man of extraordinary genius; whose birth, education, and employments had placed and kept him in a situation far below that in which the writers and readers of expensive volumes are usually found. Critics upon works of fiction have laid it down as a rule that remoteness of place, in fixing the choice of a subject, and in prescribing the mode of treating it, is equal in effect to distance of time;—restraints may be thrown off accordingly. Judge then of the delusions which artificial distinctions impose, when to a man like Doctor Currie, writing with views so honourable, the *social condition* of the individual of whom he was treating, could seem to place him at such a distance from the exalted reader, that ceremony might be discarded with him, and his memory sacrificed, as it were, almost without compunction. The poet was laid where these injuries could not reach him; but he had a parent, I understand, an admirable woman, still surviving; a brother like Gilbert Burns!—a widow estimable for her virtues; and children, at that time infants, with the world before them, which they must face to obtain a maintenance; who remembered their father probably with the tenderest affection;—and whose opening minds, as their years advanced, would become conscious of so many reasons for admiring him.—Ill-fated child of nature, too frequently thine own enemy,—unhappy favourite of genius, too often misguided,—this is indeed to be 'crushed beneath the furrow's weight!'

Why, sir, do I write to you at this length, when all that I had to express in direct answer to the request, which occasioned this letter, lay in such narrow compass?—Because having entered upon the subject, I am unable to quit it!—Your feelings, I trust, go along with mine; and, rising from this individual case to a general view of the subject, you will probably agree with me in opinion that biography, though differing in some essentials from works of fiction, is nevertheless, like them, an *art*,—an art, the laws of which are determined by the imperfections of our nature, and the constitution of society. Truth is not here, as in the sciences, and in natural philosophy, to be sought without scruple, and promulgated for its own sake, upon the mere chance of its being serviceable; but only for obviously justifying purposes, moral or intellectual.

Silence is a privilege of the grave, a right of the departed: let him, therefore, who infringes that right, by speaking publicly of, for, or against, those who cannot speak for themselves, take heed that he opens not his mouth without a sufficient sanction. De mortuis nil nisi bonum, is a rule in which these sentiments have been pushed to an extreme that proves how deeply humanity is interested in maintaining them. And it was wise to announce the precept thus absolutely; both because there exist in that same nature, by which it has been dictated, so many temptations to disregard it,—and because there are powers and influences, within and without us, that will prevent its being literally fulfilled—to the suppression of profitable truth. Penalties of law, conventions of manners, and personal fear, protect the reputation of the living; and something of this protection is extended to the recently dead,—who survive, to a certain degree, in their kindred and friends. Few are so insensible as not to feel this, and not to be actuated by the feeling. But only to philosophy enlightened by the affections does it belong justly to estimate the claims of the deceased on the one hand, and of the present age and future generations, on the other; and to strike a balance between them.—Such philosophy runs a risk of becoming extinct among us, if the coarse intrusions into the recesses, the gross breaches upon the sanctities, of domestic life, to which we have lately been more and more accustomed, are to be regarded as indications of a vigorous state of public feeling—favourable to the maintenance of the liberties of our country.—Intelligent lovers of freedom are from necessity bold and hardy lovers of truth; but, according to the measure in which their love is intelligent, is it attended with a finer discrimination, and a more sensitive delicacy. The wise and good (and all others being lovers of licence rather than of liberty are in fact slaves) respect, as one of the noblest characteristics of Englishmen, that jealousy of familiar approach, which, while it contributes to the maintenance of private dignity, is one of the most efficacious guardians of rational public freedom.

The general obligation upon which I have insisted, is especially binding upon those who undertake the biography of *authors*. Assuredly, there is no cause why the lives of that class of men should be pried into with the same diligent curiosity, and laid open with the same disregard of reserve, which may sometimes be expedient in composing the history of men who have borne an active part in the world. Such thorough knowledge of the good and bad qualities of these latter, as can only be obtained by a scrutiny of their private lives, conduces to explain not only their own public conduct, but that of those with whom they have acted. Nothing of this applies to authors, considered merely as authors. Our business is with their books,—to understand and to enjoy them. And, of poets more especially, it is true—that, if their works be good, they contain within themselves all that is necessary to their being comprehended and relished. It should seem that the ancients thought in this manner; for of the eminent Greek and Roman poets, few and scanty memorials were, I believe, ever prepared; and fewer still are preserved. It is delightful to read what, in the happy exercise of his own genius, Horace chooses to communicate of himself and his friends; but I confess I am not so much a lover of knowledge, independent of its quality, as to make it likely that it would much rejoice me, were I to hear that records of the Sabine poet and his contemporaries, composed upon the Boswellian plan, had been unearthed among the ruins of Herculaneum. You will interpret what I am writing, *liberally*. With respect to the light which such a discovery might throw upon Roman manners, there would be reasons to desire it: but I should dread to disfigure the beautiful ideal of the memories of those illustrious persons with incongruous features, and to sully the imaginative purity of their classical works with gross and trivial recollections. The least weighty objection to heterogeneous details, is that they are mainly superfluous, and therefore an incumbrance.

But you will perhaps accuse me of refining too much; and it is, I own, comparatively of little importance, while we are engaged in reading the Iliad, the Eneid, the tragedies of Othello and King Lear, whether the authors of these poems were good or bad men; whether they lived happily or miserably. Should a thought of the kind cross our minds, there would be no doubt, if irresistible external evidence did not decide the question unfavourably, that men of such transcendent genius were both good and happy: and if, unfortunately, it had been on record that they were otherwise, sympathy with the fate of their fictitious personages would banish the unwelcome truth whenever it obtruded itself, so that it would but slightly disturb our pleasure. Far otherwise is it with that class of poets, the principal charm of whose writings depends upon the familiar knowledge which they convey of the personal feelings of their authors. This is eminently the case with the effusions of Burns;—in the small quantity of narrative that he has given, he himself bears no inconsiderable part, and he has produced no drama. Neither the subjects of his poems, nor his manner of handling them, allow us long to forget their author. On the basis of his human character he has reared a poetic one, which with more or less distinctness presents itself to view in almost every part of his earlier, and, in my estimation, his most valuable verses. This poetic fabric, dug out of the quarry of genuine humanity, is airy and spiritual:—and though the materials, in some parts, are coarse, and the disposition is often fantastic and irregular, yet the whole is agreeable and strikingly attractive. Plague, then, upon your remorseless hunters after matter of fact (who, after all, rank among the blindest of human beings) when they could convince you that the foundations of this admirable edifice are hollow; and that its frame is unsound! Granting that all which has been raked up to the prejudice of Burns were literally true; and that it added, which it does not, to our better understanding of human nature and human life (for that genius is not incompatible with vice, and that vice leads to misery—the more acute from the sensibilities which are the elements of genius—we needed not those communications to inform us) how poor would have been the compensation for the deduction made, by this extrinsic knowledge, from the intrinsic efficacy of his poetry—to please, and to instruct!

In illustration of this sentiment, permit me to remind you that it is the privilege of poetic genius to catch, under certain restrictions of which perhaps at the time of its being exerted it is but dimly conscious, a spirit of pleasure wherever it can be found,—in the walks of nature, and in the business of men.—The poet, trusting to primary instincts, luxuriates among the felicities of love and wine, and is enraptured while he describes the fairer aspects of war: nor does he shrink from the company of the passion of love though immoderate—from convivial pleasure though intemperate—nor from the presence of war though savage, and recognized as the hand-maid of desolation. Frequently and admirably has Burns given way to these impulses of nature; both with reference to himself and in describing the conditions of others. Who, but some impenetrable dunce or narrow-minded puritan in works of art, ever read without delight the picture which he has drawn of the convivial exaltation of the rustic adventurer, Tam o' Shanter? The poet fears not to tell the reader in the outset that his hero was a desperate and sottish drunkard, whose excesses were frequent as his opportunities. This reprobate sits down to his cups, while the storm is roaring, and heaven and earth are in confusion;—the night is driven on by song and tumultuous noise—laughter and jest thicken as the beverage improves upon the palate—conjugal fidelity archly bends to the service of general benevolence—selfishness is not absent, but wearing the mask of social cordiality—and, while these various elements of humanity are blended into one proud and happy composition of elated spirits, the anger of the tempest without doors only heightens and sets off the enjoyment within.—I pity him who cannot perceive that, in all this, though there was no moral purpose, there is a moral effect.

> 'Kings may be blest, but Tam was glorious
> 'O'er a' the *ills* of life victorious.'

What a lesson do these words convey of charitable indulgence for the vicious habits of the principal actor in this scene, and of those who resemble him!—Men who to the rigidly virtuous are objects almost of loathing, and whom therefore they cannot serve! The poet, penetrating the unsightly and disgusting surfaces of things, has unveiled with exquisite skill the finer ties of imagination and feeling, that often bind these beings to practices productive of so much unhappiness to themselves, and to those whom it is their duty to cherish;—and, as far as he puts the reader in possession of this intelligent sympathy, he qualifies him for exercising a salutary influence over the minds of those who are thus deplorably enslaved.

Not less successfully does Burns avail himself of his own character and situation in society, to construct out of them a poetic self,—introduced as a dramatic personage—for the purpose of inspiriting his incidents, diversifying his pictures, recommmending his opinions, and giving point to his sentiments. His brother can set me right if I am mistaken when I express a belief that, at the time when he wrote his story of 'Death and Dr. Hornbook,' he had very rarely been intoxicated, or perhaps even much exhilarated by liquor. Yet how happily does he lead his reader into that track of sensations! and with what lively humour does he describe the disorder of his senses and the confusion of his understanding, put to test by a deliberate attempt to count the horns of the moon!

> 'But whether she had three or four
> He could na' tell.'

Behold a sudden apparition that disperses this disorder, and in a moment chills him into possession of himself! Coming upon no more important mission than the grisly phantom was charged with, what mode of introduction could have been more efficient or appropriate?

But, in those early poems, through the veil of assumed habits and pretended qualities, enough of the real man appears to shew that he was conscious of sufficient cause to dread his own passions, and to bewail his errors! We have rejected as false sometimes in the letter, and of necessity as false in the spirit, many of the testimonies that others have borne against him:—but, by his own hand—in words the import of which cannot be mistaken—it has been recorded that the order of his life but faintly corresponded with the clearness of his views. It is probable that he would have proved a still greater poet if, by strength of reason, he could have controlled the propensities which his sensibility engendered; but he would have been a poet of a different class: and certain it is, had that desirable restraint been early established, many peculiar beauties which enrich his verses could never have existed, and many accessary influences, which contribute greatly to their effect, would have been wanting. For instance, the momentous truth of the passage already quoted, 'One point must still be greatly dark,' &c. could not possibly have been conveyed with such pathetic force by any poet that ever lived, speaking in his own voice; unless it were felt that, like Burns, he was a man who preached from the text of his own errors; and whose wisdom, beautiful as a flower that might have risen from seed sown from above, was in fact a scion from the root of personal suffering. Whom did the poet intend should be thought of as occupying that grave over which, after modestly setting forth the moral discernment and warm affections of its 'poor inhabitant,' it is supposed to be inscribed that

> '—Thoughtless follies laid him low,
> 'And stained his name.'

Who but himself,—himself anticipating the too probable termination of his own course? Here is a sincere and solemn avowal—a public declaration *from his own will*—a confession at once devout, poetical, and human—a history in the shape of a prophecy! What more was required of the biographer than to have put his seal to the writing, testifying that the foreboding had been realized, and that the record was authentic?— Lastingly is it to be regretted in respect to this memorable being, that inconsiderate intrusion has not left us at liberty to enjoy his mirth, or his love; his wisdom or his wit; without an admixture of useless, irksome, and painful details, that take from his poems so much of that right—which, with all his carelessness, and frequent breaches of self-respect, he was not negligent to maintain for them—the right of imparting solid instruction through the medium of unalloyed pleasure.

You will have noticed that my observations have hitherto been confined to Dr. Currie's book: if, by fraternal piety, the poison can be sucked out of this wound, those inflicted by meaner hands may be safely left to heal of themselves. Of the other writers who have given their names, only one lays claim to even a slight acquaintance with the author, whose moral character they take upon them publicly to anatomize. The Edinburgh reviewer—and him I single out because the author of the vindication of Burns has treated his offences with comparative indulgence, to which he has no claim, and which, from whatever cause it might arise, has interfered with the dispensation of justice—the Edinburgh reviewer thus writes:* 'The *leading vice* in Burns's character, and the *cardinal deformity*, indeed, of ALL his productions, was his contempt, or affectation of contempt, for prudence, decency, and regularity, and his admiration of thoughtlessness, oddity, and vehement

---

* From Mr Peterkin's pamphlet, who vouches for the accuracy of his citations; omitting, however, to apologize for their length.

sensibility: his belief, in short, in the dispensing power of genius and social feelings in all matters of morality and common sense;' adding, that these vices and erroneous notions 'have communicated to a great part of his productions a character of immorality at once contemptible and hateful.' We are afterwards told, that he is *perpetually* making a parade of his thoughtlessness, inflammability, and imprudence; and, in the next paragraph, that he is *perpetually* doing something else; i.e. 'boasting of his own independence.'—Marvellous address in the commission of faults! not less than Cæsar shewed in the management of business; who, it is said, could dictate to three secretaries upon three several affairs, at one and the same moment! But, to be serious. When a man, self-elected into the office of a public judge of the literature and life of his contemporaries, can have the audacity to go these lengths in framing a summary of the contents of volumes that are scattered over every quarter of the globe, and extant in almost every cottage of Scotland, to give the lie to his labours; we must not wonder if, in the plentitude of his concern for the interest of abstract morality, the infatuated slanderer should have found no obstacle to prevent him from insinuating that the poet, whose writings are to this degree stained and disfigured, was 'one of the sons of fancy and of song, who spent in vain superfluities the money that belongs of right to the pale industrious tradesman and his famishing infants; and who rave about friendship and philosophy in a tavern, while their wives' hearts,' &c. &c.

It is notorious that this persevering Aristarch,* as often as a work of original genius comes before him, avails himself of that opportunity to re-proclaim to the world the narrow range of his own comprehension. The happy self-complacency, the unsuspecting vain-glory, and the cordial *bonhommie*, with which this part of his duty is performed, do not leave him free to complain of being hardly dealt with if any one should declare the truth, by pronouncing much of the foregoing attack upon the intellectual and moral character of Burns, to be the trespass (for reasons that will shortly appear, it cannot be called the venial trespass) of a mind obtuse, superficial, and inept. What portion of malignity such a mind is susceptible of, the judicious admirers of the poet, and the discerning friends of the man, will not trouble themselves to enquire; but they will

---

* A friend, who chances to be present while the author is correcting the proof sheet, observes that Aristarchus is libelled by this application of his name, and advises that 'Zoilus' should be substituted. The question lies between spite and presumption; and it is not easy to decide upon a case where the claims of each party are so strong: but the name of Aristarch, who, simple man! would allow no verse to pass to Homer's which he did not approve of, is retained, for reasons that will be deemed cogent.

wish that this evil principle had possessed more sway than they are at liberty to assign to it, the offender's condition would not then have been so hopeless. For malignity *selects* its diet; but where is to be found the nourishment from which vanity will revolt? Malignity may be appeased by triumphs real or supposed, and will then sleep, or yield its place to a repentance producing dispositions of good will, and desires to make amends for past injury; but vanity is restless, reckless, intractable, unappeasable, insatiable. Fortunate is it for the world when this spirit incites only to actions that meet with an adequate punishment in derision; such, as in a scheme of poetical justice, would be aptly required by assigning to the agents, when they quit this lower world, a station in that not uncomfortable limbo—the Paradise of Fools! But, assuredly, we shall have here another proof that ridicule is not the test of truth, if it prevent us from perceiving, that *depravity* has no ally more active, more inveterate, nor, from the difficulty of divining to what kind and degree of extravagance it may prompt, more pernicious than self-conceit. Where this alliance is too obvious to be disputed, the culprit ought not to be allowed the benefit of contempt—as a shelter from detestation; much less should he be permitted to plead, in excuse for his transgressions, that especial malevolence had little or no part in them. It is not recorded, that the ancient, who set fire to the temple of Diana, had a particular dislike to the goddess of chastity, or held idolatry in abhorrence: he was a fool, an egregious fool, but not the less, on that account, a most odious monster. The tyrant who is described as having rattled his chariot along a bridge of brass over the heads of his subjects, was, no doubt, inwardly laughed at; but what if this mock Jupiter, not satisfied with an empty noise of his own making, had amused himself with throwing fire-brands upon the house-tops, as a substitute for lightning; and, from his elevation, had hurled stones upon the heads of his people, to shew that he was a master of the destructive bolt, as well as of the harmless voice of the thunder!—The lovers of all that is honourable to humanity have recently had occasion to rejoice over the downfall of an intoxicated despot, whose vagaries furnish more solid materials by which the philosopher will exemplify how strict is the connection between the ludicrously, and the terribly fantastic. We know, also, that Robespierre was one of the vainest men that the most vain country upon earth has produced;—and from this passion, and from that cowardice which naturally connects itself with it, flowed the horrors of his administration. It is a descent, which I fear you will scarcely pardon, to compare these redoubtable enemies of mankind with the anonymous conductor of a perishable publication. But the moving spirit is the same in them all; and, as far as difference of circumstances, and disparity of powers, will allow, manifests itself in the same way; by professions of reverence for truth, and concern for duty—carried to the giddiest heights of ostentation, while practice seems to have no other reliance than on the omnipotence of falshood.

The transition from a vindication of Robert Burns to these hints for a picture of the intellectual deformity of one who has grossly outraged his memory, is too natural to require an apology: but I feel, sir, that I stand in need of indulgence for having detained you so long. Let me beg that you would impart to any judicious friends of the poet as much of the contents of these pages as you think will be serviceable to the cause; but do not give publicity to any *portion* of them, unless it be thought probable that an open circulation of the whole may be useful.* The subject is delicate, and some of the opinions are of a kind, which, if torn away from the trunk that supports them, will be apt to wither, and, in that state, to contract poisonous qualities; like the branches of the yew, which, while united by a living spirit to their native tree, are neither noxious, nor without beauty; but, being dissevered and cast upon the ground, become deadly to the cattle that incautiously feed upon them.

To Mr. Gilbert Burns, especially, let my sentiments be conveyed, with my sincere respects, and best wishes for the success of his praiseworthy enterprize. And if, through modest apprehension, he should doubt of his own ability to do justice to his brother's memory, let him take encouragement from the assurance that the most odious part of the charges owed its credit to the silence of those who were deemed best entitled to speak; and who, it was thought, would not have been mute, had they believed that they could speak beneficially. Moreover, it may be relied on as a general truth, which will not escape his recollection, that tasks of this kind are not so arduous as, to those who are tenderly concerned in their issue, they may at first appear to be; for, if the many be hasty to condemn, there is a re-action of generosity which stimulates them—when forcibly summoned—to redress the wrong; and, for the sensible part of mankind, *they* are neither dull to understand, nor slow to make allowance for, the aberrations of men, whose intellectual powers do honour to their species.

I am, dear Sir,
respectfully yours,
WILLIAM WORDSWORTH

Rydal Mount, January, 1816

* It was deemed that it would be so, and the letter is published accordingly.

APPENDIX

THESE passages of meditative verse cannot stand as independent poems, but are too important to be omitted in an edition which aims both to include W's finest poetry and to exemplify the range of his power and ambitions. They are all entered in Dove Cottage MS 16 and belong to the period in 1798 when W was contemplating *The Recluse*, fired by conversations with Coleridge on philosophy, religion, and politics. For the scope of W's plans see note to 'Home at Grasmere' below, pp. 695–6 and the introduction to Darlington's edition cited there. Each of these passages draws on W's knowledge of eighteenth-century thought (for which see H. W. Piper, *The Active Universe*, 1962, and Jonathan Wordsworth, *The Music of Humanity*, 1969, especially 171–258), but what is important is that they are an attempt to convey philosophical positions through the medium of the language of passion and imagination. They should be considered together with 'Tintern Abbey', The Ruined Cottage' and *The Prelude* and with C's comment in mind: 'I dare affirm that [Wordsworth] will hereafter be admitted as the first and greatest philosophical Poet—the only man who has effected a compleat and constant synthesis of Thought and Feeling . . .' (15 January 1804).

Passage (*a*) was incorporated into *The Excursion* (1814), Book ix. Passage (*b*), later incorporated into *The Excursion*, Book iv, is a discarded conclusion to MS B of 'The Ruined Cottage'. The opening lines are quoted by C in a very important letter of *c.*10 March 1798. Passage (*c*) was used in *The Excursion*, Book viii.

(*a*)

There is an active principle alive in all things;
In all things, in all natures, in the flowers
And in the trees, in every pebbly stone
That paves the brooks, the stationary rocks,
The moving waters and the invisible air.
All beings have their properties which spread
Beyond themselves, a power by which they make
Some other being conscious of their life,
Spirit that knows no insulated spot,
No chasm, no solitude, from link to link   10
It circulates the soul of all the worlds.
This is the freedom of the universe,
Unfolded still the more, more visible,
The more we know, and yet is reverenced least
And least respected in the human mind,
Its most apparent home. The food of hope
Is meditated action; robbed of this

Her sole support, she languishes and dies.
We perish also, for we live by hope
And by desire; they are the very blood   20
By which we move, we see by the sweet light
And breathe the sweet air of futurity;
And so we live, or else we have no life;
And 'tis expressed in colours of the sun
That we were never made to be content
With simple abstinence from ill, for chains,
For shackles and for bonds, but to be bound
By laws in which there is a generating soul
Allied to our own nature; and we know
That when we stand upon our native soil,   30
Unelbowed by such objects as constrain
Our active powers, those powers themselves become
Subversive of our noxious qualities,
And by the substitution of delight
And by new influxes of strength suppress
All evil; then the being spreads abroad
His branches to the wind and all who see
Bless him, rejoicing in his neighbourhood.
There is one only liberty, 'tis his,
Who by beneficence is circumscribed;   40
'Tis his to whom the power of doing good
Is law and statute, penalty, and bond,
His prison, and his warder; his who finds
His freedom in the joy of virtuous thoughts.
Then sorrow to the many, they in whom
We look for health, from seeds which have been sown
In sickness, and for increase in a power
That works but by extinction. On themselves
They cannot lean, or turn to their own hearts
To know what they must do; their wisdom is   50
To look into the eyes of others, thence
To be instructed what they must avoid,
Or let us rather say how least observed,
How with most quiet and most silent death,
With the least taint and injury to the air
The rich man breathes, their human form divine
And their eternal soul may waste away.
Oh, never was this intellectual power,
This vital spirit, in its essence free
As is the light of heaven, this mind that streams   60
With emanations like the blessed sun,
Oh, never was this [   ] existence formed

For wishes that debilitate and die
Of their own weakness, fears that live by search
Of knowledge which they cannot find, for hopes
That have no blessing in them, [   ]
And such desires as do but stir the heart
To waken consciousnesses of despair,
For hesitations, pining, languors, cold
And dead suppressions, all the subtle host   70
Of feverish infirmities, that give
Sad motion to the pestilential calm
Of negative morality, and feed
From day to day their never-ending life
In the close prison-house of human laws.

(b)

Not useless do I deem
These quiet sympathies with things that hold
An inarticulate language, for the man
Once taught to love such objects as excite
No morbid passions, no disquietude,
No vengeance and no hatred, needs must feel
The joy of that pure principle of love
So deeply that, unsatisfied with aught
Less pure and exquisite, he cannot choose
But seek for objects of a kindred love   10
In fellow-natures, and a kindred joy.
Accordingly he by degrees perceives
His feelings of aversion softened down,
A holy tenderness pervade his frame,
His sanity of reason not impaired,
Say rather all his thoughts now flowing clear
—From a clear fountain flowing—he looks round,
He seeks for good and finds the good he seeks;
Till execration and contempt are things
He only knows by name, and if he hears   20
From other mouths the language which they speak
He is compassionate, and has no thought,
No feeling, which can overcome his love.
And further, by contemplating these forms
In the relations which they bear to man
We shall discover what a power is theirs
To stimulate our minds, and multiply
The spiritual presences of absent things.

Then weariness will cease—We shall acquire
The [   ] habit by which sense is made   30
Subservient still to moral purposes,
A vital essence and a saving power;
Nor shall we meet an object but may read
Some sweet and tender lesson to our minds
Of human suffering or of human joy.
All things shall speak of man, and we shall read
Our duties in all forms, and general laws
And local accidents shall tend alike
To quicken and to rouze, and give the will
And power which by a [   ] chain of good   40
Shall link us to our kind. No naked hearts,
No naked minds, shall then be left to mourn
The burthen of existence. Science then
Shall be a precious visitant; and then,
And only then, be worthy of her name.
For then her heart shall kindle, her dull eye,
Dull and inanimate, no more shall hang
Chained to its object in brute slavery,
But better taught and mindful of its use
Legitimate, and its peculiar power,   50
While with a patient interest it shall watch
The processes of things, and serve the cause
Of order and distinctiness; not for this
Shall it forget that its most noble end,
Its most illustrious province, must be found
In ministering to the excursive power
Of Intellect and thought. So build we up
The being that we are. For was it meant
That we should pore, and dwindle as we pore,
Forever dimly pore on things minute,   60
On solitary objects, still beheld
In disconnection, dead and spiritless,
And still dividing, and dividing still,
Break down all grandeur, still unsatisfied
With our unnatural toil, while littleness
May yet become more little, waging thus
An impious warfare with the very life
Of our own souls? Or was it ever meant
That this majestic imagery, the clouds,
The ocean, and the firmament of heaven,   70
Should be a barren picture on the mind?
Never for ends of vanity and pain
And sickly wretchedness were we endued

Amid this world of feeling and of life
With apprehension, reason, will and thought,
Affections, organs, passions. Let us rise
From this oblivious sleep, these fretful dreams
Of feverish nothingness. Thus disciplined
All things shall live in us, and we shall live
In all things that surround us. This I deem   80
Our tendency, and thus shall every day
Enlarge our sphere of pleasure and of pain.
For thus the senses and the intellect
Shall each to each supply a mutual aid,
Invigorate and sharpen and refine
Each other with a power that knows no bound,
And forms and feelings acting thus, and thus
Reacting, they shall each acquire
A living spirit and a character
Till then unfelt, and each be multiplied,   90
With a variety that knows no end.
Thus deeply drinking in the soul of things
We shall be wise perforce, and we shall move
From strict necessity along the path
Of order and of good. Whate'er we see,
What'er we feel, by agency direct
Or indirect, shall tend to feed and nurse
Our faculties and raise to loftier heights
Our intellectual soul. The old man ceased.
The words he uttered shall not pass away.   100
They had sunk into me, but not as sounds
To be expressed by visible characters;
For while he spake my spirit had obeyed
The presence of his eye, my ear had drunk
The meanings of his voice. He had discoursed
Like one who in the slow and silent works,
The manifold conclusions of his thought,
Had brooded till Imagination's power
Condensed them to a passion whence she drew
Herself new energies, resistless force.   110

(c)

There is a law severe of penury
Which bends the cottage boy to early thought,
To thought whose premature necessity
Blocks out the forms of nature, preconsumes

The reason, famishes the heart, shuts up
The infant being in itself and makes
Its very spring a season of decay.
Oh miserable lot! condition sad!
Which terminates the hour of careless joy
So soon that it is lost to memory,   10
To the old man a time that never was.
And even if on some week-day festival
Or by the sabbath fire the parent's heart
Turn with a fond good-humoured tenderness
To days that are long past, the stripling hears
The tale of that sweet season, what he said
And what he did, his marvellous feats and feaks,
His wisdom and his wit, he hears them all
With languid interest, as a thing detached
From his own life—Oh miserable state!   20
Then liberty is not and cannot be,
But wheresoe'er he turns his steps the boy
Is still a prisoner, when the wind is up
Among the clouds, and in the antient woods,
Or when the sun is rising in the heavens
Quietly calm.

[After a gap in the manuscript the passage continues]

      Are these the looks
Is this the countenance or such the port
Of no mean being, one who should be clothed
In dignity befitting his proud hope,   30
Who in his very childhood should appear
Sublime from present purity and joy?
The limbs increase but liberty of mind
Is gone for ever and, the avenues
Of sense impeded, this organic frame,
So joyful in its motions, soon becomes
Dull, to the joy of its own motions dead,
And even the touch so exquisitely poured
Through the whole body with a languid will
Performs its functions, in the basking hour   40

[One line missing]

Scarce carrying to the brain a torpid sense
Of what there is delightful in the breeze,
The sunshine or the changeful elements.

NOTES

NOTES have been kept to a minimum. Date of composition and publication are always included, as are many of the notes which Wordsworth himself added to his poems. I have quoted generously from the notes composed late in Wordsworth's life, called the Fenwick Notes after his friend and amanuensis Isabella Fenwick. Because they contain occasional errors of fact and some rewriting of history the Fenwick Notes have been too little valued. They are, in fact, Wordsworth's last major prose work, an invaluable and often moving apologia for the poetry of a dedicated lifetime. I have given information only where it is essential for understanding the meaning of a passage, but have been more liberal with references to the responses of Wordsworth's friends.

The notes have been kept as uncluttered as possible by limiting references to letters, diary and notebook entries simply to date or entry number. Full citation of the standard editions used will be found in the list of abbreviations. A statement of the date of publication, e.g. 1807, always refers to one of Wordsworth's principal volumes of poetry. If there is any possibility of confusion the full title is given. Editions referred to, and from which texts are drawn for the majority of poems in this selection, are:

1793	*An Evening Walk*
1798	*Lyrical Ballads, with a Few Other Poems* (1 vol.)
1800	*Lyrical Ballads, with Other Poems* (2 vols.)
1807	*Poems, in Two Volumes*
1815	*Poems* (2 vols. Wordsworth's first Collected Edition)
1820	*The Miscellaneous Poems of William Wordsworth* (4 vols.)
1820	*The River Duddon . . . and Other Poems* (1 vol.)
1822	*Ecclesiastical Sketches* (1 vol.)
1822	*Memorials of a Tour on the Continent. 1820* (1 vol.)
1827	*The Poetical Works of William Wordsworth* (5 vols.)
1835	*Yarrow Revisited, and Other Poems* (1 vol.)
1836	*The Poetical Works of William Wordsworth* (6 vols.)
1842	*Poems, Chiefly of Early and Late Years* (1 vol.)
1849–50	*The Poetical Works of William Wordsworth* (6 vols.)

ABBREVIATIONS

C	Samuel Taylor Coleridge
DW	Dorothy Wordsworth
IF note	Notes by W, compiled in 1843 by Isabella Fenwick
JW	John Wordsworth
Journal	*Journals of Dorothy Wordsworth*, ed. Mary Moorman (1971).
Moorman	Mary Moorman, *William Wordsworth: A Biography. The Early Years* (Oxford, 1957); *The Later Years* (Oxford, 1965)

MW	Mary Wordsworth
Notebooks	The Notebooks of Samuel Taylor Coleridge, ed. Kathlccn Coburn (1957–)
PW	The Poetical Works of William Wordsworth, ed. E. de Selincourt and Helen Darbishire (Oxford, 1940–9)
Prose	The Prose Works of William Wordsworth, ed. W. J. B. Owen and Jane Worthington Smyser (Oxford, 1974)
Recollections	'Recollections of a Tour Made in Scotland', in Journals of Dorothy Wordsworth, ed. E. de Selincourt (1941)
Reed	Mark L. Reed, Wordsworth: The Chronology of the Early Years 1770–1799 (Cambridge, Mass., 1967); Middle Years 1800–1815 (Cambridge, Mass., 1975)
W	William Wordsworth
Wordsworth's Hawkshead	T. W. Thompson, Wordsworth's Hawkshead, ed. Robert Woof (1970)

Letters of W, DW and C are identified in the introduction and notes by date only. Texts can be found in: Letters of William and Dorothy Wordsworth, ed. E. de Selincourt; The Early Years, 1787–1805, revised Chester L. Shaver (Oxford, 1967); The Middle Years, 1806–11, revised Mary Moorman (Oxford, 1969); 1812–20, revised Mary Moorman and Alan G. Hill (Oxford, 1970); The Later Years, 1821–50, revised Alan G. Hill (Oxford, 1978–); Collected Letters of Samuel Taylor Coleridge, ed. Earl Leslie Griggs, 6 vols. (Oxford, 1956–71).

POEMS

1 *An Evening Walk.* Composed 1788–9. Published 1793. W noted: 'The young Lady to whom this was addressed was my Sister. It was composed at school, and during my two first College vacations. There is not an image in it which I have not observed; and now, in my seventy-third year, I recollect the time and place where most of them were noticed . . . the plan of [the poem] has not been confined to a particular walk or an individual place; a proof (of which I was unconscious at the time) of my unwillingness to submit the poetic spirit to the chains of fact and real circumstance. The country is idealized rather than described in any one of its local aspects' (IF note). The whole of this long note should be consulted, *PW*, i. 318–19.

An Evening Walk established W as a skilled practitioner in a major eighteenth-century genre and brought him to C's attention, even before the two poets had met. For the form, see R. A. Aubin, *Topographical Poetry in Eighteenth-Century England* (NY, 1936). It was a mark of the genre that it should advertise its literary texture and thus the pages of the poem when first printed were embellished with W's own footnotes. These are printed below, verbatim, marked '—W', but no attempt has been made to annotate them further. To amplify W's notes would make this, unwarrantably, the most heavily annotated poem in the volume. For further help see *PW*, i. 320–4. A full edition is forthcoming in the Cornell Wordsworth Series.

l. 19. W's quotation marks draw attention to borrowing from Charlotte Smith's sonnet '*To the South Downs*', l. 1.

l. 26. 'In the beginning of winter, these mountains, in the moonlight nights, are covered with immense quantities of woodcocks; which, in the dark nights, retire into the woods'—W.

2 l. 47. In 1793 this line reads: 'The ray the cot of morning trav'ling nigh'. Emended by de Selincourt, *PW*, ii. 6, for the sake of sense. It is worrying, however, that in the extensive erratum sheet to 1793 W did not alter this line.

3 l. 65. 'The word *intake* is local, and signifies a mountain-inclosure'—W.

l. 72. 'Gill is also, I believe, a term confined to this country. Glen, gill, and dingle, have the same meaning'—W.

l. 83. 'The reader, who has made the tour of this country, will recognize in this description the features which characterize the lower waterfall in the gardens of Rydale'—W.

4 l. 114. ' "vivid rings of green." Greenwood's *Poem on Shooting*'—W.

l. 116. ' "Down the rough slope the pond'rous waggon rings." Beattie'—W.

l. 117. 'These rude structures, to protect the flocks, are frequent in this country: the traveller may recollect one in Withburne, another upon Whinlatter'—W.

l. 129. ' "Dolcemente feroce." Tasso. In this description of the cock, I remembered a spirited one of the same animal in l'Agriculture, ou Les Géorgiques Françoises of M. Rossuet'—W.

5 l. 171. 'Not far from Broughton is a Druid monument, of which I do not recollect that any tour descriptive of this country makes mention. Perhaps this poem may fall into the hands of some curious traveller, who may thank me for informing him, that up the Duddon, the river which forms the aestuary at Broughton, may be found some of the most romantic scenery of these mountains'—W.

l. 173. 'From Thomson: see Scott's Critical Essays'—W.

6 l. 187. 'See a description of an appearance of this kind in Clark's "Survey of the Lakes", accompanied with vouchers of its veracity that may amuse the reader'—W.

l. 217. 'This is a fact of which I have been an eye witness'—W.

7 l. 224. 'The lily of the valley is found in great abundance in the smallest island of Winandermere'—W.

ll. 241–56. For analogues to the passage and an important discussion see Mary Jacobus, *Tradition and Experiment in Wordsworth's Lyrical Ballads 1798* (Oxford, 1976), 144.

9 l. 317. ' "Sugh," a Scotch word, expressive, as Mr Gilpin explains it, of the sound of the motion of a stick through the air, or of the wind passing through the trees. See Burns' Cotter's Saturday Night'—W.

l. 333. 'Alluding to this passage of Spenser—

> "Her angel face
> As the great eye of Heaven shined bright,
> And made a sunshine in that shady place" '—W.

10 l. 361. ' "So break those glittering shadows, human joys." Young'—W.

11 l. 378. ' "Charming the night calm with her powerful song". A line of one of our older poets'—W.

13 *Salisbury Plain*. Composed Summer 1793–May 1794. Revised and enlarged 1795 as 'Adventures on Salisbury Plain'; further revised and published 1842 as 'Guilt and Sorrow; or, Incidents upon Salisbury Plain'. A version of 226–324, 352–94 published 1798 as 'The Female Vagrant'. For all three texts and an account of composition see Stephen Gill, ed., *The Salisbury Plain Poems of William Wordsworth* (Ithaca, 1975).

'Salisbury Plain' is a memorial of one of the most turbulent periods of W's life. In February 1793 war was officially declared between Britain and France. Hostile to national policy, penniless, anxious about Annette and Caroline in France, W's feelings are described in *The Prelude*, x, esp. 251–75. In July–August W walked over Salisbury Plain and, as recalled in *The Prelude*, xii. 312–53, seems to have found in its dreary waste a heightening to his already overwrought imagination. In the poem, W's most sustained use of the Spenserian stanza, the wretchedness of the poor in a so-called civilized age is compared with conditions suffered by primitive man.

15 l. 92. Stonehenge, where, W later recalled, 'Overcome with heat and fatigue I took my Siesta' (letter to John Kenyon, summer 1838).

21 l. 258. W's note 1798: 'Several of the Lakes in the north of England are let out to different Fishermen, in parcels marked out by imaginary lines drawn from rock to rock.'

l. 261. See Z. S. Fink, *The Early Wordsworthian Milieu* (Oxford, 1958), 88–9, 134–5, for a story of local oppression, known to W, in which an old couple are tyrannized because they will not sell a field to a large landowner.

22 l. 306. *devoted*. doomed to die.

26 ll. 424–7. W calls on the belief that the Druids made human sacrifices locking victims in a giant wicker effigy of a man and burning it.

28 l. 509. Echoes Milton's sonnet 'On the Lord General Fairfax at the Siege of Colchester', l. 10.

29 *Old Man Travelling*. Composed April–June 1797. Published 1798. From 1800 the title became 'Animal Tranquillity and Decay, a Sketch', the last two words being dropped in 1845. Lines 15–20 were omitted after *Lyrical Ballads* (1805). Surviving MSS corroborate W's note: 'If I recollect right these verses were an overflowing from the old Cumberland Beggar' (IF note).

Lines left upon a Seat in a Yew-tree. Composed April–June 1797. Published

1798. The tree, W recalled in the IF note, was on 'my favourite walk in the evening during the latter part of my school-time'. For an account of the disappointed man, Revd William Braithwaite, see *Wordsworth's Hawkshead*, 256–64, but note Woof's important caution (p. 264) against over-literal identification of this and other figures with real people. C clearly alludes to the poem in a letter *c.*17 July 1797: 'I am as much a Pangloss as ever—only less *contemptuous*, than I used to be, when I argue how unwise it is to feel contempt for any thing—.'

30 ll. 32–3. See DW *Journal*, 26 Feb. 1798: 'We lay sidelong upon the turf, and gazed on the landscape till it melted into more than natural loveliness.'

31 *The Ruined Cottage.* Composed April 1797–March 1798. Revised and developed 1802 and 1804. Published with further revision as Book One of *The Excursion* (1814). The history of composition of 'The Ruined Cottage' (and verse not published here, 'The Pedlar') is far too complex for discussion in this note. See James Butler, ed., *The Ruined Cottage and The Pedlar* (Ithaca, 1979) and Jonathan Wordsworth, *The Music of Humanity* (1969). A brief outline is, however, necessary. 'The Ruined Cottage' began as a narrative account of the sufferings and death of Margaret. In 1798 the narrative was framed by the introduction of the Pedlar, a philosophical wanderer whose origins and powers soon engrossed W, so much so that DW could write, 5 March 1798, that 'The Pedlar's character now makes a very, perhaps the *most* considerable part of the poem'. For the MS D version printed here passages on the Pedlar's education as a favoured child of Nature were excised (used later in *The Prelude*'s account of W's own childhood), but a very important passage was added to conclude the poem, ll. 493–538. In a later MS W attempted to reunite the poem's two interests, the sufferings of Margaret and the Pedlar's instruction in how to read them. Even after publication in 1814 revision did not end. Changes to *The Excursion* in 1845 transform the poem's conclusion. See also the passage 'Not useless do I deem' in the Appendix and W's IF note to *The Excursion*, *PW*, v. 373–6.

32 l. 45. In the IF note W compared Southey's passions for *books* with his own for *wandering* and said 'had I been born in a class which would have deprived me of what is called a liberal education, it is not unlikely that, being strong in body, I should have taken to a way of life such as that in which my Pedlar passed the greater part of his days. At all events, I am here called upon freely to acknowledge that the character I have represented in his person is chiefly an idea of what I fancied my own character might have become in his circumstances . . .'

33 l. 99. 'All that relates to Margaret and the ruined cottage etc., was taken from observations made in the South-West of England' (IF note). Early on in their life in the south-west DW reported that 'The peasants are miserably poor . . .' (30 November 1795).

37 l. 232. An important statement of narrative intent. W was to use the phrase 'moving accident' from *Othello*, i. iii. 135 again for similar purposes in 'Hart-Leap Well', 97. See p. 171.

l. 264. *purse of gold.* a bounty to encourage men to enlist.

38 l. 295. W's quotation marks draw attention to a borrowing from Burns's *To W. S.* – – – – *n Ochiltree*, xv. 3.

39 ll. 330–6. See DW's Alfoxden *Journal*, 4 Feb. 1798: 'The moss rubbed from the pailings by the sheep that leave locks of wool, and the red marks with which they are spotted, upon the wood.'

42 ll. 460–2. Butler, op. cit. 70, points out that Bridport, near the W's home at Racedown, was a centre for the manufacture of twine for fishing nets. He explains how the spinner walked to and from the spinning wheel with the flex tied round her waist.

44 [*A Night-Piece.*] Composed Jan.–March 1798. Published 1815. This text follows Beth Darlington, 'Two Early Texts: *A Night-Piece* and *The Discharged Soldier*', in *Bicentenary Wordsworth Studies*, ed. Jonathan Wordsworth (Ithaca and London, 1970), 425–48, which the reader interested in the composition of the poem should consult. Wordsworth noted: 'Composed on the road between Nether Stowey and Alfoxden, extempore' (IF note). DW's *Journal*, 25 Jan. 1798 records the occasion: 'The sky spread over with one continuous cloud, whitened by the light of the moon, which, though her dim shape was seen, did not throw forth so strong a light as to chequer the earth with shadows. At once the clouds seemed to cleave asunder, and left her in the centre of a black-blue vault. She sailed along, followed by multitudes of stars, small, and bright, and sharp. Their brightness seemed concentrated, (half-moon).'

45 [*The Discharged Soldier*]. Composed Jan.–March 1798. Not published by W, but incorporated into *Prelude*, iv. 364–504. This text follows Darlington, noted above. The fact that the description was conceived as an independent poem, before W's plans for *The Recluse* or *The Prelude* had taken shape, justifies its printing here as a discrete work. For the place of the meeting above the Windermere Ferry see *Wordsworth's Hawkshead*, 139–41 and 375. DW's *Journal*, 27 and 31 Jan. 1798, records impressions used in the poem ll. 7–9 and 135–6. W's account of the soldier, 'Neglected and ungratefully thrown by | Even for the very service he [had] wrought' (*Prelude*, ii. 545–6) is further evidence to add to that in *An Evening Walk*, 'Salisbury Plain' and 'The Ruined Cottage' of his awareness of the impact of Britain's military operations on common people.

49 *The Old Cumberland Beggar.* Composed Jan.–March 1798. Published 1800. Originally a 'Description of a Beggar' (see Reed, i. 27 and 342–3) the poem developed to voice some of W's lifelong convictions. In the Postscript to 'Yarrow Revisited' (1835) he attacked the degrading effects of the amended Poor Laws and continued the theme in the 1843 IF note to this poem, composed, he says, when 'The political economists were . . . beginning their war upon mendicity in all its forms, and by implication, if not directly, on Almsgiving also.' See whole note *PW*, iv. 445–6, and *Wordsworth's Hawkshead*, 377. The best way of dealing with the poor was a very live issue in the 1790s, as the war and agricultural failures led to a great increase in

vagrancy. W remained opposed to sweeping the poor out of sight—see 'I know an aged Man', p. 372. See also the letter to Fox cited in note to 'Michael', p. 700.

54 *Lines Written at a Small Distance from my House.* Composed 1–10 March 1798. Published 1798. From 1845 entitled 'To My Sister'. W noted: 'Composed in front of Alfoxden House. My little boy messenger on this occasion was the son of Basil Montagu' (IF note). He was also called Basil in fact, not Edward, and appears again in 'Anecdote for Fathers'. This poem, no less than the more complex 'Tintern Abbey' published in the same volume of *Lyrical Ballads*, expresses some of the fundamental convictions on which the whole of W's poetry is based.

56 *Goody Blake and Harry Gill.* Composed 7–13 March 1798. Published 1798. For the incident W drew on Erasmus Darwin's *Zoönomia; or, the Laws of Organic Life* (1794–6), which he had borrowed from Cottle, his publisher friend, in March 1798. See Jacobus, 234–40 for quotation from Darwin and discussion. W was aware, of course, at first hand of the distress of the peasantry. See DW's letter of 30 Nov. 1795: 'The peasants are miserably poor; their cottages are shapeless structures (I may almost say) of wood and clay—indeed they are not at all beyond what might be expected in savage life.'

59 *The Thorn.* Composed *c.*19 March 1798. Published 1798. W noted that the poem 'Arose out of my observing, on the ridge of Quantock Hill, on a stormy day, a thorn which I had often passed in calm and bright weather without noticing it. I said to myself, "Cannot I by some invention do as much to make this Thorn an impressive object as the storm has made it to my eyes at this moment." I began the poem accordingly and composed it with great rapidity' (IF note). For form and subject W was indebted to William Taylor's translation of Gottfried Bürger's *Des Pfarrer's Tochter von Taubenhain* and possibly to a Scottish ballad also. See Jacobus, 217–32 and 277–88 for a full discussion of Bürger's great popularity and influence and for a text of Taylor's translations. See *PW*, ii. 513–14 for the Scottish ballad.

In the *Advertisement* to *Lyrical Ballads* 1798 W pointed out that 'The Thorn' 'is not supposed to be spoken in the author's own person: the character of the loquacious narrator will sufficiently shew itself in the course of the story' and in the 1800 edition added a further lengthy note which has been printed here, pp. 593–4, with W's other critical prose.

From its earliest appearance, 'The Thorn' has been the subject of critical disagreement. See Stephen Maxfield Parrish, *The Art of Lyrical Ballads* (Cambridge, Mass., 1973).

66 *'A whirl-blast from behind the hill'.* Composed *c.*18 March 1798. Published 1800. Lines 24–7 were cut after 1805. W noted: 'Observed in the holly grove at Alfoxden, where these verses were written . . .' (IF note). DW's *Journal*, 18 March 1798 records: 'The Coleridges left us. A cold, windy morning. Walked with them half way. On our return, sheltered under the hollies, during a hail-shower. The withered leaves danced with the hailstones. William wrote a description of the storm.'

67 *The Idiot Boy.* Composed late March 1798. Published 1798. It is now clear from evidence of composition that both W and C tended in later life to impute to *Lyrical Ballads* (1798) a greater ideological coherence than it, in fact, possessed. There is no reason, however, to doubt that this poem was composed under the intention that W should choose 'subjects . . . from ordinary life; the characters and incidents were to be such, as will be found in every village and its vicinity, where there is a meditative and feeling mind to seek after them, or to notice them, when they present themselves' (*Biographia Literaria*, ch. xiv). Jacobus, op. cit. p. 684, discusses the poem's subversion of the genre represented by Bürger (see 219–24; 250–61).

In his important defence of the *Lyrical Ballads* in the letter to John Wilson of 7 June 1802, printed here pp. 620–5, W discusses the poem and declares: 'I wrote the poem with exceeding delight and pleasure . . .'. He also recalled it when looking back to the *annus mirabilis* in *The Prelude*, xiii. 399–402.

80 *Lines written in Early Spring.* Composed *c.*12 April 1798. Published 1798. The poem should be read not only with the other *Lyrical Ballads* but with the meditative verse of 1798, pp. 676–81. W's note, composed more than forty years after the poem, indicates his astonishing power of recall for such moments as are the basis of this poem: 'Actually composed while I was sitting by the side of the brook that runs down from the *Comb*, in which stands the village of Alford, through the grounds of Alfoxden. It was a chosen resort of mine. The brook fell down a sloping rock so as to make a waterfall considerable for that country, and, across the pool below, had fallen a tree, an ash if I rightly remember, from which rose perpendicularly boughs in search of light intercepted by the deep shade above. The boughs bore leaves of green that for want of sunshine had faded into almost lily-white; and, from the underside of this natural sylvan bridge depended long and beautiful tresses of ivy which waved gently in the breeze that might poetically speaking be called the breath of the waterfall. This motion varied of course in proportion to the power of water in the brook' (IF note).

81 *Anecdote for Fathers.* Composed April–May 1798. Published 1798. For the fuller context of the poem see note to 'The Tables Turned', p. 691. On 7 March 1796 W reported amusingly of little Basil Montagu, the child of the poem: 'Basil is quite well quant au physique mais pour le moral il-y-a bien à craindre. Among other things he lies like a little devil.'

83 *We Are Seven.* Composed April–May 1798. Published 1798. W noted 'The little Girl who is the heroine I met within the area of Goodrich Castle in the year 1793. Having left the Isle of Wight and crost Salisbury Plain . . . I proceeded by Bristol up the Wye, and so on to N. Wales to the Vale of Clwydd . . . I composed it while walking in the grove of Alfoxden. My friends will not deem it too trifling to relate that while walking to and fro I composed the last stanza first, having begun with the last line. When it was all but finished, I came in and recited it to Mr Coleridge and my Sister, and said, "A prefatory stanza must be added, and I should sit down to our little tea-meal with greater pleasure if my task was finished." I mentioned in substance

what I wished to be expressed, and Coleridge immediately threw off the stanza thus:

A little child, dear brother Jem,—

I objected to the rhyme, dear brother Jem, as being ludicrous, but we all enjoyed the joke of hitching in our friend James Tobin's name, who was familiarly called Jem' (IF note).

The whole note, too long to be printed here, is of great importance, for in it W recalls the circumstances in which *Lyrical Ballads* was conceived, and the composition of 'The Ancient Mariner'. See *PW*, i. 360–2. See also W's note to *Ode* ('There was a time'), p. 713.

85 *Simon Lee, the Old Huntsman*. Composed April–May 1798. Published 1798. Greatly revised in later editions. W noted: 'This old man had been huntsman to the Squires of Alfoxden . . . The old man's cottage stood upon the common a little way from the entrance to Alfoxden Park . . . It is unnecessary to add, the fact was as mentioned in the poem, and I have, after an interval of 45 years, the image of the old man as fresh before my eyes as if I had seen him yesterday. The expression when the hounds were out, "I dearly love their voices" was word for word from his own lips' (IF note). Simon Lee followed the hounds on foot.

88 *The Last of the Flock*. Composed April–May 1798. Published 1798. According to W's IF note 'The incident occurred in the village of Holford, close by Alfoxden', but not to W, as a letter of *c*.24 Sept. 1836 makes clear: 'But for my own part, notwithstanding what has here been said in verse, I never in my whole life saw a man weep *alone* in the roads; but a friend of mine *did* see this poor man weeping *alone*, with the Lamb, the last of his flock, in his arms.'

'The Last of the Flock', 'Goody Blake and Harry Gill', 'Simon Lee' are not merely embodiments of the literary theory outlined in the *Advertisement* to *Lyrical Ballads* (1798), but examples of the growing distresses afflicting the rural poor in the years after the outbreak of war in 1793. Harvests failed, prices rose, and an increase in vagrancy led to intensified demands for a reform of the Poor Laws. Many of the *Lyrical Ballads* sustain the social protest, based on observation, which is expressed most stridently in 'Salisbury Plain' and W's *Letter to the Bishop of Llandaff* (see *Prose*, i. 29–66). 'The Last of the Flock' anticipates 'Michael' in dramatizing W's conviction that the dignity of the poor depends on their being able to maintain an independent life (see notes to 'Michael', pp. 700–1).

91 *Peter Bell*. Composed April–May 1798. Published in revised form 1819. This text from MS. The important IF note is too long to quote here and should be consulted in *PW*, ii. 527. The dedication in 1819 looks back to W and C in 1798 and to the account of the 'plan' of *Lyrical Ballads* C had given in *Biographia Literaria* (1817), ch. xiv, as W declares: 'The Poem . . . was composed under a belief that the Imagination not only does not require for its exercise the intervention of supernatural agency, but that, though such agency be excluded, the faculty may be called forth as imperiously, and for

kindred results of pleasure, by incidents within the compass of poetic probability, in the humblest departments of daily life.' The poem was ridiculed and parodied when it first appeared, but Henry Crabb Robinson, who saw the MS, declared it 'one of the most delightful of Wordsworth's tales: with infinite imagination, and a great deal of profound psychology interspersed with exquisite description, psychological and natural' and was impatient with Lamb's failure to see that the slowness of the narrative is 'the *art* of the poet' (see *Henry Crabb Robinson on Books and Their Writers*, ed. Edith J. Morley, 3 vols., 1938, i. 96; 103). C referred to 'Wordsworth's most wonderful as well as admirable Poem, *Peter Bell*' (see *Notebooks* entry 2584).

116 ll. 876–900. W was probably indebted to C for this passage: 'A Lady once asked me if I believed in Ghosts and Apparitions, I answered with truth and simplicity: *No, Madam! I have seen far too many myself.* I have indeed a whole memorandum Book filled with records of these Phaenomena, many of them interesting as facts and data for Psychology, and affording some valuable materials for a Theory of Perception and its dependence on the memory and Imagination' (see *The Friend*, ed. Barbara E. Rooke, 2 vols., 1969, ii. 118).

123 l. 1099. In the IF note W says 'Benoni, or the child of sorrow, I knew when I was a school-boy. His mother had been deserted by a gentleman in the neighbourhood, she herself being a gentlewoman by birth. The circumstances of her story were told me by my dear old Dame, Anne Tyson, who was her confidante.' T. W. Thompson gives full details in *Wordsworth's Hawkshead*, 65–9.

129 l. 1313. Leeming Lane is a village in Yorkshire, where the Ws spent the night, 4 October 1802.

Expostulation and Reply. Composed *c*.23 May 1798. Published 1798. In the *Advertisement* to *Lyrical Ballads* (1798) W says that this and the following poem 'arose out of conversation with a friend who was somewhat unreasonably attached to modern books of moral philosophy'. This is usually taken to refer to William Hazlitt (1778–1830), who records in his splendid essay *My First Acquaintance with Poets* that, while visiting Alfoxden in May–June 1798, he 'got into a metaphysical argument with Wordsworth . . . in which we neither of us succeeded in making ourselves perfectly clear and intelligible'. By 1798 W had fully thrown off the influence of Godwin (see especially *Prelude*, x–xii) and had begun an *Essay on Morals* in which he declares: 'I know no book or system of moral philosophy written with sufficient power to melt into our affections, to incorporate itself with the blood and vital juices of our minds, and thence to have any influence worth our notice . . .' (*Prose*, i. 99–107).

ll. 13–15. The scene is in the Lake District and not Somerset. For Matthew see the note to 'If Nature, for a favorite Child', p. 693.

130 *The Tables Turned*. Composed *c*.23 May 1798. Published 1798. See note to previous poem. This poem is so central that reference from it could be made to almost all of W's mature work. In 1797–8 the Wordsworths and Coleridge were concerned not only with questions of perception, which is obvious from

C's 'conversation poems', from 'Tintern Abbey' and the description of the Pedlar in 'The Ruined Cottage', but especially with the question of how best to educate a young mind. The Wordsworths were looking after Basil Montagu and were bringing him up, as DW explained in a letter of 19 March 1797, in a system 'so simple that in this age of systems you will hardly be likely to follow it. We teach him nothing at present but what he learns from the evidence of his senses. He has an insatiable curiosity which we are always careful to satisfy to the best of our ability. It is directed to everything he sees, the sky, the fields, trees, shrubs, corn, the making of tools, carts, etc. . . .' For an extended later statement of W's unshaken faith in Nature as wise teacher see his 'Reply to "Mathetes" ' (1809–10), *Prose*, ii. 1–41. In 1797 it was suggested that W should oversee Thomas Wedgwood's scheme for educating a genius through strict control of sensory experience. For an account of this bizarre suggestion see Moorman, i. 332–7 and W's attack on infant prodigies in *The Prelude*, v. 290–449.

131 *Lines written a few miles above Tintern Abbey*. Composed 11–13 July 1798. Published 1798. W noted: 'No poem of mine was composed under circumstances more pleasant for me to remember than this. I began it upon leaving Tintern, after crossing the Wye, and concluded it just as I was entering Bristol in the evening, after a ramble of 4 or 5 days, with my sister. Not a line of it was altered, and not any part of written down till I reached Bristol' (IF note). In his edition of *Lyrical Ballads, 1798* (Oxford, 1969), W. J. B. Owen suggests some qualification to this statement (pp. 149–50), but it is clearly essentially correct. In the 1800 edition of *Lyrical Ballads* W added the note: 'I have not ventured to call this Poem an Ode; but it was written with a hope that in the transitions, and in the impassioned music of the versification would be found the principal requisites of that species of composition.'

l. 1. W visited Tintern in August 1793 (see note to 'Salisbury Plain', p. 685) and returned 10–13 July 1798.

132 l. 18. Moorman, i. 402, points out that William Gilpin, *Observations on the River Wye . . . Relative Chiefly to Picturesque Beauty* (1782), observes: 'Many of the furnaces, on the banks of the river consume charcoal, which is manufactured on the spot; and the smoke, which is frequently seen issuing from the sides of the hills; and spreading its thin veil over a part of them, beautifully breaks their lines, and unites them with the sky' (p. 12).

133 l. 49. C's *Notebooks* entry 921 meditates on the meaning of this line.

ll. 64–6. Not a new idea for W. While in the Alps in 1790 he had rejoiced that 'At this moment when many of these landscapes are floating before my mind, I feel a high enjoyment in reflecting that scarce a day of my life will pass in which I shall not derive some happiness from these images' (letters 6 and 16, September 1790).

ll. 67–84. See *The Prelude*, xi. 186–94.

ll. 74–5. See *The Prelude*, i–ii, for description of these pleasures.

134 l. 97. 'Interfused' is used in a similar context in C's *Religious Musings* (1796), 423.

l. 107. W notes the borrowing from Edward Young's *Night Thoughts* (1742–5), vi. 426: 'And half create the wondrous World they see'.

135 l. 129. In a poem of such joyous confidence the reference in 'evil tongues' to the Milton of *Paradise Lost*, vii. 25–6 may seem odd. But see the description of the poet amidst 'this time of dereliction and dismay' which closes *The Prelude*, ll. 435–66.

136 *To a Sexton*. Composed Oct. 1798–Feb. 1799. Published 1800. A sexton looks after the fabric of a church, rings bells and digs graves.

137 *'If Nature, for a favorite Child'*. Composed Oct. 1798–Feb. 1799. Published 1800. Titled 'Matthew' from 1836–7. W noted: 'Such a tablet as is here spoken of continued to be preserved in Hawkshead School, though the inscriptions were not brought down to our time. This and other poems connected with Matthew would not gain by a literal detail of facts. Like the Wanderer in *The Excursion*, this schoolmaster was made up of several both of his class and men of other occupations' (IF note). W's caution against over-literalness is important, but T. W. Thompson's attempt in *Wordsworth's Hawkshead* to identify possible originals for Matthew give a fascinating glimpse into the world of the schoolboy Wordsworth. See pp. 151–66.

138 *The Fountain*. Composed Oct. 1798–Feb. 1797. Published 1800. See note to poem above.

140 *The Two April Mornings*. Composed Oct. 1798–Feb. 1799. Published 1800. See note to poem above.

141 l. 30. River Derwent flows through Cockermouth, W's birthplace in the north of the Lake District.

142 [*Five Elegies*] Overall title mine. These poems survive in MS 16 of the Wordsworth Library, entered in fair copy as completed poems. For his volume of 1842 W reworked V and took over some passages added in margins of the MS for the poem 'Address to the Scholars of the Village School of——'. W's *Essays Upon Epitaphs* (1810), *Prose*, ii. 42–119 should be read.

147 *'A slumber did my spirit seal'*. This and the three following poems were composed late 1798–early 1799 and published 1800. Much useless speculation has focused on these 'Lucy' poems in attempts to identify the original girl and to unravel W's psyche. In fairness it has to be said, however, that C started it, in a letter of 6 April 1799: 'Some months ago Wordsworth transmitted to me a most sublime Epitaph ["A slumber . . ."] whether it had any reality, I cannot say.—Most probably in some gloomier moment he had fancied the moment in which his Sister might die.'

149 *Lucy Gray*. W noted: '. . . founded on a circumstance told me by my sister of a little girl who, not far from Halifax in Yorkshire, was bewildered in a snowstorm. Her footsteps were traced by her parents to the middle of the

lock of a canal. The way in which the incident was treated, and the spiritualising of the character, might furnish hints for contrasting the imaginative influences which I have endeavoured to throw over common life with Crabbe's matter-of-fact style of treating subjects of the same kind' (IF note).

l. 20. In 1816 Crabb Robinson recorded W's explanation that 'He removed from his poem [*Lucy Gray*] all that pertained to art, and it being his object to exhibit poetically entire *solitude*, he represents his child as observing the day-*moon* which no town or village girl would ever notice' (*Henry Crabb Robinson on Books and their Writers*, ed. Edith J. Morley, 3 vols. 1938, i. 190).

151   *A Poet's Epitaph*. Composed Oct. 1798–Feb. 1799. Published 1800. Terms for branches of knowledge have changed and may confuse today's reader: 'Doctor' l. 11 is a clergyman or theologian; 'Philosopher' l. 18 is a scientist; 'Moralist' l. 25 is a moral philosopher. The poem sweeps broadly and must not be taken too seriously (Charles Lamb objected to the coarseness of some of the satire in a letter of 30 January 1801), but with it should be read the passage from the *Preface* to *Lyrical Ballads* beginning, 'Aristotle, I have been told, hath said, that Poetry is the most philosophic of all writing: it is so: its object is truth . . .' (see p. 605).

153   *Nutting*. Composed Oct.–Dec. 1798. Published 1800. The textual history of 'Nutting' before its publication is too complicated to go into here. See Reed, i. 331–2. W recalled that the poem was 'intended as part of a poem on my own life, but struck out as not being wanted there' (IF note). DW sent a text to C in a letter of 14 or 21 December 1798 in which she also sent *The Prelude* descriptions of skating and stealing the boat. In MS 16, in use at this time, a text of 'Nutting' also exists in which the active episode is prefaced by a meditative address to 'Lucy', clearly connected in thought with the two passages printed here, pp. 676–80. This text is printed in *PW*, ii. 504–6.

l. 9. *my frugal Dame* was Ann Tyson, with whom W lodged whilst at Hawkshead School. See *Wordsworth's Hawkshead*, Part One, 'Hugh and Ann Tyson and their Boarders'.

154   '*Three years she grew in sun and shower*'. Composed Feb. 1799. Published 1800. See note to 'A slumber did my spirit seal', p. 693.

155   *The Brothers*. Composed 1800. Published 1800. As so many of W's poems, this originates in a story told to W in an encounter while wandering. In November–December W, C and, until 5 November, John Wordsworth, toured the Lake District. On 12 November in Ennerdale they heard the story of James Bowman who 'broke his neck . . . by falling off a Crag—supposed to have layed down and slept—but walked in his sleep, and so came to this crag, and fell off—This was at Proud Knot on the mountain called Pillar up Ennerdale—his Pike staff stuck midway and stayed till it rotted away' (C notebook entry 541). For the imaginative hold such stories always had on W see *The Prelude*, viii, *passim*: 'But images of danger and distress | And suffering, these took deepest hold on me | Man suffering among awful powers and forms' (211–13). As Derek Roper points out in his

edition of *Lyrical Ballads*, 2nd edn. (1976), 363, W intended in this and other poems to renew the genre of the Pastoral by writing about real shepherds, whose virtues he described to Fox, quoted in notes to 'Michael', p. 700. W's own notes to the poem in 1800 are quoted verbatim below, as '—W'.

l. 1. 'This Poem was intended to be the concluding poem of a series of pastorals, the scene of which was laid among the mountains of Cumberland and Westmoreland. I mention this to apologise for the abruptness with which the poem begins' W.

157 ll. 53–62. 'This description of the calenture is sketched from an imperfect recollection of an admirable one in prose by Gilbert, author of *The Hurricane*'—W. *The Hurricane* (1796), by William Gilbert (?1760–?1825).

159 ll. 137–43. 'The impressive circumstance here described actually took place some years ago in this country, upon an eminence called Kidstow Pike, one of the highest of the mountains that surround Haweswater. The summit of the pike was stricken by lightning; and every trace of one of the fountains disappeared, while the other continued to flow as before'—W.

160 ll. 180–1. 'There is not anything more worthy of remark in the manners of the inhabitants of these mountains than the tranquillity, I might say indifference, with which they think and talk upon the subject of death. Some of the country churchyards, as here described, do not contain a single tombstone, and most of them have a very small number'—W.

164 ll. 305–7. 'The Great Gavel—so called, I imagine, from its resemblance to the gable end of a house—is one of the highest of the Cumberland mountains. It stands at the head of the several vales of Ennerdale, Wastdale and Borrowdale. The Leeza is a river which flows into the Lake of Ennerdale; on issuing from the lake it changes its name and is called the End, Eyne, or Enna. It falls into the sea a little below Egremont'—W.

168 *Hart-Leap Well.* Composed early 1800. Published 1800. W noted: 'The first eight stanzas were composed extempore one winter evening in the cottage; when, after having tired myself with labouring at an awkward passage in "The Brothers", I started with a sudden impulse to this to get rid of the other, and finished it in a day or two. My sister and I had past the place a few weeks before in our wild winter journey from Sockburn on the banks of the Tees to Grasmere. A peasant whom we met near the spot told us the story so far as concerned the name of the well, and the hart, and pointed out the stones' (IF note). W and DW saw the spot 17 December 1799. See also the account in *Home at Grasmere*, 236–56. Mary Jacobus, *Tradition and Experiment in Wordsworth's Lyrical Ballads 1798* (Oxford, 1976), 232, points to the poem's formal origins in Bürger's *Der wilde Jäger*.

171 l. 97. See *Othello*, I. iii. 135. For W's exploitation of narrative *not* garnished with event see, e.g. 'Simon Lee', 'Michael', ll. 16–39 and 'The Idiot Boy'.

174 l. 98. De Selincourt, *PW*, ii. 515, suggests that 'curl' is a misprint for 'curd' and cites *Hamlet*, I. v. 69 and *All's Well*, I. iii. 144.

Home at Grasmere. Composed 1800. Not published by W. Lines 959–1048 published in the Preface to *The Excursion* (1814) as a 'Prospectus' to *The Recluse*. Revised version of whole poem published 1888 as *The Recluse*. No poem of comparable weight in the Wordsworth canon poses such problems of dating. See Beth Darlington, ed., *Home at Grasmere, Part first, Book First of the Recluse* (Ithaca, 1977) and Jonathan Wordsworth, 'On Man, On Nature, and On Human Life', *Review of English Studies*, NS xxxi (1980), 2-28. On MS and other evidence the composition of *Home at Grasmere* has been assigned to 1800-6. Jonathan Wordsworth's argument is accepted here that '*Home at Grasmere* is, almost in its entirety, a poem of 1800' (p. 28). This text is the earliest complete one, MS B.

In 1798, at the height of the intimacy of the two poets, C suggested that W was uniquely fitted to write a philosophical poem. The project for *The Recluse* was eagerly embraced by W (see letters of 6 and 11 March 1798) and verse such as 'The Old Cumberland Beggar' and 'The Ruined Cottage' was probably thought to fall within the scope of the plan. Preparatory self-examination produced the two-part *Prelude* of 1799 and composition after W had made his home in Grasmere from the end of 1799 became *Home at Grasmere*. The grand design of *The Recluse*, however, was not to be fulfilled. Only *The Excursion* (1814) was published, bearing the subtitle 'Being a Portion of *The Recluse*', and a Preface in which W revealed his ambitions for the whole.

It is probable that a version of ll. 959-1048 was composed as a separate effusion, in the same spirit that moved W to write the 'Glad Preamble' to *The Prelude* in November 1799, and only later became the conclusion to *Home at Grasmere*. In the 1814 Preface to *The Excursion* W printed them 'as a kind of *Prospectus* of the design and scope of the whole Poem [*The Recluse*]'. The significance of the *Prospectus* is ably discussed by M. H. Abrams in *Natural Supernaturalism* (1971), 17-70; 463-79, and Jonathan Wordsworth, *William Wordsworth: The Borders of Vision* (1982), 98-148; 387-90.

l. 1. The Wordsworths arrived at Dove Cottage, Grasmere, on 20 December 1799, after the journey across Yorkshire referred to in ll. 218-56. 'Emma' in the poem is DW.

178   ll. 171-9. W and DW were separated in childhood after the deaths of their parents. They were reunited in 1794 and from 1795, when they lived in Dorset, remained together. On 25 June 1832 W referred to C and DW as 'the two Beings to whom my intellect is most indebted'.

180   l. 257. See note to 'Hart-Leap Well', p. 695.

191   l. 739. Helvellyn stands to the north-east of Grasmere.

195   l. 864. John Wordsworth stayed with W and DW January to September 1800. For notes on him see pp. 700, 715.

ll. 869-70. W refers to Mary Hutchinson his future wife, her sisters Sara and Joanna and to Coleridge.

197   ll. 972-4. See Milton's invocation to Urania, *Paradise Lost*, vii. 30-1. For this whole passage see also W's discussion of possible themes for his life's work in *The Prelude*, i. 169-234. Its climax expresses W's 'last and favorite

aspiration', 'some philosophic song | Of truth that cherishes our daily life | With meditations passionate from deep | Recesses in man's heart . . .'.

198 ll. 1001–14. These lines do not appear in the first version of the *Prospectus* and almost certainly belong not to 1800 but to 1806. For the significance of this addition see Jonathan Wordsworth, op. cit., 111–14.

199 *Poems on the Naming of Places*. The following five poems were composed between December 1799 and October 1800 and grouped together under one title in *Lyrical Ballads* (1800). Although not written in the order in which they were presented (Reed orders: v, iii, i, iv, ii) they were composed in a sufficiently short span to warrant departure from the strictest chronological ordering for this edition. I have therefore retained W's grouping. In 1800 the following *Advertisement* introduced the sequence: 'By Persons resident in the country and attached to rural objects, many places will be found unnamed or of unknown names, where little Incidents will have occurred, or feelings been experienced, which will have given to such places a private and peculiar interest. From a wish to give some sort of record to such Incidents or renew the gratification of such Feelings, Names have been given to Places by the Author and some of his Friends, and the following Poems written in consequence.'

'*It was an April Morning: fresh and clear*'. W recalled: 'This poem was suggested on the banks of the brook that runs through Easedale, which is, in some parts of its course, as wild and beautiful as brook can be. I have composed thousands of verses by the side of it' (IF note). Easedale is immediately to the west of Grasmere village.

200 l. 11. *various*. W's italics draw attention to his consciously literary use of the word, which means progressively changing.

l. 39. Emma is DW.

201 *To Joanna*. Joanna Hutchinson (1780–1843), sister of Mary whom W was to marry 4 October 1802. The fact that Joanna did not live her early life 'Amid the smoke of cities' emphasizes that these poems are exercises of the imagination and not merely recitals of fact. For a MS note by W see *PW*, ii. 487. In the 1800 *Lyrical Ballads* W appended the following note: 'In Cumberland and Westmoreland are several Inscriptions upon the native rock which from the wasting of Time and the rudeness of the Workmanship had been mistaken for Runic. They are without doubt Roman.

The Rotha, mentioned in this poem, is the River which flowing through the Lakes of Grasmere and Rydale falls into Wyndermere. On Helm-Crag, that impressive single Mountain at the head of the Vale of Grasmere, is a Rock which from most points of view bears a striking resemblance to an Old Woman cowering. Close by this rock is one of those fissures or Caverns, which in the language of the Country are called Dungeons. The other Mountains either immediately surround the Vale of Grasmere, or belong to the same Cluster.'

203 '*There is an Eminence,—of these our hills*'. W pointed out that 'It is not accurate that the eminence here alluded to could be seen from our orchard-seat. It

rises above the road by the side of Grasmere lake, towards Keswick, and its name is Stone-Arthur' (IF note).

l. 14. See W's other tributes to DW in *The Prelude*, vi. 207–18; x. 908–20; xiii. 211–36.

'*A narrow girdle of rough stones and crags*'. W's IF note establishes that the incident took place with DW and C on the eastern shore of Grasmere.

204   l. 16. *wreck*. Northern form of 'wrack'.

l. 36. *Osmunda named*. royal moonwort, *Osmunda regalis*.

l. 38. *Naiad*. Naiad, goddess of river or spring.

205   *To M.H.* Mary Hutchinson, whom W married on 4 October 1802. W's IF note places the scene in the Upper Park at Rydal Hall, just south of Grasmere. Other parts of the Park were well known to the 'travellers' of l. 16, for Rydal Falls was a noted halting place for searchers after the picturesque.

206   *Rural Architecture*. Composed and published 1800. W appended the following note to the poem: 'Great How is a single and conspicuous hill, which rises towards the foot of Thirlmere, on the western side of the beautiful dale of Legberthwaite, along the high road between Keswick and Ambleside.' For an account of finding such a 'man' see C's letter of 18 October 1800.

l. 12. W records seeing effigies of Gog and Magog in London, 'the Giants of Guildhall', in *The Prelude*, vii. 131. Biblical in origin, they appear in legends about prehistoric Britain.

207   *The Childless Father*. Composed and published 1800. W noted: 'The huntings on foot in which the old man is supposed to join, as here described, were of common, almost habitual occurrence in our vales when I was a boy; and the people took much delight in them' (IF note).

l. 9. In 1800 W noted: 'In several parts of the North of England, when a funeral takes place, a bason full of Sprigs of Box-wood is placed at the door of the house from which the Coffin is taken up, and each person who attends the funeral ordinarily takes a Sprig of this Box-wood, and throws it into the grave of the deceased.'

208   *Inscription: For the Spot where the Hermitage stood*. Written and published 1800. The inscription—lines of admonition or tribute associated with a particular site—was a popular eighteenth-century genre and favoured by W. See Geoffrey H. Hartmann, 'Wordsworth, Inscriptions, and Romantic Nature Poetry', in *From Sensibility to Romanticism*, eds. Frederick W. Hilles and Harold Bloom (NY, 1965), 389–413; reprinted in his *Beyond Formalism* (1970).

Derwentwater is the lake on which Kewsick (home of C and Southey) stands. The Lodore falls, l. 13, are nearby. The story that St Herbert retired to an island on Derwentwater goes back to Bede. St Cuthbert, Bishop of Lindisfarne, died 687.

' '*Tis said, that some have died for love*'. Composed and published 1800.

210 *Lines: Written with a Slate-Pencil.* Composed and published 1800.

l. 8. Sir William Fleming of Rydal Hall, d. 1736.

211 l. 31. In *A Guide through the District of the Lakes*, called in its first edition of 1820 *Topographical Description of the Country of the Lakes in the North of England*, W explains his hostility to obtrusive new buildings not 'gently incorporated with the works of nature' and his insurmountable objections to whitewash on houses. See *Prose*, ii, 211–17.

The Oak and the Broom. Composed 1800, by 4 August. Published 1800. W noted: 'Suggested upon the mountain pathway that leads from Upper Rydal to Grasmere. The ponderous block of stone, which is mentioned in the poem, remains, I believe, to this day, a good way up Nab-Scar. Broom grows under it and in many places on the side of the precipice' (IF note). Moorman, i. 480 suggests that W had in mind John Langhorne's *Fables of Flora* (1771), which contains poems with such titles as 'The Sunflower and the Ivy', 'The Violet and the Pansy', 'The Wilding and the Broom'. W valued Langhorne (1735–79), like himself a native of the Lakes, as one who, in *The Country Justice*, had 'fairly brought the Muse into the Company of common life' (letter 15 Jan. 1837).

214 *The Waterfall and the Eglantine.* See note above. The IF note locates the scene 'nearer to Grasmere on the same mountain track. The eglantine remained many years afterwards, but is now gone.'

216 *The Two Thieves.* Composed and published 1800. W noted: 'This is described from the life as I was in the habit of observing when a boy at Hawkshead School. Daniel was more than eighty years older than myself when he was daily thus occupied, under my notice. No book could have so early taught me to think of the changes to which human life is subject, and while looking at him I could not but say to myself: "We may any of us, I, or the happiest of my playmates, live to become still more the object of pity than this old man, this half-doting pilferer" ' (IF note). T. W. Thompson identifies the two thieves as Daniel and Dan Mackreth, *Wordsworth's Hawkshead*, 191–3.

l. 1. Thomas Bewick (1755–1828) wood-engraver of Newcastle-upon-Tyne. Particularly admired for his vignettes which portray with great fidelity incidents from rustic life.

l. 11. Presumably refers to moral pictures hanging in an inn, which W would replace with his own equally instructive picture from life.

217 *The Idle Shepherd-Boys.* Composed and published 1800. In the IF note W recalled triumphantly: 'When Coleridge and Southey were walking together upon the fells, Southey observed that if I wished to be considered a faithful painter of rural manners I ought not to have said that my shepherd-boys trimmed their rustic hats as described in the poem. Just as the words had passed his lips two boys appeared with the very plant entwined round their hats.'

Dungeon-Gill is in Langdale. W's note in 1800 explained: 'Gill in the dialect of Cumberland and Westmoreland is a short and for the most part a steep narrow valley, with a stream running through it. Force is the word universally employed in these dialects for Waterfall.'

220 '*When first I journeyed hither*'. Composed 1800–4. Published as 'When to the Attractions of the Busy World' 1815. This text from MS. W recalled that 'The grove was a favourite haunt with us all while we lived at Town-End' (IF note).

ll. 1–5. W and DW arrived in Grasmere to begin life there on 20 December 1799. 'John's Grove' was just above Town-End, the little community just outside the main village where Dove Cottage is situated. John Wordsworth stayed with them Jan.–Sept. 1800.

221 ll. 41–9. John Wordsworth (1772–1805), who also attended Hawkshead School, joined the East India Company's *Earl of Abergavenny* in 1789. He was drowned when this ship went down on 5–6 February 1805. For a biographical account see *The Letters of John Wordsworth*, ed. Carl H. Ketcham (Ithaca, NY, 1969).

222 ll. 85–91. After JW's death DW wrote (15–17 March 1805) that 'he had so fine an eye that no distinction was unnoticed by him, and so tender a feeling that he never noticed anything in vain'. W's description of JW here strikingly resembles C's letter of 13 July 1802 about the sensuous apprehension of a true poet.

223 *A Character*. Composed Sept.–Oct. 1800. Published 1800. In the IF note W recalled: 'The principal features are taken from that of my friend Robert Jones.' C thought that the poem sketched 'certain *parts*, and *superficies*' of his own character and in 'A Note on Wordsworth's *A Character*', *Review of English Studies*, NS iv (1953), 57–63, E. L. Griggs persuasively argues that C was not mistaken. Robert Jones (1769–1835) was the undergraduate friend with whom W toured the Continent in 1790. He remained a lifelong friend.

224 *Michael*. Composed Oct.–Dec. 1800. Published 1800. In the first edition 'By a shameful negligence of the printer' (W 9 April 1801) lines 202–16 of the text were omitted. Very important related verse published *PW*, ii. 479–84 and *The Prelude*, viii. 222–311. W noted: 'The Sheepfold, on which so much of the poem turns, remains, or rather the ruins of it. The character and circumstances of Luke were taken from a family to whom had belonged, many years before, the house we lived in at Town-End, along with some fields and woodlands on the eastern shore of Grasmere. The name of the Evening Star was not in fact given to this house but to another on the same side of the valley more to the north' (IF note).

The poem was very important to W. He sent a copy of *Lyrical Ballads* (1800) to Charles James Fox, the statesman, and in a long letter of 14 January 1801 singled out 'The Brothers' and 'Michael' for special mention: 'You have felt that the most sacred of all property is the property of the Poor. The two poems I have mentioned were written with a view to shew that men who do not wear fine cloaths can feel deeply.' W's letter to his old friend Thomas Poole of 9 April 1801 also describes his intentions in the poem: 'I have attempted to give a picture of a man, of strong mind and lively sensibility, agitated by two of the most powerful affections of the human heart; the parental affection, and the love of property, *landed* property, including the feelings of inheritance, home, and personal and family independence.'

l. 2. *Green-head Gill* is a mountain stream to the north east of Grasmere. It runs through the area still known as Forest-side, l. 40. Dunmal-Raise, l. 141, is the pass north towards Keswick and Easedale, l. 141, runs westwards out of Grasmere.

229 l. 179. W's note 1800: 'Clipping is the word used in the North of England for shearing.'

231 l. 268. 'The story alluded to here is well known in the country. The chapel is called Ings Chapel; and is on the right hand side of the road leading from Kendal to Ambleside'—W's note 1800. Robert (not Richard) Bateman, a successful merchant, provided the money for the rebuilding of the Chapel of his birthplace. See *Prose*, ii. 266 textual apparatus and 430–1. DW describes the marble floor sent by Bateman in her *Journals*, ed. Mary Moorman (1971), 160, entry October 1802.

233 l. 334. W's 1800 note: 'It may be proper to inform some readers, that a sheep-fold in these mountains is an unroofed building of stone walls, with different divisions. It is generally placed by the side of a brook, for the convenience of washing the sheep; but it is also useful as a shelter for them, and as a place to drive them into, to enable the shepherds conveniently to single out one or more for any particular purpose.'

237 '*I travelled among unknown Men*'. Composed early 1801. Published 1807. Originally intended for the 3rd edition of *Lyrical Ballads* (1802). W sent a copy to Mary Hutchinson 29 April 1801, saying that it was to be read after 'She dwelt among th'untrodden ways'.

Louisa. Composed early 1802. Published 1807. Identified with Joanna Hutchinson, but Ernest de Selincourt argued persuasively that 'Dorothy was chiefly in W's thoughts as he wrote' (*PW*, ii. 4–71).

238 l. 19. W's quotation marks draw attention to *King Lear*, IV. vi. 26–7.

To a Sky-Lark. Composed March–July 1802. Published 1807. It seems likely that this poem was amongst a number which C commented on to Southey, 29 July 1802, as being 'very excellent Compositions, but here and there a daring Humbleness of Langauge and Versification, and a strict adherence to matter of fact, even to prolixity . . .'. In a letter of 24 October 1828 W told Barron Field that 'Coleridge used severely to condemn, and to treat contemptuously' this poem.

239 *The Sparrow's Nest*. Composed March–April 1802. Published 1807. W noted: 'At the end of the garden at my Father's house at Cockermouth was a high terrace that commanded a fine view of the River Derwent and Cockermouth Castle. This was our favourite play-ground. The terrace-wall, a low one, was covered with closely-clipt privet and roses, which gave

an almost impervious shelter to birds that built their nests there' (IF note). 'Emmeline' is, of course, DW.

The Sailor's Mother. Composed 11–12 March 1802. Published 1807. W noted: 'I met this woman near the Wishing-Gate, on the high-road that then led from Grasmere to Ambleside. Her appearance was exactly as here described, and such was her account, nearly to the letter' (IF note). C discusses the poem (and 'Anecdote for Fathers', 'Simon Lee', 'Alice Fell', 'The Beggars') in ch. xviii of *Biographia Literaria* and doubts the suitability of such subjects for metrical treatment. He also remarks that in the stanzas which record the woman's words is 'the only fair instance that I have been able to discover in all of Mr. Wordsworth's writings, of an *actual* adoption, or true imitation, of the *real* and *very* language of *low and rustic life*, freed from provincialisms.'

241 *Alice Fell.* Composed 12–13 March 1802. Published 1807. DW's *Journal* 16 February 1802 records the origin of the poem: 'Mr. Graham [Robert Grahame, solicitor of Glasgow] said he wished Wm had been with him the other day—he was riding in a post chaise and he heard a strange cry that he could not understand, the sound continued and he called to the chaise driver to stop. It was a little girl that was crying as if her heart would burst. She had got up behind the chaise and her cloak had been caught by the wheel and was jammed in and it hung there. She was crying after it. Poor thing. Mr. Graham took her into the chaise and the cloak was released from the wheel but the child's misery did not cease for her cloak was torn to rags; it had been a miserable cloak before, but she had no other and it was the greatest sorrow that could befal her. Her name was Alice Fell. She had no parents, and belonged to the next Town. At the next Town Mr. G. left money with some respectable people in the town to buy her a new cloak.' For C's criticism of the poem see note above. W dropped it from the canon from 1820, but restored it, after C's death, in the 1836–7 edition.

243 *Beggars.* Composed 13–14 March 1802. Published 1807. The poem shows the fascinating relationship between DW's *Journal* and W's poems at this time. On 13 March 1802 W finished 'Alice Fell' (see above) and, DW says, 'wrote the Poem of the Beggar woman taken from a Woman whom I had seen in May—(now nearly 2 years ago) . . .'. In the evening, however, 'I read to William that account of the little Boys belonging to the tall woman and an unlucky thing it was for he could not escape from those very words, and so he could not write the poem'. W completed it the next morning. DW's description of the beggar boys on 10 June 1800 is too long to quote here, but it should be consulted. W told Crabb Robinson in March 1808 that he had written the poem as 'a poetical exhibition of the power of physical beauty and the charm of health and vigour in childhood even in a state of the greatest moral depravity' (*The Correspondence of Henry Crabb Robinson with the Wordsworth Circle*, ed. Edith J. Morley, 2 vols. 1927, i. 53).

l. 18. *Weed of glorious feature.* See Spenser, *Muiopotmos, or The Fate of the Butterflie*, l. 213.

244 *To a Butterfly* (*'Stay near me'*). Composed 14 March 1802. Published 1807. See note above. W completed 'Beggars' on 14 March and the memory of Spenser's poem *The Fate of the Butterflie* must have prompted the conversation and composition. DW records: W 'wrote the Poem to a Butterfly! He ate not a morsel, nor put on his stockings but sate with his shirt neck unbuttoned, and his waistcoat open while he did it. The thought first came upon him as we were talking about the pleasure we both always feel at the sight of a Butterfly, I told him that I used to chase them a little but that I was afraid of brushing the dust off their wings, and did not catch them—He told me how they used to kill all the white ones when he went to school because they were frenchmen.'

245 *To the Cuckoo*. Composed March–June 1802. Published 1807. W discussed the function of imagination in this poem in the *Preface* to *Poems* (1815), (see p. 632).

246 *'My heart leaps up when I behold'*. Composed 26 March 1802. Published 1807. In 1815 W printed ll. 7–9 as an epigraph to 'Ode: Intimations of Immortality', the very lines C had emphasized when he printed the poem in *The Friend*, Essay v, as an expression of the truth that 'Men are ungrateful to others only when they have ceased to look back on their former selves with joy and tenderness. They exist in fragments' (see *The Friend*, ed. Barbara E. Rooke, 2 vols. Princeton and London, 1969, i. 40). In *Coleridge and Wordsworth: The Poetry of Growth* (Cambridge, 1970) Stephen Prickett points out, p. 6, that the Rainbow had especial significance. Newton's prism experiments in *Opticks* (1704) seemed to some, e.g. Keats, to destroy the unity of beauty, but to others, e.g. Thomson and Akenside, understanding the rainbow pointed to the marriage of imaginative and scientific modes of perception.

To H.C., Six Years Old. Composed March–June 1802. Published 1807. Date of composition uncertain. See Reed, ii. 180 n. 55. C describes his son on 14 October 1803 and quotes l. 12: 'Hartley is what he always was—a strange strange Boy—*"exquisitely wild"*! An utter Visionary! like the Moon among thin Clouds, he moves in a circle of Light of his own making—he alone, in a Light of his own. Of all human Beings I never yet saw one so utterly naked of *Self*—he has no Vanity, no Pride, no Resentment, and tho' *very passionate*, I have never yet saw him *angry with* any body.' Reed, loc. cit., points out the close connection between stanzas v–viii of the 'Ode: Intimations' and this poem.

l. 6. In 1807 W referred the reader in a note to Jonathan Carver, *Travels through the interior parts of North America* (1778), 132–3.

247 *'Among all lovely things my Love had been'*. Composed 12 April 1802. Published 1807. DW's account of the writing, *Journal* 20 April 1802, confirmed by W's letter of 16 April 1802, gives a fascinating glimpse of W's absorption in composition: '. . . when William came to a well or a Trough which there is in Lord Darlington's Park he began to write that poem of the glow-worm. Not being able to write upon the long Trot. Interrupted in going

through the Town of Staindrop. Finished it about 2 miles and a half beyond Staindrop. He did not feel the jogging of the horse while he was writing but when he had done he felt the effect of it and his fingers were cold with his gloves.' The poem, which W said recorded an incident in 1795, was ridiculed on its appearance in 1807 and not reprinted by W.

248 *Written in March.* Composed 16 March 1802. Published 1807. DW's *Journal* entry 16 April 1802 is itself a very beautiful account of the circumstances of the composition of this poem and should be consulted. DW leaves W sitting on the bridge at Brothers water, a lake near Patterdale and Ullswater, and when she returns she finds him 'writing a poem descriptive of the sights and sounds we saw and heard'.

The Green Linnet. This and the following three poems were composed April–June 1802 and published 1807. In a note 1807 and in the much later IF note W grouped them together as he remembered their composition. As Ernest de Selincourt, following Hutchinson, pointed out, *PW*, ii. 490–1, these poems all reflect W's study of the Elizabethan poets in Robert Anderson's *Works of the British Poets* (1792–5). In the IF note to 'Yarrow Visited' W paid tribute to this collection: 'but for this same work, I should have known little of Drayton, Daniel, and other distinguished poets of the Elizabethan age and their immediate successors, till a much later period of my life'. De Selincourt points to the influence of Jonson and Drayton on the metre of these poems, but the affinities between W's poems and the Elizabethans are so extensive that they cannot be documented here. The reader should see, as a beginning, Jared R. Curtis, *Wordsworth's Experiments with Tradition: The Lyric Poems of 1802* (Ithaca and London, 1971), especially chapters 2–5.

250 *To the Daisy* ('*In youth*'). See note above.

252 *To the Daisy* ('*With little here*'). See note above.

253 l. 25. *Cyclops.* Giants with one eye in the middle of the forehead, on Sicily. Odysseus encounters the chief, Polyphemus, in Homer's *The Odyssey.*

To the Same Flower ('*Bright Flower*'). See note above.

254 *To a Butterfly* ('*I've watched you*'). Composed 20 April 1802. Published 1807.

255 '*These chairs they have no words to utter*'. Composed *c*.22 April 1802. Not published by W. First published *PW*, iv. 365. DW's *Journal* 22 April 1802: 'A fine mild morning. We walked into Easedale . . . [I] sate upon the grass till they [W and C] came from the Waterfall. I saw them there and heard Wm flinging stones into the River whose roaring was loud even where I was. When they returned William was repeating the poem "I have thoughts that are fed by the Sun". It had been called to his mind by the dying away of the stunning of the waterfall when he came behind a stone.'

l. 19. Cf. Chaucer, *The Knight's Tale*, l. 2779.

256 *The Tinker.* Composed 27–29 April 1802. Not published by W. See *PW*, iv. 266. A tinker travelled the countryside mending pots and pans.

257 *To the Small Celandine.* Composed 30 April–1 May 1802. Published 1807. W

noted: 'It is remarkable that this flower, coming out so early in the Spring as it does, and so bright and beautiful, and in such profusion, should not have been noticed earlier in English verse. What adds much to the interest that attaches to it is its habit of shutting itself up and opening out according to the degree of light and temperature of the air' (IF note).

259 *To the Same Flower* ('*Pleasures newly found*'). Composed 1 May 1802. Published 1807. See note above.

260 *Resolution and Independence*. Composed May–July 1802. Published 1807. W noted: 'This old man I met a few hundred yards from my cottage at Town-End, Grasmere; and the account of him is taken from his own mouth. I was in the state of feeling described in the beginning of the poem, while crossing over Barton Fell from Mr Clarkson's, at the foot of Ullswater, towards Askam. The image of the hare I then observed on the ridge of the Fell' (IF note). DW's *Journal*, 3 October 1800, describes the meeting. W crossed Barton Fell on 7 April 1802.

The first version of 'The Leech Gatherer', as the poem was known in the Wordsworth circle, underwent extensive revision, prompted by criticism to which W replies in a letter of 14 June 1802. For a text and discussion see Jared R. Curtis, *Wordsworth's Experiments with Tradition: The Lyric Poems of 1802* (Ithaca, 1971), 97–113 and 186–95.

262 l. 43. Thomas Chatterton (1752–70), author of purportedly fifteenth-century poems of Thomas Rowley. Killed himself in despair at poverty and lack of recognition. Became a symbol of the poet whose creative gifts are at once a blessing and a destructive power. This poem follows the metre of Chatterton's 'An Excelent Balade of Charitie'.

ll. 45–6. Robert Burns (1759–96), still a farmer when he wrote some of his finest work. Burns was thought to have hastened his early death through dissipation. The fact that he left at his death wife and children without support is also in W's mind at this time when his own marriage was approaching.

ll. 64–72. W analysed the play of imagination in these lines in the Preface to *Poems* (1815). See p. 633. On the melancholy and desolation of mountain pools see *Prose*, ii. 186–7.

264 l. 119. See *The Prelude*, vii. 622 where W gazes on the blind beggar 'As if admonished from another world'.

265 *Travelling*. Composed *c*.4 May 1802. Published *PW*, iv. 423. This text from MS. See DW's *Journal* 4 May 1802.

'*Within our happy Castle there dwelt one*'. Composed May 1802. Published 1815 as 'Stanzas written in my Pocket-Copy of Thomson's "Castle of Indolence" '. This text from MS. James Thomson's poem (1748) was important in fostering the Spenserian stanza in the eighteenth century and was to C 'that most lovely Poem' (10 March 1795). W employed the stanza for narrative in 'Salisbury Plain' (1793).

In the IF note W said: 'Composed in the Orchard, Grasmere, Town-End.

Coleridge was living with us much at the time; his son Hartley has said, that his father's character and habits are here preserved in a livelier way than anything that has been written about him.'

Despite some confusion caused by Arnold (see *PW*, ii. 470–1), it has been generally agreed that the first portrait is of W and the second of C. Both are highly literary in origin, however, drawing not just on Thomson but on Beattie's *The Minstrel* (1771–4) and even *Troilus and Criseyde*, passages of which W had translated in December 1801, and, as Lucy Newlyn has pointed out in a penetrating discussion of the poem, they do not distinguish the poets but on the contrary merge and blur their separate identities. See 'Wordsworth, Coleridge and The "Castle of Indolence" Stanzas', *Wordsworth Circle*, xii (1982), 106–13.

267　'*I grieved for Buonaparte*'. Composed 21 May 1802. Published *Morning Post* 16 Sept. 1802. and 1807. W noted: 'In the cottage of Town End, one afternoon in [1802], my Sister read to me the Sonnets of Milton. I had long been well acquainted with them, but I was particularly struck on that occasion by the dignified simplicity and majestic harmony that runs through most of them—in character so totally different from the Italian, and still more so from Shakespeare's fine Sonnets. I took fire, if I may be allowed to say so, and produced three Sonnets the same afternoon. . . . Of these three, the only one I distinctly remember is "I grieved for Buonaparte" ' (IF note). In a letter of 20 April 1822 W lamented having written so many Sonnets in moments which 'might easily have been better employed', but, in fact, the form was important to him. He produced many fine sonnets, especially on national themes, thought deeply about the form (see his letter to Alexander Dyce of *c*.22 April 1833), and in 1838 gathered his production into a single volume.

　　Napoleon Buonaparte (1769–1821). General-in-chief of French army 1796–9. First Consul of the Republic 1799. Proclaimed himself Emperor 1804. Not finally defeated until 1815 at Waterloo.

268　*On the Extinction of the Venetian Republic*. Composed May 1802–early 1803. Published 1807. It is difficult to fix the date of composition of many of the sonnets. Reed's evidence in vol. ii of the *Chronology* must be consulted by the advanced student. Napoleon entered Venice 16 May 1797 and declared the Republic, which had reached the climax of its power in the fifteenth and sixteenth centuries, at an end.

　　ll. 7–8. Each Ascension Day the Doge of Venice dropped a ring into the Adriatic, symbolizing the wedding of the city and the sea.

　　'*How sweet it is, when mother fancy rocks*'. Composed between May 1802–March 1804. Published 1807.

269　'*I am not One who much or oft delight*'. Composed May 1802–March 1804. Published 1807. Titled 'Personal Talk' from 1820.

　　l. 6. Cf. *A Midsummer-Night's Dream*, i. i. 76–8 and *Comus*, 743 (de Selincourt).

　　ll. 25–6. See William Collins, *The Passions. An Ode for Music*, 60.

270 ll. 41–2. References to *Othello* and *The Faerie Queene*.

'*The world is too much with us*'. Composed May 1802–March 1804. Published 1807. Lines 11–14 allude to 'Colin Clout's come home again', 244–5, 283, and *Paradise Lost*, iii. 603–4.

271 *To the Memory of Raisley Calvert*. Composed May 1802–March 1804. Published 1807. Raisley Calvert (1773–5), brother of W's schoolfriend William Calvert (1771–1829) recognized the poet's promise and left W a legacy. W stayed with and attended Calvert in the months up to his death. For a later tribute see *Prelude*, xiii. 349–67.

'*Where lies the Land to which yon Ship must go?*' Composed May 1802–March 1804. Published 1807. Crabb Robinson recorded in his diary 3 June 1812 that W said this poem 'expressed the delight he had felt on thinking of the first feelings of men before navigation had so completely made the world known, and while a ship exploring unknown regions was an object of high interest and sympathy' (*Henry Crabb Robinson on Books and Their Writers*, ed. Edith J. Morley, 3 vols. 1938, i. 94).

272 '*With Ships the sea was sprinkled far and nigh*'. Composed and published as above. At l. 8 W referred in 1807 to Skelton's 'Bowge of Court', 36-8. W was upset by criticism of this poem when it first appeared and defended it in a letter of 21 May 1807.

'*It is no Spirit who from Heaven hath flown*'. Composed late 1802–April 1803. Published 1807. W noted: 'I remember the instant my sister S.H. [Sara Hutchinson], called me to the window of our Cottage, saying, "Look how beautiful is yon star! It has the sky all to itself." I composed the verses immediately' (IF note).

273 '*Methought I saw the footsteps of a throne*'. Composed May–Dec. 1802. Published 1807. The opening recalls Milton's sonnet 'Methought I Saw My Late Espoused Saint'.

'*Are souls then nothing?*' Composed May–Dec. 1802. Published 1836–7, considerably revised, as 'What if our numbers barely could defy'. This text from MS.

274 ' "*Beloved Vale!*" *I said,* "*when I shall con*" '. Composed May–Dec. 1802. Published 1807. The poem refers to the Vale of Esthwaite, where W passed his schooldays at Hawkshead.

'*Brook, that hast been my solace days and weeks*'. Composed May–Dec. 1802. Published as 'Brook! whose society the Poet seeks' in 1815. This text from MS.

l. 9. *Naiad*. Goddess of fountain and stream in classical mythology.

275 '*Dear Native Brooks your ways have I pursued*'. Composed May–Dec. 1802. Published in the *River Duddon* volume, 1820, as 'Return, Content! for fondly I pursued'. W recalls the beloved river of his childhood, the Derwent, and appropriately alludes to C's 'Sonnet to the River Otter' which begins: 'Dear native Brook!' This text from MS.

'*England! the time is come when thou shouldst wean*'. Composed May–Dec. 1802. Published 1807. W's ambivalent attitude towards his country as the bastion of Liberty—which becomes hostility to its territorial ambitions—should be compared with a similar ambivalence in his presentation of the French Revolution and Britain's response to it in *The Prelude*, x.

276 '*Great Men have been among us*'. Composed May–Dec. 1802. Published 1807. In this roll-call of English Republicans W refers to Algernon Sidney (1622–83), author of *Discourse concerning Civil Government*; Andrew Marvell (1621–78); James Harrington (1611–77), author of *Commonwealth of Oceana*; Sir Henry Vane the younger (1613–62). See Zera S. Fink, 'Wordsworth and the English Republican Tradition', *Journal of English and Germanic Philology*, xlvii (1948), 107–26.

'*It is not to be thought of that the Flood*'. Composed May–Dec. 1802. Published *Morning Post* 16 April 1803 and 1807.

l. 4. W's quotation marks draw attention to a borrowing from Daniel's *Civil Wars*, ii. 7.

277 '*There is a bondage which is worse to bear*'. Composed May–Dec. 1802. Published 1807.

'*When I have borne in memory what has tamed*'. Composed May–Dec. 1802. Published *Morning Post* 17 Sept. 1803 and 1807.

278 '*Farewell, thou little Nook of mountain ground*'. Composed May–June 1802. Published 1815 as 'Composed in the Year 1802'. From 1827 titled 'A Farewell'. This text from MS. On 9 July 1802 W and DW set off for Gallow Hill to join Mary Hutchinson, whom W was to marry in October. They returned to Grasmere on 6 October. In a letter of 14 June 1802, in which W sends Mary revisions to the poem, he refers to it as a 'Spenserian poem'.

l. 3. Fairfield dominates the mountains just north-east of Grasmere.

ll. 9–10. W uses the same image in his earlier poem of domestic contentment, 'I am not One who much or oft delight' (see p. 270, ll. 49–50).

280 '*The Sun has long been set*'. Composed 8 June 1802. Published 1807. DW's *Journal* 8 June records: 'After tea William went out and walked and wrote [this poem] . . . he walked on our own path and wrote the lines—he called me into the orchard and there repeated them to me—he then stayed there till 11 o'clock.'

ll. 10–11. W's quotation marks draw attention to allusion to Burns's 'The Twa Dogs', 153–4.

Calais, August, 1802. Composed Aug. 1802. Published *Morning Post* 13 Jan. 1803 and 1807. The Peace of Amiens established in March 1802 brought a brief respite to the war. In August Napoleon became First Consul for life, with the right to appoint his successor. Politicians crossed the channel to meet him. The curious, among them Hazlitt, went in thousands to Paris to see the new Republic and the Louvre, enriched by the spoils of the Italian campaign. W and DW went to France to meet Annette Vallon and Caroline and to make settlements before W's imminent wedding.

281 *Composed by the Sea-Side, near Calais.* Composed Aug. 1802. Published 1807. DW's *Journal* entry for the month includes: 'We had delightful walks after the heat of the day was passed away—seeing far off in the west the Coast of England like a cloud crested with Dover Castle, which was but like the summit of the cloud. The Evening star and the glory of the sky.'

'*It is a beauteous Evening, calm and free*'. Composed Aug. 1802. Published 1807. The 'Dear Child' is Caroline, daughter of W and Annette Vallon, although it could be construed as an address to DW. 'Abraham's bosom', see Luke 16: 22, the repose of the happy after death, suggests that W is thinking of the child's transition from 'God, who is our home' to this world in the terms developed in 'Ode: Intimations of Immortality'.

282 *To Toussaint L'Ouverture.* Composed Aug. 1802. Published *Morning Post* 2 Feb. 1803 and 1807. François Dominique Toussaint, surnamed L'Ouverture, was the son of a Negro slave. He was imprisoned in Paris in June 1802 because he resisted, as Governor of Haiti, Napoleon's edict re-establishing slavery. He died in imprisonment in April 1803.

l. 14. 'unconquerable mind' is a direct quotation from Gray's 'The Progress of Poesy', l. 65.

To a Friend. Composed early Aug. 1802. Published 1807. Titled 'Composed near Calais ...' from 1840. In 1790 W walked through France to Switzerland, as he describes in *The Prelude*, vi. 338 ff. *Descriptive Sketches* (1793) is also a memorial of the tour. W's companion 'A fellow student ... he too | A mountaineer' was Robert Jones (1769–1835), whom W was to describe in a note to this poem in 1837 as 'one of my earliest and dearest friends'. They landed in France on 13 July 1790, the eve of the Fête de la Fédération, marking the King's acceptance of the new constitution. In *The Prelude*, vi. 352–4 W describes the time as 'when Europe was rejoiced, | France standing on the top of golden hours, | And human nature seeming born again'. Between 1790 and 1802 had come the Terror, the French wars of conquest and the rise of Napoleon.

283 *Calais, August 15th, 1802.* Composed 15 Aug. 1802. Published *Morning Post* 26 Feb. 1802 and 1807. Napoleon became Consul for life on 2 August 1802. For W's earlier visit see note above.

September 1st, 1802. Composed 29 Aug.–1 Sept. 1802. Published as 'The Banished Negroes' in *Morning Post* 11 Feb. 1803 and with title above 1807. From the edition of 1827 on W printed as headnote: 'Among the capricious acts of Tyranny that disgraced those times, was the chasing of all Negroes from France by decree of the Government: we had a Fellow-passenger who was one of the expelled.'

284 *Composed in the Valley, near Dover.* Composed 30 Aug. 1802. Published 1807. This poem was in DW's mind as she made up her *Journal of a Tour of the Continent* (1820): 'When within a mile of Dover, saw crowds of people at a Cricket-Match, the numerous combatants dressed in "white-sleeved shirts", and it was in the very same field where, when we "trod the grass of England" once again, twenty years ago, we had seen an Assemblage of

Youths engaged in the same sport, so very like the present that all might have been the same' (*Journal*, 10 July 1820).

September, 1802. Composd *c*.30 Aug. 1802. Published 1807. DW's *Journal* 30 August records: 'We both bathed and sate upon the Dover Cliffs and looked upon France with many a melancholy and tender thought. We could see the shores almost as plain as if it were but an English Lake.'

285 *Composed Upon Westminster Bridge*. Composed 31 July 1802–3 Sept. 1802. Published 1807. W noted that the poem was 'Composed on the roof of a coach on my way to France Sept 1802' (IF note), but W and DW left on 31 July and returned to London 1 September. (The confusion is increased by the fact that all editions through 1836 date the poem 'Sept. 3 1803'.) It seems likely that W drafted the poem on the outward journey and completed it on 3 September. DW's *Journal*, 31 July, records: 'We mounted the Dover Coach at Charing Cross. It was a beautiful morning. The City, St. Paul's, with the River and a multitude of little Boats, made a most beautiful sight as we crossed Westminster Bridge. The houses were not overhung by their cloud of smoke and they were spread out endlessly, yet the sun shone so brightly with such a pure light that there was even something like the purity of one of nature's own grand spectacles.' For another poem which celebrates the transfigured city see 'St Paul's', p. 332.

Written in London, September, 1802. Composed September 1802. Published 1807. In the IF note W explained the tone of this and the next poem: 'written immediately after my return from France to London, when I could not but be struck, as here described, with the vanity and parade of our own country, especially in great towns and cities, as contrasted with the quiet, and I may say the desolation, that the revolution had produced in France. This must be borne in mind, or else the reader may think that in this and the succeeding sonnets I have exaggerated the mischief engendered and fostered among us by undisturbed wealth.' This is an interesting comment, coming as it does from the 73-year-old W, usually regarded as a dyed-in-the-wool Tory having no connection with the youthful author of the radical *Letter to the Bishop of Llandaff* and imitator of 'Juvenal Satire VIII'.

l. 9. Allusion to Milton's sonnet 'On the Lord General Fairfax at the Siege of Colchester', 13–14.

286 *London, 1802*. Composed Sept. 1802. Published 1807. See note above. Milton was, of course, the supreme example to W: a poet of austere and principled life and art. In November 1802 he wrote in a letter: 'Milton's Sonnets I think manly and dignified compositions, distinguished by simplicity and unity of object and aim, and undisfigured by false or vicious ornaments. They are in several places incorrect, and sometimes uncouth in language, and, perhaps, in some, inharmonious; yet, upon the whole, I think the music exceedingly well suited to its end, that is, it has an energetic and varied flow of sound crowding into narrow room more of the combined effect of rhyme and blank verse than can be done by any other kind of verse I know of.'

'*Nuns fret not at their Convent's narrow room*'. Composed *c.* late 1802. Published 1807. See note above. Furness, l. 6, is the south-western part of the Lake District.

287 *Composed after a Journey across the Hamilton Hills.* Composed 4 Oct. 1802. Published 1807. In editions after 1827 'Hamilton' was changed to the correct 'Hambleton'. Written on the evening of W's marriage. Compare DW's *Journal*, written after arriving back at Grasmere: 'Before we had crossed the Hambledon hills and reached the point overlooking Yorkshire it was quite dark. We had not wanted, however, fair prospects before us, as we drove along the flat plain of the high hill, far far off us, in the western sky, we saw shapes of Castles, Ruins among groves, a great, spreading wood, rocks, and single trees, a minster with its tower unusually distinct, minarets in another quarter, and a round Grecian Temple also—the colours of the sky of a bright grey and the forms of a sober grey, with a dome.'

'*These words were uttered in a pensive mood*'. Composition uncertain, between 4 Oct. 1802–March 1804. Published 1807. See note above.

288 *The Small Celandine.* Composed 1803 to March 1804. Published 1807. See note to 'To the Small Celandine', p. 704.

289 *Sonnet. September 25th, 1803.* Composed 25 Sept.–Nov. 1803. Published 1815 as 'On Approaching Home: After a Tour in Scotland. 1803'. This text from MS. From 15 August to 25 September 1803 W, DW and C visited Scotland, a holiday recorded in DW's *Recollections of a Tour Made in Scotland A.D. 1803* and many of the poems which follow this one. The tour fed W's imagination in the years after their return and hence many poems which purport to have been composed on the journey (e.g. 'The Solitary Reaper') were actually written later than this one, which was appropriately placed last in the series when W gathered together the selection 'Memorials of a Tour in Scotland, 1803' in his collected poems from 1827 on. The baby of l. 9 is John Wordsworth, born 18 June 1803.

To the Men of Kent. Composed Sept.–Oct. 1803. Published 1807. De Selincourt suggests, *PW*, iii. 456, that W owed to Drayton's *The Baron's Wars*, i. 323–4, knowledge of a tradition that the men of Kent were not conquered by the Normans but received from them a confirmation of their charters.

290 *Anticipation.* Composed Oct. 1803. Published in the *Courier*, 28 Oct. 1803 and 1807. At this time invasion was expected. On 3 October W enlisted with the men of Grasmere in the Volunteers. By 15 January 1804 W could write: 'We have given over even thinking about Invasion though our Grasmere Volunteers do walk past the door twice a week in their Red Coats to be exercised at Ambleside.'

Yarrow Unvisited. Composed Oct.–Nov. 1803. Published 1807. During their tour of Scotland W and DW came close to visiting the Yarrow, but, as DW writes in her *Recollections*, 'debated concerning it, but came to the conclusion of reserving the pleasure for some future time' (18 September 1803). W later confessed in the IF note to *Yarrow Visited* that their reasons for not visiting 'this celebrated stream [were] not altogether . . . for the reasons assigned in the poem on the occasion'. W said to Scott, 16 January 1805, that he had written the poem 'not without a view of pleasing you'.

l. 6. From 'The Braes of Yarrow' (1724) by William Hamilton of Bangour (1704–54). In a note to l. 35 in 1807 W also acknowledges indebtedness to this poem.

291 l. 20. *Lintwhites*. linnets. In this stanza W is, of course, referring to topographical attractions of the area near the Yarrow.

l. 37. *Strath*. valley.

l. 42. *Burn-mill meadow*. In the letter to Scott of 16 January 1805 W says of these verses: 'they are in the same sort of metre as the *Leader Haughs*, and I have borrowed the name Burnmill meadow from that poem, for which I wish you would substitute something that may really be found in the Vale of Yarrow'. 'Leader Haughs and Yarrow' by Nicol Burne, also echoed in l. 64, was one of Scott's favourite poems of the Border region. Like 'The Braes of Yarrow' above, it was printed in Allan Ramsay's *The Tea-Table Miscellany: or, Allan Ramsay's Collection of Scots Sangs* (1730), 183–6; 141–2, frequently reprinted.

292 '*She was a Phantom of delight*'. Composed Oct. 1803–March 1804. Published 1807. W noted that 'The germ of this poem was four lines composed as part of the verses (*To a Highland Girl*). Though beginning in this way, it was written from my heart, as is sufficiently obvious' (IF note). Christopher Wordsworth, *Memoirs of William Wordsworth*, 2 vols. (1851), ii. 306, cites Mr Justice Coleridge's record that W said the poem 'was written on "his dear wife"', of whom he spoke in the sweetest manner; a manner full of the warmest love and admiration, yet with delicacy and reserve'.

293 *October, 1803* ('*One might believe*'). Composed Oct. 1803–Jan. 1804. Published 1807. For the fear of a French invasion see note to 'Anticipation', p. 711, and Moorman's excellent account of the mood of the time, i. 599–603.

294 *October, 1803* ('*When, looking on*'). As note above.

October, 1803 ('*These times*'). As note above. Moorman, i. 601 cites C's letter 2 October 1803: 'These, dear Brother! are awful Times; but I really see no reason for any feelings of Despondency. If it be God's will, that the commercial Gourd should be canker-killed—if our horrible Iniquities in the W. India Islands and on the coasts of Guinea call for judgment on us—God's will be done! . . . Now bad as we may be, we assuredly are the best among the nations . . .'.

295 *October, 1803* ('*Six thousand Veterans*'). Composed Oct. 1803. Published 1807. DW's *Recollections*, 8 September 1803, read: 'Before breakfast we walked to the Pass of Killicrankie. A very fine scene; the river Garry forcing its way down a deep chasm between rocks, at the foot of high rugged hills covered with wood, to a great height . . . Everybody knows that this Pass is famous in military history. When we were travelling in Scotland an invasion

was hourly looked for, and one could not but think with some regret of the times when from the now depopulated Highlands forty or fifty thousand men might have poured down for the defence of the country, under such leaders as the Marquis of Montrose or the brave man who had so distinguished himself upon the ground where we were standing.'

W's note in 1807 reveals that he had read Sir Walter Scott's note to 'The Battle of Bothwell Bridge' in his collection *Minstrelsy of the Scottish Border* (1802–3). John Graham of Claverhouse, Viscount Dundee, was victorious at the Battle of Killicrankie, 17 July 1689, although he died himself. Scott says that a soldier in the battle of Sheriff-muir told him that 'a veteran chief . . . came up to the Earl of Mar, and earnestly pressed him to order the Highlanders to charge . . . Mar repeatedly answered, it was not yet time; till the chieftain turned from him in disdain and despair, and, stamping with rage, exclaimed aloud, "O for one hour of Dundee!" '

Ode to Duty. Composed 1804–early 1807. Published 1807. Motto from Seneca added 1836–7 edition. The history of the composition of this poem is too complex for discussion here. Between the first version of 1804 and the published text of 1807 W made many significant changes. See discussion and text in Jared Curtis, *Poems, in Two Volumes, and Other Poems, 1800–1807* (Ithaca, 1983), 30–2, 104–10. W noted: 'This Ode . . . is on the model of Gray's Ode to Adversity which is copied from Horace's Ode to Fortune' (IF note).

l. 1. See *Paradise Lost*, ix. 652–4. Eve explains:

> God so commanded, and left that command
> Sole daughter of his voice; the rest, we live
> Law to our selves, our reason is our law.

296 ll. 41–8. Excised after 1807.

l. 46. Echoes Milton's dedication to *The Doctrine and Discipline of Divorce* (1644), 'empty and over-dignified precepts'.

ll. 49–56. B. R. Schneider, *Wordsworth's Cambridge Education* (Cambridge, 1957), 171 suggests that W recalls here Newton's idea, expressed in the scholium at the end of *Principia*, that God preserves and maintains the universe: 'Lest the systems of the fixed Stars should, by their gravity, fall on each other mutually, he hath placed those systems at immense distances one from another.'

297 ll. 57–64. Glossed by W in 'Reply to "Mathetes" ' (1809–10): 'in his character of Philosophical Poet, having thought of Morality as implying in its essence voluntary obedience, and producing the effect of order, he transfers, in the transport of imagination, the law of Moral to physical Natures, and, having contemplated, through the medium of that order, all modes of existence as subservient to one spirit, concludes his address to the power of Duty in the following words [this stanza]' (*Prose*, ii. 24–5).

Ode. ('*There was a time*'). Composed March 1802–March 1804. Published 1807. History of composition uncertain, but seems probable that stanzas i–iv belong to 1802 and the rest to 1804. See Reed, ii. 27 and Curtis, op. cit. p. 271. In 1807 this ode was set apart as the culminating poem in the volumes and was generally distinguished through typographical lay-out in later editions. It is clearly W's major achievement in the genre. The title from 1815 became: 'Ode: Intimations of Immortality From Recollections of Early Childhood'. From 1815 three lines from 'My heart leaps up' were added as epigraph. The epigraph in 1807, from Virgil's *Eclogues*, IV. i, translates: 'Let us sing a loftier strain'.

In his long IF note W describes the poem's origins in his childhood's 'sense of the indomitableness of the spirit within me'. See *PW*, iv. 463–4. C's 'Dejection: An Ode' (1802) engages in dialogue with stanzas i–iv and is, in turn, answered by the development of W's poem.

299   ll. 58 et. seq. In the IF note W explains his poetic use of this fiction: ' . . . a pre-existent state has entered into the popular creeds of many nations; and, among all persons acquainted with classic literature, is known as an ingredient in Platonic philosophy . . . I took hold of the notion of pre-existence as having sufficient foundation in humanity for authorizing me to make for my purpose the best use of it I could as a Poet.'

300   l. 103. W's quotation marks acknowledge a borrowing from Daniel's *Musophilus* in the sonnet to Fulke Greville, l. 1.

ll. 117–23. On our early 'intimation or assurance within us, that some part of our nature is imperishable' see *Essays upon Epitaphs* (1810), i. *Prose*, ii. 50. See also *Biographia Literaria*, ch. xxii, where C discusses the passage and objects to 'the frightful notion of lying *awake* in the grave'. W cut ll. 121–4 after 1807. See also DW's *Journal* entry 29 April 1802 for the idea of lying in the grave 'to hear the *peaceful* sounds of the earth . . .'.

301   l. 144. See important anecdotal recollections *PW*, iv. 467.

l. 156. An echo of l. 50 of 'An Address to Silence' published in the *Weekly Entertainer*, 6 March 1797, which W knew. Later recalled in his own 'On the Power of Sound', see note to p. 358.

303   '*Who fancied what a pretty sight*'. Composed March 1804–April 1807. Published 1807.

'*I wandered lonely as a Cloud*'. Composed March 1804–April 1807, Published 1807. On 15 April 1802 W and DW saw the daffodils along the western shore of Ullswater. DW records in her *Journal*: 'I never saw daffodils so beautiful, they grew among the mossy stones about and about them, some rested their heads upon these stones, as on a pillow, for weariness and the rest tossed and reeled and danced and seemed as if they verily laughed with the wind that blew upon them over the lake, they looked so gay ever glancing ever changing.' In the IF note W said: 'The two best lines in it [15–16] are by Mary.' W was particularly sensitive to misreading of this poem. See his letter of 4 Nov. 1807 and to Beaumont Feb. 1808.

304   *The Matron of Jedborough and Her Husband*. Composed March 1804–Nov. 1805. Published 1807. When W and DW reached Jedburgh on 20 September 1803, in the last days of their Scottish tour, they could not find

accommodation and so were lodged in a private house. For DW's description of their hostess and her infirm husband see *Recollections*, i. 398–9.

306 *To the River Duddon*. Composed Oct. 1804–March 1806. Published 1807. The Duddon, which flows into the sea in the south-west of the Lake District, was the subject of W's sonnet sequence *The River Duddon* (1820), in which this became xiv. W was particularly fond of the river and recommended it to his readers as early as 1793 in a footnote to l. 171 of *An Evening Walk*.

307 *To the Daisy* ('*Sweet Flower!*'). This and the following two elegies were composed late May–July 1805, and exist in fair copies in one MS notebook. 'To the Daisy' was published 1815. A revision of 'I only looked for pain and grief' was published as 'Elegiac Verses, in Memory of my Brother, John Wordsworth' in 1842. 'Distressful gift!' was not published by W and appeared in *PW*, iv. 372–3.

John Wordsworth (1772–1805) went down with his ship the *Earl of Abergavenny* on 5–6 February 1805. See notes to 'When first I journeyed hither' above, p. 700. It was hoped that John Wordsworth would make enough money to become independent. Carl Ketcham in the introduction to *The Letters of John Wordsworth* (Ithaca, 1969) gives an account of the voyages W refers to in the poem.

ll. 15–28. In a letter of 7 August 1805 W said that the poem 'was written in remembrance of a beautiful letter of my Brother John, sent to us from Portsmouth . . .'. On 2–9 April 1801 John had written: 'I have been on shore this afternoon to stretch my legs upon the Isle of White . . . the evening Primroses are beautiful—and the daisies after sunset are like little *white* stars upon the dark green fields . . . We are painting the ship and making all as smart. Never ship was like us—indeed we are not a *little* proud.'

308 ll. 36–42. JW's body was recovered 20 March 1805. A committee of enquiry cleared him of blame for the wreck.

'*I only looked for pain and grief*'. See note above.

l. 6. W's lengthy note in 1842 identifies the plant as moss campion (*Silene Acaulis*). W had acquired in 1801 William Withering, *An Arrangement of British Plants . . . and an Introduction to the Study of Botany*, and a botanical microscope.

309 l. 41. DW's *Journal* 29 Sept. 1800 records: 'John left us. Wm. and I parted with him in sight of Ulswater.' In 1843 W could remember the spot exactly: 'The point is 2 or 3 yards below the outlet of Grisedale Tarn on a foot-road by which a horse may pass to Patterdale, a ridge of Helvellyn on the left, and the summit of Fairfield on the right' (IF note). JW did not return to Grasmere.

311 '*Distressful gift! this Book receives*'. Ketcham, pp. 62–3, speculates that the poem 'seems to commemorate the transcribing of the other two poems [see above] into a book originally meant to accompany John on his vogages'.

ll. 38–43. See W's letter about John, 23 February 1805: 'I trust in God that I shall not want fortitude but my loss is great, and irreparable.'

312 *Glen-Almain.* Composed May–June 1805. Published 1807. DW's *Recollections* for 9 September 1803 records their visit to Glenalmond: '. . . the road led us down the glen, which had become exceedingly narrow, and so continued to the end: the hills on both sides heathy and rocky, very steep, but continuous; the rocks not single or overhanging, not scooped into caverns or sounding with torrents: there are no trees, no houses, no traces of cultivation, not one outstanding object . . .'. DW concludes her entry with this poem 'written by William on hearing of a tradition relating to it, which we did not know when we were there.'

l. 2. Ossian, legendary Gaelic warrior and bard. Brought into prominence by James Macpherson (1736–96), who published *Fingal* (1762) and *Temora* (1763), epic poems purporting to be translations from Ossian.

313 *Stepping Westward.* Composed 3 June 1805. Published 1807. DW's *Recollections*, 11 September 1803, describes the meeting rather as W does in the headnote and concludes: 'I cannot describe how affecting this simple expression was in that remote place, with the western sky in front, *yet* glowing with the departed sun.' In the MS of *Recollections* DW has written: 'The poem . . . was written this day while W and I and little Dorothy were walking in the green field, where we are used to walk, by the [river] Rothay. June 3 1805.'

314 *Rob Roy's Grave.* Composed Sept. 1805–Feb. 1806. Published 1807. On 12 September 1803, at Glengyle on Loch Ketterine, W and DW were wrongly informed that Rob Roy was buried there. DW's *Recollections* record that they 'went up to the burying-ground that stood so sweetly near the water-side. The ferryman told us that Rob Roy's grave was there, so we could not pass on without going up to the spot. There were several tomb-stones, but the inscriptions were either worn-out or unintelligible to us, and the place was choked up with nettles and brambles.'

l. 1. Literary and personal connections come together here. A note to Scott's 'Lay of the Last Minstrel' (1805) quotes Drayton's lines on Robin Hood. Drayton was in W's mind in 1803 (see *Recollections* 18 August 1803), and Scott read some of the *Lay* to W and DW on 20 September.

l. 5. Rob Roy was Robert MacGregor, a Highland outlaw (1671–1734). W noted for l. 10 in 1807: 'The people of the neighbourhood of Loch Ketterine, in order to prove the extraordinary length of their Hero's arm, tell you that "he could garter his Tartan Stockings below the knee when standing upright". According to their account he was a tremendous Swordsman; after having sought all occasions of proving his prowess, he was never conquered but once, and this was not until he was an Old Man.'

317 l. 95. France's 'present Boast' was Napoleon.

318 *Address to the Sons of Burns.* Composed Sept. 1805–Feb. 1806. Published 1807. Enlarged version published 1827. On the importance of Burns to W

see his 1842 note, *PW*, iii. 441–2, and, most important, W's 'Letter to a Friend of Robert Burns' (1816) pp. 663–75.

The occasion of this poem is described in *Recollections*, in an entry, too long to quote, for 18 August 1803. W and DW visited the grave of Burns and his son and afterwards 'We talked of Coleridge's children and family . . . and our own new-born John . . . while the grave of Burns' son, which we had just seen by the side of his father, and some stories heard at Dumfries respecting the dangers his surviving children were exposed to, filled us with melancholy concern, which had a connexion with ourselves.' The fate of Burns had moved W to similar thoughts before. See 'Resolution and Independence', ll. 45–6 and note, pp. 262 and 705.

319 *The Solitary Reaper.* Composed 5 Nov. 1805. Published 1807. DW's *Recollections* 13 September 1803 record: 'It was harvest time, and the fields were quietly—might I be allowed to say pensively?—enlivened by small companies of reapers. It is not uncommon in the more lonely parts of the Highlands to see a single person so employed.' A note in 1807 identified the origin of the poem in a sentence from Thomas Wilkinson's *Tours to the British Mountains* (1824), which had been known to the Wordsworths in MS. It reads: 'Passed by a Female who was reaping alone: she sung in Erse as she bended over her sickle; the sweetest human Voice I ever heard: her strains were tenderly melancholy and felt delicious, long after they were heard no more' (p. 12). Both *Recollections* and the poem were, of course, written after the tour itself.

320 *Character of the Happy Warrior.* Composed Dec. 1805–early Jan. 1806. Published 1807. W's note in 1807 reads: 'The above Verses were written soon after tidings had been received of the Death of Lord Nelson, which event directed the Author's thoughts to the subject. His respect for the memory of his great fellow-countryman induces him to mention this; though he is well aware that the Verses must suffer from any connection in the Reader's mind with a Name so illustrious.' In the later IF note, which is too long to quote here, W links the life and death of Nelson (d. 21 October 1805) with that of his brother (d. 5–6 February 1805): 'many elements of the character here portrayed were found in my brother John . . .'. See also de Selincourt's valuable notes, *PW*, iv. 420.

322 *Star Gazers.* Composed April–Nov. 1806. Published 1807. W noted: 'Observed by me in Leicester Square as here described' (IF note).

323 *Power of Music.* Composed April–Nov. 1806. Published 1807. W noted: 'Taken from life, 1806' (IF note). Orpheus, l. 1, was a legendary pre-Homeric poet, with exceptional command of the lyre. The Pantheon, l. 3, was built in 1772 as a place of entertainment for the gentry. It stood on the south side of Oxford Street.

325 *'By their floating Mill'.* Composed April–Nov. 1806. Published 1807. From 1820 titled 'Stray Pleasures'. W noted: 'Suggested on the Thames by the sight of one of those floating mills that used to be seen there. This I noticed on the Surrey side between Somerset House and Blackfriars Bridge.

Charles Lamb was with me at the time; and I thought it remarkable that I should have to point out to *him*, an idolatrous Londoner, a sight so interesting as the happy group dancing on the platform' (IF note).The edge to W's recollection comes from the fact that Lamb did not disguise his preference for London over the Lake District. See his letters of 29 November 1800, 30 January 1801, 7 February 1801, 27 February 1801: *The Letters of Charles and Mary Lamb*, ed., Edwin W. Marrs, Jr. (Ithaca and London, 1975–), i.

326 ll. 33–4. See Drayton, *The Muse's Elysium* (Nymphal vi, 4–7).

Elegiac Stanzas. Composed May–June 1806. Published 1807. In this poem, more than in any other save *The Prelude*, past and present, life and art, interact. Peele Castle is off the southernmost coast of the Lake District, opposite Rampside, where W stayed in late summer 1794. John Wordsworth died 5–6 February 1805. See notes to 'To the Daisy' ('Sweet Flower!'), p. 715. Sir George Beaumont's painting, 'A Storm: Peele Castle' was exhibited in 1806, and W probably saw it at the Royal Academy Private View 2 May 1806. The painting, which depicts a ship labouring past Peele Castle in very heavy seas, was engraved as the frontispiece for volume two of W's *Poems* (1815). The contrast between a calm and a stormy sea is also used in a very striking passage in W's second *Essays upon Epitaphs* (1810), *Prose*, ii. 63–4.

328 '*Yes! full surely 'twas the Echo*'. Composed *c.*15 June 1806. Published 1807. W noted: 'The echo came from Nab-Scar, when I was walking on the opposite end of Rydal Mere. . . . On my return from my walk I recited these verses to Mary, who was then confined with her son Thomas' (IF note). In a very fine passage on the sights and sounds of early summer in the *Guide* W mentions: 'an imaginative influence in the voice of the cuckoo, when that voice has taken possession of a deep mountain valley, very different from any thing which can be excited by the same sound in a flat country' (*Prose*, ii. 228).

329 *Lines, Composed at Grasmere*. Composed early Sept. 1806. Published 1807. The statesman Charles James Fox, b. 24 January 1749, died 13 September 1806. W sent a copy of *Lyrical Ballads* (1800) to Fox, with a letter, 14 January 1801, which gives an idea of his estimation of the man.

l. 10. W's note in 1807 refers to the opening of Michelangelo's Sonnet 103, which W translated twice. The second version was published in *Memorials of a Tour in Italy 1837* (1842), xix. For important note see *PW*, ii. 500–1.

330 *A Complaint*. Composed *c*. Dec. 1806. Published 1807. W noted: 'Suggested by a change in the manner of a friend' (IF note). Almost certainly C, who stayed with the Wordsworths at Sir George Beaumont's Dec. 1806–Jan. 1807. His personal distress (C had decided finally to separate from his wife and family) deeply affected the Wordsworths. See Moorman, ii. 92–6.

Thought of a Briton on the Subjugation of Switzerland. Composed Oct. 1806–Feb. 1807. Published 1807. This sonnet, which W considered 'as being the best I had written' (27 September 1808), was composed 'while pacing to and fro between the Hall of Coleorton, then rebuilding, and the principal farm-house of the Estate, in which we lived for nine or ten months'

(IF note). C reprinted it in *The Friend*, 21 December 1809, 'having always thought it one of the noblest sonnets in our Language'. The Swiss, who symbolized Liberty for W as early as *Descriptive Sketches* (1793), were first subjugated by the French in 1798. They were invaded again in 1802. J. C. Maxwell discusses exactly what W had in mind in 'Wordsworth and the Subjugation of Switzerland', *Modern Language Review*, lxv (1970), 16–18.

331 *November, 1806.* Composed Oct.–Dec. 1806. Published 1807.

l. 2. Prussia was defeated at the battle of Jena, 14 October 1806.

l. 10. Pitt died 23 January and Fox 13 September 1806. Lord Grenville became Prime Minister and Lord Howick Foreign Secretary.

ll. 13–14. W's note in 1807 identifies these lines as from ch. 8 of Fulke Greville's *The Life of . . . Sir Philip Sidney* (1652). The passage is quoted *PW*, iii. 456–7.

'*O Nightingale! thou surely art*'. Composed Feb.–April 1807. Published 1807.

l. 2. From *Henry VI, Part 3*, 1. iv. 87.

l. 13. W discussed the line in the *Preface* to *Poems* (1815): 'a metaphor expressing the love of *seclusion* by which this Bird is marked; and characterising its note as not partaking of the shrill and the piercing, and therefore more easily deadened by the intervening shade; yet a note so peculiar and withal so pleasing, that the breeze, gifted with that love of the sound which the Poet feels, penetrates the shades in which it is entombed, and conveys it to the ear of the listener' (see p. 632).

332 *Gipsies.* Composed *c.*26 February 1807. Published 1807. W noted: 'I had observed them, as here described, near Castle Donnington, on my way to and from Derby' (IF note). In an essay called 'On Manner' of 27 August 1815, later collected in *The Round Table* (1817). Hazlitt objected to what he called the 'Sunday-school philosophy' of the poem, an objection which elicited penetrating criticism from Keats: 'I think Hazlitt is right and yet I think Wordsworth is rightest. Wordsworth had not been idle he had not been without his task—nor had the Gipseys—they in the visible world had been as picturesque an object as he in the invisible. The Smoke of their fire—their attitudes—their Voices were all in harmony with the Evening—It is a bold thing to say and I would not say it in print—but it seems to me that if Wordsworth had thought a little deeper at that Moment he would not have written the Poem at all—I should judge it to have been written in one of the most comfortable Moods of his Life—it is a kind of sketchy intellectual landscape—not a search after Truth—nor is it fair to attack him on such a subject' (28–30 Oct. 1817).

St Paul's. Composed April–early autumn 1808. Not published by W. See *PW*, iv. 374–5. The 'Friend', l. 2, is C, and W describes his experience after leaving him 3 April 1808 in a letter of 8 April, which should be consulted.

333 *Characteristics of a Child three Years old.* Composed most probably Jan. 1813–May 1814. Published 1815. The child is Catherine Wordsworth, b. 6 September 1808, d. 4 June 1812. See 'Surprized by joy', p. 334.

ll. 12–13. See *Paradise Lost*, ix. 429.

334 'Surprized by joy—impatient as the Wind'. Composed 1813–Oct. 1814. Published 1815. W noted: 'This was in fact suggested by my daughter Catherine, long after her death' (IF note). See note above. Catherine was a much loved child, though 'the *arrantest* Mischief that ever lived' (MW, 1 August 1810). See *The Love Letters of William and Mary Wordsworth*, ed. Beth Darlington, (Ithaca, 1981), *passim*, for accounts of her, and Moorman, ii. 212–14.

Yew-Trees. Composed 1811–14. Published 1815. W visited the Lorton Vale yew-tree in late 1804 and composition may have begun then, but no MS evidence exists to support this attractive idea. The earliest extant version of the poem, composed after June 1811 (see Curtis pp. 605–6 and Reed, ii. 37–8) reads:

> —That vast eugh-tree, pride of Lorton Vale,
> Which to this day stands single in the midst
> Of its own darkness as it stood of yore;
> Nor those fraternal four in Borrowdale,
> Joined in one solemn and capacious grove;
> Huge trunks, and each particular trunk a mass
> Of intertwisted fibres serpentine
> Upcoiling and inveterately convolved,
> Nor uninformed with phantasy, and looks
> That threaten the profane, a pillared shade
> On whose [   ] floor, beneath whose sable roof
> Of boughs, as if for festal purpose, decked
> With unrejoicing berries, ghostly shapes
> May meet at noontide,—Fear, and trembling Hope,
> Silence, and Foresight, Death the skeleton
> And Time the shadow,—there to celebrate,
> As in a natural temple scattered o'er
> With altars undisturbed of mossy stone,
> United worship, or in mute repose
> To lie and listen to the mountain flood
> Murmuring from Glaramara's inmost caves;
> Pass not the place unnoticed—ye will say
> That Mona's druid oaks composed a fane
> Less awful than this grove, as Earth so long
> On its unwearied bosom has sustained
> The undecaying pile, as drouth and frost,
> The fires of heaven, have spared it, and the storms,
> So in its hallowed uses may it stand
> Forever spared by Man.

In the IF note W said: 'Calculating upon what I have observed of the slow growth of this tree in rocky situations, and of its durability, I have often thought that the one I am describing must have been as old as the Christian era.' Clearly it was the yew's identity as a mute survivor which moved W's imagination to include in revision references to English warriors of the fourteenth century and to famous battles of the Hundred Years War. 'Yew-Trees' was one of the poems C chose to demonstrate that 'in imaginative power [W] stands nearest of all modern writers to Shakespeare and Milton; and yet in a kind perfectly unborrowed and his own' (*Biographia Literaria*, ch. xxii).

Lorton Vale and Borrowdale are in the western-central part of the Lake District, as is the mountain Glaramara.

335 *'Yarrow Visited'*. Composed Sept. 1814. Published 1815. See note to 'Yarrow Unvisited', p. 711. W visited the Yarrow on 1 September 1814, in the company of James Hogg (see *Extempore Effusion*, p. 370 and note) and Robert Anderson, to whose collection of *British Poets* W was so indebted and to which he pays tribute in the IF note to this poem. The note, which is too long to quote here, should be read in *PW*, iii. 450–1.

On 23 November 1814 W wrote: 'Second parts, if much inferior to the first, are always disgusting, and as I had succeeded in *Yarrow Unvisited*, I was anxious that there should be no falling off; but that was unavoidable, perhaps from the subject, as imagination almost always transcends reality.' This comment should be compared with *The Prelude*, vi. 452–61.

337 l. 55. A graceful tribute to Scott. Newark's Towers are the scene of his 'Lay of the Last Minstrel'.

338 *Composed at Cora Linn*. Composed in part 25 July 1814. Completed by 1820. Published 1820 in *River Duddon*. Epigraph from *The Prelude*, i. 213–19 (whole poem not published till 1850). W noted: 'I had seen this celebrated waterfall twice before. But the feelings to which it had given birth were not expressed till they recurred in presence of the object of this occasion' (IF note). W visited it in 1801 and 1803. This occasion was 25 July 1814.

339 l. 20. Another tribute to Scott. The phrase 'Wallace Wight' is from *Marmion* (1808), ii. 113 and *passim*. William Wallace (?1272–1305), Scottish patriot and national hero of wars against England.

l. 41. Leonidas, King of Sparta (491–480 BC) held the Pass of Thermopylae against the invasion of Xerxes.

l. 42. *devoted*. doomed to die.

l. 46. William Tell, legendary hero of the liberation of Switzerland from Austria. Uri was his Canton.

340 *To B. R. Haydon, Esq*. Composed late Nov. 1815. Published 1 April 1816 in *The Champion* and 1820. W declared, 21 December 1815, that the poem was inspired by Haydon's letter of 27 November, in which he said: 'I shall ever remember with secret delight the friendship with which you honour me, and the interest you take in my success. God grant it ultimately be assured! I will bear want, pain, misery and blindness, but I will never yield one step I have gained on the road I am determined to travel over' (*Benjamin Robert Haydon: Correspondence and Table Talk*, ed. Frederic Wordsworth Haydon, 2 vols. 1876, ii. 19). For Haydon's private response to the sonnet: 'It is impossible to tell how I felt, after the first blaze of joy, feeling as it were lifted up in the

great eye of the World, and feeling nothing more could be said of one . . .' see *The Diary of Benjamin Robert Haydon*, ed. Willard Bissell Pope, 5 vols. (Cambridge, Mass., 1960–3), i. 491–2 and for his reply to W: 'You are the first English poet who has ever done complete justice to my delightful Art' see *Correspondence*, op. cit., ii. 20–2, 29 Dec. 1815.

Haydon (1786–1846) attempted to maintain the prestige of historical painting. In a letter of 10 January 1818 Keats declared Haydon's pictures to be one of the 'three things to rejoice at in this Age', but they met with little success and eventually Haydon took his own life.

November 1, 1815. Composed early Dec. 1815. Published 28 January 1816 in *The Examiner* and 1820. W noted: 'Suggested on the banks of the Brathay by the sight of the Langdale Pikes. It is delightful to remember these moments of far-distant days, which probably would have been forgotten if the impression had not been transferred to verse' (IF note).

341 *'While not a leaf seems faded'*. Composed early Dec. 1815. Published 11 February 1816 in *The Examiner* and 1820. W said that the poem 'notices a . . . sensation which the revolution of the seasons impressed me with last Autumn' (21 December 1815), but noted later in the IF note that the conclusion 'has more than once, to my great regret, excited painfully sad feelings in the hearts of young persons fond of poetry and poetic composition, by contrast of their feeble and declining health with that state of robust constitution which prompted me to rejoice in a season of frost and snow as more favourable to the Muses than summer itself.'

Ode.–1817. Composed *c.*17 April 1817. Published 1820 in *River Duddon*. Titled 'Vernal Ode' from Collected Edition of 1820 on. W noted that the poem was 'Composed to place in view the immortality of succession where immortality is denied, as far as we know, to the individual creature' (IF note). Compare with Tennyson's *In Memoriam* (1850).

343 ll. 67–8. Urania is the muse of astronomy, Clio of history.

344 l. 120. Tartarus was one of the regions of Hades where the most guilty were doomed to punishment.

345 *Ode. The Pass of Kirkstone*. Composed 27 June 1817. Published in *River Duddon* (1820). W noted that the poem embodied 'Thoughts and feelings of many walks in all weathers by day and night over this pass, alone and with beloved friends' (IF note). The Kirkstone Pass joins the valley in which Grasmere and Ambleside lie with Patterdale and Ullswater.

347 *Ode. Composed Upon an Evening . . . Beauty*. Composed 1817. Published in *River Duddon* (1820). Titled 'Evening Ode' in Collected Editions 1820–32. W noted: 'Felt and in a great measure composed upon the little mount in front of our abode at Rydal' (IF note). W's note at the end of the text in 1820 reads: 'The multiplication of mountain-ridges, described, at the commencement of the third stanza of this Ode, as a kind of Jacob's Ladder, leading to Heaven, is produced either by watery vapours, or sunny haze—in the present instance by the latter cause. See the account of the Lakes at the end of this volume. The reader, who is acquainted with the Author's Ode,

intitled, "Intimations of Immortality, etc." will recognize the allusion to it that pervades the last stanza of the foregoing Poem.' In the *River Duddon* volume W printed his second edition of *Topographical Description of The Country of the Lakes*, where pp. 221-2 deal in particular with effects of light. In a note to the 1820 Collected Edition W acknowledged indebtedness to the painting 'Jacob's Dream' by Washington Allston (1779-1843).

350 *Sequel to [Beggars]*. Composed 1817. Published 1817 as 'Sequel to the Foregoing'—'Beggars' being printed before it. See p. 243.

l. 1. Recollection of *King Lear*, IV. i. 38.

l. 2. *dædal*. varied. See *Faerie Queene*, IV. x. 45.

351 *The River Duddon: Conclusion*. Composed 1818-20. Published 1820. The conclusion of 'The River Duddon' sonnet sequence. See the IF note to the whole which is too long to quote here, *PW*, iii. 503-5. See note to 'To the River Duddon', p. 715. This sonnet has been selected as the finest of the sequence and the one best able to stand alone.

l. 5. See *Home at Grasmere*, p. 174, l. 384. Cf. also C's description of a waterfall, 25 August 1802: ' . . . the continual *change* of the *Matter*, the perpetual *Sameness* of the *Form*—it is an awful Image and Shadow of God and the World'.

352 *Bruges* ('*Bruges I saw*'). Composed Nov. 1820–Nov. 1821. Published 1822. DW wrote, 16 January 1822, that W 'began . . . with saying, "I will write some Poems for your journal", and I thankfully received them as a tribute to the journal which I was making from notes, memoranda taken in our last summer's journey on the Continent; but his work has grown to such importance . . . that I have long ceased to consider it in connection with my own narrative.' W published his *Memorials of a Tour on the Continent, 1820* in 1822. The Tour lasted July–October 1820. See *PW*, iii. 467-8 for W's note on Bruges, too long to quote here. See also DW's *Journal* for 13 July 1820: 'We entered Bruges by a long gently-winding street . . . W . . . walked out immediately, eager to view the City in the warm light of the setting sun' (*Journals of Dorothy Wordsworth*, ed. E. de Selincourt, 2 vols., 1941, ii. 17).

Bruges ('*The Spirit of Antiquity*'). See note above. Same *Journal* entry: 'Early as it was, people of all ages were abroad, chiefly on their way to the churches . . . Such figures might have walked through these streets two hundred years ago; streets bearing no stamp of progress or of decay. One might fancy that as the city had been built so it had remained.'

353 *Mutability*. Composed 1821. Published 1822 in *Ecclesiastical Sketches*. Line 14 is a fine example of W's total recall of his own verse. He had first written, but not published, the line in 1796 in a 'Gothic Tale' of which only a fragment survives. See Robert Osborn, ed., *The Borderers* (Ithaca, 1982), 752, l. 68.

To the Torrent at the Devil's Bridge. Composed Sept. 1824. Published 1827. In September 1824 W revisited North Wales and met again Robert Jones to revisit places seen in 1791 and 1793. W wrote 20 September: 'It rained heavily in the night, and we saw the waterfalls in perfection. While Dora was attempting to make a sketch from the chasm in the rain, I composed by her side the following address to the torrent.' Mary Wordsworth declared the day 'a sublime finale to the whole' (See *The Letters of Mary Wordsworth*, ed. Mary E. Burton, 1958, 116).

l. 4. Pindus, mountain range in Northern Greece. W refers to the Greek War of Independence (1821-6).

ll. 7-8. In the letter quoted above W writes: 'If the remembrance of 34 years may be trusted, this chasm bears a strong likeness to that of Viamala in the Grisons, thro' which the Rhine has forced its Way.' W had visited the spot in August 1790 and refers to it in *Descriptive Sketches* (1793), 184-5. *PW*, i. 52.

Composed Among the Ruins of a Castle. Composed Sept. 1824. Published 1827. See letter quoted in note above: 'We . . . breakfasted . . . at Carnarvon. We employed several hours in exploring the interior of the noble castle, and looking at it from different points of view in the neighbourhood.'

354 *To*—('*O dearer far*'). Composed 1824. Published 1827. W's IF note establishes that the poem was addressed to Mary Wordsworth. De Selincourt, *PW*, ii. 474, says that the reflections in the poem were prompted by the lingering illness of Thomas Monkhouse, MW's cousin, who died 26 February 1825. He was, W said, 19 November 1824, 'an example of a Man upright in all his dealings and a most affectionate friend'.

l. 8. W's quotation marks refer to *Comus*, 263.

To—('*Let other Bards*'). Composed 1824. Published 1827. To Mary Wordsworth. The nature of W's relationship with his wife has been the subject of ill-natured speculation. For an idea of what W's marriage meant to both see *The Love Letters of William and Mary Wordsworth*, ed. Beth Darlington (Ithaca, 1981).

355 '*Once I could hail* . . .' Composed 1826. Published 1827.

l. 15. Diana is both the moon and the goddess of the moon.

356 l. 18. Proserpine, daughter of Zeus and Demeter. She was carried off to the underworld and made Queen, but allowed to return to earth for six months of each year.

'*Scorn not the Sonnet*'. Date of composition unknown, but published 1827. W said the poem was 'Composed, almost extempore, in a short walk on the western side of Rydal Lake' (IF note). See 'Nuns fret not' p. 286 and note. For W on the sonnet form see *The Critical Opinions of William Wordsworth*, ed. Markham L. Peacock (Baltimore, 1950), 147-9.

357 *Incident at Bruges*. Composed after July 1828. Published 1835. W noted: 'This occurred in Bruges in the year 1828 . . . Dora and I, while taking a walk along a retired part of the town, heard the voice as here described, and were afterwards informed that it was a Convent in which were many English. We were both much touched, I might say affected, and Dora moved as appears in the verses' (IF note).

358 *On the Power of Sound.* Composed 1828–late 1829. Published 1835. W wrote to Alexander Dyce on 23 December 1837: 'I cannot call to mind a reason why you should not think some passages in "The Power of Sound" equal to anything I have produced; when first printed in Yarrow Revisited [1835], I placed it at the end of the Volume, and in the last edition of my poems [1836–7], at the close of the Poems of Imagination, indicating thereby my *own* opinion of it.'

359 l. 14. See Gray's 'Elegy', 39–40.

360 l. 76. See Milton's 'L'Allegro', 136.

362 l. 126. Orpheus freed Eurydice from the underworld by the power of his music.

ll. 129–31. Amphion founded Thebes by charming stones with his music.

ll. 131–2. Arion was a legendary poet and musician. Thrown overboard by sailors he was carried to land by a dolphin, charmed by his song.

ll. 134–6. See *A Midsummer Night's Dream*, II. i. 150–1.

l. 146. *Maenalian.* Arcadian.

363 ll. 150–1. See Gray's 'The Progress of Poesy', 34.

364 ll. 199–202. W said in the IF note that these lines 'were suggested near the Giant's Causeway, or rather at the promontory of Fairhead where a pair of eagles wheeled above our heads and darted off as if to hide themselves in a blaze of sky made by the setting sun'. W visited Ireland in September 1829.

ll. 217–18. See 'Ode: Intimations', 155–6.

365 *Yarrow Revisited.* Composed Autumn 1831. Published 1835. W noted: 'In the autumn of 1831, my daughter and I set off from Rydal to visit Sir Walter Scott before his departure for Italy . . . How sadly changed did I find him from the man I had seen so healthy, gay, and hopeful, a few years before . . . On Tuesday morning [20 September] Sir Walter Scott accompanied us and most of the party to Newark Castle on the Yarrow. When we alighted from the carriages he walked pretty stoutly, and had great pleasure in revisiting those favourite haunts. Of that excursion the verses "Yarrow revisited" are a memorial. Notwithstanding the romance that pervades Sir W's works and attaches to many of his habits, there is too much pressure of fact for these verses to harmonise as much as I could wish with the two preceding Poems ['Yarrow Unvisited' and 'Yarrow Visited', pp. 290 and 335]' (IF note). Only a small section of W's long note is quoted here. See *PW*, iii. 524–6.

l. 2. See note to 'Yarrow Unvisited', p. 290.

l. 8. The 'Great Minstrel of the Border' is, of course, Scott, whose 'Lay of the Last Minstrel', 26–32, is alluded to in ll. 100–4.

366 ll. 49–56. Illness forced Scott abroad in search of a better climate. He left Abbotsford on 23 September 1831. He returned a very sick man and died 21 September 1832.

368 *On the Departure of Sir Walter Scott.* Composed Autumn 1831. Published in

the *Literary Souvenir* of 1833 and 1835. In the IF note to 'Yarrow Revisited', quoted above, W writes of this poem: 'On our return [from Newark Castle] in the afternoon we had to cross the Tweed directly opposite Abbotsford. The wheels of our carriage grated upon the pebbles in the bed of the stream, that there flows somewhat rapidly; a rich but sad light of rather a purple than a golden hue was spread over the Eildon hills at that moment; and thinking it probable that it might be the last time Sir Walter would cross the stream, I was not a little moved, and expressed some of my feelings in [this] sonnet . . . At noon on Thursday we left Abbotsford, and in the morning of that day Sir W. and I had a serious conversation, *tête-à-tête*, when he spoke with gratitude of the happy life which upon the whole he had led.'

l. 14. Parthenope is Virgil's name for Naples, Scott's destination.

369 *'Calm is the fragrant air, and loth to lose'*. Composed 1832. Published 1835. In one MS titled 'Twilight by the side of Grasmere Lake'. This late poem should be compared with the evocation of the sights and sounds of evening in *An Evening Walk* (1793).

Airey-Force Valley. Composed Sept. 1835. Published 1842. Aira Force is on the western shore of Ullswater. 'Force' is the northern word for waterfall. In *A Guide Through the District of the Lakes* W declares Ullswater 'As being, perhaps, upon the whole, the happiest combination of beauty and grandeur, which any of the Lakes affords . . . Ara-force thunders down the Ghyll on the left . . .' (*Prose*, ii. 165–6).

370 *Extempore Effusion Upon the Death of James Hogg*. Composed Nov. 1835. Published 12 December 1835 in the *Athenaeum* and 1836–7. W's very long IF note begins: 'These verses were written extempore, immediately after reading a notice of the Ettrick Shepherd's death . . . The persons lamented in these verses were all either of my friends or acquaintance.' See for whole *PW*, iv. 459–62. The poem laments the following writers: James Hogg (1770–1835), called 'The Ettrick Shepherd', remembered now for his *Confessions of a Justified Sinner*; Sir Walter Scott (1771–1832), famous in his day as poet as well as novelist, 'The Lay of the Last Minstrel' being his best-known poem; Samuel Taylor Coleridge (1771–1834), the poet and thinker to whom W said he was most intellectually indebted (25 June 1832) and to whom *The Prelude* (1805) was addressed; Charles Lamb (1775–1834), best known for his *Essays of Elia*; George Crabbe (1754–1832), poet, author of 'The Village' and 'The Borough'; Felicia Hemans (1793–1835), a very popular poet, now largely forgotten.

ll. 1–5. See 'Yarrow Visited' and 'Yarrow Revisited', pp. 335 and 365. Hogg was with W when they visited the Yarrow on 1 September 1814. Scott was their companion when Yarrow was revisited on 20 September 1831.

l. 10. Scott was buried in Dryburgh Abbey.

l. 12. Hogg was born in the Borders region of Ettrick Forest and was a shepherd in his early life.

l. 19. An allusion tying the poets together. Lamb is called 'gentle-hearted' in

C's 'This Lime-Tree Bower my Prison', written in 1797 when C, W, and Lamb were all enjoying intense friendship. W presumably did not know that Lamb objected strongly—see his very funny letter of 14 August 1800.

371 *November, 1836*. Composed November 1836. Published 1837. Printed on facing page to 'Methought I saw' (see p. 273), to which the opening lines refer. The IF note establishes that this sonnet was written after the death of W's sister-in-law Sara Hutchinson on 23 June 1835, with the memory that she was particularly fond of the latter part of 'Methought I saw'. On 24 June 1835 W wrote to Southey: 'O, my dear Southey, we have lost a precious friend; . . . I saw her within an hour after her decease, in the silence and peace of death, with as heavenly an expression on her countenance as ever human creature had. Surely there is food for faith in these appearances; for myself, I can say that I have passed a wakeful night, more in joy than sorrow, with that blessed face before my eyes perpetually.' Sara had lived with the Wordsworths throughout their married life and was very much loved.

372 *'I know an aged Man constrained to dwell'*. Composed Jan. 1846. Published 1849–50. This poem demonstrates the unity of so much of W's work. It looks back to the 'Old Cumberland Beggar' of 1798 (see p. 49). The reader should also consult W's Postscript to 'Yarrow Revisited' (1835), which attacks the 1834 Poor Law Amendment Act for violating the 'most sacred claims of civilised humanity' through blind adherence to a system of political economy (*Prose*, iii, 240–59).

THE PRELUDE

375 Composed 1798–1850. A poem in two books was completed in 1799. The thirteen-book version printed here was completed by 1805. The fourteen-book poem, published and given its title by W's widow and executors on his death in 1850, was essentially ready by 1839. For all three texts and a full account of the history of composition, see Jonathan Wordsworth, M. H. Abrams, Stephen Gill, eds., *The Prelude 1799, 1805, 1850* (NY and London, 1979).

During the summer of 1798, towards the end of his period of greatest intimacy with C, W conceived the plan for *The Recluse*, the philosophical poem discussed in the notes to *Home at Grasmere*, pp. 695–6. *The Prelude*, never so called by W, began as a work of self-analysis and intellectual and emotional stock-taking, addressed to C. See i. 640–74; ii. 466–84. In 1803, *The Recluse* languishing, W returned to his autobiographical poem and greatly enlarged its scope, including now a fuller treatment both of his own life and of Romantic aesthetics. The poem's structure underwent many changes, as W expanded it from a two to a five-book version and then further to the thirteen-book poem printed here, but throughout its development it is clear that the ascent of Snowdon which opens Book xiii was designed as the climax of the whole.

The Prelude refers to W's own experiences, to historical events, to aesthetic and philosophic concepts, to other literature. For full annotation see Wordsworth, Abrams, Gill ed. cit. above and to vol. ii of Raymond Dexter

Havens, *The Mind of a Poet* (Baltimore, 1941). The notes below confine themselves to identifying people, places, and events and to giving only such textual information as contributes to an understanding of the growth of the poem's structure.

Book One

ll. 1–115. The opening celebrates W's sense of release and purposefulness when he went to Grasmere in late 1799. Allusions at ll. 6–7 and ll. 15–19 to Exodus 13: 3 and the concluding lines of *Paradise Lost* establish the literary rather than the geographically specific nature of the passage and in particular of the 'city' of l. 7.

376 l. 46. *redundant.* superfluous, overflowing.

377 l. 82. The Wordsworths moved to Dove Cottage, Grasmere on 20 December 1799.

l. 104. Named after Aeolus, God of Winds, the Aeolian harp, a set of strings across a sounding box designed to catch the winds, was seen in the eighteenth century as an emblem of the responsive poetic mind. See C's poem 'The Aeolian Harp'.

378 l. 121. *self-congratulation.* rejoicing.

ll. 151–2. See *Paradise Lost*, i. 19–22.

379 l. 180. See *Paradise Lost*, ix. 25–41.

ll. 186–8. Mithridates (131–63 BC), King of Pontus, defeated by Pompey in 66 BC, associated by Gibbon in *Decline and Fall of the Roman Empire* with Odin, who led his tribe northwards, awaiting vengeance on the Romans.

l. 190. Sertorius, Roman general (*c.*112–72 BC) who ruled Spain. On his assassination his followers were said to have fled to the Canaries, where they survived until conquered by the Spaniards in the fifteenth century.

380 l. 205. A note in 1850 refers to 'Dominique de Gourges, a French gentleman who went in 1568 to Florida to avenge the massacre of the French by the Spaniards there'.

l. 211. Gustavus I of Sweden (1496–1560), who lifted the Danish yoke in 1521–3, by raising revolt in the mining region of Dalecarlia.

l. 213. William Wallace (*c.*1272–1305), Scottish patriot warrior, executed by Edward I.

381 l. 234. Orpheus, legendary singer of early Greece, was famed as a philosopher as well as a musician.

l. 270. See the parable of the false steward, Matthew 25: 14–30.

l. 271. The 1799 two-part *Prelude* began with this abrupt question.

382 l. 278. W was born at Cockermouth in the northern Lake District; 'sweet birthplace' alludes to C's 'Frost at Midnight', l. 28.

l. 309. W entered Hawkshead Grammar School in May 1779. The region around Hawkshead and the lake Esthwaite is the setting for many of the childhood incidents described.

383 l. 317. *springes*. snares.

384 l. 376. *Patterdale*. the western side of Ullswater

387 l. 497. *characters*. distinguishing marks, signs.

389 l. 570. *Bothnic main*. the northern Baltic.

391 l. 645. The first of many tributes to C in the poem. See especially vi. 269 ff.

l. 653. W has in mind the great task of writing *The Recluse*.

Book Two

393 l. 39. Hawkshead Town Hall, built in 1790.

394 l. 82. The Sabines were noted for frugality.

l. 96. *fountain*. spring.

395 l. 108. Furness Abbey in the south of the Lake District.

l. 141. *breathed*. allowed our horses to regain breath.

396 l. 151. W refers to the White Lion at Bowness and the still surviving house built on Belle Isle in the early 1780s.

l. 174. Robert Greenwood, later Senior Fellow of Trinity College, Cambridge. See T. W. Thompson, *Wordsworth's Hawkshead*, 78–80.

398 l. 228. The image is of classifying objects or specimens as in a collection.

400 l. 314. W draws attention to an echo of *Paradise Lost*, ix. 249.

401 l. 349. School began at 6 a.m. in summer and 7 a.m. in winter. The friend was John Fleming.

l. 381. *plastic*. shaping.

403 l. 448. See C's letter of *c.* 10 September 1799 in which he urgently entreats W to write a poem which might counter the tendency of the times towards reaction and depravity.

Book Three

404 l. 1. W entered St John's College, Cambridge, in October 1787.

405 l. 37. W refers to the fashion for powdering the hair.

406 l. 63. *Recusants*. those who resist authority.

409 l. 182. W invokes Milton who had declared in *Paradise Lost*, ix. 28–9, that his 'heroic argument' was as worthy of epic treatment as the themes of classical epic.

411 l. 274. Cincinnatus was said to have been ploughing when summoned to be Roman dictator in 458 BC.

l. 276. A reference to Chaucer's *Reeve's Tale* set in Trumpington.

l. 286. In tribute to Milton W echoes *Paradise Lost*, vii. 27.

412 l. 312. Cassandra repeatedly prophesied the fall of Troy, but was not listened to.

415 l. 427. *Science*. learning, knowledge.

416 ll. 452–4. An image, which reminds one of the range of W's reading in books of travel, drawn from William Bartram's *Travels Through North and South Carolina* (1791).

l. 486. Belisarius, a fallen Byzantine general, was said to have begged 'Date obolum Belisario'.

417 l. 488. The most famous early sixteenth-century scholars.

Book Four

422 l. 11. W describes returning to Hawkshead and, at l. 15, to meeting again Ann Tyson, with whom he had lodged while at school. She died in 1796, aged 83.

427 l. 237. *those fair Seven*. The Pleiades or Seven Sisters. W was born under the planet Jupiter on 7 April.

429 l. 318. *promiscuous rout*. without modern overtones, means a varied company.

430 l. 335. *Grain-tinctured*. W recalls Milton's 'Sky-tinctured grain' of *Paradise Lost*, v. 285; 'grain' means 'fast-dyed'.

l. 361. The meeting with the Discharged Soldier was originally written as an independent poem. See notes, p. 687.

Book Five

435 l. 25. W draws attention to a borrowing from Shakespeare's Sonnet 64, l. 14.

436 l. 60. *Don Quixote* (1605), which W read as a child.

l. 71. The dream is a reworking of one experienced by Descartes in 1619. It is generally agreed that C drew W's attention to it.

438 l. 172. *ingrate*. ungrateful.

439 l. 201. *numerous*. rhythmical, as used in *Paradise Lost*, v. 150 by Milton, who is referred to in the following lines.

440 l. 238. Here and in following section W refers to the current interest in educational theory and to books of moral education for the young. See notes to 'The Tables Turned', p. 691.

l. 256. W's mother died in March 1778.

441 l. 271. *virtual*. powerful.

442 l. 307. *notices*. remarks, observations.

l. 322. *terms of art*. technical language, jargon.

l. 332. *cunning*. arts, necessary knowledge.

443 l. 362. *pinfold*. pound, enclosure.

ll. 364–7. Reference to heroes of romance. Fortunatus's magical cap would take him wherever he wished. Jack the Giant-killer's coat made him invisible. Robin Hood led the band of outlaws who robbed the rich to give to the poor. Sabra was rescued from a dragon by St George and became his wife. See C's declaration, 16 October 1797, of the importance of letting children read 'Romances, and Relations of Giants and Magicians, and Genii'.

444   l. 383. *engines*. machines.

l. 389. W interweaves memories of himself and a schoolfriend William Raincock. The episode was first cast in the first person, amongst the early drafts for the 1799 version of the poem, but put into the third person when published as 'There was a boy' in *Lyrical Ballads* (1800).

446   l. 470. The drowned man was James Jackson, schoolmaster, who died 18 June 1779.

449   l. 584. John Fleming, mentioned ii. 352.

l. 598. *inordinate*. unordered.

Book Six

450   l. 1. Furness is the ancient name, still used, for the south-western area of the Lake District.

l. 6. *Granta*. Cambridge, from a name for the River Cam.

451   ll. 25–6. 1788–90.

452   l. 60. W's birthday was 7 April 1804. He had recently completed the 'Ode: Intimations' in which he declares: 'The thought of our past years in me doth breed | Perpetual benedictions'.

453   ll. 130–4. In *Biographia Literaria*, ch. i, C points out the dangers of composition in classical languages which was forced on schoolboys.

454   ll. 160–74. DW had copied out in 1798–9 the passage on which W draws from John Newton's *Authentic Narrative* (1784)

455   ll. 200–2. James Thomson, *The Castle of Indolence* (1748), I. xv.

456   l. 216. W and DW were reunited in summer 1787, DW having been living with relatives since the death of their mother.

l. 220. Brougham Castle stands to the east of Penrith where the rivers Emont and Lowther join. Sidney did not, in fact, visit it. His *Arcadia* was written for his sister's delight.

l. 233. *Another Maid*. Mary Hutchinson (1770–1859), who became W's wife in 1802.

l. 242. The Border Beacon stands above Penrith and is the site of the episode related at xi. 278–315.

ll. 249–260. C set off for the Mediterranean in April 1804.

457   l. 260. *gales Etesian*. north-westerly summer winds in the Mediterranean.

l. 276. C was at Christ's Hospital in London, a school noted for its blue-coat uniform, 'livery'.

l. 282. *thy native Stream*. The River Otter. W alludes in these lines to C's own 'Sonnet to the River Otter'.

l. 292. C entered Jesus College, Cambridge in 1791. After a very troubled period he left in 1794 without a degree.

458 l. 309. *Schoolmen*. medieval philosophers.

459 l. 339. *Fellow Student*. Robert Jones.

l. 357. *federal Day*. 13 July 1790. The eve of the anniversary of the Fall of the Bastille.

460 l. 404. See Genesis 18: 1–15.

l. 412. The so-called 'Glorious Revolution' of 1688.

464 l. 572. Echoes Milton's description of God in *Paradise Lost*, v. 165: 'Him first, him last, him midst, and without end'.

465 l. 587. *Locarno's Lake*. Lake Maggiore.

ll. 601–2. In *Descriptive Sketches* (1793), on which this whole description of W's Alpine experiences draws.

467 l. 691. Troops of the 'États Belgiques Unis' opposing Emperor Leopold II.

Book Seven

468 l. 4. In October 1804 W refers back to the composition of i. 1–54, in November 1799.

l. 8. Scawfell and Blencathara are mountains in the Lake District.

ll. 13–20. Before C's departure for the Mediterranean W had been confident that *The Prelude* was nearly completed. The 'outward hindrance' of l. 20 included the birth of a daughter in August.

469 l. 50. For W's favourite grove, 'John's grove', see 'When first I journeyed hither', p. 220.

l. 58. W took his BA degree in January 1791.

470 l. 95. Philip Braithwaite. See T. W. Thompson, *Wordsworth's Hawkshead*, p. 42.

471 l. 117. In the story Dick Whittington, about to quit the city, hears the bells say 'Turn again Whittington | Lord Mayor of London'.

l. 123. Pleasure gardens on the Thames.

l. 131. The 'Giants' were carved figures of Gog and Magog.

l. 132. *Bedlam*. the Bethlehem hospital for the insane, which had statues of maniacs at its gates.

l. 135. The London Monument commemorates the fire of London of 1666. The Armoury is in the Tower of London.

472 l. 183. Robert Boyle (1627–91), chemist John Graham (1745–94), who opened a Temple of Health at the Adelphi in 1779.

473 l. 190. *raree-show*. a peep-show.

l. 220. In his essay 'A Complaint of the Decay of Beggars in the Metropolis' Charles Lamb describes the crippled 'King of the Beggars', Samuel Horsey. Lamb guided W through London's variety in September 1802.

474   ll. 255–80. W refers to Panorama exhibitions.

475   l. 289. Sadler's Wells in Islington was 'half-rural' in the 1790s.

476   l. 313. Thespis was the sixth-century BC founder of Greek tragedy.

l. 322. In 1803 a melodrama at Sadler's Wells told the story of Mary Robinson, daughter of the innkeeper of Buttermere in the Lake District, who was seduced into a bigamous marriage by one John Hatfield.

477   l. 346. The River Cocker flows from Buttermere to W's birthplace Cockermouth.

478   l. 399. Shadrach, Meshach and Abednego. See Daniel 3: 23–6.

l. 416. W's journey to Cambridge, October 1787.

479   l. 441. *lustres.* chandeliers.

481   l. 528. See *Henry V*, IV. iii. 51–5.

l. 533. *Aurora.* goddess of the dawn.

482   ll. 560–2. The preacher quotes from Solomon Gessner's *The Death of Abel* (1758), Edward Young's *Night Thoughts* (1742–5) and the Gaelic poems, supposedly by Ossian, actually constructed by James Macpherson in 1760–3. 'Morven' is the north-west coast of Scotland in Ossian.

483   l. 603. W refers to the Lake District legend about ghostly horsemen in *An Evening Walk*, 179–87.

484   l. 651. St Bartholomew's Fair was held annually at Smithfield, where Protestants were martyred in Queen Mary's reign.

485   l. 675. *salt-box.* A rudimentary instrument, in which salt or similar substance was rattled.

l. 686. Madame Tussaud's wax-work collection opened in London in 1802.

l. 689. *Promethean.* inventive, creative. In Greek myth Prometheus fashioned man out of clay.

Book Eight

487   l. 1. Helvellyn is a peak a little to the north-east of Grasmere and here looks down on the annual Grasmere fair.

488   l. 75. *complacency.* without modern overtones, means tranquil satisfaction.

489   l. 86. *redounding.* eddying, swirling.

490   l. 123. Pleasure gardens of the Chinese emperor, details taken from John Barrow's *Travels in China* (1804).

491   ll. 183–91. W refers to literary presentation of pastoral life in Greek and Latin poetry; 'Arcadia', in Shakespeare's *As You Like It* and *The Winter's Tale* and in Spenser's *The Shepheard's Calendar*.

492 l. 221. *Household Dame*. Ann Tyson. Her tale was originally for 'Michael' in late 1800.

ll. 229–43. W refers to the range of mountains and valleys to the east and north-east of Grasmere.

494 ll. 314–24. W again invokes poetic celebration of pastoral life. Galesus and Clitumnus are rivers mentioned in Virgil's Georgics. Lucretilis is the hill overlooking Horace's Sabine farm, mentioned in *Odes*, i. 17.

495 l. 339. *flagelet*. a pipe like the modern recorder.

ll. 349–53. Over the winter of 1798–9 W and DW stayed at Goslar, once the seat of the emperor of the Franks, near the Hartz, 'Hercynian', mountains.

496 ll. 366–7. In this passage W alludes to Thomson's *The Seasons*. Here the reference is to 'Winter', l. 16 and below at l. 401 to 'Autumn', ll. 727–9. The allusions are appropriate in that Thomson's enormously popular poem (1728–30) influenced much eighteenth-century nature poetry.

497 ll. 420–2. Corin and Phyllis are common names in pastoral poetry. '*Coronal*'. usually a circlet or crown, here a ring.

499 l.507. W draws attention to a borrowing from 'I'll never love thee more', by James Graham, first Marquis of Montrose (1612–50). I owe this information to Jonathan Wordsworth.

504 l. 681. An echo of 'Lycidas', 104–6.

l. 713. *Antiparos*. An island in the Aegean. *Yordas*. a cave in north-west Yorkshire, visited by W in May 1800.

506 l. 763. *punctual*. confined to one spot.

l. 771. *popular*. republican, i.e. ruled by the people.

507 ll. 819–23. W draws attention to borrowing from *Paradise Lost*, xi. 203–7.

Book Nine

509 l. 31. *A year*. W actually only passed January–May 1791 in London.

510 l. 39. W reached Orleans in December 1791 and moved to Blois, the home town of Annette Vallon, in early 1792.

ll. 43–7. Just as W had visited the famous sights in London, so in Paris he toured places made famous since the Revolution of 1789. He mentions the 'field of Mars' where the anniversary of the fall of the Bastille had been celebrated, 14 July 1790; the Pantheon, the 'Dome of Geneviève'; the National Assembly and the Jacobin Club.

511 l. 78. *Le Brun*. Charles Le Brun (1619–90). His 'Magdalene' is now in the Louvre.

513 l. 179. *Carra*, *Gorsas*. Girondin deputies executed under Robespierre's Reign of Terror in October 1793.

516 l. 294. Michael Beaupuy (1755–96). Though wounded in the Vendée, he did not die there, as W thought, l. 431–2, but on the eastern front in 1796.

518 ll. 368–7. The sense is compressed. It means: 'making social life as just and pure as individual life is in the wise and good'.

519 ll. 399–40. Lake District rivers: The Rothay at Grasmere, the Greta at Keswick, the Derwent at Cockermouth.

ll. 416–24. Dion liberated Sicily in 357 from the rule of Dionysius the Younger. According to Plutarch, Dion was supported in negotiation by Plato and in campaign by others of philosophical bent such as Eudemus and Timonides.

520 ll. 454–6. *Angelica . . . Erminia*. From Ariosto's *Orlando Furioso* and Tasso's *Gerusalemme Liberata*.

521 l. 483. Romorantin, once a provincial capital, near Blois.

l. 493. *Chambord*. A magnificent château in the Loire valley built by Francis I.

522 l. 555. For the story of Vaudracour and Julia W may have drawn on a story he heard. F. M. Todd in *Politics and the Poet* (1957), 217–28 gives evidence that W was also indebted to an episode in Helen Maria Williams's *Letters Written in France . . .* (1790). In the story W deals in an oblique way with some aspects of his relationship with Annette Vallon, who bore him a daughter in 1792. W was separated from Annette by the outbreak of war between England and France and did not meet her again until 1802, the year of his marriage to Mary Hutchinson.

523 l. 580. *outside*. surface.

525 ll. 638–42. See *Romeo and Juliet*, III. v. 2.

l. 667. A 'lettre de cachet', an order for imprisonment without trial.

Book Ten

532 l. 4. W left Orleans at the end of October 1792 and arrived in England by late December.

ll. 9–13. Louis XVI was deposed on 10 August 1792, and the armies of Austria and Prussia repelled at Valmy on 20 September 1792.

533 l. 31. 22 September 1792 saw the proclamation of the Republic.

ll. 46–8. The Swiss Guard of the Palace of the Tuileries killed many insurgents before being themselves slaughtered. The corpses were burnt in the Place de Carrousel in front of the Tuileries.

534 l. 65. In September 1792 many prisoners were executed after summary trial.

ll. 70–6. W echoes *As You Like It*, I. i. 13–16 and *Macbeth*, II. ii. 35–6.

535 l. 103. Louvet accused Robespierre of aiming at supreme power on 29 October 1792.

536 ll. 165–7. Harmodius and Aristogiton attempted to free Athens from tyranny in 504 BC. Both perished. Brutus took part in the assassination of Julius Caesar in 44 BC.

537 ll. 205–10. A bill to abolish slave trading had been passed by the Commons in 1792 but 'baffled' by the Lords.

538 l. 230. On 1 February 1793 France declared war on Britain, now allied with Austria and Prussia.

540 l. 297. W spent late June–early August 1793 on the Isle of Wight.

l. 310–12. Robespierre achieved supreme power in July 1793 and unleashed the Reign of Terror, ostensibly to rid the Republic of its enemies within.

ll. 318–20. Notre Dame was established as the Temple of the Goddess of Reason on 10 November 1793.

541 ll. 352–4. Madame Roland's famous last words before she was guillotined in November 1793 were, 'Oh Liberty, what crimes are committed in thy name'.

l. 362. Hercules, while still in his cradle, throttled two snakes sent to kill him.

544 l. 455. W and Jones had stayed at Arras, the birthplace of Maximilien Robespierre, on 16 July 1790.

l. 468. 'Moloch, horrid king besmeared with blood / Of human sacrifice', *Paradise Lost*, i. 392–3.

ll. 471–5. W was at Rampside on the south-west coast of the Lake District, near the estuary of the river Leven, Aug.–Sept. 1794.

545 l. 492. William Taylor (1754–86), headmaster of Hawkshead Grammar School, buried at Cartmel Priory.

546 l. 535. Robespierre was executed 28 July 1794.

l. 548. One of the labours of Hercules was the cleaning of the stables of King Augeas. He did it by diverting the rivers Alpheus and Peneus.

l. 549. *their own helper*. the guillotine.

ll. 559–66. A reference back to the boyhood episode of ii. 99–144.

547 l. 600. W did not imagine that the worst spirits would become dominant in the French cause and that a war of defence would become one of territorial gain, as at 791.

548 l. 618. *Babel-like*. See Genesis 9: 3–9.

ll. 645–56. For W's contemporary attack upon the repressive and (as the radicals saw it) war-mongering Pitt government see his *Letter to the Bishop of Llandaff* and 'Salisbury Plain', pp. 13–28.

553 l. 810. Almost certainly a reference to William Godwin's *Enquiry Concerning Political Justice* (1793). In this passage W selects only one aspect of Godwin's complex work, his emphasis on the power of human reason if fearlessly employed.

555 l. 905. W met C in September 1795. They corresponded and by 13 May 1796 C could refer to W as 'A very dear friend of mine, who is in my opinion the best poet of the age'.

l. 908. DW lived with W at Racedown House in Dorset from September 1795.

556 l. 940. Napoleon summoned Pope Pius VII to crown him Emperor on 2 December 1804.

l. 950. Timoleon drove Dionysius the Younger from Syracuse in 343 BC.

557 l. 982. In 1804, the time of writing, Britain has now become the only hope for liberty against the French 'become oppressors in their turn' (791).

l. 1003. See *Paradise Lost*, iv. 268–71.

558 ll. 1012–14. Empedocles (*c.*493–*c.*433 BC), supposed to have thrown himself into Etna. Archimedes (*c.*287–212 BC), mathematician, born at Syracuse.

ll. 1015–26. Theocritus, Sicilian pastoral poet (*c.*310–250 BC). The story of Comates is told in *Idyll*, vii. 78–83.

l. 1033. *Arethuse*. A spring at Syracuse, often mentioned in pastoral poetry.

l. 1036. *gratulatest*. rejoice over.

l. 1037. *Votary*. worshipper.

Book Eleven

559 l. 31. *distracted times*. W refers both largely, to the years of tension and repression following the outbreak of war in 1793, and personally, to his own period of instability described in the previous book. Lines 40–136 recapitulate that period.

561 l. 108. *appanage*. endowment.

562 ll. 155–63. W refers to the late eighteenth-century cult of the picturesque.

563 ll. 187–94. See 'Tintern Abbey', ll. 68–71.

564 l. 199. *A Maid*. Mary Hutchinson, who became W's wife on 4 October 1802.

565 l. 258. The two 'spots of time', 257–315, 344–88, were composed in early 1799 for the two-part version of *The Prelude*, where they appeared naturally amongst other memories of childhood. The lines which now make a transition between them were written in early 1804 and have clear links with the 'Ode: Intimations', completed then.

566 l. 305. *The beacon*. A signal beacon on a hill above Penrith.

l. 317. *two dear Ones*. Mary Hutchinson and DW.

568 l. 366. W's father, John Wordsworth, died 30 December 1783.

l. 367. *two brothers*. Richard and John.

Book Twelve

571 ll. 78–80. *Statists*. political theorists, such as Adam Smith whose *Inquiry into the Nature and Causes of the Wealth of Nations* (1776) is alluded to here.

573 l. 168. *vulgar*. ordinary, without modern class connotation.

576 l. 315. See notes to 'Salisbury Plain', p. 685, for W's experience at this time. W draws on his earlier poem for this description and refers to it as 'some imperfect verse' at 358.

578 l. 365. C read the revised poem, 'Adventures on Salisbury Plain', early in 1796 and records this response to it in *Biographia Literaria*, ch. iv.

Book Thirteen

l. 5. W made a pedestrian tour of North Wales with Robert Jones in the summer of 1791. 'Bethkelet': Beddgelert.

579 l. 11. *glaring*: clammy. See James Maxwell, ed., *The Prelude* (1971), 564 for discussion of this word.

581 l. 113. For the distinction see *Paradise Lost*, v. 487–90.

587 l. 349. Wales was the home of W's walking companion Robert Jones.

l. 350. Raisley Calvert, brother of W's schoolfriend William Calvert, died in January 1795. W had been with him during his decline from consumption and received a legacy of £900. See also W's 'To the Memory of Raisley Calvert', p. 271.

588 ll. 386–90. W once again refers to *The Recluse*, whose projected substantiality was to justify this extended personal work.

ll. 393–8. W refers to 1798 when he and C lived in the Quantocks in northern Somerset and wrote the poems alluded to here: 'The Ancient Mariner', 'Christabel' (Part I), 'The Idiot Boy', 'The Thorn'.

589 l. 416. *a private grief*: the death of John Wordsworth, 5–6 February 1805.

PROSE

The critical essays which W wrote for *Lyrical Ballads* and the 1815 *Poems* were addressed to readers not only familiar with much verse that is now little read but also with eighteenth-century discussion about the nature and function of poetry. Full annotation would therefore be voluminous and beyond the scope of this volume. The reader should consult the commentary in the edition of Wordsworth's *Prose Works* by W. J. B. Owen and J. W. Smyser and for the historical context W. J. B. Owen, *Wordsworth as Critic* (1969) and M. H. Abrams, *The Mirror and the Lamp* (1953). W's own notes are included in the printed text.

591 *Advertisement to Lyrical Ballads (1798)*. Written between April and 13 September 1798, when it appeared as the opening to *Lyrical Ballads, with a Few other Poems*. The friend alluded to in the last sentence is thought to be Hazlitt.

593 *Note to The Thorn (1800)*. Probably written late summer 1800. Published in *Lyrical Ballads, with Other Poems* (1800). Robert Southey, a friend who ought to have understood the aim of the poem, had described 'The Thorn' as a failure—'he who personates tiresome loquacity, becomes tiresome himself'—in the *Critical Review*, October 1798. In this note W defends his narrative method and the poem's purpose.

595 *Preface to Lyrical Ballads ... (1802)*. For the second edition of *Lyrical Ballads*

in 1800—enlarged to two volumes and unlike the one volume of 1798 announcing the name of the poet—W wrote his first sustained critical essay. Lamb thought it a mistake to print the *Preface* together with the poems, as its dogmas 'associate a *diminishing* idea with the Poems which follow, as having been written for *Experiment* on the public taste, more than having sprung (as they must have done) from living and daily circumstances' (30 January 1801), but W did not adopt his idea of publishing a separate critical treatise and for the next edition of 1802 he both revised the *Preface* and added an *Appendix* enlarging on his ideas about Poetic Diction.

The two Prefaces, 1800 and 1802, ought to be read as independent statements and ideally should be printed in parallel, as in Paul M. Zall's edition, *Literary Criticism of William Wordsworth* (1966). Here the major additions of 1802 have been enclosed in square brackets, much the most important being the passage between p. 602 and p. 608. On the significance of the changes W made between 1800 and 1802 see Owen's *Wordsworth as Critic* cited above.

'Wordsworth's Preface is half a child of my own Brain' was C's description of the 1800 Preface in a letter of 29 July 1802, and undoubtedly it does reflect the intellectual intimacy which gave birth to the great poetry of 1797–8. The additions to 1802, however, indicate the growing self-confidence of the poet who had completed the first version of his autobiography and declared his poetic aims at the end of *Home at Grasmere*. In the letter just cited C declared that 'I am far from going all lengths with Wordsworth. . . . On the contrary, I rather suspect that somewhere or other there is a radical Difference in our theoretical opinions respecting Poetry—this I shall endeavour to go to the Bottom of . . .'. Much of *Biographia Literaria* (1817) consists of that endeavour.

620 *Letter to John Wilson (7 June 1802)*. John Wilson (1785–1854), later noted for his contributions to *Blackwood's Magazine* as 'Christopher North', was a student when he wrote a lengthy and discerning letter to W about *Lyrical Ballads*, especially 'The Idiot Boy'. It is printed in Mary Gordon. '*Christopher North': A Memoir of John Wilson* (1862), i. 39–48. W's reply, which indicates his readiness to respond to considered criticism, is one of his most important letters. The surviving MS draft, which is the basis of the text in *Letters . . . Early Years*, 352–8, from which this text is taken, is defective.

Adam Smith's opinion is recorded in the *European Magazine*, xx (August 1791), 135 and noted by C in 1800, *Notebooks* entry 775. W refers to C's 'The Nightingale', to Cowper's *The Task*, i. 205–6 and to the Bible, Ephesians 3: 9 and Colossians 3: 3.

626 *Preface to Poems (1815)*. The two handsome volumes W published in 1815 were his first Collected Works and in them he presented his poems in classifications of his own which, however much varied in the many Collected Editions that followed, remained his preferred method of arrangement. The 'Preface', W's most extended critical statement since 1802, dwells particularly on two matters which had long concerned him: the distinction between powers of mind, chiefly Fancy and Imagination, predominant in the

composition of particular poems, and the need so to arrange the poems as to 'assist the attentive Reader in perceiving their connection with each other'.

The 'Preface' and the 'Essay, Supplementary to the Preface', which was published at the end of the first volume of *Poems* (1815), were both written about January 1815. An account of composition, a commentary, and identification of allusions, will be found in *Prose*, iii. 23–107. W. J. B. Owen discusses the aesthetics of the 'Preface' in *Wordsworth as Critic*.

663 *A Letter to a Friend of Robert Burns* (*1816*). The circumstances of the composition of this open letter to James Gray are complicated. Robert Burns died in 1796 and in 1800 an edition of his works appeared with a prefatory 'Life' by Dr James Currie. In 1815 this 'Life' was reissued by Alexander Peterkin, with a preface which moderated the view of Burns given by Currie. A further edition was called for, to be superintended by the poet's brother Gilbert Burns, and he, through their mutual friend Gray, made contact with W, 'exceedingly desirous', according to Gray, of obtaining W's opinion 'as to the best mode of conducting the defence' of his defamed brother. W's letter was transmitted to Gilbert Burns, who read it, Gray says, 'with feelings of unmingled pleasure' and was published in 1816, the year of its composition.

Because of its attack on Francis Jeffrey the 'Letter' was taken by many to be merely a pretext for W to hit back at the influential critic who had savaged *The Excursion* and 'The White Doe of Rylstone'. This judgement is unfair, however, for two reasons. W was genuinely concerned for the appreciation of a poet who had been important to him ever since his youth. He was also, and not improperly, concerned to lay down principles for the proper evaluation of a poet's work, in opposition especially to Jeffrey who had mounted his attack on 'the Lake School' in increasingly personal terms.

FURTHER READING

FULL citation for the authoritative editions of Wordsworth's letters, prose, and poems, and for DW's *Journals* will be found on pp. 682–3. Scholarly works cited there are not mentioned again in the list below, in which the titles are given of further standard editions and recommended critical and scholarly studies.

EDITIONS

The Cornell Wordsworth is a multi-volume project which will be the authoritative edition of the poems when complete. Volumes published so far are:

The Salisbury Plain Poems, ed. Stephen Gill (Ithaca, 1975)
The Prelude, 1798–99, ed. Stephen Parrish (Ithaca, 1977)
Home at Grasmere, ed. Beth Darlington (Ithaca, 1977)
The Ruined Cottage and The Pedlar, ed. James Butler (Ithaca, 1979)
Benjamin the Waggoner, ed. Paul F. Betz (Ithaca, 1981)
The Borderers, ed. Robert Osborn (Ithaca, 1982)
Poems in Two Volumes, ed. Jared R. Curtis (Ithaca, 1983)

Other editions which will be of use are, in alphabetical order:

Samuel Taylor Coleridge, *Letters*, ed. E. L. Griggs (Oxford, 1956–71)
Sara Hutchinson, *Letters 1800–1835*, ed. Kathleen Coburn (London, 1954)
Henry Crabb Robinson, *Correspondence . . . with the Wordsworth Circle*, ed. E. J. Morley (Oxford, 1927)
Henry Crabb Robinson, *Henry Crabb Robinson on Books and Their Writers*, ed. E. J. Morley (London, 1938)
John Wordsworth, *Letters*, ed. Carl H. Ketcham (Ithaca, 1969)
William and Mary Wordsworth, *The Love Letters*, ed. Beth Darlington (Ithaca, 1981)
William Wordsworth, *The Critical Opinions of*, ed. Markham L. Peacock, Jr. (Baltimore, 1950)
William Wordsworth, *Literary Criticism*, ed. W. J. B. Owen (London, 1974)
William Wordsworth, *Literary Criticism*, ed. Paul M. Zall (Lincoln, Nebraska, 1966)
William Wordsworth, *Lyrical Ballads 1798*, ed. W. J. B. Owen (Oxford, 1967, 1969)
William Wordsworth, *Lyrical Ballads 1805*, ed. Derek Roper (London, 1968)
William Wordsworth, *The Prelude 1799, 1805, 1850*, eds. Jonathan Wordsworth, M. H. Abrams, Stephen Gill (New York and London, 1979)
William Wordsworth, *The Prose Works*, ed. Alexander B. Grosart (London, 1876)—includes Fenwick Notes.

CRITICISM, BIOGRAPHY, SCHOLARSHIP

M. H. Abrams, *Natural Supernaturalism* (New York, 1971)

M. H. Abrams, ed., *Wordsworth: A Collection of Critical Essays* (Englewood Cliffs, NJ, 1972)

Matthew Arnold, *Poems of Wordsworth* (London, 1879) and in *Essays in Criticism: Second Series* (London, 1888)

James Averill, *Wordsworth and Human Suffering* (Ithaca, 1980)

A. C. Bradley, *Oxford Lectures on Poetry* (London, 1909)

C. C. Clarke, *Romantic Paradox* (London, 1962)

Jared R. Curtis, *Wordsworth's Experiments with Tradition: The Lyric Poems of 1802* (Ithaca, 1971)

Thomas De Quincey, essays collected in *Recollections of the Lakes and the Lake Poets*, ed. David Wright (Harmondsworth, 1970) and in *De Quincey as Critic*, ed. John E. Jordan (London, 1973)

W. J. Harvey and R. Gravil, eds., *Wordsworth: The Prelude* (London, 1972)

Geoffrey H. Hartman, *Wordsworth's Poetry 1787–1814* (New Haven, 1964)

John O. Hayden, *The Romantic Reviewers 1802-1824* (London, 1969)

William Hazlitt, Essays in *Works*, ed. P. P. Howe (London, 1930–4): vols. xix. 9–25; iv. 111–25; v. 143–68; xvii. 106–22; xi. 86–95. For the essay from *The Spirit of the Age* see the edition by E. D. Mackerness (London, 1969)

Mary Jacobus, *Tradition and Experiment in Wordsworth's Lyrical Ballads 1798* (Oxford, 1976)

J. Jones, *The Egotistical Sublime* (London, 1954)

Alec King, *Wordsworth and the Artist's Vision* (London, 1966)

Herbert Lindenberger, *On Wordsworth's Prelude* (Princeton, 1963)

W. J. B. Owen, *Wordsworth as Critic* (Oxford, 1969)

Thomas McFarland, *Romanticism and the Forms of Ruin* (Princeton, 1981)

Graham McMaster, ed., *William Wordsworth* (Harmondsworth, 1972)—Penguin Critical Anthologies Series

James Maxwell and Stephen Gill, 'Wordsworth' in *English Poetry: Select Bibliographical Guides*, ed. A. E. Dyson (Oxford, 1971)

Mary Moorman, *William Wordsworth: A Biography. The Early Years* (Oxford, 1957); *The Later Years* (Oxford, 1965)

Richard J. Onorato, *The Character of the Poet: Wordsworth in The Prelude* (Princeton, 1971)

Stephen Maxfield Parrish, *The Art of the Lyrical Ballads* (Ithaca, 1973)

Robert Rehder, *Wordsworth and the Beginnings of Modern Poetry* (London, 1981)

Christopher Salvesen, *The Landscape of Memory* (London, 1965)

Ben Ross Schneider, Jr., *Wordsworth's Cambridge Education* (Cambridge 1957)

Paul Sheats, *The Making of Wordsworth's Poetry 1785–98* (Cambridge, Mass., 1973)

Elsie Smith, *An Estimate of William Wordsworth by his Contemporaries 1793–1822* (Oxford, Basil Blackwell, 1932)

Leslie Stephen, 'Wordsworth's Ethics' (1876) in *Hours in a Library: Third Series* (London, 1879)

F. M. Todd, *Politics and the Poet* (London, 1957)

Jonathan Wordsworth, ed., *Bicentenary Wordsworth Studies* (Ithaca, 1970)

Jonathan Wordsworth, *The Music of Humanity* (London, 1969)

Jonathan Wordsworth, *William Wordsworth: The Borders of Vision* (Oxford, 1982)

INTELLECTUAL, POLITICAL, AND SOCIAL CONTEXT

M. H., Abrams, *The Mirror and the Lamp* (New York, 1953)

M. H. Abrams, 'English Romanticism: The Spirit of the Age', in *Romanticism Reconsidered*, ed. Northrop Frye (New York, 1962), 37–72

Marilyn Butler, *Romantics, Rebels and Reactionaries: English Literature and its Background 1760–1830* (Oxford, 1981)

Ian R. Christie, *Wars and Revolutions: Britain 1760–1815* (London, 1982)

James Engell, *The Creative Imagination: Enlightenment to Romanticism* (Cambridge, Mass., 1981)

E. J. Hobsbawm, *The Age of Revolution 1789–1848* (London, 1962)

Hugh Honour, *Romanticism* (London, 1982)

H. W. Piper, *The Active Universe: Pantheism and the Concept of the Imagination in the English Romantic Poets* (London, 1962)

Thomas McFarland, *Coleridge and the Pantheist Tradition* (Oxford, 1969)

Basil Willey, *The Eighteenth-Century Background* (London, 1940)

Carl Woodring, *Politics in English Romantic Poetry* (Cambridge, Mass., 1970)

INDEX OF TITLES AND FIRST LINES

To offer a note on the index may seem over cautious, but it is essential here. In revising his poems Wordsworth did not scruple to alter titles. I have, of course, retained the first publication title, or the title in manuscript, and where a poem was untitled I have generally left it so, using for a heading the first line. In a few cases I have used a title in common use in critical discussion, e.g. 'The Discharged Soldier', but have put it in square brackets to indicate that the title is not Wordsworth's. As readers already familiar with the poetry, however, will know the titles which appear in the 1849–50 volumes and in all subsequent collected editions, I have listed in the index both the original title and first line and the 1849–50 received title, so that the reader ought always to be able to find a poem, even if the text of it when found is unfamiliar. 'Old Man Travelling' is thus also indexed under 'Animal Tranquillity and Decay'. 'Lines Written at a Small Distance from My House' also appears in its later title as 'To My Sister'. Since the index is designed simply to help readers and does not aim to be a textual record of Wordsworth's revisions, I have, of course, used common sense. For example: the 1849–50 first line 'Yes it was the mountain echo', is not far enough removed from the 1807 'Yes! full surely 'twas the Echo' to prevent a reader finding the poem with only the one, 1807, entry.

Address to the Sons of Burns	318, 716 n.
A famous Man is Robin Hood	314, 716 n.
After-thought, see *River Duddon, The (Conclusion)*	
Age! twine thy brows with fresh spring flowers!	304, 714 n.
Airey-Force Valley	369, 726 n.
Alice Fell	241, 702 n.
Amid the smoke of cities did you pass	201, 697 n.
Among all lovely things my Love had been;	247, 703 n.
A narrow girdle of rough stones and crags,	203, 698 n.
And is this—Yarrow?—*This* the Stream	335, 721 n.
Anecdote for Fathers	81, 689 n.
Animal Tranquillity and Decay, see *Old Man Travelling*	
An Orpheus! An Orpheus!—yes, Faith may grow bold,	323, 717 n.
Another year!—another deadly blow!	331, 719 n.
Anticipation	290, 711 n.
Are souls then nothing? Must at length the die	273, 707 n.
Art thou a Statesman, in the van	151, 694 n.
A simple child, dear brother Jim,	83, 689 n.
A slumber did my spirit seal;	147, 693 n.
A trouble, not of clouds, or weeping rain	368, 725 n.
A whirl-blast from behind the hill	66, 688 n.
Beggars	243, 702 n.
Begone, thou fond presumptuous Elf	214, 699 n.
Behold her, single in the field	319, 717 n.
'Beloved Vale!' I said, 'when I shall con'	274, 707 n.
Beneath the concave of an April sky,	341, 722 n.

Bright Flower, whose home is everywhere!   253, 704 n.
Brook, that hast been my solace days and weeks   274, 704 n.
Brook! whose society, *see* Brook, that hast been
Brothers, The   155, 694 n.
Bruges ('Bruges I saw')   352, 723 n.
Bruges I saw attired with golden light   352, 723 n.
Bruges ('The Spirit of Antiquity')   352, 723 n.
By their floating Mill   325, 717 n.

Calais, August, 1802   280, 708 n.
Calais, August 15th, 1802   283, 709 n.
Calm is the fragrant air, and loth to lose   369, 726 n.
Calvert! it must not be unheard by them   271, 707 n.
Carved, Mathew, with a master's skill   145, 693 n.
Character, A   223, 700 n.
Character of the Happy Warrior   320, 717 n.
Characteristics of a Child three Years old   333, 719 n.
Childless Father, The   207, 698 n.
Complaint, A   330, 718 n.
Composed after a Journey across the Hamilton Hills   287, 711 n.
Composed Among the Ruins of a Castle   353, 724 n.
Composed at Cora Linn   338, 721 n.
Composed by the Sea-Side, near Calais   281, 709 n.
Composed in the Valley, near Dover   284, 709 n.
Composed near Calais, on the Road . . . August 7 1802, see *To a Friend*
Composed upon an Evening of Extraordinary Splendor, see *Ode, Composed
   Upon . . .*
Composed Upon Westminster Bridge   285, 710 n.
Could I the priest's consent have gained,   142, 693 n.

Dear fellow Traveller! here we are once more.   284, 709 n.
Dear Native Brooks your ways have I pursued   275, 707 n.
Dirge   146, 693 n.
[*Discharged Soldier, The*]   45, 687 n.
Distressful gift! this Book receives   311, 715 n.

Earth has not any thing to shew more fair: 285, 710 n.
Elegiac Stanzas   326, 718 n.
Elegiac Verses, see I only looked for pain and grief
Elegy ('Remembering how')   144, 693 n.
England! the time is come when thou shouldst wean   275, 708 n.
Ere we had reached the wished-for place, night fell: 287, 711 n.
Evening Walk, An   1, 683 n.
Even so for me a Vision sanctified   371, 727 n.
Expostulation and Reply   129, 691 n.
Extempore Effusion Upon the Death of James Hogg   370, 726 n.

Fair Star of Evening, Splendor of the West,   281, 709 n.
Farewell, A, see Farewell, thou little Nook
Farewell, thou little Nook of mountain ground,   278, 708 n.

Far from my dearest friend, 'tis mine to rove   1, 683 n.
Festivals have I seen that were not names: 283, 709 n.
[*Five Elegies*]   142, 693 n.
Fly, some kind Spirit, fly to Grasmere Vale!   289, 711 n.
Five years have passed; five summers, with the length   131, 692 n.
Fly, some kind Harbinger, to Grasmere-dale!, see *Sonnet. September 25th, 1803*
For the Spot Where the Hermitage Stood, see *Inscription: For the Spot where . . .*
Fountain, The   138, 693 n.
From low to high doth dissolution climb   353, 723 n.
From Stirling Castle we had seen   290, 711 n.

Gipsies   332, 719 n.
Glen-Almain   312, 716 n.
Goody Blake and Harry Gill   56, 688 n.
Great Men have been among us; hands that penned   276, 708 n.
Green Linnet, The   248, 704 n.
Guilt and Sorrow, see *Salisbury Plain*   13, 685 n.

Had this effulgence disappeared   347, 722 n.
Hard is the life when naked and unhouzed   13, 685 n.
Hart-Leap Well   168, 695 n.
High is our calling, Friend!—Creative Art   340, 721 n.
His simple truths did Andrew glean   211, 699 n.
Home at Grasmere   174, 695 n.
How art thou named? In search of what strange land   353, 723 n.
How clear, how keen, how marvellously bright   340, 722 n.
How sweet it is, when mother Fancy rocks   268, 706 n.

I am not One who much or oft delight   269, 706 n.
I bring ye little noisy crew!   146, 693 n.
Idiot Boy, The   67, 689 n.
Idle Shepherd-Boys, The   217, 699 n.
If from the public way you turn your steps   224, 700 n.
If nature, for a favorite Child   137, 693 n.
If thou in the dear love of some one friend   208, 698 n.
I grieved for Buonaparte, with a vain   267, 706 n.
I have a boy of five years old,   81, 689 n.
I heard a thousand blended notes   80, 689 n.
I know an aged Man constrained to dwell   372, 727 n.
I love to walk   45, 687 n.
I marvel how Nature could ever find space   223, 700 n.
I met Louisa in the shade;   237, 701 n.
In Brugès town is many a street   357, 724 n.
Incident at Bruges   357, 724 n.
In distant countries I have been,   88, 690 n.
Inland, within a hollow Vale, I stood,   284, 710 n.
Inscription: For the Spot where the Hermitage stood   208, 698 n.
I only looked for pain and grief   308, 715 n.

In the sweet shire of Cardigan,   85, 690 n.
In this still place, remote from men,   312, 716 n.
In youth from rock to rock I went,   250, 704 n.
I saw an aged Beggar in my walk,   49, 687 n.
Is it a Reed that's shaken by the wind,   280, 708 n.
I thought of Thee, my partner and my guide,   351, 723 n.
It is a beauteous Evening, calm and free;   281, 709 n.
It is the first mild day of March: 54, 688 n.
It is no Spirit who from Heaven hath flown   272, 707 n.
It is not to be thought of that the Flood   276, 708 n.
I travelled among unknown Men,   237, 701 n.
It seems a day,   153, 694 n.
I've watched you now a full half hour,   254, 704 n.
It was an April Morning: fresh and clear   199, 697 n.
I wandered lonely as a Cloud   303, 714 n.
I was thy Neighbour once, thou rugged Pile!   326, 718 n.

Jones! when from Calais southward you and I   282, 709 n.
Just as the blowing thorn began   143, 693 n.

Last of the Flock, The   88, 690 n.
Let other Bards of Angels sing,   354, 724 n.
Let thy wheel-barrow alone.   136, 693 n.
Lines, Composed at Grasmere   329, 718 n.
Lines left upon a Seat in a Yew-Tree   29, 685 n.
Lines Written a few miles above Tintern Abbey   131, 692 n.
Lines Written at a Small Distance from my House   54, 688 n.
Lines written in Early Spring   80, 689 n.
Lines Written on a Tablet in a School, see If nature, for a favorite
    Child
Lines: Written with a Slate-Pencil   210, 699 n.
London, 1802   286, 710 n.
Look, five blue eggs are gleaming there!   239, 701 n.
Lord of the Vale! astounding Flood!   338, 721 n.
Loud is the Vale! the Voice is up   329, 718 n.
Loving she is, and tractable, though wild;   333, 719 n.
Louisa   237, 701 n.
Lucy Gray   149, 693 n.

Matron of Jedborough and Her Husband, The   304, 714 n.
Matthew, see If nature, for a favorite Child
Methought I saw the footsteps of a throne   273, 707 n.
Michael   224, 700 n.
Milton! thou should'st be living at this hour: 286, 710 n.
Mutability   353, 723 n.
My heart leaps up when I behold   246, 703 n.

—Nay, Traveller! rest. This lonely yew-tree stands   29, 685 n.
[Night-Piece, A]   44, 687 n.
Not a breath of air   369, 726 n.

November 1, 1815   340, 722 n.
November, 1806   331, 719 n.
November, 1836   371, 727 n.
Nuns fret not at their Convent's narrow room   286, 711 n.
Nutting   153, 694 n.

Oak and the Broom, The   211, 699 n.
O blithe New-comer! I have heard,   245, 703 n.
October, 1803 ('One might believe')   293, 712 n.
October, 1803 ('Six thousand Veterans')   295, 712 n.
October, 1803 ('These times')   294, 712 n.
October, 1803 ('When looking on')   294, 712 n.
O dearer far than light and life are dear,   354, 724 n.
Ode, Composed Upon an Evening of Extraordinary Splendor and Beauty   347, 722 n.
Ode.—1817   341, 722 n.
Ode: Intimations of Immortality, see *Ode* ('There was a time')
Ode. The Pass of Kirkstone   345, 722 n.
Ode ('There was a time')   297, 713 n.
Ode to Duty   295, 713 n.
O Friend! I know not which way I must look   285, 710 n.
Oft had I heard of Lucy Gray   149, 693 n.
Oh there is blessing in this gentle breeze   375, 727 n.
Oh! what's the matter? what's the matter?   56, 688 n.
Old Cumberland Beggar, The   49, 687 n.
Old Man Travelling   29, 685 n.
O mountain Stream! the Shepherd and his Cot   306, 715 n.
Once did She hold the gorgeous East in fee;   268, 706 n.
Once I could hail (howe'er serene the sky)   355, 724 n.
Once on the brow of yonder Hill I stopped   174, 695 n.
One might believe that natural miseries   293, 712 n.
One morning (raw it was and wet,   239, 702 n.
O Nightingale! thou surely art   331, 719 n.
O now that the genius of Bewick were mine,   216, 699 n.
On the Departure of Sir Walter Scott   368, 725 n.
On the Extinction of the Venetian Republic   268, 706 n.
On the Power of Sound   358, 725 n.
O Thou! whose fancies from afar are brought;   246, 703 n.
Our walk was far among the ancient trees: 205, 698 n.

Pansies, Lilies, Kingcups, Daisies,   257, 704 n.
Pass of Kirkstone, The, see *Ode. The Pass of Kirkstone*
Personal Talk, see I am not One who much or oft delight
Peter Bell   91, 690 n.
Pleasures newly found are sweet   259, 705 n.
Poems on the Naming of Places   199, 697 n.
Poet's Epitaph, A   151, 694 n.
Power of Music   323, 717 n.
Prelude (1805), The   375, 727 n.
Pressed with conflicting thoughts of love and fear   332, 719 n.

Recluse, The, see *Home at Grasmere*   174, 695 n.
Remembering how thou didst beguile   144, 693 n.
Resolution and Independence   260, 705 n.
Return, Content! for fondly I pursued, see Dear Native Brooks your
    ways . . .
River Duddon, The (Conclusion)   351, 723 n.
Rob Roy's Grave   314, 716 n.
Ruined Cottage, The   31, 686 n.
Rural Architecture   106, 698 n.

Sailor's Mother, The   239, 702 n.
St Paul's   332, 719 n.
Salisbury Plain   13, 685 n.
Scorn not the Sonnet;   356, 724 n.
September 1st, 1802   283, 709 n.
September, 1802   284, 710 n.
September, 1815, see While not a leaf seems faded
Sequel to [Beggars]   350, 723 n.
She dwelt among th'untrodden ways   147, 693 n.
She had a tall Man's height, or more;   243, 702 n.
She was a Phantom of delight   292, 712 n.
Shout, for a mighty Victory is won!   290, 711 n.
Simon Lee, the Old Huntsman   85, 690 n.
Six thousand Veterans practised in War's game   295, 712 n.
Small Celandine, The   288, 711 n.
Solitary Reaper, The   319, 716 n.
Song ('She dwelt among th'untrodden ways')   147, 693 n.
Sonnet, In the Pass of Killicranky, see *October, 1803* ('Six thousand
    Veterans')
Sonnet. September 25th, 1803   289, 711 n.
Sparrow's Nest, The   239, 701 n.
Stanzas: Written in my Pocket-Copy, see Within our happy Castle
Star Gazers   322, 717 n.
Stay near me—do not take thy flight!   244, 703 n.
Stepping Westward   313, 716 n.
Stern Daughter of the Voice of God!   295, 713 n.
Strange fits of passion I have known   148, 693 n.
Stranger! this hillock of misshapen stones   210, 699 n.
Stray Pleasures, see By their floating Mill
Surprized by joy—impatient as the Wind   334, 720 n.
Sweet Flower! belike one day to have   307, 715 n.

Tables Turned, The   130, 691 n.
The cock is crowing,   248, 704 n.
The gallant Youth, who may have gained,   365, 725 n.
The Knight had ridden down from Wensley moor   168, 695 n.
The little hedge-row birds   29, 685 n.
The May is come again:—how sweet   248, 704 n.
The Post-boy drove with fierce career,   241, 702 n.
There's George Fisher, Charles Fleming, and Reginald Shore,   206, 698 n.

There is a bondage which is worse to bear   277, 708 n.
There is a change—and I am poor;   330, 718 n.
There is a Flower, the Lesser Celandine,   288, 711 n.
There is an Eminence,—of these our hills   203, 697 n.
There is a thorn; it looks so old;   59, 688 n.
There is a Yew-tree, pride of Lorton Vale,   334, 720 n.
There's something in a flying horse,   91, 690 n.
There was a roaring in the wind all night;   260, 705 n.
There was a time when meadow, grove, and stream,   297, 713 n.
These chairs they have no words to utter,   255, 704 n.
These times touch moneyed Worldlings with dismay: 294, 712 n.
These Tourists, Heaven preserve us! needs must live   155, 694 n.
These words were uttered in a pensive mood,   287, 711 n.
The sky is overspread   44, 687 n.
The Spirit of Antiquity, enshrined   352, 723 n.
The Sun has long been set: 280, 708 n.
The valley rings with mirth and joy.   217, 699 n.
The world is too much with us; late and soon,   270, 707 n.
This is the spot:—how mildly does the sun   265, 705 n.
Thorn, The   59, 688 n.
Thought of a Briton on the Subjugation of Switzerland   330, 718 n.
Three years she grew in sun and shower,   154, 694 n.
Through shattered galleries, 'mid roofless halls,   353, 724 n.
Thy functions are etherial,   358, 725 n.
Tinker, The   256, 704 n.
'Tis eight o'clock,—a clear March night,   67, 689 n.
'Tis said, that some have died for love: 208, 698 n.
To —— ('Let other Bards')   354, 724 n.
To —— ('O dearer far')   354, 724 n.
To a Butterfly ('Stay near me')   244, 703 n.
To a Butterfly ('I've watched you')   254, 704 n.
To a Friend, Composed near Calais   282, 709 n.
To a Sexton   136, 693 n.
To a Sky-Lark   238, 701 n.
To B. R. Haydon, Esq   340, 721 n.
To H.C., Six Years Old   246, 703 n.
To Joanna   201, 697 n.
To M.H.   205, 698 n.
To My Sister, see *Lines Written at a Small Distance*
To the Cuckoo   245, 703 n.
To the Daisy ('Bright Flower!'), see *To the Same Flower* ('Bright Flower')
To the Daisy ('In youth')   250, 704 n.
To the Daisy ('Sweet Flower!')   307, 715 n.
To the Daisy ('With little here')   252, 704 n.
To the Memory of Raisley Calvert   271, 707 n.
To the Men of Kent   289, 711 n.
To the River Duddon   306, 715 n.
To the Same Flower ('Bright Flower')   253, 704 n.
To the Same Flower ('Pleasures newly found')   259, 705 n.
To the Small Celandine   257, 704 n.

To the Torrent at the Devil's Bridge   353, 723 n.
To Toussaint L'Ouverture   282, 709 n.
Toussaint, the most unhappy Man of Men!   282, 709 n.
Travelling   265, 705 n.
'Twas summer and the sun was mounted high.   31, 686 n.
Two April Mornings, The   140, 693 n.
Two Thieves, The   216, 699 n.
Two Voices are there; one is of the Sea,   330, 718 n.

Up, Timothy, up with your Staff and away!   207, 698 n.
Up! up! my friend, and clear your looks,   130, 691 n.
Up with me! up with me into the clouds!   238, 701 n.

Vanguard of Liberty, ye Men of Kent,   289, 711 n.
Vernal Ode, see *Ode.—1817*

Yarrow Revisited   365, 725 n.
Yarrow Unvisited   290, 711 n.
Yarrow Visited   335, 721 n.
Ye now are panting up life's hill!   318, 716 n.
Yes! full surely 'twas the Echo   328, 718 n.
Yet are they here?—the same unbroken knot   332, 719 n.
Yew-Trees   334, 720 n.

Waterfall and the Eglantine, The   214, 699 n.
We Are Seven   83, 689 n.
We had a fellow-Passenger who came   283, 709 n.
We talked with open heart, and tongue   138, 693 n.
We walked along, while bright and red   140, 693 n.
What crowd is this? what have we here! we must not pass it by;   322, 717 n.
What if our numbers barely could defy, *see* Are souls then nothing?
'What you are stepping westward?'—'Yea'   313, 716 n.
When first, descending from the moorlands,   370, 726 n.
When first I journeyed hither, to a home   220, 700 n.
When I have borne in memory what has tamed   277, 708 n.
When, looking on the present face of things,   294, 712 n.
When to the attractions of the busy world, *see* When first I journeyed
    hither
Where are they now, those wanton Boys?   350, 723 n.
Where lies the Land to which yon Ship must go?   271, 707 n.
While not a leaf seems faded,—while the fields,   341, 722 n.
Who fancied what a pretty sight   303, 714 n.
Who is the happy Warrior? Who is he   320, 717 n.
Who leads a happy life   256, 704 n.
Why William on that old grey stone,   129, 691 n.
Within our happy Castle there dwelt one   265, 705 n.
Within the mind strong fancies work,   345, 722 n.
With little here to do or see   252, 704 n.
With Ships the sea was sprinkled far and nigh,   272, 707 n.

Written in London, September, 1802   285, 710 n.
Written in March   248, 704 n.
Written with a Slate Pencil upon a Stone, see *Lines: Written with a
    Slate-Pencil . . .*